Acknowledgments

CAUTION: Professionals and amateurs are hereby warned that these plays and translations, being fully protected under the copyright laws of the United States of America, the British Commonwealth, including the Dominion of Canada, and all other countries which are signatories to the Universal Copyright Convention and the International Copyright Union, are subject to royalty. All rights, including professional, amateur, motion picture, recitation, lecturing, public reading, radio broadcasting, and television, are strictly reserved. All inquiries for rights must be addressed to the copyright owners.

ACKNOWLEDGMENT is made to copyright holders and publishers for permission to reprint the following:

Wilhelm Tell by Friedrich von Schiller. Professor Gilbert J. Jordan's verse translation of Friedrich Schiller's *Wilhelm Tell* was originally published in "The Library of Liberal Arts" series by the Bobbs-Merrill Company, Inc., Indianapolis & New York, in 1964. Permission was granted by the author-translator for its inclusion in the present volume.

Faust, Part 1 by Johann von Goethe. Translated by Charles E. Passage. Copyright © 1965. Reprinted by permission of the publisher, Bobbs-Merrill Company, Inc.

Woyzeck by Georg Büchner. Translated by Theodore Hoffman. Copyright © 1955 by Theodore Hoffman. All performance rights: Samuel French, Inc., 45 West 25th Street, New York, N.Y. 10010.

The Glass of Water by Eugène Scribe. Translated by Sharon Parsell. Copyright © 1984. Reprinted by permission of the translator.

Thérèse Raquin by Émile Zola. Translated by Sharon Parsell. Copyright © 1984. Reprinted by permission of the translator.

Peer Gynt by Henrik Ibsen. Translated by Rolf Fjelde. Second edition. University of Minnesota Press, Minneapolis. Copyright © 1980 by Rolf Fjelde. Reprinted by permission.

Hedda Gabler by Henrik Ibsen from *Henrik Ibsen: The Complete Major Prose Plays*, translated by Rolf Fjelde. Copyright © 1965, 1970, 1978 by Rolf Fjelde. Reprinted by arrangement with New American Library, New York, N.Y.

The Lower Depths by Maxim Gorky. Translated by Alexander Bakshy. Reprinted by permission of Yale University Press from *Seven Plays of Maxim Gorky*, translated by Alexander Bakshy in collaboration with Paul S. Nathan. Copyright © 1945 by Yale University Press.

The Cherry Orchard by Anton Chekhov. Translated by Michael Henry Heim. Copyright © 1979. Reprinted by permission of Michael Henry Heim and the Pittsburgh Public Theater.

Our Dramatic Heritage
VOLUME 4

Our Dramatic Heritage

VOLUME 4: *Romanticism and Realism*

Edited by Philip G. Hill

Rutherford • Madison • Teaneck
Fairleigh Dickinson University Press
London and Toronto: Associated University Presses

© 1989 by Associated University Presses, Inc.

Associated University Presses
440 Forsgate Drive
Cranbury, NJ 08512

Associated University Presses
25 Sicilian Avenue
London WC1A 2QH, England

Associated University Presses
P.O. Box 488, Port Credit
Mississauga, Ontario
Canada L5G 4M2

The paper used in this publication meets the requirements
of the American National Standard for Permanence of Paper
for Printed Library Materials Z39.48-1984.

Library of Congress Cataloging-in-Publication Data

(Revised for vol. 4)

Our dramatic heritage.

   Contents: v. 1. Classical drama and the early
Renaissance — v. 2. The Golden Age —   — v. 4.
Romanticism and realism.
   1. European drama. I. Hill, Philip G. (Philip
George), 1934– .
PN6111.087   1983   808.82   81-65294
ISBN 0-8386-3106-1 (v. 1)
ISBN 0-8386-3267-X (v. 4)

PRINTED IN THE UNITED STATES OF AMERICA

Contents

Acknowledgments	7
Introduction	9
Wilhelm Tell (Friedrich von Schiller)	13
Faust, Part 1 (Johann von Goethe)	78
Woyzeck (Georg Büchner)	151
The Glass of Water (Eugène Scribe)	168
Thérèse Raquin (Émile Zola)	209
Peer Gynt (Henrik Ibsen)	244
Hedda Gabler (Henrik Ibsen)	320
Cyrano de Bergerac (Edmond Rostand)	365
The Lower Depths (Maxim Gorky)	434
The Cherry Orchard (Anton Chekhov)	474

Introduction

Late in the eighteenth century, there emerged in Germany a group of playwrights known as "romanticists"; early in the twentieth century, the rising tide of realism culminated in the work of the finest playwright Russia has yet produced—Anton Chekhov. Between these two landmarks lies the rich and varied dramatic literature of nineteenth-century Europe. Increasingly, this century offers the anthologizer new problems: not so much what to include as what to omit. Complete play scripts from this era survive in such abundance that difficult choices must be made among many good plays and fine playwrights; no longer is it possible to include at least one play by everyone whose work was truly important. A theatrically rich movement like romanticism must be represented by only three or four playwrights, whereas occasionally less satisfying works must be included in order to illustrate the development of a new trend.

The movement still most keenly felt (if sometimes only as a force to react against) in the twentieth century is realism, and thus the roots of realism are traced somewhat more fully in this volume than are those of the earlier movements. No sooner was romanticism fully established in Europe than a newer, younger "avant-garde" sprang up, determined to replace ideas already grown stale with new approaches that would be scientific, objective, and fully lifelike. The first great master of this new form was Henrik Ibsen, and traditionally the study of modern drama begins with Ibsen's major realistic works. But it in no way diminishes Ibsen's magnificent achievement to note that he too was in part a product of the forces at work in his time, and that earlier nineteenth-century playwrights may also be said to have had a great deal to do with the shape and direction of modern drama. More than a century having now passed since Ibsen turned his attention from romantic plays to realistic ones, it is also time to note that much of what he and his realistic colleagues did was violently rejected by those who came after him, and that much of twentieth-century drama is not so much a celebration of Ibsenism as a reaction against it. That will be the theme of subsequent volumes of *Our Dramatic Heritage*.

With one exception (to keep Ibsen's two plays together), the plays in this volume are arranged chronologically. They include three new translations published here for the first time, as well as several other plays not frequently anthologized. Together, they represent the richness of a century that both triumphed with major theatrical works of the highest intrinsic merit and nutured an even richer and more varied drama that was to emerge in the twentieth century. Romanticism and realism were the twin pillars upon which nineteenth-century drama rested.

Our Dramatic Heritage
VOLUME 4

Wilhelm Tell

Friedrich von Schiller

While critics, especially in France, fought to maintain neoclassic standards in serious European drama, and while popular drama increasingly depended on bourgeois tastes and bourgeois characters, there was an "avant-garde" movement in drama that emerged in Germany in the late eighteenth century that was to sweep Europe in the nineteenth. This force was romanticism. It is not possible here to trace all of the roots of the romantic movement, but by the time Goethe and Schiller wrote their finest plays, romanticism was a major force and these two playwrights its greatest interpreters. In fact, as with so many such movements, the leading figures in romanticism transcended its more extravagant aspects; Goethe's and Schiller's works are more than simply romantic plays—they can stand for what was best in that style. Schiller was ten years younger than Goethe, but he died young and his plays had thus been completed before Goethe published his master work.

Johann Christoph Friedrich von Schiller was born in Marbach, Württemberg, on November 10, 1759. His father was an officer in the army of the duke of Württemberg, and when the autocratic duke insisted that young Friedrich be enrolled in the military academy that the duke personally supervised, the Schiller family felt that they had no choice. Thus, Friedrich spent eight years enduring stern military discipline, and despite his own inclination toward literature was trained in medicine and became an assistant medical officer in the duke's army. Deeply rankled by this control over his life, Schiller nevertheless did his best work and wrote only in his spare time. While still a student, he began his first play, *The Robbers,* publishing it in 1781 and arranging for its first production at the National Theater in Mannheim, where it opened on January 13, 1782. Schiller slipped away from his medical duties without leave to attend opening night as well as a subsequent performance, and the duke, invoking military discipline, forbade him to write more plays. Upon this provocation, Schiller deserted, living a hand-to-mouth existence for several years while attempting to establish himself in a literary career. For a year he served as resident playwright at the theater in Mannheim, and for several years he was supported by friends. During this time, he wrote *Fiesco* (1784), *Love and Intrigue* (1784), and *Don Carlos* (1787). He also wrote poetry and history, and, upon the recommendation of Goethe, received an appointment as professor of history at the University of Jena. During the 1790s he worked on his Wallenstein trilogy (*Wallenstein's Camp. The Piccolomini,* and *Wallenstein's Death*) which was finally produced at Weimar in 1799.

In 1790, Schiller had married Charlotte von Lengefeld, and he became the father of two sons and two daughters. In 1791, however, he was stricken with tuberculosis; he struggled with the disease for fourteen years before succumbing to it on May 9, 1805. By 1799, he moved to Weimar, then the cultural center of Germany, where he could continue his friendship with Goethe and the other artistic leaders of the day and work with them on his many literary enterprises.

During the last five years of his life, he turned more intensively to playwriting, producing four of the major works for which he is remembered: *Maria Stuart* (1800), *The Maid of Orleans* (1801), *The Bride of Messina* (1803), and *Wilhelm Tell*, his last completed work. It is reported that so intent was he upon finishing as much work as possible that he worked all night, with his feet plunged in ice water to keep awake. Despite this heroism, he died at the age of forty-five, one of the great figures in Germanic literature.

Critics vary in their selection of Schiller's finest work, but in terms of stage history there can be little choice. *Wilhelm Tell* was a tremendous popular success when it opened at Weimar on March 17, 1804, and again in its Berlin production beginning on July 4 of the same year. Through the middle of the nineteenth century, the play was produced to great excitement all over Europe; as realism replaced romanticism as the dominant mode of European drama, *Wilhelm Tell* naturally received fewer productions, but it has continued to hold the stage to the present day. It is produced annually at Altdorf and Interlaken, Switzerland, where Tell is the national folk hero; the play adapts especially well to outdoor production there, with large casts, mountain scenery, and horseback action.

Although *Wilhelm Tell* is a history play (as were most of Schiller's), one needs little knowledge of Swiss history to appreciate it. In fact, Schiller took poetic license with the details of history anyway, and was interested in the theatrical effect of his work rather than in historical accuracy. There is no certain evidence that Wilhelm Tell ever lived, much less that he shot an apple from his son's head, but he had been a widely known Swiss legend for several centuries before Schiller turned his attention to the story. The Swiss cantons were a part of the Holy Roman Empire in the thirteenth century; the Empire was a loose confederation of kingdoms, duchies, and principalities formed in 843 after the death of Charlemagne and governed by an Emperor elected from among the leading noble houses within the confederation. The Swiss cantons of Uri, Schwyz, and Unterwalden enjoyed relative independence under direct charter from the Emperor and owing fealty only to the Emperor, but the Hapsburg rulers of Austria aspired to make the Swiss their vassals. Thus, when a Hapsburg was elected Emperor, the Swiss were in trouble. An extended struggle for "independence" ensued, although what the Swiss were seeking was simply a renewal of the several charters maintaining their direct allegiance to the Emperor without obligation to any intermediate ruler. The events in the play concern only one part of this struggle, but it was a decisive part that led directly to the formation of a Swiss union and eventually to the development of modern Switzerland. Many of the persons in the play are historical figures, but their characters do not necessarily correspond with historical fact and many of the incidents of the plot either did not occur at all or did not occur in the time sequence and proximity portrayed. Thus, the play must finally be judged, as any other play must be, as a work of theatrical art and not as a historical document. Historical details are of little importance here.

The historical spirit is of great importance, however. Schiller portrays a time when the spirit of freedom and independence ran strong in the Swiss people; it is a well-chosen mirror of the times in which Schiller wrote, when America's struggle for independence had inspired the world, France had recently exploded in its own revolution, and the threat of Napoleon hung over Europe. Napoleon took control of Switzerland in 1802, and the spirit of freedom seemed in danger everywhere. Schiller's love of freedom, no doubt nurtured by the harshness of his own military experience, pervades *Wilhelm Tell* and is its predominant theme. The play's wide-ranging plot, its simplistic all-good and all-bad characters, and its soaring poetry are all designed to reinforce this inspirational theme in a manner that later realists were to find objectionable, but generations of theatergoers have been emotionally stirred as Schiller intended them to be. That thematic content might best be transmitted by emotional rather than intellectual means was a fundamental tenet of romanticism; the great mysteries of life were not, in the romantic view, subject to satisfactory explanation through reason but might only be apprehended through feeling. The ultimate measure of success of a play like *Wilhelm Tell* was whether it could stir up such powerful feelings, and in the theater it regularly does.

Tell himself is a character too totally good to be believable in a realistic context, but as a romantic hero he sweeps one along with the spirit of the play. Furthermore, although he may be without the baser motivations of more believable human beings, he is not totally without psychological struggles. Schiller is careful to portray Tell as the rugged individualist who prefers not to get involved in the troubles of his neighbors, but who will finally risk his life for a neighbor when there is no other solution available for his problems. Then, Tell is placed in a severe moral dilemma, first in having to become involved in political matters at all and finally in undertaking a murder of great political significance in order to protect his family. Tell is perfectly aware that he is commiting murder, and the attitude of the Swiss people in rejecting murder except as a last resort is made very clear in the play, but Tell's moral dilemma is also explored in order that the audience may see that, in extreme cases such as the defense of liberty, murder too may be justified. The last scene, in which Tell's act of murder is contrasted with Parricida's, is an important final link in this chain, for Parricida has killed for personal ambition, an act that can under no circumstances be justified. Tell is compassionate, and willing to help Parricida as a fellow human being in distress, but he rejects completely any comparison between his own blow for freedom and Parricida's selfish act. To play a scene like this is difficult, especially in the modern theater grown accustomed to searching for a Freudian subtext in every line, but the thorough establishment of Tell's good character earlier in the play then makes this last scene not only possible but emotionally moving. Unreservedly good and bad characters, though eschewed in realistic plays, are nevertheless extremely powerful in certain other styles of theater when well drawn. This was the usual approach of the romantic theater.

Reinforcing the moral purity of the characters, Schiller creates a play world permeated by these same moral values. Thus, even the animals have "reason," an instinct to preserve their freedom and safety, and nature itself rebels against a great wrong, as seen especially in act 4, scene 1. God is pictured regularly on the side of the right, and when Tell does finally murder Gessler, his arrow catches him in the very act of another dastardly miscarriage of justice. Tell's values are clearly those of the play, and ultimately those of the author—values made clear when he asserts, "I . . . only can enjoy my life completely / When I must work to win it every day" (act 3, scene 1).

The German romanticists were greatly influenced by Shakespeare, first available in German prose and later translated into highly effective poetic versions by August Schlegel between 1797 and 1801. Shakespeare's approach to dramatic structure is evidenced in *Wilhelm Tell*, as Schiller follows three different plot threads, bringing them effectively together into a single fabric by the end of the play. The story of Wilhelm Tell, rugged individualist, is only one of these plot lines, though it is the most memorable one. There is also the story of the Swiss nobles and their sense of identity with the Swiss people, with Ulrich von Rudenz's love for Berta von Bruneck as the unifying element. Finally, there is the story of the Swiss people uniting against tyranny, the story in which Schiller is ultimately interested and which provides the underlying connections for the other stories. In neo-Shakespearean fashion, Schiller deals first with one of these plots and then another, interconnecting them so that they finally form a unified dramatic whole. Furthermore, Schiller's use of iambic pentameter was so successful that it became established as the standard poetic line for German drama as it previously had for English; of course Goethe and the other romanticists share with Schiller the credit for popularizing this style.

Although romanticism is a style long out of fashion in the theater, Schiller remains one of the two or three greatest German playwrights. His romantic techniques are notable, but finally his genius rises above any one style to become fine theatrical art. Schiller's passionate commitment to free will and freedom of choice was an important contribution not only in a thematic sense, but also as a theatrical technique encouraging the depiction of heroic figures who are not the victims of blind fate. Tell may be too good to be totally human, but he is also too humanly inspiring to be forgotten.

N.B. The footnotes for *Wilhelm Tell* were written by the translator and have been slightly abridged and edited by the present editor. Professor Jordan's complete notes, as well as his introduction, may be found in *Wilhelm Tell*, translated by Gilbert J. Jordan (Bobbs-Merrill, 1964).

Wilhelm Tell

Translated by Gilbert J. Jordan

Characters

Hermann Gessler, imperial governor or viceroy in Schwyz and Uri
Werner, Baron von Attinghausen, banneret and free noble
Ulrich von Rudenz, his nephew

Werner Stauffacher
Konrad Hunn
Itel Reding
Hans auf der Mauer } countrymen of Schwyz
Jörg im Hofe
Ulrich der Schmied
Jost von Weiler

Walter Fürst
Wilhelm Tell
Rösselmann, the priest
Petermann, the sacristan } countrymen of Uri
Kuoni, the herdsman
Werni, the hunter
Ruodi, the fisherman

Arnold vom Melchtal
Konrad Baumgarten
Meier von Sarnen
Struth von Winkelried } countrymen of Unterwalden
Klaus von der Flüe
Burkhard am Bühel
Arnold von Sewa

Pfeifer von Lucerne
Kunz von Gersau
Jenni, fisherman's (Ruodi's) son
Seppi, herdsman's (Kuoni's) boy servant
Gertrud, Stauffacher's wife
Hedwig, Tell's wife, Fürst's daughter
Berta von Bruneck, a rich heiress

Armgard
Mechthild } countrywomen
Elsbet
Hildegard

Walter } Tell's sons
Wilhelm
Friesshard } soldiers
Leuthold
Rudolf der Harras, Gessler's Master of the Horse
Johannes Parricida, Duke of Swabia
Stüssi, the ranger
Hornblower, the Ox of Uri
A Royal Courier
Overseer
Head Mason, Journeymen, Laborers
Public Criers
Brothers of Mercy (monks of the Order of Charity)
Troopers of Gessler and Landenberg
Many Countrymen and Women from the Forest Cantons

Act 1

Scene 1

A steep and rocky shore of Lake Lucerne,[1] opposite Schwyz. The lake forms an inlet into the land. Not far from the shore is a hut. The FISHERMAN'S SON *is rowing about in his boat. Across the lake are seen the green meadows, the villages, and the farmhouses of Schwyz in bright sunlight. To the spectator's left are the peaks of the Haken, covered with clouds; to the right, in the distant background, ice-capped mountains are visible. Before the curtain rises, the Kuhreihen, Alpine cowherd's melody,[2] and the harmonious sound of cowbells are heard. These sounds continue for some time after the curtain rises.*

FISHERMAN'S SON. [*Singing in the boat.*]
   Alpine Cowherd's Melody

The waters are smiling, inviting the
   land;
The boy lies asleep upon the green
   strand;
   He hears a sweet music
   Like flutes in the skies,
   Like voices of angels
   In paradise.
And when he awakens in blissful joy,
The waters are playing, caressing the
   boy.
   He hears in the distance
   A call from the sea:
   You are mine, dear sleeper,
   I'll draw you to me.
HERDSMAN. [*On the mountain.*]
   Variation of the Alpine Cowherd's Melody

   Farewell, sunny meadows;
   Farewell, you green grasses!
   The herdsman must leave you;
   The summer soon passes.
We'll come back to these mountains,
   return every spring,
When the cuckoo calls, when the world
   wakes to sing,
When the flowers are clothing the earth
   anew,
When the brooks are flowing, and
   fields are in dew.
   Farewell, sunny meadows;
   Farewell, you green grasses!
   The herdsman must leave you;
   The summer soon passes.
ALPINE HUNTER. [*Appearing on the opposite side on the top of the cliff.*]
   Second Variation

The mountains are rumbling and
   shaking the trail;
The hunter fears nothing, his footing
   won't fail;
   He strides along boldly
   On fields of sheer snow;
   No springtime is dawning;
   No grasses will grow.
And under his feet a nebulous sea,
Where cities and men he no longer can
   see.
   But a break in the clouds
   Gives a glimpse of a scene:
   Far down by the water,
   The meadows of green.[3]

The landscape changes, and a muffled roaring is heard from the mountains. Shadows of clouds pass over the scene. RUODI, *the fisherman, comes out of the hut.* WERNI, *the hunter, climbs down from the cliff.* KUONI, *the herdsman, comes with a milk pail on his shoulder.* SEPPI, *his boy servant, follows him.*

RUODI. Hurry, Jenni! Pull in the boat
   and come!
I see the fog and hear the glacier rumbling;
The Mythenstein[4] is putting on its
   shroud,
And from the weatherhole[5] the wind is
   blowing.
I think the storm will come before we
   know it.
KUONI. It's going to rain all right; my
   sheep are grazing
More eagerly, and Watcher paws the
   ground.
WERNI. The fish are leaping, and the
   water hen
Is diving down. A storm is on the way.
KUONI. [*To the boy.*] See, Seppi, that our
   cattle are not straying.
SEPPI. I hear brown Lisel's bell not far
   from here.
KUONI. Then none is gone, because she
   goes the farthest.
RUODI. Melodious bells you have there,
   master herdsman.
WERNI. And splendid cattle, too. Are
   they your own?
KUONI. I'm not so rich. They are my
   gracious Lord
Von Attinghausen's, and only in my
   charge.
RUODI. Just see that cow; she wears her
   collar proudly.
KUONI. She knows quite well that she
   must lead the herd;
If I should take it off, she would not
   graze.
RUODI. That makes no sense! A stupid
   animal—
WERNI. Hold on! The animals have reason, too.
We hunters learn that when we're hunting chamois.
When they go out to graze, they wisely
   post
A sentinel to prick his ears and warn,
With piercing call, whenever hunters
   come.

RUODI. [*To the* HERDSMAN.] You're driving home your herd?
KUONI. The pasture's bare.
WERNI. Good luck then, friend!
KUONI. I wish the same for you!
Some hunters don't return from trips like yours.
RUODI. Look, who's the man that's running in such haste?
WERNI. I know him well; it's Baumgart from Alzellen. [KONRAD BAUMGARTEN *dashes in, breathless.*]
BAUMGARTEN. For God's sake, boatman, take me in your boat!
RUODI. Here now, what is the hurry?
BAUMGARTEN. Untie the boat!
Save me from death! Take me across the lake!
KUONI. What is the matter, friend?
WERNI. Who's after you?
BAUMGARTEN. [*To the* FISHERMAN.]
Hurry, hurry, they're close upon my heels!
The viceroy's horsemen, they are after me!
If they should catch me, it would mean my death.
RUODI. But tell me, why are the troopers after you?
BAUMGARTEN. Just save me first, and then I'll answer questions.
WERNI. You're stained with blood. What in the world has happened?
BAUMGARTEN. The emperor's bailiff at the Rossberg castle—
KUONI. That's Wolfenschiessen! Is he after you?
BAUMGARTEN. He cannot harm me now, for I have killed him.
ALL. [*Shrinking back.*] May God be merciful! What have you done?
BAUMGARTEN. What any free man in my place would do.
Defended fairly, as it was my right,
The honor of my home and of my wife.
KUONI. You mean the bailiff has assailed your honor?
BAUMGARTEN. He would have carried out his evil purpose
If God and my good ax had not forestalled it.
WERNI. You struck the man and killed him with your ax?
KUONI. Oh, let us hear it all; you still have time
Before he can untie the boat from shore.
BAUMGARTEN. I had been felling trees in nearby woods,
When suddenly my frightened wife came running
And said the bailiff was at home and had
Commanded her to draw the bath for him,
And that he then expressed insulting wishes.
But she escaped to seek me out and tell me.
I then ran quickly home, just as I was,
And with my ax I blessed him in his bath.
WERNI. And you did right; no man can blame you for it.
KUONI. That tyrant! Now he has his just reward,
So long deserved from Unterwalden's people!
BAUMGARTEN. My deed was talked about, and now I am
Pursued—God! while we talk, I'm losing time! [*It begins to thunder.*]
KUONI. Be quick now, boatman, ferry him across!
RUODI. It can't be done. A heavy storm is coming.
You'll have to wait.
BAUMGARTEN. Oh, holy God! You must.
I cannot wait. The least delay means death.
KUONI. [*To the* FISHERMAN.] Trust God and try! We have to help a neighbor.
The same might happen any time to us. [*Roaring and thunder.*]
RUODI. The storm is here. Look how the lake is rising!
I cannot row against the wind and waves.
BAUMGARTEN. [*Throwing his arms around* RUODI's *knees.*] May God reward you, as you pity me.
WERNI. His life's at stake. Be merciful to him!
KUONI. He is a family man with wife and children! [*Repeated claps of thunder.*]
RUODI. What do you mean? I also have a life
To lose, a wife and child at home like his.
Just see the waters break and surge and

whirl
And boil up from the bottom of the lake.
I'd gladly try to save the good man's life,
But you can see it is impossible.
BAUMGARTEN. [*Still on his knees.*] Then I must fall into the tyrant's hands,
With safety on the other shore in sight.
Yes, there it lies. My eyes behold it clearly;
My pleading voice can even reach the haven.
There is the boat to ferry me across,
And I must stay here, helpless and despairing.
KUONI. Who's coming over there?
WERNI. It's Tell from Bürglen. [TELL *enters with his crossbow.*]
TELL. Who is this man that's asking you for help?
KUONI. He's from Alzellen, and to save his honor
He had to kill the tyrant Wolfenschiessen,
The royal bailiff from the Rossberg castle.
The viceroy's men are close upon his heels.
He begs the boatman to be ferried over,
But this man fears the storm and will not go.
RUODI. Look, here is Tell! He is a boatman too,
And he can say if I should risk the passage.
TELL. When there's a need, then all things must be risked. [*Violent claps of thunder, as the lake surges up.*]
RUODI. I am to leap into the jaws of hell?
No man in his right mind would try it now.
TELL. The true man thinks about his neighbor first.
Rely on God, and rescue this poor man.
RUODI. It's easy to advise when safe in harbor.
Well, here's the boat and there's the lake! You try it!
TELL. The lake may help, but not the governor. Try it, boatman.
HERDSMEN *and* HUNTER. Save him! Save him! Save him!
RUODI. If he were my own brother or my child,
It could not be. This is St. Simon's Day,
And Jude's;[6] the sea will have its sacrifice.
TELL. We can accomplish nothing here by talking.
The hour is pressing and the man needs help.
Speak, boatman, are you going?
RUODI. No, not I.
TELL. Well then, for God's sake, give the boat to me.
I will attempt it with what strength I have.
KUONI. How brave!
WERNI. Just like the hunter that he is!
BAUMGARTEN. My rescuer and guardian angel, Tell!
TELL. Well may I rescue you from tyrant's power;
A mightier arm must save you from the storm.
But rather fall into the hand of God
Than in the hands of men. [*To the* HERDSMAN.] Console my wife
If human fate should find me on this passage.
I've done what I could never leave undone. [*He jumps into the boat.*]
KUONI. [*To the* FISHERMAN.] You are a master oarsman, yet you would not
Attempt to do what Tell has undertaken?
RUODI. And better men than I can't equal Tell;
No other man is like him in these mountains.
WERNI. [*Who has climbed on the cliff.*] He's shoving off. God help you, gallant boatman!
See how his boat is tossing on the waves!
KUONI. [*On the shore.*] The waves have swallowed it. It's out of sight.
But wait, I see it now! With all his might
The brave man fights his way against the breakers.
SEPPI. Here come the viceroy's troopers at a gallop.
KUONI. God knows you're right. That help came just in time. [*A band of Landenberg's troopers appears.*]
FIRST TROOPER. Give up the murderer that you are hiding!
SECOND TROOPER. He came this way. It

does no good to hide him.
KUONI *and* RUODI. Whom do you mean?
FIRST TROOPER. [*Discovering the boat.*]
Oh, damn it all, I see him!
WERNI. [*Above.*] You want that fellow in the boat? Ride on.
Ride fast, and you may overtake him still.
SECOND TROOPER. Confound it! Gone.
FIRST TROOPER [*To the* HERDSMAN *and* FISHERMAN]. You helped him get away.
You'll pay for this. Go kill their herds and flocks!
Destroy their cabins—burn them to the ground! [*They dash off.*]
SEPPI. [*Following them.*] My little lambs!
KUONI. [*Following him.*] They're killing all my cattle!
WERNI. Those murderers!
RUODI [*Wringing his hands.*] This cries to heaven for justice!
When will a savior come to help our land? [*He follows them.*]

Scene 2

Steinen in Schwyz. A linden tree in front of STAUFFACHER'*s house on the highway, near a bridge.* WERNER STAUFFACHER *and* PFEIFER VON LUCERNE *enter, engaged in conversation.*
PFEIFER. Yes, yes, Herr Werner, it is as I said,
Don't swear allegiance to the Austrians;
Hold firmly to the Empire, as before.
May God protect you in your ancient freedom. [*He presses* STAUFFACHER'*s hand cordially and is about to leave.*]
STAUFFACHER. Do stay until my wife returns. You are
My guest in Schwyz, as in Lucerne I'm yours.
PFEIFER. No, thanks. I'm on my way to Gersau now.
Whatever hardships you may have to bear
From greed and insolence of governors,
Endure in patience. Things can quickly change;
Another emperor might rule the realm.
Once joined to Austria, you're bound for good. [*He leaves. Sorrowfully,*
STAUFFACHER *sits down on a bench under the linden tree.* GERTRUD, *his wife, finds him like this, stands beside him, and looks at him for a while without speaking.*]
GERTRUD. So solemn, Werner? I no longer know you.
For days I have observed in silence how
This gloomy melancholy makes you frown.
You bear a silent sorrow in your heart.
Confide in me. I am your faithful wife,
And I demand that I may share your sorrow. [STAUFFACHER *gives her his hand in silence.*]
What is it that can grieve your heart? Tell me.
Your diligence is blessed: your fortune grows;
The barns are full; your well-fed herds of cattle
And teams of horses, thoroughbred and sleek,
Have all been driven home from mountain pastures
To spend the winter in the spacious stables.
There stands your house, as fine as any castle,
Now newly built of costly seasoned timber
And put together by the rule and square;
From many windows gleams a homelike splendor;
It's gaily painted with our coat of arms
And words of wisdom, that the wanderer
May read and contemplate their deeper meaning.
STAUFFACHER. The house is fashioned and constructed well,
But oh, the ground on which it's built is shaking.
GERTRUD. My Werner, tell me what you mean by this.
STAUFFACHER. Not long ago I sat beneath this linden
With pleasant thoughts of our completed work,
When all at once the governor rode up.
He came from Küssnacht castle with his troopers
And halted in surprise before this house.
But I stood up respectfully and walked,
As it is due and proper, toward the

lord
Who represents the king's judicial power
Within our lands. "Whose house it this?" he asked
With evil purpose, for he knew it well.
But, thinking very quickly, I replied,
"This house, sir, is the emperor's, my lord
As well as yours, and is a fief." He said,
"I am the regent in the emperor's name,
And do not want you farmers to build houses
Upon your own decision, and suppose
That you can live as free as lords yourselves.
I plan to put a stop to all this freedom."
And then he rode away defiantly
And left me standing there with troubled mind,
Reflecting on the words that he had spoken.
GERTRUD. My own dear lord and husband, will you hear
A candid word from me, your trusting wife?
I'm proud that I am noble Iberg's daughter;
He was a man of much experience.
We sisters sat the long nights spinning wool
When leaders of the people came to father,
And met and read together ancient charters
From former rulers, and then with thoughtful words
Discussed our country's welfare and condition.
I listened to those wise deliberations,
What prudent men advise and good men wish,
And quietly I kept them in my heart.
So listen to me now and weigh my words.
I've known for many days what's troubling you.
The viceroy holds a grudge, would like to harm you
Because he thinks you are the one to blame
That men from Canton Schwyz will not submit
To Austrian rule; instead they stand and cling
In loyalty and firmness to the Empire,
Just as our fathers always did before us.
Is this not true? You tell me if I'm wrong.
STAUFFACHER. It's true, all right; that's Gessler's grudge against me.
GERTRUD. He envies you because he sees you live
A free man on your own inheritance,
For he has none. You hold your house in fief
Directly from the Empire and may show it
As well as royal princes show their lands.
You recognize no overlord above you
Except the highest one in Christendom.[7]
He is a younger son of his own house,
Possessing nothing but his cloak of knighthood,
And therefore looks on every good man's fortune
With envious eyes and a malicious mind.
He plotted for your downfall long ago.
You stand here still unharmed, but will you wait
Till he takes out his evil spite on you?
The wise man takes precautions.
STAUFFACHER. What can I do?
GERTRUD. [*Moving closer to him.*] Will you take my advice? You know how, here
In Canton Schwyz, all honest men complain
About the viceroy's greed and cruelty.
I do not doubt that people over there
In Unterwalden and in Canton Uri
Are also weary of the hard oppression;
For just as Gessler plays the tyrant here,
So Landenberger rules across the lake.
No fishing boat comes over to our shores
That doesn't bring us word of some fresh evil,
Some new injustice by the governors.
It would be well, I think, if some of you
Good citizens would quietly take counsel
How we can best escape from this oppression.
I feel convinced that God would not forsake you
And would be gracious to a righteous cause.
Have you no one in Uri, no close friend

To whom you may disclose your heart completely?
STAUFFACHER. Indeed I know some loyal men in Uri
And influential men of high repute
Whom I can trust in any secret matter. [*He stands up.*]
Oh, what a storm of dangerous thoughts you waken
Within my quiet mind and heart! You shed
The light of day upon my inmost thoughts;
And what I silently forbade myself
To think, you speak right out with daring tongue.
Have you considered well what you advise?
You'll call a wild discord and sound of weapons
Into this peaceful valley of our land.
How can we helpless country people dare
To start a war against a mighty nation?
They're only waiting for a pretext now
To loose their raging hordes of men upon us,
To overrun and take our little land
And rule it as the spoils of victory,
And under semblance of just punishment
Destroy the ancient charters of our freedom.
GERTRUD. You too are men, and you can use the ax;
And God will always help courageous men.[8]
STAUFFACHER. Oh, Gertrud, warfare is a raging horror:
It will destroy our herds and kill our herdsmen.
GERTRUD. We must endure whatever heaven sends us,
But noble hearts will never bear injustice.
STAUFFACHER. This house that we have built delights you now.
But war, this monstrous war, will burn it down.
GERTRUD. If ever I felt chained to earthly goods,
I'd throw the firebrands in with my own hands.
STAUFFACHER. Your faith is in humanity, but war
Will not spare even babies in the cradle.
GERTRUD. Yet innocence still has a friend in heaven.
Look only forward, Werner, not behind.
STAUFFACHER. We men can bravely fight, and fighting die;
But you must know what women's fate will be.
GERTRUD. The final choice lies open to the weakest;
A leap into the water makes me free.
STAUFFACHER. [*Embracing her.*] Who presses such a heart against his breast
Can fight with pleasure for his hearth and home
And never fear the royal army's might.
I'm going to Uri now, just as I am;
A trusted friend lives there. He's Walter Fürst,
And his opinions are the same as mine.
I'll also find the noble banneret
Lord Attinghausen. Though of higher rank,
He loves the people and respects our customs.
I will take counsel now with these two men
To plan defense against our enemies.
Good-by, and while I am away from home,
Conduct the business of our household wisely.
Give generous gifts and hospitality
To pilgrims going to the house of God
And to the monks collecting for the cloister.
Stauffacher's house is not concealed. It stands
Right out beside the road, a welcoming roof
For all the wanderers who come our way. [*As they move backstage,* WILHELM TELL *and* BAUMGARTEN *enter at the front.*]
TELL. [*To* BAUMGARTEN.] And now you have no further need of me.
Go to this house and enter. It's the home
Of Stauffacher, a friend of the oppressed.
But there he is himself—come, follow me! [*They walk toward him; the scene changes.*]

Scene 3

A public square at Altdorf.[9] *On a hill in the background a fortress is seen under con-*

struction, so far advanced that the shape of the whole can be made out. The back is finished, but the front is still being constructed. The scaffolding on which workmen are climbing up and down is still in place. The slater is perched on the highest point of the roof. Everybody is in motion and at work.*

OVERSEER. [*Driving the workmen with his staff.*][10] Don't stop so long! Come one! Let's have the stones!
Be quick! And now bring up the lime and mortar!
When the viceroy comes, he's got to see
Results. You're slower than a pack of snails. [*To two laborers carrying loads.*]
Is that a load? Go carry twice as much!
Such lazy idlers, always slacking off!

FIRST WORKMAN. This is too much, that we must carry stones
To build the dungeon to imprison us.

OVERSEER. What are you grumbling there? A sorry gang
That's fit for nothing but to milk the cows
Or loaf about and wander in the hills.

OLD MAN. [*Stopping to rest.*] I can't go on.

OVERSEER. [*Shaking him.*] Get up, old man, and work!

FIRST WORKMAN. Have you no heart at all, that you drive on
To heavy work a man who's barely able
To drag himself along?

HEAD MASON *and* WORKMEN. It is outrageous!

OVERSEER. Go mind your business. Here, I am in charge.

SECOND WORKMAN. Say, overseer, what will they call this fortress
That we're building?

OVERSEER. The Uri fortress. And you
Will bend your stubborn necks beneath this yoke.

WORKMEN. The Uri fortress!

OVERSEER. What's so funny now?

SECOND WORKMAN. You plan to keep down Uri with this hut?

FIRST WORKMAN. Let's see how many molehills of this kind
You'd have to pile up till a mountain grows
That's equal to the smallest one in Uri. [*The* OVERSEER *walks to the back.*]

HEAD MASON. I'll throw my hammer in the deepest lake
Because I used it on this cursed place.

[TELL *and* STAUFFACHER *enter.*]

STAUFFACHER. I wish I'd never lived to see such things.

TELL. It isn't good to stop here. Let's go on.

STAUFFACHER. Am I in Uri, in the land of freedom?

HEAD MASON. Oh, sir, if you could see the dungeons deep
Below the towers! Whoever's kept down there
Will never hear the cock crow in the morning.

STAUFFACHER. Oh God![11]

HEAD MASON. Just see the bastions, see the buttresses,
So strongly built they'll stand eternally.

TELL. What hands built up, hands can tear down again. [*He points at the mountains.*]
This house of freedom God himself created. [*A drum is heard, and people enter, carrying a hat on a pole. A* PUBLIC CRIER *follows them. Women and children press tumultuously after.*]

FIRST WORKMAN. Why do they beat the drum? Look there!

HEAD MASON. What circus
Parade is this, and why the pole and hat?

CRIER. In the emperor's name! Give heed!

WORKMEN. Be still and listen!

CRIER. Look at this hat, you men of Uri, look!
It will be raised upon a towering pole
In Altdorf, at the highest spot in town.
And this is what the governor decrees:
Give honor to the hat as though to him;
By kneeling down and taking off your hats
Show that you honor it. By this the king
Will see just how obedient you are.
If any one of you defies this order,
His life and goods are forfeit to the king. [*The people laugh out loud, the drum is heard, and they pass by.*]

FIRST WORKMAN. What new outrageous scheme has he thought up
This time? We should give honor to a hat!
Has anybody heard of such a thing?

HEAD MASON. We are to bend our knees before a hat!
What kind of joke is this to play on

people?
FIRST WORKMAN. Now if it were the royal crown—but no,
It is the Austrian hat; I saw it hang
Above the throne, where fiefs are handed out.
HEAD MASON. The hat of Austria! It is a trick
That will betray us to the Austrians.
WORKMEN. No honest man submits to such an outrage.
HEAD MASON. Come, let us talk it over with the others. [*They go to the back of the stage.*]
TELL. [*To* STAUFFACHER.] You see now how things are. Good-by, friend Werner.
STAUFFACHER. Where are you going, Tell? Don't hurry off.
TELL. My family needs me now. I'll say good-by.
STAUFFACHER. My heart is full of things to say to you.
TELL. A heavy heart will not grow light from words.
STAUFFACHER. And yet our words could lead us on to action.
TELL. Our only course is patience now, and silence.
STAUFFACHER. Shall we then bear what is unbearable?
TELL. Hotheaded rulers never last for long.
When sudden storms arise within these gorges,
We put our fires out, the boats all come
To harbor, and the mighty spirit moves
Across the land without a trace of harm.
Let everyone stay quietly at home,
For peace is granted to the peaceful man.
STAUFFACHER. You think so?
TELL. A snake strikes only when provoked.
They will at last grow weary by themselves
When they see all the country staying calm.
STAUFFACHER. We could do much if we would stand together.
TELL. In shipwreck each does best to save himself.
STAUFFACHER. Can you so coldly leave the common cause?
TELL. It's safest to rely upon oneself.
STAUFFACHER. United will the weak grow mighty too.
TELL. The strong man will be strongest when alone.
STAUFFACHER. Your fatherland, then, cannot count on you
When in despair it turns to self-defense?
TELL. [*Giving him his hand.*] Tell saves a missing lamb from the abyss,
And yet you think he will forsake his friends?
Don't call me into your debates or ask
Me for my views; I cannot weigh and compare.
But if you need me for a special task,
Then call on Tell. He will not fail you there. [*They leave on different sides. A sudden tumult starts around the scaffolding.*]
HEAD MASON. [*Rushing over.*] What happened?
FIRST WORKMAN. [*Coming forward, calling.*] The slater slipped and tumbled from the roof. [BERTA *enters with her attendants and runs up.*]
BERTA. Has he been badly hurt? Hurry! Save him!
If I can help you rescue him, here's gold! [*She throws her jewelry among the people.*]
HEAD MASON. Your gold! You nobles think all can be bought
For gold! When you have torn away a father
From his children, a husband from his wife,
When you have brought down misery on the world,
You think you can repay with gold! Get out!
We all were happy men before you came.
With you, despair has come into our land.
BERTA. [*To the* OVERSEER, *who is returning.*] Is he alive? [*The* OVERSEER *shakes his head.*] Unlucky fortress built
With curses, curses will inhabit you!
[*Exeunt.*]

Scene 4

WALTER FÜRST's *dwelling.* WALTER FÜRST *and* ARNOLD VOM MELCHTAL *enter at*

the same time from opposite sides.
MELCHTAL. Herr Walter Fürst—
WALTER FÜRST. You must remain in hiding.
We are beset by spies. What if you're seen?
MELCHTAL. Is there no news from Unterwalden yet?
No news from Father?—I cannot endure
To lie here idly like a prisoner.
What have I done that is so criminal
That I must hide out like a murderer?
I broke that rascal's finger with my staff
When he, upon the governor's command,
Attempted to unhitch my yoke of oxen
And right before my eyes to drive them off.
WALTER FÜRST. You are too rash. He was the viceroy's man,
And he was sent upon your lord's command.
You had been judged at fault and had to yield
To their decision, hard as it might be.
MELCHTAL. Was I to stand and listen while that brute
Brazenly taunted me, and said a farmer
Who wanted bread could pull the plow himself?
It cut me to the heart when he unyoked
And took the splendid oxen from the plow.
They butted with their horns and bellowed low,
As if they had a feeling of injustice.
Then I was overcome with righteous anger,
And losing self-control, I struck the servant.
WALTER FÜRST. If we old men can scarcely hold our peace,
How can these younger men control themselves?.
MELCHTAL. All my concern is for my father now.
He needs my care, and I am far away.
I know the viceroy holds a grudge against him
Because he always fought for right and freedom.
For this they will abuse the poor old man,
With no one there to shield him from mistreatment.
Whatever happens, I must go to him.
WALTER FÜRST. Just wait and try to bide your time in patience
Until some news is brought to us from Kernwald—[12]
Get back! I hear a knocking at the door.
Perhaps the viceroy's messenger has come.
You are not safe from Landenberger's power,
For tyrants give assistance to each other.
MELCHTAL. They're teaching us what we should do.
WALTER FÜRST. Go in.
I'll call you back when it is safe again.
[MELCHTAL *goes in.*]
Poor boy, I do not dare confess to him
What dark suspicions trouble me.
Who's knocking?
Each time I hear a knock, I fear the worst.
Deceit, suspicion lurk on every side.
The messengers of violence intrude
Upon the privacy of homes. It seems
That we must fit our doors with locks and bolts. [*He opens the door and starts back surprised when* WERNER STAUFFACHER *enters.*]
Whom do I see? You, Werner! Well, by heaven!
A dear and honored guest. No better man
Has ever stepped across this threshold yet.
You have a hearty welcome in this house!
What brings you here? What do you seek in Uri?
STAUFFACHER. [*Extending his hand to him.*] The good old times and good old Switzerland.
WALTER FÜRST. That's what you bring with you. It does me good;
The very sight of you can warm my heart.
Sit down, my friend, and tell me how you are,
And how you left your wife, your gracious Gertrud,
Whom all know well as Iberg's prudent daughter.
All wanderers from German lands who go

To Italy by Meinrad's monastery
Sing praises of your hospitable house.
But tell me, did you come here straight from Flüelen,
Or did you take a look at other places
Before you set your foot upon this threshold?
STAUFFACHER. [*Sitting down.*] I did indeed behold a new construction,
Displeasing and astonishing to me.
WALTER FÜRST. Yes, you have seen things clearly at one glance.
STAUFFACHER. It's never been like this in Canton Uri.
We've never heard of any fortresses;
The only stronghold here has been the grave.
WALTER FÜRST. It is a grave of freedom. You have named it.
STAUFFACHER. Herr Fürst, I tell you frankly why I came.
It was not idle curiosity.
No, worry weighs upon me now. I left
Behind oppression, and I find it here.
What we have suffered is intolerable,
And there's no end to all this tyranny.
For centuries we Swiss have prized our freedom,
And we are used to being treated well.
Such things were never known in all this land,
As long as herdsmen drove their herds to pasture.
WALTER FÜRST. What they are doing is without example.
Our noble Lord von Attinghausen, too,
Who saw and still recalls the good old days,
Has said himself that we cannot endure it.
STAUFFACHER. In Unterwalden serious things have happened,
And are repaid in blood. Herr Wolfenschiessen,
The royal bailiff at the Rossberg castle,
Expressed desires for forbidden fruit;
And when he tried to wrong most shamefully
The wife of Baumgarten who lives in Alzellen,
The husband killed the fellow with an ax.
WALTER FÜRST. The judgments of the Lord are always just.
Baumgarten, did you say? A moderate man.
I trust he has been saved and hidden well.
STAUFFACHER. Your son-in-law delivered him from danger.
I'm keeping him in hiding now in Steinen.
And he has told me something still more dreadful
That happened lately near the town of Sarnen.
It makes the heart of any good man bleed.
WALTER FÜRST. [*Attentive.*] Go on and tell me.
STAUFFACHER. Well, there lives in Melchtal,
Just where you enter, coming up from Kerns,
An honest man named Heinrich von der Halden,[13]
Whose voice has weight in his community.
WALTER FÜRST. We know him well. But tell me what has happened.
STAUFFACHER. When Landenberger, for some small offense,
Inflicted punishment upon the son
And ordered that his oxen be unyoked,
The son knocked down the servant and escaped.
WALTER FÜRST. [*In great excitement.*] But tell me now—what happened to the father?
STAUFFACHER. Then Landenberger summoned him and said
That he must bring the son to him at once.
And when the old man truthfully declared
That he knew nothing of the fugitive,
The viceroy had his torturers come in—
WALTER FÜRST. [*Springing forward and trying to take him to the other side.*] Be quiet!
STAUFFACHER. [*With rising voice.*]
"Though your son escaped, I still
Have you!" he said, and had the man held down;
And then they pierced his eyes with sharpened spikes.
WALTER FÜRST. Merciful heaven!
MELCHTAL. [*Running in.*] They pierced his eyes, you say?
STAUFFACHER. [*Astonished, to* WALTER FÜRST.] Who is this man?

MELCHTAL. [*Seizing him with convulsive violence.*] They pierced his eyes? Speak up!
WALTER FÜRST. Oh, pitiable man.
STAUFFACHER. Who is he then? [WALTER FÜRST *signals to him.*] It is the son? Almighty God!
MELCHTAL. And I
Cannot be with him now. And both his eyes?
WALTER FÜRST. Control yourself! Endure it like a man.
MELCHTAL. It's all on my account. The guilt is mine.
He's blind? He's really blind—completely blinded?
STAUFFACHER. It's true. The springs of sight have all run dry.
He'll never see again the sunlight's splendor.
WALTER FÜRST. Oh, spare his heartache!
MELCHTAL. Never see again! [*He presses his hand to his eyes and is silent for a few moments; then he turns from one to the other and speaks in a gentle voice, choking with tears.*]
Our eyesight truly is a precious gift
From heaven above. All creatures on the earth,
All happy living beings, seek the light;
Even the plants turn gladly toward the sun.
But he must sit and grope in endless darkness,
Eternal night, and never be refreshed
By dark green meadows and by gorgeous flowers,
Nor ever see the glaciers' reddish glow.
To die is nothing—but live, and never see!
That's misery. Why do you look at me
So pityingly? I have two seeing eyes
And cannot give them to my blinded father—
No single ray of all this sea of light
That floods into my eyes with blinding brilliance.
STAUFFACHER. And now I must increase your grief still more,
Instead of healing it. He's even more
In need, for they took everything he had.
The viceroy left him nothing but his staff,
To wander blindly now from door to door.
MELCHTAL. The poor old man has nothing but his staff.
They stole it all, and took his eyesight too,
This common prize of even the poorest man.
Don't talk to me of waiting now, or hiding.
Oh, what a wretched coward I have been
That I just thought of *my* security
And not of yours! I let you stay behind,
A hostage in the hands of cruel tyrants.
All cowardly precaution, leave me now!
I'll think of nothing but of bloody vengeance.
I will go home. No one can hold me back!
I'll find the governor among his troopers
And will demand my father's eyes from him.
My life and safety do not matter now,
If I can cool my burning, monstrous pain
And ease it in the lifeblood of this tyrant. [*He starts to leave.*]
WALTER FÜRST. Stay here! What can you do? He lives in Sarnen,
Where he's secure within his lordly castle
And only laughs at all our helpless rage.
MELCHTAL. And if he lived up yonder on the ice
Of Schreckhorn peak, or higher, where the Jungfrau
Is veiled eternally in mist,[14] I'd make
My way to him. With twenty of my friends
Who think as I, I'll crack his fortress open.
And if no one will follow me, if you,
Concerned about your houses and your herds,
Will bend your necks beneath the tyrant's yoke,
I'll call together herdsmen in the mountains
And there, beneath the canopy of heaven,
Where men think clearly and their hearts are sound,
I'll tell them of this great atrocity.
STAUFFACHER. [*To* WATER FÜRST.] It's gone too far. Do we intend to wait

Until the worst—
MELCHTAL. What worst is there to come
That we should fear, when eyes no longer see—
No longer are secure within their sockets?
Are we defenseless then? Why did we learn
To draw the crossbow, swing the battle-ax?
Why, every creature's furnished with a weapon
That he may use in fear and desperation.
The baited stag will show his dreaded antlers
And hold at bay a pack of barking hounds;
The chamois hurls the hunter down the chasm;
The docile and domesticated ox,
That friend of man, who bends his burdened neck
So patiently beneath the yoke, will leap
When he is angered, whet his mighty horns,
And throw his enemy up toward the clouds.
WALTER FÜRST. If all three cantons thought as we three do,
We might be able to accomplish something.
STAUFFACHER. If Uri calls, if Unterwalden helps,
We men of Schwyz will stand by our alliance.
MELCHTAL. In Unterwalden I have many friends.
Each one would gladly risk both life and limb
If others stand by him and give support.
You are the trusted fathers of our country,
And next to you I'm no more than a boy.
Therefore I must in modesty refrain
From speaking at our council of the cantons.
But don't reject my judgment and advice
Because I'm young and inexperienced.
I'm not impelled by hot, impetuous blood,
But by the power of a painful grief
So great that it might move the stones to pity.
You too are heads of families, and fathers,
And you must wish to have a virtuous son
Who wants to honor and respect his father,
To take good care of him and guard his eyes.
Oh, just because you have not suffered harm
In person or in property, because
Your eyes move in their sockets bright and sound,
You must not stand aloof from our distress.
The tyrant's sword hangs over you as well.
You turned the land against the Austrians;
My father's crime was nothing more than that.
You share his guilt; you'll have his punishment.
STAUFFACHER. [*To* WALTER FÜRST.] If you'll decide, then I'm prepared to follow.
WALTER FÜRST. First let us hear the noblemen's advice,
The lords of Sillinen and Attinghausen.
Their influential names will win us friends.
MELCHTAL. Where is a name in all these mountain ranges
More highly held than your name—or than yours?
The people put their trust in names like these;
They stand for honest worth in all the land.
You have a rich inheritance of virtue,
And you've increased this store abundantly.
Why hear the nobles? Let us alone take action.
I think we must rely upon ourselves,
For then we can control our own defense.
STAUFFACHER. The nobles are not pressed so hard as we.
The torrent that is raging in the valleys
Has not engulfed the highlands even now.
But they will not withhold their help from us
Once they have seen the country take

up arms.

WALTER FÜRST. Were there a judge between us and our foe,
Then right and law would govern the decision.
But our oppressor also is our emperor
And highest court. Our God must help us now
Through our own strength. You search out men in Schwyz,
And I will go and rally friends in Uri.
But whom are we to send to Unterwalden?

MELCHTAL. Send me. No one is more concerned than I.

WALTER FÜRST. I cannot let you leave. You are my guest,
And I must answer for your safety now.

MELCHTAL. No, let me go. I know the secret paths
And I have friends enough who'll give me shelter
And gladly hide me from our enemies.

STAUFFACHER. Oh, let him go. There are no traitors there,
For tyranny is so despised and dreaded
That no man will become a tyrant's tool.
And in the lower part of Unterwalden
Baumgarten can win adherents for our cause.

MELCHTAL. But how can we communicate in safety
And not arouse suspicions in the tyrants?

STAUFFACHER. It would be best to meet at Treib or Brunnen,
Where many trading ships go in and out.

WALTER FÜRST. We cannot do our work so openly.
Hear my suggestion. By the western shore,
On our left hand when going down to Brunnen,
Close to the Mythenstein, a meadow lies
Right in the woods; the herdsmen call it Rütli
Because the forest was uprooted here.[15] [*To* MELCHTAL.]
The borders of our cantons meet up there, [*To* STAUFFACHER.]
And in a short and easy passage, too,
A boat can carry you from Canton Schwyz.
We can go there by lonely mountain trails,
And quietly deliberate at night.
Let each of us bring ten well-trusted men
Who are at one with us and with our plans.
This way we can discuss the common cause
And with God's help decide what's to be done.

STAUFFACHER. That's what we'll do. Now let me have your hand,
And Melchtal, give me yours; and as we three
Now join our hands, united in assurance
That we will stand together honestly,
So may our cantons stand together too,
Through life and death for our defense of freedom.

WALTER FÜRST *and* MELCHTAL. Through life and death! [*They hold their hands clasped together in silence for some moments.*]

MELCHTAL. Father, my blinded father!
You cannot see the day of freedom dawn,
But you shall hear it. When from peak to peak
The signal fires send out their flaming message,
And tyrants' castles fall into our hands,
The Swiss will come as pilgrims from these lands
And bring to you the news of freedom won.
Then in your night shall dawn the rising sun.[16] [*They part.*]

Act 2

Scene 1

The castle of BARON VON ATTINGHAUSEN.[17] *A Gothic hall, decorated with coats of arms and helmets. The* BARON, *an old man of eighty-five, tall and noble in stature, leans on a staff tipped with chamois horn, and is dressed in a fur coat.* KUONI *and six other vassals are standing around him with rakes and scythes.* ULRICH VON RUDENZ *enters in a knight's costume.*

RUDENZ. I'm here, Uncle. Tell me what you want.
ATTINGHAUSEN. First let me by our ancient custom share
The morning cup with my good servants here. [*He drinks from a cup which is then passed around.*]
Time was when I could be in field and wood,
Directing them at work with my own eyes,
Just as my banner led them into battle;
But now I only play the overseer,
And if the warming sun won't come to me,
I can no longer seek it on the mountains.
And thus, in small and ever smaller circles,
I'm slowly moving toward the last and smallest,
Where all of life will cease. I'm nothing more
Than my own shadow now; soon just a name.
KUONI. [*Going to* RUDENZ *with the cup.*] I pledge you, sir! [RUDENZ *hesitates to accept the cup.*] Don't hesitate to drink.
One cup, one heart—that is the saying here.
ATTINGHAUSEN. Go, children, and tonight when work is done,
We'll talk about political affairs. [*The vassals leave.*]
ATTINGHAUSEN. [*To* RUDENZ.] I see you armed and dressed as for a journey;
You're on your way to Altdorf to the castle?
RUDENZ. Yes, Uncle, and I cannot linger now.
ATTINGHAUSEN. [*Sitting down.*] In such a hurry? Is your time of youth
So meagerly prescribed and measured out
That you can't spare a moment for your uncle?
RUDENZ. I see my presence is not needed here.
I have become a stranger in this house.
ATTINGHAUSEN. [*After having looked at him intently for some time.*] Indeed you are a stranger here. Your home
Is now a foreign place. Oh, Uli, Uli!
I hardly know you. You strut about in silk,
And wear a peacock feather for display,
And throw a purple cloak around your shoulders;
You look disdainfully upon the peasant
And turn aside, ashamed at cordial greetings.
RUDENZ. I'll gladly show him the respect that's due him,
But I deny the rights that he demands.
ATTINGHAUSEN. Our country suffers from the king's displeasure,[18]
And all good men are troubled in their hearts
At such tyrannical abuse of power
As we must suffer. You alone remain
Unmoved by all our common grief and pain.
You turn away, disloyal to your people,
And stand among our country's enemies,
Scorning our cares and seeking idle pleasures,
Courting the princes' favors, while here at home
Your fatherland lies badly scourged and bleeding.
RUDENZ. The land is much oppressed. But why, my uncle?
Who is it that has plunged it into trouble?
You only need to speak an easy word
To be released at once from all oppression
And gain a gracious emperor as well.
But woe to those who shut the people's eyes
And lead them to oppose the country's welfare.
These men, for their own gain, prevent the cantons
From swearing any Austrian allegiance,
As all around the other lands have done.
It flatters them to sit among the nobles.
They want to call the emperor their lord
In order not to have a lord at all.
ATTINGHAUSEN. Must I hear such a thing—and from your lips?
RUDENZ. You urged me on to speak; then let me finish.
What role is it that you yourself are playing?

Have you no higher pride than to live here
As banneret or village magistrate
And be the ruler of these lowly herdsmen?
Would it not be more laudable a choice
To render homage to our royal lord,
Ally yourself with all his brilliant court,
Than stay at home, the peer of your own vassals,
And play the magistrate among the peasants?
ATTINGHAUSEN. Oh, Uli, Uli! I can see it all;
The tempter's voice has reached your willing ears
And sent a vicious poison to your heart.
RUDENZ. Yes, I will not pretend. My very soul
Is deeply hurt by strangers' taunts and scoffing,
When they refer to us as peasant nobles.
I cannot bear to see all noble youths
Win honors under Hapsburg's royal banners,
While I must stay here on our property
In idleness, day in, day out, and waste
The springtime of my life in common chores.
In other places glorious deeds are done;
A world of fame stirs just beyond these mountains.
My helmet and my shield hang rusting here.
The thrilling sound of martial drums and trumpets,
The herald's call, inviting to the lists,
Will never press into these mountain valleys
Where I can only hear the herdsman's songs,
And cowbells ringing in monotony.
ATTINGHAUSEN. Poor blinded boy, seduced by empty splendor—
Renounce your native land, and be ashamed
Of good and ancient customs of your fathers!
The day will come when you, with bitter tears,
Will yearn for home and for your native mountains.
And then the herdsman's simple melody,
Which fills you now with boredom and contempt,
Will overwhelm your heart with painful longing
When you are hearing it in distant places.
Oh, mighty is the love of fatherland!
The foreign, evil world is not for you,
For at the proud imperial court you'll be
A stranger to yourself and to your heart.
The world demands a different sort of virtue
From that which you've acquired within these valleys.
But go then if you must, and sell your soul;
Take land in fief and be a prince's vassal
When you could be a ruler and a prince
Upon your own inheritance and soil.
Oh, Uli, Uli! Stay among your people
And do not go to Altdorf. Don't forsake
The sacred causes of your fatherland.
I am the last one of my line. My name
Will end with me. There hang my shield and helmet;
They will be put beside me in the grave.[19]
And must I think, when breathing out my life,
That you are only waiting for my death
To go in haste before the feudal court,
And as a fief receive from Austria
The noble lands that I received from God?
RUDENZ. It's useless to resist the kaiser's will.
The world belongs to him. Will we alone
Be stubborn and persist in our attempt
To break the mighty chain of his possessions
That he has powerfully drawn around us?
The courts of law are his. So are the markets.
The highways too are his, and every pack horse
That crosses the St. Gotthard pass is taxed.
We are entangled as within a net,

Encircled by his spreading lands and
  power.
And will the Empire shield us? Can it
  even
Defend itself against the Austrians?
If God will not, no emperor can help
  us.
How can we trust in any emperor's
  word
If he, when pressed for money or the
  needs
Of war, may pawn or even sell the
  towns
That went for refuge to his royal ea-
  gle?[20]
No, Uncle, it is wisdom and precaution,
In days of great dissension and disor-
  der,
To be allied with such a mighty leader.
The emperor's crown will pass from
  house to house—
It has no memory of faithful service.
But gaining favor of hereditary
Lords is sowing seed for future harvest.
ATTINGHAUSEN. Are you so wise? And
  do you claim to see
More clearly than your noble sires, who
  fought
With life and fortune for the gem of
  freedom?
Sail to Lucerne and ask the people
  there
How Austrian rulers weigh the cantons
  down!
Soon they will come and count our
  sheep and cattle,
And measure off and tax our mountain
  pastures.
They'll take the hunting rights for all
  the game
In our own woods, and place the toll-
  gate barrier
Across our bridges and beside our
  gates,
Impoverish us to purchase more pos-
  sessions
And fight their battles with our life and
  blood.
If we must shed our blood, then let it
  be
For our own cause. Then we will buy
  our freedom
Far cheaper than their bondage.
RUDENZ. What can we do,
A tribe of herdsmen, against the hosts
  of Albrecht?

ATTINGHAUSEN. First learn to know this
  tribe of herdsmen, boy.
I know my people well. I led them on
In battles, and I saw them take Faenza.
Just let the Austrians try to force on us
A yoke we are determined not to bear!
Oh, learn to see what is your heritage.
Don't throw away the pearl of your
  own value
In vain exchange for worthless show
  and glitter.
To be the leader of a freeborn people,
Who give you their devotion out of
  love,
Whose loyalty will stand through life
  and death—
Take pride in that. Boast that nobility.
Tie fast the native bonds and cling to
  them.
Hold firm and true to your dear fa-
  therland
And cherish it with all your heart and
  soul.
The sturdy roots of all your strength
  are here.
Out in the foreign world you'll stand
  alone,
A swaying reed that any storm can
  break.
Come now, you have not seen us for so
  long,
Just try to spend one day with us. Don't
  go
To Altdorf, Uli. Hear? Don't go today.
Just give yourself, today, to your own
  people. [*He takes his hand.*]
RUDENZ. I gave my word; I'm bound.
  Leave me alone.
ATTINGHAUSEN. [*Releasing his hand,
  speaking earnestly.*] Yes, you are surely
  bound, unlucky boy.
You're bound indeed, but not by word
  and oath;
You're tied securely by the bonds of
  love. [RUDENZ *turns away.*]
Conceal it as you will, it is the Lady
Berta von Bruneck who draws you to
  the court
And chains you to the emperor and his
  service.
You think that you can win the noble
  lady
By leaving us. Do not deceive yourself.
She's held before you as a lure and
  snare,
But she's not destined for your inno-

cence.
RUDENZ. Enough! I've heard enough. I'm going now. [*Exit.*]
ATTINGHAUSEN. Stay here, my foolish boy! Well, he is gone.
I could not hold him back. I could not save him.
In this same way the bailiff Wolfenschiessen
Deserted us, and others will desert.
The foreign charm that's come into our mountains
Will draw away our youth with its allurements.
Oh, hour of grief, when strange and novel ways
Descended on our calm and happy valleys
And overturned our simple mode of life.
The new is sweeping in relentlessly;
The old gives way, and other times are coming.
Another race and other thoughts prevail.
Why am I here? They all are dead and buried,
With whom I lived and labored here so long.
My time is also buried. Fortunate
Is he who need not live to see the new. [*Exit.*]

Scene 2

A meadow surrounded by high cliffs and woods. On the cliffs are paths with railings and ladders by which the countrymen later are seen descending. In the background appears the lake, over which a moon rainbow is seen as the scene begins. The view is closed by lofty mountains, behind which ice-covered peaks tower still higher. The scene is dark, but the lake and the white glaciers gleam in the moonlight.[21] MELCHTAL, BAUMGARTEN, WINKELRIED, MEIER VON SARNEN, BURKHARD AM BÜHEL, ARNOLD VON SEWA, KLAUS VON DER FLÜE, *and four other countrymen are arriving; all are armed.*

MELCHTAL. [*Offstage.*] The pathway widens; quickly, follow me.
I know the mountain and the cross marked on it.
We've reached our goal. Here is the Rütli. [*They enter with torches.*]
WINKELRIED. Listen!
SEWA. All clear.
MEIER. There's no one here as yet. We men
Of Unterwalden are the first to come.
MELCHTAL. How late is it?
BAUMGARTEN. The watchman called out two
Just now, up in the town of Selisberg. [*The ringing of a bell is heard in the distance.*]
MEIER. Be still!
AM BÜHEL. Across the lake in Schwyz the bells
Ring out for matins in the forest chapel.
VON DER FLÜE. The air is pure and bears the sound across.
MELCHTAL. Go gather brushwood, men, and light a fire,
That it may brightly burn to greet the others. [*Two countrymen exit.*]
SEWA. It is a fair and glorious moonlit night.
The lake is calm and smooth, just like a mirror.
AM BÜHEL. They'll have an easy crossing now.
WINKELRIED. [*Pointing at the lake.*] But look!
Just look there! Don't you see it?
MEIER. What? Why, yes!
A rainbow in the middle of the night!
MELCHTAL. It is the moonlight that created it.
VON DER FLÜE. This is a wonderful and curious sign.
There're many men who never saw the like.
SEWA. It's double. Look, a paler one above it.
BAUMGARTEN. I see a boat that's passing right beneath it.
MELCHTAL. That must be Stauffacher and men from Schwyz.
He's prompt and doesn't make us wait for him. [*He goes with* BAUMGARTEN *to the shore.*]
MEIER. The men from Uri are the slowest ones.
AM BÜHEL. They have to take a longer mountain path
In order to elude the viceroy's spies.
[*Meanwhile two countrymen have kindled*

a fire in the middle of the site.]
MELCHTAL. [*On the shore.*] Who's there? Give us the word!
STAUFFACHER. [*From below.*] Friends of our country. [*All go upstage toward the newcomers.* STAUFFACHER, ITEL REDING, HANS AUF DER MAUER, JÖRG IM HOFE, KONRAD HUNN, ULRICH DER SCHMIED, JOST VON WEILER *and three other countrymen, all armed, come out of the boat.*]
ALL. [*Crying out.*] We welcome you!
[*While the others remain at the rear of the stage and exchange greetings,* MELCHTAL *and* STAUFFACHER *come forward*]
MELCHTAL. My friend, I saw my father.
I saw the one who could not look at me.
I placed my hand upon his blinded eyes
And drew a burning impulse for revenge
From the extinguished sunlight of his face.
STAUFFACHER. Don't speak of vengeance. Don't avenge the past.
We want to fight the threat of future evil.
But tell me what you did in Unterwalden;
Say how you won adherents for our cause,
And what the people think, how you yourself
Escaped the snares of those who would betray you.
MELCHTAL. Across Surennen pass, through fearful mountains,
And over vast and lonely fields of ice
Where only hungry birds of prey were croaking,
I reached the Alpine pastures, where the herdsmen
From Canton Uri and from Engelberg
Shout friendly greetings and graze their herds together.
And as I went along I quenched my thirst
With glacier water flowing in the gullies,
Found lodging in the solitary huts,
Where I was host and guest alike, until
I came again to hospitable houses.
Reports of the atrocity had spread
By then among all people in the valleys,
And my misfortune gained respect for me
At every door to which I went and knocked.
I found those good and honest men enraged
About the tyranny of this regime.
Just as their pastures grow the selfsame plants
From year to year, and all their springs are flowing
Steadily, and even winds and clouds
Move in familiar paths across the sky,
So have the ancient customs stood unchanged
From generation unto generation.
These people will not bear rash innovation
In the accustomed pattern of their lives.
They gave me willingly their hardened hands,
And from the walls took down their rusty swords;
And in their eyes there shone a joyous courage
When I spoke out your name and Walter Fürst's,
Which are esteemed by every countryman.
They vowed to do whatever you might think
Was right and best, and swore to stand by you
And faithfully to follow you till death.
I hurried on from farm to farm, protected
By sacred laws of hospitality.
And when I came into my native valley,
Where I have many kinsmen living near,
And when I found my father, robbed and blind,
Compelled to live in strangers' homes, dependent
On others' charity—
STAUFFACHER. Merciful God!
MELCHTAL. I did not cry at all. I did not waste
The strength of burning grief in useless tears;
I kept it as a treasure, deep and sure
Within my heart, and set my mind on action.
I wandered through the winding mountain paths
And searched out every isolated valley;
Up to the icy edges of the glaciers
I looked for men and found them in their huts.

And in each place to which I came I
  found
The selfsame hatred of all tyranny;
For even to the highest boundaries
Of vegetation, where the frozen soil
Refuses growth, the viceroy's greed has
  reached.
I stirred the spirits of these honest
  men,
Aroused them with my fiery, stinging
  words,
And they are on our side with all their
  hearts.
STAUFFACHER. You have accomplished
  much in this short time.
MELCHTAL. That isn't all. The country
  people fear
The Rossberg and the Sarnen for-
  tresses;
Secure behind their walls of stone, our
  foe
Finds safety while he ravages the land.
With my own eyes I wanted to inspect
  them.
I went to Sarnen and surveyed the
  castle.
STAUFFACHER. You dared to go into the
  tiger's cave?
MELCHTAL. I went there well disguised
  in pilgrim's dress;
Now judge yourself, do I have self-
  control?
I saw the viceroy revel at a feast.
I saw our foe and did not murder him.
STAUFFACHER. You surely had good luck
  in all your boldness. [*Meanwhile the
  other countrymen have come forward, and
  they join the two.*]
But tell me now, who are these friends
  of yours,
These good and loyal men who fol-
  lowed you?
Let us be introduced, that we may
  speak
With open hearts in trust and con-
  fidence.
MEIER. Who doesn't know you, sir, in all
  these lands?
My name is Meier von Sarnen, and this
  man is
My sister's son, named Struth von
  Winkelried.
STAUFFACHER. That is no unfamiliar
  name to me.
It was a Winkelried who killed the
  dragon
Beside the Weiler swamp, and lost his
  life
In that great fight.
WINKELRIED. He was my grandfather.
MELCHTAL. [*Pointing at two countrymen.*]
  These two are workmen from the
  monastery
Of Engelberg. I hope you'll not reject
  them
Because they're only bondsmen and
  can't live
As free men on their own inheritance.
They love the land, and everyone re-
  spects them.
STAUFFACHER. [*To the two men.*] Give me
  your hands. Let him who is not
  bound
Consider it good fortune for himself;
But honesty may thrive in any class.
KONRAD HUNN. This is Herr Reding,
  our former magistrate.
MEIER. I know him well. In court he's
  my opponent
In legal action for a piece of land.
Herr Reding, we are enemies in court,
But here we are agreed. [*He shakes*
  REDING's *hand.*]
STAUFFACHER. That's nobly said.
WINKELRIED. They're coming! Listen to
  the horn of Uri! [*To the right and left,
  armed men are seen climbing down the
  cliffs with torches.*[
AUF DER MAUER. I see the reverend min-
  ister himself
Climb down the cliff with them. He
  spares no hardship
And has no terror of the trip by night,
A faithful shepherd caring for his peo-
  ple.
BAUMGARTEN. I see the sacristan and
  Walter Fürst,
But I do not find Tell among the party.
[WALTER FÜRST, RÖSSELMANN *the pastor,* PETERMANN *the sacristan,* KUONI *the
  herdsman,* WERNI *the hunter,* RUODI *the
  fisherman, and five other countrymen enter. The whole group of men, thirty-three
  in all, come forward and take their places
  around the fire.*]
WALTER FÜRST. In secret we must meet
  on our own soil,
Which we obtained in freedom from
  our fathers,
Convening furtively like murderers
At night, when darkness lends its cloak
  to crimes

And to conspirators who fear the light.
Thus must we seek out justice for ourselves—
A thing that is as pure and bright and fair
As is the radiance of the light by day.
MELCHTAL. What's plotted in the darkness of the night
Shall joyfully and freely come to light.
RÖSSELMANN. Now hear, confederates, what God reveals.
We're meeting here instead of in assembly,
And we can rightly represent the people.
So let us then hold session as is proper,
As we have always done in peaceful days;
And though the meeting is not strictly legal,
These troubled times will surely sanction it.[22]
For God is surely there where justice rules,
And we're assembled underneath his heaven.
STAUFFACHER. Yes, let us hold our meeting by old custom.
Though it is night, our rights are clear as day.
MELCHTAL. And if we're few, the hearts of all our people
Are with us here; the leaders are assembled.
KONRAD HUNN. Although we do not have our ancient books,
Their words have been engraved upon our hearts.
RÖSSELMANN. All right, let's form our circle, and in it plant
Our swords as symbols of authority.
AUF DER MAUER. Now let our magistrate sit in his place,
With his two bailiffs standing at his side.
SACRISTAN. There are three cantons represented here.
To whom belongs the honor of presiding?
MEIER. Let Schwyz contest with Uri for this honor.
We men from Unterwalden yield to you.
MELCHTAL. Yes, we will yield. We are the suppliants
Who're seeking help from you, our mighty friends.
STAUFFACHER. Then let the men from Uri take the sword;
Their banner led us when we went to Rome.[23]
WALTER FÜRST. The honor of the sword should go to Schwyz,
For we are all descendants of that race.[24]
RÖSSELMANN. May I resolve the friendly competition?
In council Schwyz will lead; in battle, Uri.
WALTER FÜRST. [*Handing the swords to* STAUFFACHER.] Here, take them.
STAUFFACHER. No, to older men this honor.
IM HOFE. Ulrich der Schmied is oldest of us all.
AUF DER MAUER. He's brave indeed, but not a freeborn man.
A serf can't be a judge in Canton Schwyz.
STAUFFACHER. But here's Herr Reding, our former magistrate.
Where could we find a more respected man?
WALTER FÜRST. Let him be magistrate and chairman here.
If you agree to this, raise up your hands. [*All raise their right hands.*]
REDING. [*Stepping to the center.*] I cannot take my oath upon the books,
So I will swear by all the stars above
That I will never turn aside from justice. [*Two swords are set up before him. The circle is formed around him, Schwyz in the center, Uri to the right, and Unterwalden to the left. He stands leaning on his battle sword.*]
What is it that has brought the people here
From all these mountain cantons to assemble
At midnight on inhospitable shores?
What shall the purpose be of our new union
That we establish here beneath the stars?
STAUFFACHER. [*Stepping into the circle.*] The union we establish is not new.
It is our fathers' ancient covenant
We now confirm. Mark well, confederates,
Although the lake, although the mountains part us,

And every canton rules itself at home,
We're all one tribe and race, we're all one blood,
And all descendants of a common homeland.
WINKELRIED. Then it is true, as we have heard in songs,
Our fathers came from far into this land?
Please tell us everything you know, so that
The old alliance makes the new one stronger.
STAUFFACHER. Then hear the tale the herdsmen tell each other.
There dwelt a mighty people in the north,
But they were struck by famine and hard times.
In this distress, the people's council voted
That of the citizens one-tenth must leave
As chosen by the lot. And this was done.
The men and women left with lamentation,
A mighty host of people going south,
And fought their way across the German lands
Up to the highlands of these forest mountains.
The great migration did not stop or tire
Until they came into the lonely valley
Where now the Muotta flows across the meadows.
Here they could see no trace of human life
Except a hut that stood beside the lake.
There sat a man who tended an old ferry.[25]
But since the surging lake could not be crossed,
They looked around, surveyed the pleasant land,
And saw there an abundance of fine timber;
Soon they discovered springs that flowed good water.
So they were satisfied and felt at home,
And they resolved to settle in that place.
They founded there the ancient town of Schwyz,
And many days were filled with bitter struggles
As they dug out entangled roots of forests.
And when the soil no longer could support
The many people living there, they moved
On farther to the forest-covered mountains,
And reached the fields of snow, beyond whose walls
Another people speak another language.
They built the town of Stanz beside the Kernwald,
And Altdorf in the valley of the Reuss.
But always they remembered their beginnings.
From all the foreign tribes who later settled
Inside their borders and within their midst,[26]
The men of Schwyz can recognize each other;
Their hearts, their blood, will make themselves be known. [*He stretches out his hands to the right and left.*]
AUF DER MAUER. Yes, we are one in heart and one in blood!
ALL. [*Clasping each other's hands.*] Yes, one we are, and we shall act together.
STAUFFACHER. The other nations bear a foreign yoke
Because they yielded to the conqueror,
And even some within our country's borders
Are serfs who still bear foreign obligations.
Their bondage is transmitted to their children.
But we, who are the true and ancient Swiss,
Have always treasured and preserved our freedom.
We did not bend our knees before the princes;
We freely chose the emperor's protection.
RÖSSELMANN. We freely chose the Empire's shield and shelter;
It's written so in Emperor Frederick's grant.
STAUFFACHER. For even free men have an overlord.
There must be government, a highest judge,

To render justice when there are disputes;
And in their lands, which they had wrested from
The wilderness, our fathers gladly gave
This honor to the emperor, who's called
The lord of Germany and Italy.
And like the other free men of his realm
They pledged themselves to military service,
For this must be the freeman's only duty:
To shield the realm that is his own defense.
MELCHTAL. And anything beyond would mark the slave.
STAUFFACHER. And when the army summons came, they joined
The royal banners and fought the kingdom's wars.
They went along to Italy in armor
To place the Roman crown upon his head.
But they were free to rule themsleves at home
According to their laws and ancient customs;
The kaiser's only right was penal justice.
For this he named some great and noble count
Whose residence was in another land.
When murder cases came, they called him in,
And under clear and open skies he stood
And fearlessly he spoke his rightful verdict.
What traces do you find of serfdom here?
If any of you disagrees, speak out.
IM HOFE. No. Everything is just as you have said.
We never tolerated despotism.
STAUFFACHER. And we refused obedience to the kaiser
When he abused our rights to help the priests.
For when Einsiedeln monastery's men
Laid claim to pastures that belonged to us,
Which we had used for grazing many years,
And when the abbot then produced a letter
That gave the unclaimed wilderness to him
(For our existence there had been suppressed),
We said, "That letter was obtained by fraud!
No emperor can give away what's ours;
And if we get no justice in the Empire,
We'll do without the Empire in our mountains."
Thus spoke our fathers then. How can we now
Endure the shamefulness of this new yoke
And tolerate from foreign underlings
The things that emperors don't dare to do?
This soil we have created for ourselves
By our own hands and by our diligence.
The woods that were the wild abode of bears
We have transformed for human habitation;
We drained the swamps to kill the dragon's brood
That sent out pestilence and noxious vapors;[27]
We tore apart the shroud of mist that hung
In constant gray about this wilderness;
We broke the rock, and for the wanderer
We built a sturdy bridge across the gorge.
This soil is ours by a thousand years' possession.
And shall some foreign lord, himself a vassal,
Now dare us to come and fasten us in chains
And put us to disgrace on our own soil?
Is there no help against such harsh oppression? [*There is a great commotion among the countrymen.*]
There must be limits to such tyranny:
When the oppressed can find no justice here,
And when his burdens grow unbearable,
He'll reach with confidence right up to heaven
And draw from there his everlasting rights,

Which still abide on high, inalienable
And indestructible as are the stars.
The ancient state of nature now returns,
When man stands face to face with hostile man;
And as a last resort, when nothing else
Avails, he has his sword to draw in battle.
It is our dearest treasures we defend
Against oppression. We'll stand for our own land,
We'll stand for our own homes, our wives and children.
ALL. [*Clashing their swords.*] We'll stand for our own homes, our wives and children.
RÖSSELMANN. [*Stepping into the circle.*] Before you draw the sword, consider well
That you might make a peaceful compromise.
It costs you but one word, and soon the tyrants,
Who now oppress, will coax and flatter you.
Accept what they have often offered you;
Renounce the Empire, swear to Austria.
AUF DER MAUER. What are you saying? Swear to Austria!
AM BÜHEL. Don't listen, men!
WINKELRIED. A traitor counsels this, Our country's foe!
REDING. Be still, confederates!
SEWA. Give homage in disgrace to Austria?
VON DER FLÜE. Let them extort from us by violence
What we denied to kindness?
MEIER. Then we'd be,
And would deserve to be, no more than slaves.
AUF DER MAUER. Let us expel from rights in Switzerland
Whoever wants to yield to Austria.
I stand on this and I demand it, chairman.
Let it become the first new law we make.
MELCHTAL. So be it, then. Whoever speaks of yielding
To Austria shall lose his rights and honor.
And let no man receive him in his home.
ALL. [*Raising their right hands.*] Agreed. Let this be law.
REDING [*After a pause.*] It is the law.
RÖSSELMANN. Now you are free; by this new law you're free.
The Austrians shall not extort by force
What they did not obtain by friendly means.
JOST VON WEILER. Proceed with business now.
REDING. Confederates,
Has every gentle means been sought and tried?
Perhaps the emperor has never known,
Perhaps it's not his will that we should suffer.
We must attempt this last resort as well,
And lay our grievances before his throne
Before we take up swords. For horrible
Is violence, although the cause is just.
God only helps when men can help no more.
STAUFFACHER. [*To* KONRAD HUNN.] Now you must speak and give us your report.
KONRAD HUNN. I was in Rheinfeld at the kaiser's palace
To lodge complaints against the viceroys' acts
And claim our covenant of ancient freedom,
Which every king confirmed when he took office.
I found the envoys there from many cities,
From Swabia and lands along the Rhine;
They all received the charters they requested,
And they returned well pleased to their own lands.
But they sent me, your envoy, to advisers,
Who sent me on with empty consolations.
They said the kaiser had no time right now;
Another day he might consider us.
And as I walked in sadness through the halls,
I saw Duke John of Swabia stand weeping
Beside a balcony, and round him stood
The noble lords of Wart and Tegerfeld,

Who called to me and said: "Defend yourselves!
You'll get no justice from the emperor.
Does he not rob his own dear brother's child,
Withhold from him his just inheritance?
The duke is asking for his mother's share;
His plea is that he is of age and now
It's time for him to rule his land and people.
What answer did he get? The kaiser placed
A wreath on him—'to ornament his youth.'"
AUF DER MAUER. You've heard it now. Do not expect the kaiser
To grant us rights. We must defend ourselves.
REDING. We have no other course. Now let us plan
A strategy by which we might succeed.
WALTER FÜRST. [*Stepping into the circle.*]
We want to drive away despised oppression,
And thus preserve the ancient rights and freedom
That were our fathers' legacy to us,
But we'll not reach for new things unrestrained.
We'll render unto Caesar what is Caesar's.
Who has a lord should render faithful service.
MEIER. I hold my land in fief from Austria.
WALTER FÜRST. Continue to discharge your feudal duties.
JOST VON WEILER. I pay my dues to the lords of Rappersweil.
WALTER FÜRST. Continue to remit your tithes and taxes.
RÖSSELMANN. I am a vassal of Our Lady of Zurich.
WALTER FÜRST. Then render to the cloister what's the cloister's.
STAUFFACHER. I hold my land directly from the Empire.
WALTER FÜRST. We'll do what must be done, but nothing more!
We'll drive away the viceroys and their soldiers,
Attack the fortresses and break them down;
But if it's possible, let's shed no blood.
The king shall see that only through compulsion
Do we cast off our sacred duties to him.
And if he sees us act with due restraint,
Perhaps he'll wisely overcome his anger;
For any nation gains a just respect
If it restrains itself with sword in hand.
REDING. But let us hear. How shall we manage it?
Our enemy has weapons in his hand,
And surely he will never yield in peace.
STAUFFACHER. He will when he has seen us with our weapons.
We'll take him by surprise before he's ready.
MEIER. That is far easier said than it is done.
Two mighty fortresses stand in our country;
They'll shield our enemy and threaten us
If ever royal troops invade our country.
Rossberg and Sarnen castles must be taken
Before we draw the sword in our three cantons.
STAUFFACHER. If you delay that long, our foe is warned.
There are too many men who share our secret.
MEIER. There are no traitors in these forest cantons.
RÖSSELMANN. Our very zeal, though good, can well betray us.
WALTER FÜRST. If we delay, the Uri fortress will
Be finished and the governor secure.
MEIER. You're thinking of yourselves.
SACRISTAN. And *you're* unjust.
MEIER. [*Starting up.*] Unjust? Can Uri men say that to us?
REDING. Be quiet, by your oath.
MEIER. All right, if Schwyz
Agrees with Uri, we must indeed be silent.
REDING. I must reproach you in the assembly's name,
For you disturb our peace with words of anger.
Don't we all stand united for one cause?
WINDELRIED. Let us postpone it until Christmas time,
When, by our custom, all the serfs will come

To Sarnen castle to bring the viceroy gifts;
Then ten or twelve of our confederates
Can meet without suspicion in the castle.
They'll take along some spearheads secretly,
Which they can quickly fasten to their staffs,
For no one gets into the castle armed.
A larger troop will wait in nearby woods;
Then, when the men inside have seized the gates,
They'll blow a horn to signal for the charge,
And those in ambush will attack in force.
The castle will be ours with little effort.
MELCHTAL. I'll undertake to climb up Rossberg's walls.
One of the castle maids is fond of me,
And I'll persuade her easily to lower
A light rope ladder for a nighttime visit.
And once I'm in, I'll pull my friends up too.
REDING. Is it your will that we should put it off? [*The majority raise their hands.*]
STAUFFACHER. [*Counting the votes.*] A count of twenty for, and twelve against!
WALTER FÜRST. And when the castles fall as we have planned,
We'll send our signals out with smoke and fire
From mountaintop to mountaintop. The call
To arms will be proclaimed in every town.
And when the governors have seen us armed,
Believe me, they will gladly quit the fight
And readily accept a peaceful escort
In order to escape beyond our borders.
STAUFFACHER. But I'm afraid that Gessler will resist us.
He is protected by his dreaded troopers;
He will not yield without first shedding blood.
Although he's driven out, he'll threaten us.
It's rash and almost dangerous to spare him.
BAUMGARTEN. Wherever it is dangerous, send *me!*
I owe my life to Tell—he rescued me—
And I will risk it gladly for my country.
Thus I appease my heart and guard my honor.
REDING. With time comes wisdom. We must wait in patience.
Some things are best decided at the moment.
But look, while we are meeting here by night,
The morning dawns upon the highest mountains
And sets its beacon lights above. Let's leave
Before the light of day surprises us.
WALTER FÜRST. Don't fear. The night leaves slowly from the valleys. [*All have removed their hats and are watching the breaking of dawn in quiet meditation.*]
RÖSSELMANN. By this new light that greets us first, before
All other people living far below
Where they must breathe the stale air of the towns,
Let us now swear the oath of our new union.
We want to be a nation of true brothers,
And stand as one in danger and distress. [*They all repeat his words with three fingers raised.*]
We will be free, just as our fathers were,
And we will die before we'll live as slaves. [*They all repeat as before.*]
We want to place our trust in God most high,
And never fear the might of mortal man. [*They all repeat again and embrace each other.*]
STAUFFACHER. Now let each man go calmly on his way
To his own friends and his community.
Whoever is a herdsman, tend your herds
And quietly win friends for our new union.
Endure what you must suffer until then,
And let the tyrants' debts to us increase
Until the day of reckoning is here,
And they must pay those debts to each and all.

Let everyone restrain his righteous
  rage
And hold his vengeance back, to serve
  the whole;
For if one man thinks only of himself,
He robs our common welfare and our
  goal. [*As they go away in three different
  directions in profound silence, the orchestra strikes up a splendid flourish. The
  empty stage remains open for a while and
  shows the spectacle of the sun rising above
  the glaciers.*]

Act 3

Scene 1

The yard in front of TELL's *house.*[28] TELL *is
busy with his ax, and* HEDWIG, *his wife,
is engaged in housework.* WALTER *and*
WILHELM *are playing with a small
crossbow in the background.*

WALTER. [*Singing.*] With his bow and
  arrow
Over hill and vale
Strides the fearless hunter
Early on the trail.

As the soaring eagle
Rules his wide domain,
So among the mountains
Does the hunter reign.

His is all the vastness
Where his arrows strike;
His is all the quarry,
Bird and beast alike.[29]
[*He comes running.*] My string is broken.
  Fix it for me, Father.
TELL. Not I. A real hunter helps him-
  self. [*The boys withdraw.*]
HEDWIG. The boys are starting young to
  take up shooting.
TELL. This early practice makes for
  mastery.
HEDWIG. I wish to God they wouldn't
  learn at all.
TELL. They should learn everything,
  and learn it well.
Whoever wants to make his way
  through life
Must be prepared.
HEDWIG. And neither one will be
  Content to stay at home.
TELL. I can't be either.
I was not born to be a herdsman, Hed-
  wig;
I always have to chase some fleeting
  goal,
And only can enjoy my life completely
When I must work to win it every
  day.[30]
HEDWIG. But you are not concerned
  about my fears—
How I may worry, waiting here for
  you;
For I am terrified at what they tell
About your daring trips and risky ven-
  tures.
At each farewell my trembling heart is
  sure
That you will not come back to me
  again.
I see you lost in wild and icy moun-
  tains,
Or failing in your leap from crag to
  crag;
I see the frightened chamois jumping
  back
To drag you down with him into the
  gorge;
I see you buried by an avalanche;
I see the glacier's treacherous abyss
Split under you, and see you falling
  down,
Interred alive in such a dreadful grave!
For death, in a hundred changing
  forms, pursues
And snatches at the daring Alpine
  hunter.
Yours is indeed a miserable calling
That takes you to the very brink of
  death.
TELL. Whoever looks around with open
  eyes
And trusts in God and his own ready
  strength
Can keep himself from danger and
  distress.
He fears no mountains who was born
  among them. [*He has finished his work
  and lays aside his tools.*]
I think that gate will last a good long
  time.
An ax at home will save the carpenter.
  [*He takes his hat.*]

HEDWIG. Where are you going?
TELL. To Altdorf, to your father.
HEDWIG. You're up to something dangerous. What is it?
TELL. What gave you such a thought?
HEDWIG. I hear of plots
Against the governors. There was a meeting
Held at the Rütli. You were at it too.
TELL. I wasn't there; but when my country calls,
I'll not hold back, or hesitate to serve.
HEDWIG. They'll put you where the danger is the greatest.
Your task will be the hardest one, as always.
TELL. We'll all be taxed according to our talents.
HEDWIG. There was that Underwalden man you took
Across the lake—it was a miracle
That you escaped. And did you never think
Of wife and children then?
TELL. I thought of you.
That's why I saved that father for his children.
HEDWIG. To venture out on such tempestuous seas—
I call that tempting God, not trusting him.
TELL. Who thinks too long will not accomplish much.
HEDWIG. You're kind and friendly, helping everyone,
But there'll be none to help when you're in trouble.
TELL. God grant that I may never need their help. [*He takes up his crossbow and arrows.*]
HEDWIG. Why do you take your bow? Just leave it here.
TELL. My arm is missing when I am without it. [*The boys return.*]
WALTER. Where are you going, Father?
TELL. To Altdorf, Son,
To Granddad. Do you want to come?
WALTER. Of course!
HEDWIG. The governor is there. Don't go to Altdorf.
TELL. He'll leave today.
HEDWIG. Then wait until he's gone.
He bears a grudge against us; don't remind him.
TELL. His malice isn't apt to injure me.
I do what's right and fear no enemy.
HEDWIG. Those who do right are just the men he hates.
TELL. Because he cannot touch them. So I think
This knight will surely let me go in peace.
HEDWIG. Are you so sure of that?
TELL. Not long ago
I was out hunting in the wild ravines
Of Schächen Valley, on deserted trails.
A precipice rose high and steep above me,
While down below the Schächen River roared.
And as I walked alone upon a ledge
Too narrow for a man to step aside,
[*The boys press close on his right and left and look up at him with eager curiosity.*]
There coming toward me was the governor,
Alone as I, and thus we faced each other,
Just man to man, with the abyss below.
And when his lordship found me there before him,
And recognized me as the man he'd punished
Severely for slight cause not long before,
And when he saw me with my stately weapon
Come striding up to him, his face turned pale,
His knees gave way, and I began to think
That he would fall unconscious down the cliff.
I pitied him, so I stepped up to him
And just said modestly, "It's I, your Lordship."
But he could never bring a single word
To pass his lips, and so he raised his hand
And dumbly motioned me to go away.
Then I went on and sent him his attendants.
HEDWIG. He trembled there before you; that is bad.
He'll not forgive you that you saw him weak.
TELL. I shun him now, and he won't look for me.
HEDWIG. Then stay away from there today; go hunting.
TELL. What has come over you?
HEDWIG. I am afraid.

TELL. How can you be so worried without reason?
HEDWIG. Because I have no reason. Tell, stay here!
TELL. I gave my word that I'd be there today.
HEDWIG. Well, if you must, then go—but leave the boy.
WALTER. No, Mother, I'm going along with Father.
HEDWIG. But Walter, surely you won't leave your mother.
WALTER. I'll bring you something pretty back from Granddad. [*He leaves with his father.*]
WILHELM. See, Mother, I will stay with you.
HEDWIG [*Embracing him.*] You are
My precious child, and you are all I have. [*She goes to the yard gate and looks with anxious eyes after the two who are leaving.*]

Scene 2

A forest surrounded by cliffs, from which water falls in fine spray.[31] BERTA *enters in hunting dress,* RUDENZ *following her.*
BERTA. He's following me. Here is my chance to speak.
RUDENZ. [*Enters hurriedly.*] At last, my lady, we are all alone,
Surrounded by a precipice of stone.
No one can hear us in this wilderness.
I'll break this endless silence, and profess—
BERTA. But are you sure the hunt won't follow us?[32]
RUDENZ. The hunting party went in that direction.
It's now or never; I must use this moment.
I want to hear my fate decided now,
Though it should mean that I must give you up.
But do not fortify your gentle eyes
With such a stern expression! Who am I
To look at you with bold and hopeful thoughts?
I have achieved no fame; I cannot yet
Be numbered with the noble knights who come,
Renowned in victory, to pay you court,
While I bring only love and loyalty.
BERTA. [*Earnestly and with severity.*] How can you speak of love and loyalty—
You who are faithless in your closest duties? [RUDENZ *steps back.*]
The slave of Austria, who sells himself
To foreigners, oppressors of his people?
RUDENZ. From you, my lady, must I hear this censure?
Whom was I seeking on that side but you?
BERTA. You thought to find me on the side of treason?
No, I would rather give my hand to Gessler,
The tyrant and oppressor of our land,
Than to a son of Switzerland who turns
A renegade and is the tyrant's tool.
RUDENZ. Oh God, what must I hear?
BERTA. Just tell me then,
What's closer to a man than his own people?
What finer duties for a noble heart
Than the protection of the innocent
And the defense of those who are oppressed?
My heart is bleeding for your patient people;
I suffer with them, for I've come to love them
Because they are so modest in their strength.
My mind and soul are drawn to them completely,
And every day I must esteem them higher.
But you, whom nature and your knightly duties
Have marked to be their natural defender,
You who forsake them, join the enemy
And forge the fetters for your native land—
It's you who hurt and grieve me, and I must
Restrain my heart to keep from hating you.
RUDENZ. Am I not thinking of my people's welfare?
Beneath the scepter of the Austrians
There's peace—
BERTA. What you prepare for them is serfdom.
You'd drive out freedom from the final stronghold
That's left to it on earth. The people

know
Much better where their true advantage lies;
They're not misled by false appearance.
But you've been caught; you're taken in the net.
RUDENZ. You surely hate me, Berta. You despise me.
BERTA. I wish I could; that would be better. But now—
To see the one I'd like to love despised,
To see him worthy of contempt—
RUDENZ. Oh, Berta!
You let me catch a glimpse of heavenly bliss
And that same moment fling me down the abyss.
BERTA. Your noble qualities are not yet stifled;
They are asleep. I want to wake them up.
I think that you have tried, by force of will,
To kill the innate goodness of your heart,
But it is mightier than you yourself.
In spite of all, I see you're good and noble.
RUDENZ. You still have faith in me! Believe me, Berta,
Your love can make me be and do all things.
BERTA. Just be what nature destined you to be.
Fulfill the duties she assigned to you,
By standing with your people and your country
To fight for justice and your sacred rights.
RUDENZ. How can I win you, have you as my own,
If I resist the power of the kaiser?
Don't your own kinfolk rule your hand and fate
According to their powerful designs?
BERTA. My own estates lie in these forests cantons,
And if the Swiss are free, then I am free.
RUDENZ. Oh, what a prospect you have opened up!
BERTA. Don't hope to win me by a Hapsburg favor.
They're stretching out their hands for my possessions,
Which they intend to join to their great holdings.
The greed for land that would devour your freedom
Is threatening to take my freedom too.
Yes, I have been selected as a victim
To be bestowed upon some favorite;
They want to drag me to the royal court,
Where intrigue rules, deceit of every sort.
There hateful marriage fetters wait for me,
And only love, your love, can set me free.
RUDENZ. Could you decide to spend your lifetime here
And be my own, in my own fatherland?
What was my yearning after distant places
Except my striving to be near to you?
For you were what I sought on paths of glory,
And my ambition was but love for you.
If you could isolate yourself with me
In this calm land, resigning worldly splendor,
Then I would reach the end of all my striving;
Then let the waters of the troubled world
Surge up against the mountain shores around us.
I have no further transient desires
To search for in the distant realms of life.
Now may these rocky cliffs spread far and wide
Impenetrable walls on every side;
May this enclosed and blissful valley be
Illumined from above for you and me.
BERTA. Now you are what my hoping heart surmised
And dreamed about. My faith did not deceive me.
RUDENZ. Now leave me, vain delusion that beguiled me.
I'll find my happiness in my own home.
Here where I spent my boyhood joyfully,
Where thousands of bright memories surround me,
Where springs and trees have come to life around me,
In our own fatherland, you will be mine.
I've always loved this country of my

birth;
I'd long for it through all the joys of earth.
BERTA. Where could we ever find the Blessed Isles
If not in this fair land of innocence?
Here where the ancient loyalties yet live,
Where falsehood still has never found its way,
No envy can obscure our happiness;
The hours will pass and fill each shining day.
In true and manly worth I see you there,
The first among these free and equal men;
You'll be revered with homage, and you'll share
The privilege of king and citizen.
RUDENZ. I see you there, the queen of womankind,
In charming feminine activity.
You'll make my home a heaven and I'll find
That as the flowers of spring adorn the lea,
So will your life and charms adorn me too,
And everything will always thrive near you.
BERTA. You see, Rudenz, why I was sad and worried
When I saw you destroy your happiness
Yourself. I thought of what my fate would be
If I should have to marry the oppressor
And follow him into his gloomy castle.
There is no fortress here. There are no walls
To part me from a people I would help.
RUDENZ. How can I save myself, how break the noose
Which foolishly I placed around me neck?
BERTA. Just tear it off with brave determination.
Whatever comes, stand firmly by your people.
That is where you belong. [*Hunting horns are heard in the distance.*] I hear the hunt
Come near. Let's go; we'll have to leave each other.
Fight for your fatherland and fight for love.
There is one foe before whose might we tremble;
There is one freedom that will free us all. [*Exeunt.*]

Scene 3

A meadow near Altdorf.[33] *In the foreground are trees; in the background, the hat on a pole. The view is bounded by the Bannberg, over which snow-covered mountains tower.* FRIESSHARD *and* LEUTHOLD *are standing guard.*

FRIESSHARD. We keep our watch in vain. No one will come
This way and pay his homage to the hat.
It used to be just like a fair out here,
But now the village green is all deserted
Since they have hung this scarecrow on the pole.
LEUTHOLD. Yes, only riffraff lets itself be seen
And, just to vex us, doffs those ragged caps.
All decent people turn away and take
A long detour halfway around the town
To keep from bowing down before the hat.
FRIESSHARD. Some people had to cross this place at noon
When they were coming from a townhall meeting,
So I was sure I'd make a catch, because
Their minds were far from greeting any hat.
But Rösselmann the priest, who just then came
From visiting a sick man, saw it all
And held the Host[34] up high before the pole.
The sacristan then had to ring his bell,
And all fell on their knees—including me—
And reverenced the Host, but not the hat.
LEUTHOLD. Look here, Friesshard, it seems to me sometimes
As if we're standing in the pillory.
It surely is a shame for any trooper
To stand on guard before an empty hat,

And every decent fellow must despise
  us.
To tell the truth, it is a foolish order
To ask that men pay homage to a hat.
FRIESSHARD. Why not pay homage to a
  hollow hat?
You've often bowed before a hollow
  skull. [HILDEGARD, MECHTHILD, *and*
  ELSBET *enter with their children and
  stand around the pole.*]
LEUTHOLD. I tell you, you are one of-
  ficious scoundrel
Who'd like to get good people into
  trouble
Let those who will walk by before the
  hat;
I'll close my eyes or look the other way.
MECHTHILD. There hangs the governor.
  Pay homage, boys.
ELSBET. I wish to God he'd go, and
  leave his hat.
Our country wouldn't be the worse for
  it.
FRIESSHARD. [*Driving them away.*] Get out
  of here! Confounded pack of
  women!
Who sent for you? Go home and send
  your husbands,
If they have the courage to defy the
  order. [*The women leave.*] [TELL *enters
  with his crossbow, leading his son by the
  hand. They walk past the hat without
  noticing it and go toward the front of the
  stage.*]
WALTER. [*Pointing at the Bannberg.*] Say,
  Father, is it true the trees up there
Upon the mountain bleed if someone
  strikes
Them with an ax?
TELL. Who says such things, my boy?
WALTER. The master herdsman told us;
  and he said
The trees were all enchanted, and the
  hand
That injured them would grow out
  from the grave.[35]
TELL. The trees are all enchanted, that
  is true.
You see the glaciers there, the icy peaks
That fade away and melt into the sky?
WALTER. Those are the peaks that
  thunder in the night
And send the avalanches down the
  mountains.
TELL. That's right, and they would long
  ago have covered
The little town of Altdorf with their
  mass
If those same forests were not standing
  there,
A mighty bulwark for our town's pro-
  tection.
WALTER. [*After thinking a while.*] And are
  there countries with no mountains,
  Father?
TELL. If you go down from our high
  mountain peaks,
Keep going lower as the rivers run,
You'll reach a great and level piece of
  land
Where forest streams no longer rush
  and foam,
And rivers calmly flow in beds of sand.
There all around you is the heaven's
  dome,
And you will see the fertile fields of
  grain
Spread out like garden spots across the
  plain.
WALTER. But Father, why don't we go
  down at once
And live in this fine land you talk
  about,
Instead of staying here with so much
  worry?
TELL. The land is fair and gracious like
  the heavens;
But they who till the soil do not enjoy
The crops that they have planted.
WALTER. Don't they live
As free as you upon their own posses-
  sions?
TELL. The bishop and the king own all
  the land.
WALTER. But surely they go hunting in
  the forests?
TELL. The overlord owns all the hunt-
  ing rights.
WALTER. But surely they go fishing in
  the rivers?
TELL. The king owns all the streams,
  the seas, the salt.
WALTER. Who is this king that every-
  body fears?
TELL. He is the one who guards and
  feeds them all.
WALTER. But aren't they brave? Why
  can't they guard themselves?
TELL. No neighbor dares to trust his
  neighbor there.
WALTER. Oh, Father, I'd feel cramped
  in that wide land.

I'd rather live beneath the avalanche.
TELL. It's better to have glaciers at your back,
My son, than evil men whom you can't trust. [*They are about to pass by.*]
WALTER. Look, Father, see the hat hung on the pole.
TELL. What is the hat to us? Come, let's go on. [*As he is about to leave,* FRIESSHARD *approaches him with leveled pike.*]
FRIESSHARD. By the kaiser's orders, halt! I tell you, halt!
TELL. [*Laying hold of the pike.*] What do you want? Why are you stopping me?
FRIESSHARD. You've disobeyed the order. Come with us.
LEUTHOLD. You failed to pay your homage to the hat.
TELL. Friend, let me go.
FRIESSHARD. Away with him to prison.
WALTER. My father go to prison? Help! Help! [*He calls toward the wings.*]
Come quickly, people! Someone come and help!
They'll capture him and take him off to prison! [RÖSSELMANN *the priest and* PETERMANN *the sacristan enter, with three other men.*]
SACRISTAN. What's happening?
RÖSSELMANN. Why did you seize this man?
FRIESSHARD. He is the kaiser's enemy, a traitor.
TELL. [*Seizing him violently.*] A traitor, I?
RÖSSELMANN. You're wrong, my friend. This man
Is Tell, an honest, loyal citizen.
WALTER. [*Seeing* WALTER FÜRST *and running up to him.*] Grandfather, help! They want to take my father.
FRIESSHARD. Away to prison!
WALTER FÜRST. [*Hurrying forward.*] Wait, I'll offer bail.
For heaven's sake, what's happened to you, Tell? [MELCHTAL *and* STAUFFACHER *enter.*]
FRIESSHARD. He has despised the viceroy's sovereign power,
And still refuses to acknowledge it.
STAUFFACHER. You claim that Tell did that?
MELCHTAL. You're lying, fellow.
LEUTHOLD. He did not pay his homage to the hat.
WALTER FÜRST. And just for that you're taking him to prison?
Here, friend, accept my bail and set him free.
FRIESSHARD. You'd better keep your bail to save yourself.
We're doing our duty here. Away with him!
MELCHTAL. [*To the people.*] This is an outrageous wrong. Shall we endure it,
And let them drag him off before our eyes.?
SACRISTAN. We are the stronger. Friends, do not allow this.
We'll stand as one and back each other up.
FRIESSHARD. Who dares resist the governor's command?
THREE OTHER COUNTRYMEN. [*Running in.*] We'll help you. What has happened? Knock them down!
[HILDEGARD, MECHTHILD *and* ELSBET *return.*]
TELL. Go on, good people, I can help myself.
Don't think, if I should want to use my strength,
That I would ever fear those pikes of theirs.
MELCHTAL. [*To* FRIESSHARD.] Just dare to take this man away from us.
WALTER FÜRST *and* STAUFFACHER. Calm down. Stay quiet.
FRIESSHARD. [*Screaming.*] Riot and rebellion! [*Hunting horns are heard.*]
WOMEN. Here comes the viceroy.
FRIESSHARD. [*Raising his voice.*] Mutiny! Rebellion!
STAUFFACHER. Scream till you burst, you scoundrel!
RÖSSELMANN *and* MELCHTAL. Keep still, can't you?
FRIESSHARD. [*Screaming louder.*] Help us! Help the servants of the law!
WALTER FÜRST. The governor! What will he do to us? [*Enter* GESSLER, *on horseback and holding a falcon on his fist,* RUDOLPH DER HARRAS, BERTA, *and* RUDENZ, *with a large train of armed attendants who form a circle of pikes around the whole stage.*]
RUDOLF HER HARRAS. Make way there for his lordship!
GESSLER. Disperse the crowd!
Why are they gathered here? Who called for help? [*General silence.*]

Who was it? I want to know who called.
[*To* FRIESSHARD.] Come here!
Say who you are and why you hold this
man. [*He gives the falcon to a servant.*]
FRIESSHARD. My noble lord, I am your
man-at-arms,
Your soldier, duly named to guard the
hat.
This man I apprehended in the act
Of passing by the hat without obeisance.
I started to arrest him as you ordered,
But now the crowd would rescue him
by force.
GESSLER. [*After a pause.*] Look, Tell, do
you despise your kaiser so,
And me, who rule as viceroy in his
place,
That you refuse your homage to the
hat
Which I put up to test obedience here?
You have revealed to me your bad intentions.
TELL. Forgive me, sir. It was through
oversight,
And not contempt for you, that this
thing happened.
Were I discreet, my name would not be
Tell.[36]
I ask your mercy. I'll not offend again.
GESSLER. [*After a silence.*] You are a master with the crossbow, Tell.
They say you are a match for any
archer.
WALTER TELL. And that's the truth, sir.
Father shoots an apple
Right off the tree, a hundred steps
away.
GESSLER. Your son, I take it, Tell?
TELL. Yes, noble lord.
GESSLER. Is this your only child?
TELL. I have two boys.
GESSLER. And of the two, which one do
you love more?
TELL. Both boys are dear to me alike,
my lord.
GESSLER. Look, Tell, because they say
you shoot an apple
Down from the tree a hundred paces
off,
You'll have to prove your skill. Now
take your bow—
You seem to keep it handy—and prepare
To shoot an apple from your own son's
head.
But let me warn you, take your aim so
well
You'll hit the apple on your first attempt,
For if you miss, your head shall be the
forfeit. [*All give signs of horror.*]
TELL. But sir, what monstrous thing is
this you ask?
You say I am to shoot at my own son—
No, no, my lord, you surely cannot
mean that.
May God forbid! You could not seriously
Demand this thing from any loving
father.
GESSLER. You'll have to shoot the apple
from his head.
This I demand, and I will see it done.
TELL. You say I am to take my bow and
aim
At my own precious child? I'd rather
die.
GESSLER. Unless you shoot, the boy and
you *both* die.
TELL. Am I to be the murderer of my
child?
My lord, you have no children; you
don't know
What stirs and throbs within a father's
heart.
GESSLER. Now suddenly it seems you've
grown discreet!
They told me that you were a dreamer,
Tell,
And that you shunned the ways of
other men.
You love unusual things; so I selected
A special, daring deed just made for
you.
Another man would think it over first,
But you will blindly tackle it, and
boldly.
BERTA. My lord, don't play with these
poor people's lives.
You see them stand before you, pale
and trembling,
So little are they used to jests from you.
GESSLER. Who says that I am jesting?
[*He grasps a branch that hangs overhead.*] Here's the apple.
Make room there now, and let him take
his distance
As is the custom. I give him eighty
steps,
No more, no less. He proudly made his
boast

That he could hit his man at a hundred paces.
Now, archer, aim, and see that you don't miss.
RUDOLF DER HARRAS. My God, this has grown serious. Quickly, boy,
Kneel down and beg the governor for your life.
WALTER FÜRST. [*Aside to* MELCHTAL, *who can hardly control his impatience.*] Control yourself. Keep calm, I beg of you!
BERTA. [*To the* GOVERNOR.] That is enough, my lord. It is inhuman
To jest like this with any father's fears.
And even if this man had forfeited
His life and limb to pay for his offense,
He must have suffered tenfold death by now.
Release him, then. Let him go home in peace.
He knows you now; he'll not forget this hour.
He will remember, and his children's children.
GESSLER. Clear the way. Be quick! Why hesitate?
Your life is forfeited, and I can kill you;
But see, I mercifully place your fate
In your own skilled and highly practiced hand.
You can't complain and call the sentence harsh
If you are made the master of your fate.
You boasted of your steady aim. All right!
Now, archer, is your chance to show your skill.
The mark is worthy and the prize is great.
Another man can hit a bull's-eye too,
But I consider only him a master
Who trusts his skill in any situation,
Whose heart does not affect his eye and hand.
WALTER FÜRST. [*Prostrating himself before him.*] My lord, we recognize your sovereignty;
But now let justice be replaced by mercy.
Take half of what I have, or take it all,
But spare this father such a dreadful deed.
WALTER TELL. Don't kneel before that wicked man, Grandfather.
Just tell me where to stand. I'm not afraid.
My father even hits a bird in flight;
He will not miss his aim and hit his son.
STAUFFACHER. Are you not touched by this child's innocence?
RÖSSELMANN. Remember that there is a God in heaven
To whom you must account for all your deeds.
GESSLER. [*Pointing at the boy.*] Go, bind him to the linden tree.
WALTER TELL. Bind me?
No, I will not be bound, I will hold still
Just like a lamb, and will not even breathe.
But if you bind me, then I can't be still;
I'll fight against my bonds until I'm free.
RUDOLF DER HARRAS. But you must let them blindfold you, my boy.
WALTER TELL. Why blindfold me? Don't think I'll fear an arrow
From my own father's hand. I'll firmly stand
And wait for it, and never blink an eye.
Quick, Father, show how good a shot you are.
He doesn't know; he thinks he'll ruin us.
To spite the tyrant; shoot, and hit your mark. [*He goes to the linden tree, and the apple is placed on his head.*]
MELCHTAL. [*To the countrymen.*]
What, shall this crime take place before our eyes?
Why did we swear the oath to stand together?
STAUFFACHER. It's all in vain because we have no weapons.
Just see the pikes, as thick as trees around us.
MELCHTAL. If only we'd attacked them on the spot.
May God forgive the ones who urged delay.
GESSLER. [*To* TELL.] Get at it now! You don't bear arms for nothing.
It's dangerous to bear a deadly weapon,
And arrows may spring back upon the archer.
This right the peasants arrogantly claim
Offends the highest sovereign of the land.
Let none be armed except the overlord.

But if you people like to bear the bow,
All right, then I'll provide you with a mark.
TELL. [*Bending the bow and fitting on an arrow.*] Clear the way! Make room!
STAUFFACHER. What, Tell? You mean to shoot! No! Never!
Your hands are trembling and your knees are shaking.
TELL. [*Lowering his crossbow.*] I'm feeling faint and dizzy.
WOMEN. God in heaven!
TELL. [*To the* GOVERNOR.] Release me from this shot. Here is my heart. [*He tears his clothing from his breast.*]
Command your troopers now to strike me down.
GESSLER. I do not want your life, I want the shot.[37]
There's nothing you can't do; you're not afraid.
You're skilled with oars as well as with the bow;
You fear no storms when there's someone to save.
Now, savior, save yourself; you save all others. [TELL *stands in terrible inner struggle, with trembling hands, turning his eyes alternatively to the* GOVERNOR *and to heaven. Suddenly he takes a second arrow from his quiver and puts it in his doublet. The* GOVERNOR *notes all these actions.*]
WALTER TELL. [*Under the linden tree.*]
Shoot, Father, I am not afriad.
TELL. I must. [*He controls himself and takes aim.*]
RUDENZ. [*Who has been standing all the while, in a state of intense excitement barely restraining himself, now stepping forward.*] My lord, you will not force this matter further.
You'll *not* do that, for it was just a test.
You have achieved your end. Severity,
When pushed too far, is sure to miss its aim,
Just as the bow will break when bent too far.
GESSLER. Keep silent till you're asked to speak!
RUDENZ. I *will* speak!
I have a right to speak. The royal honor
Is sacred, but a rule like yours breeds hate.
I know this isn't what the king intends.
My people don't deserve such cruelty,
And you have no authority for this.
GESSLER. You're growing bold, young man.
RUDENZ. I've held my tongue
Too long about the dreadful things I've seen.
I shut my eyes to what I knew went on;
My overflowing and rebellious heart
I kept subdued within my troubled breast.
But further silence would be treachery
Against my country and against my king.
BERTA. [*Flinging herself between him and the* GOVERNOR.] Keep still; you'll only rouse his fury more.
RUDENZ. I turned against my people and renounced
My kinsmen, tore apart all bonds of nature
In order to attach myself to you.
I thought I furthered what was best for all
When I helped fortify the kaiser's power.
But now the mist has cleared before my eyes,
And shuddering I see the precipice.
You have confused my independent judgment—
Deceived my honest heart. With best intentions
I was about to wreck my land and people.
GESSLER. Insolent boy, such language to your lord?
RUDENZ. The emperor is my lord, not you. I'm free
As you by birth, and I can vie with you
In every knightly virtue and achievement.
And if you did not represent the kaiser,
Whom I respect even when he is disgraced,
I'd throw the gauntlet down. You'd have to give
An answer by our knightly rule and custom.[38]
Yes! Beckon to your troopers now. I'm not
Unarmed like them. [*He points at the people.*] I have a sword, and who Approaches me—
STAUFFACHER. [*Cries out.*] Look there! The apple's fallen! [*While all have turned their attention to the side of the*

stage where BERTA *has thrown herself between* RUDENZ *and the* GOVERNOR, TELL *has shot his arrow.*]³⁹

RÖSSELMANN. The boy's alive!

MANY VOICES. The apple has been hit. [WALTER FÜRST *staggers and is about to fall.* BERTA *supports him.*]

GESSLER. [*Astonished.*] He shot the arrow? What? The man is crazy.

BERTA. The boy's unharmed. Compose yourself, good father.

WALTER TELL. [*Comes running with the apple.*] The apple, Father, here's the apple. I knew it!
I knew you wouldn't miss and injure me. [TELL *stands leaning forward, as if he wanted to follow the arrow. His crossbow drops from his hand. When he sees the boy coming, he hurries to meet him with open arms, lifts him up, and presses him fervently to his heart. From this position he falls down exhausted. All the people remain still, deeply moved.*]

BERTA. Oh, gracious God in heaven!

WALTER FÜRST. [*To father and son.*] Children, my children!

STAUFFACHER. God be praised!

LEUTHOLD. I say, that was some shot!
They'll speak of it forever and a day.

RUDOLF DER HARRAS. They will be talking of this archer Tell
As long as mountains stand on their foundations. [*He hands the apple to the* GOVERNOR.]

GESSLER. By heaven! The apple pierced right through the center!
That was a master shot. I have to praise it.

RÖSSELMANN. The shot was good, that's true, but woe to him
Whose malice drove this man to tempting God.

STAUFFACHER. Come to your senses, Tell. You have redeemed
Yourself, and you are free to go back home.

RÖSSELMANN. Come, take the boy back to his mother now. [*They start to take him away.*]

GESSLER. One moment, Tell!

TELL. [*Coming back.*] What is it, sir?

GESSLER. You put
A second arrow in your doublet. Oh yes,
I noticed that. What was the arrow for?

TELL. [*Embarrassed.*] It's just a custom, sir, among us hunters.

GESSLER. No, Tell, I cannot let that answer pass.
I think there must have been some other reason.
Don't hesitate. Just speak the candid truth;
No matter what, I'll guarantee your life.
Say, why the second arrow?

TELL. All right then, sir,
Because you've promised not to take my life,
I'll tell you all the truth, straight from my heart. [*He draws the arrow from his doublet and looks at the* GOVERNOR *with a frightful gaze.*]
This second arrow would have pierced through *you*
If I had hit my own beloved child.
And you, yes, truly—I could not have missed.

GESSLER. All right then, Tell! I guaranteed your life.
I gave my knightly word, and I will keep it.
But since I recognize your evil thoughts,
I'll have you taken off and put in prison
Where neither moon nor sun will shine on you,
So that I may be safe from flying arrows.
Arrest him, men, and bind his hands. [*They bind him.*]

STAUFFACHER. What, sir!
You dare to treat like this a man on whom
God's hand has been so visibly revealed?

GESSLER. Let's see if it will rescue him again.
Now take him to my boat; I'll follow you.
I'll carry him myself to Küssnacht castle.

RÖSSELMANN. You can't do that, nor can the emperor.
That violates the freedom in our charters.

GESSLER. Where are they? Has the emperor confirmed them?
Indeed he hasn't. This favor you must first
Deserve by your complete obedience.
You're rebels all against the kaiser's power,

And secretly you're plotting insurrection.
I know you men. I see through all of you.
This time I'm taking only one away,
But you are all involved and share his guilt.
Learn to obey in silence, if you're clever. [*He leaves.* BERTA, RUDENZ, HARRAS, *and the troopers follow.* FRIESSHARD *and* LEUTHOLD *stay behind.*]
WALTER FÜRST. [*In violent anguish.*] Now it is done. He has resolved to bring
Destruction down on me and all my house.
STAUFFACHER. [*To* TELL.] Why did you have to irritate the tyrant?
TELL. Let those who felt my pain control themselves.
STAUFFACHER. Now all is over; everything is lost.
We too are chained and bound along with you.
COUNTRYMEN. [*Surrounding* TELL.] With you, our hope, our last resort is gone.
LEUTHOLD. [*Approaching him.*] I'm sorry, Tell, I must obey the order.
TELL. Farewell!
WALTER TELL. [*Clinging to him in great anguish.*] Oh Father, Father, my dear father!
TELL. [*Raising his arms toward heaven.*] Up yonder is your Father. Call on him.
STAUFFACHER. Can I take any message to your wife?
TELL. [*Pressing the boy fervently to his breast.*] The boy's unhurt, and God will help me too. [*He tears himself away abruptly and follows the guards.*]

Act 4

Scene 1

The east shore of Lake Lucerne.[40] *Steep and strangely shaped cliffs close the prospect to the west. The lake is agitated; there is violent roaring and rushing of wind, accompanied by lightning and thunder.* KUNZ VON GERSAU, *the* FISHERMAN, *and the* FISHERMAN's SON *are talking.*[41]

KUNZ. I saw it all. With my own eyes I saw it.
It happened as I've said; you can believe me.
FISHERMAN. Our Tell a prisoner on his way to Küssnacht—
Our country's bravest man, its strongest arm
If ever there should be a fight for freedom.
KUNZ. The governor himself is taking him
By boat. They were about to go on board
As I myself was putting out from Flüelen.
But then this storm that's breaking over us,
Which made me put to shore so hurriedly,
May well have hindered them in their departure.
FISHERMAN. Tell is in chains and in the viceroy's power!
Believe me, he will be entombed so deep
He'll never see the light of day again,
For Gessler surely fears the just revenge
Of someone he has wronged and angered so.
KUNZ. They say the noble Lord von Attinghausen,
Our former magistrate, is near his death.
FISHERMAN. We've lost the final anchor of our hope.
He was the only one who still spoke out,
Defending justice and the people's rights.
KUNZ. The storm is getting worse. I must be off.
I'll stop and seek my shelter in the village,
For it's impossible to leave today. [*Exit.*]
FISHERMAN. Our Tell a prisoner, and the baron dead!
Now, tyranny, raise up your haughty brow.
Cast shame aside! The voice of truth is stilled;

The eyes that saw the right are blinded
  now;
The arms that were to save us are in
  chains.
FISHERMAN'S SON. It's hailing, Father.
  Come into the house.
You shouldn't be outside in such a
  storm.
FISHERMAN. Blow winds! You lightning
  bolts, flash down your fire![42]
And burst, you clouds! Pour waterfalls
  and streams
From heaven, drown the land in floods!
  Destroy
The germ of generations yet unborn!
You raging elements, be masters here!
Return, wild beasts, you bears and
  wolves, return!
To you belongs the land, the wilder-
  ness.
Who wants to live here now without his
  freedom?
FISHERMAN'S SON. The wind is raging on
  the cliff. Just listen!
There never was such roaring in this
  gorge.
FISHERMAN. To aim directly at his own
  child's head—
Such things were never asked of any
  father.
No wonder then that nature should
  rebel
In savage wrath. And it would not sur-
  prise me
If all these cliffs would plunge into the
  lake,
If all these mighty peaks and towers of
  ice
That since creation day have never
  melted
Should thaw and topple from their
  lofty crests,
If mountains should crash down, the
  ancient crags
Collapse, a second Deluge swallow up
The habitations of all living men. [*The
  ringing of bells is heard.*]
FISHERMAN'S SON. The bells are ringing
  on the mountain. Listen!
Somebody must have seen a boat in
  danger,
And rings the bells that we may pray
  for it. [*He ascends a knoll.*]
FISHERMAN. I pity any boat that's caught
  out there
To rock and sway in such a fearful
  cradle.
The helmsman and his helm are
  useless then;
The storm is master. Man is tossed
  about
Just like a ball by wind and waves. No
  bay
Can offer him protection near or far.
Inhospitable cliffs rise steeply up;
They stare at him, without a ledge to
  grasp,
And show him only steep and stony
  breasts.
FISHERMAN'S SON. [*Point to the left.*] Fa-
  ther, a boat! It's coming down from
  Flüelen.
FISHERMAN. May God have mercy on
  those wretched men!
When storms become entangled in
  these gorges,
They roar and rage like captive beasts
  of prey
And fling themselves against the iron
  bars.
Howling, they try to find escape in
  vain,
For all around the cliffs imprison them
And wall them up inside the narrow
  pass. [*He climbs up on the knoll.*]
FISHERMAN'S SON. It is the viceroy's boat
  from Uri, Father.
I recognize its red deck and its flag.
FISHERMAN. By God's eternal judgment!
  That's his boat.
The governor himself is sailing there
And has on board the burden of his
  crime.
How quickly the avenger's arm has
  reached him!
Now he must feel a stronger lord than
  he.
The wind and waves will not obey his
  voice;
These cliffs will not bend down or bow
  their heads
Before his hat. Oh no, my son, don't
  pray.
Don't stay the arm of judgment with
  your prayers.
FISHERMAN'S SON. Oh, I don't pray to
  save the governor.
I pray for Tell, who's also on the boat.
FISHERMAN. Oh, folly of the sightless
  elements—
Must you, to strike the only one who's
  guilty,

Destroy the boat together with the
  boatmen?
FISHERMAN'S SON. Look, they had safely
  passed the Buggisgrat,
But now the power of the storm rebounding
Upon them from the mighty Teufelsmünster
Is hurling them against the Axenberg.[43]
I cannot see them any more.
FISHERMAN. There stands
Hackmesser cliff that's broken many a
  boat.
If they do not steer wisely past those
  rocks,
Their boat will dash to pieces on the
  crag
That slopes down sharply to the water's
  edge.
But they've on board a good and practiced steersman;
If anyone can save them, Tell's the
  man.
But surely they have chained his arms
  and hands. [WILHELM TELL *enters, with
  his crossbow. He comes in rapidly, looks
  around in surprise, and shows the most
  violent agitation. When he reaches the
  center of the stage he falls upon his knees,
  stretching out his hands first toward the
  earth, then toward heaven.*].
FISHERMAN'S SON. [*Observing him.*] Look,
  Father, who's the man that's kneeling
  there?
FISHERMAN. He's clutching at the earth
  with both his hands.
He looks as if he were beside himself.
FISHERMAN'S SON. [*Coming closer.*] What's
  this I see? Come, Father, come and
  look!
FISHERMAN. [*Approaching.*] Who is it?
  God in heaven, is it Tell?
How did you get here? Speak!
FISHERMAN'S SON. Weren't you just now
  A prisoner on that boat, and bound in
  chains?
FISHERMAN. And weren't they taking
  you across to Küssnacht?
TELL. [*Getting up.*] I have escaped.
FISHERMAN *and* BOY. Escaped! A miracle!
FISHERMAN'S SON. Where did you come
  from?
TELL. From the boat there.
FISHERMAN. What?

FISHERMAN'S SON. [*At the same time.*]
  Where is the viceroy?
TELL. Tossing on the waves.
FISHERMAN. How is it possible that you
  escaped
Both from your bonds and from the
  stormy sea?
TELL. Through God's almighty providence. Now hear me.
FISHERMAN *and* BOY. Yes, tell us everything!
TELL. You heard what happened
Today in Altdorf?
FISHERMAN. Yes, I know it all.
TELL. The viceroy captured me and
  had me bound.
He planned to take me on to Küssnacht
  castle.
FISHERMAN. And that he then embarked
  with you at Flüelen—
We know all that. But how did you
  escape?
TELL. I lay on deck, securely tied with
  ropes,
Defenseless and resigned. I had no
  hope
Of looking at the shining sun again
Or on the faces of my wife and children,
And with despair I viewed the watery
  waste.
FISHERMAN. Unhappy man.
TELL. And so we moved along,
The governor and Rudolf and their
  men.
My quiver and my crossbow lay astern,
Right at the helm, beside the steersman's place—
And just as we had reached the Axenberg,
Below the Lesser Axen, God decreed
That suddenly a dreadful storm break
  out
And beat upon us from St. Gotthard's
  gorge,
So that our oarsmen all lost heart and
  hope
And thought we faced a miserable
  drowning.
Then one attendant of the governor
Approached him, and I heard him
  speak these words:
"You see your danger and ours too, my
  lord,
And that we hover on the brink of
  death.

Our oarsmen are confused from growing fear
And don't know what to do, for they're not used
To steering in the storm. But there is Tell,
A mighty man who steers a boat with skill.
What if we were to use him in our danger?"
Then spoke the viceroy: "Tell, if you could help,
And felt that you could save us from this storm,
I might consent to free you from your bonds."
I answered, "Yes, my lord, with help from God
I feel that I could get us out of this."
So I was freed from bonds and took my place
Beside the helm and steered a steady course.
But from the corner of my eye I saw
My weapon lying near, and watched the shore
For any spot where I might leap to freedom.
And when I saw a flat and rocky crag
That jutted like a ledge into the lake—[44]
FISHERMAN. I know it well. It's at the Greater Axen,
But I should think it's much too high and steep
To reach by leaping out of any boat.
TELL. I shouted to the men to row with force
Till we could reach and pass the rocky ledge.
The worst would be behind us there, I cried.
And as we came upon it, rowing stoutly,
I prayed to God for mercy, braced myself,
And pressed with all my strength to force the stern
To shore and toward the rocky precipice.
Then quickly I snatched up my near-by weapon
And leaped upon the rocky ledge above.
And as I jumped I gave a mighty shove,
To thrust the boat adrift upon the lake.
There let it ride the waves as God decrees.
Thus I am freed from violence of storms
And from the greater violence of men.
FISHERMAN. The Lord has truly wrought a miracle
For you! I scarcely can believe my eyes.
But tell me, where do you intend to go?
There can be no security for you
If Gessler should escape this storm alive.
TELL. I heard him say, when I still lay aboard
In bonds, that he would put to shore at Brunnen
And take me to his fort by way of Schwyz.
FISHERMAN. You think that he will make the trip by land?
TELL. That's what he plans.
FISHERMAN. Then you must hide at once.
Don't count on God to save you from him twice.
TELL. Which is the shortest way to Arth and Kússnacht?
FISHERMAN. The public road goes there by way of Steinen,
But there's a shorter and more secret path
My son can guide you on, by way of Lowerz.
TELL. [Shaking his hand.] May God reward you for your kindness. Good-by. [As he is leaving, he turns back.]
Did not you also take the Rütli oath?
I think I heard them mention you.
FISHERMAN. I did.
I was with them and took the oath of union.
TELL. Then do a favor for me. Go to Bürglen
Quickly and find my wife, who's in despair.
Tell her that I escaped and that I'm safe.
FISHERMAN. But shall I tell her where you've gone to hide?
TELL. You'll find her father there at home with her,
And others, too, who took the Rütli oath.
Tell them they must be brave and resolute,

For I am free and master of my
  strength,
And soon they will hear further news
  from me.
FISHERMAN. What do you have in mind?
  Come, won't you tell?
TELL. You'll hear about it after I am
  through. [*Exit.*]
FISHERMAN. Show him the way. May
  God protect him well.
Whatever he has planned, he'll surely
  do. [*Exeunt.*]

Scene 2

The baronial castle of Attinghausen. The
  BARON *is in an armchair, dying.* WALTER
  FÜRST, STAUFFACHER, MELCHTAL, *and*
  BAUMGARTEN *are busy around him.*
  WALTER TELL *is kneeling before the dying
  man.*

WALTER FÜRST. It's over with him now.
  He's passed away.
STAUFFACHER. He isn't lying like a dead
  man. Look,
The feather at his lips is moving still.
His sleep is calm; his features smile in
  peace. [BAUMGARTEN *goes to the door
  and speaks with someone.*]
WALTER FÜRST. [*To* BAUMGARTEN.] Who's
  at the door?
BAUMGARTEN. [*Coming back.*] Your
  daughter, Hedwig Tell.
She wants to speak with you and see
  the boy. [WALTER TELL *get up.*]
WALTER FÜRST. How can I comfort her
  when *I* need comfort?
Is every sorrow heaped upon my head?
HEDWIG. [*Forcing her way in.*] Where is
  my child? You have to let me see him.
STAUFFACHER. Be calm. Remember
  death is in this house.
HEDWIG. [*Running to the boy.*] My little
  Walter! You are safe!
WALTER TELL. [*Clinging to her.*] Poor
  Mother!
HEDWIG. It's really true? You're sure
  you are not hurt? [*She gazes at him
  with anxious solicitude.*]
And is it possible? He aimed at you?
How could he do it? Oh, he has no
  heart!
How could he shoot an arrow at his
  child?
WALTER FÜRST. It was in grief and an-
  guish that he acted.
He was compelled; their lives were in
  the balance.
HEDWIG. Oh, if he had a father's heart
  within him,
He would have sooner died a thousand
  deaths.
STAUFFACHER. You should be grateful
  for God's providence
That guided things so well—
HEDWIG. Can I forget
What could have happened? God in
  heaven; if I
Should live a hundred years,[45] I'd al-
  ways see
My boy stand bound, his father aiming
  at him,
And always would the arrow pierce my
  heart.
MELCHTAL. If you knew how the viceroy
  taunted him!
HEDWIG. The cruel hearts of men! Of-
  fend their pride,
And nothing matters to them any
  more.
In furious contest they will blindly risk
Their children's heads and break a
  mother's heart.
BAUMGARTEN. Is not your husband's
  fate severe enough
Without your wounding him with your
  reproach?
Have you no feeling left for his ordeal?
HEDWIG. [*Turning and staring at him.*]
  And you? Have you but tears for his
  misfortune?
And where were all of you when they
  put bonds
On this good man? How did you help
  him then?
You just looked on, and let the horror
  happen.
You made no protest when they
  dragged your friend
Right from your midst. Is that how he,
  how Tell
Has treated you? Did he just stand
  there too,
And only sympathize when in pursuit
The troopers threatened, and the an-
  gry lake
Surged up before you? He didn't show
  his pity
With idle tears. Forgetting wife and
  children,
He leaped into the boat and rescued

WALTER FÜRST. How could we try to rescue him by force?
For that we were too few, and none was armed.
HEDWIG. [*Flinging herself upon his breast.*] You too have lost him, Father, and you'll miss him.
Our country, all of us, have lost him now.
We'll miss him sorely, and he'll miss us too.
May God deliver him from cold despair!
No friends' consoling words will penetrate
That lonely dungeon. If he fell sick in there!
Yes, in the damp and darkness of that prison
He will be sick. Just as the Alpine rose
Must fade and die in low and swampy air,
There is no life for him but in the light,
In sunlight and in gentle mountain air.
Imprisoned! He! His breath of life is freedom.
He cannot breathe the prison air and live.
STAUFFACHER. Now calm yourself. We all will act together
To break the prison doors and set him free.
HEDWIG. What can you do without his help, you men?
As long as Tell was free, there still was hope;
Then innocence still had a champion,
And persecuted people had a helper.
Tell could have saved you all, but all of you
Together cannot free him from his chains. [*The* BARON *wakes up.*]
BAUMGARTEN. He's moving. Quiet.
ATTINGHAUSEN. [*Raising himself up.*] Where is he?
STAUFFACHER. Who?
ATTINGHAUSEN. I miss him.
He has deserted me in my last moments.
STAUFFACHER. He means his nephew. Have they sent for him?
WALTER FÜRST. They sent for him, my lord. Be comforted.
He found his heart at last and he is ours.

ATTINGHAUSEN. And has he spoken for his fatherland?
STAUFFACHER. With heroism.
ATTINGHAUSEN. But why is he not here
To take my final blessing? I can feel
The end come on; my life will soon be over.
STAUFFACHER. No, my good lord, don't talk that way. Your sleep
Has much refreshed you, and your eyes are clear.
ATTINGHAUSEN. All pain is life, yet that has left me too.
My suffering is gone, as is my hope.
[*He notices* WALTER TELL.]
Who is the boy?
WALTER FÜRST. Please bless him, noble sir.
He is my grandson, and he's fatherless.
[HEDWIG *kneels down with the boy before the dying man.*]
ATTINGHAUSEN. And fatherless I leave you all behind.
What wretched fate, that in these final moments
My eyes have seen the ruin of my country.
To think that I have reached this ripe old age
To see my every hope depart with me.
STAUFFACHER. [*To* WALTER FÜRST.] How can we let him die in hopeless grief?
Why can't we ease his final hour of life
By giving him a ray of hope? My lord,
Lift up your spirits; we are not forsaken.
We are not lost beyond deliverance.
ATTINGHAUSEN. Who will deliver you?
WALTER FÜRST. We will, ourselves.
We men in these three cantons pledged our word
That we will drive the tyrants from the land.
We formed a union, and a sacred oath
Unites us all. Before the present year
Has run its course, we'll take concerted action.
Your dust will lie at rest in a free land.
ATTINGHAUSEN. It's really so? The union has been formed?
MELCHTAL. Yes, all three forest cantons will rise up
On the appointed day. Our plans are all
In readiness; the secret's closely kept
Until this hour, though hundreds share

its knowledge.
The ground beneath the tyrant's feet is hollow.
The days of this regime are numbered. Soon
There'll be no trace remaining of their rule.
ATTINGHAUSEN. But what about their strongholds on our soil?
MELCHTAL. They all will fall on the appointed day.
ATTINGHAUSEN. And do the nobles share in this new union?
STAUFFACHER. We count on their assistance, should we need it.
As yet none but the countrymen have sworn.
ATTINGHAUSEN. [*Raising himself up in great astonishment.*] If countrymen have dared so bold a deed
All by themselves, without the aid of nobles,
Relied so much on their own strength and means,
Good—then we nobles are no longer needed,
And we can meet our death with confidence
That life goes on, that mankind's glory will
Hereafter be maintained by other hands. [*He lays his hand upon the head of the child who is kneeling before him.*]
From this child's head, on which the apple lay,
Shall spring your new and better liberty.
The old is falling down, and times are changing;
A better life is rising from the ruins.
STAUFFACHER. [*To* WALTER FÜRST.] Look what a light is shining in his eyes!
That's not the fading of the flame of life;
It is the radiance of new life and hope.
ATTINGHAUSEN. The nobles are descending from their castles
And swearing their allegiance to the cities.
In Üchtland and in Thurgau it has started,
And noble Bern lifts up her sovereign head,
And Freiburg is a fortress of the free,
While busy Zurich calls her guilds to arms
To form a warlike army. The power of kings
Is broken on their everlasting walls. [*He speaks the following lines in a prophetic tone, his voice rising in enthusiasm.*]
I see the ruling princes and the knights
Come riding up, all clad in steel and armor,
To wage a cruel war on harmless herdsmen.
There'll be a fight for life and death, and fame
Will come to many a pass in bloody combat.
A peasant will advance with naked breast
And willingly confront a host of lances;
He'll shatter them, and knighthood's flower will fall
And freedom's flag be raised in victory. [*He grasps* WALTER FÜRST's *and* STAUFFACHER's *hands.*]
Hold fast together then, forever fast.
Let no free canton stand apart from others.
Set beacon lights and watches on your mountains
So that your members may assemble quickly.
United, be united . . . united. . . . [*He falls back upon his pillow. His lifeless hands continue to grasp the others'.*
FÜRST *and* STAUFFACHER *look at him for some moments in silence. Then they step aside, each given over to his sorrow. Meanwhile the vassals have quietly come in. They approach, some showing calm, others violent grief. Some kneel down by his side and weep over his hand. During the wordless scene the castle bells are rung.*]
RUDENZ. [*Entering hurriedly and joining the others.*] Is he alive? Can he still hear me speak?
WALTER FÜRST. [*With his face turned aside, gesturing toward the dead man.*] You are our liege lord and protector, sir,
And now this castle bears another name.
RUDENZ. [*Gazing at the body with deep emotion.*] Oh God! Does my repentance come too late?
Why couldn't he have lived a moment longer
To see the change within my heart?
I once disdained his true and prudent

voice
When he yet moved in light upon the earth.
Now he is gone forever, and he leaves
A heavy debt that I must pay for him.
But tell me, did he die still angry with me?
STAUFFACHER. Before he died, he heard what you had done
And praised and blessed the courage of your speech.
RUDENZ. [*Kneeling by the dead man.*] Yes, hallowed body of a worthy man,
You lifeless corpse, upon your death-cold hand
I take an oath that I have torn away
All foreign bonds and freed myself forever.
I have been given back to my own people.
I am a Swiss and always will be one
With all my heart and soul— [*He rises.*] Mourn for our friend,
Our common father, yet do not despair.
It's not his wealth alone that I inherit;
I feel his heart, his spirit, rise in me,
And in the vigor of my youth I'll do
The tasks he left unfinished in old age.
Give me your hand, you venerable father.[46]
And give me yours. You too, Melchtal, your hand.
Don't hesitate or turn away from me.
Receive my oath, accept my loyal pledge.
WALTER FÜRST. Give him your hands. The heart that has returned
Deserves our trust.
MELCHTAL. You once despised the peasant.
How can we look to you and trust you now?
RUDENZ. Don't hold in mind the errors of my youth.
STAUFFACHER. [*To* MELCHTAL.] "Be united!" Those were our father's words.
Let us remember that.
MELCHTAL. Here is my hand.
A peasant's handclasp is a true man's word,
My noble sir. What is the knight without us?
The peasant's rank is older, too, than yours.

RUDENZ. I give it honor, and my sword shall guard it.
MELCHTAL. My lord, the arm that clears and cultivates
The stubborn soil to make it more productive
Can also shield the human breast.
RUDENZ. Then you
Shall be the shield for me, and I for you;
So shall we each grow stronger through the other.
But why this talking, when our fatherland
Is still a prey to foreign tyranny?
When we have swept away our enemy,
We'll reconcile our differences in peace.
[*After pausing a moment.*]
You do not speak? You have no word for me?
What, do I still deserve distrust from you?
Then I am forced to go against your wishes
And pry into the secrets of your union.
You met and took your oath on Rütli meadow.
I know it all; I know what was agreed.
And though you would not let me share your secret,
I've guarded it just like a sacred trust.
I never was my country's enemy,
And never would I have opposed your cause.
But it was wrong to put off your revolt.
The hour is pressing; we must act at once.
Already Tell's a victim of delay.
STAUFFACHER. We swore that we would wait till Christmas time.
RUDENZ. I wasn't there. I did not take the oath.
Wait if you must, but I will act.
MELCHTAL. You would—?
RUDENZ. I count myself among my country's leaders,
And my first duty now is to protect you.
WALTER FÜRST. Your first and your most sacred duty is
To lay these dear remains into the grave.
RUDENZ. When we have set our country free, we'll place
Our new-won victory wreath upon his bier.

Dear friends, it's not your cause alone
  that moves me;
I have my own to settle in this fight
Against the tyrant. Hear me now, and
  know
My Berta's disappeared; they dragged
  her off
From us by secret means, with shame-
  less boldness.
STAUFFACHER. You say the tyrant dared
  such violence
Against a lady, free and born a noble?
RUDENZ. Dear friends, I gladly prom-
  ised you assistance,
And now I come imploring help from
  you.
The one I love was stolen, dragged
  away,
And who knows where that madman's
  hiding her,
Or with what crime and outrage they
  make bold
To force her heart to some detested
  marriage.
Do not forsake me; help me rescue her.
She loves you, and deserves from her
  own land
That all should take up arms in her
  behalf.
WALTER FÜRST. What course do you
  propose?
RUDENZ. I do not know.
In this dark mystery that hides her fate,
In this anxiety of monstrous doubts
When I cannot lay hold of certainty,
One thing is clear as daylight in my
  mind:
We'll free her only if we rescue her
Out of the ruins of the tyrant's power.
We'll have to take the castles, one and
  all,
And press into her dungeon when they
  fall.
MELCHTAL. Come, lead us on! We'll fol-
  low. Why put off
Until tomorrow what we can do today?
When we assembled on the Rütli, Tell
Was free. The monstrous thing had not
  yet happened.
But time brings other laws and other
  measures.
Who is the coward that is still afraid?
RUDENZ. [*To* STAUFFACHER *and* WALTER
  FÜRST.] Meanwhile take up your
  arms, prepared to strike,
And wait for fiery signals on the moun-
  tains;
For faster than a boat can bring dis-
  patches,
The message of our victory shall reach
  you.
And when you see the welcome light of
  flames,
Then strike our foe with lightning
  speed and thunder,
And break the house of tyranny
  asunder. [*All leave.*]

Scene 3

The Hohle Gasse, *a deep and narrow road near Küssnacht.*[47] *The road slopes down steeply from the back between rocks, and wayfarers are seen on the high point before they appear on the stage. Rocks and cliffs enclose the entire scene. On one of the ridges closest to the front is a ledge overgrown with brushwood.*
TELL. [*Entering with his crossbow.*] He has
  to go along this narrow road.
There is no other way that leads to
  Küssnacht.
I'll do it here; the place is favorable.
The elderbush will hide me over there,
And from that point my arrow's flight
  can reach him.
The narrow road will hinder the pur-
  suers.
Now, viceroy, settle your account with
  heaven.
You have to go, for time's run out on
  you.
I led a harmless, quiet hunter's life.
My bow was bent for woodland game
  alone,
My mind was free from any thoughts
  of murder.
You frightened me away from peaceful
  ways;
You changed the natural milk of
  human kindness
To rankling, bitter poison in my breast.
You have accustomed me to monstrous
  things.
A man who had to aim at his own child
Can surely hit his adversary's heart.
I must protect my faithful wife, my
  children,
Against your awful anger, Governor.
When I was forced as punishment to
  draw

The bow and level it with trembling hands,
When you with such infernal glee compelled me
To take my aim at my beloved child,
When I was pleading helplessly before you—
I vowed then, deep within my heart and soul,
A dreadful oath that only God could hear,
That I would aim my bow and arrow next
Straight at your heart. The promise that I made
Amid the hellish torments of this day
Is now a sacred debt which I will pay.
You are my lord, my kaiser's governor;
But even he, the king, would not have dared
What you have done. He sent you to this country
To deal out justice sternly, for he's angry,
But not with fiendish pleasure to make bold
To do such wrong unpunished, uncontrolled.
There is a God to punish and avenge.
Come now, you messenger of bitter pain,
My dearest jewel and my greatest treasure.
I'll set a mark for you that until now
No fervent plea could ever penetrate,
But you shall pierce it irresistibly.
And you, my trusted bowstring, you so often
Have served me faithfully in joyous sport;
Do not desert me in this dreadful hour.
Hold fast this one more time, my faithful string,
Who often sped my bitter arrow's flight.
If it should feebly from my fingers fly,
I have no second one with which to try.
[*Wayfarers pass across the stage.*]
I'll sit down here upon this bench of stone
Constructed for the travelers' rest and comfort,
For there's no home out here. Each wanderer
Goes past the others quickly and estranged,
And doesn't ask about their pains and cares.
The worried, anxious merchant passes by;
The pious monk, the lightly-laden pilgrim,
The sullen thief and then the jolly minstrel,
The pack-horse driver, with his burdened beast,
Who hails from distant lands—they come and go,
For every road leads somewhere at the last.
Each has his business; each goes on his way.
My way and business are to kill today.
[*He sits down.*]
There was a time when you rejoiced, dear children,
At Father's safe return from hunting trips,
For when he came, he always brought a gift.
Sometimes it was a pretty Alpine flower,
Sometimes a curious bird or ammonite
Such as the travelers find upon the mountains.
But now he's on the hunt for other game;
He sits beside this road with thoughts of murder
And waits to kill his enemy from ambush.
But still he thinks of you alone, dear children,
And only to protect your innocence
Against the vengeance of a mighty foe,
He will take aim to kill, and draw his bow. [*He rises.*]
I lie in wait for noble game. The hunter
Will never weary when he roams about
For days in winter's bitter cold and frost.
He risks his life in leaps from rock to rock,
And climbs the steep and slippery mountainsides
And clings to them, glued on with his own blood,
So he can hunt a paltry chamois down.
But now I seek a far more precious prize:
My mortal enemy, who seeks my ruin.

[*In the distance is heard lively music, coming closer.*]
Throughout my life I've always used the bow;
I've trained and practiced by the rules of archers.
I often hit the bull's-eye of the target
And won a pretty prize to carry home
From matches. But today I want to make
My master-shot and win the greatest prize
In all the broad expanses of these mountains. [*A bridal party passes across the stage and goes up the narrow road.* TELL *watches it pass, leaning on his bow.* STÜSSI, *the ranger, joins him.*]
STÜSSI. That is the overseer of Mörlischachen[48]
And that's his wedding party. He is rich
And owns ten herds of cattle in the Alps.
He's taking home his bride from Immensee.
And there will be a feast tonight at Küssnacht.
Come with us. Every honest man's invited.
TELL. A gloomy guest is not for wedding feasts.
STÜSSI. If worry weighs you down, throw it aside.
Accept what comes your way; the times are hard,
So make the most of pleasure when it comes.
Here is a feast and elsewhere burial.
TELL. And often one comes right behind the other.
STÜSSI. So goes the world; misfortune everywhere.
In Canton Glarus there has been a landslide;
One side of Glärnisch peak has fallen down.
TELL. Are even mountains tottering and falling?
There's not a thing on earth that's standing firm.
STÜSSI. One hears of strange things happening everywhere.
I spoke, for instance, with a man from Baden;
He said a knight was on his way to court,
And on the way, a swarm of hornets came
And settled on his horse, attacking it
With painful stings until it fell down dead.
So he went on and came to court on foot.
TELL. The weak are also furnished with a sting. [ARMGARD *enters with several children and takes her position at the entrance of the narrow pass.*]
STÜSSI. They say it means disaster for our land—
Unnatural and dreadful happenings.
TELL. Such things are happening each day somewhere;
No supernatural acts need make them known.
STÜSSI. Well, lucky he who tills his field in peace
And sits at home among his own, untroubled.
TELL. The most devout cannot abide in peace
If it's displeasing to his evil neighbor.
[TELL *often looks with restless expectation toward the high point of the road.*]
STÜSSI. Good-by. Are you expecting someone here?
TELL. I am.
STÜSSI. A happy homeward journey then.
You are from Uri? Our viceroy was up there,
And we're expecting his return today.
A TRAVELER. [*Entering.*] Do not expect the governor today.
The streams are flooded from the heavy rains,
And all the bridges have been washed away. [TELL *rises.*]
ARMGARD. [*Coming forward.*] He will not come.
STÜSSI. You want to ask for something?
ARMGARD. Indeed I do.
STÜSSI. But why then stand around
In narrow roads where you obstruct his way?
ARMGARD. He can't escape me here. He has to listen.
FRIESSHARD. [*Coming down the narrow road hastily, calling toward the stage.*]
Make way! My gracious lord, the governor,
Is close behind me, riding down the pass. [TELL *leaves.*]
ARMGARD. [*Excitedly.*] The governor is

coming. [*She goes toward the front of the stage with her children.* GESSLER *and* RUDOLF DER HARRAS *appear on horseback at the high point of the road.*]

STÜSSI. [*To* FRIESSHARD.] How could you cross
The stream when every bridge is swept away?

FRIESSHARD. We fought a battle with the lake, my friend;
So now we're not afraid of Alpine streams.

STÜSSI. You were afloat in that terrific storm?

FRIESSHARD. We were. I will remember that forever.

STÜSSI. Do stay and tell me!

FRIESSHARD. I can't. I must go on
And tell them that the governor is coming. [*He leaves.*]

STÜSSI. If decent folk had been aboard that ship,
It surely would hae sunk with all on board,
But men like these are safe from fire and water. [*He looks around.*]
Where is that hunter I was talking to? [*Exit.*] [GESSLER *and* RUDOLF DER HARRAS *enter on horseback.*]

GESSLER. Say what you will, I am the kaiser's servant
And must consider how to please him best.
He didn't send me here to flatter people
And deal too gently with them. He expects
Obedience. The question here is whether
The peasant or the kaiser will be master.

ARMGARD. Now is the moment. Now I'll make my plea. [*She approaches fearfully.*]

GESSLER. I didn't hang the hat for fun in Altdorf,
Nor even as a test of people's hearts.
I know them all too well. I put it up
That they might learn to bend their stubborn necks
Which now they carry proudly and erect.
I placed this inconvenient device,
Exactly in their way, where they must pass,
So that they have to see it there and be
Reminded of their lord, whom they forget.

RUDOLF. But sir, the people also have some rights.

GESSLER. It's not the time to weigh and settle those.
Great matters are in progress. The royal house
Desires to grow, and what the father started
So gloriously, his noble son will finish.[49]
This country is a stone upon our path.
One way or other, these cantons must submit. [*They start to pass on, but* ARMGARD *throws herself down before the* GOVERNOR.]

ARMGARD. Have mercy, Governor! My lord, have mercy!

GESSLER. Why block my passage on this public road?
Get back, I say!

ARMGARD. My husband lies in prison;
These hungry orphans cry for bread. My lord,
Have pity on our terrible distress!

RUDOLF. Who are you anyway? And who's your husband?

ARMGARD. A gatherer of hay from Rigi Mountain
Who mows the wild free grass above the chasm,
Along the steep and rugged precipice
Where even cattle do not dare to climb—

RUDOLF. [*To the* GOVERNOR.] A pitiful and miserable life.
I beg you, set this wretched fellow free.
Whatever the offense he has committed,
His dreadful work is punishment enough. [*To the woman.*]
You shall have justice, woman. Make your plea
Inside the castle; this is not the place.

ARMGARD. No, no, I will not leave this spot until
The governor will set my husband free.
He's been in prison for the past six months
And waits in vain to get the judge's verdict.

GESSLER. You want to force me, woman? Get away!

ARMGARD. I plead for justice, Governor! You sit
As judge in place of emperor and God,

So do your duty here and give us justice
As you expect it for yourself from heaven.
GESSLER. Remove these shameless people from my sight!
ARMGARD. [*Seizing the reins of the horse.*] Oh no, you won't! I've nothing more to lose.
You will not leave this place, Lord Governor,
Until you've granted justice. Roll your eyes,
Wrinkle your forehead, and scowl just as you please;
Our misery is so extreme that we
Don't fear your anger any more.
GESSLER. Make room,
Unless you want my horse to step on you.
ARMGARD. Then let it step on me. [*She pulls her children to the ground and throws herself down beside them in his way.*] I'll lie right here
With my own children. There now—let your horse
Tread underfoot and kill these helpless orphans.
It will not be the worst thing that you've done.
RUDOLF. Are you completely mad?
ARMGARD. [*Continuing with greater vehemence.*] You've long been trampling
The kaiser's country underneath your feet.
I'm just a woman, but if I were a man,
I'd know a better thing to do than lie
Before you in the dust. [*The former music is heard again from the high point of the road, but more softly.*]
GESSLER. Where are my men?
Take her away before I lose my head
And do in anger something I'll regret.
RUDOLF. Your men cannot get through just now, my lord.
The road's obstructed by a wedding party.
GESSLER. I'm still too mild a ruler for these people;
Their idle tongues remain too free. They still
Are not completely tamed, as they should be.
But things are going to change, I give my word.
I'm going to break this stubborn mind of theirs;
This daring spirit of freedom I will crush.
I will proclaim a new and strict decree
In all these lands. I will—[*An arrow pierces him. He puts his hand on his heart and is about to fall from his horse. His voice is feeble.*] O God, have mercy.
RUDOLF. My lord! Oh God, what's this? Where did it come from?
ARMGARD. [*Getting up.*] It's murder, murder! He's falling down! He's hit!
The arrow struck the center of his heart.
RUDOLF. [*Jumping from his horse.*] What a dreadful thing! Oh God! My gracious lord,
Cry out to God and pray to him for mercy.
You are a dying man.
GESSLER. That was Tell's shot. [*He has slid from his horse into the arms of RUDOLF DER HARRAS, who lays him down on the bench.*]
TELL. [*Appearing above on the cliff.*] You know the archer; you needn't search for others.
Our homes are free and innocence is safe.
You'll do no further damage to our country. [*He disappears from the cliff. People rush in.*]
STÜSSI. [*Running in ahead of the people.*] What is the matter? What has happened here?
ARMGARD. Someone has shot the viceroy with an arrow.
PEOPLE. [*Running in.*] Who has been shot? [*While the first of the wedding party are coming on the stage, those in the rear are still on the height. The music continues.*]
RUDOLF DER HARRAS. He's going to bleed to death.
Get help somewhere! Pursue the murderer!
Poor helpless man, so you must die like this.
You would not listen to my words of warning.
STÜSSI. Come look how pale and lifeless he is now.
MANY VOICES. Who did this thing?
RUDOLF DER HARRAS. Are all these people crazy,
That they make music for a murder?

Silence! [*The music breaks off suddenly. People continue to flock in.*]
My lord, speak if you can. Is there no message
You would entrust to me? [GESSLER *makes signs with his hands, repeating them vehemently when they are not understood.*] Where should I go?
To Küssnacht? I can't understand. Don't be
Impatient, and don't think of earthly things;
Consider how to make your peace with heaven. [*All the people of the wedding party stand around the dying man in cold horror.*]
STÜSSI. Oh, look, how pale he is! Now death has struck
His heart. His eyes are growing dim and closing.
ARMGARD. [*Lifting up one of her children.*] Look, children! This is how a tyrant dies.
RUDOLF DER HARRAS. You crazy women, haven't you any feeling,
That you can feast your eyes on such a horror?
Come help me! Lend a hand! Will no one help
To pull the painful arrow from his breast?
WOMEN. [*Stepping back.*] What, touch the man whom God himself has struck?
RUDOLF DER HARRAS. Oh, curse you. Damn you! [*He draws his sword.*]
STÜSSI. [*Seizing his arm.*] Don't dare to do this, sir!
Your rule is past. The tyrant of our land
Is dead. We will no longer tolerate
Your violence, for we are free men now.
ALL THE PEOPLE. [*tumultuously.*] Our land is free!
RUDOLF HER HARRAS. And has it come to this?
Obedience and fear so quickly ended? [*To the soldiers and armed attendants who are pressing in.*]
You men all see this monstrous act of murder
Committed here. All help is now too late;
It does no good to hunt the murderer.
We're pressed by other worries. On to Küssnacht!
We'll try to save that fortress for the king.
For in this single moment are dissolved
All bonds of order and obedience,
And we can trust in no man's loyalty.
[*While he is leaving with the soldiers, six members of the order of the Brothers of Mercy enter.*]
ARMGARD. Make room, make room!
Here come the Brothers of Mercy.
STÜSSI. The victim's dead, and so the ravens come.
BROTHERS OF MERCY. [*Form a semicircle around the body and sing in solemn tones.*][50] Death comes to us before our time
   And grants no respite from his power;
He cuts us down in life's full prime
   And drags us off at any hour.
Prepared or not to go away,
   We have to face our judgment day.

[*While they repeat the last two lines, the curtain falls.*]

Act 5

Scene 1

A public square at Altdorf. In the right background is the Uri fortress with the scaffold still standing, as in the third scene of act 1. To the left the view opens upon many mountains, on all of which signal fires are burning. It is daybreak, and bells are heard ringing at several distances. RUODI, KUONI, WERNI, *the* HEAD MASON *and many other countrymen enter, accompanied by women and children.*]
RUODI. You see the signal fires upon the mountains?
HEAD MASON. And do you hear the bells beyond the forest?
RUODI. Our foes are driven out.
HEAD MASON. The castles are taken.
RUODI. And we in Canton Uri still endure

The tyrant's fortress on our native soil?
Are we the last to claim our liberty?
HEAD MASON. We let this yoke of bondage, meant for us,
Still stand? Let's tear it down!
ALL. Yes, tear it down!
RUODI. Where is the Ox of Uri?[51]
HORNBLOWER. Here. What is it?
RUODI. Climb to the mountain watch, and blow your horn
So loud that it will sound from peak to peak
And waken every echo in the gorges
To call together quickly all the men
From Uri's mountains. [HORNBLOWER *leaves.* WALTER FÜRST *enters.*].
WALTER FÜRST. Wait, my good friends, wait!
We haven't heard from Schwyz and Unterwalden
What's happened there. Let's wait for messengers.
RUODI. Why should we wait? The tyrant of the land
Is dead. The day of freedom has arrived.
HEAD MASON. Are not these flaming messengers enough,
That blaze on every mountain peak around?
RUDOI. Come, everybody, men and women! Come
And break the scaffold; tear the arches down!
Destroy the walls! Don't leave a stone in place!
HEAD MASON. Come on, you men! We built it, didn't we?
We know how to destroy it!
ALL. Tear it down! [*They attack the building from all sides.*]
WALTER FÜRST. It's under way. I cannot stop them now. [*Enter* MELCHTAL *and* BAUMGARTEN.]
MELCHTAL. You let this fortress stand, when Sarnen lies
In ashes and Rossberg has been stormed?
WALTER FÜRST. Oh, Melchtal, is it you? Do you bring freedom?
Are all the cantons rescued from the foe?
MELCHTAL. [*Embracing him.*] The land is free. Rejoice with me, my friend.
Right at this very moment, while we're talking,
There's not a tyrant left in Switzerland.
WALTER FÜRST. How did you take the castles? Go on, tell us!
MELCHTAL. Young Rudenz boldly stormed the Sarnen castle
And conquered it in one courageous effort.
I'd scaled the Rossberg's walls the night before.
But hear what happened. When we had driven out
The enemy and set the place on fire,
And crackling flames were leaping to the sky,
Then Diethelm, Gessler's page, dashed out and cried
That Berta von Bruneck would be burned to death.
WALTER FÜRST. Oh gracious God! [*The beams of the scaffold are heard falling.*]
MELCHTAL. She *was* in there. She'd been
Locked up in secrecy by Gessler's order.
Then Rudenz rushed in madly, for we heard
The falling beams, the crash of heavy timbers,
And through the fire and smoke the lady crying
Piteously for help.
WALTER FÜRST. And was she saved?
MELCHTAL. That was the time for action and decision.
If he'd been nothing more than feudal lord
To us, we would have thought of our lives first;
But he was our confederate, and Berta
Esteemed the people. So cheerfully we risked
Our lives for them and rushed into the fire.
WALTER FÜRST. But was she saved?
MELCHTAL. She was. Rudenz and I
Together brought her from the fire and saved her,
While close behind the timbers cracked and crashed.
And when she realized she had been saved
And raised her eyes and saw the light of heaven,
The baron clasped me to his breast, and there
A silent vow was sworn between us two,
A vow that will withstand the trials of

fate
Because it's been annealed by glowing fire.
WALTER FÜRST. Where's Ladenberg?
MELCHTAL. Across the Brünig pass.[52]
It's not my fault that he has kept his sight—.
This man who had my father's eyes put out.
I followed him and caught him as he fled,
And then I dragged him to my father's feet.
I had already drawn my sword above him,
But through the mercy of the blind old man
I spared his life as he lay pleading there.
He swore a sacred oath he'd not return
And he will keep his word, for he has felt
Our might.
WALTER FÜRST. How good you've chosen not to stain
Our victory with blood.
CHILDREN. [*Running across the stage with fragments of the scaffold.*] We're free! We're free! [*The horn of Uri is blown with a mighty blast.*]
WALTER FÜRST. See what a celebration! These children will
Recall this happy day when they are old. [*Girls bring in the hat on a pole. The whole stage is filling with people.*]
RUODI. Here is the hat to which we had to bow.
BAUMGARTEN. What do you think we ought to do with it?
WALTER FÜRST. Oh God! My grandson stood beneath this hat.
SEVERAL VOICES. Destroy this emblem of the tyrant's power!
Let's burn it up!
WALTER FÜRST. No, let us keep the thing.
It used to be the sign of tyranny;
Now let it be the symbol of our freedom. [*The countryfolk, men, women, and children, are standing and sitting on the beams of the wrecked scaffold, grouped picturesquely in a large semicircle.*]
MELCHTAL. We stand here joyously upon the ruins
Of tyranny, and what we swore at Rütli
Has come to pass today most gloriously.

WALTER FÜRST. The work has just begun, it isn't finished.
We need great courage now, and unity.
You can be sure the emperor won't wait
To avenge the death of his appointed ruler
And reinstate the one we drove away.
MELCHTAL. The let him come with all his mighty army!
Now that we have expelled the foe within,
We are prepared to meet the foe without.
RUODI. Not many passes lead into our land,
And those we will defend with our own bodies.
BAUMGARTEN. We are united by a lasting bond,
And all his armies cannot make us fear.
[RÖSSELMANN *and* STAUFFACHER *enter.*]
RÖSSELMANN. [*Speaking as he enters.*]
These are the dreadful judgments from above.
COUNTRYMEN. What is the matter?
RÖSSELMANN. What times we're living in!
WALTER FÜRST. Speak up, what's wrong? Oh, Werner, is it you?
What is the matter?
COUNTRYMEN. What is it?
RÖSSELMANN. Astounding news.
STAUFFACHER. We're liberated from the gravest fear.
RÖSSELMANN. The emperor has been murdered.
WALTER FÜRST. Gracious God! [*The countrymen are agitated and crowd around* STAUFFACHER.]
ALL. Murdered? What? The emperor was murdered?
MELCHTAL. Impossible! Where did you get such news?
STAUFFACHER. It's true. King Albrecht was assassinated
Near Bruck. A truthful man, Johannes Müller,
Brought us the awful message from Schaffhausen.[53]
WALTER FÜRST. Who dared to do so horrible a thing?
STAUFFACHER. The man who did it makes the act more dreadful.
It was his nephew, son of his own brother,
Duke John of Swabia, who carried out

the deed.
MELCHTAL. What drove him to this act of parricide?
STAUFFACHER. The emperor kept back the inheritance
Of this impatient man. And it was said
He wanted to retain it for himself,
And then appease him with a bishopric.
However this may be, the duke inclined
His ear to bad advice from friends in arms,
And with the noble lords von Eschenbach,
Von Tegerfeld, von Palm and von der Wart,
Decided, since he could not get his rights,
That he would take revenge, with his own hand.
WALTER FÜRST. Tell us, how did they do this dreadful thing?
STAUFFACHER. The king was riding from his Baden castle,[54]
En route to Rheinfeld, where he held his court;
With him were Princes John and Leopold[55]
And quite a train of noble gentlemen.
And when they reached the landing at the Reuss,
Where you must get across the stream by ferry,
Assassins forced their way into the boat
And cut the kaiser off from his attendants.
Then as the king was riding onward through
A cultivated field (where it is said
A city used to stand in pagan times),
Within clear sight of ancient Hapsburg castle,[56]
The birthplace of his royal lineage,
Duke John rushed at the king and plunged his dagger
Into his throat, von Palm thrust with his spear,
And Eschenbach came in to split his skull.
And so he fell and lay in his own blood,
By his own kinsmen killed, on his own land.
Those on the other bank could see the crime
But, separated by the stream, could give
No help, but only cries of futile anguish.
There by the wayside sat a poor old woman,
And in her arms the kaiser bled to death.
MELCHTAL. So he who took all things, but never gave,
Has only dug his own untimely grave.
STAUFFACHER. A monstrous fear hangs over all the land.
The passes in the mountains are blockaded
And all the borders of the cantons guarded.
Old Zurich even closed her city gates,
Which stood unlocked and open thirty years,
In fear of murderers, and worse—avengers.
For now stern Agnes, Queen of Hungary,[57]
Who has no trace of woman's tenderness,
Comes armored with the ban of outlawry
And would avenge her father's royal blood
Upon the families of the murderers,
Upon their servants, children, children's children,
And even on the stones of all their castles.
She's sworn an awful oath to sacrifice
Whole generations on her father's grave
And bathe in blood as in the dew of May.
MELCHTAL. You know which way the murderers have fled?
STAUFFACHER. They left right after they had done the deed
And took their flight in different directions,
So that they'll never meet on earth again.
It's said Duke John is wandering in the mountains.
WALTER FÜRST. And so their crime will bear no fruit for them,
For vengeance bears no fruit. It is itself
Its own repulsive food, its sole delight
Is murder, and its satisfaction, dread.
STAUFFACHER. Their crime will profit the assassins nothing,
But we will pluck with clean and unstained hands

The blessed fruit their bloody deed produced,
For now we are released from greatest fear.
The strongest foe of liberty has fallen,
And it's reported that the crown will pass
From Hapsburg's hands into another house.
The Empire will affirm its free election.[58]
WALTER FÜRST *and* SEVERAL OTHERS. Whom will they choose?
STAUFFACHER. The Count of Luxemburg
Is favored most by the majority.
WALTER FÜRST. It's good that we were loyal to the Empire;
There's reason now to hope for right and justice.
STAUFFACHER. Yes, each new ruler needs to have brave friends,
And he will shield us from all Hapsburg vengeance. [*The countrymen embrace each other. The* SACRISTAN *and a* ROYAL COURIER *enter.*]
SACRISTAN. Here are the honored leaders of our country.
RÖSSELMANN *and* SEVERAL OTHERS. What have you there?
SACRISTAN. A courier brings this letter.
ALL. [*To* WALTER FÜRST.] Quick, open it and read.
WALTER FÜRST. [*Reading.*] "To her good people
Of Uri, Schwyz, and Unterwalden, Queen
Elizabeth sends grace and all good wishes."
MANY VOICES. What does she want with us? Her reign is over.
WALTER FÜRST. [*Reading.*] "In her great pain and widow's heavy sorrow,
In which the bloody passing of her lord
Has plunged the queen, she still bears in her mind
The ancient faith and love of Switzerland."
MELCHTAL. She never thought of us in her good fortune.
RÖSSELMANN. Be still, let's hear the rest.
WALTER FÜRST. [*Reading.*] "And she expects of all these loyal people
That they will feel a deep and just abhorrence
Against the perpetrators of this crime.
Therefore, she now expects of all three cantons
That they will give no aid to the assassins,
But rather that in fealty they will help her
Commit them to the hands of the avenger,
Remembering the love and former favors
They have received from Rudolf's royal house." [*The countrymen show indignation.*]
MANY VOICES. The love and favors!
STAUFFACHER. True, we received some favors from the father;
But what have we to boast of from the son?
Did he confirm the charter of our freedom
Like all the other emperors before him?
Did he speak righteous verdicts or allow
Protection for mistreated innocence?
Did he so much as listen to the men
We sent to him as envoys in our anguish?
Not one of all these things the king has done;
And if we had not by ourselves secured
Our rights by our own hands, courageously,
Our needs would not have touched him. Gratitude?
He sowed no gratitude within these valleys.
He stood upon so high a place of power
He could have been a father to his people,
But he preferred to care just for his own.
Let those whom he has favored weep and moan.
WALTER FÜRST. Let's not rejoice about his fall. Let's not
Remember now the wrongs that we endured.
May that be far from us. But that we should
Avenge his death, who never did us good,
And hunt down those who never did us harm,
Does not befit us, and surely can't be

right.
For love must be a freewill offering,
And death releases from enforced demands.
We owe him no more duties in these lands.
MELCHTAL. And though the queen is weeping in her chambers,
Lamenting in her wild despair to heaven,
You see a people here released from anguish,
And giving thanks to that same heaven above.
Who would reap sympathy must first sow love. [*Exit* COURIER.]
STAUFFACHER. [*To the people.*] But where is Tell? Must he alone be absent,
The man who is the founder of our freedom?
He did the most, endured the hardest lot.
Let's go as pilgrims to his house and call
Our praises out to him who saved us all! [*All leave the stage.*]

Scene 2

The main room of TELL's *house. A fire is burning in the fireplace. The open door shows the scene outside. Present are* HEDWIG, WALTER, *and* WILHELM.]
HEDWIG. Your father's coming home today, my boys.
He is alive and free; we all are free.
Your father is the one who saved our country.
WALTER. Now, Mother, don't forget I was there too.
They'll have to mention me. My father's arrow
Came very close, but I was not afraid
And didn't tremble.
HEDWIG. [*Embracing him.*] Yes, you're given back
To me again. I've borne you twice, my son.
The pains of birth I've suffered twice for you.
But now it's past. I have you both again,
And your dear father is coming home today. [*A* FRIAR *appears in the doorway.*]
WILHELM. Look, Mother, look, a friar's standing there.
He must have come to ask us for a gift.
HEDWIG. Go bring him in, so that we can refresh him,
And let him feel this is a happy house. [*She leaves, returning soon afterward with a cup.*]
WILHELM. [*To the* FRIAR.] Come in, good man; my mother's bringing something.
WALTER. Come in and rest, and go away refreshed.
FRIAR. [*Glancing around fearfully with a wild, haggard look.*] Where am I? Tell me, what's the town and country?
WALTER. You must have lost your way if you don't know.
You are in Bürglen, sir, in Canton Uri.
This is the entrance to the Schächen Valley.
FRIAR. [*To* HEDWIG *as she enters.*] Are you alone, or is your husband here?
HEDWIG. I'm expecting him. But what is ailing you?
You look as if you brought us nothing good.
Whoever you are, though, you're in need. Take this. [*She offers him the cup.*]
FRIAR. However much I'm longing for refreshment,
I'll not take anything until you've promised—
HEDWIG. Don't touch my dress! Don't come too close to me.
Stay farther back if you want me to listen.
FRIAR. Oh, by this hospitable fire, and by
Your children's precious heads I here embrace,
I beg of you— [*He takes hold of the boys.*]
HEDWIG. What do you want? Get back
And leave my boys alone! You're not a friar!
You're not! These robes are meant to harbor peace,
But there's no sign of peace in your expression.
FRIAR. I am the most unfortunate of men.
HEDWIG. Misfortune calls the heart to sympathy,
But your appearance freezes all my feeling.
WALTER. [*Jumping up.*] Look, Mother, Father's here! [*He rushes out.*]

HEDWIG. Heavens! [*She starts to follow, trembles, and holds onto the door post.*]
WILHELM. [*Running after* WALTER.] It's Father!
WALTER. [*Outside.*] Now you are home again!
WILHELM. [*Outside.*] Father, Father!
TELL. [*Outside.*] Yes, I'm home again. But where's your mother? [*They enter the house.*]
WALTER. She's standing by the door and can't get farther,
Because she's trembling so from fright and joy.
TELL. Oh, Hedwig! Hedwig! Mother of my children!
Our God has helped. No tyrant parts us now.
HEDWIG. [*Clinging to him.*] Oh, Tell, Tell! I suffered anguish for you! [*The* FRIAR *becomes attentive.*]
TELL. Forget it now, and live for joy alone.
I'm home with you again! This is my house,
And I am standing in my place once more!
WILHELM. But Father, where's your crossbow? I don't see it.
Where is it?
TELL. You'll not see it again, my son. I've had it put inside a holy place;
It won't be used for hunting any more.
HEDWIG. Oh, Tell! Tell! [*She steps back, letting go of his hand.*]
TELL. Why are you frightened, dear?
HEDWIG. But how have you come back to me? Oh God!
How do I dare to hold this hand? This hand—
TELL. [*With warmth and spirit.*] Defended you and also saved our country.
With conscience clear I raise it up to heaven. [*The* FRIAR *starts up suddenly.* TELL *catches sight of him.*]
Who is this friar?
HEDWIG. I had forgotten him.
You speak with him, I'm frightened in his presence.
FRIAR. [*Coming nearer.*] Are you the Tell who killed the governor?
TELL. I am. I don't intend to hide the fact.
FRIAR. So you are Tell. It must be Providence
That's brought me here to you, beneath your roof.
TELL. [*Looking at him closely.*] You aren't a friar. Who are you then?
FRIAR. You killed
The governor who wronged you. I too have killed
An enemy who kept my rights from me.
He was your enemy as well as mine.
I freed this country from its foe.
TELL. [*Starting back.*] You are—
How dreadful! Children! Children, go in there.
Go with them, Hedwig. Go! You wretched man,
You must be—
HEDWIG. Heavens, who is it?
TELL. Don't ask.
Just go away. The children mustn't hear it.
Go from the house. Go far. You mustn't stay
A moment here beneath this roof with him.
HEDWIG. Oh God! What is it? Come. [*She leaves with the children.*]
TELL [*To the* FRIAR.] You are the duke
Of Austria. That's who you are! You've killed
The emperor, your uncle and your lord.
JOHANNES PARRICIDA. He robbed me of my legacy.
TELL. You've killed
Your emperor, your uncle! And the earth
Still bears your weight? The sun still shines on you?
PARRICIDA. Tell, hear my side—
TELL. You're dripping with the blood
Of murdering your kinsman and your kaiser.
How dare you step into my decent house?
How dare you show your face to honest men
And claim the right of hospitality?
PARRICIDA. I hoped to find compassion in your house.
You too have taken vengeance on your foe.
TELL. You dare confuse ambition's bloody guilt
With a father's necessary self-defense?
Did you defend your children's heads from harm

And guard the sanctuary of the home,
Or shield your own against the greatest wrongs?
I'll raise my guiltless hands to heaven above
And curse you and your deed, for I avenged
The laws of nature; you dishonored them.
I share no guilt with you. Your act was murder,
But I defended what's most dear to me.
PARRICIDA. You cast me off, uncomforted, despairing?
TELL. I'm overcome with horror as we talk.
Away! Go on your dreadful road alone,
And let this house of innocence be pure.
PARRICIDA. [*Turning around, ready to leave.*] I cannot and I will not live like this.
TELL. And yet I must have pity. God in heaven!
You're still so young, from such a noble house,
The grandson of my former kaiser Rudolf—
And now a fugitive assassin, pleading,
Despairing, at my door—a poor man's door. [*He turns aside.*]
PARRICIDA. If you can weep, lament my awful fate.
It's horrible. I am a prince—or was one—
And surely could have lived in happiness
If I had curbed my own impatient wishes.
But envy always gnawed my heart, because
I saw the youth of cousin Leopold
Endowed with honors and enriched with lands,
While I was kept like a dependent boy,
Although I was of equal age with him.
TELL. Unlucky man, your uncle knew you well
When he withheld from you those lands and subjects.
You have yourself confirmed his wise decision
With your impulsive, shocking act of madness.
Where are your bold accomplices in crime?

PARRICIDA. Wherever the avenging spirits drove them.
I haven't seen them since the woeful deed.
TELL. You know the ban of outlawry forbids
Your friends to help and gives your foes free hand.
PARRICIDA. That's why I must avoid all public roads
And do not dare to knock at any door.
I turn my footsteps to the wilderness;
A terror to myself, I roam the mountains
And shudder at the sight of my own image
Whenever it's reflected in a brook.
If you have sympathy of human kindness—[*He falls down before* TELL.]
TELL. [*Turning aside.*] Get up! Get up!
PARRICIDA. Not till you give your hand to me in help.
TELL. How can I help? Can any sinful man?
But stand up now. Whatever dreadful thing
You've done, you are a man, and so am I.
No one shall go uncomforted from Tell.
I'll do for you what's in my power.
PARRICIDA. [*Jumping to his feet and grasping* TELL's *hand vigorously.*] Oh, Tell,
You save my trembling soul from stark despair.
TELL. Let go my hand. You have to leave. You can't
Remain here undiscovered, and if discovered,
You can't expect protection. Where will you go?
Where will you look for peace?
PARRICIDA. I do not know.
TELL. Then hear what God suggests to me. You have
To go to Rome, the city of St. Peter,
And fall upon your knees before the pope,
Confess your guilt, and thus redeem your soul.
PARRICIDA. But won't he give me up to the avenger?
TELL. Whatever he does, accept it as from God.
PARRICIDA. How can I reach this unfamiliar land?

I do not know the roads or where they lead,
And can't risk joining other travelers.
TELL. I will describe the road that you must follow.
You'll have to go upstream along the Reuss
That rushes wildly down the mountain gorges.
PARRICIDA. [*Frightened.*] The Reuss? It was the witness of my crime.[59]
TELL. The road leads you beside the gorge. Along
Its course are many crosses to remind you
Of travelers entombed by avalanches.
PARRICIDA. I'm not afraid of nature's threats and terrors
If I can tame the anguish in my heart.
TELL. At every cross kneel down, and there confess
Your sins with fervent tears of penitence.
And when you've passed this road of horrors[60] safely,
And if the icy mountain doesn't send
An avalanche of snow to bury you,
You'll reach the Devil's Bridge, which hangs in spray.
If it does not give way beneath your guilt,
Then when you've safely left the bridge behind,
A rocky gate will lead you to a tunnel—
As black as night, where daylight never reaches—
And it will take you to a pleasant valley.
But you must hurry on with rapid steps;
You cannot stay where peace and joy abide.
PARRICIDA. Oh, Rudolf, noble ancestor, like this
Your grandson comes into your royal realm.
TELL. Then, climbing still, you'll reach St. Gotthard's heights
Where you will see the everlasting lakes
That draw their water from the streams of heaven.
There you will say farewell to German lands;
From there another lively stream will lead you
Into your promised land of Italy. [*The Alpine cowherd's melody, sounded on alpenhorns, is heard.*]
I hear the people coming. You must leave.
HEDWIG. [*Rushing in.*] Where are you, Tell? My father's coming. And there's
A whole parade of fellow countrymen.
PARRICIDA. [*Hiding his face.*] I cannot stay among these happy people.
TELL. Go, Hedwig, give this man some food and drink,
And give abundantly. His road is long
And he'll not find an inn along the way.
Hurry now. They're coming.
HEDWIG. Who is he?
TELL. Don't ask.
And when he leaves us turn away your eyes
So that you will not see the road he follows. [PARRICIDA *goes quickly toward* TELL, *but the latter motions him to stay back and leaves. When the two have left the stage in different directions, the scene changes, showing the*

Last Scene

The whole valley before TELL's *house and the heights that enclose it are crowded with countrymen who are grouped in a picturesque tableau. Other countrymen are coming along a high pathway and crossing a footbridge over the Schächen.* WALTER FURST *with the two boys,* MELCHTAL, *and* STAUFFACHER *come forward. Others crowd behind them. When* TELL *appears, all greet him with shouts of joy.*]
ALL. Love live our Tell, deliverer and archer! [*While those in front are crowding around* TELL *and embracing him,* RUDENZ *and* BERTA *appear, the former embracing the countrymen, the latter embracing* HEDWIG. *The music from the mountain accompanies this wordless scene. When it has stopped,* BERTA *walks to the center of the crowd of people.*]
BERTA. Confederates and countrymen, receive me
Into your union, the first so fortunate
To find protection in this land of freedom.
I put my cause into your valiant hands.
Will you protect me as your citizen?
COUNTRYMEN. We will indeed, with life and property.

BERTA. Then I will give to this young man my hand,
To live in liberty in this free land.
RUDENZ. And I declare my serfs and vassals free. [*While the music begins to sound again, the curtain falls.*]

1. In German *Vierwaldstättersee*, or "Lake of the Four Forest Cantons." The four cantons bordering on the lake are Lucerne *(Luzern)*, Schwyz, Uri, and Unterwalden. Only the last three are involved in the fight for freedom treated in the play.
2. The *Kuhreihen*, literally "cow dance," is a sort of folk tune without words that can be played on the alpenhorn. It is used again to herald the celebration at the end of the play.
3. The three parts of the lyrical prelude were set to music by Franz Liszt in three songs titled "The Fiserman's Son," "The Herdsman," and "The Alpine Hunter" (Opus 292, 1845 and 1855). Each of the parts has been given at least one other musical setting: the first by Edward MacDowell, "The Fisher Boy" (Opus 27, No. 3, 1890); the second by Robert Schumann, "The Herdsman's Farewell" (Opus 79, No. 22); and the third by Franz Schubert (Opus 37, No. 2, 1817).
4. A steep but not very high rock on the shore of Lake Lucerne, near the locale of the scene. Schiller evidently meant one of the Mythenstock peaks.
5. A literal translation of *Wetterloch*, a term applied to gorges, caves, or crevices in the mountains from which the wind blows before a storm.
6. St. Simon's and St. Jude's Day is October 28 and sets the date of the scene. The year in 1307.
7. The emperor of the Holy Roman Empire of the German nation.
8. This dialogue in couplets is an adaptation of the Greek single-line speeches called *stichomythia*.
9. The chief town in Canton Uri. This canton is the setting of all but two of the fifteen scenes of the play.
10. Schiller calls the overseer a *Fronvogt*, that is to say, a man who oversees the *Frondienst*, the compulsory labor performed, instead of payment of taxes, by vassals for the feudal lord.
11. One of several short lines in the original.
12. In German the word is *Walde* ("forest"), but obviously Kernwald (Forest of Kerns) is meant. Melchtal lives near Kerns at the edge of the Kernwald.
13. Melchtal's father.
14. The Schreckhorn and the Jungfrau are two of the highest peaks in the Bernese Oberland. In Schiller's day these peaks were considered inaccessible.
15. The name comes from the verb *roden*, meaning "to uproot" or "clear the trees"; hence, a clearing or meadow.
16. When Goethe read the first act, he said, "That really is not a first act, but a whole play, and truly first rate" (Karl Berger, *Schiller. Sein Leben und seine Werke* [Munich, 1923], 2: 667).
17. The ruins of the castle may still be seen near Attinghausen on the Reuss River, south of Altdorf in Uri. The date of this episode seems to be November 8, 1307, ten days after act 1.
18. Albrecht, who is called king, as well as emperor or kaiser, is displeased because the Swiss cantons have resisted his private (Hapsburg) claims.
19. The burial of shield and helmet with the last of a line was an old custom.
20. The questions are real enough. The emperor did not always have as much power as some of the dukes and ruling princes within the Empire, and he might give the cities over to some powerful vassal in exchange for troops or money.
21. The time is probably the night after the preceding scene, at 2:00 A.M., November 9, 1307.
22. The meeting is not legal because it is not public and is held at night and without the statute books.
23. The trips to Rome were made in order that the pope might crown the newly elected German kings as Holy Roman emperors.
24. Tradition has it that Schwyz was settled first and gave the name to all of Switzerland *(die Schweiz)*; see Stauffacher's oral history beginning thirty lines subsequently.
25. The contradiction between the man at the ferry and "no trace of human life" is found in the folk songs.
26. Other Teutonic tribes such as the Franks, the Burgundians, and some of the Goths.
27. Another dragon story, like that of Winkelried's grandfather, but this time Schiller makes dragon-killing symbolic of the draining of the swamps.
28. Tell's house is in Bürglen, Uri, and the date is apparently November 20, 1307.
29. Robert Schumann set Walter's song to music in "The Boy Archer's Song" (Opus 79, No. 25, 1849). There is also a setting by B. A. Weber, "The Archer."
30. Compare Goethe's *Faust*, Part 2, lines 11,575–11,576: "He only earns his freedom and existence, / Who daily conquers them anew" (tr. Bayard Taylor [Boston: Houghton Mifflin Company, 1870], 2:294). [Also quoted below, page 80].
31. The setting is near Altdorf, and the time seems to be about the same as in the previous scene (November 20, 1307).
Schiller meant to give this scene a lyrical tone. This accounts for the rhymes at the beginning and again later in the scene. Most of these rhymes were retained in the translation for the same reason.
32. This is Gessler's hunting expedition, from which he returns in the next scene.
33. The setting "near Altdorf" disagrees with the crier's earlier proclamation "in Altdorf" and the suggestion of a *Platz* or plaza which the people

cross when coming from the town hall. Tradition sets the locale on the town square of Altdorf. Schiller may have been influenced by old woodcuts that show the apple-shooting near the town.

34. The Eucharistic wafer used in the sacrament of the Lord's Supper.

35. The superstition about the trees is apparently derived from the word *Bannberg* itself. The German verb *bannen* has a double meaning: "to be charmed, enchanted," and "to protect by law, put under the ban." Folklore prefers the idea of enchantments, but actually the trees *protect* the town from avalanches, as Tell points out.

36. There have been various attempts to explain the name Tell. One theory would associate the word with the German *toll* ("mad, crazy") and the English cognate "dull"; another (by Grimm), with the Latin *telum* ("arrow"). Here Schiller follows Tschudi, who inferred some such attribute as foolishness, simplicity, or lack of discretion. See also act 1, scene 3, where Tell is depicted as a plain man of action rather than a reflective person.

37. Actually Gessler does not want the shot, as is seen by his reaction when Tell shoots. His purpose is to humiliate Tell publicly.

38. Rudenz is talking about a challenge to a duel.

39. The skillful diversion of attention from Tell and Walter simplifies the technical aspects of the shot. Moreover, on the stage, the people can crowd around Walter so that he cannot be seen during the shooting, and a pierced apple can be produced in place of the other one.

40. There are various indications that the locale is near Sisikon.

41. The Fisherman, not named, is Ruodi, and he addresses the boy by the name "Jenni," as in Act I, scene 1. The name was deleted in the translation for reasons of meter and rhyme.

42. In this passage Schiller was influenced by the famous storm speech in Shakespeare's *King Lear*, act 3, scene 2.

43. The Buggisgrat and Hackmesser are steep cliffs of the Axenberg or Axen Mountain; the Teufelsmünster is a steep rock on the opposite shore.

44. The ledge is now called "Tells Platte." Here a small chapel now stands, with frescoes depicting scenes from the play.

45. The German reads "eighty years," a general expression like the English "hundred years."

46. Walter Fürst.

47. Küssnacht is on the northern end of Lake Lucerne. It is now in Canton Lucerne, but at the time of the events of the play it was in Schwyz, one of the two cantons (Schwyz and Uri) over which Gessler ruled.

48. A monastery.

49. Rudolf of Hapsburg (reigned 1273–91) and his son Albrecht (reigned 1298–1308).

50. This song of the monks is meant to function like the chorus in Greek tragedy. There is a musical setting by Beethoven, "Gesang der Mönche" ("Song of the Monks").

51. A literal translation of *Stier von Uri*. He is the official hornblower and his horn is supposed to be made of the horn of the ure-ox (*Auerochs*, "aurochs, bison"). Tradition derives the name Uri from the old word "ure-ox," and the seal of the canton shows the head of an ox or bull.

52. On the southwest border of Unterwalden.

53. Bruck is north from Zurich, with the old Hapsburg castle not far away. Müller was a Swiss historian from Schaffhausen whose writings served as one of Schiller's sources.

54. Baden is in Canton Aargau, in northern Switzerland.

55. Leopold was Emperor Albrecht's son.

56. The *Habichtsburg* or "Hawk's Castle." The name developed into Habsburg by elision.

57. Albrecht's oldest daughter.

58. The German emperors of the Holy Roman Empire were chosen by the electoral princes of the realm.

59. Tell means the upper part of the Reuss that flows from the south into Lake Lucerne. Parricida is referring to that part of the Reuss that flows from the lake northward into the Aare and thence to the Rhine.

60. The road along the Reuss is called the *Schreckensstrasse*.

Faust, Part 1

Johann von Goethe

Despite a good deal of modern reevaluation, Johann Wolfgang von Goethe is still widely regarded as the preeminent figure in German literature and one of the great minds in the western tradition. As a practical playwright, he was not the equal of Schiller, and his great masterpiece *Faust* has been the despair of those attempting to bring it within the confines (and technical capabilities) of an ordinary theater, but *Faust* is so consummate an expression not only of romantic ideals, but also of mankind's eternal striving that it demands consideration in any orderly review of the development of European drama.

Goethe was born in Frankfurt on August 28, 1749, the son of upper-middle-class parents who could afford to put him in touch with the best in European culture. He received his early education from his father; later, he studied at Leipzig and, following an extended illness, at Strasbourg. It was intended that he should pursue a legal career, but the liberalizing influence of the universities further opened his mind to art, literature, philosophy, science—indeed, to virtually all branches of human knowledge. Goethe was the last of the true Renaissance men, with both an interest and a solid education in all of the major areas of human endeavor. In a lifetime of research, writing, and contemplation, Goethe was to make significant contributions in many fields, of which the theater was only one.

By 1771, Goethe had become an attorney in Frankfurt, but he was already devoting more time to literature than to law. *Götz von Berlichingen*, his first play of significance, was produced in Berlin in 1774. It was an important landmark in the so-called storm and stress movement, a radical form of romanticism just than reaching its height in Germany. *Clavigo* (1775) and *Stella* (1776) were somewhat less successful plays of this period. At the same time, Goethe published his novel, *The Sorrows of Young Werther* (1774), which took Europe by storm. The suicide of the romantic young hero at the end was so affecting that young men all over Europe dressed in Werther-like costumes and attempted to kill themselves.

Having attracted the attention of all Europe as a young man of genius, Goethe was invited by the young Duke Karl August of Weimar in November 1775, to join his court; as it turned out, he spent the rest of his life there (except for journeys abroad). For a number of years he busied himself about the duties assigned him by the duke, rising eventually to the equivalent of prime minister, with responsibility for organizing the army, carrying out irrigation projects, inspecting mines, and a great deal more. Following an extended trip to Italy (1786–88), however, Goethe decided to renounce a number of these official duties in order to devote himself more fully to literature and the arts; fortunately, the duke was willing to support him in these endeavors, and in 1791 Goethe became the director of the Weimar Theater (having already directed amateur productions in Weimar during earlier years). In the meantime, several plays on which he had been working for a number of years received their first productions: *Egmont* (1789), *Iphigenia in Tauris* (1802), and *Torquato Tasso* (1807) all showed a far more classical orientation with less insistence on the romantic tenets of Goethe's youth. Although Goethe wrote a number of shorter plays and fragments of little enduring value, these six plays, in addition to *Faust*, constitute the principal body of his dramatic work. He retired as director of the Weimar Theater in 1817.

No brief sketch of Goethe's life can do justice to the breadth of interest, intelligence, and accomplishment that he evidenced. His research in botany and physiology was of major significance in his day. His published work in physics and in philosophy attracted wide attention. His poetry and other literary efforts made him the leading man of letters in Europe, as well as the object of almost daily visits by hundreds of admirers who journeyed to Weimar to seek him out. He met and impressed Napoleon (in 1808) and Beethoven (in 1812), and his friendship with Schiller was perhaps the major influence in the lives of both of these important German writers. His numerous love affairs were a public scandal and yet a source of endless literary stimulation, but he eventually married his housekeeper, Christiane Vulpius, who was already the mother of his seventeen-year-old son. She died in 1816, but Goethe lived until March 22, 1832, creating new works and renewing his vision to the very end of his life.

Faust was, in a very real sense, the work of Goethe's entire lifetime. It was begun when, as a young man, he was a leader of the storm and stress movement, and the earliest scenes (primarily the Gretchen story) reveal this youthful influence. Fortunately, a manuscript of this earliest version survives because a young lady of the Weimar court had occasion to copy it; it was published in 1886. Goethe worked again on the manuscript during his extended sojourn in Italy, and published it under the title *Faust: A Fragment* in 1790. Under Schiller's influence, Goethe went back to work in earnest on *Faust* around the turn of the century, and finally published *Faust, Part 1* (the work translated here) in 1808. During the next quarter of a century, Goethe labored to complete *Part 2*, finally finishing it only a few months before his death and sealing it in an envelope to be published posthumously. Thus, only after Goethe's death did the complete work become available.

Only as a complete work is *Faust* truly comprehensible. It is a common expedient to reprint only *Part 1*, as it is the more stageable segment, but clearly a work that begins with a wager in heaven between The Lord and Mephistopheles cannot logically end with no further mention of the wager and with the death of a pitiful girl in prison. *Part 2*, which is 63 percent longer than *Part 1*, continues the fortunes of Faust and Mephistopheles through the "great world" following the small one of *Part 1*; at the end, Faust wins his bet and his immortal soul is saved. Although occasional attempts have been made to stage the entire work, it is clear that Goethe, who had many years of experience in the practical theater and certainly knew what was stageable and what was not, never intended *Faust* as a theater work. He chose to express himself in dramatic terms, and isolated scenes are vividly theatrical in the sense of evoking striking images in the mind of the reader, but the whole work is simply not a play. *Part 1* was fully produced as a separate work in 1829 and it has frequently been restaged since, although its incompleteness is bound to make of it a less than fully satisfying theatrical experience. The Gretchen story is so deeply moving, and offers such a unifying element in itself, that this no doubt accounts for the work's success as a separate play. Unquestionably it contains moments of the highest theatrical excitement.

The Faust legend goes back at least as far as the fifteenth century, when a magician, seer, and conjurer by that name actually lived in Germany. Some of the legends surrounding this personage were printed in the *Faust Book* in 1587; the main outlines of the story were used by Christopher Marlowe in his version of *Dr. Faustus* and were widely imitated by other writers throughout Europe. The Marlowe play toured widely on the Continent and, in debased and caricatured versions, became a series of puppet shows which Goethe saw in his youth. In the meantime, many other printed versions of the story were in circulation, all sharing the traditional ending in which Faust was damned, having sold his soul to Mephistopheles. Goethe's important predecessor Gotthold Lessing outlined but never completed a Faust play in which Faust would be saved at the end because of his noble striving and thirst for knowledge, qualities that were to stir a romantic age, and evidently this notion especially appealed to Goethe's imagination.

What he made of it almost defies description. *Faust* is a work of dramatic (if not strictly theatrical) art expressing a total world view, a concept of life as continual striving but never total satisfaction. Faust's pact with Mephistopheles is summed up in these lines:

> If I to any moment say:
> Linger on! You are so fair!
> Put me in fetters straightaway,
> Then I can die for all I care!

Mephistopheles then devotes many years to giving Faust the fullest possible realization of human life, cramming all human experience into a single lifetime and yet failing ever so to satisfy Faust as to create in him a willingness to stop striving. With his dying breath near the end of *Part 2,* Faust pictures a giant reclamation project in which the draining of a swamp will provide a Utopian land on which future generations may build a new society. He concludes:

> Freedom and life belong to that man solely
> Who must reconquer them each day.
> Thus child and man and old man will live here
> Beset by peril year on busy year.
> Such in their multitudes I hope to see
> On free soil standing with a people free.
> Then to that moment I could say:
> Linger on, you are so fair!

This is the same philosophy expressed by Wilhelm Tell in act 3, scene 1, of Schiller's play, and is an excellent distillation of the romantic view of life. Goethe's own life was devoted to such an ideal, and *Faust* is more than incidentally autobiographical in its reflection of Goethe's mind if not the details of his activities.

Part 1 as a separate stage work focuses inevitably on the Gretchen love story. If the plot is not structurally complete, it is nevertheless tender and touching, and Gretchen's prison scene is one of the most pitiful and powerful mad scenes anywhere in drama. All of the play's principal characters are interesting and well-rounded ones, but Faust and Mephistopheles are supreme evocations of affirmation and negation, respectively. Some critics even see them as opposing halves of a single personality, as Faust zestfully reaches for all that life has to offer and Mephistopheles is the eternal cynic and nay-sayer. Mephistopheles' supernatural power is somehow enhanced by his humanity, and one senses the pervading life-denying force in everything he is and does. The magnificence of these character creations is matched by the brilliance of Goethe's poetry, which quite revolutionized German literature and, as usual, cannot fully be rendered in another language. Additionally, Goethe effectively and playfully embroiders his piece with complex and occasionally arcane references that require lengthy footnotes, which hinder the reader and which cannot possibly be conveyed fully in today's theater. Yet the richness of this embroidery, as indeed of the whole play, well repays the reader willing to linger over it.

Faust is so important a piece of literature to the romantic movement and to European culture that it must be experienced. Attempts to stage even *Part 1* may never be fully satisfying, but are nevertheless well worth the effort. As a piece of dramatic literature, *Faust* occupies a unique place in the development of European civilization and the European theater.

N.B. The footnotes for *Faust, Part 1*, were written by the translator and have been somewhat abridged by the present editor. Professor Passage's complete notes, as well as his introduction and interpretive guide, may be found in *Faust*, translated by Charles E. Passage (Bobbs-Merrill, 1965). Professor Dennis J. Spininger, co-executor of Professor Passage's estate, has kindly provided several emendations for the Walpurgis Night scene. Certain stage directions, here enclosed in braces {}, have been added by the present editor.

Faust, Part 1

Translated by Charles E. Passage

Characters
Theater Manager
Dramatic Poet
Comic Character
Faust
Wagner
Mephistopheles
Frosch ⎫
Brander ⎬ *drinking companions*
Siebel ⎪
Altmayer ⎭
Margaret or Gretchen
Martha, Margaret's neighbor
Lieschen, Margaret's friend
Valentine, Margaret's brother
The Lord
Archangels
Spirits
Witches
Apes
Servants, apprentices, students, etc.

Prologue in the Theater[1]

{*Enter* THEATER MANAGER, DRAMATIC POET, COMIC CHARACTER.}
MANAGER. You two who often stood by me
In times of trouble and distress,
What hopes have you for our success
With this work here in Germany?
I'd like to please the crowd that has collected,
Since they both live and let live. As we meet,
The posts are set, the stage has been erected,[2]
And everyone expects a special treat.
They sit there in their seats with eyebrows raised
And patiently prepare to be amazed.
I know what gets the public interest
And yet I've never been in such a spot;
True, they are not accustomed to the best,
But all the same they've read an awful lot.
What can be done to make things fresh and new
Yet have them meaningful and pleasant too?
It really pleases me, to tell the truth,
To see the crowds come streaming toward our place,
Wave after wave flood toward our ticket booth
To squeeze in through the narrow gate of grace.[3]
In broad daylight, before the hour of four
They fight their way with blows up to the wicket
And much like starvelings begging bread at baker's door,
They almost break their necks to get a ticket.
The poet's miracle alone can sway
Such various minds; perform it, friend, today!
POET. O speak not of the motley multitude!
My spirit flies in horror from the sight.
Conceal from me that milling, jostling brood
That sucks us down the whirlpool by their might.
No, guide me to some holy solitude
Where pure joy blooms for poets' sole delight,
Where love and friendship in divine hands bear

Our hearts' true bliss and give it loving care.
Ah, what welled up from deep within our breast,
What our lips hesitantly tried for sound,
Now badly put, now haply well expressed,
Is in the moment's frenzy lost and drowned.
And often only years will pass the test
In which the form's perfection can be found.
What dazzles, fills an instant and is gone;
The true will for posterity live on.

COMIC CHARACTER. Don't talk posterity to me!
What if *I* talked posterity,
Who would provide *this* world with fun?
They want it and it shall be had.
The presence of a fine and sterling lad
Means something too, I think. And one
Who is engaging will not ever be
Embittered by the audience's moods;
To stir them more effectively
He craves to play to multitudes.
Just have good will and show your competence,
Let Fantasy with all her choirs be heard—
Emotion, passion, reason, and good sense—
But not without some nonsense, mark my word!

MANAGER. Above all, let there be enough live action!
They like to watch, and that's the chief attraction.
With lots of things before their eyes displayed
For crowds to stare and gape in wonder of,
There's most of your success already made
And you're the man whom they will love.
By mass alone the masses can be won,
Each picks out something for himself. Provide
A lot, provide for many, and everyone
Will leave the house and go home satisfied.
In staging any piece, stage it in pieces!
With hash like that your chance of luck increases;
It's served as easily as it's invented.
Why fuss to get a perfect whole presented?
The public only pick it all to pieces.

POET. How bad such hackwork is you do not seem to feel!
How ill it fits with real artistic mind!
The trash in which these bunglers deal
You turn into a principle, I find.

MANAGER. At such reproaches I take no offense.
To make a thing and get results with it
A man must use the best implements.
Remember it's soft wood you have to split.
See who they are for whom you write today!
One comes to while an hour away,
Another's overfull from dinner scenes,
And what is worst of all, I say,
So many come from reading magazines.
They come here scatterbrained, as to a masquerade,
Steps winged by curiosity alone;
The ladies treat us to themselves and gowns, unpaid,
And stage a show all of their own.
What are your poet's dreams up there on high?
Why does a full house put you in good mood?
Observe your patrons from close by:
Half are indifferent, half are crude.
One wants a game of cards after the show.
One wants a wild night in a wench's arms.
Why should you poor fools trouble so,
For ends like this, to court the Muses' charms?
I tell you, give them more and more and yet more still,
You won't go wrong with such a plan of action;
Just see you give the people some distraction,
For satisfy them, that you never will—
What ails you? Is this rapture or distress?

POET. Then find some other man to write your play!
Why should the poet lightly fling away
His highest right, the right that Nature lent

Him, just for your sake and in frivolousness?
How does he move all hearts to tenderness?
How does he conquer every element?
If not by harmony that wells forth from his heart
And takes the world back down into his heart?
When Nature, listless at her spinning, skeins
Around her spindle endless threads of life,
When unharmonious creatures of all strains
Clash in encounters of vexatious strife:
From that monotonous line in endless prolongation
Who singles portions out for rhythmic words?
Who summons things unique to general consecration
So that they may resound as splendid chords?[4]
Who whips the tempest's rage to passion's wrath?
Makes sunsets burn in high solemnity?
Who strews all springtime's blossoms winsomely
Upon the sweet beloved's path?
Who twines the green leaves of no consequence
To crowns that merit wins in every test?
Unites the gods, gives high Olympus sure defense?[5]
The might of man in poets manifest.
COMIC CHARACTER. Then use the powers that in you lie
And ply the trade that poets ply
The way you carry on a love affair.
By chance one meets, one feels, one lingers there,
And step by step one is involved;
Joy grows, and then by trouble is resolved;
One is enraptured, then along comes grief,
Before you know it there's a novel sketched in brief.
O let us also give just such a play!
You need but reach into life's full array!
All men lead lives, and though few realize it,
Their lives hold interest, anywhere one tries it.
In bright-hued pictures little clarity,
Much error and a glint of verity,
That is the way to make the best of brew
To cheer the world and edify it too.
Then to your play will come youth's fairest bloom
Harkening as to an oracle that speaks,
And from your work all tender souls consume
The melancholy food that each one seeks;
Now one and now another will be roused
And each find what in his own heart is housed.
They can be brought to tears or laughter with great ease,
They love illusion, have respect for ardent animation:
With finished men there's nothing that will please,
But boundless thanks will come from those still in formation.
POET. Then give me back the former times
When I myself was still a-growing
And when the spring of songs and rhymes
Uninterruptedly was flowing,
When mists concealed the world from me,
When buds enclosed miraculous powers,
And when I picked the thousand flowers
That filled all dales abundantly.
With nothing, I still had enough with youth,
Joy in illusion and the urge for truth.
Give me back the ardors of
Deep, painful happiness that I had then,
The force of hate, the might of love,
O give me back my youth again!
COMIC CHARACTER. You do need youth, good friend, in any case
When enemies in battle round you press,
When pretty girls their arms enlace
Around your neck with fond duress,
When victors' crowns allure your glance
From hard-won goals still far away,
When after whirlings of the dance
You dine and drink the nights away.
But taking up the well-known lyre
And playing it with strength and grace,

Approaching a goal that *you* desire
With amiably digressive pace,
That, elder Sirs, should be your aim,
And we accord it no less reverence.
Age does not make us childish, as they claim,
But finds us children in a truer sense.
MANAGER. Sufficient speeches have been made,
Now let me see some actions done!
While all these compliments were paid
Some useful goal could have been won.
Why talk about poetic mood?
It never goes with hesitancy.
If you are poets, well and good,
Then take command of Poetry.
You're well aware of what we need.
We want strong drink, it is agreed;
Then brew me some without delay!
Tomorrow will not see what is not seen today,
And not one day must go to waste;
Resolve must seize occasion fast
By forelock, and do so with haste;
Then it will hold on to the last
And move ahead because it must.
You know on German stages we
All try experiments today,
So do not stint in any way
On sets and stage machinery.
Use both sky-orbs, the large one and the small,
Be lavish with the stars, be free
With water, fire, and mountain wall,
Have birds and beasts in quantity.
Thus all creation will appear
Within our narrow wooden confines here,
Proceeding by Imagination's spell
From heaven, through the world, to hell.[6] {*Exeunt.*}

Prologue in Heaven

{*Enter* THE LORD, *the heavenly hosts,*[7] MEPHISTOPHELES; *the three* ARCHANGELS *step forward.*}
RAPHAEL. The sun sings as it sang of old
With brother spheres in rival sound,[8]
In thundrous motion onward rolled
Completing its appointed round.
The angels draw strength from the sight,
Though fathom it no angel may;
The great works of surpassing might
Are grand as on Creation day.
GABRIEL. And swift beyond conception flies
The turning earth, now dark, now bright,
With clarity of paradise
Succeeding deep and dreadful night;
The sea in foam from its broad source
Against the base of cliffs is hurled,
And down the sphere's eternal course
Both cliff and sea are onward whirled.
MICHAEL. And storms a roaring battle wage
From sea to land, from land to sea,
And forge a chain amid their rage,
A chain of utmost potency.
There blazing lightning-flashes sear
The path for bursting thunder's way—
And yet thy heralds,[9] Lord, revere
The mild procession of thy day.
ALL THREE. The angels draw strength from the sight,
Though fathom it no angel may;
The great works of surpassing might
Are grand as on Creation day.
MEPHISTOPHELES. Since you, O Lord, approach again and see
These people here and ask us how we do,
And since you used to like my company,
Behold me also here among this crew.
Excuse me, I can not be eloquent,
Not even if I'm scorned by all your staff;
My grand style would provoke your merriment
If you had not forgotten how to laugh.
Of suns and worlds there's nothing I can say;
How men torment themselves is what I see.
The little earth-god stays the same perpetually
And still is just as odd as on Creation day.
He would be better off at least
If you had not endowed him with the heavens' light;
He terms it Reason and exerts the right

To be more brute than any beast.
He seems like—craving pardon of Your
  Grace—
One of the spindle-shank grasshopper
  race
That flit around and as they hop
Sing out their ancient ditty where they
  stop.
He should stay in the grass where he
  has sung!
He sticks his nose in every pile of dung.
THE LORD. Is there no more that you
  could add?
Is finding fault all you can do?
Is nothing on earth ever right with
  you?
MEPHISTOPHELES. No, Lord! I find
  things there, as always, downright
  bad.
The human race in all its woes I so
  deplore
I hate to plague the poor things any
  more.
THE LORD. Do you know Faust?
MEPHISTOPHELES. The Doctor?
THE LORD. And my servant.
MEPHISTOPHELES. He serves you in a
  curious way, I think.
Not earthly is the poor fool's food and
  drink.
An inner ferment drives him far
And he is half aware that he is mad;
From heaven he demands the fairest
  star,
From earth all peaks of pleasure to be
  had,
And nothing near and nothing far
Will calm his troubled heart or make it
  glad.
THE LORD. Though now he serves me
  but confusedly,
I soon shall guide him on toward what
  is clear.
The gardener knows, when green
  comes to the tree,
That flowers and fruit will deck the
  coming year.
MEPHISTOPHELES. What will you bet you
  lose him if you give
Me your permission now to steer
Him gently down my path instead?
THE LORD. As long as he on earth may
  live,
To you such shall not be gainsaid.
Man errs as long as he can strive.
MEPHISTOPHELES. Thank you for that;
for with the dead
I never hankered much to be.
It is the plump, fresh cheeks that mean
  the most to me.
I'm out to corpses calling at my house;
I play the way the cat does with the
  mouse.
THE LORD. Good, then! The matter is
  agreed!
Divert this spirit from his primal
  source,
And if you can ensnare him, lead
Him with you on your downward
  course;
And stand abashed when you have to
  confess:
A good man harried in his dark dis-
  traction
Can still perceive the ways of righteous-
  ness.
MEPHISTOPHELES. All right! It won't be
  any long transaction.
I have no fears at all for my bet's sake.
And once I've won, let it be understood
You will admit my triumph as you
  should.
Dust shall he eat, and call it good,
Just like my aunt, the celebrated snake.
THE LORD. There too feel wholly free to
  try;
Toward your kind I have borne no
  hate.
Of all the spirits that deny,
The scoffer burdens me with slightest
  weight.
Man's activeness can all too easily go
  slack,
He loves to be in ease unqualified;
Hence I set a companion at his side
To goad him like a devil from the back.
  But you, true sons of gods,[10] may
  you
Rejoice in beauty that is full and true!
May that which is evolving and alive
Encompass you in bonds that Love has
  wrought;
And what exists in wavering semblance,
  strive
To fix in final permanence of thought.
  [*The heavens close, the* ARCHANGELS
  disperse.]
MEPHISTOPHELES. From time to time I
  like to see the Boss,
And with him like to keep things on
  the level.
It's really nice in one of such high class

To be so decent with the very Devil.
{*Exit.*}

Night

FAUST *restless in his chair at his desk in a narrow and high-vaulted Gothic room.*
FAUST. I've read, alas! through philosophy,
Medicine and jurisprudence too,
And, to my grief, theology
With ardent labor studied through.
And here I stand with all my lore,
Poor fool, no wiser than before!
I'm Master, I'm Doctor, and with my reading
These ten years now I have been leading
My scholars on wild-goose hunts, out
And in, cross-lots, and round about—
To find that nothing can be known!
This burns my very marrow and bone.
I'm shrewder, it's true, than all the tribes
Of Doctors and Masters and priests and scribes;
Neither doubts nor scruples now can daunt me,
Neither hell nor devils now can haunt me—
But by the same token I lose all delight.
I don't pretend to know anything aright,
I don't pretend to have in mind
Things I could teach to improve mankind.
Nor have I lands nor treasure hoards,
Nor honors and splendors the world affords;
No dog would want to live this way!
And so I've yielded to magic's sway,
To see if spirits' force and speech
Might not bring many a mystery in reach;
So I no longer need to go
On saying things that I don't know;
So I may learn the things that hold
The world together at its core,
So I may potencies and seeds behold,[11]
And trade in empty words no more.

O if, full moon, you did but shine
Your last upon this pain of mine,
Whom I have watched ascending bright
Here at my desk in mid of night;
Then over books and papers here,
Sad friend, you would come into view.
Ah, could I on some mountain height
Rove beneath your mellow light,
Drift on with spirits round mountain caves,
Waft over meadows your dim light laves,
And, clear of learning's fumes, renew
Myself in baths of healing dew!
   Am I still in this prison stall?
Accursed, musty hole-in-the-wall,
Where the very light of heaven strains
But dully through the painted panes!
   By these enormous book-piles bounded
Which dust bedecks and worms devour,
Which are by sooty charts surrounded
Up to the vaultings where they tower;
With jars shelved round me, and retorts,
With instruments packed in and jammed,
Ancestral junk together crammed—
Such is your world! A world of sorts!
   Do you still wonder why your heart
Is choked with fear within your breast?
Why nameless pain checks every start
Toward life and leaves you so oppressed?
Instead of Nature's living sphere
Wherein God placed mankind of old,
Brute skeletons surround you here
And dead men's bones and smoke and mold.
   Flee! Up! And out into the land!
Does not this mystic book indeed,
From Nostradamus' very hand,[12]
Give all the guidance that you need?
Then you will recognize the courses
Of stars; within you will unfold,
At Nature's prompting, your soul's forces
As spirits speech with spirits hold.[13]
In vain this arid brooding here
The sacred signs to clarify—
You spirits who are hovering near,
If you can hear me, give reply! [*He opens the book and glimpses the sign of the macrocosm.*][14]
Ha! Suddenly what rapture at this view

Goes rushing through my senses once
   again!
I feel a youthful joy of life course new
And ardent through my every nerve
   and vein.
Was it a god who wrote these signs
   whereby
My inward tempest-rage is stilled
And my poor heart with joy is filled
And with a mystic impulse high
The powers of Nature all around me
   are revealed?
Am I a god? I feel so light!
In these pure signs I see the whole
Of operative Nature spread before my
   soul.
Now what the wise man says I
   understand aright:
"The spirit world is not locked off from
   thee;
Thy heart is dead, thy mind's bolt
   drawn!
Up, scholar, and bathe cheerfully
They earthly breast in rosy dawn!" [*He
   contemplates the sign.*]
How all things interweave to form the
   Whole,[15]
Each in another finds its life and goal!
How each of heaven's powers soars and
   descends
And each to each the golden buckets
   lends;
On fragrant-blessed wings
From heaven piercing to earth's core
Till all the cosmos sweetly rings!
   O what a sight!—A sight, but nothing
      more!
Where can I grasp you, Nature without
   end?
You breasts, where? Source of all our
   lives,[16]
On which both heaven and earth
   depend,
Toward you my withered heart so
   strives—
You flow, you swell, and must I thirst in
   vain? [*Impatiently he turns pages of the
   book and glimpses the sign of the Earth
   Spirit.*][17]
How differently I am affected by this
   sign!
You, Spirit of the Earth, are nearer me,
I feel more potent energy,
I feel aglow as with new wine.
I feel the strength to brave the world,
   to go
And shoulder earthly weal and earthly
   woe,
To wrestle with the tempests there,
In shipwreck's grinding crash not to
   despair.
Clouds gather over me—
The moon conceals its light—
The lamp has vanished!
Mists rise!—Red lightnings dart and
   flash
About my head—Down from
The vaulted roof cold horror blows
And seizes me!
Spirit implored, I feel you hovering
   near.
Reveal yourself!
O how my heart is rent with fear!
With new emotion
My senses riot in wild commotion!
My heart surrenders to you utterly!
You must! You must! though it cost life
   to me! [*He seizes the book and mystically
   pronounces the sign of the Spirit. A
   reddish flame flashes. The* SPIRIT *appears
   in the flame.*]

SPIRIT. Who calls me?
FAUST. [*Cowering.*] Ghastly shape!
SPIRIT. With might
You have compelled me to appear,
You have long sucked about my
   sphere,[18]
Now—
FAUST. No! I cannot bear the sight!
SPIRIT. You begged so breathlessly to
   bring me near
To hear my voice and see my face as
   well;
I bow before your strong compulsive
   spell,
And here I am!—What childish fear
Besets you, superman![19] Where is the
   soul that cried?
Where is the heart that made and bore
   a world inside
Itself and sought amid its gleeful pride
To be with spirits equal and allied?
Where are you, Faust, whose voice
   called out to me,
Who forced yourself on me so
   urgently?
Are you the one who, having felt my
   breath,
Now tremble to your being's depth,
A terrified and cringing worm?
FAUST. Shall I give way before you,
   thing of flame?

I am your equal. Faust is my name!
SPIRIT. In tides of life, in action's storm
I surge as a wave,
Swaying ceaselessly;
Birth and the grave,
An endless sea,
A changeful flowing,
A life all glowing:
I work in the hum of the loom of time
Weaving the living raiment of godhead sublime.
FAUST. O you who roam the world from end to end,
Restless Spirit, I feel so close to you!
SPIRIT. You are like the spirit you comprehend,
Not me! [*Disappears.*]
FAUST. [*Overwhelmed.*] Not you? Whom then?
I, image of the godhead!
Not even rank with you! [*A knock.*]
God's death! I know who's there—my famulus—[20]
This puts an end to my great joy!
To think that dry-bones should destroy
The fullness of these visions thus!
[*Enter* WAGNER *in a dressing gown and nightcap, a lamp in his hand.* FAUST *turns around impatiently.*]
WAGNER. Excuse me! I heard you declaiming;
It surely was a Grecian tragedy?
There I would like some more proficiency,
Today it gets so much acclaiming.
I've sometimes heard it said a preacher
Could profit with an actor for a teacher.
FAUST. Yes, if the preacher is an actor too,
As may on some occasions be the case.
WAGNER. Oh, cooped up in one's museum[21] all year through
And hardly seeing folks except on holidays,
Hardly by telescope, how can one find
Persuasive skills wherewith to guide mankind?
FAUST. Unless you feel it you will not succeed;
Unless up from your soul it wells
And all your listeners' hearts compels
By utmost satisfaction of a need,
You'll always fail. With paste and glue,
By grinding others' feasts for hash,
By blowing your small flame up too
Above your paltry pile of ash,
High praise you'll get in apes' and children's sight,
If that's what suits your hankering—
But heart with heart you never will unite
If from your heart it does not spring.
WAGNER. Delivery makes the speaker's real success,
And that's just where I feel my backwardness.
FAUST. Try for an honest win! Why rail
Like any bell-loud fool there is?
Good sense and reason will prevail
Without a lot of artifice.
If you have serious things to say,
Why hunt for words out of your way?
Your flashy speeches on which you have pinned
The frilly cutouts of men's artistry
Are unrefreshing as the misty wind
That sighs through withered leaves autumnally!
WAGNER. Oh Lord! How long is art,
How short our life! And ever
Amid my work and critical endeavor
Despair besets my head and heart.
How difficult the means are to come by
That get one back up to the source,[22]
And then before one finishes mid-course,
Poor devil, one must up and die.
FAUST. Is that the sacred font, a parchment roll,
From which a drink will sate your thirst forever?
Refreshment will delight you never
Unless it surges up from your own soul.
WAGNER. But what delight there is in pages
That leads us to the spirit of the ages!
In seeing how before us wise men thought
And how far glorious progress has been brought.
FAUST. O yes, up to the furthest star!
My friend, the eras and past ages are
For us a book with seven seals.[23]
What you the spirit of the ages call
Is only those men's spirits after all
Held as a mirror that reveals
The times. They're often just a source of gloom!
You take one look at them and run away.

A trash can and a littered storage room,
At best a plot for some heroic play[24]
With excellent pragmatic saws
That come resoundingly from puppets' jaws.
WAGNER. But then the world! The mind and heart of man!
To learn about those things is our whole aim.
FAUST. Yes, call it learning if you can!
But who dares call a child by its right name?
The few who such things ever learned,
Who foolishly their brimming hearts unsealed
And to the mob their feelings and their thoughts revealed,
Were in all ages crucified or burned.
But it is late into the night, my friend,
We must break off now for the present.
WAGNER. I would have liked to stay awake and spend
The time in talk so learned and so pleasant.
But since tomorrow will be Easter Day,
I'll ask some further questions if I may.
I have industriously pursued my studying;
I know a lot, but would like to know everything. [*Exit.*]
FAUST. [*Alone.*] Why hope does not abandon all such brains
That cling forever to such shallow stuff!
They dig for treasure and are glad enough
To turn up angleworms for all their pains!
   May such a human voice presume to speak
Where spirits closed around me in full ranks?
And yet for this one time I give you thanks,
Of all earth's sons the poorest and most weak.
You pulled me back from the despair and panic
That threatened to destroy my very mind.
That vision loomed so vast and so titanic
That I felt dwarfed and of the dwarfish kind.
   I, image of the godhead, who supposed
Myself so near eternal verity,
Who reveled in celestial clarity,
My earthly substance quite deposed,
I, more than cherub, whose free strength presumed
To flow through Nature's veins, myself creating,
Thereby in godlike life participating,
How I must pay for my expostulating!
There by a word of thunder I was consumed!
Your equal I dare not pretend to be;
If I had power to make you come to me,
I did not have the power to make you stay.
In that brief moment's ecstasy
I felt so small and yet so great;
You thrust me backwards cruelly
To my uncertain human fate.
Who will instruct me? What must I not do?
Should I give every impulse play?
Alas, our very actions, like our sorrows too,
Build obstacles in our life's way.
   On the most glorious things mind can conceive
Things strange and ever stranger force intrusion;
Once we the good things of this world achieve,
We term the better things cheat and delusion.
The noble feelings that conferred our life
Are paralyzed amid our earthly strife.
   If Fantasy once soared through endless space
And hopefully aspired to the sublime,
She is content now with a little place
When joys have foundered in the gulf of time.
Deep down within the heart Care builds her nest
And causing hidden pain she broods,
And brooding restlessly she troubles joy and rest;
Assuming ever different masks and moods,
She may appear as house and home, as child, as wife,
As poison, dagger, flood, or fire;
You dread what never does transpire,
And what you never lose you grieve for

all your life.
   I am not like the gods! Too sharp I feel that thrust!
I am more like the worm that burrows in the dust,
That living there and finding sustenance
Is crushed beneath a passing foot by chance.
   Is all of this not dust that these walls hold
Upon their hundred shelves oppressing me?
The rubbish which with nonsense thousandfold
Confines me in this world of moths distressfully?
Should I find *here* the things I need?
When in perhaps a thousand books I read
That men have been tormented everywhere,
Though one may have been happy here and there?—
What is your grinning message, hollow skull,
But that your brain, like mine, once sought the day
In all its lightness, but amid the twilight dull,
Lusting for truth, went miserably astray?
And all you instruments make fun of me
With wheel and cog and drum and block:
I stood before the door, you should have been the key;
Your wards are intricate but do not turn the lock.
Mysterious in broad daylight,
Nature's veil can not be filched by you,
And what she keeps back from your prying spirit's sight
You will not wrest from her by lever or by screw.
You old contrivances unused by me,
You served my father's needs, hence here you stay.
You, ancient scroll, have blackened steadily
As long as dull lamps on this desk have smoked away.
Better if I had squandered my small estate
Than sweat and by that little be oppressed!
Whatever you inherit from your late Forebears, see that it is possessed.
Things unused are a burden of great weight;
The hour can use what it alone creates, at best.
   But why does my gaze fix on that spot over there?
Is that small bottle then a magnet to my eyes?
Why is all suddenly so bright and fair
As when in a dark wood clear moonlight round us lies?
   Rare phial, I salute you as I draw
You down with reverence and with awe.
In you I honor human skill and art.
You essence of all lovely slumber-flowers,
You extract of all subtle deadly powers,
Unto your master now your grace impart!
I see you, and my suffering is eased,
I clasp you, and my strugglings have ceased,
The flood tide of my spirit ebbs away.
To open seas I am shown forth by signs,
Before my feet the mirror-water shines,
And I am lured to new shores by new day.
   A fiery chariot comes on airy pinions[25]
Down toward me! I feel ready now and free
To rise by new paths unto aether's wide dominions,
To newer spheres of pure activity.
This higher life! This godlike ecstasy!
And you, but now a worm, have you acquired such worth?
Yes, only turn your back decisively
Upon the lovely sun of earth!
By your presumptuous will, fling wide the portals
Past which each man would rather slink away.
Now is the time to prove by deeds that mortals
Yield not to gods in dignity's array:
To shrink not back from that dark cavern where
Imagination sees itself to torment damned,
To press on toward that thoroughfare
Around whose narrow mouth all hell is

spanned:
To take that step with cheer, to force egress—
Though at the risk of passing into nothingness.
    Come down, you glass of crystal purity,
Come forth out of your ancient case to me
Who have not thought of you these many years.
You used to gleam amid my father's feasts
And used to gladden earnest guests
As you were passed from hand to hand with cheers.
Your gorgeous braid of pictures deftly twined,
The drinker's pledge to tell of them in rhyme
And drain your hollow rondure at one time,
These bring back many youthful nights to mind;
I shall not this time pass you to a neighbor,
To prove my wit upon your art I shall not labor;
Here is a juice that makes one drunk with no delay.
Its brownish liquid streams and fills your hollow.
This final drink which now shall follow,
Which I prepared and which I choose to swallow,
Be it a festive high salute to coming day! [*He lifts the glass to his lips.*] [*A peal of bells and choral song.*]
CHORUS OF ANGELS.[26] Christ is arisen!
Joy to the mortal
Whom the pernicious
Lingering, inherited
Dearths encompassed.
FAUST. What bright clear tone, what whirring drone profound
Makes me put this glass from my lips away?
Do you deep bells already sound
The solemn first hour of the Easter Day?
Do you choirs sing the song that once such comfort gave
When angels sang it by the darkness of a grave
Assuring a new covenant that day?
CHORUS OF WOMEN. With spices embalmed
Here we had carried Him,
We, His devoted,
Here we had buried Him;
With winding cloths
Cleanly we wrapped Him;
But, alas, we find
Christ is not here.
CHORUS OF ANGELS. Christ is arisen!
Blessed the loving
Who stood the troubling,
Stood the healing,
Chastening test.
FAUST. Why seek here in the dust for me,
You heavenly tones so mighty and so mild?
Ring out around where gentle souls may be.
I hear your tidings but I lack for faith,
And Miracle is Faith's most favored child.
As high as to those spheres I dare not soar
Whence sound these tidings of great joy;
Yet by these sounds, familiar since I was a boy,
I now am summoned back to life once more.
Once there would downward rush to me the kiss
Of heavenly love in solemn Sabbath hour;
Then plenitude of bell tones rang with mystic power
And prayer had the intensity of bliss;
Past comprehension sweet, a yearning
Drove me to wander field and forest where
Amid a thousand hot tears burning
I felt a world arise which was most fair.
The merry games of youth are summoned by that song,
And free delight of springtime festival;
And by that memory with childlike feeling strong
I am kept from this final step of all.
Sing on, sweet songs, in that celestial strain!
A teardrop falls, the earth has me again!
CHORUS OF DISCIPLES. If from the dead He has ascended,
Living, sublime,
Glorious on high,

If He in His growth[27]
Nears creative joy,
We, alas, are still here
On the bosom of earth.
He has left His own
Behind here to languish;
Master, we mourn
Thy happiness.
CHORUS OF ANGELS. Christ is arisen
From the womb of decay;
Bonds that imprison
You, rend gladsome away!
For you as you praise Him,
Proving your love,
Fraternally sharing,
Preaching and faring,
Rapture proclaiming,
For you the Master is near,
For you He is here.[28]

Outside the City Gate

All sorts of people coming out for a walk.
SEVERAL APPRENTICES. But why go up the hill?
OTHERS. We're going to the Hunting Lodge up there.
THE FIRST ONES. We'd rather walk out to the Mill.
ONE APPRENTICE. I'd suggest you go to the Reservoir.
THE SECOND. It's not a pleasant walk, you know.
OTHERS. How about you?
A THIRD. I'll go where the others go.
A FOURTH. Come on to Burgdorf! There you're sure to find good cheer,
The prettiest girls and also first-rate beer,
And the best fights you'll ever face.
A FIFTH. You glutton, do you itch to go
For your third drubbing in a row?
I have a horror of that place.
SERVING GIRL. No, no! I'm going back now, if you please.
ANOTHER. We'll surely find him standing by those poplar trees.
THE FIRST GIRL. For me that's no great lucky chance;
He'll walk at your side and he'll dance
With none but you upon the lea.
What good will your fun be to me?
THE OTHER GIRL. He won't be there alone today; he said
He'd bring along the curlyhead.
SCHOLAR.[29] Damn! How those lusty wenches hit their stride!
Brother, come on! We'll walk it at their side.
Strong beer, tobacco with a bite,
A girl decked in her best, just suit my appetite.
GIRL OF THE MIDDLE CLASS. Just see those handsome boys! It certainly
Is just a shame and a disgrace;
They could enjoy the very best society,
And after serving girls they chase.
SECOND SCHOLAR. [*To the* FIRST.] Don't go so fast! Behind us are two more,
Both very nicely dressed;
One is my neighbor from next door
In whom I take an interest.
They walk demurely, but you'll see
How they will overtake us finally.
THE FIRST. No, Brother, I don't like things in my way.
Quick! Let's not lose these wildfowl on our chase.
The hand that wields the broom on Saturday
On Sunday will provide the best embrace.[30]
CITIZEN. No, this new burgomaster, I don't care for him,
And now he's in, he daily gets more grim.
And for the city, what's he done?
Don't things get worse from day to day?
More rules than ever to obey,
And taxes worse than any yet, bar none.
BEGGAR. [*Sings.*] Kind gentlemen and ladies fair,
So rosy-cheeked and gay of dress,
Be good enough to hear my prayer,
Relieve my want and my distress.
Let me not vainly tune my lay.
Glad is the giver and only he.
Now that all men keep holiday,
Be there a harvest day for me.
ANOTHER CITIZEN. There's nothing better for Sunday or a holiday
Than talk about war and war's alarms,
When off in Turkey people up in arms

Are battling in a far-off fray.
You sip your glass, stand by the window side,
And down the river watch the painted vessels glide,
Then come home in the evening all at ease,
Blessing peace and the times of peace.
THIRD CITIZEN. Yes, neighbor, that's the way I like it too:
Let them beat out each other's brains,
Turn everything up wrong-end-to,
So long as here at home our good old way remains.
OLD WOMAN. [*To the* MIDDLE-CLASS GIRLS.] Heydey! How smart! My young and pretty crew!
Now who could help but fall for you?—
But don't act quite so proud. You'll do!
And what you're after, I could help you to.
MIDDLE-CLASS GIRL. Come, Agatha! I don't want to be seen
In public with such witches. It's quite true
My future lover last Saint Andrew's E'en
In flesh and blood she let me view—[31]
THE OTHER GIRL. She showed me mine too in her crystal glass,
A soldier type, with dashing friends behind him;
I look for him in every one I pass
And yet I just don't seem to find him.
SOLDIERS. Castles and towers,
Ramparts so high,
Girls of disdainful
Scorn-casting eye,
I'd like to win!
Keen is the contest,
Grand is the pay!
  We'll let the trumpets
Sound out the call,
Whether to joy
Or to downfall.
There's an assault!
That is the life!
Maidens and castles
Surrender in strife.
Keen is the contest,
Grand is the pay!
And then the soldiers
Go marching away. [*Enter* FAUST *and* WAGNER.]
FAUST. From ice are released the streams and brooks
At springtime's lovely, life-giving gaze;
Now hope smiles green down valley ways;
Old Winter feebly flees to nooks
Of rugged hills, and as he hies
Casts backward from him in his flight
Impotent showers of gritty ice
In streaks over meadows newly green.
But the sun permits of nothing white,
Everything is growth and striving,
All things are in colors reviving,
And lack of flowers in the countryside
By gay-clad humans is supplied.
Turn and from these heights look down
And backwards yonder toward the town.
From the hollow, gloomy gate
Streams a throng in motley array.
All want to sun themselves today.
The Lord's resurrection they celebrate
For they are themselves new risen from tombs:
From squalid houses' dingy rooms,
From tradesman's and apprentice' chains,
From crushing streets and choking lanes,
From roof's and gable's oppressive mass,
From their churches' everlasting night,
They are all brought forth into the light.
See now, just see how swiftly they pass
And scatter to fields' and gardens' grass
And how so many merry boats
The river's length and breadth there floats,
How almost sinking with its load
That last barque pushes from the quay.
From even the hillside's distant road
Bright costumes glimmer colorfully.
Sounds of village mirth arise,
Here is the people's true paradise.
Both great and small send up a cheer:
"Here I am human, I can *be* human here!"
WAGNER. Doctor, to take a walk with you
Is an honor and a gain, of course,
But come here alone, that I'd never do,
Because I am foe of all things coarse.
This fiddling, shouting, bowling, I detest
And all that with it goes along;
They rage as if by fiends possessed

And call it pleasure, call it song!
[*Peasants under the linden tree. Dance and song.*]
SINGERS. The shepherd for the dance got dressed
In wreath and bows and fancy vest,
And bravely did he show.
Beneath the linden lass and lad
Were dancing round and round like mad.
Juchhe! Juchhe!
Juchheisa! Heisa! He!
So went the fiddlebow.
  In through the crowd he pushed in haste
And jostled one girl in the waist
All with his sharp elbow.
The buxom lass, she turned her head,
"Well, that was stupid, now!" she said.
Juchhe! Juchhe!
Juchheisa! Heisa! He!
"Don't be so rude, fine fellow!"
  The ring spun around with all its might,
They danced to left, they danced to right,
And see the coattails go!
And they got red, and they got warm,
And breathless waited arm in arm,
Juchhe! Juchhe!
Juchheisa! Heisa! He!
A hip against an elbow.
  "Don't be so free! How many a maid
Has been betrothed and been betrayed
By carrying on just so!"
And yet he coaxed her to one side,
And from the linden far and wide
Juchhe! Juchhe!
Juchheisa! Heisa! He!
Rang shout and fiddlebow.
OLD PEASANT. Doctor, it's really nice of you
Not to shun our mirth today,
And such a larnèd master too,
To mingle with the folk this way.
Therefore accept our finest stein
Filled with cool drink and let me first
Present it with this wish of mine:
May it not only quench your thirst—
May all its count of drops be added to
The sum of days that are allotted you.
FAUST. I take the cooling drink you offer me
And wish you thanks and all prosperity.
[*The people gather around in a circle.*]
OLD PEASANT. Indeed it was most kind of you
On this glad day to come here thus,
For in the evil days gone by
You proved a friend to all of us.
Many a man is here alive
Because your father in the past
Saved him from raging fever's fury
When he had stemmed the plague at last.
And as a young man you went too
Among the houses of the pest;
Many a corpse they carried out
But you came healthy from the test.
You bore up under trials severe;
The Helper yonder helped the helper here.
ALL. Good health attend the proven man,
Long may he help, as help he can!
FAUST. Bow to Him yonder who provides
His help and teaches help besides. [*He walks on with* WAGNER.]
WAGNER. What feelings must be yours, O noble man,
Before the veneration of this crowd!
O fortunate indeed is one who can
So profit from the gifts with which he is endowed!
The fathers show you to their sons,
Each asks and pushes in and runs,
The fiddle stops, the dancer waits,
They stand in rows where you pass by,
And all their caps go flying high:
A little more and they would bend the knee
As if there passed the Venerabile.[32]
FAUST. Only a few steps more now up to yonder stone
And we shall rest from our long walk. Up there
I often used to sit and brood alone
And rack myself with fasting and with prayer.
Then rich in hope, in faith secure,
By wringing of hands, by tears and sighs,
I sought the plague's end to assure
By forcing the Lord of the skies.
Praise sounds like mockery on the people's part.
If you could only read within my heart
How little father and son
Were worthy of the fame they won!
My father was a man of honor but obscure

Who over Nature and her holy spheres
   would brood
In his own way and with capricious
   mood,
Though wholly upright, to be sure.
With other adepts of the art he locked
Himself in his black kitchen and from
   lists
Of endless recipes sought to concoct
A blend of the antagonists.[33]
There a Red Lion—a wooer to aspire—
Was in a warm bath with the Lily wed,
And both were then tormented over
   open fire
From one into the other bridal bed.
If the Young Queen was then espied
In rainbow hues within the flask,
There was our medicine; the patients
   died,
And "Who got well?" none thought to
   ask.
Thus we with hellish tonics wrought
   more ills
Among these valleys and these hills,
And raged more fiercely, than the pest.
I gave the poison out to thousands with
   my hand;
They withered, and I have to stand
And hear the ruthless killers blessed.
WAGNER. How can such things make
   you downcast?
Has not a good man done sufficient
In being conscientious and proficient
At skills transmitted from the past?
If you respect your father in your
   youth,
You will receive his fund of knowledge
   whole;
If as a man you swell the store of truth,
Your son can then achieve a higher
   goal.
FAUST. O happy he who still can hope
To rise out of the sea of errors here!
What one most needs to know exceeds
   his scope,
And what one knows is useless and
   unclear.
But let us not spoil hours that are so
   fair
With these dark melancholy thoughts
   of mine!
See how beneath the sunset air
The green-girt cottages all shine.
The sun moves on, the day has spent
   its force,
Yonder it speeds, new day eliciting.

O that I am swept upward on no wing
To follow it forever in its course!
Then I would see by deathless evening
   rays
The silent world beneath my feet,
All valleys calmed, all mountaintops
   ablaze,
And silver brooks with golden rivers
   meet.
No mountains then would block my
   godlike flight
For all the chasms gashed across their
   ways;
And soon the sea with its warmed bays
Would open to my wondering sight.
But now the goddess seems to sink
   down finally;
But a new impulse wakes in me,
I hasten forth to drink her everlasting
   light,
With day in front of me and at my back
   the night,
With waves down under me and over
   me the sky.
A glorious dream, dreamed while the
   day declined.
Alas, that to the pinions of the mind
No wing corporeal is joined as their
   ally.
And yet inborn in all our race
Is impulse upward, forward, and
   along,
When overhead and lost in azure space
The lark pours forth its trilling song,
When over jagged pine tree heights
The full-spread eagle wheels its flights,
And when across the seas and plains
Onward press the homing cranes.
WAGNER. I have had moody hours of
   my own,
But such an impulse I have never
   known.
The spectacle of woods and fields soon
   cloys,
I'll never envy birds their pinionage;
But how we *are* borne on by mental
   joys
From book to book, from page to page!
How sweet and fair the winter nights
   become,
A blessed life glows warm in every
   limb,
And oh! if one unrolls a noble
   parchment tome,
The whole of heaven then comes down
   to him.

FAUST. By one impulse alone are you possessed,
O may you never know the other!
Two souls abide, alas, within my breast,[34]
And each one seeks for riddance from the other.
The one clings with a dogged love and lust
With clutching parts unto this present world,
The other surges fiercely from the dust
Unto sublime ancestral fields.
If there are spirits in the air
Between the earth and heaven holding sway,
Descend out of your golden fragrance there
And to new life of many hues sweep me away!
Yes, if a magic mantle were but mine,
And if to far-off lands it bore me,
Not for all costly raiment placed before me
Would I exchange it; kings' cloaks I would decline!
WAGNER. Do not invoke that well-known troop
That stream above us in the murky air,
Who from all quarters down on mankind swoop
And bring the thousand perils they prepare.
With whetted spirit fangs down from the north
They pitch upon you with their arrowy tongues;
Out of the morning's east they issue forth
To prey with parching breath upon your lungs;
And if the south up from the desert drives
Those which heap fire upon your brain,
The west brings on the swarm that first revives
Then drowns you as it drowns the field and plain.
They listen eagerly, on mischief bent,
And to deceive us, willingly comply,
They often pose as being heaven sent
And lisp like angels when they lie.
But let us go. The world has all turned grey,
The air is chill, mist closes out the day.
With nightfall one enjoys a room.—
Why do you stand and stare with wondering gaze?
What so arrests you out there in the gloom?
FAUST. Do you see that black dog that through the stubble strays?
WAGNER. He looks quite unremarkable to me.
FAUST. Look close! What do you take the beast to be?
WAGNER. A poodle, searching with his natural bent
And snuffing for his master's scent.
FAUST. Do you see how he spirals round us, snail-shell-wise, and ever closer on our trail?
And if I'm not mistaken, he lays welts
Of fire behind him in his wake.
WAGNER. I see a plain black poodle, nothing else;
Your eyes must be the cause of some mistake.
FAUST. I seem to see deft snares of magic laid
For future bondage round our feet somehow.
WAGNER. I see him run about uncertain and afraid
Because he sees two strangers, not his master now.
FAUST. The circle narrows, he is near!
WAGNER. You see! It's just a dog, no phantom here.
He growls, he doubts, lies belly-flat and all,
And wags his tail. All doggish protocol.
FAUST. Come here! Come join our company!
WAGNER. He's just a foolish pup. You see?
You stop, and he will wait for you,
You speak to him, and he'll jump up on you,
Lose something, and he'll fetch it quick,
Or go in water for a stick.
FAUST. You must be right, I see there's not a trace
Of spirits. It's his training he displays.
WAGNER. A sage himself will often find
He likes a dog that's trained to mind.
Yes, he deserves your favor totally,
A model scholar of the students, he.
[*They go in through the city gate.*]

Study Room

FAUST *entering with the poodle.*
FAUST. From field and meadow I withdraw
Which deepest darkness now bedecks,
With holy and foreboding awe
The better soul within us wakes.
Asleep now are my wild desires,
My vehement activity;
The love of mankind now aspires,
The love of God aspires in me.
   Be quiet, poodle! Why should you romp and rove?
What are you snuffing there at the sill?
Go and lie down behind the stove,
I'll give you my best pillow if you're still.
Out there on the hill-road back to town
You amused us by running and frisking your best;
Now accept your keep from me; lie down
And be a welcome and quiet guest.
   Ah, when in our close cell by night
The lamp burns with a friendly cheer,
Then deep within us all grows bright
And hearts that know themselves grow clear.
Reason begins once more to speak
And hope begins to bloom again,
The brooks of life we yearn to seek
And to life's source, ah! to attain.
   Stop growling poodle! With the sacred tones that rise
And now my total soul embrace,
Your animal noise is out of place.
We are accustomed to having men despise
What they do not understand;
The good and the beautiful they misprize,
Finding it cumbersome, they scowl and growl;
Must a dog, like men, set up a howl?
   But alas! with the best of will I feel no more
Contentment welling up from my heart's core.
Why must the stream so soon run dry
And we again here thirsting lie?
These things experiences familiarize.
But this lack can find compensation,
The supernatural we learn to prize,
And then we long for revelation,
Which nowhere burns more nobly or more bright
Than here in the New Testament. Tonight
An impulse urges me to reach
Out for this basic text and with sincere
Emotion make its holy meaning clear
Within my own beloved German speech. [*He opens a volume and sets about it.*]
It says: "In the beginning was the *Word*."35
Already I am stuck! And who will help afford?
Mere word I cannot possibly so prize,
I must translate it otherwise.
Now if the Spirit lends me proper light,
"In the beginning was the *Mind*" would be more nearly right.
Consider the first line with care,
The pen must not be overhasty there!
Can it be mind that makes and shapes all things?
It should read: "In the beginning was the *Power*."
But even as I write down this word too,
Something warns me that it will not do.
Now suddenly the Spirit prompts me in my need,
I confidently write: "In the beginning was the *Deed*!"
   If I'm to share this room with you,
Poodle, that howling must be curbed.
And stop that barking too!
I cannot be disturbed
By one who raises such a din.
One of us must give in
And leave this cell we're in.
I hate to drive you out of here,
But the door is open, the way is clear.
But what is this I see?
Can such things happen naturally?
Is this reality or fraud?
My poodle grows both long and broad!
He rises up with might;
No dog's shape this! This can't be right!
What phantom have I harbored thus?
He's like a hippopotamus
With fiery eyes and ghastly teeth.
O, I see what's beneath!
For such a mongrel of hell
The key of Solomon works well.36
SPIRITS. [*In the corridor.*]
Captive inside there is one of us,
Stay out here, follow him none of us.
Like a fox in an iron snare

A lynx of hell is cornered in there.
But take heed!
Hover to, hover fro,
Above, below,
And pretty soon he'll be freed.
If you can help him in aught
Don't leave him caught.
Many a turn he has done
Helping us every one.

FAUST. To deal with the beast before
Me, I'll use the spell of the four:[37]
  Salamander shall kindle,
Undine shall coil,
Sylph shall dwindle,
Kobold shall toil.
  Lacking the lore
Of the elements four,
Not knowing aright
Their use and might,
None shall be lord
Of the spirit horde.
  Vanish in flame,
Salamander!
Together rush and stream,
Undine!
In meteor glory gleam,
Sylph!
Bring help to the house,
Incubus! Incubus!
Step forth and make an ending! Thus!
  None of the four
Lurks in the beast.
He lies and grins at me as before,
I have not harmed him in the least.
You'll hear me tell
A stronger spell.
  Do you, fellow, live
As hell's fugitive?
See this sign now[38]
To which they bow,
The black hordes of hell!
  With hair abristle he starts to swell.
  Forfeiter of bliss,
Can you read this?
The never-created
Of name unstated,
Diffused through all heavens' expanse.
Transpierced by the infamous lance?[39]
  Back of the stove he flees from my
    spells,
There like an elephant he swells,
He fills the room entire,
He melts like a mist of sleet.
Rise ceilingwards no higher!
Fall down at your master's feet.
You see that mine is no idle threat.
With sacred flame I will scorch you yet.
Await not the might
Of the triply burning light![40]
Await not the sight
Of my arts in their fullest measure! [*As the mist falls away,* MEPHISTOPHELES *steps forth from behind the stove, dressed as a traveling scholar.*][41]

MEPHISTOPHELES. Why all the fuss?
What is the gentleman's pleasure?

FAUST. So this was what was in the cur!
A traveling scholar? That's the best joke
  I've heard yet.

MEPHISTOPHELES. I salute you, learned
  Sir.
You had me in a mighty sweat.

FAUST. What is your name?[42]

MEPHISTOPHELES. For one so
    disesteeming
The word, the question seems so small
  to me,
And for a man disdainful of all
  seeming,
Who searches only for reality.

FAUST. With gentlemen like you, their
    nature is deduced
Quite often from the name that's used,
As all too patently applies
When you are named Corrupter, Liar,
  God of Flies.[43]
All right, who are you then?

MEPHISTOPHELES. Part of that Force
    which would
Do evil ever yet forever works the
  good.

FAUST. What sense is there beneath that
    riddling guise?

MEPHISTOPHELES. I am the Spirit that
    constantly denies!
And rightly so; for everything that's
  ever brought
To life deserves to come to naught.
Better if nothing ever came to be.
Thus all that you call sin, you see,
And havoc—evil, in short—is meant
To be my proper element.

FAUST. You call yourself a part, yet
    stand quite whole before me there?

MEPHISTOPHELES. It is the modest truth
    that I declare.
Now folly's little microcosm, man,
Boasts *him*self whole as often as he
  can. . . .
I am part of the part which once was
  absolute,
Part of the Darkness which gave birth

    to Light,
The haughty Light, which now seeks to
    dispute
The ancient rank and range of Mother
    Night,
But unsuccessfully, because, try as it
    will,
It is stuck fast to bodies still.
It streams from bodies, bodies it makes
    fair,
A body hinders its progressions; thus I
    hope
It won't be long before its scope
Will in the bodies' ruination share.
FAUST. I see your fine objectives now!
Wholesale annihilation fails somehow,
So you go at it one by one.
MEPHISTOPHELES. I don't get far, when
    all is said and done.
The thing opposed to Nothingness,
This stupid earth, this Somethingness,
For all that I have undertaken
Against it, still remains unshaken;
In spite of tempest, earthquake, flood,
    and flame
The earth and ocean calmly stay the
    same.
And as for that damned stuff, the
    brood of beasts and man,
With them there's nothing I can do.
To think how many I have buried too!
Fresh blood runs in their veins just as it
    always ran.
And so it goes. Sometimes I could
    despair!
In earth, in water, and in air
A thousand growing things unfold,
In dryness, wetness, warmth, and cold!
Had I not specially reserved the flame,
I wouldn't have a thing in my own
    name.
FAUST. So you shake your cold devil's
    fist
Clenched in futile rage malign,
So you the endless Power resist,
The creative, living, and benign!
Some other goal had best be sought,
Chaos' own fantastic son!
MEPHISTOPHELES. We really shall give
    this some thought
And talk about it more anon.
Right now, however, might I go?
FAUST. Why you should ask, I don't
    quite see.
Now that we've made acquaintance,
    though,
Come any time to visit me.
Here is the window, there are the
    doors,
The chimney too is practical.
MEPHISTOPHELES. Must I confess? To
    leave this room of yours
There is a trifling obstacle.
The witch's foot there on the sill—[44]
FAUST. The pentagram distresses you?
But tell me now, O son of hell,
If that prevents you, how did you get
    through?
Could such a spirit be so blind?
MEPHISTOPHELES. Observe it carefully.
    It's ill designed.
One point there, facing outward as it
    were,
Is just a bit disjoined, you see.
FAUST. Now what a lucky chance for me!
And so you are my prisoner?
And all by merest accident!
MEPHISTOPHELES. The poodle did not
    notice when in he went.
Things now take on a different shape:
The Devil's caught and can't escape.
FAUST. But why not use the window to
    withdraw?
MEPHISTOPHELES. With devils and with
    spirits it's a law:
Where they slipped in, they must go
    out.
The first is up to us, the second leaves
    no doubt:
There we are slaves.
FAUST. So hell has its own law?
I find that good, because a pact could
    then
Perhaps be worked out with you gen-
    tlemen?
MEPHISTOPHELES. What once is prom-
    ised, you will revel in,
No skimping and no spreading thin.
But such things can't be done so fast,
We'll speak of that when next we meet.
And now I beg you first and last
To let me make my fair retreat.
FAUST. Just for a single moment yet
    remain
And tell me of some pleasant news.
MEPHISTOPHELES. No, let me go now!
    I'll come back again,
Then you can ask me all you choose.
FAUST. I never had a plan so bold
As capturing you. You walked into the

snare.
Whoever holds the Devil, let him hold!
A second time he will not have him there.
MEPHISTOPHELES. I am quite ready, if you choose,
To keep you company and stay,
But on condition that I use
My worthy skills to while the time away.
FAUST. I'd like to see them, so feel free,
Just so the skills work pleasantly.
MEPHISTOPHELES. Your senses will, my friend, gain more
In this hour than you've known before
In one whole year's monotony.
And what my dainty spirits sing you,
The lovely images they bring you
Will be no empty magic play.
Your sense of smell shall be delighted,
Your sense of taste shall be excited,
And feelings will sweep you away.
No preparation shall we need;
We are assembled, so proceed!
SPIRITS.[45] Vanish, you gloomy
Vaultings above!
Lovelier hue
Of aether's blue
Be shed in here!
O might the darkling
Clouds melt for once!
Stars begin sparkling;
Mellower suns
Shine now in here.
Sons of the air,
Of beauty rare,
Hover thronging,
Wafting in light.
Ardent longing
Follows their flight.
Raiment in strands
Shed as streamer bands
Cover the lands,
Cover the groves
Where lovers vow,
Lost in reverie,
Lifelong loves.
Arbors on arbors!
Lush greenery!
Masses of grapes
Tumble from vines
Into presses and vats,
Gush now as brooks
Of foaming wines,
Trickle as rills
Through gorges that wind,

Leaving the hills
Far behind,
Widening to lakes
Around the abundance
Of verdant heights.
And then the birds
Drink delight,
Fly to the sun,
Fly to the bright
Islands that gleam
Drifting and glittering
Upon the stream;
There we hear choirs
Of jubilant throngs,
See them on meadows
At dances and songs,
Disporting free
In festivity;
Climbing, some,
Over the peaks,
Skimming, some,
Over the lakes,
Still others fly;
All toward the high
Joy of existence,
All toward the distance
Of loving stars.[46]
MEPHISTOPHELES. He is asleep. Well done, my dainty, airy youngsters!
You lulled him loyally, my songsters!
I am much in your debt for such a concert.
You are not yet the man to hold the Devil fast!
Around him your sweet dream illusions cast
And steep him in a sea of fancy;
But now I need a rat's tooth to divest
This threshold of its necromancy.
No lengthy incantation will be needed,
Here comes one rustling up, and my word will be heeded.
The Master of the rats and mice,
Of bedbugs, flies, and frogs and lice,
Commands you boldly to appear
And gnaw this carven threshold clear
Where he has daubed a jot of oil—[47]
Ah, there you scamper up to toil!
Get right to work! I'm hemmed in by the wedge
That's right there on the outer edge.
Just one more bite and then it's done.—
Now, till we meet again, Faustus, dream on!
FAUST. [*Waking.*] Have I been once

again betrayed?
The spirit throng has fled so utterly
That I but dreamed the Devil came and stayed
And that a poodle got away from me?

Study Room [2]

FAUST. A knock? Come in! Who now comes bothering me?
MEPHISTOPHELES. It's I.
FAUST. Come in!
MEPHISTOPHELES. A third call there must be.
FAUST. Come in, then!
MEPHISTOPHELES. That's the way I like to hear you.
We shall, I trust, get on quite well,
For I have come here to dispel
Your moods, and as a noble squire be near you,
Clad all in scarlet and gold braid,
With my short cape of stiff silk made,
A rooster feather on my hat,
A long sharp rapier at my side,[48]
And I advise you to provide
Yourself a costume just like that,
So you, untrammeled and set free,
Can find out just what life can be.
FAUST. No matter what might be my own attire,
I would feel life cramped anyway.
I am too old merely to play,
Too young to be without desire.
What can the world give me? Renounce,
Renounce shalt thou, thou shalt renounce!
That is the everlasting song
Dinned in our ears throughout the course
Of all our lives, which all life long
Each hours sings until it's hoarse.
Mornings I wake with horror and could weep
Hot tears at seeing the new sun
Which will not grant me in its sweep
Fulfillment of a single wish, not one,
Which mars anticipated joys
Themselves with willful captiousness
And with a thousand petty frets destroys
My eager heart's creativeness.
At nightfall I must lie down ill at ease
Upon my couch of misery where
There will be neither rest nor peace,
Wild dreams will terrify me even there.
The god that in my heart abides
Can stir my soul's profoundest springs;
He over all my energies presides
But cannot alter outward things.
Existence is a weight by which I am oppressed,
With death desired, life something to detest.
MEPHISTOPHELES. And yet Death never is a wholly welcome guest.
FAUST. O happy he around whose brow Death winds
The blood-stained wreath in victory's radiance,
Or he whom in a girl's embrace Death finds
After the hectic whirling of the dance!
O, had I in my exultation sunk
Down dead before the lofty Spirit's power!
MEPHISTOPHELES. And yet a brownish potion was not drunk
By someone on a certain midnight hour.
FAUST. Spying, it seems, amuses you.
MEPHISTOPHELES. I dare
Not claim omniscience, but of much I am aware.
FAUST. If from that harrowing confusion
A sweet familiar tone drew me away,
Belied me with a child's profusion
Of memories from a former day,
I now curse everything that holds the soul
Enchantged by the lures of sorcery
And charms it in this dreary hole
By sweet illusion and duplicity!
Cursed be the lofty self-opinion
With which the mind itself deludes!
Cursed be phenomena's dominion
Which on our senses so intrudes!
Cursed be the cheating dream obsessions
With name and fame that have us so beguiled!
Cursed be what we have deemed possessions:
Servant and plow, and wife and child!

Cursed be old Mammon[49] when with treasure
He lures to deeds adventurous
Or when for idleness and pleasure
He spreads the pillows soft for us!
Cursed be the nectar of the grape!
Cursed be love at its happiest!
And cursed be hope! And cursed be faith!
And cursed be patience more than all the rest!
CHORUS OF SPIRITS. [*Invisible.*] Woe! Woe!
You have destroyed
The beauteous world
With mighty fist;
It crumbles, it collapses!
A demigod has shattered it!
We carry
The fragments to the void,
We grieve
For beauty so destroyed.
More mightily,
Son of earth,
More splendidly
Bring it to birth,
Rebuild it in the heart of you!
Begin a new
Life course
With senses clear,
And may new songs
Hail it with cheer![50]
MEPHISTOPHELES. These are the minions
From my dominions.
Precociously wise,
Deeds and desires they now advise.
Out of solitude
Where senses and saps are glued,
To the wide worlds' view
They lure and summon you.
  Cease toying with your sorrow then,
Which tears your life as vulture-talons tear;
The worst of company makes you aware
You are a man with other men.
This does not indicate
That you're to run with the pack;
I am not one of the great,
But if you want a track
Through life together with me,
I'll adapt myself quite willingly
To be yours right here and now.
I am your fellow,
If it suits you, to the grave,
I am your servant and your slave.
FAUST. And what am I supposed to do for you?
MEPHISTOPHELES. There's lots of time before that's due.
FAUST. No, no! The Devil is an egoist
And does not willingly assist
Another just for God's sake.[51] I insist
You make all your conditions clear;
Such a slave is one to fear.
MEPHISTOPHELES. I'll bind myself to be your servant *here*
And at your beck and call wait tirelessly,
If when there in the *yonder* we appear
You will perform the same for me.
FAUST. The yonder is of small concern.
Once you have smashed this world to pieces,
The other one may come to be in turn.[52]
It is out of this earth that my joy springs
And this sun shines upon my sufferings;
Once free of them, this trouble ceases;
Then come what may and as time brings.
About all that I do not wish to hear,
Whether in future there is hate and love
And whether in that yonder sphere
There is a new beneath and new above.
MEPHISTOPHELES. In this mood you dare venture it. Just make
The compact, and I then will undertake
To turn my skills to joy. I'll give you more
Than any man has ever seen before.
FAUST. Poor, sorry Devil, what could you deliver?
Was human mind in lofty aspiration ever
Comprehended by the likes of you?
Do you have food that does not satisfy? Or do
You have red gold that will run through
The hand like quicksilver and away?
A game that none may win who play?
A girl who in my very arms
Will pledge love to my neighbor with her eyes?
Or honor with its godlike charms
Which like a shooting star flashes and

dies?
Show me the fruit that rots right on the tree,
And trees that every day leaf out anew!
MEPHISTOPHELES. Such a demand does not daunt me,
Such treasures I can furnish you.
But still the time will come around, good friend,
When we shall want to relish things in peace.
FAUST. If ever I lie down upon a bed of ease,
Then let that be my final end!
If you can cozen me with lies
Into a self-complacency,
Or can beguile with pleasures you devise,
Let that day be the last for me!
This bet I offer!
MEPHISTOPHELES. Done!
FAUST. And I agree:[53]
If I to any moment say:
Linger on! You are so fair!
Put me in fetters straightaway,
Then I can die for all I care!
Then toll bells for my funeral,
Then of your service you are free,
The clock may stop, the clock hand fall,
And time be past and done for me!
MEPHISTOPHELES. Consider well, we shall remember this.
FAUST. And that would be quite right of you.
I have committed no presumptuousness.
I am a slave no matter what I do,
Yours or another's, we may dismiss.
MEPHISTOPHELES. I will begin right with your doctoral feast[54]
And be your slave this very day.
For life and death's sake, though, just one thing, if I may:
Just write a line or two at least.
FAUST. You ask for written forms, you pedant? Can
You never have known man, or known the word of man?
Is it not enough that by the word I gave
The die of all my days is finally cast?
Does not the world down all its rivers rave,
And should a promise hold me fast?
But this illusion in our hearts is set
And who has ever wanted to uproot it yet?
Happy the man whose heart is true and pure,
No sacrifice he makes will he regret!
A parchment, though, with seal and signature,
That is a ghost at which all people shy.
The word is dead before the ink is dry
And wax and leather hold the mastery.
What, evil spirit, do you want from me?
Bronze, marble, parchment, paper? And then
Am I to write with stylus, chisel, or a pen?
The choice is yours and wholly free.
MEPHISTOPHELES. Why carry on so heatedly
And force your eloquence so high?
Just any little scrap will do;
You sign it with a drop of blood.
FAUST. If that is satisfactory to you,
We'll let it stand at that absurdity.
MEPHISTOPHELES. Blood is a juice of very special kind.
FAUST. I'll honor this pact, you need not be afraid!
The aim of all my strength and mind
Will be to keep this promise I have made.
I puffed myself up far too grand;
In your class I deserve to be.
The mighty Spirit spurned me and
Nature locks herself from me.
The thread of thought is snapped off short,
Knowledge I loathe of every sort.
Let us now sate our ardent passion
In depths of sensuality!
Let miracles of every fashion
Be brought in veils of mystery!
Let us plunge in the flood of time and chance,
Into the tide of circumstance!
Let grief and gratification,
Success and frustration
Spell one another as they can;
Restless doing is the only way for man.
MEPHISTOPHELES. There is no goal or limit set. Snatch tidbits as impulse prompts you to,
Take on the wing whatever you can get!
And may you digest what pleases you.
Just help yourself and don't be coy.
FAUST. But I tell you there is no talk of joy.
I vow myself to frenzy, agonies of gratification,

Enamored hatred, quickening frustration.
Cured of the will to knowledge now, my mind
And heart shall be closed to no sorrow any more
And all that is the lot of human kind
I want to feel down to my senses' core,
Grasp with my mind their worst things and their best,
Heap all their joys and troubles on my breast,
And thus my self to their selves' limits to extend,
And like them perish foundering at the end.
MEPHISTOPHELES. Believe me, many a thousand year
I've chewed this rugged food, and I well know
That from the cradle to the bier
No man digests this ancient sourdough.
This whole, believe the likes of us,
For deity alone was made.
He dwells in timeless radiance glorious,
Us he has relegated to the shade,
You, day and night alone can aid.
FAUST. But I am set on it.
MEPHISTOPHELES. Easy said!
There's just one thing that could go wrong:
Time is short and art is long;
You could, I think, be taught and led.
Choose a poet for your associate,
Let the gentleman's thoughts have their free bent
To heap upon your reverend pate
All noble qualities he can invent:[55]
The lion's nobility,
The fleetness of the hind,
The fiery blood of Italy,
The Northman's steadfast mind.[56]
Have him for you the secret find
Of magnanimity and guile combined,
Then make you fall in love by plan
While youthful passions are in flame.
I'd like myself to meet just such a man,
I'd give him "Sir Microcosm" for a name.
FAUST. What am I then, if seeking to attain
That toward which all my senses strain,
The Crown of mankind, is in vain?
MEPHISTOPHELES. You're after all—just what you are.
Wear wigs of a million ringlets as you will,[57]
Put ell-thick soles beneath your feet, and still
You will remain just what your are.
FAUST. I feel that I have fruitlessly amassed
All treasures of the human mind,
And now when I sit down at last
No fresh strength wells within my heart, I find;
I'm not one hair's breadth taller nor one whit
Closer to the infinite.
MEPHISTOPHELES. These matters, my good Sir, you see
Much in the ordinary light;
We must proceed more cleverly
Before life's joys have taken flight.
What the Devil! You've got hands and feet,
You've got a head, you've got a prat;
Are all the things that I find sweet
Less mine for all of that?
If I can buy six stallions, can
I not call their strength also mine?
I race along and am a proper man
As if their four-and-twenty legs were mine.
Come on, then! Let this brooding be!
And off into the world with me!
I tell you, any speculative fellow
Is like a beast led round and round
By demons on a heath all dry and yellow
When on all sides lies good green pasture ground.
FAUST. But how do we begin?
MEPHISTOPHELES. First we will get away.
What kind of dungeon is this anyway?
What kind of life do you lead if
You bore yourself and bore the youngsters stiff?
Leave that to Neighbor Sleek-and-Slow.
Why go on threshing straw? There is no doubt
The best things that you know
You dare not tell the boys about.
I hear one now out in the hall.
FAUST. I simply cannot see him now.
MEPHISTOPHELES. The poor lad has been waiting, after all,
And must not go uncomforted somehow.
Come, lend your cap and gown to me;
The mask will suit me admirably. [*He changes clothes.*]

Just trust my wits and I'll succeed.
A quarter of an hour is all I need.
Meanwhile get ready for your travels with all speed. [*Exit* FAUST.]
MEPHISTOPHELES. [*In* FAUST's *long gown.*]
Scorn reason and the lore of mind,
Supremest powers of mankind,
Just let the Prince of Lies endow
Your strength with his illusions now,
And I will have you unconditionally—
Fate has conferred on him a mind
That urges ever onward with incontinency,
Whose eager striving is of such a kind
That early joys are overleaped and left behind.
I'll drag him through wild life at last,
Through shallow insipidity,
I'll make him wriggle, stultify, stick fast,
And in his insatiety
His greedy lips will find that food and drink float past.
He will vainly beg refreshment on the way.
Had his lot not been with the Devil cast,
He would go to the Devil anyway.
  [*Enter a* STUDENT.]
STUDENT. I've been here just a short time, Sir,
And come to you with deference
To meet a man, and see and hear,
Of whom all speak with reverence.
MEPHISTOPHELES. I must approve your courtesy.
A man like other men you see.
Have you inquired around elsewhere?
STUDENT. Take me, I entreat you, in your care.
I come with fresh blood, spirits high,
And money in tolerable supply.
My mother was loath to have me go,
But I would like to learn and know.
MEPHISTOPHELES. Then this is just the place to come.
STUDENT. Frankly, I'd rather be back home.
I feel confined within these walls,
I'm ill at ease amid these halls,
The space is cramped, you never see
Green country or a single tree,
And in these rooms with benches lined
I lose my hearing, sight, and mind.
MEPHISTOPHELES. It all depends on habit. Right at first
The infant will not take its mother's breast,
But then it finds relief from thirst
And soon it feeds away with zest.
So you to Wisdom's breast will turn
And every day more strongly yearn.
STUDENT. I'll hang upon her neck with all affection
If you will set me in the right direction.
MEPHISTOPHELES. First tell me, before we go on,
What course have you decided on?
STUDENT. I want to be quite erudite;
I'd like to comprehend aright
What all there is on earth, in heaven as well,
In science and in nature too.
MEPHISTOPHELES. You're on the right track, I can tell;
Just see that nothing distracts you.
STUDENT. With body and soul it shall be done.
But to be frank, I would like in some ways
A little freedom and some fun
On pleasant summer holidays.
MEPHISTOPHELES. Make good use of your time, so fast it flies.
You'll gain time if you just will organize.
And so, dear friend, I would advise
First off *collegium logicum*.[58]
There you will get your mind well braced
In Spanish boots so tightly laced[59]
That it will henceforth toe the taut
And cautiously marked line of thought
And not go will-o'-the-wisping out
And in, across, and round about.
They will spend days on teaching you
About how things you used to do—
Like eating, drinking—just like that,
Need One! Two! Three! for getting at.
For with thought-manfacturies
It's like a weaver's masterpiece:
A thousand threads one treadle plies,
The shuttles dart back to and fro,
Unseen the threads together flow,
A thousand knots one movement ties;
Then comes the philosopher to have his say
And proves things have to be this way:
The first being so, the second so,
The third and fourth are so-and-so;
If first and second were absent, neither
Would third and fourth be present either.

All scholars find this very clever,
None have turned weavers yet, however.
Whoever wants to know and write about
A living thing, first drives the spirit out;
He has the parts then in his grasp,
But gone is the spirit's holding-clasp.
Encheiresin naturae chemists call it now,[60]
Mocking themselves, they know not how.
STUDENT. I don't just get all you imply.
MEPHISTOPHELES. It will go better by and by,
Once you have all these things principified
And properly classified.
STUDENT. I feel as dazed by all you've said
As if a mill wheel spun inside my head.
MEPHISTOPHELES. Above all else you next must turn
To metaphysics. See that you learn
Profoundly and with might and main
What does not fit the human brain.
For what fits in—or misfits—grand
Resounding phrases are on hand.
But this semester most of all
Keep schedule, be punctual.
You'll have five classes every day;
Be in there on the stroke of the bell.
See that you are prepared as well,
With paragraphs worked up in such a way
That you can see with just a look
There's nothing said but what is in the book
And take your notes with dedication
As if the Holy Ghost gave the dictation!
STUDENT. No second time need I be told,
I see its usefulness all right;
What one gets down in black and white
One can take home and feel consoled.
MEPHISTOPHELES. But name your field of concentration!
STUDENT. I don't feel law is just the thing for me.
MEPHISTOPHELES. I cannot blame you there especially,
Well do I know the law school situation.[61]
Laws are perpetrated like disease
Hereditary in some families;
From generation to generation they are bred
And furtively from place to place they spread.
Sense turns to nonsense, wise works to a mire.
Woe that you are a grandson and born late!
About the legal right that is innate
In man, they do not so much as inquire.
STUDENT. You make my own aversion still more great.
He whom you teach is fortunate.
I'd almost take theology, in a way.
MEPHISTOPHELES. I wouldn't want to lead you astray.
That branch of learning, once you do begin it,
It's so hard to avoid the path of sin,
There's so much hidden poison lurking in it
And you can hardly tell this from the medicine.
Again it's best to follow only one man there
And by that master's statements swear.
Cling hard and fast to words, in sum;
Then through sure portals you will come
To Certainty's own tempted home.
STUDENT. But words must have ideas too behind them.
MEPHISTOPHELES. Quite so! But just don't fret too much to no avail,
Because just when ideas fail
Words will crop up, and timely you will find them.
With words you can most excellently dispute,
Words can a system constitute,
In words you can put faith and not be shaken,
And from a word not one iota can be taken.
STUDENT. Forgive me for so importuning you,
But I must trouble you again.
Would you say just a telling word or two
About the course in medicine?
Three years is a short time, and O my God!
The field itself is far too broad.
With just a little hint alone
One feels it would not seem to great.

MEPHISTOPHELES. [*Aside.*] I've had enough of this dry tone,
I've got to play the Devil straight. [*Aloud.*]
The gist of medicine is grasped with ease;
You study through the great world and the small
To let it go on after all
As God may please.
In vain you'll go a-roving scientifically,
There each learns only what he can;
But one who grasps the moment, he
Is truly the right man.
You've got a good build on the whole,
And you won't lack for imprudence;
If you just have self-confidence
You'll have the trust of many a soul.
And learn to manage women, of that make sure;
For all their endless Ah!'s and Oh!'s
And thousand woes
Depend on one point only for their cure,
And if you're halfway decent about that,
You'll have them all under your hat.
First, by a title win their confidence
That your skills many skills transcend,
Then you can finger every little thing and be
Welcome where others wait for years on end.
Know how to take her little pulse, and grasp her
With slyly passionate glances while you clasp her
Around her trim and slender waist
To see how tightly she is laced.
STUDENT. Now that's more like it! The where and how I see!
MEPHISTOPHELES. Grey, my dear friend, is all of theory,
And verdant is life's golden tree.
STUDENT. I swear it's all just like a dream to me.
Might I come back another time to sound
Your wisdom to its depths profound?
MEPHISTOPHELES. I'll gladly do anything I may.
STUDENT. It's just impossible to go away
Unless you take my album here and sign.
Would you do me the honor of a line?
MEPHISTOPHELES. With pleasure. [*He writes and gives the album back.*]
STUDENT. [*Reads.*] *Eritis sicut Deus, scientes bonum et malum.*[62] [*He respectfully closes the book and takes his leave.*]
MEPHISTOPHELES. Just follow that old saying and my cousin, the snake,
And you will surely tremble for your God's-likeness' sake! [*Re-enter* FAUST.]
FAUST. And where do we go now?
MEPHISTOPHELES. The choice is up to you.
We'll see the small world first, and then the great one too.
What joy, what profit will be yours
As you sail glibly through this course!
FAUST. But with this long beard on my face
I lack for easy social grace.
This bold attempt will never work with me,
I never could get on in company,
In front of others I feel small and harassed,
I'll be continually embarrassed.
MEPHISTOPHELES. Good friend, all that is needed, time will give.
Once you have confidence, you will know how to live.
FAUST. How do we travel, though, and get about?
Do you have servants, coach and pair?
MEPHISTOPHELES. All we need do is spread this mantle out
And it will take us through the air.
But see that on this daring flight
Beginning now you travel light.
A little fire gas I will now prepare[63]
Will lift us to the upper air,
And if we're light, we'll go up fast from there.
Congratulations on your new career!

Auerbach's Tavern in Leipzig[64]

A drinking bout of jolly cronies.
FROSCH.[65] Will no one drink? Will no one laugh?
I'll snap you out of your gloomy daze!
Today you're all like sodden chaff

And usually you're all ablaze.
BRANDER.[66] It's your fault, you've been keeping mum,
No horseplay and no jokes with sour scum.
FROSCH. [*pours a glass of wine over his head.*] There's both!
BRANDER. You double pork-hog, you!
FROSCH. It's what you wanted me to do!
SIEBEL. Whoever brawls here, throw him out!
Sing chorus with full chest now, drink and shout!
Ho! Holla! Ho!
ALTMAYER. Help! I've been wounded here!
Bring me some cotton, this chap's split my ear!
SIEBEL. Not till the rafters of the room
Re-echo, do you get the bass's boom.
FROSCH. That's right! Throw out the ones complaining of the noise!
A! tara lara da!
FROSCH. Our throats are tuned up, boys! [*Sings.*]
The good old Holy Roman Empire,
How does it hold together?
BRANDER. A filthy song! A song of politics!
The song's offensive. Thank God every time you wake
You need not worry for the Roman Empire's sake!
At least I count it luck that mine is not
The Emperor's or the Chancellor's lot.
But then again we mustn't be without a head,
So let's elect a Pope instead.
You know the qualities that can
Distinguish and elect a man.[67]
FROSCH. [*Sings.*] Rise, Lady Nightingale, and soar.
Greet my sweetheart ten thousand times and more.
SIEBEL. No sweetheart's greetings here! We'll have no more of that!
FROSCH. Greetings and meetings too!
You won't stop me, that's flat! [*Sings.*]
Bolt shoved back! in stilly night.
Bolt shoved back! the lover wakes.
Bolt shoved to: the morning breaks.
SIEBEL. Yes, sing away, sing on, and praise and boast of her!
My time will come for laughing too
She jilted me and she will do the same for you.

For lover may she get some filthy gnome
To dally with her where the crossroads meet,[68]
And may an old goat from the Blocksberg bleat
Good night to her as he goes galloping home.[69]
For that wench it's a lot too good
To have a stout lad with real flesh and blood.
To smash her windows in will be
The only greeting she'll get from me.
BRANDER. [*Pounding on the table.*] Attention everybody! Give me ear!
You will agree, Sirs, I know how to live.
There are some lovesick people here,
And so it's proper I should give
Them something for their good night cheer.
This song's new cut and tailored for us,
So come in loudly on the chorus: [*He sings.*]
In a cellar once there lived a rat
And all he ate was lard and butter;
He grew a gut so sleek and fat
He looked like Doctor Luther.
The cook, she put some poison out,
And then the world closed in about,
As if he had love inside him.
CHORUS. [*Shouting.*] As if he had love inside him!
BRANDER. He traveled forth, he traveled to,
He swilled from every puddle,
He gnawed, he scratched the whole house through
In fury all befuddled.
He jumped for pain to beat the band,
But soon had all that he could stand,
As if he had love inside him.
CHORUS. As if he had love inside him!
BRANDER. Into the kitchen by light of day
He ran in agony,
Dropped on the hearth and twitched and lay
And snuffled piteously.
The poisoneress, she laughed and said,
"One more squeak and then he's dead,
As if he had love inside him."
CHORUS. As if he had love inside him!
SIEBEL. Those dullard lads just relish that!
It seems a scurvy trick to me
To poison that poor helpless rat!

BRANDER. You tend to see them favorably?
ALTMAYER. Our lard-gut with the balding head
Must take the mishap much to heart;
The swollen rat he sees in his own stead
As a wholly lifelike counterpart. [*Enter* FAUST *and* MEPHISTOPHELES.]
MEPHISTOPHELES. Before all else it's up to me
To get you into jolly company
So you can see how lightly life can run.
These lads make every day a day of fun.
Long on pleasure, short on brains,
Around in narrow circles each one sails
Like kittens chasing their own tails.
When they're not nursing hangover pains,
As long as credit's on the cuff,
They're carefree and quite pleased enough.
BRANDER. Those who have been on travels, they
Act odd and dress in a peculiar way.
They haven't been an hour in this town.
FROSCH. You're right! O Leipzig, such is your renown!
It's "little Paris" and it gives its people *ton*.[70]
SIEBEL. These strangers would be what, you think?
FROSCH. Just let me have free hand. I'll worm the truth
Out of their noses with a drink,
And faster than you pull an infant's tooth.
They have the air of being nobly born,
They act dissatisfied and full of scorn.
BRANDER. I'll bet they're montebanks just come to town.[71]
ALTAMYER. Could be.
FROSCH. Watch me, I'll pin them down.
MEPHISTOPHELES. [*To* FAUST.] The Devil's never recognized by such
Even when their collar's in his clutch.
FAUST. Good evening, gentlemen.
SIEBEL. Thanks, and to you the same. [*Softly, scanning* MEPHISTOPHELES *from the side.*] The fellow drags one foot; could he be lame?[72]
MEPHISTOPHELES. Would you let us come join you where you sit?
Since decent drink is an impossibility,
The company will take the place of it.
ALTMAYER. It seems that you are very finicky.
FROSCH. You must have started out from Rippach late.
Did you stay on for supper there with Jack?[73]
MEPHISTOPHELES. We passed him on the road but didn't wait.
We walked with him the last time, a while back.
He spoke about his cousins at that meeting
And asked that we bring all of you his greeting. [*He bows to* FROSCH.]
ALTMAYER. [*Softly.*] You got it! He caught on!
SIEBEL. Cool customer, I'd say!
FROSCH. Just wait, I'll get him yet some way!
MEPHISTOPHELES. We did hear, if I am not wrong,
Trained voices singing chorus here?
This ceiling must re-echo song
Magnificently loud and clear.
FROSCH. Might you then be a virtuoso?
MEPHISTOPHELES. No, I enjoy it, but my talent's only so-so.
ALTMAYER. Give us a song.
MEPHISTOPHELES. If you like, a quantity.
SIEBEL. Be sure it's in the latest vein!
MEPHISTOPHELES. We've only just come back from Spain,
The lovely land of wine and minstrelsy. [*Sings.*]
A king once was, they tell,
Who had a big pet flea—
FROSCH. Hark! He said "flea!" Did you all catch the rest?
I find a flea a very proper guest.
MEPHISTOPHELES. [*Sings.*] A king once was, they tell,
Who had a big pet flea;
He loved him passing well,
Just like a son, they say.
His tailor he then bade,
And up the tailor goes;
"Here measure me this lad
To make a suit of clothes."
BRANDER. Just don't forget to let the tailor know
He's got to measure to a T,
Because I'll have his head if he
Makes them so any wrinkles show.
MEPHISTOPHELES. In silks and velvet dressed
He stood now in his pride,

With ribbons on his chest
And many a cross beside.
Prime Minister by station,
He wore a star of state,
And all his flea relation
Were numbered with the great
  The gentlemen and ladies
At courts were much distressed,
Both queen and maid were harried
Along with all the rest,
Yet didn't dare to scratch
However they might itch.
When we are bit, we catch
And squash them as they twitch.
CHORUS. [*Shouting.*] When we are bit, we catch
  And squash them as they twitch.
FROSCH. Bravo! Bravo! That was fine!
SIEBEL. That's what should happen to all fleas!
BRANDER. Just purse your fingers, nip, and squeeze!
ALTMAYER. Long live freedom! Long live wine!
MEPHISTOPHELES. To honor freedom I'd be glad to drink a glass
If only you had wines of somewhat better class.
SIEBEL. We'd rather not hear that again.
MEPHISTOPHELES. I fear the keeper of the inn
Might be offended, or I'd fetch the best
Our cellar offers for each worthy guest.
SIEBEL. Go to it! And on my head be the sin!
FROSCH. Come up with a good glass and our praises will be ample,
But just don't be too stingy with the sample;
If I'm to judge and not be doubtful,
I need to have a good big snoutful.
ALTMAYER. [*Softly.*] They're from the Rhine, they've got that smack.
MEPHISTOPHELES. Bring me a gimlet.
BRANDER. Why? What would you use it for?
You surely don't have casks outside the door?
ALTMAYER. The host has got a tool chest out in back.
MEPHISTOPHELES. [*Takes the gimlet. To* FROSCH.]
Now tell me, what would be most to your mind?
FROSCH. How do you mean? Do you have every kind?

MEPHISTOPHELES. To every man the choice is free.
ALTMAYER. [*To* FROSCH.] Aha! You start to lick your lips, I see.
FROSCH. If I can have my choice, it's Rhine wine any time.
My homeland turns out products in their prime.
MEPHISTOPHELES. [*As he bores a hole in the table edge at* FROSCH's *place.*] Get me some wax to use for stoppers. Quick!
ALTMAYER. Aw, this is some magician's trick.
MEPHISTOPHELES. [*To* BRANDER.] And you?
BRANDER. Champagne's the thing for me.
And let it bubble busily! [MEPHISTOPHELES *bores a hole. Someone has meanwhile made wax plugs and stops up the holes.*]
This foreign stuff you sometimes can't avoid,
Good things are often far away.
A Frenchman's something no real German can abide
But he will drink their wines with relish any day.
SIEBEL. [*As* MEPHISTOPHELES *comes to his place.*] I don't like sour wine in any case.
A glass of sweet wine, if I may.
MEPHISTOPHELES. [*Boring.*] For you at once shall flow Tokay.
ALTMAYER. No, gentlemen, now look me in the face!
You're making fun of us, I know you are.
MEPHISTOPHELES. That would be going much too far
With such distinguished company.
Quick now, speak up! What shall it be?
What kind of wine can I serve you?
ALTMAYER. Don't fuss too much, just any kind.
MEPHISTOPHELES. [*After the holes have been bored and plugged. With weird gestures.*]
Grapes the vine stem bears!
Horns the he-goat wears!
The wine is juicy, of wood, the vine,
The wooden table too gives wine.
Into the depths of Nature peer!
Have faith, a miracle is here.
  Now draw the corks and drink your

fill!
ALL. [*As they draw the corks and as the wine of their choice runs into the glass.*] O lovely fountain, flowing all for us!
MEPHISTOPHELES. Just watch that none of it should spill! [*They drink again and again.*]
ALL. [*Singing.*] We've got more fun than cannibals
Or more than five hundred sows!
MEPHISTOPHELES. Just look, they're in their glory, they are free!
FAUST. I would prefer to go away.
MEPHISTOPHELES. You watch now, bestiality
Will gloriously come into play.
SEIEBEL. [*Drinks carelessly; the wine spills on the floor and turns to flame.*] Help! Fire! Help! This flame is out of hell!
MEPHISTOPHELES. [*Addressing the flame.*] Be quiet, friendly element! All's well. [*To the fellows.*]
This time it was a drop of purgatory merely.
SIEBEL. What's this supposed to mean? You'll pay for this, and dearly!
You don't know us much, I can tell.
FROSCH. Don't you try that a second time, you hear!
ALTMAYER. I think we'd better gently ease him on his way.
SIEBEL. What, Sir! Do you presume to play
Your hocus-pocus with us here?
MEPHISTOPHELES. Quiet, old wine vat!
SIEBEL. Splindling broomstick!
You dare to add your insults yet?
BRANDER. Just wait! A rain of fists you'll get.
ALTMAYER. [*Pulls out a cork from the table; fire leaps at him.*] Help! I'm on fire!
SIEBEL. It's magic flame.
Stick him, boys! He's anybody's game! [*They draw their knives and go after MEPHISTOPHELES.*]
MEPHISTOPHELES. [*Gesturing in earnest.*]
False forms be seen,
Shift sense and scene!
Be here, be there! [*They stand in amazement and look at each other.*]
ALTMAYER. Where am I? What a lovely land!
FROSCH. And vineyards? Am I seeing right?
SIEBEL. And grapes at hand?

BRANDER. Here under this green arbor, O!
Just see what grapes and grapevines grow! [*He grabs* SIEBEL *by the nose. The others do likewise to one another and lift their knives.*]
MEPHISTOPHELES. [*As before.*] Error, slip the fetters from their view!
And see what jokes the Devil knows. [*He disappears with* FAUST. *The cronies move apart.*]
SIEBEL. What's happened?
ALTMAYER. How . . . ?
FROSCH. Was that your nose?
BRANDER. [*To* SIEBEL.] And yours is here in my hand too!
ALTMAYER. I felt a shock go through my every limb!
Give me a chair, I'm caving in.
FROSCH. Just what did happen anyway?
SIEBEL. Where is he? Let me at him just once more
And he won't live to get away!
ALTMAYER. I saw him go out through the tavern door . . .
And he was riding on a cask. . . . Why, say!
My feet are weights of lead. [*Turning toward the table.*] You don't suppose
By any chance the wine still flows?
SIEBEL. It was all cheating lies and fraud.
FROSCH. Yet I drank wine, or so I thought.
BRANDER. And what about the grapes?
ALTMAYER. Yes, what about them?
But miracles occur, you cannot doubt them!

Witch's Kitchen

A large cauldron stands over the fire on a low hearth. Amid the steam rising from it various forms are seen. A MONKEY[74] *sits by the kettle skimming it and watching that it does not boil over. The* HE-MONKEY *sits near by with the young ones, warming himself. Walls and ceiling are hung with the most bizarre paraphernalia of witchcraft.*[75]

{*Enter* FAUST *and* MEPHISTOPHELES.}
FAUST. I am revolted by this crazy witchery;
I shall be cured, you guarantee,
In this stark raving rookery?
Must I seek counsel from an aged crone?
And will her filthy cookery
Take thirty years off from my flesh and bone?
Alas for me if you can nothing better find!
Already hope has vanished, I despair.
Has neither Nature nor a wholesome mind
Devised a balm to cure me anywhere?
MEPHISTOPHELES. Ah, now, my friend, you're talking sense once more.
There is a natural way to make you young again,
But that is in another book, and on that score
It forms a curious chapter even then.
FAUST. I want to hear it.
MEPHISTOPHELES. Good! A way without recourse
To money, medicine, or sorcery:
Straight to the fields direct your course
And start to dig immediately;
There keep yourself and keep your mind
Within a circle close confined,
Eat only unadulterated food,
Live with the beasts as beast, and count it good
To strew the harvest field with your own dung;
There is no better way, believe me,
Up to age eighty to stay young.
FAUST. I am not used to that, nor could I ever stand
To take a shovel in my hand.
For me that narrow life would never do.
MEPHISTOPHELES. Well, then it's to the witch for you.
FAUST. But why just this old hag? What makes
You say that *you* can't brew the cup?
MEPHISTOPHELES. A pretty pastime that! I could put up
A thousand bridges in the time it takes.[76]
This work needs skill and knowledge, it is true,
But it requires some patience too.
A quiet mind may work for years on end
But time alone achieves the potent blend.
And as for what there may be to it,
There's many an odd ingredient.
The Devil taught her how to brew it,
But by himself the Devil cannot do it.
[*Catching sight of the* ANIMALS.]
Ah, see the cute breed by the fire!
That is the maid, that is the squire. [*To the* ANIMALS.]
Where is the lady of the house?
THE ANIMALS. Out of the house
On a carouse
Up chimney and away.
MEPHISTOPHELES. How long does she rampage today?
THE ANIMALS. Until we get our paws warm, anyway.
MEPHISTOPHELES. [*To* FAUST.] How do you like these cunning creatures?
FAUST. Repulsive to the nth degree.
MEPHISTOPHELES. No, discourse such as this one features
Is just the kind that most entrances me.
[*To the* ANIMALS.]
Now, you accursed puppets you,
Why are you paddling in that broth, pray tell?
THE ANIMALS. We're cooking up some beggars' stew.
MEPHISTOPHELES. You'll have a good big clientele.
THE HE-MONKEY. [*Coming over and fawning on* MEPHISTOPHELES.] O roll the dice
And make me nice
And rich with gains!
My lot is bad,
But if I had
Some money, I'd have brains.
MEPHISTOPHELES. How happy would this monkey be
If he could play the lottery! [*Meanwhile the young monkeys have been playing with a large globe and now roll it forward.*]
THE HE-MONKEY. That is the world;
Spun and twirled,
It never ceases;
It rings like glass,
But hollow, alas,
It breaks to pieces.
Here it gleams bright,

And here more bright,
Alive am I.
Dear son, I say
Keep far away,
For you must die.
It's made of clay,
And splinters fly.
MEPHISTOPHELES. And why the sieve?
THE HE-MONKEY. [*Takes it down.*]
I'd know you if
You were a thief.[77] [*He runs to the* SHE-MONKEY *and has her look through it.*]
Look through the sieve:
You see the thief
And name him not?
MEPHISTOPHELES. [*Going over to the fire.*]
And why the pot?
THE HE-MONKEY AND THE SHE-MONKEY.
The silly sot!
Not know the pot,
Not know the kettle?
MEPHISTOPHELES. Uncivil beast!
THE HE-MONKEY. Here, take the whisk[78]
And sit on the settle. [*He has* MEPHISTOPHELES *sit down.*]
FAUST. [*Has all this time been standing in front of a mirror, now going up to it, now stepping back away from it.*]
What do I see with form divine
Upon this magic mirror shine?
O Love, lend me the swiftest of your pinions
And take me off to her dominions!
Unless I stand right here in this one place
And do not venture to go near,
I see her misted only and unclear.—
A woman of the utmost grace!
Can any woman be so fair?
In this recumbent body do I face
The essence of all heavens here?
Is there on earth the like of it?[79]
MEPHISTOPHELES. It's natural, if a god will six whole days expend
And then himself shout bravo! in the end,
That something smart must come of it.[80]
Go right ahead and gaze your fill;
Just such a sweetheart I can well provide,
And lucky is the man who will
Then take her with him as his bride.
[FAUST *keeps right on looking into the mirror.* MEPHISTOPHELES *sprawls on the settle and toys with the whisk as he goes on speaking.*]
I sit here like a king upon his throne,
I hold a scepter, and I lack a crown alone. [*The* ANIMALS, *who have been going through all kinds of odd motions helter-skelter, bring* MEPHISTOPHELES *a crown amid loud cries.*]
THE ANIMALS. O just be so good
As with sweat and blood
To glue this crown and lime it. [*They handle the crown clumsily and break it in two pieces, then hop around with the pieces.*]
Now it is done!
We talk, look, and run,
We listen and rhyme it—
FAUST. [*Toward the mirror.*] I'm going crazy here, I feel!
MEPHISTOPHELES. [*Pointing to the* ANIMALS.] My own head now almost begins to reel.
THE ANIMALS. If we have luck
And don't get stuck
We'll make sense yet![81]
FAUST. [*As before.*] My heart is catching fire within!
Let's get away from here, and fast!
MEPHISTOPHELES. [*In his previous posture.*] This much you'll have to grant at least:
As poets they are genuine. [*The kettle, which the* SHE-MONKEY *has left unwatched, begins to boil over. A great flame flashes up the chimney. Down through the flame comes the* WITCH *with hideous screams.*]
THE WITCH. Ow! Ow! Ow! Ow!
Damnable brute! Accursed sow!
Neglect the kettle, scorch your mate!
Accursed beast! [*Catching sight of* FAUST *and* MEPHISTOPHELES.]
What have we here?
Who are you here?
What do you want?
Who has sneaked in?
Flames and groans
Consume your bones! [*She dips the skimmer into the kettle and scoops flames at* FAUST, MEPHISTOPHELES, *and the* ANIMALS. *The* ANIMALS *whimper.*]
MEPHISTOPHELES. [*Reverses the whisk he is holding and goes smashing the glasses and pots.*] Crash! And smash!
There goes your trash!
Your glassware's done!
It's all in fun,

I'm only beating time,
Carrion, to your rhyme. [*As the* WITCH *falls back in fury and horror.*]
You recognize me, Bone-bag? Skeleton?
Your know your master and your lord?
What keeps me now from going on
To pulverize you and your monkey horde!
For my red coat you have such small respect?
My rooster feather you don't recognize?
Is my face hidden? Or do you expect
I'll state my name and enterprise?
THE WITCH. O Sir, forgive this rude salute from me!
And yet no horse hoof do I see;
And then where is your raven pair?[82]
MEPHISTOPHELES. This time I'll let you get away with it.
It has been quite some while, I will admit,
Since last we met. And to be fair,
The culture that has licked the world up slick
Has even with the Devil turned the trick.
The northern phantom is no longer to be found;
Where will you see horns, tail, or claws around?
As for the foot, which I can't do without,
It would work me much social harm, I fear;
And so, like many a young man, I've gone about
With padded calves this many a long year.[83]
THE WITCH. [*Dancing.*] I'll lose my mind for jubilation
To see Squire Satan back in circulation!
MEPHISTOPHELES. Woman, I forbid that appellation!
THE WITCH. Why? What harm has it ever done?
MEPHISTOPHELES. It's long since passed to fable books and vanished.
Yet people are no better off. The Evil One
They're rid of, but their evils are not banished.
Just call me Baron, that will do.
I am a cavalier like any cavalier.
You do not doubt my noble blood, and you
Can see the coat of arms that I wear here. [*He makes an indecent gesture.*][84]
THE WITCH. [*Laughing immoderately.*] Ha! Ha! Just like you, that I'll swear!
Oh you're a rogue, just as you always were!
MEPHISTOPHELES. [*To* FAUST.] Learn this, my friend! This is the way
To handle witches any day.
THE WITCH. Now, gentlemen, how can I be of use?
MEPHISTOPHELES. A good glass of the well-known juice,
But of your oldest, is what I'm after;
It's years that put the powers in those brews.
THE WITCH. Why, sure! Here is a bottle on my shelf
From which I sometimes take a nip myself
And which no longer has a trace of stink.
I'll gladly pour you out a little glass. [*Softly.*]
But if this man here unprepared should drink,
You know he'll die before two hours pass.
MEPHISTOPHELES. He's a good friend, and I mean things to thrive with him;
Give him the best your kitchen offers, serve him well.
So draw your circle, speak your spell,
And fill his cup right to the brim. [*With bizarre gestures the* WITCH *describes a circle and places strange things inside it. Meanwhile the glasses begin to ring and the kettle to boom and make music. Finally she fetches a great book and disposes the monkeys within the circle to serve her as a lectern and to hold torches. She beckons* FAUST *to come to her.*]
FAUST. [*To* MEPHISTOPHELES.] Now tell me, what is all this leading to?
These frantic motions and this wild ado
And all of this disgusting stuff
I've known and hated long enough.
MEPHISTOPHELES. Oh, nonsense! It's just for the fun of it!
And don't be such a prig! As a physician,
She needs to hocus-pocus just a bit
So that the juice can work on your condition. [*He gets* FAUST *into the circle.*]

THE WITCH. [*Begins to declaim with great bombast out of a book.*] This must ye ken!
From one take ten;
Skip two; and then
Even up three,
And rich you'll be.
Leave out the four.
From five and six,
Thus says the witch,
Make seven and eight,
And all is straight.
And nine is one,
And ten is none.
This is the witch's one-times-one!
FAUST. I think the hag's in fever and delirium.
MEPHISTOPHELES. Oh, there is lots more still to come.
As I well know, the whole book's in that vein.
I've wasted much time going through its pages,
For total paradox will still remain
A mystery alike to fools and sages.
My friend, the art is old and new.
For ages it has been the thing to do,
By Three and One, and One and Three,
To broadcast error in guise of verity.[85]
And so they teach and jabber unperturbed;
With fools, though, who is going to bother?
Man has a way of thinking, when he hears a word,
That certainly behind it lies some thought or other.
THE WITCH. [*Continues.*] The lofty force
Of wisdom's source
Is from the whole world hidden.
Once given up thinking,
And in a twinkling
It's granted you unbidden.[86]
FAUST. What nonsense is she spouting now before us?
My head is going to split before too long.
I feel as if I'm listening to a chorus
Of fools a hundred thousand strong.
MEPHISTOPHELES. Enough, O worthy Sibyl! Pray, no more!
Bring on your potion now, and pour
A goblet quickly to the brim;
My friend is safe, your drink won't injure him.
He is a man of many titles,[87]
And many a dram has warmed his vitals. [*With many ceremonies the* WITCH *pours out the drink in a goblet. As* FAUST *raises it to his mouth a little flame arises.*]
Just drink it down. Go on! You'll love
The way it makes your heart soar higher.
What! With the Devil hand-in-glove
And boggle at a little fire? [*The* WITCH *dissolves the circle.* FAUST *steps forth.*]
Come right on out! You must not rest.
THE WITCH. And may the dram do you much good!
MEPHISTOPHELES. [*To the* WITCH.] If you have any favor to request,
Just tell me on Walpurgis, if you would.[88]
THE WITCH. Here is a spell; say it occasionally
And you'll see strange results without a doubt.
MEPHISTOPHELES. [*To* FAUST.] Just come along, entrust yourself to me.
You must perspire now necessarily
To get the force to penetrate both in and out.
I'll teach you later all the joys of indolence,
And soon to your heart's pleasure you'll commence
To feel how Cupid rises up and hops about.
FAUST. Just one more quick look in the mirror there!
That womanly form was O! so fair!
MEPHISTOPHELES. No, no! For soon, alive before you here
The paragon of women shall appear. [*Aside.*]
With that drink in you, you will find
All women Helens to your mind.

A Street

FAUST. MARGARET *passing by.*
FAUST. Fair lady, may I be so free
As offer my arm and company?
MARGARET. I'm neither a lady nor fair, and may

Go unescorted on my way. [*She disengages herself and goes on.*]
FAUST. By heaven, but that child is sweet!
Like none I ever chanced to meet.
So virtuous and modest, yes,
But with a touch of spunkiness.
Her lips so red, her cheek so bright,
I never shall forget the sight.
The shy way she cast down her eye
Has pressed itself deep in my heart;
And then the quick and short reply,
That was the most delightful part! [*Enter* MEPHISTOPHELES.]
You must get me that girl, you hear?
MEPHISTOPHELES. Which one?
FAUST. She just went by me here.
MEPHISTOPHELES. That one? She just came from the priest,
He absolved her from her sins and all;
I stole up near the confessional.
She's just a simple little thing,
Went to confession just for nothing.
On such as she I have no hold.
FAUST. And yet she's past fourteen years old.
MEPHISTOPHELES. Why, you talk just like Jack the Rake
Who wants all flowers to bloom for his sake
And fancies that no honor is,
Or favor, but the picking's his.
It doesn't always work that way.
FAUST. Dear Master Laudable, I say
Don't bother me with your legality!
And I am telling you outright,
Unless that creature of delight
Lies in my arms this very night,
At midnight we part company.
MEPHISTOPHELES. Remember there are limits! I
Need fourteen days at least to try
And find an opportunity.
FAUST. Had I but seven hours clear,
I wouldn't need the Devil near
To lead that girl astray for me.
MEPHISTOPHELES. You're talking like a Frenchman. Wait!
And don't be put out or annoyed:
What good's a thing too soon enjoyed?
The pleasure is not half so great
As when you first parade the doll
Through every sort of folderol
And knead and pat and shape her well,
The way that all French novels tell.
FAUST. I've appetite enough without it.

MEPHISTOPHELES. With no more joking now about it:
I'm telling you that pretty child
Will not be hurriedly beguiled.
There's nothing to be gained by force;
To cunning we must have recourse.
FAUST. Get me some of that angel's attire!
Lead me to her place of rest!
Get me the kerchief from her breast,
A garter for my love's desire!
MEPHISTOPHELES. Just so you see that I do heed
Your pain and serve your every need,
We shall not waste a single minute.
I'll take you to her room and put you in it.
FAUST. And shall I see her? have her?
MEPHISTOPHELES. No!
She'll be at a neighbor's when we go.
And all alone there you can dwell
Upon the fragrance of her cell
And hope for future joys as well.
FAUST. Can we go now?
MEPHISTOPHELES. It's too soon yet.
FAUST. Get me a gift for her, and don't forget. [*Exit.*]
MEPHISTOPHELES. What! Gifts so soon! That's fine! He'll be right in his glory!
I know a lot of pretty places
Where there are buried treasure cases;
I must go through my inventory! [*Exit.*]

Evening

A small, neat room. MARGARET *braiding her hair and doing it up.*
MARGARET. I'd give a good deal if I knew
Who was that gentleman today!
He had a very gallant way
And comes of noble lineage too.
That much I could read from his face—
Or he'd not be so bold in the first place.
[*Exit.*] [*Enter* FAUST *and* MEPHISTOPHELES.]
MEPHISTOPHELES. Come on! But softly. In you go!

FAUST. [*After a silence.*] I beg you, leave me here alone.
MEPHISTOPHELES. [*Peering about.*]
Not every girl's this neat, you know? [*Exit.*]
FAUST. [*Looking all around.*]
Welcome, lovely twilight gloom
That hovers in this sacred room!
Seize on my heart, sweet love pangs who
Both live and languish on hope's own dew.
How everything here is imbued
With stillness, order, and content!
Here in this poverty, what plenitude!
Here in this prison, what ravishment!
[*He throws himself into the leather armchair beside the bed.*]
O you who have both joy and sorrow known
From times gone by, clasp me too in your arms!
How often at this patriarchal throne
Children have gathered round about in swarms!
Perhaps my sweetheart, plump-cheeked, used to stand
Here grateful for a Christmas present and
Devoutly kiss her grandsire's withered hand.
I feel your spirit, maiden, playing
About me, breathing order, plenitude,
And every day in mother-fashion saying
The cloth upon the table must be fresh renewed
And underfoot clean sand be strewed.
Dear hand! so godlike! In it lies
What turns a cottage to a paradise.
And here! [*He lifts the bed curtains.*]
What chill of rapture seizes me!
Here I could linger on for hours.
Here, Nature, you with your creative powers
From light dreams brought the angel forth to be;
Here lay the child, her bosom warm
With life; here tenderly there grew
With pure and sacred help from you
The godlike image of her form.
  And you? What purpose brought you here?
How I am touched with shame sincere!
What do you want? Why is your heart so sore?
O sorry Faust! I know you now no more.
  Does magic haze surround me everywhere?
I pressed for pleasure with no least delay,
And in a love dream here I melt away!
Are we the toys of every breath of air?
If she this moment now were to come by,
What punishment your impudence would meet!
The loud-mouth lummox—O how small!—would lie
Dissolved in shame before her feet.
[*Enter* MEPHISTOPHELES.]
MEPHISTOPHELES. Quick now! I see her at the gate.
FAUST. Away! And never to come back!
MEPHISTOPHELES. Here is a casket of some weight,
I took it elsewhere from a rack.
Just put it in her clothespress there,
It'll make her head swim, that I'll swear.
I put some little baubles in it
To bait another bauble and win it
A girl's a girl and play is play.
FAUST. I wonder . . . should I?
MEPHISTOPHELES. You delay?
You wouldn't maybe want to keep the baubles?
In that case I advise Your Lust
To save my pretty daytime, just
Don't bother me with further troubles.
You are not miserly, I trust!
I scratch my head, I rub my hands—
[*He puts the casket in the clothespress and pushes the lock shut again.*]
Off and away now!
To get that lovely child to play now
Into your heart's desires and plans.
And you stand all
Poised to proceed to lecture hall,
And as if in the flesh, and grey,
Physics and Metaphysics led the way.
Come on! [*Exeunt.*] [*Enter* MARGARET *with a lamp.*]
MARGARET. It's close in here, there is no air. [*She opens the window.*]
And yet it's not so warm out there.
I feel so odd, I can't say how—
I do wish Mother would come home now.

I'm chilled all over, and shivering!
I'm such a foolish, timid thing!
[*She begins to sing as she undresses.*]
    There was a king of Thule
True even to the grave,
To whom a golden goblet
His dying mistress gave.
    Naught did he hold more dear,
He drained it every feast;
And from his eye a tear
Welled each time as he ceased.
    When life was nearly done,
His towns he totaled up,
Begrudged his heir not one,
But did not give the cup.
    There with his vassals all
At royal board sat he
In high ancestral hall
Of his castle by the sea.
    The old toper then stood up,
Quaffed off his last life-glow,
And flung the sacred cup
Down to the flood below.
    He saw it fall, and drink,
And sink deep in the sea;
Then did his eyelids sink,
And no drop more drank he. [*She opens the clothespress to put her clothes away and catches sight of the jewel casket.*]
How did this pretty casket get in here?
I locked the press, I'm sure. How queer!
What can it have inside it? Can it be
That someone left it as security
For money Mother has provided?
Here on a ribbon hangs a little key—
I think I'll have a look inside it!
What's this? O Lord in heaven! See!
I've never seen the like in all my days!
A noble lady with such jewelry
Could walk with pride on holidays.
I wonder how this chain would look on me?
Such glorious things! Whose could they be? [*She puts it on and steps up to the mirror.*]
If just these earrings could be mine!
One looks so different in them right away.
What good does beauty do, young thing? It may
Be very well to wonder at,
But people let it go at that;
They praise you half in pity.
Gold serves all ends,
On gold depends
Everything. Ah, we poor!

Promenade

FAUST *pacing up and down in thought.*
    MEPHISTOPHELES *comes to him.*
MEPHISTOPHELES. Now by the element
  of hell! By love refused!
I wish I knew a stronger oath that
  could be used!
FAUST. What's this? What's griping you
  so badly?
I've never seen a face the like of this!
MEPHISTOPHELES. Why, I'd surrender to
  the Devil gladly
If I were not the Devil as it is!
FAUST. Have you gone off your head? I
  grant
It suits you, though, to rave and rant.
MEPHISTOPHELES. Just think, those jewels for Gretchen[89] that I got,
Some priest has made off with the lot!—
Her mother got to see the things,
Off went her dire imaginings;
That woman's got some sense of smell,
She has prayerbook-sniffing on the brain,
A whiff of any item, and she can tell
Whether the thing is sacred or profane.
That jewelry she spotted in a minute
As having no great blessing in it.
"My child," she cried, "ill-gotten good
Ensnares the soul, consumes the blood.
Before Our Lady we will lay it,
With heaven's manna she'll repay it."[90]
Margretlein pulled a pouty face,
Called it a gift horse, and in any case
She thought he wasn't godless, he
Who sneaked it in so cleverly.
The mother had a priest drop by;
No sooner did he the trick espy
Than his eyes lit up with what he saw.
"This shows an upright mind," quoth he,
"Self-conquest gains us victory.
The church has a good healthy maw,
She's swallowed up whole countries,

still
She never yet has eaten her fill.
The church, dear ladies, alone has health
For digestion of ill-gotten wealth."
FAUST. That's nothing but the usual game,
A king and a Jew can do the same.
MEPHISTOPHELES. Then up he scooped brooch, chain, and rings
As if they were just trivial things
With no more thanks, if's, and's, or but's
Than if they were a bag of nuts,
Promised them celestial reward—
All edified, they thanked him for it.
FAUST. And Gretchen?
MEPHISTOPHELES. Sits lost now in concern,
Not knowing yet which way to turn;
Thinks day and night about the gems,
But more of him from whom the present stems.
FAUST. I hate to see the dear girl worry.
Get her a new set in a hurry.
The first one wasn't too much anyway.
MEPHISTOPHELES. My gentleman finds this mere child's play.
FAUST. And here's the way I want it. Go
Make friends there with that neighbor. Show
You're not a devil made of sugar water,
Get those new gems and have them brought her.
MEPHISTOPHELES. Sir, I obey with all my heart. [*Exit* FAUST.]
This fool in love will huff and puff
The sun and moon and stars apart
To get his sweetheart pastime stuff.
[*Exit.*]

The Neighbor's House

MARTHA *alone.*
MARTHA. Now God forgive my husband, he
Has not done the right thing by me.
Way off into the world he's gone,
And leaves me on the straw alone.
Yet he surely had no cause on my part,
God knows I loved him with all my heart. [*She weeps.*]
He could be dead!—If I just knew for sure!
Or had a statement with a signature! [*Enter* MARGARET.]
MARGARET. Dame Martha!
MARTHA. What is it, Gretelchen?
MARGARET. My knees are sinking under me.
I've found one in my press again,
Another casket, of ebony,
And this time it's a gorgeous set
Far richer than the first one yet.
MARTHA. This time you mustn't tell your mother,
Off it would go to church just like the other.
MARGARET. O look at them! Just see! Just see!
MARTHA. [*Putting them on her.*] You *are* a lucky creature!
MARGARET. Unfortunately
In church or on the street I do not dare
Be seen in them, or anywhere.
MARTHA. You just come over frequently,
Put on the jewels in secret here,
Walk by the mirror an hour or so in privacy,
And we'll enjoy them, never fear.
There'll come a chance, a holiday, before we're done,
Where you can show them to the people one by one,
A necklace first, pearl ear-drops next; your mother
Won't notice it, or we'll make up something or other.
MARGARET. But who could bring both caskets here?
There's something not quite right . . . [*A knock.*] Oh, dear!
Could that be Mother coming here?
MARTHA. [*Looking through the blinds.*] It's a strange gentleman—Come in! [MEPHISTOPHELES *steps in.*]
MEPHISTOPHELES. I'm so free as to step right in,
The ladies must excuse my liberty. [*Steps back respectfully before* MARGARET.]
I wish to see Dame Martha Schwerdtlein, if I may.
MARTHA. Right here! What might the gentleman have to say?

MEPHISTOPHELES. [*Aside to her.*] I know you now, that is enough for me.
You have distinguished company.
Forgive my freedom, I shall then
Return this afternoon again.
MARTHA. [*Aloud.*] Child, think of it! The gentleman takes
You for some lady! For mercy's sakes!
MARGARET. I'm just a poor young girl; I find
The gentleman is far too kind.
These gems do not belong to me.
MEPHISTOPHELES. Oh, it's not just the jewelry.
She has a quick glance, and a way!
I am delighted I may stay.
MARTHA. What is your errand then? I'm very—
MEPHISTOPHELES. I wish my tidings were more merry.
I trust you will not make me rue this meeting:
Your husband is dead and sends you greeting.
MARTHA. He's dead! That faithful heart! Oh, my!
My husband's dead! Oh! I shall die!
MARGARET. Dear lady, Oh! Do not despair!
MEPHISTOPHELES. Now listen to the sad affair.
MARGARET. I hope I never, never love.
Such loss as this I would die of.
MEPHISTOPHELES. Glad must have sad, sad must have glad, as always.
MARTHA. O tell me all about his dying!
MEPHISTOPHELES. At Padua, by Saint Anthony's
They buried him, and he is lying
In ground well sanctified and blest
At cool and everlasting rest.
MARTHA. And there is nothing else you bring?
MEPHISTOPHELES. Yes, one request and solemn enterprise:
Three hundred Masses for him you should have them sing.
My pockets are quite empty otherwise.
MARTHA. What, not a luck-piece, or a trinket such
As any journeyman deep in his pack would hoard
As a remembrance token stored
And sooner starve or beg than use it!
MEPHISTOPHELES. Madam, it grieves me very much;
Indeed he did not waste his money or lose it.
And much did he his failings then deplore,
Yes, and complained of his hard luck still more.
MARGARET. To think that human fortunes so miscarry!
Many's the Requiem I'll pray for him, I'm sure.
MEPHISTOPHELES. Ah, you deserve now very soon to marry,
A child of such a kindly nature.
MARGARET. It's not yet time for that. Oh, no!
MEPHISTOPHELES. If not a husband, then meanwhile a beau.
It's one of heaven's greatest graces
To hold so dear a thing in one's embraces.
MARGARET. It's not the custom here for one.
MEPHISTOPHELES. Custom or not, it still is done.
MARTHA. But tell me more!
MEPHISTOPHELES. I stood at his bedside—
Half-rotten straw it was and little more
Than horse manure; but in good Christian style he died,
Yet found he had still further items on his score.
"How I detest myself!" he cried with dying breath,
"For having left my business and my wife!
Ah, that remembrance is my death.
If she would just forgive me in this life!"—
MARTHA. [*Weeping.*] The good man! I long since forgave.
MEPHISTOPHELES. "God knows, though, she was more to blame than I."
MARTHA. It's a lie! And he with one foot in the grave!
MEPHISTOPHELES. Oh, he was talking through his hat
There at the end, if I am half a judge.
"I had no time to sit and yawn," he said,
"First children and then earning children's bread,
Bread in the widest sense, at that,
And could not even eat my share in peace."
MARTHA. Did he forget my love, how I

would drudge
Both day and night and never cease?
MEPHISTOPHELES. No, he remembered that all right.
"As I put out from Malta," he went on,
"I prayed for wife and children fervently;
Then heaven too disposed things favorably
So our ship took a Turkish galleon
With treasure for the great Sultan aboard.
Then bravery came in for reward
And I got, as was only fair,
My own well calculated share."
MARTHA. What! Where? Do you suppose he buried it?
MEPHISTOPHELES. Who knows where the four winds have carried it?
A pretty girl took him in tow when he
Was roaming Naples there without a friend;
She showed him so much love and loyalty
He bore the marks right to his blessed end.[91]
MARTHA. The rogue! He robbed his children like a thief!
And all that misery and grief
Could not prevent the shameful life he led.
MEPHISTOPHELES. But that, you see, is why he's dead.
Were I in your place now, you know,
I'd mourn him for a decent year and then
Be casting round meanwhile to find another beau.
MARTHA. Oh Lord, the kind my first man was,
I'll never in this world find such again.
There never was a fonder fool than mine.
Only, he liked the roving life too much,
And foreign women, and foreign wine,
And then, of course, those devilish dice.
MEPHISTOPHELES. Well, well, it could have worked out fine
If he had only taken such
Good care on his part to be nice.
I swear on those terms it is true
I would myself exchange rings with you.
MARTHA. Oh, the gentleman has such joking ways!
MEPHISTOPHELES. [Aside.] It's time for me to be pushing onward!
She'd hold the very Devil to his word. [To GRETCHEN.]
How are things with your heart these days?
MARGARET. What do you mean, Sir?
MEPHISTOPHELES. [Aside.] O you innocents!
Ladies, farewell!
MARGARET. Farewell.
MARTHA. One word yet! What I crave is
Some little piece of evidence
Of when and how my sweetheart died and where his grave is.
I've always been a friend of orderliness,
I'd like to read his death note in the weekly press.
MEPHISTOPHELES. Good woman, what two witnesses report
Will stand as truth in any court.
I have a friend, quite serious,
I'll bring him to the judge with us.
I'll go and get him.
MARTHA. Do that! Do!
MEPHISTOPHELES. This lady will be with you too?
A splendid lad, much traveled. He
Shows ladies every courtesy.
MARGARET. The gentleman would make me blush for shame.
MEPHISTOPHELES. Before no earthly king that one could name.
MARTHA. Out in the garden to the rear
This afternoon we'll expect both of you here.

A Street[92]

{Enter FAUST and MEPHISTOPHELES.}
FAUST. How is it? Will it work? Will it succeed?
MEPHISTOPHELES. Ah, bravo! I find you aflame indeed.
Gretchen is yours now pretty soon.
You meet at neighbor Martha's house this afternoon.
The woman is expressly made
To work the pimp and gypsy trade!
FAUST. Good!

MEPHISTOPHELES. Ah, but something is required of us.
FAUST. One good turn deserves another.
MEPHISTOPHELES. We will depose some testimony or other
To say her husband's bones are to be found
In Padua in consecrated ground.
FAUST. Fine! First we'll need to do some journey-going.
MEPHISTOPHELES. *Sancta simplicitas!* For that we need not fuss.
Just testify, and never mind the knowing.
FAUST. Think of a better plan, or nothing doing.
MEPHISTOPHELES. O saintly man! and sanctimonious!
False witness then you never bore
In all your length of life before?
Have you not with great power given definition
Of God, the world, and all the world's condition,
Of man, man's heart, man's mind, and what is more,
With brazen brow and with no lack of breath?
And when you come right down to it,
You knew as much about them, you'll admit,
As you know of this Mister Schwerdtlein's death!
FAUST. You are a liar and a sophist too.
MEPHISTOPHELES. Or would be, if I didn't know a thing or two.
Tomorrow will you not deceive
Poor Gretchen and then make her believe
The vows of soul-felt love you swear?
FAUST. And from my heart.
MEPHISTOPHELES. All good and fair!
Then comes eternal faith, and love still higher,
Then comes the super-almighty desire—
Will that be heartfelt too, I inquire?
FAUST. Stop there! It will!—If I have feeling,
And for this feeling, for this reeling
Seek a name, and finding none,
With all my senses through the wide world run,
And clutch at words supreme and claim
That boundless, boundless is the flame
That burns me, infinite and never done,
Is that a devilish, lying game?
MEPHISTOPHELES. I still am right!
FAUST. Mark this and heed it,
And spare me further waste of throat and lung:
To win an argument takes no more than a tongue,
That's all that's needed.
But come, this chatter fills me with disgust,
For you are right, primarily because I must.

A Garden

MARGARET *on* FAUST's *arm,* MARTHA *with* MEPHISTOPHELES, *strolling up and down.*
MARGARET. I feel, Sir, you are only sparing me
And shaming me by condescending so.
A traveler, from charity,
Will often take things as they go.
I realize my conversation can
Not possibly amuse such an experienced man.
FAUST. One glance of yours, one word delights me more
Than all of this world's wisdom-store
[*He kisses her hand.*]
MARGARET. How can you kiss it? It must seem to you
So coarse, so rough a hand to kiss.
What kinds of tasks have I not had to do!
You do not know how strict my mother is. [*They pass on.*]
MARTHA. And so, Sir, you are traveling constantly?
MEPHISTOPHELES. Business and duty keep us on our way.
Many a place one leaves regretfully,
But then one simply cannot stay.
MARTHA. It may well do while in one's prime
To rove about the world as a rolling stone,
But then comes the unhappy time,

And dragging to the grave, a bachelor,
    alone,
Was never good for anyone.
MEPHISTOPHELES. Ah, such with horror
    I anticipate.
MARTHA. Then act, dear Sir, before it is
    too late. [*They pass on.*]
MARGARET. But out of sight is out of
    mind!
Your courtesy comes naturally;
But you have friends in quantity
Who are more clever than my kind.
FAUST. Dear girl, believe me, clever in
    that sense
Means usually a close self-interest.
MARGARET. Really?
FAUST. To think simplicity and inno-
    cence
Are unaware their sacred way is best,
That lowliness and sweet humility
Are bounteous Nature's highest gifts—
MARGARET. Think only for a moment's
    time of me,
I shall have time enough to think of
    you.
FAUST. Then you are much alone?
MARGARET. Yes, our house is a little one,
And yet it must be tended to.
We have no maid, hence I must cook
    and sweep and knit
And sew, and do the errands early and
    late;
And then my mother is a bit
Too strict and strait.
And yet she has no need to scrimp and
    save this way;
We could live better far than others,
    you might say;
My father left a sizeable estate,
A house and garden past the city gate.
But I have rather quiet days of late.
My brother is a soldier,
My little sister died;
The child did sometimes leave me with
    my patience tried,
And yet I'd gladly have the trouble
    back again,
She was so dear to me.
FAUST. An angel, if like you.
MARGARET. I brought her up; she dear-
    ly loved me too.
She was born following my father's
    death.
Mother we thought at her last breath,
She was so miserable, but then
Slowly, slowly got her strength again.
It was impossible for her to nurse
The little mite herself, of course,
And so I raised her all alone
On milk and water; she became my
    own.
In my arms, in my lap she smiled,
Wriggled, and grew up to be a child.
FAUST. You must have known the purest
    happiness.
MARGARET. But many trying hours
    nonetheless.
At night her little cradle used to stand
Beside my bed, and she had but to stir
And I was there at hand,
Sometimes to feed her, sometimes to
    comfort her,
Sometimes when she would not be still,
    to rise
And pace the floor with her to soothe
    her cries,
And yet be at the washtub early, do
The marketing and tend the hearth
    fire too,
And every morrow like today.
One's spirits are not always cheerful,
    Sir, that way;
Yet food is relished better, as is rest.
[*They pass on.*]
MARTHA. Poor women! They are badly
    off indeed,
A bachelor is hard to change, they say.
MEPHISTOPHELES. Someone like you is
    all that I would need
To set me on a better way.
MARTHA. But is there no one, Sir, that
    you have found?
Speak frankly, is your heart in no wise
    bound?
MEPHISTOPHELES. The proverb says: A
    wife and one's own household
Are worth their weight in pearls and
    gold.
MARTHA. But I mean, have you felt no
    inclination?
MEPHISTOPHELES. I have met every-
    where with much consideration.
MARTHA. But has your heart in no case
    been impressed?
MEPHISTOPHELES. With ladies one must
    not presume to jest.
MARTHA. Oh, you misunderstand me!
MEPHISTOPHELES. What a shame! I find
I understand—that you are very kind.
[*They pass on.*]
FAUST. And so you did, my angel, rec-
    ognize

Me in the garden here at the first look?
MARGARET. Did you not see how I cast down my eyes?
FAUST. And you forgive the liberty I took
And all my impudence before
When you had just left the cathedral door?
MARGARET. I was confused, the experience was all new.
No one could say bad things of me.
Ah, thought I, could he possibly
Have noted something brazen or bold in you?
He seemed to think here was a girl he could
Treat in just any way he would.
I must confess that then I hardly knew
What soon began to argue in your favor;
But I was angry with myself, however,
For not becoming angrier with you.
FAUST. My darling!
MARGARET. Wait! [*She picks a star flower and plucks the petals off it one by one.*]
FAUST. What is it? A bouquet?
MARGARET. No, just a game.
FAUST. What?
MARGARET. You'd laugh at me if I should say. [*She murmurs something as she goes on plucking.*]
FAUST. What are you murmuring?
MARGARET. [*Half aloud.*] He loves me—loves me not.
FAUST. You lovely creature of the skies!
MARGARET. [*Continuing.*] Loves me—not—loves me—not—[*With delight as she reaches the last petal.*]
He loves me!
FAUST. Yes, my child! And let this language of
The flowers be your oracle. he loves you!
Do you know what that means? He loves you! [*He takes both her hands.*]
MARGARET. I'm trembling!
FAUST. O do not tremble! Let this glance
And let this pressure of my hands
Say what is inexpressible:
To yield oneself entirely and to feel
A rapture that must be everlasting!
Eternal!—Its end would be despair.
No! Without end! Without end!
[MARGARET *presses his hands, disengages herself, and runs off. He stands in thought for a moment, then follows her.*]
MARTHA. [*Coming along.*] It's getting dark.
MEPHISTOPHELES. We must be on our way.
MARTHA. I'd ask you gentlemen to stay,
But this is such a wicked neighborhood.
It seems that no one has a thing to do
Or put his mind to
But watch his neighbor's every move and stir.
No matter what one does, there's always talk.
What of our couple?
MEPHISTOPHELES. They've flown up the arbor walk.
The wanton butterflies!
MARTHA. He seems to take to her.
MEPHISTOPHELES. And she to him. Such is the world's old way.

A Summer House

MARGARET *comes running in, hides behind the door, puts her finger to her lips, and peeps through the crack.*
MARGARET. He's coming! [FAUST *comes along.*]
FAUST. Little rogue, to tease me so! I'll catch you! [*He kisses her.*]
MARGARET. [*Embracing him and returning his kiss.*] From my heart I love you so!
[MEPHISTOPHELES *knocks.*]
FAUST. [*Stamping his foot.*] Who's there?
MEPHISTOPHELES. A friend!
FAUST. A beast!
MEPHISTOPHELES. It's time for us to go.
[MARTHA *comes along.*]
MARTHA. Yes, it is late, Sir.
FAUST. May I not escort you, though?
MARGARET. My mother would—farewell!
FAUST. Ah, must I leave you then? Farewell!
MARTHA. Adieu!
MARGARET. But soon to meet again!
[*Exeunt* FAUST *and* MEPHISTOPHELES.]
Dear Lord! What things and things there can

Come to the mind of such a man!
I stand abashed, and for the life of me
Cannot do other than agree.
A simple child, I cannot see
Whatever it is he finds in me. [*Exit.*]

Forest and Cavern

FAUST *alone.*
FAUST. Spirit sublime, thou gavest me, gavest me all
For which I asked. Thou didst not turn in vain
Thy countenance upon me in the fire.
Thou gavest me glorious Nature for my kingdom,
And power to feel it and enjoy it. No
Cold, marveling observation didst thou grant me,
Deep vision to her very heart thou hast
Vouchsafed, as into the heart of a friend.
Thou dost conduct the ranks of living creatures
Before me and teachest me to know my brethren
In quiet bush, in air, and in the water.
And when the storm in forest roars and snarls,
And the giant fir comes crashing down, and, falling,
Crushes its neighbor boughs and neighbor stems,
And hills make hollow thunder of its fall,
Then dost thou guide me to safe caverns, showest
Me then unto myself, and my own bosom's
Profound and secret wonders are revealed,
And when before my sight the pure moon rises
And casts its mellow comfort, then from crags
And rain-sprent bushes there come drifting toward me
The silvery forms from ages now gone by,
Allaying meditation's austere pleasure.
That no perfection is to man allotted,
I now perceive. Along with this delight
That brings me near and nearer to the gods,
Thou gavest me this companion whom I can
No longer do without, however he
Degrades me to myself or insolently
Turns thy gifts by a breath to nothingness.
Officiously he fans a frantic fire
Within my bosom for that lovely girl.
Thus from desire I stagger to enjoyment
And in enjoyment languish for desire.
[*Enter* MEPHISTOPHELES.]
MEPHISTOPHELES. Won't you have had enough of this life presently?[93]
How can it in the long run do for you?
All well and good to try it out and see,
But then go on to something new!
FAUST. I do wish you had more to do
Than pester me on a good day.
MEPHISTOPHELES. All right, then, I won't bother you.
You dare not mean that anyway.
In you, friend, gruff, uncivil, and annoyed,
There's nothing much to lose, indeed.
The whole day long you keep my time employed!
But from my master's nose it's hard to read
What pleases him and what one should avoid.
FAUST. Now there is just the proper tone!
He wants my thanks for having been annoying.
MEPHISTOPHELES. What kind of life would you now be enjoying,
Poor son of earth, without the help I've shown?
But I have long since cured you anyhow
From gibberish your imagination talked,
And if it weren't for me you would have walked
Right off this earthly globe by now.
Why should you mope around and stare
Owl-like at cave and rock lair?
Why suck up food from soggy moss and trickling stone
Just like a toad all, all alone?

A fine sweet pastime! That stick-in-the-mud
Professor still is in your blood.
FAUST. Can you conceive the fresh vitality
This wilderness existence gives to me?
But if you could conceive it, yes,
You would be devil enough to block my happiness.
MEPHISTOPHELES. A superterrestrial delight!
To lie around on dewy hills at night,
Clasp earth and heaven to you in a rapture,
Inflate yourself to deity's great size,
Delve to earth's core by impulse of surmise,
All six days' creation in your own heart capture,
In pride of power enjoy I know not what,
In ecstasy blend with the All there on the spot,
The son of earth dissolved in vision,
And then the lofty intuition—[*With a gesture.*]
To end—just how, I must not mention.
FAUST. O vile!
MEPHISTOPHELES. That does not please you much; meanwhile
You have the right to speak your moral "Vile!"
Before chaste ears one must not talk about
What chaste hearts cannot do without.
All right: occasional pleasure of a lie
To yourself, is something I will not deny;
But you won't last long in that vein.
Soon you will be elsewhere attracted,
Or if it goes too long, distracted
To madness or to anguished pain.
Enough of this! Your sweetheart sits there in her room,
Around her everything is gloom.
You never leave her thoughts, and she
Loves you just overwhelmingly.
Passion came to flood first on your part,
As melting snow will send a brooklet running high;
You poured all that into her heart,
And now your brook is running dry.
It seems to me, instead of playing king
In woodland wilds, so great a lord
Might help the childish little thing
And give her loving some reward.
Time hangs upon her like a pall,
She stands by the window, watches the clouds along
And past the ancient city wall.
"If I were a little bird!" so goes her song
Half the night and all day long.
Sometimes cheerful, mostly sad and of
No further power of tears,
Then calm again, so it appears,
And always in love.
FAUST. Serpent! Serpent!
MEPHISTOPHELES. [*Aside.*] Admit I've got you there!
FAUST. Infamous being! Begone! And do not dare
So much as speak that lovely creature's name!
Do not arouse desire in me to where
Half-maddened senses burst in open flame!
MEPHISTOPHELES. What, then? She thinks you fled from her,
And more or less that's just what did occur.
FAUST. I am near her, and even if I were
Afar, I could not lose her or forget;
The very body of the Lord, when her
Lips touch it, rouses envy and regret.[94]
MEPHISTOPHELES. My friend, I've often envied you indeed
The twin roes that among the lilies feed.[95]
FAUST. Pander, begone!
MEPHISTOPHELES. Fine! I laugh while you rail.
The God that created girls and boys
Saw that the noblest power He enjoys
Was seeing that occasion should not fail.
Come on, then! What a shame this is!
You've going to your sweetheart's room
And not off to your doom.
FAUST. What if I do find heaven in her arms?
What if in her embrace my spirit warms?
Do I not still feel her distress?
Am I not still the fugitive, the homeless,
The monster without rest or purpose sweeping
Like a cataract from crag to crag and leaping

In frenzy of desire to the abyss?
While at one side, she, with her
    childlike mind,
Dwells in a cottage on the Alpine slope
With all her quiet life confined
Within her small world's narrow scope.
And I, the God-detested,
Had not enough, but wrested
The crag away and scattered
Its ruins as they shattered
To undermine her and her peace as
    well!
The victim you demanded, fiend of
    hell!
Help, Devil, make this time of anguish
    brief!
Let it be soon if it must be!
Let her fate crash in ruins over me,
Together let us come to grief.
MEPHISTOPHELES. Ah, now it seethes
    again and glows!
Go in and comfort her, you lout!
A head like yours beholds the close
Of doom as soon as he sees no way out.
Hurrah for men that bravely dare!
You're half bedeviled anyway;
There's nothing sillier in the world, I
    say,
Than being a devil in despair.

Gretchen's Room

GRETCHEN *at her spinning wheel, alone.*
GRETCHEN. My peace is gone,
My heart is sore,
I'll find it never
And nevermore.
    When he does not come
I live in a tomb,
The world is all
Bitter as gall.
    O, my poor head
Is quite distraught,
And my poor mind
Is overwrought.
    My peace is gone,
My heart is sore,
I'll find it never
And nevermore.
    I look from my window
Only to greet him,
I leave the house
Only to meet him.
    His noble gait
And form and guise,
The smile of his mouth,
The spell of his eyes,
    The magic in
Those eyes of his,
The clasp of his hand,
And oh!—his kiss.
    My peace is gone,
My heart is sore,
I'll find it never
And nevermore.
    My bosom aches
To feel him near,
Oh, could I clasp
And hold him here
    And kiss and kiss him
Whom I so cherish,
Beneath his kisses
I would perish!

Martha's Garden

{*Enter* MARGARET *and* FAUST.}
MARGARET. Promise me, Henry!
FAUST. If I can!
MARGARET. About religion, what do you
    feel now, say?
You are a good, warmhearted man,
And yet I fear you're not inclined that
    way.
FAUST. Leave that, my child! That I love
    you, you feel;
For those I love, my flesh and blood I'd
    give,
And no one's church or feelings would
    I steal.
MARGARET. But that is not enough! One
    must believe!
FAUST. Must one?
MARGARET. O, if I had some influence!
You do not even revere the sacraments.
FAUST. I do revere them.
MARGARET. But without desire.
It's long since you have gone to Mass or
    to confession.
Do you believe in God?

FAUST. My darling, who can say:
I believe in God?
Ask priest or sage you may,
And their replies seem odd
Mockings of the asker.
MARGARET. Then you do not believe?
FAUST. My answer, dear one, do not misconceive!
Who can name
Him, or proclaim:
I believe in Him?
Who is so cold
As to make bold
To say: I do not believe in Him?
The all-embracing,
The all-sustaining,
Does He not hold and sustain
You, me, Himself?
Does heaven not arch high above us?
Does earth not lie firm here below?
And do not everlasting stars
Rise with a kindly glance?
Do I not gaze into your eyes,
And do not all things crowd
Into your head and heart,
Working in eternal mystery
Invisibly visible at your side?
Let these things fill your heart, vast as they are,
And when you are entirely happy in that feeling,
Then call it what you will:
Heart, Fortune, Love, or God!
I have no name for it.
Feeling is everything,
Names are sound and smoke
Obscuring heaven's glow.
MARGARET. That is all very good and fair;
The priest says much the same, although
He used a different wording as he spoke.
FAUST. It is said everywhere
By all hearts underneath the sky of day,
Each heart in its own way;
So why not I in mine?
MARGARET. It sounds all right when you express it so;
There's something not quite right about it, though;
You have no Christianity.
FAUST. Dear child!
MARGARET. It has this long time troubled me
To find you keep the company you do.

FAUST. How so?
MARGARET. The person whom you have with you,
In my profoundest being I abhor,
And nothing in my life before
So cut me to the heart
As this man's face when he came near.
FAUST. My darling, have no fear.
MARGARET. His presence roils my blood, yet for my part,
People otherwise win my heart;
Much as I yearn to have you near,
This person inspires in me a secret fear,
And if I take him for a scoundrel too,
God forgive me for the wrong I do!
FAUST. Such queer fish also have to be.
MARGARET. To live with him would never do for me!
Let him but so much as appear.
He looks about with such a sneer
And half enraged;
Nothing can keep his sympathy engaged;
Upon his brow it's written clear
That he can hold no person dear.
In your embrace I feel so free,
So warm, so yielded utterly;
His presence chokes me, chills me through and through.
FAUST. O you intuitive angel, you!
MARGARET. This so overwhelms me, that when
He joins us, be it where it may,
It seems that I no longer love you then.
With him there, I could never pray.
This eats my very heart; and you,
Henry, must feel the same thing too.
FAUST. This is a matter of antipathy.
MARGARET. I must be going.
FAUST. O, when will it be
That I may for a little hour rest
In your embrace in quiet, breast to breast?
MARGARET. If I but slept alone, this very night
I'd leave the door unbolted, you realize,
But Mother's sleep is always light,
And if she took us by surprise,
I would die on the spot, I think.
FAUST. There is no need for that, my dear!
Here is a little phial. A mere
Three drops into her drink
Will shroud up Nature in deep sleep.
MARGARET. What will I not do for your

sake?
It will not harm her, though, to take?
FAUST. Would I propose it, Love, if that were so?
MARGARET. I look at you, dear man, and do not know
What so compels me to your will;
Already I have done so much for you
That there is little left for me to do.
[*Exit. Enter* MEPHISTOPHELES.]
MEPHISTOPHELES. The little monkey's gone?
FAUST. You spied again?
MEPHISTOPHELES. I could
Not help but hear it word for word:
Professor had his catechism heard;
I hope it does you lots of good.
Girls have a way of wanting to find out
Whether a man's conventionally devout.
They think: he gave in there, he'll truckle to us, no doubt.
FAUST. You, monster, do not realize
How this good loyal soul can be
So full of faith and trust—
Which things alone suffice
To make her bliss—and worry holily
For fear she must look on her best beloved as lost.
MEPHISTOPHELES. You supersensual sensual wooer,
A girl has got you on a puppet wire.
FAUST. You misbegotten thing of filth and fire!
MEPHISTOPHELES. She's mighty clever too at physiognomy:
When I am present, she feels—how, she's not just sure,
My mask bodes meaning at a hidden level;
She thinks beyond a doubt I'm a "Genie,"[96]
And possibly the very Devil.
Tonight, then—?
FAUST. What is that to you?
MEPHISTOPHELES. I have my pleasure in it too!

At the Well

GRETCHEN *and* LIESCHEN *with pitchers*.[97]
LIESCHEN. About Barbie, I suppose you've heard?
GRETCHEN. I get out very little. Not a word.
LIESCHEN. Why, Sibyl was telling me today.
She's finally gone down Fools' Way.
That's what grand airs will do!
GRETCHEN. How so?
LIESCHEN. It stinks!
She's feeding two now when she eats and drinks.
GRETCHEN. Ah!
LIESCHEN. Serves her right! And long enough
She hung around that fellow. All that stuff!
It was walk and jaunt
Out to the village and dancing haunt,
And everywhere she had to shine,
Always treating her to pastry and wine;
She got to think her good looks were so fine
She lost her self-respect and nothing would do
But she accepted presents from him too.
It was kiss and cuddle, and pretty soon
The flower that she had was gone.
GRETCHEN. O the poor thing!
LIESCHEN. Is it pity that you feel!
When our kind sat at the spinning wheel
And our mothers wouldn't let us out at night,
There she was with her lover at sweet delight
Down on the bench in the dark entryway
With never an hour too long for such play.
So let her go now with head bowed down
And do church penance in a sinner's gown![98]
GRETCHEN. But surely he'll take her as his wife!
LIESCHEN. He'd be a fool! A chipper lad
Finds fun is elsewhere to be had.
Besides, he's gone.
GRETCHEN. O, that's not fair!
LIESCHEN. If she gets him, she'll find it bad.
The boys will rip her wreath, and what's more,
They'll strew chopped straw around her door![99] [*Exit.*]
GRETCHEN. [*Walking home.*] How firmly I

could once inveigh
When any young girl went astray!
For others' sins I could not find
Words enough to speak my mind!
Black as it was, blacker it had to be,
And still it wasn't black enough for me.
I thanked my stars and was so game,
And now I stand exposed to shame!
Yet all that led me to this pass
Was so good, and so dear, alas!

Zwinger[100]

In a niche of the wall a statue of the Mater dolorosa *with jugs of flowers in front of it.*
GRETCHEN. [*Puts fresh flowers in the jugs.*]
O deign
Amid your pain
To look in mercy on my grief.
   With sword thrust through
The heart of you,
You gaze up to your Son in death.
   To Him on high
You breathe your sigh
For His and your distressful grief.
   Who knows
What throes
Wrack me, flesh and bone?
What makes my poor heart sick with fear
And what it is I plead for here,
Only you know, you alone!
   No matter where I go,
I know such woe, such woe
Here within my breast!
I am not quite alone,
Alas! I weep, I moan,
My heart is so distressed.
   The flowerpots at my window
Had only tears for dew
When early in the morning
I picked these flowers for you.
   When bright into my room
The early sun had come,
Upon my bed in gloom
I sat, with sorrow numb.
   Help! Rescue me from shame and death!
O deign
Amid your pain
To look in mercy on my grief!

Night

The street in front of GRETCHEN'*s door.*
VALENTINE, *a soldier,* GRETCHEN'*s brother.*
VALENTINE. When I used to be in a merry crowd
Where many a fellow liked to boast,
And lads in praise of girls grew loud
And to their fairest raised a toast
And drowned praise in glasses' overflow,
Then, braced on my elbows, I
Would sit with calm assurance by
And listen to their braggadocio;
Then I would stroke my beard and smile
And take my brimming glass in hand
And say: "To each his own! Meanwhile
Where is there one in all the land
To hold a candle or compare
With my sister Gretel anywhere?"
Clink! Clank! the round of glasses went;
"He's right!" some shouted in assent,
"The glory of her sex!" cried some,
And all the braggarts sat there dumb.
But now!—I could tear my hair and crawl
Right up the side of the smooth wall!—
Now every rascal that comes near
Can twit me with a jibe or sneer!
With every chance word dropped I sweat
Like one who had not paid a debt.
I'd knock the whole lot down if I
Could only tell them that they lie.
   What have we here? Who's sneaking along?
There are two of them, if I'm not wrong.
If he's the one, I'll grab his hide,
He won't get out of here alive! [*Enter* FAUST *and* MEPHISTOPHELES.]
FAUST. How from the window of that sacristy
The vigil lamp casts forth its flickering light
Sidewise faint and fainter down the night,
And darkness closes around totally.
So in my heart the darkness reigns.
MEPHISTOPHELES. And I feel like a cat with loving-pains
That sneaks up fire escapes and crawls
And slinks along the sides of walls;

I feel so cozy at it, and so right,
With a bit of thievery, a bit of rutting to
  it.
Through all my limbs I feel an ache for
The glorious Walpurgis Night.
Day after tomorrow brings us to it;
Then one knows what he stays awake
  for.
FAUST. Will it come to the top, that
  treasure
I see glimmering over there?[101]
MEPHISTOPHELES. You very soon will
  have the pleasure
Of lifting the pot to upper air.
Just recently I took a squint:
It's full of ducats shiny from the mint.
FAUST. Not a jewel, not a ring
To add to others of my girl's?
MEPHISTOPHELES. I do believe I saw a
  string
Of something that looked much like
  pearls.[102]
FAUST. That's good. I really hate to go
Without a gift to take with me.
MEPHISTOPHELES. You needn't fuss and
  trouble so
About enjoying something free.
But now that all the stars are in the sky,
You'll hear a real art work from me:
I'll sing her a moral lullaby
To befool her the more certainly. [*He
  sings to the zither.*]
What dost thou here[103]
With dawn so near,
O Katie dear,
Outside your sweetheart's door?
Maiden, beware
Of entering there
Lest forth you fare
A maiden nevermore.
    Maidens, take heed!
Once do the deed,
And all you need
Is: Good night, you poor things!
If you're in love,
To no thief give
The thing you have
Except with wedding rings.
VALENTINE. [*Steps forward.*]Who is it
  you're luring? By the Element!
You accursed rat-catcher, you!
To the Devil first with the instrument!
Then to the Devil with the singer too!
MEPHISTOPHELES. The zither's smashed,
  there's nothing left of it.
VALENTINE. And next there is a skull to
  split!
MEPHISTOPHELES. [*To* FAUST.] Don't
  flinch, Professor, and don't fluster!
Come close in by me, and don't tarry.
Quick! Whip out your feather duster!
Just thrust away and I will parry.
VALENTINE. Then parry this!
MEPHISTOPHELES. Why not?
VALENTINE. This too!
MEPHISTOPHELES. Of course!
VALENTINE. I think the Devil fights in
  you! What's this? My hand is going
  lame.
MEPHISTOPHELES. [*To* FAUST.] Thrust
  home!
VALENTINE. [*Falls.*] O!
MEPHISTOPHELES. There, the lummox is
  quite tame.
Come on! It's time for us to disappear.
Soon they will raise a murderous hue
  and cry.
With the police I always can get by,
But of the court of blood I stand in
  fear.[104]
MARTHA. [*At the window.*] Come out!
  Come out!
GRETCHEN. [*At the window.*] Bring out a
  light!
MARTHA. [*As before.*] They swear and
  scuffle, shout and fight.
PEOPLE. Here's one already dead!
MARTHA. [*Coming out.*] Where are the
  murderers? Have they fled?
GRETCHEN. [*Coming out.*] Who's lying
  here?
PEOPLE. Your mother's son.
GRETCHEN. Almighty God! I am
  undone!
VALENTINE. I'm dying! That's a tale
Soon told and sooner done.
Why do you women stand and wail?
Come close and hear me, everyone!
  [*They all gather around him.*]
My Gretchen, see! too young you are
And not yet wise enough by far,
You do not manage right.
In confidence I'll tell you more:
You have turned out to be a whore,
And being one, be one outright.
GRETCHEN. My brother! God! What do
  you mean?
VALENTINE. Leave our Lord God out of
  this farce. What's done
Is done, alas! and cannot be undone.
And what comes next will soon be seen.
You started secretly with one,

It won't be long till others come,
And when a dozen more have had you,
The whole town will have had you too.
    When shame is born, she first appears
Stealthily amid the world
And with the veil of darkness furled
About her head and ears.
First one would gladly slay her outright.
But as she grows and waxes bold,
She walks quite naked in the daylight,
But is no fairer to behold.
The uglier her visage grows,
The more by open day she goes.
    The time already I foresee
When all the decent citizenry
Will from you, harlot, turn away
As from a plague corpse in their way.
Your heart will sink within you when
They look you in the eye! No more
Golden chains will you wear then![105]
Or stand by the altar in church as before!
No more in collars of fine lace
Will you come proudly to the dancing place!
Off to a dismal corner you will slouch
Where the beggars and the cripples crouch.
And even though God may forgive,
Accursed here on earth you still will live.
MARTHA. Commend your soul to God! Will you
Take blasphemy upon you too?
VALENTINE. If I could reach your withered skin and bone,
You shameless, pandering, old crone,
I do believe that I could win
Full pardon for my every sin!
GRETCHEN. My brother! What pain of hell for me!
VALENTINE. I tell you, let your weeping be!
When you gave up your honor, you gave
The fiercest heart-stab I could know.
Now through the sleep of death I go
To God, a soldier true and brave. [*Dies.*]

Cathedral

Service, organ, and choir. GRETCHEN *among many people. An* EVIL SPIRIT *behind* GRETCHEN.
EVIL SPIRIT. How different, Gretchen, it was
When still full of innocence
You approached this altar,
From your little dog-eared prayer book
Murmuring prayers,
Half childish play,
Half God in heart!
Gretchen!
Where are your thoughts?
Within your heart
What deed of crime?
Do you pray for your mother's soul that slept
Away unto the long, long pain because of you?
Whose blood is on your doorstep?
—And underneath your heart
Does not a new life quicken,
Tormenting itself and you
With its premonitory presence?
GRETCHEN. Alas! Alas!
If I could be rid of the thoughts
That rush this way and that way
Despite my will!
CHOIR. *Dies irae, dies illa*
solvet saeclum in favilla.[106] [*The organ sounds.*]
EVIL SPIRIT. Wrath seizes you!
The trumpet sounds!
The graves shudder!
And your heart
From ashen rest,
For flames of torment
Once more reconstituted,
Quakes forth.[107]
GRETCHEN. If I were out of here!
I feel as if the organ were
Stifling my breath,
As if the choir dissolved
My inmost heart.
CHOIR. *Judex ergo cum sedebit,*
quidquid latet adparebit,
nil inultum remanebit.[108]

GRETCHEN. I cannot breathe!
The pillars of the wall
Imprison me!
The vaulted roof
Crushes me!—Air!
EVIL SPIRIT. Concealment! Sin and shame
Are not concealed.
Air? Light?
Woe to you!
CHOIR. *Quid sum miser tunc dicturus?*
Quem patronum rogaturus?
Cum vix justus sit securus.[109]
EVIL SPIRIT. The clarified avert
Their countenances from you.
The pure shudder to reach
Out hands to you.
Woe!
CHOIR. *Quid sum miser tunc dicturus?*
GRETCHEN. Neighbor! Your smelling-bottle! [*She falls in a faint.*]

Walpurgis Night

The Harz Mountains. Vicinity of Schierke and Elend.[110] {*Enter* FAUST *and* MEPHISTOPHELES.}
MEPHISTOPHELES. Now don't you long for broomstick-transportation?
I'd like the toughest he-goat there can be.
We're far yet, by this route, from destination.
FAUST. Since my legs still are holding out so sturdily,
This knotty stick will do for me.
Why take a short cut anyway?
Slinking through this labyrinth of alleys,
Then climbing cliffs above these valleys
Where streams plunge down in everlasting spray,
Such is the spice of pleasure on this way!
Springtime over birches weaves its spell,
It's sensed already by the very pine;
Why should it not affect our limbs as well?
MEPHISTOPHELES. There's no such feeling in these limbs of mine!
Within me all is winter's chill;
On my path I'd prefer the frost and snow.
How drearily the reddish moon's disc, still
Not full, is rising with belated glow
And giving such bad light that any step now
Will have us bumping into rock or tree!
I'll call a will-o'-the-wisp, if you'll allow.[111]
I see one burning merrily.
Hey, there my friend! May I request your flare?
Why flash for nothing over there?
Just be so good and light our way up here.
WILL-O'-THE-WISP. I hope sheer awe will give me mastery
Over my natural instability;
Most commonly we go a zigzag career.
MEPHISTOPHELES. Ho, ho! It's a man you want to imitate!
Now in the Devil's name, go straight!
Or else I'll blow your flicker-life right out.
WILL-O'-THE-WISP. You are the master here beyond a doubt,
And so I'll do my best to serve you nicely.
Remember, though! The mountain is magic-mad tonight,
And if you want a will-o'-the-wisp to lend you light
You mustn't take these matters too precisely.
FAUST, MEPHISTOPHELES, WILL-O'-THE-WISP. [*In alternating song.*]
Having entered, as it seems,
Realms of magic and of dreams,
Guide us well so that we may
Get along our upward way
Through the vast and empty waste.
  Tree after tree, with what mad haste
They rush past us as we go,
See the boulders bending low,
And the rocks of long-nosed sort,
How they snore and how they snort.[112]
  Athwart the turf, the stones athwart,
Brook and brooket speeds along.
Is it rustling? Is it song?
Do I hear love's sweet lament
Singing of days from heaven sent?
What we hope and what we love!
And the echo is retold
Like a tale from times of old.

To-whit! To-whoo! it sounds away,
Screech owl, plover, and the jay;
Have all these stayed wide awake?
Are those efts amid the brake?
Long of haunch and thick of paunch!
And the roots that wind and coil
Snakelike out of stone and soil
Knot the bonds of wondrous snares,
Scare us, take us unawares;
Out of tough and living gnarls
Polyp arms reach out in snarls
For the traveler's foot. Mice scurry
Thousand-colored by drove and flurry
Through the moss and through the heather!
And the fireflies in ascent
Densely swarm and swirl together,
Escort to bewilderment.
 Have we stopped or are we trying
To continue onward flying?
Everything is whirling by,
Rocks and trees are making faces,
Wandering lights in many places
Bloat and bulge and multiply.
MEPHISTOPHELES. Grab my cloak-end and hold tight.
Here's a sort of medium height
Which for our amazement shows
How Mammon in the mountain glows.[113]
FAUST. How oddly in the valley bottoms gleams
A dull glow like the break of day,
And even in the chasm's deepest seams
It probes and gropes its searching way.
There steam puffs forth, there vapor twines,
Here through the mist the splendor shines,
Now dwindling to a slender thread,
Now gushing like a fountainhead.
It fans out in a hundred veins
A long stretch of the valley run,
Then where the narrow pass constrains
Its course, it merges into one.
There sparks are gusting high and higher
Like golden sand strewn on the night.
Look! There along its entire height
The cliff-face kindles into fire.
MEPHISTOPHELES. Has not Sir Mammon done some fine contriving
To illuminate his palace hall?
You're lucky to have seen it all.
But now I scent the boisterous guests arriving.

FAUST. How the wind's bride rides the air!
How she beats my back with cuff and blow!
MEPHISTOPHELES. Grab on to this cliff's ancient ribs with care
Or she will hurl you to the chasm far below.
A mist has thickened the night.
Hark! Through the forests, what a crashing!
The startled owls fly up in fright.
Hark! The splitting and the smashing
Of pillars in the greenwood hall!
Boughs strain and snap and fall.
The tree trunks' mighty moaning!
The tree roots' creaking and groaning!
In fearful entanglement they all
Go tumbling to their crushing fall,
And through the wreckage-littered hollows
The hissing wind howls and wallows.
Do you hear voices there on high?
In the distance, or nearby?
Yes, the mountain all along
Is bathed in frenzied magic song.
WITCHES. [*In chorus.*] The witches to the Brocken ride,
The stubble is yellow, the corn is green.
There with great crowds up every side.
Seated on high, Lord Urian is seen.[114]
And on they go over stock and stone,
The he-goat stinks from the farts of the crone.
A VOICE. Old Baubo by herself comes now,[115]
Riding on a farrow sow.
CHORUS. Pay honor where honor is due!
Dame Baubo, up and on with you!
A mother astride a husky sow,
The whole witch crew can follow now.
A VOICE. Which way did *you* come?
A VOICE. By Ilsenstein crest.[116]
And I took a peep in an owlet's nest:
What eyes she made at me!
A VOICE. O go to hell!
Why must you drive so hard!
A VOICE. She skinned me alive,
I'll never survive!
WITCHES. [*Chorus.*] The way is broad, the way is long,
O what a mad and crazy throng!
The broomstick scratches, the pitchfork pokes,
The mother bursts open, the infant

chokes.
WITCHMASTERS. [*Semi-chorus.*] We creep along like a snail in his house,
The women are always up ahead.
For traveling to the Devil's house,
Women are a thousand steps ahead.
THE OTHER HALF. Why, that's no cause for sorry faces!
Women need the thousand paces;
But let them hurry all they can,
One jump is all it takes a man.
A VOICE. [*Above.*] Come on along from Felsensee there, you!
VOICES. [*From below.*] We'd like to make the top there too.
We wash and are as clean as clean can be,
And still the same sterility.
BOTH CHORUSES. The wind has died, the star has fled,
The dull moon hides, and in its stead
The whizzings of our magic choir
Strike forth a thousand sparks of fire.
A VOICE. [*From below.*] Wait! Wait! Or I'll get left!
A VOICE. [*From above.*] Who's calling from that rocky cleft?
A VOICE. [*From below.*] Take me with you! Take me with you!
Three hundred years I have been climbing
And still can't make the top, I find.
I'd like to be with my own kind.
BOTH CHORUSES. A broom or stick will carry you,
A pitchfork or a he-goat too;
Whoever cannot fly today
Is lost forever, you might say.
HALF-WITCH. [*Below.*] Here all these years I've minced along;
How did the others get so far ahead?
I have no peace at home, and yet
Can't get in here where I belong.
CHORUS OF WITCHES. The salve puts courage in a hag,[117]
A sail is made from any rag,
For a ship any trough will do;
None flies unless today he flew.
BOTH CHORUSES. And when the topmost peak we round
Just coast along and graze the ground,
So far and wide the heath will be
Hid by your swarm of witchery. [*They alight.*]
MEPHISTOPHELES. They push and shove, they bustle and gab,
They hiss and swirl, they hustle and blab!
They glow, shed sparks, and stink and burn!
The very witches' element!
Hold tight to me, or we'll be swept apart in turn.
Where are you?
FAUST. Here!
MEPHISTOPHELES. What? Swept so far so soon?
I must invoke my house-right and call the tune.
Squire Voland comes! Give ground, sweet rabble, ground![118]
Grab on to me, Professor! In one bound
We'll give this mob the slip quite easily;
It's too mad even for the likes of me.
There's something shining with a very special flare
Down in those bushes. Curiosity
Impels me. Come! We'll drop in there.
FAUST. You Spirit of Contradiction! Be my guiding light!
I think it was a move that made good sense:
We travel to the Brocken on Walpurgis Night
To isolate ourselves up here by preference.
MEPHISTOPHELES. Just see the jolly fires! Why here
A club has gathered for good cheer.
In little circles one is not alone.
FAUST. I'd rather be up there, I own.
I see the glow and twisting smoke.
The crowd streams toward the Evil One;
There many a riddle must be undone.
MEPHISTOPHELES. And many a riddle also spun.
But let the great world revel away,
Here where it's quiet we shall stay.
It is a usage long since instituted
That in the great world little worlds are constituted.
I see young witches naked and bare,
And old ones clothed more prudently;
For my sake, show them courtesy,
The effort is small, the jest is rare.
I hear some tuning up of instruments.
Damned whine and drone! One must get used to it.
Come on! Come on! Now there's no help for it,

I'll go in first and prepare your entrance,
And you will owe me for another work of mine.
This is no little space, you must admit, my friend.
Look, and your eye can hardly see the end.
A hundred bonfires burn there in a line;
There's dancing, chatting, cooking, drinking, making love;
What better things than these can you think of?

FAUST. In which of your roles will you now appear,
Magician or Devil, to introduce me here?

MEPHISTOPHELES. Most commonly I go incognito,
But on such gala days one lets one's Orders show.
I have no Garter to distinguish me,
But here the cloven hoof is held in dignity.
You see that snail that's creeping toward us there
Its feelers have already spied
My presence somehow in the air;
I couldn't hide here even if I tried.
Come on! We'll stroll along from fire to fire,
I'll be the wooer and you can be the squire. [*To some people who are sitting around some dying embers.*]
Old gentlemen, what are you doing here?
I'd praise you if I found you in the midst of cheer
Surrounded by the noise and youthful riot;
Alone at home we get our fill of quiet.

GENERAL. Who can put any faith in nations,
Do for them all you may have done?
With women and with populations
Youth is always number one.

PRIME MINISTER. They're too far off the right course now today,
I still stick with the men of old;
For frankly, when we had our way,
That was the actual Age of Gold.

PARVENU. We weren't so stupid either, you'll allow,
And often did what we should not;
But everything is topsy-turvy now
Just when we'd like to keep the things we've got.

AUTHOR. Where can you read a publication
With even a modicum of sense?
As for the younger generation,
They are the height of impudence.

MEPHISTOPHELES. [*Who suddenly looks very old.*] I feel men ripe for doomsday, now my legs
Are climbing Witches' Hill in their last climb;
And since my cask is running dregs,
The world is also running out of time.

HUCKSTER WITCH. O Sirs, don't pass me by this way!
Don't miss this opportunity!
Just give my wares some scrutiny,
All sorts of things are on display.
Across the earth you will not find
A booth like this; no item here, not one
But what has good sound mischief done
At some time to the world and human kind.
No dagger here but what has dripped with gore,
No cup but what has served to pour
Consuming poison in some healthy frame,
No jewel but what has misled to her shame
Some lovely girl, no sword but of the kind
That stabbed an adversary from behind.

MEPHISTOPHELES. Cousin, you're out of date in times like these.
What's done is past, what's past is done.
Get in a stock of novelties!
With us it's novelties or none.

FAUST. If I don't lose my mind! But I declare
This really is what I would call a fair!

MEPHISTOPHELES. The whole mad rout is pushing on above;
You're being shoved, though you may think you shove.

FAUST. Now who is that?

MEPHISTOPHELES. Observe her with some care,
For that is Lilith.

FAUST. Who?

MEPHISTOPHELES. Adam's first wife.[119]
Beware of her resplendent hair,
The one adornment that she glories in,

Once she entraps a young man in that snare,
She won't so quickly let him out again.
FAUST. That old witch with the young one sitting there,
They've kicked their heels around, that pair!
MEPHISTOPHELES. No rest for them today. Ah! They're beginning
Another dance. Come on! Let's get into the swing.
FAUST. [*Dancing with the* YOUNG WITCH.]
A lovely dream once came to me;
In it I saw an apple tree,
Two lovely apples shone upon it,
They charmed me so, I climbed up on it.
THE BEAUTY. Apples always were your craze
From Paradise to present days.
I feel joy fill me through and through
To think my garden bears them too.
MEPHISTOPHELES. [*With the* OLD WITCH.]
A dismal dream once came to me;
In it I saw a cloven tree,
It had a most enormous hole;
Yet big as it was, it charmed my soul.
THE OLD WITCH. I proffer now my best salute
To the Knight with the Horse's Hoof!
So if your rod is right, go to it,
Unless the size won't let you do it.
PROKTOPHANTASMIST.[120] Accursed mob! This is presumptuous!
Was it not long since proved to you
Ghosts do not have the same feet humans do?
And here you dance just like the rest of us!
THE BEAUTY. [*Dancing.*] And what does *he* want at our ball?
FAUST. [*Dancing.*] Oh, he turns up just anywhere at all.
What others dance, he must evaluate.
If there's a step about which he can't prate,
It's just as if the step had not occurred.
It bothers him the most when we go forward.
If you would run in circles round about
The way he does in his old mill,
He'd call it good and sing its praises still,
Especially if his opinion were sought out.
PROKTOPHANTASMIST. But you're still here! Oh! This is insolent!
Begone! Why, we brought in Enlightenment!
This Devil's pack, with them all rules are flouted.
We are so clever, yet there is no doubt about it:
There's still a ghost at Tegel. How long have I swept
Illusions out, and still I find they're kept.
THE BEAUTY. Then go away and let us have the field.
PROKTOPHANTASMIST. I tell you spirits to your faces
I will not stand for any traces
Of spirit despotism I can't wield. [*The dancing goes on.*]
I just can't win today, no matter what I do.
But I can always take a trip,[121]
And I still hope, before I'm done, to slip
One over on the devils and the writers too.
MEPHISTOPHELES. Down in the nearest puddle he will plump,
That is the best assuagement he can find;
If leeches feast upon his rump,
He will be cured of ghosts and his own mind.[122] [*To* FAUST, *who has left the dance.*]
Why do you leave that pretty girl
Who in the dance so sweetly sang?
FAUST. Because a little red mouse sprang
Out of her mouth while she was singing.
MEPHISTOPHELES. What's wrong with that? The mouse was still not grey.
Why raise such questions and be bringing
Them to a trysting hour anyway?
FAUST. Then I saw—
MEPHISTOPHELES. What?
FAUST. Mephisto, do you see
A pale girl standing over there alone?
She drags herself but slowly from the place
And seems to move with shackled feet.
I must confess she has the sweet
Look of my kindly Gretchen's face.
MEPHISTOPHELES. Let that be! That bodes well for no one.
It is a magic image, lifeless, an eidolon.
Encounters with such are not good;
The fixed stare freezes human blood

And one is turned almost to stone—
You've heard of the Medusa, I suppose.
FAUST. Indeed, a corpse's eyes are those,
Unshut by loving hand. That is the breast
That Gretchen offered for my rest,
That is the dear, sweet body I have known.
MEPHISTOPHELES. You easily misguided fool, that's magic art.
She looks to every man like his own sweetheart.
FAUST. What suffering! And what delight!
My eyes can not shift from that sight.
How oddly round that lovely throat there lies
A single band of scarlet thread
No broader than a knife has bled.
MEPHISTOPHELES. Quite right! And I can see it likewise.
Beneath her arm she also carries that same head
Since Perseus cut it off for her.
And you crave for illusion still!
Come, let us climb that little hill,
The Prater is no merrier,[123]
And if I haven't been misled,
I actually see a theater.
What's being given?
SERVIBILIS.[124] A minute yet before it starts.
A new play, last of seven in a row;
That is the number given in these parts.
A dilettant made up the show,
And dilettanti take the parts.
Forgive me, Sirs, if I now disappear;
I just delight in running up the curtain.
MEPHISTOPHELES. I'm glad to find you on the Blocksberg here,[125]
It's just where you belong, that's certain.

Walpurgis Night's Dream

Or Oberon's and Titania's Golden Wedding Intermezzo[126]

THEATER MANAGER. Loyal sons of Mieding,[127] we
Shall repose today.
Ancient hills and valleys may
Provide the scenery.
HERALD. For a marriage to be golden,
Must fifty years be ended;
I would far prefer that "golden"
Where quarrels were suspended.
OBERON. If you are a spirit crew,
Let such now appear;
King and Queen have pledged anew
Troth and marriage here.
PUCK. Puck comes leaping left and right
Tripping it and dancing;
Come to share in his delight,
Hundreds are advancing.
ARIEL. Ariel uplifts his song
In tones celestial ringing,
Luring ugly forms along
With fair ones he is bringing.
OBERON. Spouses, if you would agree,
Choose us for imitation;
Two who would forever be
In love, need separation.
TITANIA. Brooding husband, pouting wife,
Apart from them henceforth,
Off with her to southland life,
With him to furthest north.
ORCHESTRA TUTTI. [*Fortissimo.*][128] Nose of gnat and snout of fly
With all their family,
Tree toad and the cricket's cry
Make up our symphony.
SOLO. Yonder see: the bagpipe comes,
A soap bubble he blows.
Schnecke-schnicke-schnack he hums
Through his turned-up nose.
MIND IN EMBRYO. Spider-foot and hoptoad's belly
And winglets on the mite
Add up to no wee animal
But *do* to a poem-ette.
A LITTLE COUPLE. [a] Little steps and lofty leaps
Through honey-dew and light.
[b] True, you mince and mince along
But never rise in flight.
INQUISITIVE TRAVELER. Is this a masquerade? How odd!
Can I believe my eyes?
Oberon the handsome god
Here *too* beneath these skies?
ORTHODOX. Lacking claws and tail maybe,
And yet no doubt it's true:
Like the gods of Greece, so he,
He is a devil too.

NORTHERN ARTIST. What I have achieved already
Is sketchy, that is sure;
But I'm starting to get ready
For my Italian tour.
PURIST. Ah! What bad luck brings me to!
They're lewd jades here, I swear!
Of all these witches only two
Are wearing powdered hair.
YOUNG WITCH. Powder, like the petticoat,
Suits grannies old and grey,
So I sit naked on my goat
With my charms on display.
MATRON. We are too well-bred by far
To haggle with you here;
Young and tender as you are,
I hope you rot, my dear.
ORCHESTRA CONDUCTOR.[129] Nose of gnat and snout of fly,
Don't crowd the naked lady!
Tree toad and the cricket's cry,
Beat time and keep it steady!
WEATHER VANE. [*In one direction.*] Company of first-rate sort.
And nothing but sheer brides!
Bachelors to a man, besides,
To lend them proper escort.
WEATHER VANE. [*In the other direction.*]
Unless a yawning of the ground
Opens to receive them,
I will with a sudden bound
Jump into hell to leave them.
"XENIEN." As small insects we appear
With sharpened scissors here,
Showing how much we revere
Satan, our papa dear.
HENNINGS. Just see them smiling there and jesting,
So innocently too!
They will wind up yet protesting
Their hearts are tried and true.
"MUSAGET." How I'd like to be absorbed
Into these witches' crews;
I could lead them on much sooner
Than I could the Muse.
CI-DEVANT "GENIUS OF THE AGE." With proper people, one arrives,
Come, grab my coattails now!
The Blocksberg like the German Parnassus
Has a broad, lofty brow.
INQUISITIVE TRAVELER. Tell me, who's that stodgy man?
He struts about and fidgets.
He snoops as much as snoop he can.
—"He's after Jesuits."
CRANE. I like to fish in waters clear,
In troubled ones as well;
That's why you see the pious man
Mix with devils from hell.
CHILD OF THE WORLD. Yes, for pious men, believe me,
All things are vehicles;
On the Blocksberg here they hold
Their own conventicles.
DANCER.[130] What! Another chorus coming?
I hear a distant drumming—
"Have no fear! It's bitterns booming
And withered sedge grass humming."
BALLET MASTER. How each one hists his legs and jounces
And as he can, gains clearance!
The crooked jumps, the clumsy bounces.
Not caring for appearance.
FIDDLER. This rabble hate and most would like
To see each other expire;
They are united by the bagpipe
Like beasts by Orphesus' lyre.
DOGMATIST. Doubts and critics will not shout
Me out of certainty.
The Devil's real beyond a doubt,
Else how could devils be?
IDEALIST. The fantasy of my mind is
My master, willy-nilly.
Indeed, if I am all of this,
I must be pretty silly.
REALIST. Existence is a torment and
There's worse yet I must meet;
This is the first time that I stand
Unsteady on my feet.
SUPERNATURALIST. It's a pleasure to be here
Among this motley crew,
For from the devils I infer
That there are angels too.
SKEPTIC. They chase their will-o'-wisps and fancy
That buried treasure's near.
"Doubt" and "devil" start with *d*.
So I'm in my true sphere.
ORCHESTRA CONDUCTOR.[131] Tree toad and the cricket's cry,
O dilettants accursed!
Nose of gnat and snout of fly,
In music you're well versed!

THE CLEVER ONES. *Sans souci* this host is called
That merrily here treads;
Walking's no more done on feet,
So we walk on our heads.
THE AWKWARD ONES. We sponged a lot in our time, true,
Goodbye to all that, though;
Our shoes have all been danced right through,
And barefoot now we go.
WILL-O'-THE-WISPS. We come out of marshes dank
From which we first arose,
Here we are, rank after rank,
The most resplendent beaux.
SHOOTING STAR. I came shooting from on high
In starry flame and heat;
Sprawled now on the grass I lie—
Who'll help me to my feet?
BRUISERS. Gangway there! We're coming through!
The grass is bending low;
Spirits come, and spirits too
Have brawny limbs, you know.
PUCK. Don't go plowing through that way
With elephantine tramp!
Let the clumsiest one today
Be Puck himself, the scamp.
ARIEL. If mind or Nature gave you wings
And any wing discloses,
Follow where my leading brings
You to the Hill of Roses.
ORCHESTRA. [*Pianissimo.*] Gauze of mist and cloud-bank's edge
Are touched with streaks of dawn.
Breeze in branch and wind in sedge,
And everything is gone.

Gloomy Day

A field. {*Enter* FAUST *and* MEPHISTOPHELES.}
FAUST. In misery! Desperate! Long wandering pitifully upon the earth and now in prison! Locked up as a wrongdoer for ghastly torments in a jail, that lovely, unfortunate creature! To come to this! To this!—Perfidious, worthless Spirit, and this you kept from me!—Stand there, yes, stand there! Roll those devilish eyes furiously in your head! Stand and defy me with your unbearable presence! In prison! In irrevocable misery! Delivered over to evil spirits and to judging, heartless humanity! And meanwhile you lull me with insipid dissipations, conceal her increasing misery from me, and let her go helpless to destruction!
MEPHISTOPHELES. She is not the first.
FAUST. Cur! Monster of abomination!—Turn him, Infinite Spirit, turn the worm back into his canine form, the way he used to like to trot along in front of me often in time of night, and roll at the feet of the harmless traveler, and cling to the shoulders of one who fell. Turn him back into his favorite shape, so he can crawl on his belly in the sand up to me and I can kick him, the reprobate!—Not the first!—Grief! Grief beyond the grasp of any human soul, that more than one creature has sunk to the depths of such misery, that the first did not atone for the guilt of all the others in her writhing and earthly agony before the eyes of Eternal Forgiveness! It grinds through my marrow and my life, the misery of this one alone; you grin complacently over the fate of thousands!
MEPHISTOPHELES. Now we are once again at the limit of our wits, where the minds of you mortals go overboard. Why do you make common cause with us if you can't go through with it? You want to fly and are not proof to dizziness? Did we force ourselves on you, or you on us?
FAUST. Do not bare your ravening fangs at me that way! I loathe it!—Great and glorious Spirit who didst deign to appear to me, who knowest my heart and my soul, why dost thou forge me together with this infamous associate who gloats on harm and revels in destruction?
MEPHISTOPHELES. Are you through?
FAUST. Save her! Or woe to you! The ghastliest of curses upon you unto millennia!

MEPHISTOPHELES. I cannot loose the avenger's bonds, nor open his locks.—Save her!—Who was it plunged her into ruin? I or you? [FAUST *gazes wildly about.*] So you reach for thunderbolts? Lucky they were not given to you miserable mortals! To pulverize an innocent person in his path is the way of the tyrant, in order to relieve his feelings.

FAUST. Take me there! She shall be free!

MEPHISTOPHELES. And the risk you run? Remember: blood-guilt from your hand still lies upon the city. Over the place where the slain man fell hover avenging spirits in wait for the returning murderer.

FAUST. This yet from you? A world of murder and death upon you, monster! Take me there, I say, and set her free!

MEPHISTOPHELES. I will take you, and what I *can* do: hear! Do I have all power in heaven and on earth? The jailer's senses I will becloud, *you* get possession of his keys and lead her out yourself with your human hand. I will stand watch! The magic horses are ready, I will carry you away. This much I can do.

FAUST. Up and away!

Night, Open Country

FAUST, MEPHISTOPHELES, *rushing on black horses.*

FAUST. What are they doing yonder on Gallows Rock?

MEPHISTOPHELES. I don't know what they're brewing or doing.

FAUST. They soar and swoop, bending and stooping.

MEPHISTOPHELES. A crew of witches.

FAUST. They strew and bless.

MEPHISTOPHELES. On past! On past!

Dungeon

FAUST *in front of a little iron door, with a bunch of keys and a lamp.*

FAUST. A horror long unfamiliar over me crawls,
Grief seizes me, grief common to human kind.
She is imprisoned in these clammy walls,
Her crime a fond illusion of the mind.
You shrink back from her door
Afraid to see her once more!
On! Delay brings Death up from behind. [*He seizes the lock. Singing is heard from inside.*][132]
My mother, the whore,
She murdered me!
My father, the rogue,
He has eaten me!
Little sister has laid
My bones away
In a place of cool, cool shade.
And I am turned into a woodland bird;
Fly away! Fly away!

FAUST. [*Unlocking the door.*] She does not dream her lover can thus hear
Her clanking chains, her rustling straw so near. [*He enters.*]

MARGARET. [*Cowering on her pallet.*] They're coming. O how bitter it is to die!

MARGARET. [*Throwing herself at his feet.*] If you are human, feel my misery.

FAUST. You'll wake the jailer with your cry [*He takes hold of the chains to unlock them.*]

MARGARET. [*On her knees.*] Who was it, headsman, who could give
You so much power!
You take me at the midnight hour.
Have pity on me, let me live!
Is tomorrow morning not time enough? [*She stands up.*]
Am I not still so young, so young!
To die so soon!
And I was beautiful, and that was my undoing.
My friend was near, now he is near no more.

My wreath lies torn, the flowers scattered that I wore.
O do not seize me so violently!
What have I done to you? O pity me!
Let me not in vain implore,
I never saw you in my life before!
FAUST. Will I survive such misery!
MARGARET. I am now wholly in your might.
First let me nurse my child again.
I fondled it all through the night;
They took it from me just to cause me pain,
And now they saw that I have slain
My child. Now I shall never more be glad.
And they sing songs about me! How can they be
So wicked! So runs an ancient story, but who bade
Them make that tale fit me!
FAUST. [*Falling on his knees.*] A lover at your feet implores
You to come forth out of these woeful doors.
MARGARET. [*Kneels with him.*] O let us kneel and call upon the saints in prayer!
Look! Underneath that stair.
Beneath that threshold there,
Hell seethes! Beneath the floor
The Evil One
Makes ghastly noise
Of tumult and uproar!
FAUST. [*Loudly.*] Gretchen! Gretchen!
MARGARET. [*Attentively.*] That was my beloved's voice! [*She jumps up. Her chains fall off.*]
Where is he? I heard him calling me.
No one can stop me. I am free!
To his arms I will fly,
And at his heart I'll lie!
Gretchen, he called! He stood there at that door.
And through the howling din of hell's uproar,
Through the wrath of devils' mocking noise
I recognized that sweet, that loving voice.
FAUST. I *am* here!
MARGARET. You! O say that once again! [*Embracing him.*]
It *is* he! Where is anguish now, or pain?
Where is my prison's agony?
You come to set me free!

And I am saved!—
There is the street once more where I
That first time saw you passing by.
There is the cheerful garden too
With Martha and me waiting for you.
FAUST. [*Trying to lead her away.*] Come with me! Come with me!
MARGARET. O tarry!
I gladly tarry where you tarry. [*Caressing him.*]
FAUST. Hurry!
Unless you hurry,
It will cost us a bitter price.
MARGARET. What! Can you no longer kiss?
So briefly gone, so soon returned,
My friend, and kissing all unlearned?
Why am I frightened with such strange alarms,
When from your words, your glances, overwhelmingly
I once felt all of heaven in your arms,
When you would kiss as though to stifle me?
Kiss me now, or
I will kiss you! [*She embraces him.*]
Alas! your lips are cold,
And dumb.
What has become
Of your loving?
Who has robbed me of it? [*She turned away from him.*]
FAUST. Come! Follow me! My darling, be bold!
I'll love you with a passion thousandfold,
Only come with me! That's all I'd have you do!
MARGARET. [*Turning toward him.*]
But is it you? But is it really you?
FAUST. It is! But come with me!
MARGARET. You loose my chain,
And take me back into your arms again.
How is it that you do not shrink from me?—
Do you know who it is, my friend, you're setting free?
FAUST. Come! Come! Deep night will soon be done.
MARGARET. I sent my mother to her death,
I drowned my child—the one
Born to both you and me—yes, to you too.
It *is* you! I can not believe it yet.

Give me your hand! It is no dream!
Your dear hand!—O! But it is wet!
Wipe it off. But still I seem
To see blood on it.
My God! What have you done!
Put up your sword,
That much I ask!
FAUST. O let the past be past and done
Or you will be my death.
MARGARET. No, you must stay alive!
The graves I will describe for you,
And you must see to them
This coming morning;
The best spot give to my mother,
And next to her my brother;
Bury me off a little way,
But not too far away;
and the babe at my right breast.
No one else will lie by me!—
To nestle at your side so lovingly,
That was a rapture sweet and blest!
But for me that will never come again.
It seems as if I had to force my way to you;
As if you spurned me away from you;
Yet it is you, and your look is so winsome.
FAUST. If you feel it is I, then come!
MARGARET. Out there?
FAUST. To freedom.
MARGARET. If the grave is there,
If Death is waiting, come!
From there to my eternal bed
But not one step beyond—
You go? O Henry, if I could go too!
FAUST. You can! If you but will! There is the door.
MARGARET. I cannot go! For me hope is no more.
What good is flight? They only hunt me down.
It is so wretched to have to beg,
And with an evil conscience too!
It is so wretched to wander far from home.
And they would catch me anyway!
FAUST. I will stay with you.
MARGARET. O quick! O quick!
Save your poor child.
Go up the path
That skirts the brook
And across the bridge
To the woods beyond,
Left, where the plank is
In the pond.
Catch it quick!
It tries to rise,
It struggles still!
Save it! Save it!
FAUST. Control yourself!
One step, and you are free!
MARGARET. If only we were past the hill!
There sits my mother on a stone,
And I am cold with dread!
There sits my mother on a stone
And shakes her head.
She does not beckon, does not nod, her head sinks lower,
She slept so long, she wakes no more.
She slept so we might love.
O those were happy times!
FAUST. If all things fail that I can say,
Then I must carry you away.
MARGARET. No, let me go! I will not suffer violence!
Let go the hand that murderously holds me so fast!
I did all things to please you in the past.
FAUST. The day shows grey. My love! My love!
MARGARET. Yes, daylight penetrates. The final day.
It was to be my wedding day.
Tell no one you have been with Gretchen.
Alas! rough hands
Have ripped the wreath I wore.
And we shall meet once more,
But not at the dance.
The crowd wells forth, it swells and grows
And overflows
The streets, the square;
The staff is broken, the death knell fills the air.[133]
How I am seized and bound!
I am already at the block.
The neck of every living soul around
Foresenses the ax blade and its shock.
The crowd is silent as a tomb.
FAUST. Would I were never born!
[MEPHISTOPHELES *appears outside.*]
MEPHISTOPHELES. Up! Or it is your doom.
Useless dallying! Shilly-shallying!
My horses shudder outside the door,[134]
It is the break of day.
MARGARET. What rises out of the floor?
He! He! Send him away!

What does he want in this sacred place?[135]
He comes for me!
FAUST. You shall live!
MARGARET. Judgment of God! Myself to Thee I give!
MEPHISTOPHELES. [*To* FAUST.] Come on! Come on! Or I'll leave you here with her.
MARGARET. Father, I am Thine! Deliver me!
You angels! Sacred hosts, descend!
Guard me about, protect me and defend!
Henry! I shudder to behold you.
MEPHISTOPHELES. She is condemned!
A VOICE. [*From above.*] Is saved!
MEPHISTOPHELES. [*To* FAUST.] Hither to me! [*Disappears with* FAUST.]
A VOICE. [*From within, dying away.*]
Henry! Henry!

1. Written 1802 in imitation of the prologue to Kālidāsa's *Sakuntalā* (written ca. A.D. 375), most famous of Sanskrit dramas, which Goethe read in translation.
2. In the late eighteenth century, acting companies run by a manager *(Theaterdirektor)* who was both producer and director still traveled about and performed in improvised quarters, but such sideshow booths or crude temporary platforms as are described here were then only quaint and rare survivals in provincial market squares.
3. Compare the "strait gate" of Matthew 7:13.
4. The metaphors are mixed. Nature, like the first of the three Fates, spins the endless thread of life, monotonous in its very variety. The poet selects portions of this listlessly spun, endless, formless thread, and to these portions gives literary form ("rhythmic words") and moral significance. These unique episodes take on permanent significance for all mankind ("general consecration"), e.g., the episode of the historical Macbeth is lost in the web of history, but Shakespeare's *Macbeth* has received poetic definition. The musical metaphor arises from the monotonous *sound* of the spinning-wheel, from which the poet gathers individual threads of tone into full chords.
5. "Unites the gods" *(vereinet Götter)* apparently conveys the classical notion of the poet as mythologizer, one who defines the sublimity of all gods. "Gives high Olympus sure defense" *(sichert den Olymp)* apparently means "affirms the ideal," though Witkowski believes it means "assures man's achievement of the ideal," i.e., by "scaling Olympus" or achieving heaven.
6. The allusion is not to any idea in *Faust*, but to the old multiple stage of medieval drama—such as Goethe uses in the second-last scene of *Part 2*—with heaven on the right, the world in the center, and the "jaws of hell" on the left.
7. In the manner of a medieval sovereign at a convocation of his vassals.
8. Job 38:7: "When the morning stars sang together, and all the sons of God shouted for joy." Witkowski feels that any allusion to the classical "music of the spheres" is unlikely.
9. "Heralds" *(Boten)* literally translates Greek *aggeloi* ("angels").
10. *Göttersöhne* literally translates the Hebrew *Bene Elohim* of Genesis 6:2.
11. "Potencies" *(Wirkenskraft)* and "seeds" *(Samen)* were alchemists' terms for "energy" and "primal matter," the latter being analogous to "atoms."
12. Michel de Notredame (1503–66) was a younger contemporary of the historical Faust, an astrologer, and the composer of a volume of rhymed prophecies of the future.
13. Emanuel Swedenborg (1688–1772) states in his *Arcana coelestia* that spirits communicate thoughts instantaneously without the medium of words or speech.
14. A mystic symbol representing the total universe.
15. In the difficult lines which follow, the written symbol of the macrocosm (universe) is imagined as coming alive before Faust's eyes. Essentially it is a vision of the starry sky with all the stars complexly moving by immutable laws like a cosmic watchworks. The moving parts, however, are also angels, for the metaphor is blended with Jacob's dream from Genesis 28:12: "And he [Jacob] dreamed, and behold a ladder set up on earth, and the top of it reached to heaven: and behold the angels of God ascending and descending on it." Regularly ordered movement is suggested by the passing of the golden pails from angel to angel; possibly they are fetching light from the well and source of all light, which is God. The angels, by piercing through the earth, include our planet in the cosmic vision.
16. The image is that of a mother-earth-goddess, perhaps like the ancient Diana of Ephesus, who was represented with innumerable breasts which gave suck to all creatures.
17. The much discussed Spirit is a personification of amoral Nature, Goethe's own variation of the *Archaeus terrae* of the sixteenth-century natural philosophers and Giordano Bruno's *Anima terrae*. These philosophers, and later ones as well, e.g., Swedenborg, conceived of a supernatural spirit dwelling at the earth's core and controlling all earthly life of animals, vegetables, and even minerals. Each planet had its own analogous spirit. In a jotting of 1800, reproduced by Witkowski (Vol. 1, p. 526), Goethe defined the Earth Spirit as *Welt und Thaten Genius*, the spirit of the world and of deeds.
18. According to Swedenborg, every spirit has its own "sphere"; spirits also suck, leechlike, on human heads and leave a kind of wound. Para-

celsus, one of the chief alchemists whom Goethe had read, says the senses suck reason from the sun the way a bee sucks honey from flowers.

19. "Superman" (*Übermensch*), probably the first occurrence of the word in literature.

20. Famulus, a graduate assistant to a professor.

21. Museum, literally "a haunt of the Muses," used preciously here in the sense of "study" or "private library."

22. I.e., it takes so long to master Greek and Latin in order to study the classics in the original.

23. Revelation 5:1.

24. "Heroic play" stands for the technical term *Haupt- und Staatsaktion*, which describes drama of the French classical type involving the fates of countries and their rulers, but more particularly the sorry seventeenth-century German works in that vein.

25. In 2 Kings 2:11, Elijah was taken up to heaven in a "chariot of fire."

26. Angel voices are heard in all poetic appropriateness in this scene, which is a dialogue between Faust and "spirits." On a more literal plane, a nearby church is to be assumed, where a miracle play of the Resurrection is being enacted. Angels at the empty tomb make replies to the three Marys. See Luke 24. Regarding the rhyme scheme for the Chorus of Angels, see note 28 below.

27. The word "growth" stands for the original *Werdelust* which can only be roughly paraphrased as "delight in the process of becoming."

28. In view of the intricacies of rhyme which these Easter choruses combine with uncommon verbal compression and with grammatical tours de force, the translator has chosen to render them fairly literally and line for line, with only occasional rhymes to suggest the lyric quality of the original.

29. "Scholar" in the old-fashioned sense of "student."

30. At this point the Scholars set off in pursuit of the Serving Girls, while the Middle-Class Girls remain waiting on the sidelines; the Citizens come along.

31. On November 30 Saint Andrew, the patron saint of the unwed, will, if properly invoked, grant visions of future spouses.

32. The Blessed Sacrament, i.e., the consecrated wafer contained in a round, glass-covered compartment in the center of a golden sun-burst monstrance, which is carried aloft in procession.

33. Using actual sixteenth-century terms, though a trifle freely, Goethe describes the manufacture of "the Philosopher's Stone" in an alchemist's laboratory ("black kitchen"). The male "antagonist," derived from gold and called "the Blood of the Golden Lion" or "the Red Lion" (mercuric oxide), was "wed" with the female "antagonist," derived from silver and called "the White Eagle" or "the Lily" (hydrochloric acid), in a retort ("bridal bed"); the "offspring" was "the Young Queen" or "the Philosopher's Stone."

34. The two impulses are to repose and exertion, rather than Christian flesh and spirit.

35. John 1:1, *En arkhê ēn lo logos*, in which the word *logos* ("Word") has a complex theological meaning of pre-Christian origin.

36. The *Key of Solomon* was a quasi-religious book composed in Hebrew, and enormously popular in Latin translation as *Clavicula Salomonis* from the sixteenth to the eighteenth centuries. It dealt with the rules and means for controlling spirits.

37. The "spell of the four" is Goethe's whimsical invention, based on the *Key of Solomon*. By pronouncing it, Faust seeks to compel the spirit which has assumed a dog's shape to appear in its true form: as fire, if it is a fire spirit (salamander); as water, if it is a water spirit (undine, nixie, nymph); as air—represented by a shooting star or meteor—if it is an air spirit; as personified earth (kobold, incubus, gnome, dwarf, pygmy), if it is an earth spirit. The incubi were particularly malevolent since, as nightmares, they bestrode and oppressed sleeping persons.

38. The sign INRI or JNRJ, abbreviation for "Jesus the Nazarene, King of the Jews" (*Jesus Nazarenus Rex Judaeorum*), which Pilate had inscribed on the cross that held the body of Jesus at the crucifixion (John 19:19). Faust apparently holds a crucifix over the shape-shifting spirit-beast.

39. John 19:34 states that one of the attendant soldiers thrust his lance into the side of the dead Jesus. The three previous lines refer to Christ as uncreated, i.e., existent from all time, as inconceivable in terms of any earthly name, and as "the same also that ascended up far above all heavens, that He might fill all things" (Ephesians 4:10).

40. The "sign" of the Trinity.

41. Traveling scholars were frequently rogues and adventurers.

42. To know a spirit's name was to give one "a name to conjure with," and hence put the spirit in the knower's power.

43. The "Baal-zebub the god of Ekron" of 2 Kings 1:2, usually etymologized as "the god of flies" or "the fly-god."

44. The witch's foot, identical with the pentagram of the following line, is a symbol made up of interlocking triangles to form a five-pointed star. Known also as "the sign of Christ," it was inscribed to ward off evil spirits.

45. From the corridor, where they were gathered at the beginning of the scene.

46. The spirits speak Faust's incantatory dream: the vaulted arches of the Gothic room dissolve into cloud, which in turn dissolves into starry sky (of this Easter night); a new and different day is reached by Faust's spirit on its flight accompanied by other spirits, and ardent longing projects the flight still further; the spirits "shed down" the beauties of an Arcadian landscape with many pairs of lovers in leafy shade and with the grape harvest in progress; the grapejuice spurting

from the presses becomes rivers flowing through mountain gorges to emerge as a flood that turns hills into islands; birds drink the wines and become intoxicated with rapture; the vintage festivals become a Bacchic revel on the newly made Isles of the Blessed. The dream is a wild upsurge of voluptuous desire. The Greek scene anticipates motifs to be developed in *Part 2.*

47. Mephistopheles probably dips his finger in the oil of the lamp and smears the imperfectly drawn angle of the pentagram on the threshold. Oil is bait for rodents.

48. Approximation of Spanish court costume of ca. 1500–1550, when the historical Faust (d. 1539?) was alive and when German lands formed part of the immense empire ruled by Charles V from Madrid.

49. The Aramaic word *mamona,* "richs," used by Jesus to personify the false god of riches (Matthew 6:24 and Luke 16:13).

50. Interpretations differ as to the significance of this chorus and Mephisto's identifications of the singers. Witkowski plausibly argues for this one: the spirits are benevolent; their thoughts are the author's own; Mephisto's claim to the spirits is opportunistic, as is his seizing on their words, to which he lends his own flat, utilitarian, and unbenevolent meaning.

51. "For God's sake" *(um Gottes Willen)* is the beggar's formula for asking alms.

52. If by any chance Goethe used the word *entstehn* ("come to be") in its obsolete sense of "to be lacking," the whole sense of the lines would be changed: If you smash this world to pieces, the other world may not exist either.

53. The German *(Und Schlag auf Schlag)* seems to indicate some sort of double handshake in token of both parties' agreement to the compact.

54. Goethe planned, sketched, and abandoned a "Disputation Scene" following the present one, in which Faust would defend a "thesis" before a board of examiners and receive his degree to become "Doctor Faustus." Mephistopheles dressed as a traveling scholar was to appear at the examination and defend his own "thesis" of worldly experience versus book learning. The plan called for choruses of students, a "thesis defense" by Wagner, Mephisto's intrusion, Faust's challenge to him to formalize his questions and answers, Mephisto's mocking proposals of problems in natural science, and, at some point, a speech by Faust which would culminate in the remark: "You have won no knowledge unless it springs from your own soul!" (Witkowski prints Goethe's tentative sketch of the scene and the extant fragments of text.)

55. Mephisto's ironic advice is to let an eighteenth-century tragic poet talk Faust into believing he is one of those stage heroes who are compendia of all virtues, impossible miniature universes (microcosms) in themselves.

56. Scandinavian gravity had been discussed by Lavater in a book which Goethe had reviewed.

57. The allusion is to the enormous curled wigs falling to the waist, worn in the seventeenth-century by tragic actors. The following line refers to the "elevator shoes" worn by the same actors, though the word used is "sock" (the *soccus* of the ancient Roman stage).

58. A course in logic.

59. The Spanish boot was an instrument of torture, consisting of metal greaves fastened to the victim's leg and screwed tighter and tighter.

60. "Nature's hand-hold," a pretentious Greek-plus-Latin term of J. R. Spielmann in his *Institutiones chemiae* (1763), signifying the elusive factor that holds biological components together in a living organism.

61. Goethe took a law degree at the University of Strasbourg in 1771 and served briefly in the hopelessly antiquated law court of the Holy Roman Empire at Wetzlar in 1772.

62. ". . . ye shall be as gods, knowing good and evil" (Genesis 3:5). This is the serpent's temptation to Eve in the Garden of Eden, slightly misquoted from the Vulgate Bible—*Deus* (God) instead of *dii* (gods)—doubtless from recollection of Luther's *Gott.*

63. The brothers Montgolfier made the first balloon ascension in 1783.

64. Auerbach's Tavern was an actual tavern in Leipzig, allegedly frequented by the historical Faust. Goethe probably visited the tavern while at the University of Leipzig. This stage direction is unique in the poem for its geographical specificity.

65. The common noun "frog," but in dialect, "schoolboy."

66. Suggestive of *Brandfuchs* (literally "brant fox"), the term for a second-semester student.

67. The leader of a drinking bout was called "the Pope"; his "qualities" were his capacity for liquor.

68. Crossroads, from time immemorial, have been considered places dear to evil spirits.

69. The Blocksberg, highest peak of the Harz Mountains, was the traditional scene of devils' orgies on St. Walpurga's Night, April 30. Goat form was a popular guise to assume for the occasion.

70. Leipzig's proud boast in the mid-eighteenth century.

71. The Leipzig Fair attracted all sorts of comers to the city.

72. Folklore attributed a limp to the Devil.

73. Frosch hopes to catch the traveling stranger with an allusion to a local joke. Rippach, a village near Leipzig, was, since at least 1710, the alleged home of Jack Ass (Hans Arsch), alias Jack Dull (Hans Dumm). Frosch expects Mephisto to inquire innocently, "Jack who?"

74. The text terms the beast a *Meerkatze,* a "long-tailed monkey," literally a "sea-cat."

75. See the title page from Lavater's *De spectris,* illustrations.

76. "Devil's bridges" are both bizarre rock formations and "underhanded methods."

77. Folklore claimed a thief became recognizable as such when viewed through a sieve.

78. A thick-handled dusting instrument.

79. The magic mirror reveals an ideal female nude, such as Giorgione's *Venus*.

80. The refrain in Genesis, especially Genesis 1:31: "And God saw that it was good."

81. The monkeys speak both as French revolutionists and as German Romantic lyric poets who sacrificed sense for sound.

82. The "northern" or Germanic Devil, as opposed to the Mediterranean one, inherited the ravens attendant upon Wotan as well as a horse hoof instead of a human foot, horse sacrifices having been made to Wotan.

83. Knee breeches left the lower leg cased in skintight silk stockings to the disadvantage of some persons; padding supplied "muscles" to the calf of the leg.

84. The gesture is usually identified as "the fig" (Italian *fico*), thumb between forefingers, though sixteenth-century male costume would easily enable Mephisto to display the reality in lieu of the symbol.

85. A jibe at the Trinity.

86. A jibe at blind faith in revelation as opposed to eighteenth-century Reason.

87. Magister, Doctor, Professor; or in modern terms, B.A., M.A., Ph.D.

88. See above, note 69.

89. Diminutives of Margaret include (Mar)gretchen, Margretlein, Gretel, Gretelchen, etc.

90. Revelation 2:17: "To him that overcometh will I give to eat of the hidden manna."

91. Syphilis, *le mal de Naples*.

92. The present rendezvous of Faust and Mephisto is in the city and nearer Margaret's home, whereas their former one was in the "suburb" beyond the walls of an eighteenth-century town, as the stage direction "Promenade" indicated. Goethe originally wrote *Allee*, i.e., a tree-shaded walk, impossible in towns until ca. 1800.

93. Mephisto's words are a *reply* to the monologue on which he has eavesdropped. More strikingly than any other Faust-Mephisto interchange in the poem, this passage sounds like a dialogue of the divided self.

94. Witkowski suggests that the crucifix is meant, not the Eucharistic wafer.

95. Song of Solomon 4:5: "Thy two breasts are like two young roes that are twins, which feed among the lilies."

96. The French word *génie* ("genius")—pronounced with an initial "sh" sound and with the accent on the second syllable—was German jargon of the 1770s for a young fellow of mighty passions and insensitive conscience, something between Casanova and a Byronic hero.

97. "Lieschen" would be similar to our "Lizzy." "Barbie" (the text calls her Bärbelchen) is a familiar form for Barbara. The diminutives designate girls of the lower class who are fetching water from the public well.

98. Unwed mothers were required by law to do church penance publicly in a prescribed costume of humiliation. As early as 1763 the Weimar government considered repeal of the law in order to reduce the high incidence of infanticide. Repeal was enacted on May 15, 1786, partly at Goethe's urging, and over the objections of Herder! (Herder, five years older than Goethe and Goethe's most famous teacher, was a distinguished philosopher and, upon Goethe's recommendation, had been appointed official chaplain to the Weimar court.)

99. Like other details in this connection, to be understood quite literally. In the language of the flowers, broken straw means broken agreement.

100. *Zwinger* is an untranslatable term for the open space between the last houses of a town and the inside of the city walls, sometimes the open space between two parallel city walls. Gretchen has sought the most out-of-the-way spot in the city for her private devotions. The *Mater dolorosa* is a statue of Mary, the mother of Jesus, in an attitude of grief as she beholds the crucifixion; in accordance with Luke 2:35 her visible heart is pierced with a sword. The text freely adapts the famous thirteenth-century hymn, *Stabat mater dolorosa* probably by Jacopone da Todi though sometimes attributed to Pope Innocent III:

Stabat mater dolorosa	The sorrowful mother was standing
juxta crucem lacrimosa	beside the cross in tears
dum pendebat filius;	while her Son hung [there],
cuius animam gementem	[she] whose soul grieving
contristantem et dolentem	compassionating and sorrowing,
pertransivit gladius.	a sword pierced through.

The hymn has a total of sixty lines.

101. Abruptly and not altogether felicitously Goethe brings in the motif of buried treasure working its way up through the ground under the force of the Devil's magical presence. The motif is frequent in the background readings which Goethe did in preparation for the "Walpurgis Night" scene.

102. In the language of gems, pearls represent tears.

103. The song is imitated from Ophelia's song in *Hamlet*, 4.5:

> And I a Maid at your Window,
>   To be your Valentine.
> Then up he rose, & don'd his clothes,
>   & dupt the chamber dore,
> Let in the Maid, that out a Maid,
>   Never departed more.

104. With the lower courts Mephistopheles could "arrange" most matters; but in the "court of

blood" *(Blutbann),* originally under the jurisdiction of no one less than the emperor or king, where capital crimes were tried and where the death sentence was passed "in the name of God," he is out of his depth.

105. As Goethe had observingly read, a Frankfurt police ordinance of the fifteenth-century forbade fallen women to wear jewelry, silk, satin, or damask, and denied them the use of a pew in church. This latter requirement would force them to remain at the rear with the "beggars and cripples."

106. The opening of the greatest of medieval hymns, the *Dies irae,* composed before 1250, probably by Thomas of Celano, and used in Masses of the dead:

> The day of wrath, that day
> Shall dissolve the world in fire. . . .

Through nineteen three-line stanzas the hymn describes the end of the world and the Last Judgment.

107. The Evil Spirit paraphrases stanzas three and four of the same hymn:

Tuba mirum spargens sonum	The trumpet scattering wondrous sound
per sepulchra regionum	Through the sepulchers of the lands
coget omnes ante thronum.	Will drive everyone up before the throne.
Mors stupebit et natura	Death and nature will stand aghast
cum resurget creatura	When the creature shall resurrect
judicanti responsura.	In answer to the Judge's call

The Evil Spirit's lines also refer to the doctrine that from death until the Last Judgment the soul will be either in heaven, in hell, or in purgatory, while the body will be in its grave; at the sound of the last trumpet, however, the body will resurrect, be rejoined with its soul, submit to judgment, and then, together with the soul, be assigned either to heaven or to hell for all eternity. (Purgatory will be abolished on the Last Day.)

108. Stanza six:

> Therefore when the Judge shall sit,
> Whatever is hidden shall appear,
> Nothing shall remain unavenged.

109. Stanza seven:

> What shall I, wretched, say?
> What patron shall I call upon?
> When scarcely the just man is safe.

110. Saint Walpurgis (Walpurga, Walburga, Valburg, d. 780), was a niece of Saint Boniface and herself a missionary to Germany. By coincidence, her church calendar day, April 30, fell together with the pagan festivals on the eve of May Day, the end of winter and the beginning of summer. Under the Christian dispensation those festivals, like the Hallowe'en festivals (Oct. 31) at the end of summer and the beginning of winter, passed into folklore as devils' orgies. Folklore further localized those orgies on the Brocken, highest peak of the Harz Mountains in central Germany. From the village of Elend a two- or three-hour walk leads past the village of Schierke to a desolate plateau and finally to the top of the Brocken.

111. A will-o'-the-wisp (*ignis fatuus*, Jack-o'-Lantern) is a conglomeration of phosphorescent gas from decayed vegetation in swamps. By night it resembles an eerily swaying lantern.

112. The Snorer *(Schnarcher)* is a curious rock formation near the Brocken.

113. "Mammon" here is gold.

114. Urian is a name for the Devil.

115. In classical mythology Baubo was Demeter's nurse; she is the archetype of the lascivious old woman.

116. The Ilsenstein is the topmost point on the Brocken.

117. Witches rub a special salve over their whole bodies in preparation for an expedition.

118. Voland is another name for the Devil.

119. Lilith (Hebrew, "she of the night") figures in medieval Jewish folklore as Adam's first wife from whom demons were begotten. Genesis 1:27 speaks of God's creation of humans "male and female" *before* the creation of Eve described in chap. 2. The name is taken from Isaiah 34:14, though the King James version translates it as "screech owl."

120. Proktophantasmist (Greek, "buttocks-mage") is an allusion to Friedrich Nicolai, the tedious and superannuated writer-publisher-"philosopher" who denounced every innovation in German thought and letters after 1770 (including Kant). In the midst of the popularity of Goethe's novel *The Sorrows of Young Werther,* he published a silly parody called *The Joys of Young Werther* and somehow conceived the notion that *Faust* was a parody of him by way of retaliation. The specific allusions here, however, are recondite to the point where only a few people understood them in 1808. Nicolai had long denounced belief in ghosts, but in 1797 seriously announced that a certain castle in Tegel was haunted. Then he compounded his self-contradictions by saying that he himself had been plagued by ghosts back in 1791, but had found an effective antidote in the application of leeches to his buttocks.

121. Alludes sarcastically to Nicolai's twelve-volume *Description of a Trip through Germany and Switzerland in 1781,* published 1783–96.

122. The untranslatable pun on *Geist* as "ghost," and *Geist* as "mind," "intelligence," may echo

Friedrich Schlegel's caustic comment in an issue of the *Athenäum* to the effect that Nicolai was looking for a vision of his own *Geist*.

123. The Prater is a famous park in Vienna.

124. Latin, "officious."

125. Blocksberg is an alternate name for the Brocken.

126. The subtitle "Intermezzo" is inappropriately retained from an earlier plan of the "Walpurgis Night," where it came between the witch passages and the orgiastic finale. (Fragments preserved from the originally planned finale indicate that it would have been a monstrous travesty of the Last Judgment.)

127. Johann Martin Mieding was stage manager of the Weimar theater.

128. Group 1 (next 40 lines), miscellaneous and social. Orchestra Tutti: a transition stanza; the insect orchestra plays throughout. Solo: a soap bubble playing like a bagpipe—any loud and empty person. Mind in Embryo: some trivial eclectic poet (unidentified) who puts together incongruous oddments. A Little Couple: (a) "I write poems that soar"; (b) "You don't get off the ground." Inquisitive Traveler: Nicolai (see above, note 120). Orthodox: Count Friedrich Leopold von Stolberg, who had attacked Schiller's poem *The Gods of Greece* for its paganism. Northern Artist: the native German painter waiting until he gets to Italy to begin serious work. Purist: an academic critic insisting on the neoclassical rules. Young Witch, Matron: female representatives of the younger and older generations.

129. Group 2 (next 40 lines), miscellaneous and personal. Orchestra Conductor: a transition stanza; the insect musicians are distracted by the Young Witch. Weather Vane: an insincere flatterer of both factions; possibly Orchestra Conductor Reichardt, possibly Weimar Rector Böttiger (who has also been proposed for Servibilis, note 124). "Xenien": the title of a collection of satirical quatrains by Goethe and Schiller. The present scene is the outgrowth of Goethe's plan for a larger and artistically ordered collection of such quatrains. Hennings: the Danish critic August von Hennings, a determined foe of Goethe and Schiller. "Musaget": *Der Musaget* (Latin, *Musagetes*, "Leader of the Muses"), title of a two-volume poetry anthology published by Hennings in 1798–99. Ci-devant "Genius of the Age": *Genius of the Age (Genius der Zeit)* was the title of Hennings' magazine—the vehicle of his attacks on Goethe and Schiller—up to 1800; from 1800 to 1802 it was called *Genius of the Nineteenth Century*, hence the use of *ci-devant*, "formerly." Inquisitive Traveler: Nicolai again, as traveler and as baiter of Jesuits. Crane: Lavater, the phrenologist and Goethe's onetime friend; his walk was awkward like that of a crane. Child of the World: Goethe himself; see the poem "Dîné zu Coblenz," which begins, "Between Lavater and Basedow" (another onetime friend of Goethe), and ends:

Prophets to the right, prophets to the left,
The child of the world in between.

130. Group 3 (next 32 lines), schools of philosophy. Dancer, Ballet Master, Fiddler: transition stanzas describing the arriving philosophers. The latter state in turn their conflicting opinions on the existence of devils. The Idealist represents the school of Fichte: only the ego actually exists and all things are its moment-to-moment creations. The Supernaturalist represents the followers of Friedrich Jacobi. The Skeptic represents the tradition of Hume.

131. Group 4 (to end of scene), political types from the era of the French Revolution; finale. Orchestra Conductor: a transition stanza. The Clever Ones: "shrewd operators," political opportunists who change sides blithely *(sans souci)* as the tides of politics shift. The Awkward Ones: "weak sisters," émigrés stranded without capacity for earning their living. Will-o'-the-wisps: upstarts "made" by the Revolution. Shooting Star: a leader who rose from obscurity, had his day, and fell. Bruisers: brutal demagogues. Finale: Puck spurns the Bruisers; Ariel bids all the spirits follow him to the Hill of Roses, which, as was well known to readers of Wieland's *Oberon*, was the site of Oberon's palace; the Orchestra, playing to an empty stage, concludes the "scherzo."

132. Margaret sings a distorted form of the song in the old fairy tale of the juniper tree, which Goethe knew long before it was set down as No. 47 in Grimm's Fairy Tales in 1812. In *Von dem Machandelboom* a bird, representing the ghost of the boy slain by his wicked stepmother, sings:

Mein' Mutter der mich schlacht'	My mother who slew me,
Mein' Vater der mich ass,	My father who ate me,
Mein' Schwester der Marlenichen	My sister, little Marlene,
Sucht' alle meine Benichen,	Gathered up all my bones,
Bind't sie in ein seiden Tuch,	Tied them up in a silken cloth,
Legt's unter den Machandelbaum.	And buried them beneath the juniper tree.
Kywitt, Kywitt, wat vör'n schöön Vagel bün ik!	To-whit, to-whit, what a fair bird am I!

133. After reading the death sentence, the judge broke a staff to symbolize the forfeiture of the condemned person's life; the death knell was rung throughout the execution ceremony.

134. They are magic horses of the night and cannot bear the light of day.

135. A condemned person's place of confinement was inaccessible to evil spirits; that Mephisto dares intrude is a sign of his desperation lest he lose Faust.

Woyzeck

Georg Büchner

It is not at all uncommon for poets and painters of extraordinary genius to work for a lifetime without recognition, then to be "discovered" some years after their deaths. Some showed little interest in bringing their work to the attention of a wider public; others were in some sense ahead of their time and thus remained unappreciated until changes in society suddenly made their work seem more relevant. Playwrights almost never are "discovered" by a later age in this fashion, however. It is the nature of a playwright's work to collaborate with a group of other artists (the actors and technicians) and to create a work that is shared by an audience. If the audience's experience is in any way noteworthy, the public at large quickly learns about it, and the playwright works to improve his technique based in part upon what he learns by contact with audiences. It is not the case that every popularly successful playwright is a great artist, but historically it has almost always been true that great playwrights have enjoyed a considerable measure of popular success in their own day.

Georg Büchner is a notable exception to this generalization. Struck down by typhus at the age of only twenty-three, Büchner had no opportunity to develop his talent as presumably he might have had he been granted a normal life span. Caught up in revolutionary activities, hiding from the police, and attempting to complete university studies, he found no opportunity for active involvement with a producing theater, the process by which most playwrights hone their skills. His three surviving plays were never produced until decades after his death, yet their influence on twentieth-century drama has been so profound that Büchner must be counted among the most important European playwrights of the nineteenth century. He spanned in a remarkable fashion the romantic and realistic theaters, and looked forward to twentieth-century dramatic modes otherwise undreamed of in his own time.

Georg Büchner was born in Geddelau, Hesse, on October 17, 1813, and shortly thereafter his family moved to Darmstadt. Georg was the eldest of six children in an apparently happy and well-balanced family. His father was a physician, scientist, and political activist, and his mother took a deep interest in literature and the arts; Georg was raised in a liberalizing environment and educated in the Darmstadt schools. Upon his graduation from Darmstadt's *Gymnasium,* Büchner was sent to the University of Strasbourg to study medicine, and this sophisticated Germanic city on French soil further opened his mind to the liberal and revolutionary currents still flowing in Europe following the French Revolution. Apparently Büchner had some involvement with radical political groups in Strasbourg, but after two years there he was compelled to transfer to the University of Giessen because of a law requiring Hessian citizens to do at least two years of their university training at a Hessian school. The sense of political oppression that Büchner felt at Giessen quickly led to his active participation with a radical group attempting to stir up open revolt among the people; Büchner was coauthor of a tract that the group printed and attempted to distribute, but an informer within the group betrayed them to the police. In the absence of direct evidence linking him to the conspiracy, Büchner was able for a time to avoid arrest; he returned to his parents' home where, in an attempt to raise money for an escape from the country, he wrote his first play, *Danton's Death* (written early in 1835). Büchner sent his play to Karl Gutzkow, a young liberal literary figure who did, in fact, arrange for its publication, but in the meantime Büchner had escaped to Strasbourg.

During the next eighteen months in Strasbourg, Büchner completed a dissertation (in French) on the nervous system of the barbel and was awarded his doctorate. He also translated two of Victor Hugo's plays, *Lucrece Borgia* and *Marie Tudor,* into German (although he did not care at all for their romantic excesses); completed three important papers in natural history; and worked on three more plays. *Leonce and Lena* was completed in 1836 and submitted to a German playwriting contest, but arrived too late for consideration. It was returned to him unopened. *Pietro Aretino* may or may not have been completed, but its manuscript has never been found. He began work on *Woyzeck* in 1836, and was still working on it at the time of his death.

In the fall of 1836, Büchner secured an appointment as lecturer at the University of Zurich. Apparently disillusioned with politics and convinced that Germany was not ready for the revolution he thought was needed, Büchner lived quietly in Zurich that winter. His fiancée, Wilhelmine Jaegle, the daughter of a Protestant minister, remained in her home at Strasbourg, but she was summoned to his bedside in February 1837, when he was stricken with typhus. He died on February 19.

Büchner's papers, including his diary and correspondence, became the property of his family and his fiancée upon his death. Miss Jeagle never married, and before her death in 1880 she destroyed everything of Büchner's in her possession, evidently scandalized by his radical outlook and earthy language. A fire in the Büchner family home destroyed other papers, but a Viennese scholar, Karl Emil Franzos, collected and published in 1879 all of the work of Büchner that he could find. *Leonce and Lena* was first produced in Munich in 1885, *Danton's Death* in Berlin in 1902, and *Woyzeck* in Munich in 1913.

There may have been a finished draft of *Woyzeck* among the papers Miss Jaegle destroyed, but the manuscripts from which Franzos worked were in a sad state of disarray. The play is structured in short scenes anyway, and the manuscripts do not reveal in what order Büchner intended for them to occur nor which were to be kept and which discarded. Scholars have reached some measure of concensus with respect to the order of the early scenes, but there is little agreement regarding the play's ending. The version printed here seems theatrically effective and consistent with the rest of the play, but there is no way to be certain that it is what Büchner intended. Some have even speculated that, in a much lengthened play, Büchner planned to depict Woyzeck's trial.

In fact, the play is based on a highly publicized murder committed by one Johann Woyzeck on June 21, 1821, in Leipzig. Woyzeck, aged forty-one, killed his mistress, aged forty-six. Freely admitting his crime, Woyzeck was brought to trial, found guilty, and eventually beheaded on August 27, 1824—the first public execution in Leipzig in over thirty years. There was a great deal of evidence that Woyzeck experienced hallucinations and other manifestations of insanity, and a public outcry and extended investigations delayed the execution by nearly two years. The reports of psychiatric examinations by Dr. Johann Clarus of the University of Leipzig were published, and Büchner used a great many details from these reports in his play. The real Woyzeck, when he was about thirty years old, had taken another mistress by whom he had a child, and Büchner increases the pathos of the case by identifying the stabbing with this earlier liaison. In other respects, however, the character created by Büchner is remarkably close to that emerging from Dr. Clarus's reports.

Liberal groups in Germany had argued vigorously that the real Woyzeck was a victim of a corrupt system and of social forces beyond his control; because of Büchner's politics, it has frequently been assumed that the fictional Woyzeck serves these same political arguments. Although it is true that Woyzeck is a victim, and that he has little control over the social forces that manipulate him, these facts alone do not account for his vicious act of murder. Here, as well as in other works, Büchner is interested in probing what factors in the human psyche drive one to lying, stealing, fornication, and murder; the almost clinical presentation of Woyzeck allows the probing of these factors in him, but offers no final answers to the eternal questions that challenged Büchner. Thus, in a single stroke Büchner created what many regard as the first proletarian tragic hero, though one may argue over the meaning of both "tragedy" and "hero" in this context. Certainly one factor that marks Büchner as years ahead of his time is his realistic and sympathetic portrayal of proletarian characters. Only in the 1890s, when realism had been firmly established in European drama, did playwrights begin to realize how revolutionary Büchner had been some sixty years earlier.

Perhaps even more remarkable than Büchner's character development is the structural pattern he employed. Romanticism had established the practice of constructing plays in a series of short scenes, but Büchner made of them mere fragments, like flashes of light reflected in a broken mirror, briefly illuminating a subject and then dying again into blackness. This erratic, dreamlike quality inherent in the play's structure was not to be seen again until the expressionists "invented" it before World War I and Brecht turned it into a high order of theatrical art. Both Brecht and the expressionists have acknowledged their important debt to Büchner's early work. Furthermore, the language with which Büchner works is integrally related to this structural form, for he depends not simply on proletarian diction, but specifically on the disjointed syntax and fragmentary forms of distracted, hopeless people or of ideas only half perceived. No doubt had his plays been produced in his own time the audience would have been shocked, but today such an approach to dramatic dialogue seems congruent with the best in twentieth-century drama.

At the most fundamental level, however, it is Büchner's world view, his thematic outlook underlying the play, that makes him seem so modern. Reacting against the essential optimism of the romanticists and their eternal striving, yet sharing their view that an upheaval of the social order was the key to improvement in man's condition, Büchner found himself despairing and frustrated by the inertia that seemed to him to stand in the way of progress in Germany. As an incipient realist, he pictured people (especially the lower classes) as they actually were, but he despaired of the possibility of any improvement in the human condition. Accordingly, he arrived at a position of absurdity, of finding no meaning in human life and no explanation for the evil and sloth that infects mankind. The post–World War II playwrights were to find in Büchner the precursor of everything important that they were trying to say, and thus again Büchner was recognized as a genius out of his time.

In twenty-three years and four months of life, Georg Büchner wrote at least three extraordinary plays. Had he lived to see them produced, no doubt the theater would have undergone a remarkable upheaval in the middle of the nineteenth century that would totally have changed the outlook of the playwrights that came after him. Since in fact his work was virtually unknown until the end of the century, it has remained for the twentieth century to recognize Büchner's genius and to pursue the new directions that he had opened. His plays suffer from weaknesses inevitably associated with lack of practical theater experience, but they are nevertheless truly remarkable achievements.

Woyzeck

Translated by Theodore Hoffman

Characters
*Woyzeck**
The Captain
Andres
Marie
Margret
Drum-Major
Marie's child
Barker
An Old Man
A Young Boy
Sergeant
The Doctor
First Apprentice
Second Apprentice
The Jew
Fool
An Old Woman
Three Little Girls
Käthe (pronounced pretty much like Katey)
Innkeeper
Two Men
Policeman
Horse, Monkey, Court Clerk, Doctor, Judge, Soldiers, Children, Apprentices, Students, Ordinary People.

The action apparently takes place in Leipzig, 1824.

*Pronounced: Voyt-seck. (The form Wozzeck—pronounced Votseck—is still widely current. It has its origin in a misreading of the MS by its first editor.)

1 At the Captain's

The CAPTAIN *in a chair;* WOYZECK *shaving him.*
CAPTAIN. Easy, Woyzeck, take it easy. One thing after the other! You're making me dizzy. You'll finish up early and what'll I do with ten minutes on my hands? Use your head, Woyzeck. You've got thirty years to live! Thirty! That's three hundred sixty months. And days! Hours! Minutes! What are you going to do with that horrible stretch of time? Figure it out for yourself, Woyzeck!
WOYZECK. Yes sir, Captain.
CAPTAIN. When I think about eternity, Woyzeck, this world gets me worried. Our task, Woyzeck! Our task is eternal. It's eternal, eternal! You know that? And then again, it's not so eternal. It's just a passing moment. Yes, a passing moment. Woyzeck, I get upset when I think it takes a whole day for the world to turn around just once. What a waste of time! And where does it get us? Woyzeck, I can get melancholy just looking at a millwheel.
WOYZECK. Yes sir, Captain.
CAPTAIN. Woyzeck, you always look so moody. A good man doesn't look moody; a good man is someone with a good conscience. Well, say something, Woyzeck! How's the weather today?
WOYZECK. Nasty, Captain, nasty. Wind.
CAPTAIN. Yes, I felt it before. It's really whizzing around. A wind like that has the same effect on me a mouse does. [*Slyly.*] I think the wind's from the north-south.
WOYZECK. Yes sir, Captain.
CAPTAIN. Ha! Ha! Ha! north-south! Ha! Ha! Ha! Are you dumb! Disgustingly dumb! [*Touched, but condescending.*] Woyzeck, you're a good man, but [*With dignity.*] you have no morals. Morals! That's what a man's got who

154

behaves morally! Understand? It's a good word. You went and got yourself a child without the blessing of the Church, as our right reverend chaplain put it. "Without the blessing of the Church." Now, I didn't invent the phrase.

WOYZECK. Captain, the Good Lord's not going to be hard on the little worm, just because no one said Amen before they made him. The Lord said, "Suffer little children to come unto me."

CAPTAIN. What did you say? What kind of crazy answer is that? It's got me all confused, and by "it" I mean "you"! See?

WOYZECK. You see, Captain—with us poor people—it's money, money! If you don't have money . . . Well, you just can't have morals when you're bringing someone like yourself into the world. We're only flesh and blood. People like us can't be holy in this world—or the next. If we ever did get into heaven, they'd put us to work on the thunder.

CAPTAIN. Woyzeck, you have no virtue. You are not a virtuous man. Flesh and blood? Why, when I lie by my window after the rain and I see those white stockings flashing over the sidewalk—damn it, Woyzeck, then I know what love is too! I'm flesh and blood, too, Woyzeck. But virtue! Virtue! The things I could waste my time on! But I say to myself "You're a virtuous man!" [*Moved.*] A good man, a good man.

WOYZECK. Yes, Captain. Virtue. I don't have much of that. But you see, what happens to us ordinary people— that's just nature. Now, if I was a gentleman and wore a hat and a watch and a cane, and could talk smooth—well, I'd like to be virtuous too. It must be fine to be virtuous, Captain, but I'm just ordinary.

CAPTAIN. You're good, Woyzeck. You're a good man. But you think too much. It wears you out. You're always so moody. Well, this conversation has exhausted me too. You can go. But don't run. Take it easy, nice and easy, out into the street.

2 An Open Field, the Town in the Distance

WOYZECK *and* ANDRES *cut kindling wood in the bushes.* ANDRES *is whistling.*

WOYZECK. You know, Andres, there's a curse on this place. You see that light spot on the grass down there, where the toadstools are sprouting? At night a head rolls around there. Someone picked it up once. Thought it was a hedgehog. Three days, three nights, and he was lying in a wooden box. [*Low.*] Andres, that was the Freemasons. I get it! The Freemasons!

ANDRES. [*Singing.*]

And there did sit two hares, Sir,
A-tearing up the green, the greenest grass.

WOYZECK. Quiet. Listen, Andres, listen! Something's moving.

ANDRES.

A-tearing up the green, the greenest grass,
Until the ground was bare, Sir.

WOYZECK. It's moving behind me. Under me. [*He stamps on the ground.*] Hollow. Listen! It's all hollow under here. The Freemasons!

ANDRES. I'm scared.

WOYZECK. It's so queer, and quiet. Makes you want to hold your breath . . . Andres!

ANDRES. What?

WOYZECK. Say something! [*Stares around him.*] Andres, look how bright it is. It's all shiny over the city. There's a fire running around the sky, and a sound coming down like trumpets. It's closing in on us!—Come on. Don't look back! [*Pulls him into the shrubbery.*]

ANDRES. [*After a pause.*] Woyzeck! You still hear it?

WOYZECK. Quiet. Everything's quiet. Like the world was dead.

ANDRES. Listen! There's the drum. We've got to get back.

3 The Town

MARIE *with her child at the window,* MARGRET. *The Retreat passes, the* DRUM-MAJOR *in front.*
MARIE. [*Dandling her child.*] Hey, boy! Ta-ra-ra-ra! Hear them? Here they come!
MARGRET. What a man! Built like a tree.
MARIE. He handles himself like a lion. [*The* DRUM-MAJOR *salutes her.*]
MARGRET. Ooh, he's giving you the glad eye, neighbor. I hardly expected it of you.
MARIE. [*Singing.*]

Oh, soldiers are such handsome guys.

MARGRET. Your eyes are still shining.
MARIE. Who cares? If you took yours to the pawnbroker's and had them polished up, maybe they'd shine enough to be sold for a couple of buttons.
MARGRET. What's that? Why, you! Listen, Mrs. Virginity, I'm at least respectable. But you, everyone knows you could stare your way through seven pairs of leather pants.
MARIE. You bitch! [*Slams the window.*] Come on, little fellow. What do people want, anyhow? Maybe you are just a poor whore's kid, but your illegitimate little face still brings joy to your mother. Da, da, dum. [*Singing.*]

Girlie, what's wrong in this house?
You've got a kid but no spouse.
Night-time I sing me a song.
Why let a man do me wrong?
Hush-a-bye, baby; baby, hurrah!
Let the men stay where they are.

Hansel, harness your six horses up.
They'd like to drink and to sup.
Oats they won't eat for you,
Water won't drink for you.
But lovely cool wine would do fine. Hurrah!
But lovely cool wine would do fine.
  [*A knock at the window.*]

Who's there? That you, Franz? Come on in.
WOYZECK. Can't. Got roll call.
MARIE. Get the wood cut for the Captain?
WOYZECK. Yes. Marie.
MARIE. What's the matter, Franz? You look upset.
WOYZECK. Marie, it happened again. Plenty. Doesn't the good book say, "And behold, there was a smoke coming up from the land like the smoke of an oven?"
MARIE. Oh, you . . . [*With pity.*]
WOYZECK. It followed me all the way into town. Something we can't understand, that drives you out of your senses. What's going to happen?
MARIE. Franz!
WOYZECK. I've got to go. See you tonight at the fair grounds. I saved something up. [*He goes.*]
MARIE. That man! He's seeing things. Didn't even notice his own child. He'll crack up with these ideas of his. Why so quiet, little fellow? Are you scared? It's getting so dark it's like going blind. Only that street light shining in. It gives me the creeps.

4 Fair Booths, Lights, People

OLD MAN *singing and* CHILD *dancing to a barrel-organ.*

Everything on earth fades fast,
Death will take us all at last,
That's a truth we know won't pass.

WOYZECK. Yahoo! A poor old man and a poor little boy. Fun and trouble!
MARIE. Good God, if fools make sense, then we're all fools. What a crazy world! What a beautiful world! [*Both move on to a barker.*]
BARKER. [*In front of a booth, with his wife in trousers and a monkey in costume.*] Ladies and gentlemen, if you looked at this creature as God made him, you'd see nothing, absolutely nothing! Ah, but Art, look what Art has done for him! He walks upright, wears a fancy jacket and tight trousers, and carries a sword. This here monkey is a soldier! He is no longer

in the lowest ranks of the masculine gender. Here, take a bow. There you are, the perfect gentleman. Give us a kiss. [*The monkey trumpets.*] The kid is really musical. Ladies and gentlemen, inside you will also see the little love birds and the astronomical horse. Favorite of the crowned heads of Europe. Can tell any one of you your age, number of children, and physical ailments. The show is about to begin. We're going to begin at the beginning. This is just the introduction to the introduction.
WOYZECK. Want to?
MARIE. It's all right with me. It should be good. Did you see the tassels on the man, and the wife wearing pants? [*Both go in.*]
DRUM-MAJOR. Hey, hold it! Did you see her? What a piece!
SERGEANT. And how! Made for breeding whole regiments of cavalry.
DRUM-MAJOR. And reproducing Drum-Majors!
SERGEANT. Look at the way she holds her head up. You'd think all that black hair would weigh her down. And those eyes!
DRUM-MAJOR. Like looking into a well, or staring up a chimney. Let's go! After her!

5   Inside the Brightly Lighted Booth

MARIE. What lights!
WOYZECK. Yeah, Marie. Black cats with burning eyes. Oh, what a night!
BARKER. [*Leading a horse.*] Show your talent! Show your brute reason! Put human society to shame! Ladies and gentlemen, the animal you see here, four hoofs on the ground and a long tail on his body, is a member of all the learned societies, a professor here at our university, where he teaches the students to ride and to fence. There's simple intelligence for you. But he also thinks with double reason. Show what you do when you use double reasoning. For instance, among this learned company do you see one single donkey? [*The nag shakes his head.*] Now do you see the double reasoning? That's physiognomy for you. Yes, this is no mere specimen of a dumb animal. This is a human being! No, a human beast! But still a beast. [*The horse mounts up indecently.*] All right, put society to shame! This beast, as you can see for yourselves, is still in a state of nature—not ideal nature of course . . . Take a lesson from him. But first consult your doctor. It may prove highly dangerous. Now, we have been told, be natural! You are created from dust, sand, and dung. Do you want to be more than dust, sand, and dung? See? What a mind! He can do arithmetic, even if he can't count on his fingers. Why? He just can't express himself, he just can't explain. He's a metamorphosed human being. Tell the audience what time it is. Have any of you ladies and gentlemen got a watch? A watch?
SERGEANT. A watch? [*Pulling a watch out of his pocket with great deliberation and dignity.*] There you are, sir.
MARIE. I'm not going to miss this. [*She climbs on the front bench. The* SERGEANT *helps her.*]
DRUM-MAJOR. What a piece!

6   Marie's Room

MARIE. [*Sitting, the child in her lap, a piece of mirror in her hand. She looks at herself.*] Don't the stones shine! What kind did he say they were? Sleep, baby. Close your eyes, tight. [*The child covers his eyes with his hands.*] Tighter yet. That's it. Stay like that—or he'll get you. [*Sings.*]

Quick, girl, lock the shutter tight.
A gypsy's on the road tonight.
He'll take you by the hand
Straight into gypsyland.
          [*Looking at herself again.*]

They must be gold. Wonder how I'd look dancing in them? Maybe people like us may only have a little corner of the world and a little piece of mirror, but my lips are as red as the finest ladies', with their top to bottom mirrors, and handsome gentlemen kissing their hands. And I'm just a common woman. [*The child raises himself.*] Quiet, boy. Close your eyes. There's the sandman running across the wall.
[*She flashes the mirror.*] Close your eyes, or he'll look into them and strike you blind! [WOYZECK *walks in, behind her. She jumps up, her hands over her ears.*]
WOYZECK. What have you got?
MARIE. Nothing.
WOYZECK. It's shinging through your fingers.
MARIE. An earring. I found it.
WOYZECK. I never found anything that way, two at a time.
MARIE. I'm only human.
WOYZECK. Forget it, Marie. Look at the way that kid sleeps. Lift him up under the arms. The chair's hurting him. Those shiny drops on his forehead. Everything under the sun is work. Sweat, even in our sleep. Us poor people! Here's some more money, Marie. My pay and something from the Captain.
MARIE. You're too good, Franz.
WOYZECK. I have to go. See you tonight, Marie. Good bye.
MARIE. [*Alone, after a pause.*] I'm such a rotten creature. I could stab myself. What the hell! Everything is going to the devil anyhow.

7   At the Doctor's

WOYZECK, *the* DOCTOR.
DOCTOR. And what do I see, Woyzeck? You! A man of your word!
WOYZECK. What's that, doctor?
DOCTOR. I saw you, Woyzeck. You were pissing in the street. You were pissing against the wall, like a dog! Three groschen a day and board for that! Woyzeck, that was bad. The world's going bad, very bad.
WOYZECK. But, Doctor, when Nature calls.
DOCTOR. When Nature calls! When Nature calls! Nature! Didn't I prove that the *musculus constrictor vesicae* can be controlled by the will? Woyzeck, Man is free! Through Man alone shines the individual's will to freedom! Can't hold his water! [*Shakes his head, puts his hands behind his back, paces up and down.*] Have you been eating your peas, Woyzeck? Nothing but peas. *Cruciferae.* Remember that! This will cause a revolution in scientific thought, I'll blow it to bits! Urea, o.10., Ammonium hydrochlorate, hyperoxidic. Woyzeck, can't you piss again? Go in there again and try.
WOYZECK. Can't do it, doctor.
DOCTOR. [*Upset.*] Pissing against a wall! Tsk, Tsk, tsk! I have it in writing, the agreement's right here. And what do I see? With my own eyes I saw it. I stick my nose out the window, letting the sun's rays hit it to observe the process of sneezing, and what do I see? Did you bring me any frogs? Tadpoles? Fresh water polyps? *Cristatellum?* Keep away from the microscope. I've got the thick back tooth from an infusorium under it. I'll blow them to bits, all of them! Pissing against a wall indeed! And I saw it! [*Bearing down on him.*] No, Woyzeck. I'm not getting angry. Anger is unhealthy, it's unscientific. I'm calm, perfectly calm. My pulse is beating its regular 60, and I'm addressing you in an absolutely cold-blooded manner. Why get angry with a man, God forbid? A man! Now if a Proteus should fail on you . . . But, Woyzeck, you shouldn't have been pissing against that wall.
WOYZECK. Don't you see, Doctor? Some people are built like you say—they have character, you might say. But it's something else with Nature. You see, with Nature, [*He snaps his fingers.*] it's like that. How can I explain? For instance . . .
DOCTOR. Woyzeck, you're philosophizing again.
WOYZECK. Nature. Yes, doctor, when

Nature gives way . . .

DOCTOR. Nature. What's that? When Nature gives way?

WOYZECK. When Nature gives way. That is, when Nature gives way. The world gets dark and you have to feel around with your hands, and everything keeps slipping, like in a spider's web. That's the way it is when something's there but really isn't, when it's all dark with only a red glow in the west, like from a furnace. [*He paces the room.*]

DOCTOR. You feel around with your feet as if you were a spider!

WOYZECK. Doctor, did you ever see anything with a double nature? When the sun stops at noon, and it's like the whole world's caught on fire? That's when a terrible voice spoke to me.

DOCTOR. Woyzeck, you have an *aberratio*.

WOYZECK. [*Putting his finger to his nose.*] In the toadstools, doctor, that's where it is. Did you ever notice the signs toadstools make growing in the grass? If only you could figure out what they mean!

DOCTOR. Woyzeck, you have the most beautiful *aberratio mentalis partialis*, secondary order, nicely developed. Woyzeck, you're getting a raise. *Idée fixe*, of the second highest rank, but with a tractable disposition. Doing everything as usual? Shaving the Captain?

WOYZECK. Yes sir.

DOCTOR. Eating your peas?

WOYZECK. Everything's regular, doctor. The money goes to Marie for the house.

DOCTOR. Going on duty?

WOYZECK. Yes, sir.

DOCTOR. You're an interesting case. Woyzeck, you're getting a raise. Behave yourself. Let's feel your pulse. Yes.

8 Marie's Room

MARIE, *the* DRUM-MAJOR.

DRUM-MAJOR. Marie!

MARIE. [*Looking at him intently.*] Stand up there!—a chest like a bull and a beard like a lion. In a class by himself—no woman is prouder than I am.

DRUM-MAJOR. But Sunday, when I'm wearing my white gloves and the hat with the plume in it, hot damn! The Prince always says, "By God, there's a real man!"

MARIE. [*Mockingly.*] Does he? [*Steps up before him.*] A real man!

DRUM-MAJOR. And you're a real piece of woman, too. Hell's bells, let's raise a race of Drum-Majors. Eh? [*He embraces her.*]

MARIE. [*Moody.*] Let me go!

DRUM-MAJOR. You wildcat!

MARIE. [*Violently.*] Just touch me!

DRUM-MAJOR. You've got the devil in your eyes.

MARIE. What's the difference?

9 The Street

The CAPTAIN, *the* DOCTOR. *The* CAPTAIN *comes panting along the streets, stops, pants, looks around.*

CAPTAIN. Don't run so fast, Doctor. Stop paddling your cane in the air like that. You're chasing your own death. A good man, with a clear conscience, doesn't run so fast. A good man . . . [*He seizes the* DOCTOR *by the coat.*] Doctor, permit me to save a human life.

DOCTOR. I'm in a hurry, Captain, a hurry.

CAPTAIN. Doctor, I'm feeling low. I get so sentimental. When I look at my coat hanging on the wall, I start crying.

DOCTOR. Puffy, fat, thick neck, apoplectic constitution. You're headed straight for *Apoplexia Cerebria*. You'll probably just get it on one side. Paralyzed down one side. Or, if you're lucky, just lose your mental faculties and go on vegetating. Those are your prospects for the next four weeks. I can assure you, you'll be a most interesting case. And if God wills that your tongue only gets half paralyzed, our experiments are immortal.

CAPTAIN. Don't frighten me, Doctor. People have died of fright, just plain fright!—I can see them already, with flowers in their hands. But they'll say: He was a good man, a good man—you coffin-nail devil!

DOCTOR. [*Showing him his hat.*] Do you know who that is, Captain? That's Mr. Emptyhead, my dear Drill-killer.

CAPTAIN. [*Showing a button hole.*] Do you know who this is, Doctor? That's Mr. Hole-in-the-Head, my dear Coffin-nail. Hahahaha! No harm meant. I'm a good man, but I can play that game too. [WOYZECK *tries to hurry past.*] Hey, Woyzeck! Where are you rushing? Hang on, Woyzeck. Why, he runs through the world like an open razor, you could cut yourself on him. He runs as if he had a regiment of eunuchs to shave and would be hung while the last hair was being cut. But what about long beards, Woyzeck? How shall I put it? Woyzeck, long beards . . .

DOCTOR. A long chin beard. Now Pliny mentions that, how soldiers should be broken of the habit.

CAPTAIN. [*Continuing.*] Ah, yes, long beards. Woyzeck, how come you haven't found the hair from a beard in your soup bowl? Eh? You get it? The hair from an engineer's beard? A noncommissioned officer's? A Drum-Major's? Eh, Woyzeck? But you've got a good woman. Not like the others.

WOYZECK. Yes sir. What do you mean, sir?

CAPTAIN. What a face the man's making. Well, perhaps not in the soup, but if you run around the corner, maybe you can still find a pair of lips. A pair of lips, Woyzeck! I too have felt the love itch, Woyzeck. Why, you're white as chalk.

WOYZECK. Captain, I'm just a poor devil, and I have nothing else in the world. Captain, if you're joking . . .

CAPTAIN. Joking? Joking with you, Woyzeck?

DOCTOR. Your pulse, Woyzeck, your pulse. Short, hard, jerky, irregular.

WOYZECK. Captain, the earth is hot like hell, but to me it's ice cold, ice cold. Hell is cold. You want to bet? Impossible! God! God! Impossible!

CAPTAIN. Soldier, do you—do you want a couple of bullets in your head? You keep stabbing at me with those eyes, but I'm trying to help you, because you're a good man, Woyzeck, a good man.

DOCTOR. Facial muscles rigid, tense, occasionally jumpy. Disposition excitable, tense.

WOYZECK. I'm going. Anything can happen. God! Anything can happen. It's nice weather, Captain. A fine, clear, gray sky. A man could almost want to hammer a nail up there and hang himself on it. Just on account of that little dash between yes, and yes again, and no. Yes and no, Captain? Is no yes's fault? Or yes no's? I'll think it over. [*He leaves, taking long steps, slowly at first, then faster and faster.*]

DOCTOR. A phenomenon. [*Calling after him.*] Woyzeck, a raise!

CAPTAIN. These people make me dizzy. So fast. You know, a good man takes care of himself. A good man doesn't have courage. Only a mongrel bitch has courage. I joined the army to show myself that I have no courage.

10 Marie's Room

MARIE, WOYZECK.

WOYZECK. [*Staring straight at her and shaking his head.*] Hm! I can't see it. I

can't see it. You should be able to. You should be able to hold it in your fist.
MARIE. [*Frightened.*] What is it, Franz? You're raving, Franz.
WOYZECK. A sin, so big, and so wide. It should stink, until the angels are smoked out of heaven. You have a red mouth, Marie. No blisters on it? Marie, you're as beautiful as sin—but can mortal sin be so beautiful?
MARIE. Franz, you're talking like you had a fever.
WOYZECK. Hell! Did he stand here? Like this? Like this?
MARIE. The world is old and the day is long, so lots of people can stand in the same place, one after the other.
WOYZECK. I saw him!
MARIE. There's a lot you can see if you have two eyes, you're not blind, and the sun is shining.
WOYZECK. You whore! [*He goes for her.*]
MARIE. Just touch me, Franz! I'd rather have a knife in my ribs than your hands on me. At ten, my father didn't dare touch me. I only had to look at him.
WOYZECK. Bitch! No, it should show on you. Each one of us is a precipice. You get dizzy when you look down.— There should be! She's innocence itself. All right, innocence. You bear the mark on you. Do I know it though? Do I know it? Who does?

11 The Guard House

(Where the sentries congregate.)

WOYZECK, ANDRES.
ANDRES. [*Singing.*]

Our hostess has a merry maid,
She sits in the garden night and day,
She sits within her garden.

WOYZECK. Andres!
ANDRES. Huh?
WOYZECK. Nice weather.
ANDRES. Sunny Sunday weather. Music outside town, the bitches already there, the men sweating. Great stuff.
WOYZECK. [*Restless.*] Dancing, Andres! They're dancing!
ANDRES. At the Horse and the Star.
WOYZECK. Dancing! Dancing!
ANDRES. I don't care.

She sits within her garden,
Till twelve o'clock has chimed away,
And the infantry comes mar-arching.

WOYZECK. Andres, I can't calm down.
ANDRES. Fool!
WOYZECK. I've got to get out. It keeps turning in front of my eyes. Dancing! Dancing! Her hands will be hot. Damn her, Andres!
ANDRES. What do you want?
WOYZECK. I've got to go, got to see for myself.
ANDRES. You lunatic. On account of that bitch?
WOYZECK. I've got to get out, it's so hot in here.

12 An Inn

The windows open. Dancing. Benches in front of the house. APPRENTICES.
FIRST APPRENTICE.

This little shirt I'm wearing is not mine,
And my soul it stinks of brandy wine.

SECOND APPRENTICE. Hey, brother, let me knock a hole in your nature for friendship's sake. Forward! I'll knock a hole in his nature. I'm just as big a man, you know, and I'll slaughter ever flea on his body.
FIRST APPRENTICE. "And my soul, my soul, it stinks of brandy wine." Even money falls into decay. Forget me not, how beautiful the world is! Brother, I could fill a rain barrel with tears. I wish our noses were bottles, so we could pour them down each other's throat.
OTHERS. [*In chorus.*]

A hunter from the Rhine
Was riding through the forest fine.
Hallee, hallo, how merry are the hunting men,

*Roaming the fields so free.
A hunting life for me.*
   [WOYZECK *posts himself by the window.*
   MARIE *and the* DRUM-MAJOR *dance by,
   without noticing him.*]
WOYZECK. Him and her! Damn it to hell!
MARIE. [*Dancing by.*] Don't stop! Don't stop!
WOYZECK. [*Choking.*] Don't stop! [*He jumps up and falls back on the bench.*] Don't stop! Don't stop! [*Pounding his hands.*] Turn around! Roll on! Why doesn't God blow out the sun so they can all roll on top of each other in filth? Male and Female! Man and Beast! They'll do it on your hands, like flies! Women! That woman is hot, hot! Don't stop! [*He jumps up.*] That bastard! Look how he's feeling her up—all over her body! He's, he's got her—like I did at first. [*He slumps down, bewildered.*]
ANDRES. What are you doing here?
WOYZECK. What time is it?
ANDRES. Almost ten.
WOYZECK. I thought it was later. It should go faster.
ANDRES. Why?
WOYZECK. So it'd be over.
ANDRES. What?
WOYZECK. The fun.
ANDRES. What are you sitting by the door for?
WOYZECK. It's fine here. Some people don't know they're near the door until they're dragged out, feet first.
ANDRES. Come on with us.
WOYZECK. It's fine here.
ANDRES. You're drunk. [*He leaves with the others.*]
WOYZECK. Not enough.
FIRST APPRENTICE. [*Preaching from a table.*] Nevertheless, consider the wanderer who standeth learning by the stream of time, answereth himself with the wisdom of God, and asketh: What is Man? What is Man? Yea, verily I say unto you, On what would the farmer, the cooper, the cobbler, and the doctor live—if God had not created Man? How would the tailor live—if God had not planted a sense of modesty in men? How would the soldier live—if God had not equipped him with the urge to slaughter himself? Therefore, doubt not, everything is sweet and lovely. Yet everything on earth is evil, even money falls into decay! In conclusion, my beloved, let us now piss crisscross, so that somewhere a Jew will die. [*In the middle of the general howling* WOYZECK *wakes up.*]
FOOL. It smells.
WOYZECK. Yes, it smells! She had a red, red mouth. Is that what you smell?
FOOL. I smell blood.
WOYZECK. Blood! Everything's going red before my eyes. Like they were all rolling on top of each other in a sea of it!

13   An Open Field

WOYZECK. Don't stop! Don't stop! Hish! Hash! That's the way the flutes and fiddles go. Don't stop! Don't stop! No more music! Who's talking under there? [*He stretches out on the ground.*] What? What are you saying? Louder! Louder! Stab, stab the bitch of a goat-wolf dead? Stab, stab the bitch of a goat-wolf dead? Should I? Must I? Is it out there, too? Is the wind saying it, too? The words don't stop! Don't stop! Stab her dead! Dead!

14   A Room in the Barracks

Night. ANDRES *and* WOYZECK *in one bed.*
WOYZECK. [*Softly.*] Andres!
ANDRES. [*Murmurs in his sleep.*]
WOYZECK. [*Shaking* ANDRES.] Hey, Andres! Andres!
ANDRES. What do you want?
WOYZECK. I can't sleep. When I close my eyes, everything turns around

and I hear the fiddles saying: Don't stop! Don't stop! Then it comes out of the wall, too. Don't you hear anything?
ANDRES. Sure. Let them dance. A man gets tired. God bless us all. Amen.
WOYZECK. It keeps saying: Stab! Stab! And it pulls my eyes open, like a knife. A big, thick knife, lying on a counter in a dark narrow street, with an old man sitting behind it. That's the knife I keep seeing in front of my eyes.
ANDRES. You ought to drink some schnaps with a powder in it. That cuts the fever.
WOYZECK. Don't stop! Don't stop!
ANDRES. Go to sleep, you fool! [*He goes to sleep.*]

15   The Courtyard at the Doctor's

STUDENTS *and* WOYZECK *below, the* DOCTOR *at the garret window.*
DOCTOR. Gentlemen, I am on the roof like David when he beheld Bathsheba, but I behold only the Parisian panties of the boarding-school girls, drying in the garden. Gentlemen, we have come to the important problem of the relation between the object and the subject. Now, if we select just one of the creatures in which appears the highest organic self-affirmation of the Divine Spirit, and explore its relation to space, earth, and the planetary constellations . . . Gentlemen, if I throw this cat out the window, how will this organism react with respect to its center of gravity—its *centrum gravitationis*—and its own instincts? Hey, Woyzeck! [*Roaring.*] Woyzeck!
WOYZECK. [*Picking up the cat.*] Doctor, she's biting me!
DOCTOR. Numbskull! He handles the beast as tenderly as his grandmother. [*He comes down.*]
WOYZECK. Doctor, I've got the shakes.
DOCTOR. [*Quite delighted.*] Oh, fine, fine, Woyzeck! [*Rubs his hands. Takes the cat.*] What is this, gentlemen? A new species of chicken lice? A fine species. [*He takes out a magnifying glass. The cat gets away.*] Gentlemen, that animal has no scientific instincts! However, here's something better for you to examine. Just look at this man. For three months, he's eaten nothing but peas. Note the result. Just feel him! What an irregular pulse. And those eyes!
WOYZECK. Everything's getting black, Doctor. [*He sits down.*]
DOCTOR. Courage, Woyzeck! A couple of days and it will be over. Feel that pulse, gentlemen, feel it. [*The students fumble over his pulse, temples, and chest.*] Incidentally, Woyzeck, wiggle your ears for the gentlemen. I've been intending to show you this. He does it with two muscles. Come on, snap into it!
WOYZECK. Doctor! Oh!
DOCTOR. You brute, do I have to wiggle your ears for you? Are you going to behave like that cat? Well, gentlemen, here's a case of evolution into a donkey, which is frequently the consequence of being brought up by women. How much of your hair has your sentimental old mother been pulling out for souvenirs? It's gotten quite thin the last couple of days. Yes, gentlemen, it's those peas!

16   The Barracks Yard

WOYZECK. Heard nothing?
ANDRES. He is still in there with a pal.
WOYZECK. He said something.
ANDRES. How do you know? What do you want me to say? Well, he laughed, and he said: A luscious piece! What thighs! And red hot!
WOYZECK. [*Quite coldly.*] So that's what he said? What was I dreaming last night? Something about a knife?

What crazy dreams you can have.
ANDRES. Where you going, pal?
WOYZECK. Getting wine for my Captain. You know, Andres, she was one girl in a thousand.
ANDRES. Who was?
WOYZECK. Never mind. So long.

17 The Inn

DRUM-MAJOR. WOYZECK. PEOPLE.
DRUM-MAJOR. I'm a real man! [*Pounds his chest.*] A real man, see? Anyone looking for something? Anyone who isn't drunk as the Lord better let me alone or I'll smash his nose up his arsehole for him. I'll—[*To* WOYZECK.] Hey, you lout, get drunk! I wish the whole world was schnaps, schnaps. That guy better start drinking.
WOYZECK. [*Whistles.*]
DRUM-MAJOR. You lout! You want me to yank your tongue out of your throat and wrap it round your ribs? [*They wrestle.* WOYZECK *loses.*] You want me to leave you enough wind for an old lady's fart? Do you?
WOYZECK. [*Sits on a bench, trembling and exhausted.*]
DRUM-MAJOR. The bastard can whistle himself blue in the face.

Brandy is the drink for me
Brandy keeps your fancy free.

SOMEONE. He sure got his.
ANDRES. He's bleeding.
WOYZECK. One thing after the other.

18 Pawnshop

WOYZECK. *The* JEW.
WOYZECK. The pistol's too much.
JEW. So, are you buying or not buying? Make up your mind?
WOYZECK. How much was the knife?
JEW. It's good and sharp. Going to cut your throat with it? Make up your mind. I'm giving it to you cheap as anybody. You can die cheap, but not for nothing.
WOYZECK. It'll cut more than bread . . .
JEW. Two groschen.
WOYZECK. Here! [*Goes out.*]
JEW. Here! Like it was nothing. And it's good money! The pig!

19 Marie's Room

FOOL. [*Stretched out, telling fairy tales on his fingers.*] This one has a golden crown. He's Our Lord the King. Tomorrow I'll bring Her Royal Highness the Queen her child. . . . Pork Sausage says, "Come on, Liverwurst . . ."
MARIE. [*Leafing through the Bible.*] "And no guile is found in his mouth." Lord God, Lord God, don't look at me! [*Leafs again.*] "And the scribes and the Pharisees brought unto him a woman taken in adultery, and set her in the midst . . . And Jesus said unto her, 'Neither do I condemn thee; go, and sin no more.'" Lord God, Lord God, I can't—Lord God, give me the strength to pray! [*The child cuddles up to her.*] The child stabs me to the heart. [*To the* FOOL.] Karl! Strutting in the sun! [*The* FOOL *takes the child and becomes quiet.*] Franz hasn't been here yesterday or today. It's getting hot in here. [*She opens the window.*] "And stood at his feet weeping, and began to wash his feet with tears, and did wipe them with the hairs of her head, and kissed his feet, and annointed them with ointment." [*Beats her breast.*] Everything's dead. Saviour, Saviour! If only I could annoint Thy feet!

20 Barracks

ANDRES. WOYZECK *rummaging through his belongings.*
WOYZECK. This jacket isn't regular issue, Andres. You might be able to use it, Andres.
WOYZECK. [*Quite rigid, keeps saying.*] Sure.
WOYZECK. This cross was my sister's. The little ring, too.
ANDRES. Sure.
WOYZECK. I've got a Holy picture, with two hearts, pure gold—it was in my mother's Bible, and it said:

Lord, like thy body, red and sore,
So let my heart be, evermore.

My mother can't feel much any more, only when the sun shines on her hands. That doesn't matter.
ANDRES. Sure.
WOYZECK. [*Pulls out a document.*] Private Friedrich Johann Franz Woyzeck, Rifleman, 2nd Regiment, 2nd Battalion, Company Four. Born Feast of the Annunciation, July 20th. I'm thirty years, seven months, and twelve days old.
ANDRES. Franz, why don't you go on sick-call? You poor guy, you ought to get some schnaps with a powder in it. It'd kill the fever.
WOYZECK. Yes, Andres. When the carpenter puts that wooden box together, you never know whose head is going to lie in it.

21 The Street

MARIE, *with little girls, in front of the door.*
OLD WOMAN. *Later* WOYZECK.
GIRLS.

The sun shines bright at Candlemas.
The corn is in full bloom.
They danced across the meadow grass,
They danced it two by two.
The flutes, they marched ahead,
The fiddles in the rear,
Their stockings were the reddest red . . .

FIRST GIRL. Aw, that's no good.
SECOND GIRL. You always want to do something different.
FIRST GIRL. Marie, you sing for us.
MARIE. I can't.
FIRST GIRL. Why Not?
MARIE. Because.
SECOND GIRL. But why because?
THIRD GIRL. Grandma, tell a story.
OLD WOMAN. All right, you little crabs. Once upon a time there was a poor little girl who had no father or mother because everyone was dead and there was no one left in the whole world. Everyone was dead, and she went off and kept looking for someone night and day. And since there was no one on earth, she thought she'd go to heaven. The moon looked out at her so friendly, but when she finally got to it, it was just a piece of rotted wood. So she went on to the sun, and when she got there, it was just a dried up sunflower. And when she got to the stars, they were just little gold flies stuck up there as if they'd been caught in a spider web. And when she thought she'd go back to earth, it was just an upside down pot. And she was all alone. And so she sat down and cried. And she's still sitting there, all alone.
WOYZECK. [*Appears.*] Marie!
MARIE. [*Frightened.*] What?
WOYZECK. Marie, it's time to go.
MARIE. Where to?
WOYZECK. You think I know?

22 A Woodland Path by a Pond

MARIE *and* WOYZECK.
MARIE. The town's that way. It's dark.
WOYZECK. You're not going. Come on, sit down.
MARIE. But I have to go.

WOYZECK. Your feet will get sore running.
MARIE. You're so changed.
WOYZECK. Do you know how long it's been, Marie?
MARIE. Two years, Pentecost.
WOYZECK. Do you know how long it will last?
MARIE. I have to go and get supper.
WOYZECK. You're not freezing, Marie? No, you're warm. You've got hot lips. Hot! A hot whore's breath! And I'd still give heaven to kiss them again. Are you freezing? When your bones are cold, you don't freeze anymore. You won't freeze in the morning dew.
MARIE. What are you saying?
WOYZECK. Nothing. [*Silence.*]
MARIE. The moon's rising. It's red.
WOYZECK. Like a sword with blood on it!
MARIE. What are you going to do, Franz? You're so pale. [*He raises the knife.*] Franz, stop! For Heaven's sake! Help! Help!
WOYZECK. [*Stabbing madly.*] Take that, and that! Why can't you die? There! There! Ha! She's twitching. Still can't? Still twitching? [*Stabs again.*] Now are you dead? Dead! Dead! [*He drops the knife and runs away.*]

23   The Inn

WOYZECK. Dance, everyone dance! Don't stop! Sweat and stink! He'll get all of you in the end. [*Sings.*]

*Oh, daughter, darling daughter,
You thought it no harm
When you hung around with stable boys
And the coachmen in the barn.*

[*He dances.*] Whew, Käthe! Sit down. I'm hot, hot! [*He takes off his coat.*] That's the way it goes. The devil takes one and lets the other get away. Käthe, you're hot. How come? You'll cool off now too, Kathë. Be reasonable. Can't you sing something?
KÄTHE. [*Sings.*]

*To Swabia I'll never go,
And dresses wear down to my toe.
For dresses long and pointed shoes
A servant girl should never choose.*

WOYZECK. No, no shoes. You can get into Hell without shoes.
KÄTHE. [*Sings.*]

*No, no, my love, that was not right.
Take back your gold, sleep single tonight.*

WOYZECK. That's true. I don't want to get any blood on me.
KÄTHE. But what's that on your hand?
WOYZECK. On me? Me?
KÄTHE. Red! Blood! [*People gather round.*]
WOYZECK. Blood? Blood?
INNKEEPER. Ugh! Blood!
WOYZECK. I think, I cut myself. There, on my right hand.
INNKEEPER. How come it's on your elbow?
WOYZECK. I wiped it off.
INNKEEPER. Wiped your right hand on your right elbow? You have talent!
FOOL. And the Giant said: I smell, I smell. What do I smell? A man, a man who's bound for Hell! Pah! it stinks already!
WOYZECK. What the devil do you all want? What business is it of yours? Out of my way, or the first one who . . . Hell, do you think I did away with someone? Am I a murderer? What are you gaping at? Gawk at yourselves! Get out of my way! [*He runs off.*]

24   At the Pond

WOYZECK *alone.*
WOYZECK. The knife? Where's the knife? I left it here. It'll give me away. Nearer. Nearer yet. What place is this? What's that I hear? Something moving! No, it's quiet. Over there. Marie? Ha, Marie! You're quiet. Everything's quiet! What are you so white for, Marie? What's that red string around your neck? Who did

your sins earn that necklace from? You were black with them, black! Did I bleach you white again? Why is your black hair hanging so wild? Didn't you braid your long braids today? Here's something! Cold and wet, and still. The knife! the knife! Got it? Get rid of it! [*He runs into the water.*] There! Down it goes. [*He throws the knife in.*] It dives down into the water like a stone. The moon's like a sword with blood on it! Is the whole world going to gab about it? No, it's lying too close. When they're swimming.... [*He goes into the pond and throws it further.*] There, that's it! But, in the summer, when they're diving for mussels? Bah! it'll be rusty. Who'd recognize it—I should have broken it. Am I still bloody? I better wash up. There's a spot and there's another. [*Goes deeper into the water. Time passes. People come up.*]

FIRST PERSON. Wait up!
SECOND PERSON. You hear? Shh! Over there!
FIRST PERSON. Ugh! Over there. What a sound!
SECOND PERSON. It's the water, calling. It's been a long time since anyone was drowned. Let's go, it's not a pleasant thing to hear.
FIRST PERSON. Ugh! There it is again! Like a man, dying.
SECOND PERSON. It's eerie. So foggy, that gray mist everywhere, and the bugs humming like broken bells. Let's go!
FIRST PERSON. Wait! It's too clear, too loud. It's up there. Come on!

25   The Street

CHILDREN.
FIRST CHILD. Let's go look at Marie!
SECOND CHILD. What for?
FIRST CHILD. Don't you know? Everybody's gone out there. [*To* MARIE'S CHILD.] Hey, your mother's dead.
MARIE'S CHILD. [*Playing horsey.*] Giddyap, giddyap!
SECOND CHILD. Where is she?
FIRST CHILD. On the path to the pond.
SECOND CHILD. Hurry up! Let's get there before they bring her back.
MARIE'S CHILD. Giddyap, giddyap!

26   At the Pond

COURT CLERK. DOCTOR. JUDGE.
POLICEMAN. A real murder, a first-rate murder, a beautiful murder. As beautiful a little murder as you could ask for. It's a long time since we had one like this.

The Glass of Water

Eugène Scribe

Augustin Eugène Scribe is one of the more remarkable figures the European theater has produced. Hailed and acclaimed during his lifetime as a playwright wildly popular with the public, he has been vilified and derided since his death, blamed for all the shortcomings of the playwrights who came after him. Neither position is completely fair, for Scribe's popularity was exaggerated because of his deft manipulation of theatrical elements in order to appeal to the widest possible range of his middle-class audience, whereas his mastery of dramatic form as embodied in the "well-made play" was a legacy of incalculable importance to major writers such as Shaw and Ibsen as well as to countless hack playwrights whose potboiling works gave the well-made play a bad image. Scribe was not a great playwright, but he was a technician of genius whose work profoundly influenced the realistic playwrights of the nineteenth century and thus the development of the theater ever since.

Eugène Scribe was born in Paris on December 24, 1791, the son of a silk merchant. The father died in 1798, leaving sufficient wealth to maintain his wife and three children in modest but comfortable circumstances. As the youngest child, Eugène received only a small share of this inheritance, but he was well educated (achieving a brilliant record) at the Collège Sainte-Barbe and was destined for a legal career. His mother died in 1807, and Eugène, although nominally continuing his study of the law for several years thereafter, was in fact able to give more and more of his time to the theater. In collaboration with a friend, Scribe began to write *vaudevilles,* short verse plays with music that were a popular form of entertainment and that were to become the mainstay of his writing career. After several unsuccessful attempts, Scribe opened his first *vaudeville* on September 2, 1811, and within a few years was an established and much sought after author in this form. He was also a shrewd businessman, who used his newfound success to persuade management to grant, in addition to an initial cash payment, a royalty on box office receipts to the authors of all *vaudevilles* as well as plays. A catalog of Scribe's work lists 216 of these *vaudevilles,* most written with collaborators to whom Scribe scrupulously gave credit, though his own name on the work (and his skill in the structure) was its principal guarantee of success.

In Scribe's fifty-year career in the Parisian theater, he lived through a period of social upheaval and revolution both politically and artistically. The rise and fall of successive French governments did not significantly affect Scribe's activity; his works had little thematic content and reflected the society about him only in a frivolous and finally insignificant way. Similarly, the stirring of romanticism abroad, its eventual taking of Paris by storm with Hugo's epoch-making production of *Hernani* in 1830 (a poor play by today's standards, but a shattering event in its own time), and the gradual replacement of romanticism by realism, all left Scribe relatively untouched. His audience had little interest in the avant-garde, but sought simply light entertainment, and Scribe became a master at providing it. Attaching himself by contract to a *vaudeville* theater for which he sometimes wrote more than a dozen pieces a year, Scribe also turned his attention to light opera, ballet, and comic opera, writing 123 works in these genres.

Most important for consideration here are Scribe's legitimate plays, many of which he wrote for the Théâtre-Français and which represent the highest level of his artistic achievement. He wrote thirty-five such plays, beginning in 1816 and continuing at one or two-year intervals. Besides *The Glass of Water,* his only other work that need be mentioned here is *Adrienne Lecouvreur* (1849), which was atypical in being Scribe's only attempt at tragedy but which is still occasionally revived with success. Between 1823 and 1900, the Théâtre-Français staged more performances of Scribe's plays than of those of any other nineteenth-century playwright. These legitimate plays were for the most part light comedies and historical dramas, for Scribe never forgot the lessons he had learned in the *vaudeville* theater about keeping an audience entertained. Scribe evidenced little sense of literary style, little interest in profound thematic content, and little talent at creating complex characterizations or gaining deep insight into human nature. What he did accomplish superlatively was the structuring of theatrically effective plots out of nearly any subject matter that came to his hand, so that the "well-made play" became almost a formula that could be applied to plays for the Théâtre-Français as well as to *vaudevilles*. Scribe viewed the theater as a business and measured his own success in terms of box-office income; although this attitude strikes some as crassly commercial, it cannot be divorced totally from the fact that the cooperative presence of an audience is indeed essential for the theatrical event to take place. Alexandre Dumas *fils* once noted that the writer who understood the stage as did Scribe and the human heart as did Balzac would be a truly great dramatist.

Scribe was elected to the Académie Française in 1836. He was a major figure in all the theater capitals in Europe through the middle years of the nineteenth century. He married a widow in 1839, owned several estates, worked indefatigably throughout his lifetime, and was widely known for his generosity both with creative advice and help and with money. He died in Paris on February 20, 1861, of a sudden attack while on his way to a business appointment; his funeral was attended by over three thousand Parisians.

Because the content of Scribe's plays was so often trivial, their form has sometimes not received the attention it deserves. Scribe created an action-packed plot, based on frequent surprises and reversals, but tightly organized around a single central action and always logically consistent from beginning to end. Lesser playwrights that came after him reduced this approach to formula and ground out thousands of claptrap plays that filled the popular theaters in their own day and whose equivalents are the mainstay of commercial television today. Writers of greater merit, such as Ibsen and Shaw, decried this cheap commercialism but used Scribe's forms in a great many of their finest works. The tenets of the well-made play were taught in the early twentieth century as the right way to write any play; current theory encourages far wider options and experimentation, but many of the most successful modern writers still use what is fundamentally the well-made play form. Briefly, this form entails well-organized and logical exposition at the beginning of the play, followed by an inciting incident that gets the single central action under way. Complications are introduced through the rising action, leading to a turning point that determines the final outcome. After the turning point, falling action works out the complications that were earlier introduced, while at the same time these logical progressions build toward a climax in which the central action is finally resolved. A denouement then follows in which any remaining tangles are unraveled and any loose ends tied up. The essence of the form is an appearance of realism—a logically connected series of events that may in fact be contrived but that convinces an audience to accept them as natural. The more credulity is strained, the less effectively the form works. Scribe often built his plots around relatively unimportant actions, showing how great events might result from trifling causes. A commonplace prop or a trivial incident might thus become of major importance, as the business surrounding the glass of water provides the turning point of *The Glass of Water*. Dramatic irony abounds in such plots, as misunderstandings between characters are understood and enjoyed by the audience in eager anticipation of their resolution. Throughout all this manipulation, Scribe was a master at holding his audience's interest while not unduly straining their credulity; his plays "work" in the theater.

The Glass of Water, which opened at the Théâtre-Français on November 17, 1840, is an excellent example of Scribe's typical technique; it also happens to be among the four or five best plays he wrote and is occasionally revived today. Unlike plays with more thoughtful thematic content, which usually raise more questions than they answer, *The Glass of Water* advances a single, rather simplistic, thesis: that results of major historical importance often follow from apparently trivial causes. Bolingbroke clearly states this thesis early in the play and procedes to illustrate it in the events that follow. The central action of the play is simply to marry Masham to Abigail; the great historical events that are made to flow from this conflict are embellishments of that simple action. The key events from which the play takes its title are even more trivial, but Scribe shows how the Queen's seemingly simple request for a glass of water radically affects the lives of those about her and ultimately the fate of several nations. The events of the play amply illustrate the features of the well-made play outlined above, with the spectators' interest held by the give-and-take of political struggle and the ups-and-downs of the hero's fortune. Eventually the typical well-made play came to be written in three acts, but Scribe applied his principles equally well within any number; since five was still the classical standard in France at the time, he often wrote in five acts.

Although *The Glass of Water* is loosely based on historical occurrences, no serious knowledge of history is required to understand it. All of the play's principal characters actually lived, but Scribe changes their ages, their natures, and some of the events that happen to them in order to serve his plot. The play takes place in 1710, at which time Queen Anne was actually forty-five years old and a widow. The Duchess of Marlborough had been her girlhood friend, and it was through her influence that her husband rose to high political and military position, but he was eventually caught lining his own pockets. The Duchess in fact introduced her distant cousin Abigail Hill (not Churchill) to the Queen, only to see her eventually displace the Duchess as the Queen's favorite. It was through Abigail's influence that her husband, Samuel Masham, was created a baron. Queen Anne was weak and vascillating, but the treaty of Utrecht resulted from significant political causes, not from the Queen's dallying with any court lover. The love intrigues in the play are entirely the invention of the playwright. Bolingbroke was Tory secretary of war from 1710 to 1714, but was so opposed to the Hanover succession to the throne that he had to leave England after Queen Anne's death in 1714.

Scribe breathes enough life into these historical characters to make them viable on the stage, but he depends on the actors to give them any genuine distinction. Queen Anne is somewhat more interesting than the rest, but by and large they are two-dimensional figures jumping through the hoops of the plot. The thesis is simplistic and the language is overblown (the translation consciously retains that quality), but the play can still be entertaining theater because of its sprightly and well-contrived plot. Scribe need not be overpraised as anything more than a brilliant technician, but that distinction should not be denied him. His influence on the further development of the European theater has been profound.

The Glass of Water
or
Effects and Causes
(Le Verre d'Eau)

Translated by Sharon Parsell

Characters
Henry Saint John, Viscount Bolingbroke
Masham, ensign in the guards
The Marquis de Torcy, envoy of Louis XIV
Thompson, court usher
A Member of Parliament
Queen Anne
The Duchess of Marlborough, the Queen's favorite
Abigail, The Duchess of Marlborough's cousin
Lady Albemarle
Members of Parliament, Lords and Ladies of the Court

SCENE: *London, the Court of Saint James*

Act 1

A luxurious salon in the palace of Saint James—a door at the rear, two side doors—a table on the left—on the right, a pedestal table. DE TORCY *and* BOLINGBROKE *enter from the left.* MASHAM *is asleep in a chair, near the door on the right.*

BOLINGBROKE. Certainly, Marquis, your letter will reach the Queen. Don't worry, I will find a way, and it will be received with the honor due a letter from your great king.
DE TORCY. My trust is in you, Milord. My honor and the honor of France depend upon your loyalty.
BOLINGBROKE. Your trust is not misplaced. They say that Henry Saint John is a libertine, a rake with a quick, capricious temper, a passionate writer and a hot headed orator; and that's how I want it. No one can say that I have ever sold my influence or betrayed a friend.
DE TORCY. I know that, and for that reason I put my trust in you. [*He exits.*]
BOLINGBROKE. Oh, the fortunes of war and the destiny of conquering kings! De Torcy blocked from an audience with Queen Anne! He's reduced to sending a diplomatic note in the guise of a love letter. Poor de Torcy; should his negotiations fail, he'll die of shame. How he loves his old sovereign who still flatters himself by seeking an honorable and glorious peace. Old age is the age of error.
MASHAM. [*Dreaming.*] Oh! What a beauty!
BOLINGBROKE. And youth the age of illusion. Here's a young man to whom good things come in his sleep.
MASHAM. [*As before.*] Oh, I love you . . . I will always love you.
BOLINGBROKE. He's dreaming, poor fellow! Eh! It's young Masham; I'm among friends.
MASHAM. [*Still dreaming.*] What a blessing! What wonderful luck! It's too much for me.

BOLINGBROKE. [*Hitting him on the shoulder.*] In that case, my boy, let's share it!

MASHAM. [*Rising and rubbing his eyes.*] What? What is it? Sir, you woke me up.

BOLINGBROKE. [*Laughing.*] And ruined you also!

MASHAM. You! To whom I owe everything. A poor school boy, a poor provincial, lost in London. Two years ago I wanted to throw myself in the Thames because of twenty-five guineas, and you gave me two hundred . . . which I still owe you.

BOLINGBROKE. By God! My boy, I would happily be in your shoes, and gladly trade places with you.

MASHAM. But whatever for?

BOLINGBROKE. Because I owe a hundred times that amount.

MASHAM. Heavens! You've been unlucky.

BOLINGBROKE. Not at all! I'm ruined, that's all. But these last five years have been the happiest and freest of my life. During earlier years, rich and sated by pleasure, I went through my inheritance. I didn't concern myself with the consequences, and at twenty-six, I was a pauper.

MASHAM. Can it be?

BOLINGBROKE. I couldn't have ruined myself any faster. To put my affairs in order, I married a charming lady—impossible to live with—a million in her dowry, not to mention her faults and caprices. I returned the dowry. I would win it back! My wife shone at Court. She was in Marlborough's camp, a Whig. You see now why I became a Tory. I threw myself into the Opposition: I owed her that much; I owe her my happiness because from that day on my instincts and vocation were revealed. It was danger that my restless, inactive soul missed. In our political tournaments, in our thunderings from the gallery, I breathe, I am at peace, like a sailor at sea—at home, in my element, in my empire. Good fortune is movement, misfortune is rest! Twenty times in my idle youth and especially during my marriage I had, as you have, the idea of killing myself.

MASHAM. What!

BOLINGBROKE. Yes . . . on those days when I had to take my wife to a ball. Now, I am eager to be at Court and would hate to leave. Now I don't have enough time, not a moment to myself—a member of the House of Commons, a respected journalist. I speak in the morning and write at night. In vain does the Whig government overwhelm us with its triumphs. In vain does it dominate England and Europe. Only a few of us continue the opposition, for the vanquished often trouble the sleep of the vanquisher. Lord Marlborough, at the head of his army, trembling before a speech of Henry Saint John or an article in *The Examiner*. He has on his side Prince Eugene, Holland, and 500,000 men. I have on my side Swift, Prior, and Atterbury. For him, the sword! For us, the press! We shall see to whom the victory goes. The illustrious and miserly Marshal uses war to drain the public treasury and fill his own pockets! For my part, I want peace and industry, which will bring prosperity to England sooner than conquests. The Queen, Parliament, and the country must be made to understand this.

MASHAM. It won't be easy.

BOLINGBROKE. No, because brutal, physical force, success forced by cannons, so stuns the populace that it never occurs to them that a conquering general could be a fool—and Marlborough is one! I will expose his victorious hand slipping furtively through the public coffers.

MASHAM. You dare not!

BOLINGBROKE. I have written it, I have signed it. The article is there. I will run it again tomorrow, the day after, and as long as it takes. There is a voice that will be heard, a voice louder than trumpets and drums—Truth will out! But forgive me, I thought I was in Parliament; and I've subjected you to a political speech. You, my young friend, have other dreams in your head—dreams of fortune and love.

MASHAM. Who told you that?

BOLINGBROKE. Why you, of course. I believe you're discreet when you're awake, but when you're asleep, it's another matter.

MASHAM. How?

BOLINGBROKE. I heard you reveling in your good fortune while you slept. Tell me the name of the great lady to whom you owe your luck. Your secret will be safe with me.

MASHAM. Why?

BOLINGBROKE. In case the lady's favors . . . But then, I won't force you to reveal her name. I am discreet.

MASHAM. You're wrong. I don't know any great ladies. There is someone, I confess, who is acting as my patron. Who this person is, I can't tell you—a friend of my father's . . . you perhaps.

BOLINGBROKE. Of course not!

MASHAM. You're the only one it could be. There I was, an orphan without money, but the son of a brave gentleman killed on the field of battle, when I decided to seek a place in the Queen's household. But, how to reach the Queen, how to present my petition—that was the difficulty. At the Opening of Parliament I resolutely joined the crowd surrounding her carriage. I had almost reached it when I stumbled against an elegant dandy; and he, thinking I was a clumsy schoolboy, tweaked my nose.

BOLINGBROKE. Surely, not!

MASHAM. Indeed, sir. I can still see his insolent sneer which I will remember as long as I live. As we parted, the crowd pushed me against the Queen's carriage. It was two weeks before I received an answer to my petition and was granted an audience with Her Majesty. Oh, you can imagine how I hurried to the palace, dressed in my best—on foot, of course, because of my poverty. I was not two steps from Saint James, just across from a balcony where some ladies of the court were seated, when I was drenched from head to toe by a careening carriage. The only satin doublet I owned, ruined. And to make matters worse, I recognized in it that same insolent dandy from two weeks before. In my rage, I lunged towards him, but the carriage had, of course, disappeared. Furious and without hope, I returned to my shabby rooms. The hour of my audience had passed.

BOLINGBROKE. What happened?

MASHAM. Strange to tell, on the next day I received from an unknown benefactor an elegant court costume, and some days later a position in the Queen's household. In less than three months at Court I've received a commission as an Ensign in the Guards. My dreams are coming true!

BOLINGBROKE. That they are. And you have no idea who your mysterious patron is?

MASHAM. None. I am assured of constant favor as long as I remain worthy of it. I could ask for no more. The only condition is that I do not marry.

BOLINGBROKE. Ah hah!

MASHAM. Surely, marriage would hinder my advancement.

BOLINGBROKE. [*Laughing.*] That's the only meaning you can find in that condition?

MASHAM. Yes, of course.

BOLINGBROKE. [*Laughing.*] Ah well, my dear friend, for one of the Queen's former pages and one of her new officers, you are as innocent as a lamb.

MASHAM. What do you mean?

BOLINGBROKE. Why, your unknown patron is a woman.

MASHAM. What?

BOLINGBROKE. What great lady have you attracted?

MASHAM. No, Milord, no it can't be.

BOLINGBROKE. Why be shocked? Anne, our charming sovereign, is a decent and wise woman who gets royally bored. I must warn you, at Court everyone seeks their own pleasure. All our ladies have their protégés, young handsome officers who, without leaving the palace, earn promotion to higher ranks.

MASHAM. Sir!

BOLINGBROKE. Flattery rather than merit wins promotion.

MASHAM. What injustice! If I had known . . .

BOLINGBROKE. [*Going to sit at the table on the left.*] Perhaps I could be mistaken, and it may well be that some influential friend of your father's has arranged all this. Let's leave it at that. Hmm. This person ordered you not to marry. . . . Strange! It's clear that this person is not an enemy . . . on the contrary . . . and obeying these conditions is not at all difficult.

MASHAM. [*Standing near* BOLINGBROKE's *chair.*] No, no, when you are in love, it's quite a different matter.

BOLINGBROKE. Of course! The lady of your dreams!

MASHAM. Yes, Milord, the most lovable, the most beautiful girl in London, and she is as poor as I am, unfortunately. It is because of her that I want success. I will wait to marry her until my fortune is made.

BOLINGBROKE. You've not made much progress in that. Tell me about her.

MASHAM. She has even less than I do; she's an orphan too, a shop girl in the City in Master Tomwood's jewelry shop.

BOLINGBROKE. Good Lord!

MASHAM. Master Tomwood has just declared bankruptcy. She is without a position and without resources.

BOLINGBROKE. Abigail!

MASHAM. You know her?

BOLINGBROKE. Of course! During my marriage I was a regular customer at Tomwood's shop. My wife loved diamonds and I . . . jewels . . . You're right Masham—a charming girl—

MASHAM. Wait! Your voice indicates that you might have loved her too.

BOLINGBROKE. For a week or maybe a little longer. Time meant nothing to me then. However, now I have nothing but the purest thoughts for the young lady . . . and for the first time a twinge of remorse, not for losing my fortune but for having used it badly. I would have helped you, seen the two of you married. But now my debts, my creditors who spring up from the earth, offer no hope. The family fortune has reverted to my cousin, Richard Bolingbroke, who guards it jealously. Unfortunately, he is young and, like all fools, healthy. Perhaps we can find a place at Court for Abigail.

MASHAM. My idea, exactly—a place as a Maid of Honor with some great lady who is not too stuck up.

BOLINGBROKE. [*Shaking his head.*] That won't be easy.

MASHAM. I had thought of the old Duchess of Northumberland who, they say, needs a reader.

BOLINGBROKE. Perhaps. If only she weren't such a bore.

MASHAM. I told Abigail to present herself this morning but the very idea of coming to the Queen's palace made her tremble.

BOLINGBROKE. Don't worry; the hope of seeing you will bring her. See, see! What did I tell you? Here she is now. [*Enter* ABIGAIL.]

ABIGAIL. Milord! [*She turns to* MASHAM, *to whom she gives her hand.*]

BOLINGBROKE. My dear child, you were born under a lucky star—your first time at Court and you have found two friends—a rare occurrence in these parts.

ABIGAIL. [*Happily.*] How right you are! Today is my lucky day.

MASHAM. You have decided to approach the Duchess of Northumberland?

ABIGAIL. You don't know? That place has been filled.

MASHAM. And you're still happy?

ABIGAIL. Because I have been offered another, much nicer place.

MASHAM. To whom do you owe this good fortune?

ABIGAIL. To Luck, believe it or not.

BOLINGBROKE. That's the most generous and least demanding of patrons.

ABIGAIL. Among the elegant ladies that visited Mr. Tomwood's shop there was one who was always friendly and gracious. As I helped her select diamonds, we often chatted.

BOLINGBROKE. And Miss Abigail chats very well.

ABIGAIL. It seemed to me that this lady was not very happily married; indeed, she felt enslaved by it, for she would say again and again, "Oh, dear Abigail, how happy you are! You can do as you please." That was hardly the case. There I was bound to the shop, unable to leave it. And I only saw Mr. Masham on Sundays, after church, when he wasn't on duty. One day about a month ago, my elegant lady was struck by the exquisite workmanship of a small gold button, a mere nothing worth thirty guineas. Well, she had forgotten her purse that day, so I said, "We'll send it to your lodgings, Milady." Then my lady, somewhat embarrassed, was hesitant to give her address—undoubtedly because of her husband whom she didn't want to find out about the purchase—there are ladies like that! So, I blurted out, "Keep it, keep it, Milady, I'll take care of everything." "You trust me?" she asked with a charming smile. "Good, I will come back." But nothing, she did not return.

BOLINGBROKE. [*Laughing.*] What a wicked little trick!

ABIGAIL. I started to worry when a month went by. Mr. Tomwood's business was going badly, and the thirty guineas that I had covered were due him or his creditors. I was desolate and dared tell no one about it; so I decided to sell my possessions: my prettiest dresses—even this one which, as everyone tells me, is so becoming.

BOLINGBROKE. Indeed, it is.

ABIGAIL. You see why it was such a hard decision to make. Finally, I made up my mind. Then, last evening a carriage stopped in front of the shop door and a lady got out. It was my lady! Many things—far too many to explain—had kept her from returning; and moreover, she was not free to leave her house. She knew that it was up to her to set this matter straight. As she was talking, the tears that I had tried to hold back flowed out. She demanded that I tell her all, especially about the embarrassing position I found myself in. She was goodness itself, it seemed, in my sorrow. Finally, I told her everything—except about Mr. Masham—and when she learned that I was planning to present myself to the Duchess of Northumberland, she said, "Don't do it; you would be too unhappy there. Besides, that place is filled. But I, dear child, maintain a rather large household at Court; although I am not always mistress in my own house, let me offer you a position there. Will you take it?" I threw myself into her arms saying, "I am at your service; I will never leave you. I will share your troubles and your grief." "Present yourself at the palace tomorrow and ask to see the lady whose name I have written." She wrote two words on a piece of paper which she handed me. Here it is, and here am I.

MASHAM. Most singlular!

BOLINGBROKE: And the paper? Can we see it?

ABIGAIL. [*Handing it to him.*] Certainly.

BOLINGBROKE. [*Smiling.*] Hmm! Who else? Goodness, I should have guessed. [*To* ABIGAIL.] This was written by your new patron in your presence?

ABIGAIL. Yes, of course. By chance do you recognize the handwriting?

BOLINGBROKE. [*Coolly.*] Yes, my dear, it's the Queen's.

ABIGAIL. [*With joy.*] The Queen! Can it be?

MASHAM. [*With joy.*] The Queen is giving you a place at Court along with her friendship and protection! Your fortune is assured forever!

BOLINGBROKE. [*Stepping between them.*] Wait, my friends, wait. Don't be too overjoyed.

ABIGAIL. The Queen did this, and a queen is mistress in her own household.

BOLINGBROKE. Not this one. However sweet and good she is by nature, she is too weak and indecisive to support anyone without taking the advice of those around her. Inevitably, she allows herself to be used by her advisors and her favorites. Near her there is a woman with a determined, strong mind who clearly sees right and valor. I mean, of course, Lady Churchill, Duchess of Marlborough. She is a much greater general than her husband, more skillful than he, more valiant, more ambitious, more avaricious even than he. Indeed, she is more queen than the Queen whom she leads by the hand . . . the hand that holds the scepter.

ABIGAIL. How the Queen must love the Duchess!

BOLINGBROKE. She detests her! Although they each call the other best friend.

ABIGAIL. Why doesn't she send her away? Why does she allow such an intolerable situation?

BOLINGBROKE. That, my dear child, is hard to explain. In our country, as Masham will tell you, it is not the Queen but the majority party who rules. The Whigs, with Marlborough at their head, control not only the army but also Parliament. Their majority is a fact; and Queen Anne, whose glorious reign we celebrate, is forced to suffer ministers who displease her, a favorite who tyrannizes her, and friends who do not love her. Moreover, her most cherished interests force her to pay court to this proud duchess. Her brother, the last of the Stuarts whom the nation banished, cannot return to England except through an act of Parliament. And only the majority, that is only Marlborough, can force this act through parliament. The Duchess has agreed to support this act; therefore, all influence is yielded to her. Chief Lady-in-Waiting, she ordains, she rules, she decides, she fills all positions; and a choice made without her consent will provoke her defiance, her jealousy and perhaps, her refusal. That's why, my friends, it appears to me that the Queen has been too bold, and Abigail's appointment is in doubt.

ABIGAIL. Oh, if it depends on the Duchess, there is, I think, some hope.

MASHAM. What?

ABIGAIL. We are distant kin.

BOLINGBROKE. You, Abigail?

ABIGAIL. Indeed, the Churchills were horrified when one of them married my mother.

MASHAM. Is it true—a relative of the Duchess?

ABIGAIL. Very distant—and I've never asked her for a thing because years ago she refused to receive my mother. But I who have never asked for a thing can surely ask her not to oppose the Queen's goodness.

BOLINGBROKE. That's not reason enough for her, though you couldn't have known it. But this time, at least, I can help you. And that I intend to do. I must draw her hatred to me.

ABIGAIL. How good of you!

MASHAM. How can we ever thank you?

BOLINGBROKE. By your friendship.

ABIGAIL. That's little enough.

BOLINGBROKE. It is enough for me, a politician who believes in little enough. [*Animatedly.*] But I believe in you, and I am counting on you. [*Giving them his hand.*] Among us, from now on, an offensive and defensive alliance.

ABIGAIL. [*Smiling.*] An unbeatable alliance!

BOLINGBROKE. Stronger than you think, perhaps, and what a match we will present to them. To success! Abigail's position! And another matter dear to me—a letter that must at whatever price be delivered to the Queen this morning. How to do it is the question. Ah, if Abigail were appointed, if she were received along with the other ladies, all my messages would reach the Queen in spite of the Duchess.

MASHAM. [*Animatedly.*] Is that all? I can arrange that for you.

BOLINGBROKE. How is it possible?

MASHAM. Every morning at ten o'clock—and it's almost ten now—I bring to Her Majesty during breakfast [*Picking up the newspaper from the table in the right.*] The Gazette which she glances through during tea. She looks at the pictures and sometimes enjoys having me read the articles about the balls and parties.

BOLINGBROKE. Wonderful! What luck that the Queen reads the society newspaper. It's the only one she is allowed. [*Slipping the letter into the folds of the newspaper.*] The Marquis's letter between pictures of the latest fashions. And while we're at it . . . [*Taking a newspaper from his pocket.*]

ABIGAIL. What are you doing?

BOLINGBROKE. I'm slipping an issue of *The Examiner* under the cover. Her Majesty will see how the Duke and Duchess of Marlborough are treated. She and her whole court will be indignant. But it will give her several moments of pleasure, and she has so few of them. Well now, it's ten o'clock; go, Masham, go!

MASHAM. [*Leaving by the door on the right.*] Count on me!

BOLINGBROKE. You see, our triple alliance has already produced results. Masham is protecting us and serving us.

ABIGAIL. Maybe he is, but my part is so small.

BOLINGBROKE. Don't scorn the little things: it is thus that the big things are accomplished. You believe, as everyone, that political catastrophies, revolutions, collapsing empires result from serious, profoundly important causes. Wrong! Nations are conquered or led by heroes, by great men; however, these great men are led by their passions, their caprices, their vanities, that is, the smallest and most miserable emotions man is capable of. You don't realize that a window in the Trianon, criticized by Louis XIV and defended by Louvois, gave rise to the war that now engulfs Europe. The wounded vanity of a courtier has cost the kingdom disaster. Perhaps an even more frivolous reason will result in its deliverance. And without continuing this lesson, do you know how I, Henry Saint John, who until I was twenty-six was considered a foppish rake, incapable of serious endeavor, came to be almost overnight a statesman, a member of Parliament, and a minister in the government?

ABIGAIL. No, not at all.

BOLINGBROKE. Very well, my dear, I became a minister because I knew how to dance the saraband, and I lost power because I had a cold.

ABIGAIL. Can it be so?

BOLINGBROKE. [*Looking toward the* QUEEN's *apartment.*] I'll leave that story for another day when we have time. And now with your encouragement, I'll continue my fight in the ranks of the vanquished.

ABIGAIL. What will you accomplish?

BOLINGBROKE. I'll bide my time for the right moment.

ABIGAIL. Some great revolution?

BOLINGBROKE. Nothing like that. A chance perhaps, a kind of caprice, a grain of sand to upset the chariot of the triumphant.

ABIGAIL. Can't you create this grain of sand?

BOLINGBROKE. No, but if I come across it, I can throw it under the wheel. Talent is not competing with fate by inventing incidents but profiting from them. The more futile it appears the more it is within my reach. Great results are produced by small causes—that's my system. I have confidence in it; you'll see.

ABIGAIL. [*Looking at the door opening.*] Masham is back!

BOLINGBROKE. No! Even better! It is our triumphant, glorious Duchess!

ABIGAIL. [*In a whisper, watching the* DUCHESS *enter through the gallery on the right.*] What! It's the Duchess of Marlborough?

BOLINGBROKE. [*In the same manner.*] Your cousin, the great lady.

ABIGAIL. I've seen her before . . . at the shop. [*Aside, watching the* DUCHESS.] Ah yes, she's the elegant lady who bought those fine diamonds not long ago.

THE DUCHESS. [*Reading a newspaper as she walks, she raises her eyes and sees* BOLINGBROKE, *who bows to her.*] Milord Saint John.

BOLINGBROKE. In the flesh. Madam, what brings you here at this moment?

THE DUCHESS. You do me honor, you and your constant attacks.

BOLINGBROKE. It's the only way I can bedevil you!

THE DUCHESS. [*Showing the paper that she is holding.*] Be assured, sir, I will not soon forget today's attack.

BOLINGBROKE. You deigned to read it?

THE DUCHESS. In the Queen's chambers where I've just been.

BOLINGBROKE. [*Troubled.*] There!

THE DUCHESS. Indeed, sir, the officer on duty just brought *The Gazette*.

BOLINGBROKE. Which never prints my articles.

THE DUCHESS. [*Ironically.*] How well I know that! You no longer have any influence in *The Gazette*. I found this article from *The Examiner* and a letter

from the Marquis de Torcy.
BOLINGBROKE. Addressed to the Queen.
THE DUCHESS. Which is why I read it.
BOLINGBROKE. [*Indignantly.*] Madam!
THE DUCHESS. It's one of my duties as Chief Lady-in-Waiting. All letters are to pass through my hands first. You are aware of that, sir; and in the future when you write epigrams or witty remarks directed against me, you've only to address them to the Queen. That way, you can be sure that I'll read them.
BOLINGBROKE. I will remember that, Madam, but at least Her Majesty knows the Marquis's proposals, which was my intention.
THE DUCHESS. There you are mistaken. I read them, which was sufficient; then the fire did them justice.
BOLINGBROKE. Madam!
THE DUCHESS. [*Curtsying to him and starting to leave. She sees* ABIGAIL *who has stayed behind.*] Who is this lovely child standing here, so timid and aloof? What is her name?
ABIGAIL. [*Coming forward and curtsying.*] Abigail.
THE DUCHESS. [*Haughtily.*] Ah yes, the pretty jeweler. Now I recognize her. Didn't the Queen just mention her to me?
ABIGAIL. [*Eagerly.*] Oh! Her Majesty deigned to speak of me?
THE DUCHESS. Leaving me the choice of accepting her or turning her down. And since this nomination depends on me alone . . . I shall see . . . I shall be a fair and impartial judge of her merit.
BOLINGBROKE. [*Aside.*] We are lost!
THE DUCHESS. You understand, young lady, a title is required.
BOLINGBROKE. [*Advancing.*] She has one!
THE DUCHESS. [*Shocked.*] Sir, you are interested in this young lady?
BOLINGBROKE. From the affectionate welcome that you deigned to give her, I thought you had guessed.
THE DUCHESS. I would gladly appoint her, but to enter the Queen's service, one must come from a distinguished family.
BOLINGBROKE. That's where she shines.
THE DUCHESS. That remains to be seen. There are many who say they are noble and who are not.
BOLINGBROKE. My dear, don't be afraid of telling us. Admit answering to the name of Abigail Churchill.
THE DUCHESS. [*Aside.*] Heavens!
BOLINGBROKE. A distant relative, no doubt, but still a cousin of the Duchess of Marlborough, the Queen's Chief Lady-in-Waiting who, in strict impartiality, hesitated and asked herself if the child were from a good enough background to approach the Queen. You understand, Madam, that for me, a hackneyed, out-of-fashion writer, there might be something in the retelling of this story to put me back in favor with my readers. What fun *The Examiner* would have at the expense of the noble Duchess, cousin of the shop girl! Don't worry, Madam, your goodwill is too necessary to your young relative for me to deprive her of it. Should she be admitted to the Queen's household today, I give you my word as a gentleman that no one shall know of this anecdote, however amusing it might be. I await your decision.
THE DUCHESS. [*Proudly.*] I won't make you wait. I was about to make my recommendations about this child to the Queen. Whether she is my relative or not will not alter my decision. I will make it known to Her Majesty and no one else. As for you, sir, you know full well that I have never given in to empty threats of this sort. If you force me, I shall take action against you. When one is a journalist, sir, and especially a member of the Opposition, one should take care to manage his own affairs before trying to manage the government. That you have not done. Your debts are enormous, more than a million, which your desperate and impatient creditors have sold to me for a sixth of the total. I bought up all your debts. I who am so greedy, so money mad. You cannot accuse me of making money this time. [*Smiling.*] Because the debts are so overwhelming, they say; but they do have the advantage of forcing restraint . . . an advantage from which I can still profit. As a

member of Parliament, you realize that the session ends tomorrow. Should this spicy story appear in the morning paper tomorrow, the evening paper will announce that its witty author, Mr. Saint John, is at the moment in Newgate Prison composing a treatise on the art of piling up debts. However, I do not fear that, sir, for you are too necessary to your friends of the Opposition to want to deprive them of your presence. However painful silence may be for an orator of your eloquence, you understand as well as I the necessity of remaining silent. [*She curtsies and leaves.*]

ABIGAIL. Well? What have you to say now?

BOLINGBROKE. [*Gaily.*] Well played! By God! Very well played! It will be a fine battle. I have always said that the Duchess is a capable and efficient woman. She does not threaten, she strikes. The idea of blackmailing me by covering my debts, that's quite ingenious of her. She is doing what my best friends would not do. She has covered my debts; she must really hate me. That excites my admiration and courage. Let's go, Abigail. Courage!

ABIGAIL. No, no! I'll give it all up. You must be free.

BOLINGBROKE. [*Gaily.*] We shall see to your happiness by whatever means are possible. [*Looking at the pendulum clock on one of the panels on the right.*] Good Heavens! It's time for Parliament to be in session. I cannot miss it . . . I am to speak against the Duke of Marlborough's latest subsidies. I will prove to the Duchess that I understand economics. I won't vote a shilling. Goodbye! I am counting on Masham, on you, and on our alliance. [*He exits through the door on the left.*]

ABIGAIL. [*Ready to leave.*] A fine alliance in which Arthur will be the only victor.

MASHAM. [*Running in, pale and out of breath, from the door at the rear.*] Thank goodness, you're here. I was looking for you.

ABIGAIL. What is it?

MASHAM. I am ruined!

ABIGAIL. How?

MASHAM. In Saint James Park, on a secluded path, I suddenly found myself face to face with him.

ABIGAIL. Who?

MASHAM. My evil spirit, my fate . . . you know, the man who tweaked my nose. At first glance we recognized each other. He laughed when he looked at me. [*With anger.*] He laughed again! And then without saying a word, without even asking him his name, I drew my sword, and he, his . . . and, and, he is no longer laughing.

ABIGAIL. He's dead!

MASHAM. No, no, I don't think so; but I did see him fall. Then I heard people running toward us and remembered the strict new laws against dueling.

ABIGAIL. The death penalty!

MASHAM. That depends on the circumstances.

ABIGAIL. No matter; you must leave London.

MASHAM. I will leave in the morning.

ABIGAIL. No, tonight.

MASHAM. But what about you, what about Milord Saint John?

ABIGAIL. He is to be arrested for his debts; and I will not have my appointment. But, that's not important . . . you first, you above all else. Get away from here!

MASHAM. I will! But before I leave, I want you to know that I love no one but you. I want to see you, to hold you . . .

ABIGAIL. [*Eagerly.*] Then hurry, now!

MASHAM. [*Throwing himself into her arms.*] Ah!

ABIGAIL. [*Pulling away.*] Farewell! Farewell! If you love me, go before you are caught. [*They separate and exit.*]

Act 2

Enter QUEEN *and* THOMPSON.

THE QUEEN. Thompson, you say some members of Parliament are here?

THOMPSON. Yes, Your Majesty, they have asked for an audience with you.

THE QUEEN. [*Aside.*] More speeches and discourses . . . here I am alone; the Duchess is at Windsor. [*Aloud.*] You told them that I was reading important dispatches that just arrived?

THOMPSON. Yes, Your Majesty, that's what I always say.

THE QUEEN. And that I will not receive them . . .

THOMPSON. Before two o'clock. They gave me their petition and agreed to return at two to present their respects and demands to Your Majesty.

THE QUEEN. [*Putting the petition on the table.*] The Duchess will be there, that's her duty. She could at least spare me these burdens. I have so many. Do you know which gentlemen were present?

THOMPSON. There were four of them. I only recognized two who were former ministers. They were the spokesmen for the group.

THE QUEEN. [*Eagerly.*] Who were they?

THOMPSON. Sir Harley and Mr. Saint John.

THE QUEEN. Oh! And they have left?

THOMPSON. Yes, Your Majesty.

THE QUEEN. Oh dear! I'm sorry that I didn't receive them, especially Mr. Saint John. When he was in power all went smoothly. My mornings passed quickly, and I wasn't at all bored. Today, with the Duchess away, seeing him would be a special treat. We would have had a nice chat. Call him back.

THOMPSON. The Duchess told me as a general rule that any time Mr. Saint John presented himself . . .

THE QUEEN. Oh! That's the Duchess; this is different. Did Mr. Saint John say anything?

THOMPSON. He wrote the petition that I just handed Your Majesty.

THE QUEEN. [*Gaily, picking up the petition from the table.*] Very good. Leave me.

[THOMPSON *exits.*]

THE QUEEN. [*Reading.*] "Madam: My colleagues and I have asked for a royal audience—they, for matters of state and I for the pleasure of seeing my sovereign who for too long has banished me." Poor Sir Henry! "The Duchess may keep your political enemies from you, but her suspicions have pushed away a poor child whose tenderness and concern could relieve Your Majesty's anxieties. Her nomination is being rejected because it is said that she is without family. Believe me when I tell you that Abigail Churchill is a cousin to the Duchess of Marlborough." [*Stopping.*] Is it so? [*Reading.*] "This fact will surely profit Your Majesty; I know that you will guard this secret which has been given you by your faithful servant and subject." Yes, yes, it must be true. Henry Saint John is one of my most faithful servants. Although he is a former minister, I cannot receive him without causing suspicion and complaints from the Duchess. Ah, were I a stronger sovereign so that I could be my own mistress! Even in the choice of my friends I must seek permission from the counsellors to the crown, from Parliament, from the Majority . . . in sum, from everyone. It should not be! What an odious, hateful bondage. Here, in my own home, I don't want to be obedient. I want to be free. Whatever may come of this, my mind is made up! [*She rings;* THOMPSON *appears.*] Thompson, go immediately to Master Tomwood's shop in the City and ask for Miss Abigail Churchill. Bring her to the palace at once. I want this, I command it, I, the Queen! Go at once.

THOMPSON. Yes, Your Majesty.

THE QUEEN. We shall see whose will reigns here. And now to the Duchess, whose friendship and constant advice are beginning to bore me. Why, here she is now! [*She sits down and slips* BOLINGBROKE'*s letter into her bodice.*]

THE DUCHESS. [*Entering from the door at the rear, observes the Queen hide the letter. The* QUEEN *remains seated and turns her back to the* DUCHESS.] May I ask, how is Your Majesty today?

THE QUEEN. [*Drily.*] Badly; I am suffering, indisposed.

THE DUCHESS. Your Majesty has some complaints?

THE QUEEN. [*In the same tone.*] Several.

THE DUCHESS. My absence, perhaps . . .

THE QUEEN. Indeed, without a doubt. I do not see the necessity of your going to Windsor this morning, leaving me here burdened by matters of state, obliged to hear petitions and speeches from Parliament.

THE DUCHESS. Do you know what has happened?

THE QUEEN. No, I don't.

THE DUCHESS. A very serious matter, most upsetting.

THE QUEEN. Good Heavens!

THE DUCHESS. Which has already excited quite an uproar in town. Haven't you heard the noise?

THE QUEEN. Terrible! We had planned an outing on the Thames with my ladies this afternoon.

THE DUCHESS. Please be assured, Your Majesty, that we will see to everything. We have had a regiment of dragoons called to Windsor. They have orders to march on London at a moment's notice. The commanders, who are completely devoted to my husband and Your Majesty, assure me of this.

THE QUEEN. So that's why you were at Windsor.

THE DUCHESS. Yes, Your Majesty. Don't you trust me?

THE QUEEN. I? Madam!

THE DUCHESS. [*Smiling.*] You received me with such coldness that I thought I was in disgrace.

THE QUEEN. Don't think ill of me today, Madam. My nerves are in a terrible state.

THE DUCHESS. That's evident. Has Your Majesty received some upsetting news?

THE QUEEN. Not really.

THE DUCHESS. You won't tell me because you are afraid of upsetting me or burdening me with your problems. How well I know your goodness.

THE QUEEN. You are wrong.

THE DUCHESS. As I came in, I saw you press a letter to your bosom with such emotion that I knew at once that it must concern me.

THE QUEEN. No, Duchess, I tell you it only concerns a young girl [*Pulling the letter from her dress.*] who was recommended to me through this letter . . . a young girl whom I want . . . whom I wish to see in my service.

THE DUCHESS. [*Smiling.*] Really? Nothing more, then . . . Would Your Majesty permit . . .

THE QUEEN. [*Clutching the letter.*] No use! We've already spoken about the child. It's Abigail.

THE DUCHESS. [*Aside.*] Heavens! [*Aloud.*] And who recommends her with such vigor?

THE QUEEN. It doesn't matter. I promised not to expose him or his letter.

THE DUCHESS. Of course! It's Mr. Saint John.

THE QUEEN. [*Troubled.*] So, the truth is out.

THE DUCHESS. [*Trying to control her anger.*] Yes, presented to you by our enemies. Our Queen is betraying us just as we are fighting for her. Yes, Madam, today a bill recalling your brother to England has been presented in Parliament. Moreover, it named him as your heir. Already the hatred of the nation and the unrest of the people have been provoked by this bill. We are the ones who are supporting it against the opposition of Henry Saint John and his friends, at the risk of losing our popularity and power. This is how our sovereign repays us by carrying on a secret correspondence with our declared enemies. We are abandoned and betrayed for their sake.

THE QUEEN. [*Aside with impatience.*] More jealousy and complaints. It will be thus all day. [*Aloud.*] No, Duchess, your imagination is perverting and exaggerating the matter. This correspondence has nothing to do with politics. What it contains is of such a nature . . .

THE DUCHESS. That Your Majesty is afraid to show it to me.

THE QUEEN. [*Impatiently.*] Don't worry. [*She hands it over.*] It concerns facts that you cannot deny.

THE DUCHESS. [*Scanning the letter.*] Is this all? It's not a very vicious attack.

THE QUEEN. You are not opposed to Abigail's appointment?

THE DUCHESS. If it pleases Your Majesty.

THE QUEEN. Is the allegation that she is your cousin true?

THE DUCHESS. Yes, Madam, I admit it. I cry it aloud. The real reason I did not want Abigail appointed to your household is that for too long I have been accused of using my position as Chief Lady-in-Waiting to surround you with my friends, my relatives, my protégés, in a word, those who are devoted only to me. Naming Abigail would give them a pretext of almost slanderous proportions to use against me. Your Majesty is too fair and too generous not to understand.

THE QUEEN. [*Embarrassed and almost convinced.*] Certainly, I understand, but I only wanted dear Abigail . . .

THE DUCHESS. Don't worry about her fate. I will find her a brillant and honorable place, far from you, far from London.

THE QUEEN. Do it at once.

THE DUCHESS. I am pleased to see the interest Your Majesty has for the girl and to know that I can fulfill your desires. As for that young man, that Ensign, Your Majesty recommended to me the other day . . .

THE QUEEN. What young man?

THE DUCHESS. Young Masham whose praises you sang.

THE QUEEN. Oh yes, that's right. He's the young officer who reads me *The Gazette* every morning.

THE DUCHESS. I've arranged for him to be made an officer of the Guards. Not even the Marshal who signed the commission with scarcely a glance could doubt his qualifications. Today, the newly made captain will come to thank Your Majesty.

THE QUEEN. [*With joy.*] Oh! He's coming today?

THE DUCHESS. Yes, I have put him on the list for today's audience.

THE QUEEN. Very well! I will receive him. How can the Opposition papers claim that you are guilty of favoritism?

THE DUCHESS. Because of the Marshal . . . they see that he is paid by you.

THE QUEEN. [*Going to sit at the table on the left.*] Of course.

THE DUCHESS. [*Standing near the chair.*] You see, wherever possible, your wish is my command.

THE QUEEN. [*Seated and turning toward her.*] You are so good.

THE DUCHESS. Good Heavens, no! It is my nature to serve you, for I am so devoted to you.

THE QUEEN. [*Aside.*] After all, that's the truth.

THE DUCHESS. Sovereigns have so few true friends, friends who are not afraid of angering them, hurting them, contradicting them. What more could you ask of me? I do not know how to flatter, how to deceive. I know only how to love.

THE QUEEN. Yes, you are right, Duchess. Friendship is a sweet thing.

THE DUCHESS. How true! What does character matter; the heart is everything. [*The* QUEEN *extends her hand, which the* DUCHESS *kisses.*] Your Majesty will promise me that there will be no more questions about this matter which has caused both of us pain.

THE QUEEN. Agreed!

THE DUCHESS. The thought of it is too painful; it should be forgotten forever.

THE QUEEN. I promise you that.

THE DUCHESS. There, it's decided. You will see no more of Abigail.

THE QUEEN. Certainly. [*Enter* THOMPSON *and* ABIGAIL.]

THOMPSON. Miss Abigail Churchill. [*He exits after his announcement.*]

THE DUCHESS. [*Aside and moving away.*] Heavens!

THE QUEEN. [*Embarrassed.*] Just as we were talking about you. What luck!

ABIGAIL. Your Majesty commanded me to appear.

THE QUEEN. Commanded? I said that I wanted you, if it were convenient . . .

THE DUCHESS. It is only right for Her Majesty to tell you herself that your application has been denied.

ABIGAIL. My appointment? It wasn't my idea in the first place, but Her Majesty's.

THE QUEEN. That's true. But serious considerations, matters of policy . . .

ABIGAIL. Where is my part in this?

THE QUEEN. Please bear with me; but I must renounce a dream that would have made us both happy, Abigail. From now on, The Duchess, your cousin, will be charged with your welfare. She has agreed to find you an honorable position far from London. [*With dignity, passing by the* DUCHESS *and taking center stage.*] I agreed to this arrangement.

ABIGAIL. Heavens!

THE DUCHESS. From now on Abigail is my charge. [*To* ABIGAIL.] Wait for me, I will have a word with you after I leave the Queen, whose every wish I must obey.

THE QUEEN. [*Whispering to* ABIGAIL.] Thank her! [ABIGAIL *remains immobile, but as the* DUCHESS *reaches center stage she kisses the* QUEEN's *hand eagerly.*]

ABIGAIL. [*Aside.*] Poor woman! [*The* QUEEN *and the* DUCHESS *leave by the door on the right.*]

ABIGAIL. [*Watching the* QUEEN *leave.*] Oh, how I pity her! Mr. Saint John was right; how well he knows them. Anne is not the Queen, it is the Duchess. Now she is to protect me, I mean tyrannize me. I'd sooner die. I will refuse! Now more than ever I need friends and protectors because, since Arthur's leaving yesterday, I have not seen Mr. Saint John. I don't know what has become of him. I am completely alone. [*With dread.*] It was here in the Queen's palace that he dueled with a grand lord. It will not go easy for him. No question about that! I pray that he has reached the Continent by now. I ask nothing for myself, Dear Lord. I know it is wrong for me to complain; I accept my lot—abandonment and misery—so that he may be saved, that he may live. I will give up my happiness, my marriage to him.

BOLINGBROKE. [*Entering before the end of* ABIGAIL's *speech.*] What? Why then, by God? I intend to give up nothing.

ABIGAIL. Oh, Sir Henry, you are here. Come, come. I am so unhappy. Everyone is against me, everyone has abandoned me.

BOLINGBROKE. [*Gaily.*] My friends are usually happy to see me. Let's see, dear Abigail, what is it?

ABIGAIL. Is it about your promises to me.

BOLINGBROKE. My promises have been kept, exactly as I planned.

ABIGAIL. [*Shocked.*] What do you mean?

BOLINGBROKE. Remember my telling you of Lord Richard Bolingbroke, my cousin?

ABIGAIL. No, I don't.

BOLINGBROKE. He was the most intractable of my creditors even though we were both members of the Opposition. He sold my debts to the Duchess of Marlborough. A totally useless man!

ABIGAIL. And you are relatives?

BOLINGBROKE. He holds the family title, and therefore he controls our immense family fortune.

ABIGAIL. So, this cousin . . .

BOLINGBROKE. [*Laughing.*] Look at me, will you. Don't I look like someone who has inherited a fortune?

ABIGAIL. You, Henry Saint John?

BOLINGBROKE. Indeed! Now Lord Henry Saint John, Viscount Bolingbroke, surviving member of this famous family of matchless lineage. As such, I intend to demand justice from the Queen.

ABIGAIL. How?

BOLINGBROKE. [*Showing her the door at the rear which is opening.*] With my honorable colleagues, the principal members of the Opposition.

ABIGAIL. Why?

BOLINGBROKE. [*In a whisper.*] Besides his fortune, my cousin also left me a cause . . . that is, to incite a riot to avenge his death. It is the only service he ever did our party. He would have never been able to strike such a blow in his life. Quiet! Here's the Queen. [ABIGAIL *is on the right. Several lords and ladies of the Court are standing near her. Sir Harley and the members of the Opposition are on the left around* BOLINGBROKE. *The* QUEEN, *the* DUCHESS *and several Ladies of Honor enter from the right and take center stage.*]

BOLINGBROKE. [*Choosing his words carefully and forcing warmth.*] Madam, as a sincere friend of our nation and as a bereaved relative who carries his name in tears, I demand justice and vengeance. That defender of our liberties, Lord Richard, Viscount Bolingbroke, my noble cousin, yesterday in your palace, yes in these gardens . . .

ABIGAIL. [*Aside.*] Heavens!

BOLINGBROKE. Was struck dead in a duel. If you can call an encounter without witness a duel; and his adversary, protected through his flight, is above the law.

THE DUCHESS. Allow me . . .

BOLINGBROKE. Who is to say that those who helped him to escape are not the same ones who armed him? What of this mission? [*To the* DUCHESS *and the nobles who show their impatience by shrugging their shoulders.*] Yes, Madam, I accuse them! And the cries of the angry people speak more loudly than I. I accuse the perpetrators, their partisans, their friends. I will name no names, but I accuse them all of having sought to destroy by this treason an adversary as strong as Lord Richard Bolingbroke. I say to you, Your Majesty, that if serious trouble erupts today in your capital, it is not we, your faithful servants, who will have caused it but those who surround you and whose dismissal public opinion demands.

THE DUCHESS. [*Coldly.*] Are you finished?

BOLINGBROKE. Yes, Madam.

THE DUCHESS. Now for the truth which has been verified by reports that I received this morning.

ABIGAIL. [*Aside.*] I'm trembling.

THE DUCHESS. It is, unfortunately, all too true that yesterday Lord Richard was struck down in a duel in Saint James Park.

BOLINGBROKE. By whom?

THE DUCHESS. By a cavalier of unknown identity. Not even Lord Richard knew.

BOLINGBROKE. Your Majesty, I demand to know if this is true.

THE DUCHESS. Indeed it is. Lord Richard's last words were witnessed by some palace servants whom you can question yourself.

BOLINGBROKE. I don't doubt their answers; their positions are a sure guarantee of honesty. If, however, as the Duchess claims, the real culprit escaped without being seen—a feat which supposes a first-hand knowledge of the palace—why has no action been taken to capture the culprit?

ABIGAIL. [*Aside.*] We're done for!

BOLINGBROKE. Why, then, are we forced to stimulate the zeal, ordinarily so active, of the Duchess, who has complete control of the Queen's household? Why haven't orders been issued for pursuit?

THE DUCHESS. They have!

ABIGAIL. [*Aside.*] Heavens!

THE DUCHESS. Her Majesty has just decreed that the death penalty be invoked.

THE QUEEN. The execution of which we entrust to the Duchess and [*Turning to* BOLINGBROKE] to you Mr. Saint John . . . I mean to say Milord Bolingbroke. Your title and relationship to the deceased impose more on you than on anyone else the duty of finding the culprit.

THE DUCHESS. [*Sarcastically.*] No more need be said. I hope that we can shield him from your vengeance.

THE QUEEN. Milord and gentlemen, are you satisfied?

BOLINGBROKE. We are always satisfied when we have seen Your Majesty and listened to your words. [*The* QUEEN *indicates that the audience is over. She, the* DUCHESS, *and the ladies of the Court exit to the right.* BOLINGBROKE's *colleagues exit through the doors at the rear.* ABIGAIL *follows for a moment the Opposition who are exiting through the doors at the rear; then she comes back downstage on the left.*]

BOLINGBROKE. Wonderful! If they think they have placated me, they are mistaken. Thanks to the Queen, I will soon arrest all of England. [*Turns towards* ABIGAIL *who is trying to control herself. She falls into a chair.*] Oh, Good Lord! What's the matter with you?

ABIGAIL. Everything! You have just destroyed us!

BOLINGBROKE. How?

ABIGAIL. The culprit whom you will surrender to the vengeance of the people and the courts, the one whom you are charged to pursue, to arrest,

and to have executed . . .
BOLINGBROKE. Well?
ABIGAIL. Well, it's Arthur!
BOLINGBROKE. What? This duel, this encounter . . .
ABIGAIL. Yes, Arthur and Lord Richard, your cousin, dueled. He didn't know him but recognized him only by his insolent sneer.
BOLINGBROKE. [*Gasping.*] I see! The man who tweaked his nose. Oh, my dear, a tweak is the cause of all this—a duel, a murder, the superb speech that I just delivered, the royal decree.
ABIGAIL. Which allows you to arrest him.
BOLINGBROKE. Arrest him! Let me see . . . I owe everything to him, my title and my fortune. No, my conscience does not compel me to carry this out [*Taking the decree which he wants to tear up.*] I'd rather, By God! . . [*Stopping.*] O Good God! The whole party is counting on me, not to mention all the opposition which I loosed against this unfortunate duel. And yet, public opinion forces me because he was my relative, my cousin . . .
ABIGAIL. What is to be done? Oh, Dear Lord!
BOLINGBROKE. [*Gaily.*] By God, I'll do nothing . . . only noise, articles, and speeches until you are certain that he is safely away from England. Then I will reveal it and have him pursued all over the kingdom with a rage that will shield my true feelings and my responsibility to my cousin.
ABIGAIL. How good you are! What an ingenious solution! Since he left yesterday, he must be far away by now. [*Gasping as she sees* MASHAM.] Oh! [*Enter* MASHAM.]
BOLINGBROKE. Our plan is ruined, damn it! What brings you back; why retrace your steps?
MASHAM. [*Tranquilly.*] I never left.
ABIGAIL. Yesterday we said our farewells.
MASHAM. I had not gotten out of London when I heard hoofbeats behind me. An officer was following me, and because he was better mounted than I, he quickly caught up with me. For a moment I thought of defending myself; but I had just stabbed a man to death. Killing a second would solve nothing, you understand. I stopped and said to him [*Putting his hand on his sword.*] "Sir, I am at your command!" "Your orders," he told me, "Are here." With that, he handed me a packet which I opened with trembling hands.
ABIGAIL. And?
MASHAM. And! Strange to tell, it was my nomination as an officer of the Guards.
BOLINGBROKE. Are you certain?
ABIGAIL. What a reward!
MASHAM. After what I had just done! "Tomorrow will be time enough to thank the Queen," the young officer continued, "but today we will have a banquet with all our friends from the regiment. I will be your sponsor. Come, I'll show you the way." How to respond? I couldn't flee, that would be suspicious, betray me, show my guilt.
ABIGAIL. So you followed him?
MASHAM. To the banquet which lasted most of the night.
ABIGAIL. Unfortunately!
MASHAM. Why?
BOLINGBROKE. There is no time to explain. For the moment all you need to know is that the man who laughed at you and insulted you was Richard Bolingbroke, my cousin.
MASHAM. What are you saying?
BOLINGBROKE. That your first stroke brought me sixteen thousand pounds sterling in revenues. I only wish that the second one had brought you something. In the meantime, however, I have been charged with arresting you.
MASHAM. [*Presenting his sword.*] I am at your command.
BOLINGBROKE. No! I have neither a commission nor a banquet to offer you.
ABIGAIL. Fortunately, he has your interests at heart.
BOLINGBROKE. All I ask is that you do not betray yourself. I will look for you—not very hard, I admit—and if I find you, it will be your fault and not mine.
ABIGAIL. Lie low until the threat of suspicion has passed you by.

BOLINGBROKE. Avoid going out, stay quiet, stay at home. In a word, do not show yourself.

MASHAM. This morning I am to see the Queen.

BOLINGBROKE. You can't.

MASHAM. This letter orders me to do the opposite of what you have recommended.

ABIGAIL. What letter?

MASHAM. From my unknown patron to whom, no doubt, I owe my new commission. This letter and box were just delivered to my rooms.

THOMPSON. [*Appearing from the* QUEEN'S *apartments.*] Captain Masham!

MASHAM. The Queen awaits me. [*He hands the letter to* ABIGAIL *and the box to* BOLINGBROKE.] See for yourselves. [*Exit* MASHAM *and* THOMPSON.]

ABIGAIL. What can it mean?

BOLINGBROKE. Let's find out.

ABIGAIL. [*Reading the letter.*] "You are an officer! I kept my word; keep yours by continuing to obey me. Be in Chapel every morning and at the Queen's card game every evening. The moment when I will reveal myself to you will soon come. Until then, silence. Obey my orders; if not, it will go badly for you!" What does it mean?

BOLINGBROKE. That he cannot marry.

ABIGAIL. What a terrible price to pay for advancement.

BOLINGBROKE. Worse than you might know!

ABIGAIL. What do you mean?

BOLINGBROKE. [*Smiling.*] This mysterious protector . . .

ABIGAIL. Might be a friend of his father's, a lord!

BOLINGBROKE. [*Same tone.*] I would wager, rather, a lady!

ABIGAIL. How can that be? Arthur is such a steady person and above all, so faithful.

BOLINGBROKE. It is not his fault that someone is advancing his cause, and incognito at that.

ABIGAIL. Oh, it can't be true. Perhaps this postscript will tell us something more.

BOLINGBROKE. [*Gaily.*] Oh, is there a postscript?

ABIGAIL. [*Reading with emotion.*] "Captain Masham, let me present you with the insignia of your new rank."

BOLINGBROKE. [*Opening the box which he is holding.*] Diamond tabs of magnificent taste. . . . Not bad!

ABIGAIL. [*Looking at them.*] Heavens! I know who it is! I recognize these diamonds! I sold them last week in Mr. Tomwood's shop.

BOLINGBROKE. Tell me, who is it?

ABIGAIL. Oh, I can't. I don't dare say her name because she is too highly placed. If she loves Arthur, I am lost.

BOLINGBROKE. What does it matter to you—if he loves you, if he doesn't even suspect this other one.

ABIGAIL. I will tell him everything.

BOLINGBROKE. [*Taking her hand.*] No, believe me, he must never know what you are doing for him.

ABIGAIL. Why?

BOLINGBROKE. My poor child! You do not understand men . . . the most modest and least conceited have plenty of vanity. It is flattering to know that such a great lady loves you. Is it true that this one is so powerful?

ABIGAIL. More than I can say.

BOLINGBROKE. And who is she, then?

ABIGAIL. [*Pointing to the* DUCHESS *who is entering from the right.*] Here she is now!

BOLINGBROKE. [*Eagerly taking the letter from* ABIGAIL.] The Duchess! [*To* ABIGAIL, *whom he dismisses.*] Leave us, leave us.

ABIGAIL. She told me to wait for her.

BOLINGBROKE. [*Directing her to the door on the left.*] Too bad; it will be I whom she finds. [*Aside.*] O Lady Luck, you have given me a second chance! [*The* DUCHESS *enters daydreaming.* BOLINGBROKE *approaches her and greets her with respect.*]

THE DUCHESS. Oh, it is you, Milord. I was looking for our young friend.

BOLINGBROKE. May I have a moment of your time?

THE DUCHESS. Speak. Do you have some clues, some news about the culprit we are charged with finding?

BOLINGBROKE. None yet. And you, Madam?

THE DUCHESS. Nothing at all.

BOLINGBROKE. [*Aside.*] So much the bet-

THE DUCHESS. Well, what shall we do?
BOLINGBROKE. First, cancel my debts to you. Acknowledging them is my duty. After becoming rich, my first act was to have your banker send a million francs to pay off the two hundred thousand pounds which you so confidently claim my debts to total.
THE DUCHESS. Sir!
BOLINGBROKE. That's enough. For good reasons I would not have paid that amount. As chance would have it and in spite of you, it appears that you will earn three hundred for every one hundred. I am delighted! You see, as you were so quick to tell me, the matter is not so disastrous.
THE DUCHESS. [*Smiling.*] How true! That is, for you!
BOLINGBROKE. No, Madam. You have shown me that to succeed, the first thing a statesman must do is keep his own affairs in order. Only this leads to success which brings freedom and power. In that way, no one need sell himself and often one can buy others—This lesson is certainly worth a million! I am grateful to you and shall put your teachings to good use.
THE DUCHESS. I see! Now that you don't have to fear for your freedom, you are going to wage a much more violent war against me.
BOLINGBROKE. On the contrary. I propose peace.
THE DUCHESS. Peace between us? That's impossible!
BOLINGBROKE. Well then, a truce, a truce of twenty-four hours.
THE DUCHESS. Whatever for? You can begin the attacks against me whenever you want. I acknowledged to the Queen and all the Court that Abigail was my cousin. My honesty has forestalled your slander. I was just on my way to tell the child that I have arranged a place for her in a royal house, thirty leagues from London. A favor, I might add, that is sought by the most noble families of the kingdom.
BOLINGBROKE. How generous! I doubt that she'll accept.
THE DUCHESS. Why not, pray tell?

BOLINGBROKE. She wants to stay in London.
THE DUCHESS. [*With irony.*] Because of you, perhaps?
BOLINGBROKE. [*Conceitedly.*] It's possible!
THE DUCHESS. But of course! Now I see—the interest you've shown in her, the fervor, the warmth with which you come to her aid. [*Smiling.*] Tell me, Milord, do you love the little one?
BOLINGBROKE. Why should that be?
THE DUCHESS. [*Same tone.*] It would please me.
BOLINGBROKE. Why?
THE DUCHESS. [*Same tone.*] A statesman in love is lost; he has everything to fear.
BOLINGBROKE. I don't see it that way. I know many able politicians who mix business with pleasure, who console their busy lives with sweet thoughts and often leave the corridors of power to enter into spicy and mysterious intrigues. I know, for example, a great lady whom you might also know, who has been charmed by the youthful naïveté of a young gentleman from the country. This lady found it tantalizing and amusing—I can think of no other reason—to become the young man's invisible patron, controlling his earthly fate without revealing her name, without seeing him. She busied herself with his advancement and his fortune. [*Gesturing toward the* DUCHESS.] It's interesting isn't it, Madam? Believe me, that's not all. Finally through the influence of her husband, a great general, she had the young man named an officer of the Guards. This morning she sent him, to inform him secretly of his new rank, diamond insignia. They say that the jewels are magnificent.
THE DUCHESS. [*Embarrassed.*] It's not at all true. How can you be sure?
BOLINGBROKE. Here are the tabs, as well as the letter that accompanied them. [*In a whisper.*] You understand that we, because we are the only ones who know this secret, could destroy this lady. Promotions made in this manner are subject to the approval of Parliament, that is to say the Opposi-

tion. You would say to me that we must have evidence! This expensive present bought by her, this letter even with its disguised handwriting, these would both provoke frightful publicity. The great lady could perhaps weather the furor, but her husband . . . Such a hero would be inclined to act so that his reputation would be protected from disaster.

THE DUCHESS. [*Angrily.*] Sir!

BOLINGBROKE. [*Changing his tone.*] Madam, let me speak plainly. You understand: such evidence cannot remain in my hands. It is my intention to return it to the one to whom it belongs.

THE DUCHESS. Can it be so?

BOLINGBROKE. Between us, no promises and no threats, only facts! Abigail will be admitted to the Queen's household today, and everything will be returned to you.

THE DUCHESS. Right now!

BOLINGBROKE. No, only when Abigail begins her duties, and that depends on you—whether it is this evening or tomorrow.

THE DUCHESS. Oh, do you doubt me or my word?

BOLINGBROKE. Do I have reason to?

THE DUCHESS. Hate blinds you.

BOLINGBROKE. [*Gallantly.*] Not at all, I find you charming, and if, instead of placing us in opposite camps, heaven had united us, we would have ruled the world.

THE DUCHESS. Very well! Give me some proof before I consent.

BOLINGBROKE. What?

THE DUCHESS. How did you find out?

BOLINGBROKE. I cannot tell you without compromising someone.

THE DUCHESS. Whose identity I can guess. Now that you are rich, as you were quick to tell me a moment ago, you must have bought this secret at a handsome price, no doubt from Old William, my confidant.

BOLINGBROKE. Possibly.

THE DUCHESS. The only servant in whom I had confidence!

BOLINGBROKE. Not a word to him.

THE DUCHESS. Or to anyone.

BOLINGBROKE. This evening, Abigail's nomination.

THE DUCHESS. This evening, the letter.

BOLINGBROKE. I promise it . . . a faithful and frank truce for today!

THE DUCHESS. So be it! [*She gives him her hand which he kisses. Aside.*] And tomorrow war! [*She leaves by the door on the right and* BOLINGBROKE, *by the left.*]

Act 3

ABIGAIL *holding a book and the* QUEEN *holding a piece of needlework enter by the door on the right.* ABIGAIL *remains standing near the* QUEEN *as she sits on the right near the pedestal table.*

ABIGAIL. I cannot believe how happy I am although it's only been two days. I still cannot believe that I, lowly Abigail, have been given this opportunity to serve Your Majesty.

THE QUEEN. This did not come easily to you. You had to think, when I received you so coldly, that all was lost. But you see my dear, they underestimate me. I appear to go along with them, I give in every once in a while, but I don't lose sight of my desires. When the occasion arises, I show my character, as in your case.

ABIGAIL. You spoke to the mighty Duchess?

THE QUEEN. [*Naïvely.*] No, I said nothing to her, but she saw my coldness and that I was not pleased. Several hours later she found it within herself to come to me. With embarrassment she confessed that she had objected to your nomination and asked that I forgive her. Expressly to punish her, I hesitated for a moment; then I said forthrightly that I wanted you.

ABIGAIL. How good you are! [*Showing the book she is holding.*] Shall I read? [*The* QUEEN *indicates that she is ready to listen.* ABIGAIL *fetches a tabouret, places herself near the* QUEEN *and begins to read.*] History of Parliament.

THE QUEEN. [*With a gesture of boredom and putting her finger to her lip.*] How right I was to want you. Since you have been with me, my life has not been the same. I am no longer bored. I am free to think. I am more the Queen.

ABIGAIL. [*With the book.*] Can Queens be bored?

THE QUEEN. [*Taking the book and tossing it on the pedestal table.*] To death! Here I sit all day occupied with things that say nothing to the heart or to the imagination, dealing with people who are so adamant, so egotistical, so dry. They monopolize my time. You, on the other hand, have ideas that are youthful and fun.

ABIGAIL. Not always! Sometimes I am sad.

THE QUEEN. Oh, this sadness does not upset me. Remember yesterday, for example, when we talked of my poor exiled brother, whose love is lost to me. I, the Queen, am separated from my brother because of an act of Parliament.

ABIGAIL. How terrible!

THE QUEEN. Indeed it is! When I saw your tears, I knew at that moment that you understood me. You would be a companion, a true friend.

ABIGAIL. They are so right to call you Good Queen Anne.

THE QUEEN. Yes, I am good. They know it and abuse it. They torment me and burden me with their demands. They must have their places, they want everything that I can give them—and each the best, the most beautiful.

ABIGAIL. Very well. Give them their honors and power. For me, I only want to share your sadness.

THE QUEEN. [*Rising and tossing her work on the table.*] Oh, it is my entire reign that you ask, and that I give to you. You will take the place of those who are lost to me. We are all exiles: they in France, I, on the throne.

ABIGAIL. Why isolate yourself without love? You, who are young and free?

THE QUEEN. Hush, hush, that's what they all say. For their sake, I would have to marry someone whom I did not choose. I would have to consider matters of state and accept a marriage imposed by Parliament and the people. No, no, I prefer my freedom, my solitude and loneliness to slavery.

ABIGAIL. I see. When one is a princess, one cannot choose nor love for herself.

THE QUEEN. That is not always true.

ABIGAIL. What? In an idea, in a dream are you not permitted to be yourself?

THE QUEEN. [*Smiling.*] Parliament would forbid it.

ABIGAIL. And you would not defy them? You, the Queen, would not have the courage?

THE QUEEN. Who knows? I am perhaps more brave than you think.

ABIGAIL. At the right moment.

THE QUEEN. I jest. It is, as you said, a dream, an idea. A secret future where the imagination enjoys itself, a dream that one might not want to come true . . . even if it were possible. In a word, a novel which I compose for myself and which will never be read.

ABIGAIL. Why not? A reading for us alone . . . [*In a whisper.*] . . . only I would know the heroes.

THE QUEEN. [*Smiling.*] Later; I am not ready to tell you now.

ABIGAIL. It is some handsome lord; I am sure of it.

THE QUEEN. Perhaps! All I know is that for two or three months we've not spoken a word to one another. He doesn't dare speak to me. I am, after all, his Queen.

ABIGAIL. How difficult it must be to be Queen! With me, you must promise not to stand on ceremony. So, between us, in idle moments, we can talk of this unknown gentleman without fear of Parliament.

THE QUEEN. You are right! Here there is no danger; all there is is charming Abigail whom I love for being herself. You are not like the others who always plague me with matters of state. You, never.

ABIGAIL. Oh, goodness!

THE QUEEN. What's the matter.

ABIGAIL. I have a favor to ask of you, a very important favor for . . .

THE QUEEN. For whom?

ABIGAIL. For Lord Bolingbroke . . . oh, it's terrible, I forgot all about it and he trusted me . . . and Mr. Masham.

THE QUEEN. [*With emotion.*] Masham!

ABIGAIL. The officer who is on duty today. Consider, Madam, that some time ago Bolingbroke met a worthy gentleman in France. This friend did a great service for Lord Henry, and he, in return wanted to obtain for his friend . . .

THE QUEEN. A position, a title?

ABIGAIL. No, an audience with Your Majesty, or at least an invitation to tonight's reception.

THE QUEEN. It is the Duchess's responsibility to issue invitations. I will give her his name. [*Sitting down to write.*] What is it?

ABIGAIL. The Marquis de Torcy.

THE QUEEN. [*Quickly.*] Be quiet!

ABIGAIL. Why?

THE QUEEN. [*Still seated.*] He is a man whom I would honor and value, but he is an envoy of Louis XIV. If they knew that you had mentioned his name!

ABIGAIL. Why?

THE QUEEN. Why? That's all you need do to excite suspicions, jealousies, demands. It would be most tiresome. And if I should see the Marquis . . .

ABIGAIL. But Lord Bolingbroke is counting on it and has attached so much importance to it. He claims that all is lost if you refuse to receive the Marquis.

THE QUEEN. He does?

ABIGAIL. You are your own mistress, you are the Queen, you want this, don't you?

THE QUEEN. [*Embarrassed.*] Certainly, I want it.

ABIGAIL. [*Eagerly.*] Then promise to see him!

THE QUEEN. But that . . . Quiet!

THE DUCHESS. [*Entering through the door at the rear.*] Here, Madam, the dispatches from the Marshal. In spite of the uproar that Bolingbroke's speech has produced . . . [*She stops when she sees* ABIGAIL.]

THE QUEEN. Well, go on.

THE DUCHESS. [*Pointing to* ABIGAIL.] I'll wait until the young lady has left.

ABIGAIL. [*Turning to the* QUEEN.] Your Majesty wishes me to leave?

THE QUEEN. [*Embarrassed.*] No, I have some instructions to give you in a moment. [*With an affected dryness.*] Read a book. [*To the* DUCHESS *with a gracious tone.*] So, Duchess?

THE DUCHESS. [*Peevishly.*] So, in spite of Bolingbroke's speeches, the subsidies have been voted; and the Majority, doubtful until now, stood with us provided that the question be settled once and for all, and that all negotiations with Louis XIV be stopped.

THE QUEEN. Certainly.

THE DUCHESS. That is why de Torcy's presence in London is so dangerous. I felt quite justified in promising in your name that you would not see him and that his passport would be returned today. That was, I believe, our agreement.

ABIGAIL. [*Seated at the table on the right, dropping her book.*] Heavens!

THE DUCHESS. What's the matter?

ABIGAIL. [*Looking at the* QUEEN *with supplication.*] The book . . . it fell!

THE QUEEN. [*To the* DUCHESS.] It seems to me that I could hear the Marquis's proposals without risking anything.

THE DUCHESS. Listen to him? Receive him so that the fickle majority can turn against us and support Bolingbroke?

THE QUEEN. Would that happen?

THE DUCHESS. It would be a hundred times better to withdraw the bill and not to present it. If Your Majesty wants to assume responsibility for this and to expose herself to the general uproar that would follow. . . .

THE QUEEN. [*Appalled and peevish.*] Oh, Heavens no! Say no more. It overwhelms me. [*She sits at the table on the left.*]

THE DUCHESS. When it is appropriate, I will tell the Marshal what has happened and write de Torcy. I will submit these letters to Your Majesty for your approval and signature.

THE QUEEN. Very well.

THE DUCHESS. I will present them at three o'clock, just before Chapel.

THE QUEEN. Very good, thank you.

THE DUCHESS. [*Aside.*] Finally! [*She leaves.*]

ABIGAIL. [*Still seated at the table.*] Poor Marquis de Torcy. Our plans are ruined. [*She gets up, replaces the tabouret near the door at the rear where she found it.*]

THE QUEEN. [*On the left, taking the dispatches that the* DUCHESS *gave her.*] Oh, how bothersome! Must I always hear of this bill, of Parliament, of political discussions? The Marshal would have me read these dispatches—as if I understood these things, these terms of war. [*She leafs through the report.*]
ABIGAIL. [*To* MASHAM *who has appeared through the door at the rear of the stage.*] Oh, goodness, what do you want?
MASHAM. [*In a whisper.*] A letter from our friend.
ABIGAIL. [*Eagerly reading.*] "My dear child, may fortune smile on you. I suggest that you and Masham speak to the Queen as soon as possible about your marriage . . . while you are still in favor. As for me, I am ruined. I am here, waiting for you. Come at once. It concerns our well being." Oh, I must go to him. [*She leaves by the door at the rear, followed by* MASHAM.]
THE QUEEN. [*Still seated, turning toward the sound of footsteps.*] What is it? [MASHAM *stops.*] Oh, it's the officer of the Guards. Is that you, Mr. Masham?
MASHAM. Yes, Madam. [*Aside.*] Dare I follow Bolingbroke's suggestion and speak to her about our marriage?
THE QUEEN. What do you want?
MASHAM. A favor from Your Majesty.
THE QUEEN. As you wish. Thus far you have never said a word to me or asked a thing of me.
MASHAM. That's true, Your Majesty, until today I dared not . . .
THE QUEEN. What makes you so brave now?
MASHAM. That I am alone with you. Would you deign to spare me a few moments?
THE QUEEN. It is most difficult right now . . . these dispatches.
MASHAM. [*Respectfully.*] I will leave.
THE QUEEN. No. I must, after all, be kind to my subjects and receive their petitions and requests. Yours surely concerns your new rank.
MASHAM. No, Madam.
THE QUEEN. Your future advancement.
MASHAM. Not at all, Madam.
THE QUEEN. [*Smiling.*] What is this about?
MASHAM. Please, Madam. Perhaps I would appear less disrespectful if I dared to share my secrets with you.
THE QUEEN. [*Gaily.*] Well now, I adore secrets! Please go on. [*Giving him her hand.*] Know that you have my royal protection.
MASHAM. [*Kissing her hand.*] Oh Madam . . .
THE QUEEN. [*Withdrawing her hand with emotion.*] What is it?
MASHAM. Well, I already have a powerful protector. Why, I do not know.
THE QUEEN. [*Making a gesture of surprise.*] Pauh!
MASHAM. You are shocked?
THE QUEEN. [*Looking at him with kindness.*] No, I am not shocked.
MASHAM. This protector, whose identity remains a mystery to me, forbids me, under the severest strictures . . .
THE QUEEN. Forbids you what?
MASHAM. Ever to marry.
THE QUEEN. [*Laughing.*] You're right, it is strange but most interesting. [*With curiosity.*] Go on, go on. [*Turning peevishly toward Abigail who is entering.*] What is it? Who gave you permission to enter? Oh, it is you, Abigail. I'll talk to you later.
ABIGAIL. No, Madam, right now. A devoted friend asks to be admitted at once.
THE QUEEN. [*Peevishly.*] These constant interruptions and upsets. Not a moment to spend on important matters. Who demands entry? Who is it?
ABIGAIL. Lord Bolingbroke.
THE QUEEN. [*Frightened, standing up.*] Bolingbroke!
ABIGAIL. It concerns, he says, a most important matter.
THE QUEEN. [*Aside with impatience.*] Still more petitions, claims, discussions! [*Aloud.*] It's impossible; the Duchess is on her way now.
ABIGAIL. Then before she comes back.
THE QUEEN. I told you that I didn't want to be bothered by matters of state. Besides, the interview would be useless now.
ABIGAIL. Then see him anyway. Don't have him sent away; besides, I told him that you would see him.
THE QUEEN. What of the Duchess? She is planning to see him to tell him of

my decision. What have you done?
ABIGAIL. Punish me, Madam, because he is here.
THE QUEEN. [*Angrily, crossing the stage.*] Leave us!
ABIGAIL. [*To* BOLINGBROKE *at the rear of the stage in a whisper.*] She's angry.
MASHAM. [*Same tone.*] And there's nothing you can do about it.
BOLINGBROKE. Who knows—talent or luck. Here's to success! [ABIGAIL *and* MASHAM *exit.*]
THE QUEEN. [*Seated in the armchair at the pedestal table, to* BOLINGBROKE *as he approaches her and greets her respectfully.*] At any other time, Bolingbroke, I would happily receive you, for as you know I am always pleased to see you. But today of all days . . .
BOLINGBROKE. I come, nevertheless, to talk to you about England's future and de Torcy's departure.
THE QUEEN. [*Rising.*] I expected as much; just as I feared! I know, Bolingbroke, everything you are going to tell me. I appreciate your motives and I am grateful for them. It is, you see, impossible. The Marquis's passport has been signed.
BOLINGBROKE. It has not reached him yet. If he leaves, the war will become more terrible. It is a contest in which there is no victor. Please, deign to hear me out.
THE QUEEN. The arrangements have been made; I gave my word. I must tell you that the Duchess is bringing me the documents at three o'clock. If she should find you here . . .
BOLINGBROKE. I understand.
THE QUEEN. There would be new scenes and discussions; and I cannot take any more of that. I know the depth of your friendship for me, your devotion.
BOLINGBROKE. You are sending me away, dismissing me to receive an enemy. Please, Madam! I will acknowledge the Duchess's power; but the hour has not yet struck. Grant the few minutes that remain to my zeal and candor. I will not ask you to answer me. Just hear me out. [*The* QUEEN *falls into the chair. He looks at the clock.*] Fifteen minutes, Madam, fifteen minutes. That is all that is left to me to paint the misery of this country for you—our commerce depressed, our finances destroyed, our debts rising each day. The present is eating the future. All this because of the war, a war that serves neither our honor nor our interests. Ruining England to make Austria stronger. Paying taxes so that the Emperor can be powerful and Prince Eugene, glorious. Continuing an alliance in which they only profit. Yes, Madam, if you don't believe me, if you want facts, do you realize that the capture of Bouchain, in which our allies took all the glory, cost England seven million pounds sterling?
THE QUEEN. Go on, Milord.
BOLINGBROKE. [*Going on.*] Do you realize that at Malplaquet we lost thirty thousand soldiers and that in their glorious defeat our enemies only lost eight thousand? If Louis XIV would resist the influence of Mme de Maintenon, his Duchess of Marlborough, if instead of appointing the likes of the Duke de Villeroi from the halls of Versailles to command the armies, Louis XIV examined the battlefields and chose Vendôme or Catinat, do you know what would happen to us and to our allies? Alone against our alliances, France's armies are still the largest in Europe. We have seen their might and will see it again. Of that you can be sure!
THE QUEEN. Yes, Bolingbroke, yes, perhaps in your desire for peace, you are right; but I am only a weak woman. To achieve what you ask demands a courage that I do not possess. It must be achieved by you and those who are devoted to me . . .
BOLINGBROKE. [*Animated.*] Who mislead you, I swear it to you. I will show you their deceit.
THE QUEEN. No, no, leave me uninformed about this. It would be too painful. I cannot stand the thought of ill will.
BOLINGBROKE. [*Aside.*] Oh, how to deal with a queen who doesn't even know how to get angry. [*Aloud.*] What, Madam, if you could be convinced beyond a doubt that a part of our

subsidies enter the Duke of Marlborough's coffers and that this is his reason for continuing the war. . . ?

THE QUEEN. [*Fearing that the* DUCHESS *is about to enter.*] Quiet, I believe I heard . . . Go, Bolingbroke; someone is coming.

BOLINGBROKE. [*Continuing with passion.*] No, Madam. What if I told you about a tender secret whose exposure the Duchess fears, a disclosure that would bring the Duke back to London and to Court. . . ?

THE QUEEN. I won't believe you.

BOLINGBROKE. If you have reason to doubt my truth, just ask the young officer who was just here, Arthur Masham. Perhaps he could give you the details.

THE QUEEN. [*With emotion.*] Masham! What are you saying?

BOLINGBROKE. That the Duchess loves him.

THE QUEEN. [*Trembling.*] Masham?

BOLINGBROKE. [*About to leave.*] Yes! But what does it matter who he is?

THE QUEEN. [*Angrily.*] Does it matter, you ask? [*Getting up quickly.*] That they abuse me, that they deceive me, that they put caprices, intrigues, personal interests before matters of state. No, no, I want answers. Stay, Milord, stay. I want, I have to know everything. [*She goes and peers into the right wing, then comes back.*]

BOLINGBROKE. [*Aside during this time.*] Perhaps by chance . . . Young Masham! O, Destiny of England, where are you hiding?

THE QUEEN. [*With emotion.*] Very well, Bolingbroke, you said that the Duchess . . .

BOLINGBROKE. [*Watching the* QUEEN.] Wants the war to continue.

THE QUEEN. [*Same tone.*] To keep her husband away from London?

BOLINGBROKE. [*As above.*] Yes, Madam.

THE QUEEN. And out of love for Masham?

BOLINGBROKE. I have reason to believe so.

THE QUEEN. What!

BOLINGBROKE. [*Eagerly.*] First of all, the Duchess arranged his appointment to your household.

THE QUEEN. Can it be true?

BOLINGBROKE. [*The same tone.*] Through her influence, his commission was arranged.

THE QUEEN. Is that right?

BOLINGBROKE. Through her influence, he was named to the Guards a few days ago.

THE QUEEN. Now I see that you were right—all this under the guise that I myself wanted it. [*Eagerly.*] Now I know who Masham's unknown patron is.

BOLINGBROKE. Perhaps, patroness . . .

THE QUEEN. Who forbids him to marry . . .

BOLINGBROKE. [*Near the* QUEEN *and almost in her ear.*] It was she who created this romantic adventure to excite her lively imagination. Because she wanted to enjoy these sweet pleasures without constraints, our noble Duchess kept her husband at the head of our armies and had subsidies voted to continue the war. [*Purposefully.*] A war which gives him his glory, his fortune, and his happiness, a happiness so great that he ignored her machinations. By another quirk of fate, august personages believed that they were serving his ambitions when in fact they were serving her passions. How she must have laughed up her sleeve! [*Seeing the* QUEEN's *angry gesture.*] Yes, Madam.

THE QUEEN. Quiet! She's here!

THE DUCHESS. [*Entering proudly through the door on the right. She sees* BOLINGBROKE *and is shocked.*] Bolingbroke! [*He bows and greets her.*]

THE QUEEN. [*Trying to hide her anger, addressing the* DUCHESS *coldly.*] What is it, Madam? What do you want?

THE DUCHESS. [*Handing her the papers in her hand.*] De Torcy's passport and the letter to accompany it.

THE QUEEN. [*Drily.*] Very well. [*She throws them on the table.*]

THE DUCHESS. I brought them for Your Majesty's signature.

THE QUEEN. [*As above, going to sit at the table on the left.*] Very well, I'll read them.

THE DUCHESS. [*Aside.*] Heavens! [*Aloud.*] Your Majesty decided earlier today to sign these.

THE QUEEN. Indeed! Other considerations have, however, changed my mind.

THE DUCHESS. [*Angrily and looking at* BOLINGBROKE.] That's easy to see; and I can guess whose influence you are following.

THE QUEEN. [*Trying to contain herself.*] What do you mean? Whose influence? I heard nothing or no one. I am following only the voice of reason, of justice, and of the public welfare.

BOLINGBROKE. [*Standing near the table, to the right of the* QUEEN.] We know everything!

THE QUEEN. You can keep the truth from me, but when it reaches me, when it concerns the nation, I do not hesitate to act.

BOLINGBROKE. She speaks as a queen!

THE QUEEN. [*Animatedly.*] It is evident that the capture of Bouchain cost England seven million pounds sterling.

THE DUCHESS. Madam!

THE QUEEN. [*More and more animatedly.*] It is certain that when everything is calculated, we lost thirty thousand soldiers at the battle of Hochstadt or as we call it Malplaquet.

THE DUCHESS. Allow me.

THE QUEEN. [*Getting up.*] And you want me to sign a letter without considering the seriousness of the consequences? No, Duchess, I do not serve ambitious designs or any other for that matter. I will not sacrifice the interest of the nation for them.

THE DUCHESS. A word . . .

THE QUEEN. No! It is time we were in Chapel. [*To* ABIGAIL *who has just entered through the door on the right.*] Come, let us go.

ABIGAIL. Your Majesty is distressed?

THE QUEEN. [*In a whisper and leading her aside.*] Not without reason. There is a mystery that I want to unravel. I must see the person of whom we spoke earlier. I must question him.

ABIGAIL. [*Gaily.*] Who, our unknown favorite?

THE QUEEN. You will bring him to me; those are your instructions.

ABIGAIL. [*Same tone.*] To do that, I must know who he is.

THE QUEEN. [*Turning, sees* MASHAM *who is entering through the door at the rear. He presents the* QUEEN *her gloves and her Bible. She whispers to* ABIGAIL.] Oh, dear, he's here!

ABIGAIL. [*Frozen with surprise.*] Oh Heavens!

BOLINGBROKE. [*Coming along side her.*] The contest was superb!

ABIGAIL. It is lost!

BOLINGBROKE. It is won! [*The* QUEEN *takes the gloves and Bible from* MASHAM; *she motions* ABIGAIL *to follow. They exit. The* DUCHESS *angrily gathers up her papers and leaves.* BOLINGBROKE *looks at her with triumph.*]

Act 4

Enter the DUCHESS.

THE DUCHESS. How extraordinary! For the first time in her life she has shown some will, actual will. Are Bolingbroke's talents responsible? Or could it be the influence of that young girl? [*With bad humor.*] We shall see; I will discover the reasons for this change. I will wait until they leave the Chapel where once she and I shared loving thoughts . . . She was alone. Bolingbroke and Abigail were not there and yet she resisted. I had to use the most drastic measures— the bill for the recall of the Stuarts. I promised her that it would pass Parliament today if the Marquis was banished. Here's his passport, I have it! For tomorrow, only twenty-four more hours. As she signed it, this queen who cannot hide a thing, not even her ill will, took a tone of bitterness and dryness that was unusual even for her. There was irony, spite, and a secret anger so concentrated that she could not let it explode. [*Laughing.*]. It's a fact, she hates her favorite. How well I use her hatred to my advantage. Favor based on love melts away quickly, but when it is based on hate, it can only grow. That's the secret of my power. Who's there? Oh, our young captain. [*Enter* MASHAM.]

MASHAM. It's the Duchess. Abigail has warned me to avoid her at all costs. Why should I? Must we always be afraid to trust? [*He greets her with respect.*]

THE DUCHESS. Why, it's Mr. Masham, the newest officer of the Guards to be nominated by the Duke of Marlborough.

MASHAM. Yes, milady. [*Aside.*] Heavens! She's going to have me dismissed.

THE DUCHESS. What are your qualifications for this post?

MASHAM. Very few, if you count my virtues. As many as can be, if you count my zeal and courage.

THE DUCHESS. Well done! I like your answer, and I see that the Duke was right to nominate you.

MASHAM. I only wish he had granted me another favor.

THE DUCHESS. He will grant it, no doubt. Tell me.

MASHAM. Can it be?

THE DUCHESS. What is this favor?

MASHAM. The opportunity of showing my gratitude by calling me to serve with him in the field.

THE DUCHESS. It is as good as done. Do you trust me?

MASHAM. Oh, Madam, how good you are. They told me you were our enemy.

THE DUCHESS. What? Who?

MASHAM. They shall remain unnamed, and they shall not sway my devotion to you.

THE DUCHESS. May I count on your devotion? May I claim it as mine?

MASHAM. I am at your service.

THE DUCHESS. [*Looking at him with kindness.*] Very well, Masham, I am pleased with you. [*Motioning him to come forward.*] Come.

MASHAM. [*Aside.*] How good she is! I can't get over it.

THE DUCHESS. You did hear me, didn't you?

MASHAM. Yes, Milady. [*Aside.*] What does she want of me?

THE DUCHESS. The Queen has charged me with an important mission which caused me to think of your devotion. You will report to me each day on the results of your actions; you will consult with me, and follow my orders so that we may get to the bottom of this crime.

MASHAM. A crime?

THE DUCHESS. Yes, a bold crime, truly unworthy, took place in Saint James Palace, a few days ago. A member of the Opposition, for whom I had little respect, Richard Bolingbroke . . .

MASHAM. Heavens!

THE DUCHESS. Was murdered.

MASHAM. [*Indignantly.*] No, Madam. He was killed justly with his sword in his hand by a gentlemen whose honor had been insulted.

THE DUCHESS. Very well, if you know the murderer, hand him over to me. You promised me, and we are sworn to pursue him.

MASHAM. Pursue no one, Madam, because it is I.

THE DUCHESS. You, Masham?

MASHAM. Indeed.

THE DUCHESS. [*Quickly putting her hand over his mouth.*] Quiet, quiet! No one must know. What a storm would rage around you—attached to the Court and the Queen's household! You have nothing to feel guilty about, nothing. I'm sure that you are telling me the truth; no one could doubt your word, Masham. Our enemies will seize upon your nomination to the Guards the very day of the duel as a reward.

MASHAM. How true!

THE DUCHESS. We could no longer defend you.

MASHAM. Can it be so? What do I care!

THE DUCHESS. There's only one way to save yourself—you must join the Duke in the field. Remember how ardently you begged for this a moment ago.

MASHAM. How can I ever thank you?

THE DUCHESS. [*With emotion.*] In a few days, Masham, this affair will die down and be forgotten. You must leave tomorrow, and I want to send some dispatches for the Marshal with you. Come for them.

MASHAM. When?

THE DUCHESS. After the Queen's reception this evening. So that no one may suspect your departure, make sure

that no one sees you.
MASHAM. I give you my word! You have mystified me, you whom I feared and distrusted. In gratitude, I want to open my soul to you.
THE DUCHESS. Tonight is time enough for that. Quiet, they're coming.
ABIGAIL. [*Upset, entering by the door on the right.*] Alone with her!
THE DUCHESS. [*Aside.*] That little Abigail! I meet her everywhere! [*Aloud.*] What brings you here? What do you want? Do you have something to tell me?
ABIGAIL. [*Troubled, looking at them.*] Nothing . . . I don't know . . . I'm afraid . . . [*Collecting her thoughts.*] Oh yes, now I remember, the Queen wants to see you, Madam.
THE DUCHESS. Very well, I will see her in a little while.
ABIGAIL. Now, Madam. The Queen is waiting for you.
THE DUCHESS. [*Angrily.*] Very well, tell your mistress . . .
ABIGAIL. [*Dignified.*] I have nothing to say to anyone but you, Madam. The Queen, my mistress and yours, wishes to see you at once. [*The* DUCHESS *makes an angry gesture, collects herself, then exits.*]
MASHAM. What is bothering you, Abigail? Tell me.
ABIGAIL. Why not? I have the right. And you, sir, why are you taking her side?
MASHAM. Because of what she has done for us. You told me that she was terrible and imperious.
ABIGAIL. Wicked. I said it, and I will say it again.
MASHAM. Then you are mistaken. You do not know what I owe to her goodness and protection.
ABIGAIL. Her protection? Who told you that?
MASHAM. No one. After I confessed my part in the duel with Richard Bolingbroke, she, in her generosity, promised to defend and protect me.
ABIGAIL. [*Drily.*] Whatever from? Isn't Mr. Saint John enough? I don't see that there is a need for so much protection.
MASHAM. [*Shocked.*] Abigail! I don't recognize you! Why this anger, this emotional outburst?
ABIGAIL. What do you mean? I came running, intent on obeying the Queen. There's nothing wrong with me. But the Duchess, what did she say to you?
MASHAM. To keep me safe from danger, she wants me to join the Marshal tomorrow.
ABIGAIL. [*Gasping.*] Protecting you from danger by sending you to the battlefield? And you believe that this woman loves you? [*Catching herself.*] No, I meant to say, looks out for your interests, protects you.
MASHAM. Certainly! I told her I would take some dispatches to the Marshal. I'm meeting her this evening in her apartment.
ABIGAIL. You agreed to that! Oh dear!
MASHAM. What's the matter?
ABIGAIL. Are you going?
MASHAM. Certainly. She was so kind, so gracious to me. Just as you came in, I was going to tell her about our plans to marry.
ABIGAIL. [*Happily.*] Really! [*Aside.*] And I suspected him! [*Aloud, with emotion.*] Dear Arthur, your words have made me so happy.
MASHAM. I'm glad; and this evening I shall tell her about us.
ABIGAIL. No, no, please don't; find a reason not to follow her orders.
MASHAM. Why not? She will be offended, and our fate will be sealed.
ABIGAIL. No matter. It would be better . . .
MASHAM. Why?
ABIGAIL. [*Embarrassed.*] Because this evening at the same time the Queen asked me to invite you to her apartments. She wants to see you and talk to you. She expects you; but her plans are still uncertain.
MARSHAM. I see. I will, of course, go to the Queen.
ABIGAIL. Don't do that either.
MASHAM. Why not?
ABIGAIL. I can't tell you. Please help me; I am so upset, so unhappy.
MASHAM. What's the matter?
ABIGAIL. Listen to me, Arthur, do you love me as I love you?
MASHAM. More than my life!
ABIGAIL. My sentiments exactly! Do not

think that I am trying to hurt your advancement or your fortune, however absurd my instructions may appear to you. Give me your word that you will accept them without asking me why.
MASHAM. I promise.
ABIGAIL. To begin with, never mention our plans to the Duchess.
MASHAM. You're right. It would be better to tell the Queen.
ABIGAIL. [*Quickly.*] That would be even worse!
MASHAM. That's the reason I asked for an audience this morning. I am sure that she will protect us because she received me with such kindness and friendship.
ABIGAIL. [*Aside.*] He calls that kindness!
MASHAM. She was so gentle as I kissed her hand. [*To* ABIGAIL.] What's wrong with you? Your hand is like ice.
ABIGAIL. No! [*Aside.*] She didn't tell me about that. [*Aloud.*] I also share the Queen's good favor, I am showered with her goodness and kindness. Yet, for our happiness together, it might be better to remain poor and miserable than to live at Court in the midst of these beautiful people, surrounded by so many dangers, so many seductions.
MASHAM. [*Angrily.*] Oh, now I understand! One of the great nobles wants to separate us, tear us apart, carry you off from my love.
ABIGAIL. Yes, that's almost it! Quiet, someone is at the door. It's Bolingbroke. I sent him a note telling him to come. He's the only one that can help us now.
MASHAM. Do you think so?
ABIGAIL. Yes, and for that reason, you must leave us alone.
MASHAM. [*Shocked.*] Leave?
ABIGAIL. You promised.
MASHAM. And I pledge myself completely to you. [*He kisses her hand and exits through the door at the rear.*]
ABIGAIL. [*As he leaves, she watches him lovingly.*] Oh, Arthur, how I love you, more than before, more than ever, perhaps because they want to take you away from me. No, I would love you in any case. [*A knock at the door on the left.*] Oh, I forgot about Bolingbroke. I've lost my head! [*She opens the door for* BOLINGBROKE.]
BOLINGBROKE. [*Entering gaily.*] I came running as soon as I read your note. The Queen's new favorite! Everyone is talking about your success.
ABIGAIL. [*Without listening to him.*] Yes, yes, the Queen adores me, and nothing can happen without me. Quickly or all is lost!
BOLINGBROKE. Heavens! Has de Torcy . . . ?
ABIGAIL. [*Striking her forehead.*] Oh! It's true. I'm not thinking straight. The Dutchess came into the Queen's chambers and she signed the passport.
BOLINGBROKE. [*Frightened.*] The ambassador's passport?
ABIGAIL. That's not all, compared to Masham . . .
BOLINGBROKE. The Marquis is leaving London?
ABIGAIL. [*Not listening.*] In twenty four hours. [*With force.*] If only you knew!
BOLINGBROKE. [*Angrily.*] And the Duchess?
ABIGAIL. [*Quickly.*] The Duchess is no longer to be feared; now there is a more formidable opponent.
BOLINGBROKE. For whom?
ABIGAIL. For Masham!
BOLINGBROKE. [*Impatiently.*] Don't treat affairs of the heart as affairs of state! I told you about peace, about war, about all the interests of Europe.
ABIGAIL. And I told you of mine. Europe can go it alone. I, should you abandon me, I should die.
BOLINGBROKE. Please, my dear, please. You, first of all. Ambition, you see, is egotistical and always begins with itself.
ABIGAIL. Like love.
BOLINGBROKE. Indeed! Let's see! You say that the Queen signed the passport?
ABIGAIL. [*Impatiently.*] Yes, because of a bill that they are going to present.
BOLINGBROKE. I know about that. So, the Duchess is still in favor?
ABIGAIL. [*Same tone.*] No, the Queen hates her and is upset with her. She hasn't told me why, and I don't dare ask.
BOLINGBROKE. [*Eagerly.*] An explosion,

waiting for a spark! Only twenty-four hours! It is possible! Did you remind her that the Marquis is leaving in twenty-four hours? What would be gained by receiving him today? Nothing but respect for a great king and good politics, politics of the future. His envoy should be received with honor. Did you tell her that?

ABIGAIL. [*Distracted.*] I think so, I'm not sure—my mind was on other things.

BOLINGBROKE. I can understand your dilemma. Now, to the other matter.

ABIGAIL. Remember how terrified and desperate I was this morning when I learned of the Duchess's interest in Arthur? Well, that's nothing! Another great lady [*Embarrassed*] whose name I dare not say . . .

BOLINGBROKE. [*Aside.*] Poor child, she thinks she's telling me something I don't know. [*Aloud.*] How did you find out about this?

ABIGAIL. It's a secret that I cannot betray.

BOLINGBROKE. [*Intently.*] I applaud your discretion and will pry no further. This person, be she duchess or marquise, does she also love Masham?

ABIGAIL. It's terrible, it's not fair. They all have princes, dukes, and great lords who love them; but all I have is Arthur. How can I, a poor child, defend myself, fight for him against two great ladies?

BOLINGBROKE. Very easily. Two are less formidable than one.

ABIGAIL. [*Shocked.*] If only you could tell me how!

BOLINGBROKE. Very simply. When a great kingdom wants to conquer a little province, there are no obstacles to the conquest, and the province is lost. But when another great empire has the same idea, the province has a chance of escaping. The two great powers which watch each other, frustrate each other's plans, neutralize each other; as a result, the threatened province escapes, thanks to the number of her enemies. Do you understand?

ABIGAIL. Somewhat. The danger is still there! The Duchess has planned a rendezvous with Masham after the Queen's reception.

BOLINGBROKE. Very good!

ABIGAIL. [*Impatiently.*] No, sir, it is not very good.

BOLINGBROKE. My thoughts exactly.

ABIGAIL. At that very moment the other person, the other great lady, wants to receive him in her apartments.

BOLINGBROKE. What did I tell you? They are each destroying the other's chances. He cannot be two places at once.

ABIGAIL. In neither, I hope. Fortunately, this great lady still does not know and will not know until the last moment if she will be free to receive him. Her freedom is not her own. I cannot tell you why.

BOLINGBROKE. [*Coldly.*] Her husband?

ABIGAIL. [*Quickly.*] You might say. If she manages to get away . . .

BOLINGBROKE. She will manage, I'm sure of that.

ABIGAIL. To signal Arthur and me that all is clear for the rendezvous, she will complain in front of everyone of the heat and casually ask for a glass of water.

BOLINGBROKE. Meaning, I'm expecting you, hurry.

ABIGAIL. Word for word.

BOLINGBROKE. That's simple enough.

ABIGAIL. Too simple. I have told Arthur none of this. It's useless, isn't it? Because I don't want him to go to either rendezvous; I'd rather die, rather destroy myself.

BOLINGBROKE. What do you mean?

ABIGAIL. Oh, what do I matter? But Arthur? The more I think about it, do I have the right to destroy his future, to expose him to terrible vengeance, to powerful hate because of this or because of the duel? He could be found out and arrested. What can I do? Help me! I don't know where else to turn; my faith is in you.

BOLINGBROKE. [*Reflecting, he takes her hand.*] Your faith is well placed, dear child. Dear Abigail, calm yourself! The Marquis de Torcy shall have his invitation for this evening. He will see the Queen.

ABIGAIL. [*Impatiently.*] Sir!

BOLINGBROKE. [*Quickly.*] We are saved, even Masham! Without compromising him or destroying you. I will prevent those two rendezvous.

ABIGAIL. Oh, Bolingbroke, if you are right, I will owe you my devotion, my friendship, my entire life. The Queen is coming. Go! If someone should see you . . . !

BOLINGBROKE. [*Coldly, as he notices the* DUCHESS.] I can stay; someone has seen me. [*The* DUCHESS *enters through the door on the right; catching sight of* ABIGAIL *and* BOLINGBROKE, *she makes an ironic curtsey to* ABIGAIL. ABIGAIL *returns it and leaves.* BOLINGBROKE *remains standing between the two women.*]

BOLINGBROKE. [*Ironically.*] Praises be! Blood will finally out. You were so gracious to your cousin. There's hope for me yet!

THE DUCHESS. [*Same tone.*] How true! You predicted that one day we would end up loving each other.

BOLINGBROKE. [*Gallantly.*] I've already begun. And you, Madam?

THE DUCHESS. I still admire your shrewdness and talent.

BOLINGBROKE. You could also include my loyalty, for I have faithfully kept all the promises I made to you.

THE DUCHESS. And I, mine. I nominated that person to whom you were just speaking. There she is quite near the Queen, positioned as you wished to confound my plans and to serve yours.

BOLINGBROKE. You hold nothing back. How spirited you are!

THE DUCHESS. I have just enough spirit to disrupt your plans. Miss Abigail, on your orders, would have the Marquis de Torcy invited to tonight's reception.

BOLINGBROKE. I was wrong; I should have approached you before I asked her, Madam. That is exactly what I will do now. [*He goes to the table and picks up a printed letter.*] Here are the invitations. It is your responsibility as Chief Lady-in-Waiting to issue these. Surely, you will do me that service.

THE DUCHESS. [*Laughing.*] Truly, Milord, a service, for you!

BOLINGBROKE. Please understand that I am prepared to do a far greater one for you. It's the only way that we can get along. As with my debts and your profit of three hundred percent, the advantage is yours.

THE DUCHESS. Milord, you speak of a certain letter that you intercepted; I have taken the necessary measure to insure that such a letter never sees the light of day. I have several charming letters from Milady, the Viscountess Bolingbroke, your wife. [*In a whisper and confidentially.*] I got them from Lord Avon.

BOLINGBROKE. [*The same tone and smiling.*] At a pretty price, no doubt!

THE DUCHESS. [*Angrily.*] Sir!

BOLINGBROKE. What does it matter? You have them, and I do not intend to take them from you or threaten you in any way. On the contrary, even though the truce is over, I will act as if it is still in effect and give you some news that you should know.

THE DUCHESS. [*Ironically.*] Will it please me?

BOLINGBROKE. [*Smiling.*] I don't think so; perhaps that's why I am sharing it with you. [*In a whisper.*] You have a rival.

THE DUCHESS. [*Quickly.*] What do you mean?

BOLINGBROKE. There is a lady at Court, a great lady, who has designs on young Masham. I know everything—the hour, the place, and the signal for the rendezvous.

THE DUCHESS. [*Trembling with anger.*] You are teasing me.

BOLINGBROKE. [*Coldly.*] Indeed not! It is just as certain as the fact that you are expecting him in your apartment after the Queen's reception tonight.

THE DUCHESS. My God!

BOLINGBROKE. You should try to stop her at the reception because she will certainly fight you for him and keep him from your love. Farewell, Madam. [*He starts out the door on the left.*]

THE DUCHESS. [*Angrily, following him as far as the table on the left.*] Tell me the place of the rendezvous, the signal. Tell me!

BOLINGBROKE. [*Handing her the pen from the table.*] As soon as you have written this invitation to de Torcy. [*She eagerly sits down.*] An invitation which will honor de Torcy's mission and which will give you the opportunity to reject his proposals and to continue your war with him . . . as you have with me. [*Seeing that the letter is signed, he rings. A footman appears and he takes the letter.*] To the Marquis de Torcy, Hotel Ambassador, across from the palace. [*The footman leaves.*] He will have it in five minutes.

THE DUCHESS. Now, Milord, about this lady . . .

BOLINGBROKE. She will be at the Queen's reception this evening.

THE DUCHESS. It's Lady Albermarle or Lady Elworth, I'm sure of it.

BOLINGBROKE. [*Intently.*] I've forgotten the name, but we will all soon know it. If she is able to get away, if the rendezvous is to take place, they will exchange a signal.

THE DUCHESS. [*Impatiently.*] Go on, go on, please!

BOLINGBROKE. In a loud voice, the lady will ask Masham for a glass of water.

THE DUCHESS. Here, this evening?

BOLINGBROKE. Indeed; you will be able to see for yourself if my information is correct.

THE DUCHESS. [*Angrily.*] A pox on them! I will spare them nothing!

BOLINGBROKE. [*Aside.*] I can count on that!

THE DUCHESS. I shall unmask them before the whole Court.

BOLINGBROKE. Calm yourself! Here's the Queen and her ladies! [*The Queen, Lady Albemarle and the ladies of the Court enter from the right. The Gentlemen of the Court and members of Parliament enter from the rear. The ladies sit in a semicircle to the right.* ABIGAIL *and the Maids of honor stand behind them.* BOLINGBROKE *and the members of the Opposition are on the left.* THE DUCHESS, *watching the ladies, is on the right.* MASHAM *and several officers are on the same side.*]

THE DUCHESS. [*Aside and inspecting all the ladies.*] Which one? I can't decide who it is. [*To the* QUEEN *who is approaching her.*] I will prepare the game, Madam.

THE QUEEN. [*Seeking out* MASHAM.] Wonderful! [*Aside.*] I don't see him.

THE DUCHESS. [*Aloud.*] The Queen's game table! [*Approaching the* QUEEN *and in a whisper.*] There have been so many complaints that it was necessary to send de Torcy an invitation.

THE QUEEN. [*Not listening and still searching.*] Very good! [*Finding* MASHAM.] There he is.

THE DUCHESS. The Opposition should be pleased.

THE QUEEN. [*Looking at* MASHAM.] And Abigail too, no doubt.

THE DUCHESS. [*Ironically.*] Really? [*The* DUCHESS *gives orders for the* QUEEN'S *game table. A* MEMBER OF PARLIAMENT *approaches* BOLINGBROKE.]

MEMBER OF PARLIAMENT. Yes, gentlemen, I know for a matter of fact that all negotiations have been broken off.

BOLINGBROKE. Are you certain?

MEMBER OF PARLIAMENT. The Duchess's power is such that the Ambassador has been dismissed.

BOLINGBROKE. Extraordinary!

MEMBER OF PARLIAMENT. He leaves tomorrow without being able to see the Queen.

MASTER OF CEREMONIES. The Marquis de Torcy! [*General disbelief. Everyone gets up to greet him.* BOLINGBROKE *goes to him, takes him by the hand to present him to the* QUEEN.]

THE QUEEN. [*Graciously.*] Sir, welcome. We are pleased to receive you.

THE DUCHESS. [*Whispering to the* QUEEN.] Nothing more, please be careful.

THE QUEEN. [*Turning to* BOLINGBROKE *who is on her other side and in a whisper.*] I know you are pleased by this invitation. You see, when I want something . . .

BOLINGBROKE. [*Bowing respectfully.*] Oh, Madam, what goodness!

DE TORCY. [*Whispering to* BOLINGBROKE.] I just now received the letter at my hotel.

BOLINGBROKE. [*Same tone.*] I know.

DE TORCY. [*Same tone.*] All is going well?

BOLINGBROKE. [*Same tone.*] Better than I had hoped. And soon . . .

DE TORCY. [*Same tone.*] Some great change in the Queen's politics?

BOLINGBROKE. [*As above.*] That will depend on us.

DE TORCY. [*As above.*] On Parliament or the Ministers?

BOLINGBROKE. [*As above.*] No, on an alliance much more trivial and fragile.

The Glass of Water 201

[*Servants bring in the game table. It is arranged with an armchair and two side chairs.*]

THE DUCHESS. [*On the other side and addressing the* QUEEN.] Whom does Your Majesty choose as players?

THE QUEEN. Whomever you wish; you do the choosing.

THE DUCHESS. Lady Abercrombie?

THE QUEEN. No! [*She points to a lady near her.*] Lady Albemarle.

LADY ALBEMARLE. Thank you, Your Majesty.

THE DUCHESS. [*Aside.*] And I too! [*Watching* LADY ALBEMARLE.] This way she can't speak to him. [*Aloud.*] And the third?

THE QUEEN. The third? [*Seeing* DE TORCY, *who is approaching her.*] The Ambassador. [*General astonishment,* BOLINGBROKE *overjoyed.*]

THE DUCHESS. [*Reproaching the* QUEEN.] What a choice! Where are your loyalties?

THE QUEEN. [*Whispering.*] No matter.

THE DUCHESS. [*Whispering.*] Watch what will happen.

THE QUEEN. [*Same tone.*] You should have chosen yourself.

THE DUCHESS. [*Same tone.*] They will think . . . they will believe . . .

THE QUEEN. [*Same tone.*] Whatever they want. [DE TORCY *hands his hat to one of the gentlemen, presents his hand to the* QUEEN *who leads him to the game table. He sits between her and* LADY ALBEMARLE. *The* DUCHESS, *observing all, leaves the table and goes to the left.*]

BOLINGBROKE. [*Whispering to the* DUCHESS.] You are too generous, Duchess. How well you arranged it—the Marquis invited to the reception and chosen as the Queen's partner! It's more than I could ever ask.

THE DUCHESS. [*Spitefully.*] And more than I could ever wish.

BOLINGBROKE. I'm just sorry that you don't share my opinion. See how pleasantly he is chatting with Her Majesty.

THE DUCHESS. Really! [*She starts to move away.*]

BOLINGBROKE. [*Holding her back.*] Let's not disturb them. It would be better to watch and listen because I think the moment is at hand.

THE DUCHESS. Yes, but who is she?

THE QUEEN. [*Still playing and appearing to answer the* MARQUIS.] You are right, Marquis, the room is quite stuffy. [*With emotion, addressing* MASHAM.] Mr. Masham! [MASHAM *comes forward.*] Would you bring me a glass of water?

THE DUCHESS. [*Gasping and taking a step toward the* QUEEN.] Oh, no!

THE QUEEN. What's the matter, Duchess?

THE DUCHESS. [*Furious and trying to contain herself.*] It's just . . . it's just . . . Your Majesty, is it possible?

THE QUEEN. [*Still seated and turning toward her.*] What are you trying to say? What's wrong with you?

THE DUCHESS. Is it possible that Your Majesty has forgotten?

BOLINGBROKE and DE TORCY. [*Trying to calm her.*] Madam!

LADY ALBEMARLE. What a lack of respect for the Queen!

THE QUEEN. [*With dignity.*] What, then, have I forgotten?

THE DUCHESS. [*Troubled and trying to regain control.*] The rights, the etiquette, the privileges of the Court. This honor belongs to one of your ladies.

THE QUEEN. [*Shocked.*] Too much noise for that! [*Turning back to the game table.*] Very well, Duchess, fetch it yourself.

THE DUCHESS. [*Stupified.*] I!!

BOLINGBROKE. [*To the* DUCHESS *as* MASHAM *presents her the tray.*] I agree, Duchess, you should present it yourself. There, right in front of them; it's much more effective that way.

THE DUCHESS. [*Barely containing herself and taking the tray from* MASHAM.] Oh!

THE QUEEN. [*Impatiently.*] Well, Madam, did you hear me? You insisted on this privilege. [*The* DUCHESS, *her hand trembling with anger, presents the tray to the* QUEEN. *The glass of water slides off the tray and spills on the* QUEEN's *dress. The* QUEEN *quickly stands up.*] How awkward you are! [*Everyone stands up, and* ABIGAIL *goes to the* QUEEN.]

THE DUCHESS. That's the first time Your Majesty has spoken to me in that tone.

THE QUEEN. [*Acidly.*] That only proves

my indulgence!

THE DUCHESS. [*Acidly.*] After all I've done for you.

THE QUEEN. [*Acidly.*] Must I hear myself rebuked?

THE DUCHESS. I will not bother Your Majesty with my presence any more. I submit my resignation.

THE QUEEN. I accept it.

THE DUCHESS. [*Aside.*] Heavens!

THE QUEEN. I do not need your services any longer. My Lords and Ladies, you may leave.

BOLINGBROKE. [*To the* DUCHESS.] Duchess, the game is over.

THE DUCHESS. [*Aside, angrily.*] Never! Masham will not keep his rendezvous with her. [*Aloud to the* QUEEN.] A moment, please, Your Majesty. Along with my resignation I must also report on Your Majesty's last charge to me.

BOLINGBROKE. [*Aside.*] What is she going to do?

THE DUCHESS. [*Pointing to* BOLINGBROKE.] At the request of Milord and his colleagues of the Opposition, you ordered me to find the murderer of Richard Bolingbroke.

BOLINGBROKE. [*Aside.*] Good God!

THE DUCHESS. [*To* BOLINGBROKE.] Now it is you who must act. Arrest Mr. Masham at once! There he is!

THE QUEEN. [*Sadly.*] Masham! Is it true?

MASHAM. [*Lowering his head.*] Yes, Madam.

THE DUCHESS. [*Contemplating the* QUEEN's *sadness, whispering to* BOLINGBROKE.] I have my vengeance.

BOLINGBROKE. [*Whispering and joyfully.*] Yes, but we have won the day.

THE DUCHESS. [*Proudly.*] Not yet, Sir! [*At the* QUEEN's *gesture,* BOLINGBROKE *receives* MASHAM's *sword. The* QUEEN, *supported by* ABIGAIL, *enters her apartments. The* DUCHESS *exits through the rear door.*]

Act 5

The QUEEN's *private quarters. Two doors at the rear. On the left, a window with a balcony. On the right, the door leading to the rest of the* QUEEN's *apartment. On the left, a table and a sofa.*

BOLINGBROKE. [*Entering by the door on the left.*] "After the meeting of Parliament, in the Queen's quarters." Abigail wrote me to come at once. All doors are open before me! Does Her Majesty, my gentle ally, want to talk to me? The Duchess and the Queen are furious with each other. The explosion which was so easily set has finally taken place. It was sure to happen. These two august friends have so long only needed an occasion to tell each other of their hate. Knowing the Duchess's proud, imperious nature, I expected better of her first salvo. I was sure that she would rebuke the Queen before the Court by exposing the secret intrigue and the rendezvous; but she tricked me by stopping in time. She controlled herself. The first blows, however, have been struck! The Duchess is in disgrace, the Whigs are furious, and the bill has been rejected. A general upheaval! I am right in thinking that a glass of water has changed the government's policy. [*Reflecting.*] As soon as I am Minister . . .

ABIGAIL. [*Entering through the door on the right.*] Oh, Milord, here you are!

BOLINGBROKE. Just thinking about a Ministry . . .

ABIGAIL. Whose?

BOLINGBROKE. Mine, of course. I am eager to start; I will not be delayed.

ABIGAIL. Oh, sir, we are farther away from that than ever.

BOLINGBROKE. What has happened?

ABIGAIL. Let me tell you. While I was in the Queen's bedroom, helping her and talking about Masham—he's not in danger, is he?

BOLINGBROKE. Under house arrest in my most comfortable quarters.

ABIGAIL. And after that?

BOLINGBROKE. Nothing to fear if we are the victors.

ABIGAIL. [*Naively.*] Oh, you've frightened me.

BOLINGBROKE. [*Quickly.*] I share your fear. Now, go on!

ABIGAIL. A great lady came to the Queen's apartments. Milady, Milady . . . she is devoted to the Queen.

BOLINGBROKE. Lady Abercrombie?
ABIGAIL. Yes, that's who it was! She was accompanied by Lord Devonshire and Walpole.
BOLINGBROKE. Friends of the Duchess.
ABIGAIL. Who came on their own.
BOLINGBROKE. Meaning that they were sent by the Duchess.
ABIGAIL. To tell the Queen that the Duchess's dismissal has had terrible repercussions, that the Whigs are furious, and that the bill for the recall of the Stuarts would be rejected.
BOLINGBROKE. How did the Queen react?
ABIGAIL. She said nothing and was indecisive. From time to time she would look around the room for help, especially appealing to me for help.
BOLINGBROKE. What are their plans?
ABIGAIL. I haven't found out yet.
BOLINGBROKE. Ask some of the Queen's counsellors. What happened next?
ABIGAIL. The Queen became even more unsure of herself, then Lady Abercrombie spoke to her in a whisper.
BOLINGBROKE. What did she say?
ABIGAIL. I couldn't hear. Although I was nearby, I could only hear a name or two—Lord Avondale and Masham. [*Eagerly.*] Yes, I'm sure of that. The Queen, who had been cold and severe until then, said with warmth, "Don't say any more. If she comes, I'll see her."
BOLINGBROKE. [*Angrily.*] The Duchess! Returning to the palace as if nothing has happened.
ABIGAIL. In my confusion, I decided to write you to come at once. You must know what has happened and what has been decided.
BOLINGBROKE. What?
ABIGAIL. The Queen and these gentlemen have decided on reconciliation.
BOLINGBROKE. What?
ABIGAIL. They decided that the Duchess should meet the Queen today so that she could return the keys to the Queen's private quarters. [*Pointing to the door on the right.*] There's a key that allows her to enter the Queen's apartment at will.
BOLINGBROKE. [*Impatiently.*] I knew it!
ABIGAIL. The Queen will refuse to take it; the Duchess will then fall at her feet. The Queen will pick her up, and they will make up. The bill will pass and the Marquis de Torcy will be dismissed.
BOLINGBROKE. Oh, how weak women are! And at the very moment we had victory in our hands!
ABIGAIL. Is it over?
BOLINGBROKE. No, no, Lady Luck and I know each other too well. I flout her, and sometimes she deserts me, but she always comes back. When is the reconciliation to take place?
ABIGAIL. In half an hour.
BOLINGBROKE. I must speak to the Queen.
ABIGAIL. She is closeted with her Ministers who just arrived. That's why she sent me away.
BOLINGBROKE. [*Striking his forehead.*] My God, my God! What can we do? I have to rekindle the hatred that I produced in her. What will it take to fan it? Only half an hour to accomplish this!
ABIGAIL. [*Pointing to the door at the rear, on the left as it opens. . . .*] What luck! Here's the Queen!
BOLINGBROKE. [*Sighing.*] I knew that it was not over between Lady Luck and me! Leave us, Abigail, leave us. Watch for the Duchess and warn us when she arrives.
ABIGAIL. Yes, Milord. [*Aside.*] May God protect him! [*She exits by the door on the right.*]
THE QUEEN. [*Aside.*] Perhaps I can buy peace of mind at this price. I am resigned to it. [*Lifting her eyes, gaily.*] Ah, Bolingbroke! I am so happy to see you. I have just spent the most boring day.
BOLINGBROKE. [*Smiling ironically.*] I've heard of Your Majesty's new treaty of clemency. It is magnanimous of you to forget yesterday's scandal.
THE QUEEN. How can I forget it? Heavens above! If you only knew what I have been through since yesterday? All because of that cursed glass of water. Everything I have had to hear! My nerves are frazzled. I don't want to hear any more about it.
BOLINGBROKE. They will have you patch things up?
THE QUEEN. In spite of me, but it must

be cleared up. Because you are for peace, you will not be shocked by the sacrifices I had to make. And the poor Duchess [BOLINGBROKE *looks shocked.*] . . . I will not defend her. Heaven help me. She has been so unfairly treated this time and especially by you. [*Confused.*] I don't mean the last subsidies and the capture of Bouchain; there was no time to verify that. [*Seriously.*] What you told me about young Masham . . .

BOLINGBROKE. Well?

THE QUEEN. [*Smiling contentedly.*] Completely untrue!

BOLINGBROKE. [*Aside.*] So that's her game.

THE QUEEN. She hardly took notice of him.

BOLINGBROKE. Is that so?

THE QUEEN. [*Smiling.*] I have reason to believe her, proof that she gave me herself and that cannot be told. She's interested in Lord Avondale!

BOLINGBROKE. Your Majesty accepted this?

THE QUEEN. [*Severely.*] Certainly! [*Laughing.*] Think, Bolingbroke, would this poor Duchess—why I accused her yesterday, I don't know—had she loved Masham, have denounced him before the entire Court and had you arrest him?

BOLINGBROKE. [*In a low voice.*] If she hadn't given in to a fit of jealousy and anger, why should she repent now?

THE QUEEN. What did you say?

BOLINGBROKE. [*Laughing and still in a low voice.*] The Duchess suspected that Masham had a mysterious appointment last night.

THE QUEEN. [*Aside.*] Oh, Heavens!

BOLINGBROKE. With whom I do not know, and it's doubtful that the rumor is true. If Your Majesty wishes, I could look into it.

THE QUEEN. [*Eagerly.*] No need for that.

BOLINGBROKE. What is true is that last night after the reception the Duchess had planned a rendezvous with Masham in her apartment.

THE QUEEN. A rendezvous?

BOLINGBROKE. [*Quickly.*] Yes, Madam.

THE QUEEN. [*Angrily.*] Yesterday! With him! They had agreed! They were in this together!

BOLINGBROKE. [*Quickly and passionately.*] Look at her desperation today, her regret for having, in a moment of spite, given up her position as Chief Lady-in-Waiting. Without her power and authority, she could no longer defend Masham, my prisoner. Without access to the palace and the means of coming and going at will, she could no longer see him here under your nose without danger or suspicion. That's why she wants this reconciliation her friends have forced on you.

THE QUEEN. [*Aside.*] Never!

ABIGAIL. [*Shaken, running through the door on the right, to* BOLINGBROKE.] Milord, Milord . . .

THE QUEEN. [*Angrily.*] What is it?

ABIGAIL. The Duchess's carriage has just entered the palace courtyard.

THE QUEEN. [*Going to center stage.*] Oh? How dare she present herself to me!

ABIGAIL. She has come to apologize about yesterday's events.

THE QUEEN. I will not allow it! I can pardon personal slights but never those directed against the dignity of my crown. To think that yesterday the Duchess in all her pride schemed to be disrespectful to her sovereign.

BOLINGBROKE. That was her intention, indeed.

THOMPSON. [*Presenting himself at the door at the rear.*] Milady, the Duchess of Marlborough awaits Your Majesty's orders in the reception room.

THE QUEEN. Abigail, go and tell her this: We cannot receive her, the place she held with us has been filled, and tomorrow she is to return her patent of office and, above all, the key to our apartment. From this moment hence these quarters are forbidden to her and also our presence. Go!

ABIGAIL. [*Amazed.*] What? Is it true?

BOLINGBROKE. [*Coldly.*] Go, Miss Abigail, obey your Queen.

ABIGAIL. Yes, Milord! [*Aside.*] What a devil Bolingbroke is! [*She exits through the left rear door.*]

BOLINGBROKE. [*Approaching the* QUEEN *who has thrown herself into a chair on his right.*] Well done, my sovereign, well done!

THE QUEEN. [*Exalted and proud.*] It was well done, wasn't it? They thought I was weak, and I am not!
BOLINGBROKE. How well we see it!
THE QUEEN. [*Angrily.*] Abusing my patience was too much.
BOLINGBROKE. It was intolerable.
THE QUEEN. It could not go on like that.
BOLINGBROKE. [*Eagerly.*] We've said that for a long time. Give me you orders; my friends and I are ready to carry them out.
THE QUEEN. [*Rising.*] My orders, certainly! I will give them to you and confide in you. Now tell me, what of Masham?
BOLINGBROKE. He is still my prisoner. We will take this matter up as soon as the new government is formed, Parliament dissolved, and the Duke of Marlborough recalled.
THE QUEEN. [*Agitated.*] Very well. I will give the order to have him tried.
BOLINGBROKE. [*Eagerly.*] The Marshal?
THE QUEEN. No, Masham!
BOLINGBROKE. [*Aside.*] Masham, again!
THE QUEEN. [*Eagerly.*] And his punishment—because I want him punished—the death penalty. I want it!
BOLINGBROKE. [*Aside.*] Good God!
THE QUEEN. He has taken a relative whom you loved from you, and besides, the Duchess will be furious.
BOLINGBROKE. [*Quickly.*] On the contrary, she will be delighted since they are embroiled in a duel to the death.
THE QUEEN. [*Whose anger fades away.*] Oh, [*In a sweet voice.*] You didn't tell me that.
BOLINGBROKE. [*In a low voice and laughing.*] She discovered that Masham, without a shadow of a doubt, did not love her, never loved her, and in fact, loved another.
THE QUEEN. [*Eagerly.*] Are you sure? Who told you this?
BOLINGBROKE. [*Quickly.*] My young prisoner told me of a secret love. He loves someone at Court and cannot tell her of his love. Beyond that I know nothing.
THE QUEEN. [*Contentedly.*] That changes the matter considerably. [*Gaining control.*] Quite a bit, I would say. [*Laughing.*] We shall talk further about this.
BOLINGBROKE. Yes, Madam! [*Quickly.*] This evening, Your Majesty shall have a list of my most trusted colleagues. About the Order of Dissolution . . .
THE QUEEN. Of course.
BOLINGBROKE. [*As above.*] The preliminaries for the conference with de Torcy.
THE QUEEN. [*As above.*] Wonderful!
BOLINGBROKE. And once Your Majesty has agreed . . .
THE QUEEN. Certainly! But shouldn't we question Masham to find out more about the Duchess's projects?
BOLINGBROKE. Of course, provided that it is done in total secrecy.
THE QUEEN. Why?
BOLINGBROKE. Because I am responsible for him and cannot allow him to communicate freely with members of the Court. This evening when everyone has retired, when there is no danger of being seen . . .
THE QUEEN. I understand.
BOLINGBROKE. [*Coming upstage and approaching the door at the rear.*] I will bring my prisoner tonight so that we may question him—or rather Your Majesty may question him since I haven't the time.
THE QUEEN. [*Joyfully.*] Wonderful, wonderful! [*At this moment the* DUCHESS *half opens the door on the right.*]
THE DUCHESS. [*Seeing* BOLINGBROKE.] God, Bolingbroke! [*She slams the door.*]
THE QUEEN. [*Stopping at the noise.*] Quiet!
BOLINGBROKE. What is it?
THE QUEEN. [*Entering the apartment on the right.*] Nothing, I thought I heard something. [*Turning gaily to him.*] This evening! Soon!
BOLINGBROKE. [*Moving Away.*] Masham will be here before eleven o'clock. [BOLINGBROKE *exits through the door at the rear.*]
THE QUEEN. [*Starting to follow him, sees Abigail entering through the rear door on the right. She sits on the sofa on the left.*] Oh, there you are, my dear. What of the Duchess?
ABIGAIL. If only you knew!
THE QUEEN. [*Arranging herself.*] Come here by me. [ABIGAIL *hesitates.*] Come

now. What did she say?

ABIGAIL. Nothing. Anger and pride had frozen all her features.

THE QUEEN. [*Smiling.*] I can believe that; for the message that I entrusted to you also indicated to her whom her replacement would be.

ABIGAIL. [*Shocked.*] What do you mean?

THE QUEEN. Yes, Abigail, yes you are to replace her. You will be my confidant and friend because as of today I command, I reign. Finish your story. You said that the Duchess was furious?

ABIGAIL. Indeed. As she went down the great staircase, she spoke to the Duchess of Norfolk who was supporting her. Miss Price, who is quite reliable, overheard them. She said, "Since I have been destroyed, I will dishonor the Queen. . . ."

THE QUEEN. Heavens!

ABIGAIL. And then she added, "I am about to receive some news which can only help me." They continued on, and Miss Price could hear no more.

THE QUEEN. What news was she talking about?

ABIGAIL. Important news.

THE QUEEN. Where had she learned it?

ABIGAIL. Perhaps political news.

THE QUEEN. Or rather, the interview that we had planned for last evening.

ABIGAIL. What can that matter now?

THE QUEEN. Because if yesterday I had questioned Masham—with you present—it would have had severe consequences. Then I would have discovered the degree to which they abused me and learned, at last, the truth.

ABIGAIL. That is certainly your right, especially as Queen.

THE QUEEN. Do you think so?

ABIGAIL. It's your duty. [*Quickly.*] Besides, what could she do? You didn't see him. [*Aside.*] Thank goodness! [*With satisfaction.*] Now that he is a prisoner, it's impossible.

THE QUEEN. [*Embarrassed.*] What if it weren't?

ABIGAIL. [*Terrified.*] What do you mean?

THE QUEEN. [*With joy.*] You don't know, Abigail? He's coming, I'm waiting for him!

ABIGAIL. [*Quickly.*] Madam!

THE QUEEN. [*Taking her hand.*] What's wrong?

ABIGAIL. [*Emotionally.*] I'm shaking, I'm afraid.

THE QUEEN. [*Understanding and getting up.*] For me. Don't worry, there's no danger.

ABIGAIL. If the Duchess knew he were in the palace, in your apartment, at this hour! Your Majesty hopes in vain; Masham is Bolingbroke's prisoner and he cannot, without exposing himself, free Masham.

THE QUEEN. [*Pointing to the left rear door as it opens.*] Quiet, here he is!

ABIGAIL. [*Wanting to run to* MASHAM.] Heavens!

THE QUEEN. [*Holding her back.*] Don't leave me.

ABIGAIL. [*Jealously.*] Oh no, Madam, certainly not. [MASHAM *enters slowly, greets the* QUEEN *respectfully. She says nothing but emotionally beckons him to come forward.*]

THE QUEEN. [*Whispering to* ABIGAIL.] Close the doors, then come back. [ABIGAIL *closes the door on the right, the two rear doors and returns quickly to her place by the* QUEEN.]

MASHAM. Lord Bolingbroke sent me to give you these, Your Majesty. He said I was the most trustworthy person to bring them to you.

THE QUEEN. [*With goodness, taking the papers.*] Very well, thank you.

MASHAM. I am to return them with Your Majesty's signature.

THE QUEEN. Of course! I forgot. [*She goes to the table on the left and sits down.*] Good Heavens what have we here! [*She takes off her gloves and signs quickly without reading.* MASHAM *goes to* ABIGAIL *who is on the extreme right.*]

MASHAM. Oh! Good Lord! How pale you are, Miss Abigail.

ABIGAIL. [*Emotionally, in a whisper.*] Listen to me, Arthur. I have the power, the Duchess's power.

MASHAM. [*Joyfully.*] Is it true?

ABIGAIL. [*The same.*] Yes, the Queen's favor. I have decided to give it all up, to renounce everything.

MASHAM. [*Shocked.*] Why?

ABIGAIL. For you! If such luck came your way, would you do otherwise?

MASHAM. [*Quickly.*] How can you ask

that?
ABIGAIL. [*Trembling.*] Because, Arthur, you are loved by a great lady, the first of this kingdom.
MASHAM. What are you saying?
ABIGAIL. Quiet! [*Indicating that the QUEEN has finished and is coming to him.*] The Queen will speak to you.
THE QUEEN. I have signed the papers that Bolingbroke entrusted to you.
MASHAM. Thank you, Your Majesty. I will go tell him that he is Minister.
THE QUEEN. That is generous of you, for his first act will be, no doubt, to pursue Richard Bolingbroke's assailant.
MASHAM. I have nothing to fear. He knows how the duel happened.
THE QUEEN. Well then, you are doubly protected, by me and better still, by the Duchess. [*She sits on the sofa. MASHAM stands in front of her and ABIGAIL stands behind the sofa which she uses as a support as she looks at MASHAM.*] They told me, Masham—however I am not convinced of it because you are so discrete—they told me that you loved her.
MASHAM. I, Madam? Never?
THE QUEEN. How could you avoid it? The Duchess is so beautiful, and her power . . . her position . . .
MASHAM. What do power and position matter? One does not dream of them when one falls in love. [*Looking at ABIGAIL.*] And I love elsewhere! [*ABIGAIL looks frightened.*]
THE QUEEN. [*Lowering her eyes.*] Ah, that's different! And the one you love is indeed very beautiful?
MASHAM. [*With love and looking at ABIGAIL*]. More than I can tell you. [*Gaining control.*] I want to tell you of my love, that I am happy and proud of this love. Punish me, Madam, if even here at your feet, I dare to deny it!
THE QUEEN. [*Getting up quickly.*] Quiet! Do you hear something?
ABIGAIL. [*Pointing to the door on the right.*] Someone's knocking at the door.
MASHAM. [*Pointing to the rear doors.*] And these as well!
ABIGAIL. And the noise outside! The palace is filling up with people.
THE QUEEN. What are we to do? [*Aside with fear.*] The Duchess's threat! [*Aloud.*] If they see him here!
ABIGAIL. Hide there on the balcony! [*MASHAM dashes to the balcony on the left. ABIGAIL closes the window.*]
THE QUEEN. Very good. Go let them in.
ABIGAIL. Yes, Madam. Quickly, calm yourself, collect your thoughts.
THE QUEEN. Oh, I'm about to die!
[*ABIGAIL opens the rear doors. The DUCHESS enters with several gentlemen of the Court. BOLINGBROKE enters after them. The Maids of Honor enter through the door on the right which ABIGAIL opens.*]
THE QUEEN. Who dares? At this hour? In my apartments? Oh, goodness, the Duchess! What nerve!
THE DUCHESS. [*Looking around the apartment.*] Your Majesty will forgive me because it concerns important news about the salvation of our nation.
THE QUEEN. [*Impatiently.*]What news?
THE DUCHESS. [*Still searching the apartment.*] Rumors are sweeping the city. [*Aside, looking at the balcony.*] Of course, that's where he is! [*Aloud.*] Lord Marlborough tells me that the French armies have just attacked Prince Eugene's forces at Denain and achieved a total victory.
BOLINGBROKE. [*Coldly.*] It's true.
THE DUCHESS. [*Running to the window. ABIGAIL takes several steps toward her and finds herself standing between the QUEEN and the DUCHESS.*] Listen! Do you hear the furious cries of the crowd?
BOLINGBROKE. Who demand peace!
THE DUCHESS. [*Opening the window and gasping.*] Ah, Mr. Masham! In the Queen's apartment!
THE QUEEN. [*Aside as MASHAM appears.*] I'm done for!
ABIGAIL. [*Whispering to the QUEEN.*] No, not if I can help it! [*Falling on her knees.*] Mercy, Madam, mercy! It was I, without your permission, who sent for him tonight!
THE DUCHESS. [*Angrily.*] What nerve! You dare to tell me . . .
ABIGAIL. [*Lowering her eyes.*] The truth!
MASHAM. [*Bowing.*] May Your Majesty punish us both!
THE QUEEN. [*In a whisper to BOLINGBROKE.*] Bolingbroke, save us!
BOLINGBROKE. [*Advancing from the gen-

tlemen of the Court who are at the rear and taking center stage.] I have something to say!
THE DUCHESS. [*Turning to* BOLINGBROKE.] And I too. I want to know why a prisoner confined to Milord's safekeeping is free at this moment. What is your reason?
BOLINGBROKE. [*Turning to those assembled.*] A reason which even you would understand, Milords. Mr. Masham asked, pledging his word and his honor as a gentleman, permission to say farewell to Abigail Churchill, his wife.
THE QUEEN and THE DUCHESS. [*Gasping.*] Heavens!
THE QUEEN. [*Agitated.*] Sirs, sirs, [*Motioning them away.*] a moment please. [*They move away. The* QUEEN *and* BOLINGBROKE *are alone at stage front.*]
THE QUEEN. [*In a low voice.*] What have you done?
BOLINGBROKE. [*Same tone.*] You told me to save you. [*The* QUEEN *cannot hide her emotions.*] Can you let this young girl who just sacrificed herself for you be dishonored?
THE QUEEN. [*With courage and resolutely.*] No, I can't. [*In a whisper.*] Tell them to come here. [BOLINGBROKE *makes a sign.* ABIGAIL *and* MASHAM, *who have stood apart from the crowd, advance timidly.*]
THE QUEEN. [*With emotion and in a low voice to* ABIGAIL.] What you have just done must be—don't deny it—evidence of your devotion. I owe you my undying gratitude and friendship which until that moment were only superficial.
ABIGAIL. [*To the* QUEEN *effusively.*] Oh, Madam, if you only knew!
BOLINGBROKE. [*Cutting off her words.*] Enough! [*He makes a sign for* MASHAM *to approach the* QUEEN.]
THE QUEEN. As for you, Masham.
BOLINGBROKE. [*Whispering to* MASHAM.] Don't say a thing!
THE QUEEN. I had other plans for you, perhaps, but because of your devotion to her, your Queen demands that you marry her.
MASHAM. Madam!
THE QUEEN. She orders it! [*The two lovers bow and pass to the right of the stage.*]
THE QUEEN. [*Addressing the Court from center stage.*] My Lords, the serious events that the Duchess just related will hasten the measures that we have been considering for some time. Sir Harley, Count Oxford, and Lord Bolingbroke, my new ministers, will present their plans tomorrow. We are recalling His Grace, the Duke of Marlborough, whose talent and services will no longer be needed. Having decided on an honorable peace, we intend that with the least delay possible, a peace conference shall open in Utrecht between our plenipotentiaries and those of France.
BOLINGBROKE. [*Standing on the right between* MASHAM *and* ABIGAIL, *in a whisper to* ABIGAIL.] Well, Abigail, my system worked—Lord Marlborough deposed, Europe pacified.
MASHAM. [*Returning the papers to* BOLINGBROKE.] And Bolingbroke Minister!
BOLINGBROKE. All because of a glass of water!

Thérèse Raquin
Émile Zola

Occasionally in the theater one encounters an author who exerts great influence on future playwriting without himself being a great playwright. Eugène Scribe was one such writer, and Émile Zola is another. Zola was a novelist of major importance in nineteenth-century France. He was also something of a firebrand and an espouser of causes, as well as a theater critic of intelligence and acumen. With a lifelong interest in the theater, and a passionate commitment to reforming all the arts in accordance with what he perceived as the wave of the future, Zola argued fervently for naturalism in the arts and specifically in the theater. Challenged to dramatize his own novel, *Thérèse Raquin,* by critics who did not think he would dare, Zola not only did so, but made of his play one of the major landmarks in the development of a realistic theater. Although it remained for Ibsen to create realistic stage works of real genius, Zola and the other prophets prepared the way for Ibsen both by championing realistic playwriting and by demonstrating its potential.

Émile Édouard Charles Antoine Zola was born in Paris on April 2, 1840. His father was an engineer engaged in creating a water system for Aix-en-Provence, and Émile, an only child, therefore grew up in the south of France. His father died in 1847, and his mother, although she tried to salvage some financial security from his father's projects, was eventually forced into near destitution. Through the kindness of family friends, Émile received a reasonably good education and a scholarship at the Lycée Saint-Louis in Paris. He completed his studies there in 1859, but failed his examinations for the degree. For more than two years thereafter, he was unemployed or unsatisfactorily employed, living precariously and learning firsthand what poverty meant. Finally he landed a job with a Parisian publisher, thus providing himself with both a steady income and an important stepping stone toward a writing career; within a few years, he was supporting himself fully by writing, and eventually he became quite wealthy. It is not necessary to trace here Zola's full career as a novelist.

Between 1865 and 1887, Zola wrote five plays, none of which was a great success. Perhaps the fact that his novels were far more successful ventures influenced him to devote more time to that pursuit, but later in his life he wrote six opera librettos, and at the time of his death he had sketched out plans for a new cycle of plays; he never gave up the theater altogether. He also collaborated with other playwrights in dramatizing a number of his novels. He married Gabrielle-Alexandrine Meley in 1870; the marriage was childless, and he took a mistress in 1888 by whom he had two children (legally recognized by his wife after his death). Zola became embroiled in the celebrated court-martial of Alfred Dreyfus, championing one whom he considered an innocent victim of anti-Semitism and bureaucratic bungling. Eventually brought to trial himself for libel, Zola went into exile in England for nearly a year, returning to Paris in 1899 when Dreyfus was completely exonerated. Not unaware of his new status as a national hero, Zola threw himself into renewed literary activity, but died suddenly on September 29, 1902, of carbon monoxide poisoning resulting from a faulty flue in his bedroom fireplace. Somehow, this sudden, shocking, and mechanically ridiculous death seemed peculiarly appropriate for one who had created many such bizarre deaths in his novels and plays.

The nineteenth century in Europe was a period of rapid advancement in science and industrialization. The ideas of Darwin and of Marx were pervasively influential in turning social and artistic consciences to new views of human life. Zola was an important part of this mainstream of European thinking, championing the view that scientific objectivity must be brought to bear on the arts, and specifically on the theater, in order to show human beings as they really were rather than as the idealizations of the romanticists. A good play, then, in Zola's view, should be a "slice of life," as undistorted by the playwright's subjectivity as a detached, scientific approach could make it. Typically, Zola defended this viewpoint vigorously. In a France still reeling from the onslaught of the romanticists in 1830, Zola led a new generation of avant-garde rebels who proclaimed realism the theatrical wave of the future. History has shown that they were right, but at the time audiences were not prepared for the depiction of events that seemed to them grisly and obscene, nor for the portrayal on their stages of the lowest dregs of society about whom it was much pleasanter to forget. Most of the realistic plays were not enthusiastically received at first, and the battle to portray life as it really was extended well into the twentieth century.

Zola completed his novel entitled *Thérèse Raquin* in 1867, then adapted his own novel for the stage. The naturalistic novel had drawn the ire of some of the more conservative critics, who had dared Zola to put such "garbage" on the stage. Rising enthusiastically to the challenge, and eager to experiment with the "slice of life" technique he had been advocating, Zola opened his play in July 1873. It ran for only nine performances, and the critics thought it morbid and depressing. With several other avant-garde writers, Zola enjoyed a monthly "Dinner of the Hissed Authors," celebrating their disregard for public opinion. In fact, *Thérèse Raquin* is by far Zola's best play, and it has been revived a number of times in Europe and elsewhere since its original production. Zola took the occasion of the publication of his play to write a preface that summarizes his dramatic theories: "There should no longer be any school, no more formulas, no standards of any sort; there is only life itself," he wrote. "Given a strong man and an unsatisfied woman, [I resolved] to seek in them the beast, to see nothing but the beast, to throw them into a violent drama and note scrupulously the sensations and acts of these creatures. . . . I have simply done in two living bodies the work which surgeons do on corpses."

In fact, Zola himself was aware that no work of art is totally objective, that the consciousness of the artist inevitably imposes at least some measure of structure on the work. In the case of *Thérèse Raquin*, Zola has certainly avoided the turns and twists of plot that Scribe would have employed; the brooding mood of the play is reflected in a loose and slow-moving plot in which such sensational events as Camille's murder occur between the acts. Toward the end of the play, however, Zola has compromised with tradition, and has contrived for Madame Raquin to be stricken with paralysis at exactly the moment that she learns the truth about her son's death. He then further contrives for her to regain muscular control to a degree just sufficient to keep the audience (and the killers) in suspense as to what she will do, and finally he contrives for Thérèse and Laurent to attempt to kill each other at the same moment and to commit double suicide in a culminating act of despair and expiation. These melodramatic devices are clearly borrowed from the romantics, and would have been disdained by Zola himself had he seen them in the light that a century of realistic practice now throws on them. What is more noteworthy, however, is the fact that much of the plot is *not* contrived, that for the most part events move smoothly and naturally, growing out of the human reactions of frustrated people trapped in situations over which they feel they have little control. Zola even manages to introduce significant and effective foreshadowing in the discussions of other murders, especially in act 1, and he builds a nice sense of horror and dread in acts 2 and 3 as Laurent and Thérèse sense the presence of Camille in everything they do. Furthermore, the certain knowledge about whether Camille has been murdered or has died accidentally is neatly withheld until act 3; the audience suspects, but is not fully informed until Madame Raquin learns the truth also. Act 4 depends for its effectiveness on a skillful use of dramatic irony, as the audience shares Laurent's and Thérèse's horror at seeing the murder scheme gradually come unravelled before their eyes. All of these devices are deviations from the "slice of life" technique in its strictest sense, but most of them are used with such skill that the appearance of a slice of life is maintained while at the same time theatrical suspense is built. This is genuine theatrical artistry in a realistic mode.

Instead of depending upon a plot as the center of interest, however, as Scribe would have done, Zola is mainly concerned with exploring the effects of guilt on the characters of Thérèse and Laurent. Passionate lovers in the first act, they gradually find themselves unable to continue their affair, first out of fear of detection and then finally, once married, out of guilt and despair. On their wedding night, they find themselves unable to communicate except through masks of convention and make-believe. By the last act, their love has turned to hate, and Thérèse and Laurent torture each other with a finesse and fury not to be matched until years later in the works of Strindberg and O'Neill. This probing of the human psyche is masterfully carried out by Zola, and is the basis of the play's continued appeal. Nineteenth-century audiences were horrifed by the pubic display of such intimate matters, and probably more than a little discomfitted to find something of their own inner impulses in what was revealed. This has been the basis of both the controversy and the success of much of realism, and Zola's early efforts ring true despite the romantic trappings that he was not fully able to shed.

Thérèse Raquin has real theatrical power, but it is significantly less than a great play. Zola's other plays are today completely unknown. Still, the success achieved by Zola in this play, and by the other avant-garde playwrights espousing the cause of naturalism, was to pave the way for what many have seen as a new Golden Age of theater—a realistic theater that became the rage of Europe and the world, and upon which its greatest practitioner, Henrik Ibsen, was already at work.

Thérèse Raquin

Translated by Sharon Parsell

Characters
Camille
Laurent
Madame Raquin
Thérèse Raquin
Grivet
Michaud
Suzanne Michaud

Eight o'clock—A summer evening after supper—The table is still set; the window is half-opened. An atmosphere of peace and middle-class comfort. CAMILLE *is seated in an armchair on the right, posing. He is in a suit and is holding himself with the stiffness of a middle-class man in his Sunday best.* LAURENT *is painting, standing before his easel which is in front of the window.* THÉRÈSE *is hunched down in a low chair, daydreaming; she has her chin cupped in her hand.* MME. RAQUIN *is clearing the table.*

CAMILLE. [*After a silence.*] Can I talk? It won't bother you?

LAURENT. No at all, as long as you don't move.

CAMILLE. After supper, I must talk or I'll fall asleep. You're lucky that you have your health. You can eat anything. I've never been able to eat ice cream because it upsets my stomach. You know how tricky my stomach is. You really like it, don't you?

LAURENT. Of course; it's good and sweet.

CAMILLE. We know your tastes here. We made the ice cream especially for you even though Mother knows how it upsets me. Mother is spoiling you. Isn't she, Thérèse, isn't she spoiling Laurent?

THÉRÈSE. [*Without lifting her head.*] Yes.

MME. RAQUIN. [*Carrying a pile of dishes.*] Don't listen to them, Laurent. Camille was the one who told me that you liked vanilla ice cream, and Thérèse was the one who thought of freezing it with powdered sugar.

CAMILLE. You're selfish, Mother.

MME. RAQUIN. What, me, selfish?

CAMILLE. [*To* MME. RAQUIN *who exits smiling.*] Yes, yes! [*To* LAURENT.] She likes you because you are from Vernon too. Remember when we were kids and she used to give us money. . . ?

LAURENT. You always bought lots of apples.

CAMILLE. And you always bought little knives. We were quite lucky to find each other in Paris. It's taken my boredom away. Oh, I was so bored, bored to death. In the evenings when I came home from the office, it was so sad here. Do you have enough light?

LAURENT. Not quite, but I want to finish.

CAMILLE. It's almost eight o'clock. These summer evenings are so long. I wanted to be painted in the sunshine; that would have been prettier. You could have painted a landscape instead of that grey background. However, we barely have enough time in the mornings to gulp down our coffee before getting to the office. Surely, it can't be good for the digestion to sit still so long after a meal.

LAURENT. It's almost over; this is your last sitting. [MME. RAQUIN *enters and finishes clearing the table which she then wipes.*]

CAMILLE. At least, in the morning you'd have more light. We don't get much sun, but it shines on the wall across

the way and reflects into this room. Mother's idea to rent in the Pont Neuf arcade was stupid. It's too humid, and on rainy days, it's almost like a damp cave.
LAURENT. Yes, but you couldn't ask for a better place for a shop.
CAMILLE. I didn't say that. They have their shop to keep them busy; it doesn't interest me at all.
LAURENT. It is a comfortable apartment.
CAMILLE. Not really. There's only Mother's bedroom and this room where we must eat and sleep. The kitchen is a dark hole about as big as a closet. It's drafty and chilly here. At night a terrible draught comes through that little door leading to the stairwell. [*He points out the little door on the left.*]
MME. RAQUIN. [*Finishing her chores.*] Poor Camille, you're never happy. I came to Paris for you because you wanted to be a bookkeeper in the city. I would rather have my old shop in Vernon, but when you married your cousin, Thérèse, we had to provide for the children that you might have.
CAMILLE. I wanted to live on a busy street where I could sit at the window and watch the traffic. That would be fun! Now when I open the window, all I see is the big wall across the way and the skylights of the arcade. The wall is black, and the skylight's covered with dust and cobwebs. Our windows in Vernon were prettier, because I could see the Seine flowing past. That was always fun.
MME. RAQUIN. I've told you we can go back.
CAMILLE. Goodness no! Not now that I've found Laurent in the same office. I'm here only in the evenings after all. It doesn't bother me that the arcade is damp, if you can stand it.
MME. RAQUIN. Then don't complain about it any more. [*The shop bell rings.*] There's someone in the shop. Thérèse, go down, won't you? [THÉRÈSE *appears not to have heard and remains immobile.*] Never mind, I'll go myself. [*She exits by the spiral staircase.*]
CAMILLE. I don't want to complain; but the arcade is unhealthy. I'm afraid that a good case of pneumonia might carry me off. I'm not as strong as the rest of you. I . . . [*Silence.*] Can I take a break now? I can't feel my left arm any more.
LAURENT. As you wish; I have only a few more brush strokes.
CAMILLE. Thank goodness! I can't hold this pose any longer. I need to walk around. [*He gets up, goes upstage, then back downstage and stops in front of* THÉRÈSE.] I have never understood how she can sit like that for so long; she won't move a finger for hours on end. It is nerve-wracking to be around someone who always has her head in the clouds. Doesn't it irritate you, Laurent, to see her there, not moving an inch? Let's see; Thérèse, move! Are you having a good time there?
THÉRÈSE. [*Without moving.*] Yes.
CAMILLE. I hope you are enjoying yourself. You're like an animal! When her father, Captain Degans, left her with us, I was scared for the longest time of her huge black eyes. And the Captain. What a terrible man! He died in Africa without returning to Vernon. Isn't that so, Thérèse?
THÉRÈSE. [*Without moving.*] Yes.
CAMILLE. You'd think the cat had her tongue. [*He embraces her.*] All in all, you're a good wife. Since Mother told us to get married, we haven't had a quarrel. You don't hold that against me, do you?
THÉRÈSE. No.
LAURENT. [*Tapping* CAMILLE *on the shoulder with his maulstick.*] Come on, Camille, only ten more minutes. [CAMILLE *sits down.*] Turn your head to the left; good, now don't move.
CAMILLE. [*After a silence.*] No news from your father.
LAURENT. No, he has disowned me; besides, I won't write him.
CAMILLE. What a strange relationship between a father and son. I could never act that way.
LAURENT. Pauh! My father had his plans for me—he wanted me to be a lawyer so that I could represent him in all his petty lawsuits with the neighbors. When he found out that I had wasted my tuition money by hanging around

artists' studios he cut off my allowance. Being a lawyer wasn't my idea of fun.

CAMILLE. Still, it is a good career—you have to have some skill, and you are well paid.

LAURENT. After I met one of my old school friends, I decided to become a painter as he had.

CAMILLE. You should have kept at it, perhaps by now you would have been discovered.

LAURENT. I had to find a job because I was starving. So, I threw painting to the devil and found a job.

CAMILLE. Anyway, you did learn how to draw.

LAURENT. I'm not very good. I enjoy the craft of painting and the fact that it is relaxing. There are times that I miss that wretched studio where I started painting. There was a divan where I used to sleep off the binges we had had . . .

CAMILLE. Did you have models?

LAURENT. Certainly. Once a superb blond came . . . [THÉRÈSE *gets up slowly and goes down to the shop.*] We have shocked your wife.

CAMILLE. Oh, well if you think she was listening. She's such a simple girl, but perfection when she cares for me during my illnesses. Mother taught her how to make herbal teas.

LAURENT. She doesn't appear to like me.

CAMILLE. Oh, you know how women are! Haven't you finished yet?

LAURENT. Yes, you can look now.

CAMILLE. [*Getting up and going to look at the portrait.*] Finished, completely finished?

LAURENT. All it needs now is the frame.

CAMILLE. It's good, isn't it? [*He goes and leans over the staircase.*] Mother, Thérèse, come up, Laurent has finished!

MME. RAQUIN. What, it's finished?

CAMILLE. [*Holding the portrait in front of him.*] Yes! Come up! [MME. RAQUIN *and* THÉRÈSE *enter.*]

MME. RAQUIN. [*Looking at the portrait.*] Ah! Let me see. The mouth is certainly well done; isn't it, Thérèse?

THÉRÈSE. [*Without coming near.*] Yes. [*She goes to the window where she loses control of herself and rests her head against the frame.*]

CAMILLE. And the suit! It's my wedding suit which I've only worn four times. The lapel looks hand-tailored.

MME. RAQUIN. And the corner of the chair!

CAMILLE. Amazing! It looks like real wood! It's my chair from Vernon. [*Pointing to the other armchair.*] Mother's is blue.

MME. RAQUIN. [*To* LAURENT *who has closed up his easel and paint box and is passing on the right.*] Why did you put black under his left eye?

LAURENT. It's a shadow.

CAMILLE. [*Putting the portrait on the easel which is leaning on the walls between the bed recess and the window.*] Perhaps it would be prettier without the shadow, but no matter. I look like a distinguished visitor.

MME. RAQUIN. Dear Laurent, how can we thank you? All you asked was that Camille buy the paints.

LAURENT. He was gracious enough to pose for me.

CAMILLE. No, no, it can't go on like this. I'm going to get a bottle of something. Devil be hanged! Let's drink to your work.

LAURENT. Oh all right! If you wish! I'm going to get a frame. Today's Thursday; I want to surprise M. Grivet and the Michauds with the portrait hanging in its place. [*He leaves.* CAMILLE *takes off his coat, changes his tie, puts on an overcoat held by his mother and prepares to go out.*]

CAMILLE. [*Coming back.*] What kind of liqueur should I buy?

MME. RAQUIN. Something that Laurent likes. That dear boy is so good, he's almost like family now.

CAMILLE. Yes, he's like a brother to me. Shall I buy anisette?

MME. RAQUIN. Do you know if he likes anisette? A fine wine would be better, perhaps, with the cakes.

CAMILLE. [*To* THÉRÈSE.] You haven't suggested anything. Do you know if he likes malaga?

THÉRÈSE. [*Leaving the window and coming downstage.*] No, but I do know that he likes everything. He eats and drinks like an ogre.

MME. RAQUIN. Child!
CAMILLE. Scold her! She can't stand him. It is so obvious that Laurent has mentioned it to me. [*To Thérèse.*] I don't understand why you don't like my friends. What has he done to you?
THÉRÈSE. Nothing. He's here at almost every meal. You save him the best bites. Laurent, taste this; Laurent, try that. It irritates me, that's all. He's not funny, but a glutton and lazy.
MME. RAQUIN. Behave yourself, Thérèse. Laurent's life is not happy. He lives in that attic and is forced to eat very poorly. It pleases me to see him well fed and warm with us. He's at home here, he smokes here. All of these things please me. Poor boy, he's all alone in the world.
THÉRÈSE. As you will; in any case, you spoil him. What do my opinions matter, anyway?
CAMILLE. I've got it! I'll buy champagne, that's best of all!
MME. RAQUIN. Yes, a bottle of champagne will be an even trade for the portrait. Don't forget the cakes.
CAMILLE. It's not even eighty-thirty. Our friends won't be here until nine. They will be pleasantly surprised to find champagne. [*He exits.*]
MME. RAQUIN. [*To* THÉRÈSE.] Light the lamp, won't you? I'm going to the shop. [MME. RAQUIN *exits to the shop;* LAURENT *enters.*]
LAURENT. Thérèse!
THÉRÈSE. Oh Laurent—I knew you were going to come, my love. [*She takes his hands and leads him to the front of the stage.*] It's been a week since I've seen you. I've waited for you every afternoon, hoping that you could get away from the office. If you had not come tonight, I would have done something stupid. Tell me, why did you stay away for so long? It has been torture for me. This evening your handshake was so cold.
LAURENT. Let me explain.
THÉRÈSE. You are afraid here. What a good boy you are! Go! This is the best hiding place of all. [*She raises her voice and takes several steps.*] How can they suspect our love? Would anyone ever think to look for us in here?
LAURENT. [*Bringing her back and taking her in his arms.*] Don't you know that I'm not afraid to come here?
THÉRÈSE. Then, you're afraid of me, admit it. You're afraid that I love you too much, that I am ruining your life.
LAURENT. Why do you doubt me? Don't you know that I can't sleep because of you? I, who always made fun of women, am blinded by love. That's what bothers me, Thérèse; you have wakened from the depths of my soul a feeling that I do not understand. My peace has been shattered. It's not natural to love as I love you. I'm afraid that our love will lead us further than we could want.
THÉRÈSE. [*Her head resting on his shoulder.*] That would be an unending joy, a springtime without end.
LAURENT. [*Pulling away quickly.*] Do you hear steps on the stairs? [*They both listen.*]
THÉRÈSE. It's the humidity making the steps creak. [*They resume their former positions.*] Go on, let's love one another without fear or remorse. If you only knew what my childhood was like. I was raised in the smothering atmosphere of a sickroom.
LAURENT. My poor Thérèse!
THÉRÈSE. I was so unhappy, spending long hours hunched before the fire mindlessly watching the herbal tea boil. If I moved, Aunt would scold me. Camille could not be disturbed, you understand. I had the slurred speech and trembling movements of a little old lady; and Camille made fun of my awkward movements. On the inside, I felt strong and robust; I would not give in to my urge to break everything. They told me that my mother was the daughter of an African chief. It must be true for all too often I've dreamed of running away, barefoot, down dusty roads, begging like a gypsy. . . . You see, I'd rather be destitute than at the mercy of their hospitality! [*She raises her voice.*]
LAURENT. [*Frightened, crosses the stage to listen for footsteps.*] Not so loud; you'll bring your aunt.
THÉRÈSE. What do I care if I lie to

them? [*She leans against the table, arms crossed.*] I don't know why I agreed to marry Camille. It was agreed that once I was of age, we would marry. When I was twelve Aunt began to say to me, "You will love him, you will care for your cousin." She didn't want a wife, but a nurse, a maker of herbal tea. She adored her puny child for whom she had cheated Death at least twenty times. She trained me to be his servant. I didn't protest because they had turned me into a coward. I pitied the boy. When we played together as children my fingers dug into his wrists as if they were putty. The night of our marriage I crossed into his room instead of mine. That was the only difference. But you, dear Laurent . . .

LAURENT. Do you love me? [*He takes her in his arms and slowly sits her in the chair to the right of the table.*]

THÉRÈSE. I love you and have loved you ever since Camille pushed you into the shop, that day you found each other at work. I don't know how it happened. I revel in our passion. I love you without knowing why, at times even hating you. Seeing you irritated me, made me suffer. When you joined us, my nerves would be stretched to the breaking point, but I sought that pain as I waited for you to come. There I sat as you painted, secretly dreaming of our love, silent at your feet, on the footstool.

LAURENT. I adore you. [*Kneeling at her feet.*]

THÉRÈSE. For some reason that I can't understand that silly old fool Grivet and his crony Michaud come regularly every Thursday evening for an endless game of dominoes. They have just about driven me crazy. One Thursday after another, with no end in sight and the same half-witted company. But now I have my sweet revenge. As we sit around this table after supper, I taste the evil joys of our love. While you play dominoes, I embroider in my outwardly sour mood; inwardly, in the midst of this middle-class calm, I hug my secret memories. . . . What ecstasy, dear Laurent.

LAURENT. [*Thinking he hears some noise, he rises frightened.*] I tell you, you're talking too loud; your voice will bring her upstairs. [*He listens at the stairwell and then crosses the stage.*] Where is my hat?

THÉRÈSE. [*Getting up tranquilly.*] Pauh! You think she's on her way up? [*She goes to the stairwell and comes back whispering.*] Yes, you're right, it would be better if you left. But I want to know about tomorrow. You will come, won't you, at two o'clock?

LAURENT. No, don't expect me. I can't.

THÉRÈSE. You can't?

LAURENT. My boss has noticed my absences and is threatening to fire me.

THÉRÈSE. Very well then, we won't see each other again. Break it off! We will part because of your caution. What a coward you are!

LAURENT. [*Taking her in his arms.*] No, we can be happy. All we need to do is wait for our chance. How often I dream of having you to myself for a whole day; then my desire grows and I want you for a month of happiness, then a year, and finally my whole life. Our whole life to love each other and to be together. I would quit my job and return to my painting. You would be free to do as you please. Our love would last forever. Would that please you?

THÉRÈSE. [*Smiling, her hand on her breast.*] Oh yes, it would.

LAURENT. [*Breaking away, in a very low voice.*] What if you were a widow . . . ?

THÉRÈSE. [*Dreamily.*] We could marry. We would have nothing to fear; our dreams would come true.

LAURENT. I can see nothing in the shadows but your gleaming eyes, eyes that have driven me out of my mind. If only I had the wisdom for two . . . Now, I must say farewell, Thérèse.

THÉRÈSE. You won't come tomorrow?

LAURENT. No! Be brave! Remember, when we are apart, we are working for our happiness. [*He embraces her and exits quickly through the little door.*]

THÉRÈSE. [*Alone, after a moment of daydreaming.*] Widow . . .

MME. RAQUIN. [*Entering.*] What, you're still in the dark! Oh, you dreamer!

Wait, where's the lamp? I'll light it. [*She leaves by the door at the rear.*]

CAMILLE. [*Entering with a bottle of champagne and a box of cakes.*] Where are you? Why are you standing there in the dark?

THÉRÈSE. Aunt has gone to get the lamp.

CAMILLE. [*Shivering.*] Oh! You startled me, there in the dark. You'd better use a more natural voice; you know I don't like to be teased about the dark.

THÉRÈSE. I'm not teasing.

CAMILLE. Even though you're white as a ghost, I can barely see you. When I wake up tonight and call out that a woman in white is parading around the bed ready to strangle me, you'll have a good laugh.

THÉRÈSE. I'm not laughing.

MME. RAQUIN. [*Entering with the lamp.*] What's going on here? [*The lights go up.*]

CAMILLE. Thérèse is amusing herself by trying to scare me. A little more and I would have dropped the champagne. Three francs would have gone down the drain.

MME. RAQUIN. You only paid three francs for it? [*She takes the bottle.*]

CAMILLE. Yes, I went up to the Boulevard Saint-Michel where I had seen it advertised at that price in a grocery shop. It is as good as an eight franc bottle. Everyone knows that the merchants are a bunch of jokers; only the label is different. Here are the cakes.

MME. RAQUIN. Give them to me; I'll put everything on the table so that M. Grivet and the Michauds will have a surprise when they come in. Hand me two plates, Thérèse. [*They put the bottle between the two plates of cakes.* THÉRÈSE *goes to sit at the work table and begins to embroider.*]

CAMILLE. M. Grivet is exactness itself. In a quarter of an hour as the clock strikes nine, he'll be here. Be nice to him, won't you? He's only the assistant manager, but on occasion he can give me a good pat on the back. No doubt about it, he's a very able man. The old timers in the office say that in twenty years he has never been so much as a minute late. Laurent was wrong to tell you that he's an old stick in the mud.

MME. RAQUIN. Our friend Michaud is also very prompt. In Vernon when he was Chief of Police, he got home every evening at exactly eight o'clock. Don't you remember how we complimented him about it?

CAMILLE. Yes, but since his retirement and the move to Paris to be with his niece, he's gotten a little confused. Little Suzanne leads him around by the nose. All the same, it's pleasant to have our friends in once a week. Under other circumstances, it would cost more. Oh, I have something to tell you before they get here: I've made some plans.

MME. RAQUIN. What plans?

CAMILLE. You know, Mother, that I promised Thérèse one Sunday to take her to Saint-Ouen before bad weather comes. She doesn't like to stroll with me in the streets. I find the streets more fun that the country. She complains that I tire her out because I don't know how to walk properly. Finally, I've hit upon the idea of going to Saint-Ouen. We'll take Laurent with us.

MME. RAQUIN. That's it, my dears, go to Saint-Ouen! My legs aren't good enough to go with you, but it is an excellent idea. That way you'll be quits with Laurent for the portait.

CAMILLE. Laurent is lots of fun in the country. Remember, Thérèse, when we all went to Suresnes? He was as strong as an ox, that joker. He jumped over ditches full of water, he threw big stones to a shocking height. At Suresnes, on the carousel, he imitated a galloping jockey—the cracking of the whip, the sound of the spurs—all so well that he had an entire wedding party laughing so hard that they cried. The bride was positively sick from it all. Isn't that so, Thérèse?

THÉRÈSE. He drank enough at dinner to get tipsy.

CAMILLE. Oh, you! You don't understand what's funny. If you were the only one around to amuse me, taking you to Saint-Ouen would be a chore.

She'll sit on the ground and watch the water flow by. At least, if I take Laurent along, I'll have a good time. Where in the devil did he go to get a frame? [*The bell rings in the shop.*] There he is; M. Grivet still has seven minutes.

LAURENT. [*Entering with a frame in his hand.*] They never finish anything in that shop. [*Looking at* CAMILLE *and* MME. RAQUIN *who are chatting in a low voice.*] I'll bet you're contemplating something delicious.

THÉRÈSE. Guess!

LAURENT. You are inviting me to dinner tomorrow, and we will have chicken with rice.

MME. RAQUIN. Glutton!

CAMILLE. Better than that! Sunday I'm taking Thérèse to Saint-Ouen, and you're coming with us. Will you come?

LAURENT. Will I come! [*He takes the portrait from the easel and has* MME. RAQUIN *get him a hammer.*]

MME. RAQUIN. You must promise me to be careful. Laurent, please take care of Camille. Because you are so strong, I'm much happier knowing that you will be with him.

CAMILLE. How Mother bores me with her continual fears. Do you think that I can go to the end of the street without her imagining some terrible thing? It's awful to be treated like a little boy. We'll take a cab to the fortifications; that way, we'll only have one fare to pay. Then we'll stroll along the path, spend the afternoon on the island, and in the evening, eat fish stew on the river banks. Eh? Everyone agreed?

LAURENT. [*Downstage, putting the canvas in the frame.*] Yes, but there's one more thing that we can do.

CAMILLE. What's that?

LAURENT. [*Glancing at* THÉRÈSE.] Go boating.

MME. RAQUIN. No, no! No boats! That worries me.

THÉRÈSE. If you think for one minute that Camille would get into a boat! He's too afraid!

CAMILLE. I am afraid.

LAURENT. That's right! I forgot that you were afraid of the water. In Vernon when we used to paddle on the Seine, you stayed on the bank, shivering. Very well, we'll forget about boating.

CAMILLE. But it's not always so! I'm not afraid! We'll go boating! I'll not have you pass me off as a half-wit. Devil be hanged! We'll see who has the least fear. Thérèse is the one who's afraid.

THÉRÈSE. Oh, my poor dear, you're already pale as a ghost.

CAMILLE. Don't mock me! We shall see, we shall see.

MME. RAQUIN. Camille, dear Camille, give up this idea; do it for me.

CAMILLE. Mother, please, don't torment me. You know that it makes me sick.

LAURENT. Very well, let your wife decide.

THÉRÈSE. Accidents can happen anywhere.

LAURENT. True! In the street, your foot can slip, a tile can fall on your head.

THÉRÈSE. Besides, you know how I adore the Seine.

LAURENT. [*To* CAMILLE.] Well then, it's decided; you've won. We'll go boating!

MME. RAQUIN. [*Aside to* LAURENT.] Good Lord! I can't tell you how this upsets me. Camille is so demanding; you see how he carried on!

LAURENT. Don't be afraid; I'll be there. Ah! The portrait is ready to hang. [*He hangs it over the buffet.*]

CAMILLE. It will be a fine outing, won't it? [*The shop bell rings. The clock strikes nine.*] Nine o'clock. Here's M. Grivet!

GRIVET. [*Entering.*] I'm the first to arrive. Good evening, ladies and gentlemen.

MME. RAQUIN. Good evening, M. Grivet. May I take your umbrella? [*She takes the umbrella.*] Is it raining?

GRIVET. It's threatening rain. [*She goes to put the umbrella to the left of the fireplace.*] Not in that corner, not in that corner. You know my little habits. In the other corner, there, thank you.

MME. RAQUIN. Give me your galoshes.

GRIVET. No, no! I'll take care of it myself. [*He sits down as she comes toward him.*] I'll do my own little chores. He! He! I like everything in its own place, you understand. [*He puts the galoshes by the umbrella.*] In

that way, I don't get upset.
CAMILLE. Have you anything new to tell us, M. Grivet?
GRIVET. [*Getting up and coming center stage.*] I left the office at four-thirty, I ate at six o'clock in the Orleans dairy shop, I read my newspaper at seven o'clock in the Saturnin Café, and because today is Thursday, instead of going to bed at nine o'clock—as is my habit—I came here. [*Reflecting.*] That's all there is, I believe.
LAURENT. And you saw nothing on your way here?
GRIVET. Of course not! Wait a minute, there was a crowd in the rue Saint-André-des-Arts. I had to switch sidewalks. That mixed me up. You understand in the morning I go to work on the left side of the street, and in the evening I return on the other side.
MME. RAQUIN. The right sidewalk?
GRIVET. No, let me explain. [*Acting out the action.*] In the morning, I go this way, and when I come home . . .
LAURENT. Now I see!
GRIVET. Always the left sidewalk, you see. I keep to my left, you know, just like the railroad. That way it's easier not to lose track of the streets.
LAURENT. What was this crowd doing on the sidewalk?
GRIVET. How should I know?
MME. RAQUIN. Some accident, do doubt.
GRIVET. Goodness, that's right! It could have been an accident. That never occurred to me. My Heavens! You have set my mind to rest by suggesting that it was an accident. [*He sits down on the left of the table.*]
MME. RAQUIN. Ah, here's M. Michaud! [SUZANNE *and* MICHAUD *enter.* SUZANNE *takes off her shawl and hat and goes to chat with* THÉRÈSE *who is still seated at the work table.* MICHAUD *shakes hands with everyone.*]
MICHAUD. I believe that I am late. [*He stops before* GRIVET *who has taken out his watch to show* MICHAUD *with a triumphant air.*] I know—nine—oh-six. It's the girl's fault. [*He points to* SUZANNE.] She wants to stop in all the shops. [*He goes to put his cane next to* GRIVET's *umbrella.*]
GRIVET. No, please, that's the place for my umbrella. You know very well that I don't like to share. I left you the other side of the fireplace for your cane.
MICHAUD. All right! All right! Let's not get angry.
CAMILLE. [*In a whisper to* LAURENT.] Look, I think M. Grivet is upset because of the champagne. He has looked at the bottle three times without saying a word. I'm amazed that he's not more surprised than that.
MICHAUD. [*Turning and seeing the champagne.*] My word! You're going to send us home in a jolly mood tonight—cakes and champagne.
GRIVET. Goodness! It is champagne. I've only had it four times in my life.
MICHAUD. What saint's day are we celebrating?
MME. RAQUIN. We're celebrating Camille's portrait which Laurent has just finished. [*She takes the lamp to throw more light on the portrait.*] Look! [*Everyone follows her except* THÉRÈSE *who remains at her work table and* LAURENT *who is leaning against the fireplace.*]
CAMILLE. It's striking, isn't it? I look like a visitor.
MICHAUD. Yes, yes.
MME. RAQUIN. It's still quite fresh! You can still smell the paint.
GRIVET. That's it! I caught a whiff of the paint! A photograph, at least, has the advantage of not smelling.
CAMILLE. Once the paint is dry . . .
GRIVET. Certainly, once the paint is dry. . . . It will dry quickly enough. There is a shop on the rue de la Harpe where things take five days to dry.
MME. RAQUIN. Well, M. Michaud, how do you like it?
MICHAUD. It's very good, quite good indeed. [*They all come away, and* MME. RAQUIN *puts the lamp on the table.*]
CAMILLE. Could you get us some tea, Mother? We'll drink the champagne after the dominoes.
GRIVET. [*Sitting down again.*] Nine-fifteen. We barely have enough time for a good game.
MME. RAQUIN. All I need is five minutes. Stay, Thérèse, since you aren't feeling well.

SUZANNE. [*Gaily.*] I'm feeling well; I'll help you, Mme. Raquin, It will be fun to play housewife! [*They exit through the door at the rear.*]

CAMILLE. And you know nothing new, M. Michaud?

MICHAUD. No, nothing. I took my niece to embroider at the Luxembourg Gardens. Ah, yes, my goodness, there is something new! There is the drama in the rue Saint-André-des-Arts!

CAMILLE. What drama? On his way over M. Grivet saw a crowd in the street.

MICHAUD. It hasn't broken up since this morning! [*To* GRIVET.] They were looking up, weren't they?

GRIVET. I really couldn't say; I changed sidewalks. Then, it really was an accident? [*He puts on a skull cap and sleeve cuffs that he takes out of his pocket.*]

MICHAUD. Yes, they found the body of a woman stuffed into the trunk of a traveler at the Hôtel Bourgogne—a traveler who has since disappeared. The woman had been cut into four pieces.

GRIVET. Is it possible? Four pieces? How can you cut a woman into four pieces?

CAMILLE. That's appalling!

GRIVET. And to think that I walked by there! I remember now, they were looking up. Could they see something up there?

MICHAUD. They were looking at the window of the room where they thought the trunk had been found. They were mistaken, however, because the window of the room in question faces the courtyard.

LAURENT. Has the murderer been arrested?

MICHAUD. No, one of my former colleagues who is conducting the investigation told me this morning that the murderer got completely away. [GRIVET *sneers as he shakes his head.*] This will be a hard case to solve.

LAURENT. Has the victim's identity been established?

MICHAUD. No, the corpse was nude, and the head was not in the trunk.

GRIVET. Someone carried it off, no doubt.

CAMILLE. Please, gentlemen! This is giving me goose bumps. Your wife cut into four pieces!

GRIVET. Eh! It's fun to be afraid when you are perfectly certain that there is no risk of danger. M. Michaud's stories from his days as Chief of Police are very droll. You remember the one about the buried gendarme whose hand came up among the carrots? He told us about it last fall. That was an interesting one. Devil be hanged! We all know that there are no murderers lurking behind our backs. May the Good Lord protect this house! Now, in the woods, I don't know. If I were going through the woods with M. Michaud, I would beg him to keep quiet.

LAURENT. [*To* MICHAUD.] You think, then, that many crimes remain unpunished?

MICHAUD. Yes, unfortunately. Disappearances, slow deaths, suffocations, sudden collapses without a cry or a drop of blood. Justice passes and sees nothing. There's more than one murderer who is walking around in broad daylight.

GRIVET. [*Sneering even louder.*] You were about to laugh. And they are not caught?

MICHAUD. If they are not caught, dear M. Grivet, it is because no one knows that they have killed.

CAMILLE. Then the police are incompetent?

MICHAUD. Of course not! The police are competent, but they can't do the impossible. I'll say it again: there are murderers who are happy, who live nicely, and who are loved and respected. Don't shake your head, M. Grivet.

GRIVET. I'll shake my head if I want to. Leave me alone.

MICHAUD. Perhaps you know one of these men, and perhaps you shake his hand every day.

GRIVET. Now don't say that! It's not true! You know that it can't be true. If you like, let me tell you a story.

MICHAUD. Tell your story.

GRIVET. Certainly! I'll tell you about the magpie who was a thief. [MICHAUD *shrugs.*] Perhaps you know it already

since you know everything. Once upon a time, a servant was thrown into prison for stealing some silverware. Two months later as they were cutting down a poplar tree the silverware was found in the nest of a magpie. The magpie was the thief, the servant was released. You see now that culprits are always punished.
MICHAUD. [*Sneering.*] So, they put the magpie in prison?
GRIVET. [*Getting angry.*] The magpie in prison! Are you that stupid, Michaud?
CAMILLE. Eh! No, that's not what M. Grivet meant to say. You're confused.
GRIVET. The police are incompetent; that's all there is to it. It's immoral.
CAMILLE. Do you think that someone can kill without being found out, Laurent?
LAURENT. What? [*He crosses the stage and turns slowly toward* THÉRÈSE.] Don't you see, M. Michaud is teasing us? He wants to shock you with his stories. How can he know what he says no one knows? If there are such skillful people, so much the better for them. See here, [*Near* THÉRÈSE.] see here, your wife is less credulous than you.
THÉRÈSE. Certainly. What we don't know doesn't exist.
CAMILLE. No matter, I would rather talk about other things; how about it? Let's talk about something else.
GRIVET. I agree. Let's talk about something else.
CAMILLE. Goodness! We haven't brought up the chairs from the shop. Come on, help me. [*He goes down the spiral staircase.*]
GRIVET. [*Grumbling as he gets up.*] He calls that talking about other things—going to get the chairs.
MICHAUD. Are you coming, M. Grivet?
GRIVET. You go on ahead. The magpie in prison! The magpie in prison! Can you believe that! For a former Chief of Police, you really made a fool of yourself on that one, M. Michaud. [*They go downstairs.*]
LAURENT. [*Brusquely taking* THÉRÈSE'S *hands and lowering his voice.*] You promise you'll obey me?
THÉRÈSE. [*Same tone.*] Yes, I belong to you. Do with me as you will.
CAMILLE. [*From below.*] Hey, Laurent, you lazy bum, can't you get your own chair instead of making these gentlemen fetch it?
LAURENT. [*Raising his voice.*] I stayed here to flirt with your wife. [*Softly to* THÉRÈSE.] Have hope! We will live happily together for ever.
CAMILLE. [*From below, laughing.*] Oh! You have my permission to do that—it's your duty to please Thérèse.
LAURENT. [*To* THÉRÈSE.] Remember what you said: "What we don't know doesn't exist." [*They hear footsteps on the stairs.*] Be careful! [*They quickly separate.* THÉRÈSE *returns sourfaced to her work.* LAURENT *passes to the right. The others return, each carrying a chair and laughing.*]
CAMILLE. [*To* LAURENT.] Joker, go downstairs! Isn't he funny, the rogue? All that so that he wouldn't have to go downstairs. [MME. RAQUIN *and* SUZANNE *bring in the tea.*]
MME. RAQUIN. [*To whom* GRIVET *shows his watch.*] Yes, it took a quarter of an hour. Sit down, we'll make up for lost time. [GRIVET *sits on the left, downstage.* LAURENT *sits behind him.* MME. RAQUIN'S *chair is on the right.* MICHAUD *sits behind her.* CAMILLE *sits in his chair which is at the upstage center of the table.* THÉRÈSE *is still at her work table.* SUZANNE *goes to her after the tea is served.*]
CAMILLE. [*Sitting down.*] Well, here I am in my chair. Give me the dominoes, Mother.
GRIVET. [*Beatifically.*] What a pleasure! Thursday when I wake up I say, "Goodness! I'm going to play dominoes at the Raquin's tonight." Well now, you just can't believe . . .
SUZANNE. [*Interrupting him.*] May I sweeten your tea, M. Grivet?
GRIVET. Thank you, my dear, you are most charming. Two lumps, please. [*Starting over.*] You just can't believe . . .
CAMILLE. [*Interrupting.*] Aren't you coming, Thérèse?
MME. RAQUIN. [*Handing him the domino box.*] Let her be. You know how she suffers when we play dominoes. If

someone comes into the shop, she can go down.
CAMILLE. It's upsetting when everyone is having a good time to have a sour puss around. [*To* MME. RAQUIN.] Let's see, are you going to sit down, Mother?
MME. RAQUIN. [*Sitting down.*] Yes, yes, I'm ready.
CAMILLE. Is everybody comfortable?
MICHAUD. Certainly! This evening I'm going to beat you all hollow. Mme. Raquin, your tea is a little stronger than last Thursday. M. Grivet, did you say something?
GRIVET. I said something?
MICHAUD. Yes, you had started a sentence.
GRIVET. A sentence, are you sure? That's unusual.
MICHAUD. I can assure you that you did. Mme. Raquin, didn't M. Grivet say, "Well, you just can't believe . . ."
GRIVET. "Well, you just can't believe . . ." I don't remember that at all. If you're trying to make a joke, you must know, M. Michaud, that I don't find it very funny.
CAMILLE. Is everybody comfortable? Then let's start! [*He noisily empties the domino box. Silence while the players mix up the tiles and then divide them up.*]
GRIVET. M. Laurent didn't take any, and he can't give advice, either. There, we all take seven. Don't peek, M. Michaud, don't peek, do you understand? [*Silence.*] Ah! I'm first, I have the double six!

Act 2

Ten o'clock. The lamp is lit. A year has passed. Nothing has been changed in the room—same atmosphere, same intimacy. MME. RAQUIN *and* THÉRÈSE *are in mourning. The actors are arranged as they were at the end of Act 1:* THÉRÈSE *is at her work table with the same sour-faced detachment; her embroidery is in her lap.*
GRIVET, LAURENT, *and* MICHAUD *are at their places around the round table.* CAMILLE's *place is empty. Silence while* MME. RAQUIN *and* SUZANNE *serve the tea, repeating exactly their moves from Act 1.*
LAURENT. May I trouble you for the domino box, Mme. Raquin?
SUZANNE. May I sweeten your tea, M. Grivet?
GRIVET. Thank you, my dear, you are most charming. Two lumps, please. You are all I need for sweetening.
LAURENT. [*Holding the domino box.*] Ah, here are the dominoes. Sit down, Mme. Raquin. [*She sits.*] Are you all comfortable?
MICHAUD. Certainly, and this evening I'm going to beat you all hollow. Allow me to pour a bit of rum into my tea. [*He pours the rum into his tea.*]
LAURENT. Are you all comfortable? Then, let's start. [*He noisily empties the box. They mix up the tiles and then divide them.*]
GRIVET. What a pleasure! There, we all take seven. Don't peek, M. Michaud, don't peek, do you understand? [*Silence.*] No, today I'm not first.
MME. RAQUIN. [*Bursting into tears.*] I can't, I can't. [LAURENT *and* MICHAUD *get up.* SUZANNE *comes to the back of* MME. RAQUIN's *chair.*] When I see all of you around this table as if nothing had happened, my heart breaks. My poor Camille was here too!
MICHAUD. My God! Mme. Raquin, please get hold of yourself.
MME. RAQUIN. Forgive me, dear friend, I can't. Remember how he loved to play dominoes? He dumped out the tiles—just as Laurent did. And when I didn't sit down fast enough, he complained. I was afraid to say anything to him because it would make him sick. Oh! Those happy evenings! Now his chair is empty. Can't you understand?
MICHAUD: Dear lady, take courage or you'll end up taking to your bed.
MME. RAQUIN. You're right; I must be stronger. [*She cries.*]
GRIVET. [*Turning back his tiles.*] Then it might be better not to play. It's too bad that it has this effect on you. Your tears won't bring your son back.
MICHAUD. We are all mortal.

MME. RAQUIN. Alas!
GRIVET. We intend our visits to take your mind off Camille's death.
MICHAUD. You must stop grieving for him, my dear friend.
GRIVET. Certainly! Devil be hanged! Let's don't be sad. How about the two of us finishing the game? What do you say?
LAURENT. In a little while. Let Mme. Raquin collect herself. We all grieve for our dear Camille.
SUZANNE. Did you hear that, dear lady? We all grieve for him along with you. [*She sits on* MME. RAQUIN's *lap.*]
MME. RAQUIN. Oh, how good you are. Now don't be angry with me if I've upset the game.
MICHAUD. We're not angry with you. It's been a year since that terrible accident, and you should have gotten hold of yourself by now.
MME. RAQUIN. I haven't counted the days. I cry because the tears come to my eyes. Forgive me. I still see my poor child rolling into the choppy waters of the Seine, and then I see him as a little boy being put to bed under two blankets. What a terrible death! How he must have suffered! I had a premonition of danger; I begged him not to take that outing on the Seine. He wanted to be brave. If you knew how I cared for him in his cradle! When he had typhoid fever, I went three weeks without sleep as I cradled him in my arms.
MICHAUD. You still have your niece. What about her grief? What about the grief of Camille's kind friend who saved her and whose eternal despair is that he could not pull Camille to shore along with her? Your grief is too selfish. See, you're making Laurent cry.
LAURENT. These memories are too cruel.
MICHAUD. Eh! You did what you could. The boat capsized as it hit a pile—one of those piles that holds the eel nets, wasn't it?
LAURENT. I think so. The jolt threw all three of us into the water.
MICHAUD. Let's see: as you fell, you were able to grab Thérèse.
LAURENT. Since she was near me, I was able to grab her clothes and pull her to shore. When I dove in again, Camille had disappeared. He was in the front of the boat. I remember that he made a joke as he dipped his hands into the river by saying that the soup was cold.
MICHAUD. Don't bring up those chilling memories. You acted bravely enough by diving in three times.
GRIVET. How well I know! The day after the accident there was a superb article in my paper. It gave me goose bumps to read of how three people had fallen into the river as their dinner was waiting for them on shore. And then a week later when they found poor Camille's body, there was another article. [*To* MICHAUD.] You remember, Laurent came to ask you to go with him to identify the body.
[MME. RAQUIN *breaks into tears again.*]
MICHAUD. [*Angrily, lowering his voice.*] Really, Grivet, you'd better be quiet. Mme. Raquin is calming down now. But to go over all the details again . . .
GRIVET. [*Offended, lowering his voice.*] A thousand pardons! You started talking about the accident. As long as we're not playing, it would be better to talk about something else.
MICHAUD. [*Raising his voice little by little.*] Ah! You have told us about that article in your newspaper at least a hundred times. It's distasteful, don't you understand? See, Mme. Raquin has been crying about it for at least a quarter hour.
GRIVET. [*Standing up and shouting.*] You started it!
MICHAUD. [*Same voice.*] Oh? No, hang it! It was you!
GRIVET. [*Same voice.*] All of a sudden telling me that I am ridiculous!
MME. RAQUIN. Dear friends, don't fight! [*They go upstage, carrying on their fight wordlessly.*] I will be brave; I won't cry any more. Your conversations have comforted me because I can talk about my misfortune and be reminded of your friendship. Dear Laurent, give me your hand. Are you angry with me?
LAURENT. [*Going to her.*] Only with myself because I wasn't able to bring

them both back to you.

MME. RAQUIN. [*Taking his hand.*] You are my child now, and I love you. I pray for you every night because you tried to save my son. I ask the angels to watch over your sweet life. You see, my dear son is among them; he hears my prayers and blesses your life. Every time that you have some little joy, remind yourself that it was I who prayed for it and Camille who granted it.

LAURENT. Dear Mme. Raquin.

MICHAUD. All is well, all is well.

MME. RAQUIN. [*To* SUZANNE.] And now, little one, go back to your work. See, I'm smiling for you.

SUZANNE. Thank you! [*She gets up and embraces* MME. RAQUIN.]

MME. RAQUIN. [*Slowly returning to the game.*] Whose turn is it?

GRIVET. Are you up to it? Ah! Very good! [GRIVET, LAURENT, *and* MICHAUD *sit back down.*] Whose turn is it?

MICHAUD. Mine! There you are! [*He plays.*]

SUZANNE. [*Has gone back to the work table.*] Dear friend, shall I tell you about the blue prince?

THÉRÈSE. The blue prince?

SUZANNE. [*Taking a footstool and sitting near* THÉRÈSE.] It's quite a story. I won't speak loudly because I don't want Uncle to know about him. Once upon a time there was a young man, dressed in a blue suit and sporting a fine, brown moustache that made him quite handsome.

THÉRÈSE. Watch out; your uncle is listening! [*She half rises to look at the players.*]

MICHAUD. [*Angrily to* GRIVET.] But you passed on a five a minute ago, and now you're putting fives everywhere.

GRIVET. I passed on a five? No, you're mistaken. [MICHAUD *protests; the game continues.*]

SUZANNE. [*Making herself comfortable and continuing in a low voice.*] Uncle is so funny when he plays dominoes! This young man comes to the Luxembourg Gardens every day. Uncle always sits on the terrace, under the third tree on the left, near the newspaper kiosk. The blue prince sits under the fourth tree with a book in his hands; and he glances at me as he turns the pages. [*She stops every once in a while to look furtively at the players.*]

THÉRÈSE. Is that your story?

SUZANNE. Yes, that's what happens in the Luxembourg Gardens. Oh! I almost forgot! One day he saved me from a hoop that a little girl had flung toward me. He gave the hoop a hit to direct it to the other side; that made me laugh. I immediately thought of a lover who has thrown himself at a team of runaway horses. The same thought must have occurred to the blue prince, for ever since then he smiles as he greets me.

THÉRÈSE. Does the story end there?

SUZANNE. Of course not, it starts there. The day before yesterday, after Uncle had gone out and I was vexed because of our stupid maid, I took out the big telescope to amuse myself. You know it, Uncle brought it from Vernon. From our balcony you can see nearly all of Paris. I was looking at Saint-Sulpice, at all the pretty statues at the bottom of the great tower.

MICHAUD. [*Angrily to* GRIVET.] Very well! That's six; go on now!

GRIVET. That's six, that's six! I can see! By God! Now I have to calculate. [*The game goes on.*]

THÉRÈSE. And the blue prince?

SUZANNE. Wait a minute! I was looking at the chimneys, the oceans of chimneys. When I turned the lens a little, all the chimneys were marching, running into each other, parading double time just like soldiers. The lens was full of them! All of a sudden, what should I see between two chimneys—have you guessed?—but the blue prince!

THÉRÈSE. Is your prince a chimney sweep?

SUZANNE. [*Rising.*] Oh, no! He was on a balcony just as I was, and the funniest thing of all was that he was using a telescope too! I recognized him because of his blue suit and his moustache.

THÉRÈSE. Where does he live?

SUZANNE. I don't know because I only saw him in the telescope. Certainly, it was far away, near Saint-Sulpice. When I looked with my naked eye, everything looked grey except the blue spots of the slate roof. I even managed to lose him. The lens moved; and I had to make that terrible trip through the sea of chemneys again. I do have a landmark now— the weathervane of a house near ours.

THÉRÈSE. Have you seen him again?

SUZANNE. Yes, yesterday, today, every day. Am I doing wrong? If you could see how little and cute he is in the telescope. He's barely this tall, almost a picture. I'm not at all afraid of him. But then, I don't know where he lives, I don't even know if what you see in a telescope is real. That's all there is to it. When he does this [*She blows a kiss.*] I stand up straight and can see nothing but grey. Then I think that the blue prince didn't do that [*She repeats the gesture.*], since I can no longer see him except by staring really hard.

THÉRÈSE. [*Smiling.*] You have helped me. [*Looking at* LAURENT.] Always love your blue prince in your dreams.

SUZANNE. Oh! I hope not! Oh dear, the game is over.

MICHAUD. Let's go, the two of us, a deciding game, M. Grivet!

GRIVET. As you wish, M. Michaud! [*They mix up the tiles.*]

MME. RAQUIN. [*Pushing her chair to the right.*] Laurent, since you are up, would you please go get the basket where I keep my wool? It must be on the chest in my room. Take a lamp.

LAURENT. No need! [*He goes out through the door at the rear.*]

MICHAUD. You have a real treasure in that one. He is so easy-going.

MME. RAQUIN. Yes, he is so good to us. He does our little errands and in the evenings helps us close up the shop.

GRIVET. The other day I saw him selling needles just like a shop girl. He! He! A shop girl with a beard! [*He laughs.* LAURENT *returns quickly, haggard, as if pursued; he leans for a moment against the armoire.*]

MME. RAQUIN. What's the matter?

MICHAUD. [*Standing up.*] Are you sick?

GRIVET. Have you had an accident?

LAURENT. No, nothing's wrong, thank you—a dizzy spell. [*He goes downstage with a shaky step.*]

MME. RAQUIN. Where's my basket?

LAURENT. The basket? I don't know; I don't have it.

SUZANNE. What, a man like you afraid?

LAURENT. [*Trying to laugh.*] Afraid? Afraid of what? I didn't find the basket.

SUZANNE. Wait, I'll get it myself. If I see your ghost, I'll bring him back. [*She goes out.*]

LAURENT. [*Getting hold of himself, little by little.*] You see, it's over.

GRIVET. You're too healthy; you have too much blood.

LAURENT. [*Shaking.*] Yes, I do have too much blood.

MICHAUD. —*Sitting back down.*] You should have a refreshing herbal tea.

MME. RAQUIN. Come to think of it, you've seemed agitated for some time. I'll put a little red wine in it. [SUZANNE *comes back with the basket.*] Ah, you found it!

SUZANNE. It was on the chest. [*To* LAURENT, *who is slowly going to the left.*] M. Laurent, I didn't see your ghost; I scared him away.

GRIVET. That girl is really witty! [*The shop bell rings.*]

SUZANNE. Don't bother, I'll go. [*She goes down the spiral stairs.*]

GRIVET. A treasure, a true treasure. [*To* MICHAUD.] Let's see, I had thirty-two, and you had twenty-eight.

MME. RAQUIN. [*Rummaging around in the basket. Then she puts it on the mantle.*] No, I don't see the wool I wanted. I'll have to go to the shop. [*She goes down the spiral stairs.*]

GRIVET. [*Half rising, then lowering his voice.*] Well, the party was almost ruined a while ago. It's not as much fun as before.

MICHAUD. [*The same.*] What do you expect, when death visits a house? Cheer up; I have a plan to bring back our good old Thursdays. [*They play.*]

THÉRÈSE. [*In a whisper to* LAURENT, *who has reached her.*] You were afraid, weren't you?

LAURENT. [*Same tone.*] Yes! Do you want me to come to you tonight?

THÉRÈSE. Let's wait. Let's be careful until it's over.

LAURENT. We've been careful for a year; I haven't kissed you for a whole year. It would be so easy for me to come in through that little door. We're free now. We have nothing to fear about being together in this room.

THÉRÈSE. No, let's not spoil our future. We need lots of happiness, and we may never find enough of it.

LAURENT. Have faith! We'll give each other comfort when we are alone together. When can I come?

THÉRÈSE. On our wedding night, which is not far away. The end is in sight. Be careful, here's Aunt.

MME. RAQUIN. [*Entering.*] Thérèse, go down, dear. They need you in the shop. [THÉRÈSE *exits with an air of fatigue. All eyes follow her.*]

MICHAUD. Did you see Thérèse a moment ago? She was hanging her head and was quite pale.

MME. RAQUIN. I watch her every day—her eyes have circles under them, and her hands shake with weakness.

LAURENT. Yes, her cheeks have a consumptive flush.

MME. RAQUIN. You've made me see these alarming symptoms, dear Laurent, and now I see that they're getting worse. No sadness will be spared me!

MICHAUD. Bah! You're worrying about nothing. It's nerves. She'll get over it.

LAURENT. No. Her heart has been broken. Her long silences and pale smiles are like a farewell. She's suffering a slow death.

GRIVET. You're hardly consoling, old man. We have to cheer our dear Thérèse up instead of bringing up these sad memories.

MME. RAQUIN. Alas, my friend, Laurent is right. The hurt is in her heart, and she does not want to be consoled. Every time I try to reason with her, she becomes impatient, almost angry. She hides away like a wounded animal.

LAURENT. We must resign ourselves to it.

MME. RAQUIN. That's the last blow. She's all I have left, and I am depending on her to bury me. If she were gone, I would be alone in this shop. I would die in a corner. Oh! Please, I am too unhappy, I don't know what has happened to us. [*She cries.*]

GRIVET. [*Timidly.*] Well then, shall we continue the game?

MICHAUD. Wait a minute, hang it! [*He gets up.*] Let's see, I may have a remedy. At Thérèse age, Devil be hanged, one is not inconsolable. Did she cry a lot after the terrible catastrophe at Saint-Ouen?

MME. RAQUIN. No, it was very hard for her to cry. She had a quiet grief, a weakness of the spirit and the body; it was as if she had worked too long and hard. She was confused and became very frightened at times.

LAURENT. [*Shivering.*] Very frightened?

MME. RAQUIN. Yes, one night I heard her muffled sobs. She was babbling and didn't recognize me.

LAURENT. What a nightmare! And she spoke? What did she say?

MME. RAQUIN. I couldn't catch it. She called out Camille's name. She won't come upstairs without a light. In the morning she is exhausted and drags herself around wearily. Her empty stares break my heart. I know that she wants to join my other poor child.

MICHAUD. Thank you, dear lady! My little investigation is done. I'm going to tell you right now what I have concluded, but first [*To* LAURENT.] you must leave us.

LAURENT. Do you want to be alone with Mme. Raquin?

MICHAUD. Yes.

GRIVET. [*Getting up.*] Well, we'll leave you two alone. [*Coming back.*] Don't forget that you owe me two games, M. Michaud. Call me when you are ready to play. [LAURENT *and* GRIVET *exit by the door at the rear.*]

MICHAUD. Now, my dear friend, I am going to be a little brutal.

MME. RAQUIN. What do you advise? If only we can save her!

MICHAUD. [*Lowering his voice.*] You must marry Thérèse off!

MME. RAQUIN. Marry her off! Oh, you are cruel! I would lose my poor Camille a second time.

MICHAUD. Dear lady, I am not being at all romantic. I am a doctor, if you will.

MME. RAQUIN. No, it's impossible. You've seen her tears. She would reject such a suggestion with indignation; she has not forgotten Camille. You make me doubt your refinement, M. Michaud. Thérèse will not remarry as long as she carries her love for Camille in her heart. It would be profane!

MICHAUD. How can you say such grand words? A woman who is afraid to enter her own bedroom every night needs a husband, Devil be hanged.

MME. RAQUIN. What about this stranger we are going to introduce into our home? My old age would be plagued. We could make a bad choice and upset the little peace that remains to us. No, no, let me die with my mourning family around me. [*She sits in the chair on the right.*]

MICHAUD. No doubt we will have to find a brave heart who could be a good husband to Thérèse and a loving son to you. He would, in fact, replace Camille. In a word . . . Laurent!

MME. RAQUIN. Laurent?

MICHAUD. Indeed! Wouldn't they make a handsome couple! There, dear friend, is my advice: you must marry them to each other.

MME. RAQUIN. Thérèse and Laurent? Michaud!

MICHAUD. I knew that you would object. I have nurtured this plan for some time. Think about it; have faith in my long years of experience. If, to add a final joy to your old age, you decide to marry Thérèse off, where could you find a better husband for her than Laurent?

MME. RAQUIN. It seems to me that they are almost brother and sister.

MICHAUD. Think of yourself—although I want you all to be happy. The happy times will come back, and you will once again have two children to bury you.

MME. RAQUIN. Don't tempt me. I know you are right. I do need some consolation, but I'm afraid we'd be doing the wrong thing. My poor Camille would punish us for forgetting him so soon.

MICHAUD. Who spoke of forgetting him? Laurent is always talking about him. He won't leave the family, Devil be hanged!

MME. RAQUIN. I am quite old, my legs have given out. All I want is to die in peace.

MICHAUD. See there, you have convinced yourself. It's the only way of not introducing a stranger into your house. All you have to do is close the bonds of friendship. And soon, I hope you will be a grandmother with little tots bouncing on your knees! You were smiling; I know full well that I made you smile.

MME. RAQUIN. Oh, it's wrong! It's wrong to smile! My soul is in torment, my friend. But those two would never agree to it; they scarcely think of those things.

MICHAUD. Bah! We are rushing things. They are too reasonable not to understand that their marriage is necessary for the well-being of this house. That is how I plan to approach them. I will take care of Laurent; I will talk to him as we are closing the shop. During that time you can broach it to Thérèse. By the end of the evening, we shall have them engaged!

MME. RAQUIN. [*Getting up.*] I'm trembling all over.

MICHAUD. Bear up! Here she is; I will leave you. [*Exits.*]

MME. RAQUIN. [*To* THÉRÈSE, *who enters looking depressed.*] What's wrong, my child? You've not said a word all evening. Please try to be a little less sad. Do it for the gentlemen. [THÉRÈSE *makes a vague gesture.*] I know, you can't control your sadness. Are you in pain?

THÉRÈSE. No, I'm just tired out.

MME. RAQUIN. If you're in pain, you must tell me. I would be wrong to let you suffer without getting you some help. Do you, perhaps, have palpitations? Chest pains?

THÉRÈSE. No . . . I don't know . . . I have no pains. It seems that everything in me is asleep.

MME. RAQUIN. Dear child, you cause me so much sorrow with your silences and depressions. You are all I have left.

THÉRÈSE. How can you expect me to forget?

MME. RAQUIN. I didn't say that; I can't say that. However, it is my duty to ask you . . . to avoid imposing my grief on you . . . to know if you are consoled by our sorrow. Answer me frankly.

THÉRÈSE. I'm just tired out.

MME. RAQUIN. I want you to answer me. You are worried because you live alone, aren't you? At your age, you can't cry forever.

THÉRÈSE. What are you trying to tell me?

MME. RAQUIN. Nothing. I am asking you where your pain is. Living with a woman who is constantly in tears is not pleasant. I can understand that. Then, this room is too big, too dark, and perhaps you want . . .

THÉRÈSE. I don't want anything.

MME. RAQUIN. Listen, don't get upset; it's a stupid idea that came to us. We thought that you might get remarried.

THÉRÈSE. I? Never, never! Why do you doubt me?

MME. RAQUIN. [*Moved.*] They are right, don't you see, dear child? The house is too sad. Everyone avoids us. Go on, you'd do better to listen to them.

THÉRÈSE. Never!

MME. RAQUIN. Yes, remarry. I can't remember any more all the reasons for it; but I am convinced that it is right. I'm going to call Michaud, if you don't mind. He's better at speaking than I am.

THÉRÈSE. My mind is made up; I won't listen. Leave me alone, please. [*She goes to the left.*] Remarry! Good Lord, and to whom?

MME. RAQUIN. They've thought of everything and have even found someone! Right now Michaud is downstairs talking to Laurent.

THÉRÈSE. Laurent! Laurent is your choice? But I don't love him, I could never love him!

MME. RAQUIN. I can assure you that they are right. I agree with their choice. Laurent is almost one of the family; you know how good he is and how he helps us. At first, I was hurt, as you were; it seemed wrong to me. Then as I thought about it, I realized that you would not be unfaithful to the memory of our lost one by marrying his friend, your rescuer.

THÉRÈSE. But what about me, my tears, my need to grieve?

MME. RAQUIN. I am pleading with you because of our tears. Don't you see that they want us to be happy? They said I would once again have two children who would surround me with sweetness and happiness as I peacefully await my death. I am selfish: I need to see you smile again. Say yes; do it for me.

THÉRÈSE. But my grief! You know that I had resigned myself to it forever, and that my only desire was to please you.

MME. RAQUIN. Oh, what a good girl you are! [*Trying to smile.*] This will brighten my last years. We will make a life for ourselves, and our hearts will be warm again. Laurent will be so good to both of us. You know, it's almost as if I'll be marrying him too—I'll borrow him for my little errands, the whims of an old lady.

THÉRÈSE. Dear Aunt, I always thought that whatever happened, you would let me cry in peace.

MME. RAQUIN. You agree, then?

THÉRÈSE. Yes!

MME. RAQUIN. [*Very moved.*] Thank you, my child, you have made me so happy. [*Falling into a chair to the right of the table.*] Oh, my poor child, my poor dead boy! I was the first to betray you! [MICHAUD *enters from the shop.*]

MICHAUD. [*In a whisper to* MME. RAQUIN.] I convinced him, but hang it, it wasn't easy. He's doing it for you, you see. I pleaded your cause. He'll be up in a minute; he's locking up. And Thérèse?

MME. RAQUIN. [*Softly.*] She has agreed. [MICHAUD *goes to join* THÉRÈSE *at the left rear, and chats with her.*]

SUZANNE. [*Arriving, followed by* GRIVET, *and continuing their conversation.*] No, no, M. Grivet, you're too vain; I won't dance with you at the wedding. What, you never married because you didn't want to change your habits?

GRIVET. Certainly, missy!
SUZANNE. You silly man! You understand, not a quadrille, nothing grand like that. [*She goes to rejoin* THÉRÈSE *and* MICHAUD.]
GRIVET. Every little girl thinks it's fun to get married. [*To* MME. RAQUIN.] I tried five times. You remember the last time; it was that old maid school teacher. The banns were published, everything was going well. Then she told me that she drank coffee in the mornings. You know how I hate coffee and that I have drunk cocoa for thirty years. That would have completely upset my existence, so I broke it off. I was right, wasn't I?
MME. RAQUIN. [*Smiling.*] No doubt.
GRIVET. It's pleasant when everyone agrees. Michaud saw immediately that Laurent and Thérèse were made for each other.
MME. RAQUIN. [*Seriously.*] You are right, my friend. [*She gets up.*]
GRIVET. As the song goes:

Well matched spouses
Make a happy marriage . . .

[*Looking at his watch.*] Goodness! Five minutes to eleven! (*He sits on the right, puts on his galoshes, and takes his umbrella.*]
LAURENT. [*Coming upstairs and going to* MME. RAQUIN.] M. Michaud has just told me how happy you are. Your children want to make you happy, dear Mother.
MME. RAQUIN. [*Very moved.*] Oh, do call me Mother, dear Laurent.
LAURENT. Thérèse, shall we make a sweet and peaceful life for our mother?
THÉRÈSE. Yes, it is our duty.
MME. RAQUIN. Oh, children! [*Taking their hands and holding them close to her.*] Marry her, Laurent, make her happy. My Camille will reward you. You are giving me so much joy. I pray to the angels that we will not be punished.

Act 3

Three o'clock in the morning. The room is decorated in white. A fire in the fireplace. The lamp is lit. White cushions on the bed. The bedspread is trimmed with lace; lace doilies on the chairs. Bouquets of roses everywhere—on the buffet, the mantle, the table. THÉRÈSE, MME. RAQUIN, *and* SUZANNE, *all in their wedding finery, enter through the door at the rear.* MME. RAQUIN *and* SUZANNE *are without their shawls and hats.* THÉRÈSE *is dressed in grey silk. She goes to sit on the left wearily.* SUZANNE *stays at the door, trying to keep* MICHAUD *and* GRIVET *out. They have on black suits.*

SUZANNE. No, Uncle! No, M. Grivet! You can't come into the bridal chamber. What you're doing isn't proper. [MICHAUD *and* GRIVET *come in anyway.*]
MICHAUD. [*Whispering to* SUZANNE.] Be quiet, now, it's a joke. [*Same tone to* GRIVET.] Do you have the packet of nettles, M. Grivet?
GRIVET. Certainly, they've been in my suit pocket since this morning. I was most uncomfortable in the church and at the restaurant. [*They sneak up to the bed.*]
MME. RAQUIN. [*Smiling.*] So, gentlemen, you want to help with the undressing of the bride?
MICHAUD. The undressing of the bride! Ah! Dear lady, what a happy occasion! If you need us to hold the pins, we will gladly help. [*He goes back to* GRIVET.]
SUZANNE. [*To* MME. RAQUIN.] I have never seen Uncle so cheery; he's as rosy as an apple.
MME. RAQUIN. Let them laugh. On a wedding night, they should enjoy themselves. In Vernon they did a lot worse than this; the newlyweds could hardly close an eye the whole night.
GRIVET. [*In front of the bed.*] Hang it! This bed is really soft! See for your-

self, M. Michaud.
MICHAUD. Damn! There are at least three mattresses on it. [*Softly.*] Did you bury the nettles in it?
GRIVET. [*Same tone.*] Right in the middle.
MICHAUD. [*Laughing aloud.*] He! He! You're really a card!
GRIEVET. [*Also laughing.*] He! He! It worked out well, didn't it?
MME. RAQUIN. [*Smiling.*] The bride is waiting.
SUZANNE. See, go away now. You two are too much.
MICHAUD. All right, all right, we'll leave.
GRIVET. [*To* THÉRÈSE.] Madam, our compliments for a good night.
THÉRÈSE. [*Rising, then sitting back down.*] Thank you, gentlemen.
GRIVET. [*Shaking* MME. RAQUIN's *hand as they leave.*] You aren't too upset with us, are you, dear lady?
MME. RAQUIN. How could I be, old friend, on this wedding night? [MICHAUD *and* GRIVET *exit slowly, trying to stifle their laughter.*]
SUZANNE. [*Closing the door behind them.*] And don't come back! Only the husband has the right to enter this room and only when we let him.
MME. RAQUIN. You should get undressed, Thérèse; it's almost three o'clock.
THÉRÈSE. I'm dead tired. The ceremony . . . the carriage ride . . . that meal that took forever. Please leave me alone for a minute.
SUZANNE. Yes, it really was hot in the restaurant. I got a headache, but it went away in the cab. [*To* MME. RAQUIN.] You're the one who should be tired because of your bad legs. The doctor told you not to tire yourself out.
MME. RAQUIN. Only a painful emotion could kill me, and today I only had sweet ones. Things turned out well, didn't they? It was done properly.
SUZANNE. The mayor played his role perfectly. When he started to read his little red book, Laurent bowed his head. M. Grivet signed the register with a flourish.
MME. RAQUIN. At church the priest was very touching.
SUZANNE. Yes, everyone cried. I watched Thérèse, and she was as solemn as the rest of us, believe me. And in the afternoon, what a crowd there was on the boulevards! We rode twice from the Madeleine to the Bastille. The people were really amused by us. By the time we got to the restaurant on the Boulevard des Batignolles, half the wedding party was asleep. [*She laughs.*]
MME. RAQUIN. Thérèse, you should get undressed, child.
THÉRÈSE. Let's chat just a few minutes longer.
SUZANNE. Shall I be your maid? Wait! Let me do it. That way you won't get tired.
MME. RAQUIN. Give me your hat.
SUZANNE. [*Takes off the hat and hands it to* MME. RAQUIN *who puts it in the armoire.*] There, you see, you don't have to move at all. But you'll have to stand up if you want me to help you with your dress.
THÉRÈSE. [*Standing up.*] You're a nuisance.
MME. RAQUIN. It's late, my dear.
SUZANNE. [*Unhooking the dress, taking out the pins.*] It must be terrible to have a husband. One of my friends cried and cried after she got married. You hardly have to cinch yourself in at all, your waist is so small. You're right to wear dresses with long bodices. Ah! Here's a pin that's really stuck in good. Maybe I should call M. Grivet. [*She laughs.*]
THÉRÈSE. I'm getting a chill. Hurry up, dear.
SUZANNE. Let's go in front of the fire. [*They cross to the fireplace.*] You have a tear in your slip. What magnificent silk; it stands up by itself. Ah! How nervous you are! You're shaking just like Thisbe. Thisbe is the cat that Uncle gave me. I'll try not to poke you in the ribs.
THÉRÈSE. I have a little fever.
SUZANNE. I'm at the last hook; there. [*She lifts off the dress and hands it to* MME. RAQUIN.] I'm finished. Shall I fix your hair for bed now?
MME. RAQUIN. That's it. [*She exits through the rear door with the dress.*]
SUZANNE. [*Making* THÉRÈSE *sit in front of the fire.*] You've gotten quite red; a

moment ago you were as pale as death.

THÉRÈSE. The fire has warmed me.

SUZANNE. [*Behind her, taking her hair down.*] Lower your head a little. You have beautiful hair. Tell me, Thérèse, you know what all young girls want to know. Is your heart beating and are you trembling because of your wedding night?

THÉRÈSE. I'm not seventeen like you, my dear.

SUZANNE. I haven't made you angry, have I? All day I have thought that if I were in your place, I'd be scared, and I promised myself to see how you prepared for bed so that I wouldn't act stupidly when my turn came. You seem a little sad, but you're acting bravely. I'm afraid of sobbing like an animal.

THÉRÈSE. Is the blue prince so terrible?

SUZANNE. Don't tease me. When your hair is down you look like one of those queens in the paintings. No braids, all right? Only a coil.

THÉRÈSE. Yes, just tie it up. [MME. RAQUIN *enters and takes a white negligee from the armoire.*]

SUZANNE. [*Tying up her hair.*] If you promise not to laugh, I'll tell you what I would feel if I were in your place. I'd be happy, happier than I had ever been. And yet, I'd still be terribly afraid. To me, it would be like walking on the clouds, entering into some beautiful, yet terrifying, new place, with soft music and sweet perfumes. I'd enter in a white light, pushed in spite of myself by a joy so thrilling that I could die from it. Do you feel that way too?

THÉRÈSE. [*In a low voice.*] Music, perfumes, a great light . . . ah, the springtime of youth and love.

SUZANNE. You're shaking again.

THÉRÈSE. I've caught a chill; I can't get warm.

MME. RAQUIN. [*Coming to sit by the corner of the fireplace.*] I will warm your negligee. [*She warms it before the fire.*]

SUZANNE. [*Continuing.*] And as the blue prince waits, just as M. Laurent is waiting now, I'll be mean enough to make him wait a little longer. Finally, when he's at the door, I'd become a little silly. I'd make myself really small and I'd try to hide myself. That's all I know; it hurts to think about it.

MME. RAQUIN. [*Turning the negligee.*] Don't think about it, Suzanne. Children think of nothing but dolls, flowers, and husbands.

THÉRÈSE. Life is rougher than that.

SUZANNE. [*To* THÉRÈSE.] But isn't that what you feel?

THÉRÈSE. Yes. [*In a low voice.*] I didn't want to marry in the winter and from this room. I would have preferred Vernon in May when the acacias are in bloom, and the nights are warm.

SUZANNE. There, your hair is done. [THÉRÈSE *and* MME. RAQUIN *stand up.*] You can put on a warm negligee.

MME. RAQUIN. [*Helping* THÉRÈSE *put on the negligee.*] It almost burned my hands.

SUZANNE. You won't be cold any more, I hope.

THÉRÈSE. Thank you.

SUZANNE. [*Looking at her.*] Ah! You are lovely, you really look like a bride in that lace.

MME. RAQUIN. Now we are going to leave you alone, my child.

THÉRÈSE. Alone, alone. Wait, there's something else that I should tell you.

MME. RAQUIN. No, don't talk; I forbid you to talk. I don't want to make you cry. If you only knew what an effort today has been for me. Now, I'm going to be happy, I am happy! You saw how happy our old friend Michaud is. We should be happy.

THÉRÈSE. You're right. It was just a stupid idea. Good night.

MME. RAQUIN. Good night. [*Returning.*] Tell me, do you have some sorrow, are you hiding some grief from me? What keeps me going is the thought that we have made you happy. You will love your husband who deserves love from us. You will love him as you loved . . . No, I won't say it. We have done the best we could. I wish you lots of joy, my dear, for all the comfort that you have given me.

SUZANNE. It seems as though we're leaving poor dear Thérèse with a band of wolves, in a deep cave. The cave smells good because there are roses everywhere. It's sweet and lovely like a nest.

THÉRÈSE. You were extravagant to spend so much money on roses.

MME. RAQUIN. I know that you love springtime and I wanted to bring a little of it into your room for your wedding night. You will be able to make Suzanne's dream come true, pretend that you are visiting the gardens of paradise. See, you're smiling. Be happy, among your roses. Good night, my child. [*She embraces her.*]

SUZANNE. Won't you hug me too, dear friend? [*She hugs her.*] You've become pale all over again. The blue prince is coming. [*Looking around the room.*] Oh! How wonderful, a room filled with roses! [*They exit.* THÉRÈSE, *alone, goes to sit by the fire,* LAURENT, *still in his wedding suit, enters softly, closes the door and advances cautiously.*]

LAURENT. Thérèse, my love!

THÉRÈSE. [*Pushing him away.*] Not now; I'm cold.

LAURENT. [*After a silence.*] At last we are alone, my Thérèse, far from the others, free to love one another. This is our life, this is our room, and you are mine, my dear wife, because I have won you and because you want to give yourself to me. [*He tries to hug her.*]

THÉRÈSE. [*Pushing him away.*] No, in a little while. I'm all shivers.

LAURENT. Poor angel! Give me your feet, I'll warm them with my hands. [*He kneels before her, reaches for her feet which she draws back.*] Our time has come at last. We've waited for a year, we worked for a year for this night of love. We earned it, didn't we, with our caution and our pain and our agony?

THÉRÈSE. I know. Don't stay there. Sit for a moment; we'll talk.

LAURENT. [*Standing up.*] Why are you trembling? I closed the door, and I am now your husband. Before, when I came, you didn't tremble; you laughed, you talked out loud even at the risk of discovery. Now you talk in a whisper, as if someone were listening through the walls. Go on, we can raise our voices and laugh and love one another. On our wedding night, no one will disturb us.

THÉRÈSE. [*Terrified.*] Don't say that, don't say that. You are as pale as I, Laurent, and you stutter as you say these things. Don't play brave. We don't dare embrace each other. You're afraid you'd look like a fool, if you didn't kiss me. You're a child! We're not like other couples. Sit down, let's talk. [*He crosses behind her, leans against the fireplace as she assumes her old, familiar tone of voice.*] There was a lot of wind today.

LAURENT. A very cold wind, but it died down a little in the afternoon.

THÉRÈSE. Yes, everyone was wearing spring clothes on the boulevards. Anyway, the apricot trees had better not bloom too quickly.

LAURENT. Late freezes in March are bad for the fruit trees. In Vernon, you remember . . . [*He stops. The two dream for a moment.*]

THÉRÈSE. [*In a low voice.*] Vernon, that was child's play. [*Taking up her familiar, indifferent voice.*] Put a log on the fire; there, it's catching now. Do you think it's four o'clock yet?

LAURENT. [*Looking at the clock.*] No, not yet. [*He goes to the left and sits on the other side of the room.*]

THÉRÈSE. It's amazing how long the night is. Are you like me? I can hardly stand to ride in a cab. Nothing bores me more than riding along for hours. I hate to eat in restaurants, too.

LAURENT. It's always more comfortable at home.

THÉRÈSE. As for the country, I don't know.

LAURENT. The food is good in the country. Remember the beer gardens on the banks of the Seine? [*He gets up.*]

THÉRÈSE. [*Getting up brusquely, in a harsh voice.*] Hush! Why bring up those memories? In spite of myself I hear them beating in my head and yours. Again and again, the whole ghastly story. No, we'll not talk about it or think about it any longer. I can see the thoughts behind your words. You're remembering the accident. Stop it! [*Silence.*]

LAURENT. Thérèse, talk to me, please.

Your silence is too awful. Talk to me.
THÉRÈSE. [*Going to sit on the right, her hands pressed against her temples.*] Close your eyes. Forget you're near me.
LAURENT. No, I have to hear your voice; tell me something, anything, as you did a moment ago—the weather is bad, the night is long.
THÉRÈSE. No matter what, I remember; I can't stop remembering. You're right, the silence is bad. I should be able to force some words out. [*Trying to smile, gaily.*] The town hall was quite cold this morning; my feet were frozen. But I was able to warm them by the heater in the church. Did you see the heater? It was quite near where we were kneeling.
LAURENT. Yes, Grivet was planted in front of it during the whole ceremony. The old boy looked jubilant. He was really funny, wasn't he?
THÉRÈSE. The church was a little dark because of the weather. Did you see the lace on the altar cloth? That kind costs at least ten francs a meter. We never have that kind in our shop. The smell of the incense was so strong that it made me sick. At first I felt we were alone in the vast, empty church, and that pleased me. [*Her voice becomes more and more gloomy.*] Then I heard voices singing in the chapel on the other side of the nave.
LAURENT. [*Hesitant.*] I think I saw some people with candles.
THÉRÈSE. [*Seized by a growing terror.*] It was a funeral. When I lifted my eyes, I saw a black pall with a big white cross. [*She stands up and steps back slowly.*] The coffin passed by us as I watched. It was a cheap coffin, short, narrow and quite shabby. What a miserable way to die, destitute and barely mourned. [*She reaches* LAURENT *and throws herself against his shoulder. They shudder together. Then she begins in a low and ardent voice.*] You saw him at the morgue, didn't you, Laurent?
LAURENT. Yes.
THÉRÈSE. Had he suffered?
LAURENT. Horribly.
THÉRÈSE. His eyes were open, and he was staring at you, wasn't he?
LAURENT. The corpse was awful, all blue and bloated by the water. And he was laughing with the corner of his mouth twisted.
THÉRÈSE. He was laughing, you think? Tell me everything. Tell me what he was like. Never in my sleepless nights have I seen him clearly. I must see him, I must!
LAURENT. [*In a terrible voice, shaking* THÉRÈSE.] Be quiet! Wake up! We are both dreaming. What are you talking about? I answered you with lies. I saw nothing, nothing, nothing. What crazy game are we playing?
THÉRÈSE. In spite of us, these terrible words are pouring out just as I knew they would. Everything leads to him: the apricot trees in bloom, the beer gardens on the riverbanks, the shabby coffins passing by. Go on, there are no idle conversations for us; he haunts our every thought.
LAURENT. Hold me.
THÉRÈSE. I knew that our every word would be filled with our memories of him. We can't stop this terrible story from retelling itself over and over in our minds.
LAURENT. [*Trying to take her in his arms.*] Hold me, Thérèse. Our love will cure us. We got married to find peace in each other's arms. Hold me, and let us forget, dear wife.
THÉRÈSE. [*Pushing him away.*] Don't torment me, please. Give me a moment longer. Cheer me up; be good and cheerful like you were before. [*Silence;* LAURENT *takes several steps, then exits through the door at the rear, taken by a sudden thought.*]
THÉRÈSE. [*Alone.*] He's left me alone. Don't leave me, Laurent, I am yours. He's not there, and I'm alone now. The lamp is flickering. If it goes out, if I am to stay alone in the dark . . I don't want to be alone, I don't want night to come. Why did I refuse to let him kiss me? I don't know what came over me. My lips were ice cold, and I felt that his kiss would kill me. Where could he have gone? [*There's a knocking at the little door.*] Good God! The other one is knocking; he's come back for my wedding night! He's knocking in the wood of the bed, he's calling me from the pillows. Go away, I'm afraid! [*She remains shaking, hands*

over her eyes. New knocking. Little by little she calms down, then smiles.] No, it's the other one. It's my dear love, the one from my memories. Thank heavens for those memories. Laurent, I recognize your knock. [*She goes to admit* LAURENT. *They repeat exacty the same movements from the corresponding scene of Act 1.*]

THÉRÈSE. Oh, dear Laurent! [*She embraces his neck.*] I knew that you would come, my love. I dreamed of you. It's been so long since I have had you all to myself.

LAURENT. Do you remember how I couldn't sleep because of you and how I dreamed that we would never be separated? Tonight this beautiful dream will come true, Thérèse.

THÉRÈSE. It will be an unending joy, a springtime without end.

LAURENT. Hold me, then, dear wife.

THÉRÈSE. [*Breaking brusquely away from his arms.*] No, no, no! Why replay this comedy from the past? We don't love each other any more, that's certain. We have killed our love. How can you think that I don't feel how cold you are in my arms? Let's keep calm. It would be cruel and vile.

LAURENT. You are mine, I will have you. I will cure you in spite of your fears. It would be cruel to stop loving each other, to turn our happiness into a nightmare. Come, put your arms around my neck again.

THÉRÈSE. No, that's asking for pain.

LAURENT. You'll see how silly that is after we spend a night of love in this room. No one will come in.

THÉRÈSE. [*Fearfully.*] You already said that. Please don't say it again. He might come.

LAURENT. Are you trying to drive me crazy? [*She goes to the left, and he walks up to her.*] I bought you at too high a price for you to refuse me.

THÉRÈSE. [*Struggling.*] No! The sound of our kisses might bring him. [*As* LAURENT *tries to embrace her, he sees the portrait of* CAMILLE *hanging above the buffet.*]

LAURENT. [*Terrified, backing up, pointing at the portrait.*] There . . . there . . . Camille!

THÉRÈSE. [*Breaking clear of his grasp, standing behind him.*] I felt a cold breath on my back. Where do you see him?

LAURENT. There, in the shadow.

THÉRÈSE. Behind the bed?

LAURENT. No, to the right. He's not moving. He's looking at us deliberately, deliberately. He's just like I remember him from the morgue—pale and muddy, with that smile in the corner of his mouth.

THÉRÈSE. [*Looking.*] It's only his portrait!

LAURENT. His portrait?

THÉRÈSE. Yes, the painting that you did, remember?

LAURENT. No, I don't know any more. His portrait, are you sure? I saw his eyes move. Watch it! They're moving again! His portrait! Go, take it down. His stare is destroying us.

THÉRÈSE. No, I won't do it.

LAURENT. Then, let's turn it to the wall. That way we won't be afraid any more; then perhaps we can kiss.

THÉRÈSE. No, do it yourself.

LAURENT. I can't break his stare. I told you his eyes were following me, accusing me. [*He approaches slowly.*] I will keep my head down and when I can no longer see it . . . [*In a fit of rage, he takes the portrait down.*]

MME. RAQUIN. [*Entering.*] What's going on? I heard screaming.

LAURENT. [*Still holding the portrait, looking at it in spite of himself.*] It's terrible! He's there just as when we threw him in the water.

MME. RAQUIN. [*Advancing in a stagger.*] My God! They killed my child! [THÉRÈSE, *bewildered, screams in terror.* LAURENT, *frightened, throws the portrait on the bed and inches toward* MME. RAQUIN *who is babbling.*] Murderer, murderer! [*Wracked by spasms, she staggers to the bed, grabs one of the bed curtains tearing it down, and falls backward across the bed, panting dreadfully.* LAURENT, *haunted by her stare, crosses to the right and seeks refuge near* THÉRÈSE.]

LAURENT. The doctor warned her. The paralysis is spreading and will afflict her throat.

MME. RAQUIN. [*Advancing with a superhuman effort.*] My poor child! You scum, you scum!

THÉRÈSE. How horrible! She's all twisted! I don't dare help her.
MME. RAQUIN. [*Falling back onto the floor, dragging herself to a chair on the left.*] Oh, God! I can't . . . I can't . . . [*She remains stiff and mute, her burning eyes fixed on* THÉRÈSE *and* LAURENT, *who are shaking.*]
THÉRÈSE. She's dying!
LAURENT. No, her eyes are alive; her eyes threaten us. Only her body is paralyzed.

Act 4

Five o'clock. The room has become dank and dark again, housekeeping neglected, dust cloths on the chairs, dishes strewn over the furniture. A rolled up mattress is thrown behind one of the bed curtains. SUZANNE *and* THÉRÈSE, *at work, are seated at the work table on the right.*
THÉRÈSE. [*Gaily.*] So, you finally found out where the blue prince lives. Love doesn't make you silly, as they say.
SUZANNE. I don't know about that, but I am very cunning. You see after a while it was no longer any fun at all to watch my prince from half a league away, always pretty as a picture. Between us, too pretty, I might add.
THÉRÈSE. [*Laughing.*] You mean you would prefer a naughty lover?
SUZANNE. I don't know. For a lover to be serious, I'd have to be afraid of him. When I watched my prince from the balcony, not knowing if he was in the sky or among the chimneys, I thought he was one of those prayer book angels with clouds under their feet. Oh, how lovely it was! Unfortunately, the ending was not so pretty. On my birthday, Uncle gave me a map of Paris!
THÉRÈSE. A map of Paris!
SUZANNNE. Uncle was a bit shocked too. When I got the map, I went to work. It was hard work! I drew lines with a ruler, I took distances with a compass, I added, I multiplied. When finally I thought I had found my prince's balcony. I stuck a pin in the map. The next day I made Uncle take the street where I thought my prince's house was located.
THÉRÈSE. My dear, your story is delightful. [*Looking at the clock and suddenly become somber.*] Five o'cock already. Laurent will be home soon.
SUZANNE. What's wrong with you? You were so happy a moment ago!
THÉRÈSE. [*Changing back.*] So, your map gave you the blue prince's address?
SUZANNE. Not really; it didn't tell me everything. If you only knew where the map led me! One day it led me to a big, ugly shoe polish factory, another day to a photographer's studio, then to a seminary or maybe it was a prison. You're not laughing, even though my story is funny. Are you sick?
THÉRÈSE. No, my husband will be coming soon. I was daydreaming. When you're married, you'll have to put your pretty map aside.
SUZANNE. [*Getting up and coming to the right as she passes behind* THÉRÈSE.] But I just told you it was all for nothing. Didn't you hear me? One afternoon, I went to the flower market at Saint-Sulpice to buy some nasturtiums for our balcony. [*At the front of the stage.*] Can you guess who I saw in the middle of the market? The blue prince, covered with flowers, with pots in his pockets, pots under his arms, pots in his hands. He looked a little stupid with all those pots. Then he noticed me and followed me, still loaded down with all those pots he was buying for his balcony. Next he made friends with Uncle; then he asked for my hand; and now we are to be married. I made paper dolls out of my map and only watch the moon through the telescope. Did you hear me, dear friend?
THÉRÈSE. Of course, your story is very pretty. You are still in the clouds, still in the flowers, still in make-believe. Oh, dear child, with your beautiful blue bird, if you only knew! [*Looking at the clock.*] Five o'clock; it is five o'clock, isn't it? I must set the table.

SUZANNE. Let me help you. [THÉRÈSE *gets up.* SUZANNE *helps her set the table for three.*] It's a little cruel of me to be so happy when your happiness is so clouded by Mme. Raquin's sad situation. How is she today?

THÉRÈSE. Still mute, still paralyzed. However, she doesn't appear to suffer.

SUZANNE. The doctor warned her that she was working too hard. It's as if a thunderbolt turned her into stone, poor lady. When I see her there still and straight in her chair with her white hair and her pale hands on her lap, I think of those funeral statues that you see in churches; and for some unknown reason, I get scared to death.

THÉRÈSE. Her hands are as dead as her legs.

SUZANNE. Oh! Lord! What a shame! Uncle believes that she has lost her mind, too. He says it would be better if she didn't realize how hopeless her state was.

THÉRÈSE. He's wrong. She understands everything. She is still lucid; her eyes take everything in.

SUZANNE. You're right. I think that her eyes have gotten larger. They are huge now, all dark and terrible in her dead face. I'm not afraid, but at night when I think about the poor woman, I get the shivers. You know about those stories of people buried alive? I dream that she has been buried alive, and there she is at the bottom of a ditch with a pile of dirt on her chest that prevents her from crying out. What must go through her mind on these long days? It's horrible to be like that, always thinking, thinking . . . But you are so good to her.

THÉRÈSE. We are only doing our duty.

SUZANNE. You are the only one who understands the language of her eyes, aren't you? I can't make a thing out. M. Grivet prides himself on understanding her least wish, but he really can't understand her either. It's wonderful that she is here with you where she wants for nothing. How often I've heard Uncle say, "That house is blessed by the Good Lord." Your happiness will return, you'll see. Does the doctor offer you any hope at all?

THÉRÈSE. Very little.

SUZANNE. The last time I was here I thought I heard him say that the poor lady might regain her voice and the use of her limbs.

THÉRÈSE. Don't count on it; we don't dare think of that.

SUZANNE. No, no, try to have hope! [*They have finished setting the table, and they go downstage.*] We hardly see M. Laurent any more.

THÉRÈSE. Since he quit his job and returned to his painting, he leaves early in the morning and often doesn't come home until late. He's working so hard because he wants to enter a painting in the next Salon.

SUZANNE. M. Laurent has become so proper; he no longer laughs aloud and he looks so distinguished. You haven't had a falling out, have you? Oh good! Before, I would not have wanted him for my husband even though I now find him attractive. If you promise not to tell, I'll tell you a secret.

THÉRÈSE. I'm not a chatterbox.

SUZANNE. That's for sure; you keep everything within yourself. Yesterday as we were going down the rue Mazaraine, near your husband's studio, Uncle decided to pay him a visit. As you know, M. Laurent doesn't want to be disturbed under any circumstances, but he received us rather nicely. Do you know what he was working on?

THÉRÈSE. His painting for the Salon.

SUZANNE. Not at all; the big canvas was completely blank. Scattered around the studio were a lot of little drawings, sketches of faces. There were children's heads, women's heads, heads of old men. Uncle, who is something of an expert, was impressed. He claims that all of a sudden your husband has become a great painter. That's not flattery since before he always criticized Laurent's painting rather severely. What surprised me, however, was that all the heads looked alike. They looked . . .

THÉRÈSE. Who did they look like?

SUZANNE. [*Hesitantly.*] I'm afraid to tell

you, but they all looked like Camille.

THÉRÈSE. [*Shaking.*] No, no, you imagined that!

SUZANNE. But it's true! The children's heads, the women's heads, the heads of the old men all looked like Camille. Uncle thought that they should have been more colorful. They were all a little pale, with a smile in the corner of their mouth. [*They hear* LAURENT *at the door.*] Here's Laurent; don't say anything. Perhaps the heads are a surprise for you.

LAURENT. [*Entering.*] Good evening, Suzanne. Did the two of you work hard today?

THÉRÈSE. Yes.

LAURENT. I'm exhausted. [*He sits heavily in the chair on the right.*]

SUZANNE. You must be tired out from standing at your easel all day.

LAURENT. I didn't work today; I walked out to Saint-Cloud. That did me some good. Is dinner ready, Thérèse?

SUZANNE. I'm just leaving.

THÉRÈSE. You must wait; your uncle promised to come for you. Besides, you won't bother us.

SUZANNE. All right! I'll wait in the shop; anyway I want to pick up some tapestry needles. [*As she starts down, the shop bell rings.*] Heavens! A customer! She will surely need some help. [*She exits.*]

LAURENT. [*Pointing to the mattress at the foot of the bed.*] Why didn't you hide the mattress in the little chest? Those idiots don't need to know that we don't sleep together. [*He gets up.*]

THÉRÈSE. It was up to you to hide it this morning. I do what I please.

LAURENT. [*In a harsh voice.*] Woman, let's don't start fighting. Night has not come yet.

THÉRÈSE. If you amuse yourself outside the house by walking to exhaustion, so much the better. I am at peace, don't you see, when you are not here. As soon as you come in, hell returns. Let me, at least, dream the day away, for the night no longer belongs to us.

LAURENT. [*In a soft voice.*] Your voice is harsher than mine, Thérèse.

THÉRÈSE. [*After a silence.*] Would you go bring in Aunt for dinner? You'd better wait until the Michauds have left, for I always tremble when she is around them. For some time now I've noticed a relentless determination in her eyes. She's trying to find a way to communicate.

LAURENT. Pauh! Michaud will want to see his old friend. What could she tell him? She can't even raise her little finger. [*He exits by the door at the rear.*] [MICHAUD *and* SUZANNE *enter from the shop.*]

MICHAUD. Ah, the table is set.

THÉRÈSE. Of course, M. Michaud. [*She takes a dishtowel, a salad bowl, and a head of romaine from the buffet. She sits on the left, spreads the towel on her lap, and washes the lettuce during this scene.*]

MICHAUD. How are you all, eh? Ah, these lovers really have hellish appetites. Get your hat, Suzanne. [*Looking around him.*] And how is dear Mme. Raquin? [LAURENT *enters pushing* MME. RAQUIN *in her wheelchair; she is rigid and mute; her hair is snow white, and she is dressed all in black. He rolls her up to her place on the right of the table.*] Ah! Here's the dear lady now.

SUZANNE. [*Embracing the invalid.*] Our hearts are with you; you must be brave.

MICHAUD. Her eyes are shining; she must be happy to see us. [*To* MME. RAQUIN.] We've known each other for a long time, haven't we? Don't you remember when I was Chief of Police? As I remember, the murder in Gorge-aux-Loups had just taken place. You must recall that case: a man and a woman had killed a driver; and I arrested them myself in their hovel. They were, thank God, guillotined in Rouen.

GRIVET. [*Who enters just as* MICHAUD *is finishing.*] Ah! The story of the driver; I know that one. You told it to me, and I was very taken with it. M. Michaud has a flair for discovering rogues! Good evening, ladies and gentlemen.

MICHAUD. What are you doing here at this hour, M. Grivet?

GRIVET. Oh, I was passing by and thought I'd treat myself to a little visit with dear Mme. Raquin. You were about to sit down to dinner;

don't let me disturb you.
LAURENT. Not at all.
GRIVET. Mme. Raquin and I understand each other so well. One look and I know what she wants.
MICHAUD. You'd do well to tell me what she wants when she stares at me so fixedly.
GRIVET. Wait, I can read her eyes like a book. [*He sits by* MME. RAQUIN, *touches her arm, and waits as she slowly turns her head to him.*] There, let's chat for a moment. Do you have something to tell M. Michaud? Nothing at all? Just as I thought. [*To* MICHAUD.] You've overestimated your importance to her. She doesn't want you, don't you see, she only wants me. [*Turning to* MME. RAQUIN.] Eh? What did you say? Good, good, I understand! You're hungry.
SUZANNE. [*Perched on the back of the chair.*] Do you want us to leave, dear lady?
GRIVET. Good Lord, yes! She's hungry! Plus she invited me for a little visit this evening. A thousand pardons, Mme. Raquin, but I can't accept; you know my little habits. I'll come on Thursday, I promise you.
MICHAUD. She didn't say a thing to you, M. Grivet, whatever makes you think so! Let me have a turn at questioning her.
LAURENT. [*To* THÉRÈSE *who has stood up.*] See to your aunt. You were right, she has a terrible gleam in her eyes. [*He takes the salad bowl in which* THÉRÈSE *has washed the lettuce and puts it and the dish cloth on the buffet.*]
MICHAUD. Let's see, dear friend, you know that your wish is my command. Why are you looking at me like that? If only you could find a way to tell us what you want!
SUZANNE. You heard what Uncle said—your desires are sacred to us.
GRIVET. I just explained what she wanted. It's clear to me.
MICHAUD. [*Insistent.*] Well, could you make it clear to us? [*To* LAURENT, *who is coming to the table.*] You see, Laurent, how strangely she's looking at me.
LAURENT. No, I don't see anything unusual in her eyes.
SUZANNE. What about you, Thérèse? You must know what she wants.
MICHAUD. Do help her, please. Find out what she wants.
THÉRÈSE. You're mistaken; she doesn't want anything. There's nothing unusual in her eyes. [*She leans on the table, facing* MME. RAQUIN. *She can't stand the look in* MME. RAQUIN's *eyes.*] You don't want anything, do you? No, nothing. I'm quite sure. [*She backs off, returning to the left.*]
MICHAUD. Well, perhaps M. Grivet is right.
GRIVET. Good Lord! I must be on my way now! I know what she said: she's hungry and has invited me for a visit.
LAURENT. Why don't you stay, M. Michaud? It would be no trouble.
MICHAUD. Thank you; but I have plans for the evening.
THÉRÈSE. [*Whispering to* LAURENT.] For God's sake, get them out of here!
MICHAUD. Good evening, friends. [*He gets ready to leave.*]
GRIVET. Good evening, good evening. [*He gets up and follows* MICHAUD.]
SUZANNE. [*Who is still behind* MME. RAQUIN.] Look!
MICHAUD. [*From the spiral staircase.*] What?
SUZANNE. Look, she's moving her fingers! [MICHAUD *and* GRIVET *gasp in shock and go to* MME. RAQUIN's *chair.*]
THÉRÈSE. [*Whispering to* LAURENT.] We're done for! She has made a superhuman effort! It's our punishment. [*They stay on the left, side by side, terrified.*]
MICHAUD. [*To* MME. RAQUIN.] You've become a young girl again. Your fingers are dancing the gavotte. [*Silence as* MME. RAQUIN *continues her finger play. She fixes* THÉRÈSE *and* LAURENT *with a terrible stare.*] Look! She has succeeded in lifting her hand and putting it on the table!
GRIVET. Oh, oh! What a gadabout; her hands are everywhere!
THÉRÈSE. [*Whispering.*] She's recovering! Good Lord! Life is returning to this stone statue.
LAURENT. [*The same tone.*] Be brave! Hands don't talk.
SUZANNE. She's tracing letters with the tip of her finger.

GRIVET. Yes, that's what she's doing on the oil cloth.

MICHAUD. She's writing, don't you see? She just made a capital T.

THÉRÈSE. [*Whispering.*] Her hands are talking, Laurent.

GRIVET. She's writing, by God! [*To* MME. RAQUIN.] No, start over, I didn't follow. [*After a silence.*] It's amazing. I can read it! T-H-E-R-E-D-C. She must want that red cup.

SUZANNE. Really, M. Grivet, you don't understand at all. [*Reading.*] Thérèse and . . . Go on, Mme. Raquin.

LAURENT. [*Whispering.*] Vengeful hand, hand that is already dead, emerging from its coffin, and every finger has become a mouth. She won't get it out. I'll shut her up before she finishes it. [*He puts a knife in his pocket.*]

THÉRÈSE. [*Holding him back whispering.*] Be careful, you'll destroy us!

MICHAUD. It's so clear, I can read it. "Thérèse and Laurent are . . ." She's written your name, my friends.

GRIVET. Your two names, word of honor. It's uncanny.

MICHAUD. [*Reading.*] "Thérèse and Laurent are . . ." What are they, these dear children?

GRIVET. Oh dear! She's stopped! Go on, go on!

MICHAUD. Finish the sentence; just a little more effort. [MME. RAQUIN *stares at* THÉRÈSE *and* LAURENT, *then slowly turns her head.*] You have looked at each of us; now we want to know the end of your sentence. [*She remains still for a moment, relishing the terror of the murderers. Then she lets her hand fall.*] Oh! You let your hand fall!

SUZANNE. [*Touching her hand.*] It's glued to her lap again like a piece of marble. [*The three gather behind her chair where they talk eagerly.*]

THÉRÈSE. [*Whispering.*] I was sure she would betray us; then her hand fell silent. We are saved, aren't we?

LAURENT. Be careful; don't faint. Lean on my shoulder. I'm suffocating.

GRIVET. [*Continuing his conversation aloud.*] It's a pity she didn't finish the sentence.

MICHAUD. Yes, I was reading it along. What could she have meant?

SUZANNE. That she is happy with the care that Thérèse and Laurent provide.

MICHAUD. This child is smarter than both of us. "Thérèse and Laurent are my beloved children." Isn't that it, Mme. Raquin? You want to praise your children. [*To* THÉRÈSE *and* LAURENT.] You are two brave souls who merit a reward in this world as well as the next.

LAURENT. You'd do the same.

GRIVET. They've already been blessed. Don't you know that they call them the turtledoves in the neighborhood?

MICHAUD. Eh! And because of us, they married. Come, M. Grivet. We must let them eat at last. [*Going to* MME. RAQUIN.] Be patient, dear lady. Your little hands and then your feet will come back. Being able to move your fingers was a good sign—a cure is near. Goodbye!

SUZANNE. [*To* THÉRÈSE.] I'll see you tomorrow, dear friend.

GRIVET. [*To* MME. RAQUIN.] There! I knew that we would understand each other wonderfully. Be brave, we will have our Thursdays again, and we will beat M. Michaud, the two of us; yes, we'll beat him. [*As he leaves, to* THÉRÈSE *and* LAURENT.] Goodbye, turtledoves! Yes, you are two turtledoves. [*As* MICHAUD, SUZANNE, *and* GRIVET *exit by the spiral staircase,* THÉRÈSE *exits for a moment by the rear door and comes back with a soup tureen. During this scene,* MME RAQUIN's *face reflects her emotions: anger, horror, cruel joy, and relentless vengeance. She follows the murderers with her burning eyes, through all their quarrels and their hysteria.*]

LAURENT. She spared us.

THÉRÈSE. Be quiet; leave her alone. [*She serves herself and* LAURENT *some soup.*]

LAURENT. [*Sitting on the upstage side of the table.*] Would she spare us if she could talk? Michaud and Grivet were strangely pleased with themselves when they talked about our happiness. They'll find out in the long run. Grivet had his hat down around his ears, didn't you see?

THÉRÈSE. [*Putting the soup tureen on the hearth.*] Yes, I saw it.

LAURENT. He buttoned up his coat and put his hand in his pocket as he left just like in the office when he wanted to appear important. And how he said, "Goodbye, turtledoves!" He's a terrible, sinister old idiot.

THÉRÈSE. [*Returning to the table.*] Hush! Don't blow it up, don't add that to our nightmares.

LAURENT. When he smiles that stupid smile, I know that he's mocking us. I can't stand people who act so stupid. I can tell that he must know everything.

THÉRÈSE. They're too naïve. That would put an end to it, if they betrayed us; but they don't understand what they see. They will continue to come into the horror of our lives with their humdrum middle-class ways. [*She sits on the left of the table.*] Let's talk about something else. Whatever possesses you to talk about it when she is with us?

LAURENT. I don't have a spoon. [THÉRÈSE *gets a spoon from the buffet, gives it to him and sits back down.*] You haven't fed her yet, have you?

THÉRÈSE. I will when I finish my soup.

LAURENT. [*Tasting the soup.*] It's terrible as usual. You put too much salt in it. [*He pushes his bowl away.*] Another of your nasty tricks! You know I don't like salt.

THÉRÈSE. Laurent, please don't provoke me. I'm exhausted, can't you see that? My emotions will destroy me soon enough.

LAURENT. Go on, tell me you're exhausted; torture me with your petty grievances.

THÉRÈSE. You want us to quarrel, don't you?

LAURENT. I don't want you to talk to me like that.

THÉRÈSE. So, that's it! [*In a harsh voice, pushing the soup bowl away.*] As you wish; we won't eat this evening but tear each other apart while Aunt watches us. It's a treat that we give her every day now.

LAURENT. Aren't you forgetting your attacks on me? You spy on me, you try to wound me to the quick, and you are happy when my pain drives me crazy.

THÉRÈSE. I was not the one who found the soup salty. All you need is some ridiculous pretext to turn your impatience into a towering rage. Admit it, you are happy to argue the night away so that you can dull your nerves and sleep a bit.

LAURENT. You sleep more than I do.

THÉRÈSE. Oh! You have made my life a hell. As soon as night falls, we shiver in fear. And you know why. Oh, the agonies of this room!

LAURENT. It's your fault.

THÉRÈSE. My fault? Is it my fault that your life is intolerable, and filled with unspeakable horrors instead of the wonderful life that you envisioned?

LAURENT. Yes, it is your fault.

THÉRÈSE. Let me be! I'm not an idiot! Do you think that I don't know you? You have always been a cheap gambler. You took me as your mistress because I cost you nothing. Don't you dare deny it! Can't you see that I hate you?

LAURENT. Is it you or I who is provoking a quarrel now?

THÉRÈSE. I hate you! You killed Camille.

LAURENT. [*Getting up, then sitting down.*] Be quiet! [*Pointing to* MME. RAQUIN.] You just told me to hold my tongue in front of her. Don't make me remind you of the facts, to tell you once again in her presence.

THÉRÈSE. What if she hears it, what if she is suffering? Don't I have a right to suffer too? The truth is that you killed Camille.

LAURENT. You're lying; admit you're lying. I threw him into the water because you pushed me into murdering him.

THÉRÈSE. I? I?

LAURENT. Yes, you! Don't play the innocent with me. Don't force me to choke a confession out of you. I want you to accept your share of the crime. That will make me feel better; that will give me peace.

THÉRÈSE. But I wasn't the one who killed Camille.

LAURENT. Yes, a thousand times, yes! You were on the riverbank when I whispered to you, "I'm going to throw him into the water." Then you agreed to it by getting into the boat. You know full well that you killed him with me.

THÉRÈSE. It's not true. I was out of my mind. I didn't know what I was doing. I never wanted to kill him.

LAURENT. And in the middle of the Seine, when I made the boat capsize, didn't I warn you? You clutched at my neck and let him drown like a dog.

THÉRÈSE. It's not true! You killed him!

LAURENT. And in the cab on the way home, didn't you put you hand in mine? It burned right through to my heart.

THÉRÈSE. You killed him!

LAURENT. You don't remember, you don't want to remember. You bewitched me with your caresses, here, in this room. You turned me against your husband. You wanted to be rid of him. He didn't please you, he was shaking with fever, you said. For three years that was all I thought about. Was I a criminal? I was an honest man, I hurt no one, nothing, not even a fly.

THÉRÈSE. You killed him!

LAURENT. Twice you've made me a cruel brute. I was cautious, I was peaceful, and look now how I tremble before a shadow as if I were a timid child. My nerves are as shattered as yours. I'm suffocating. You led me into adultery, into murder, without my recognizing it. Every day as I come home, I'm faced with what I have done. I see with a shudder, in a dream, the police, the trial, the guillotine. [*He gets up.*] You'd better be careful. At night I can hear your teeth chattering in terror. You know that when the ghost comes, he'll strangle you first.

THÉRÈSE. [*Standing up.*] Don't say that! You killed him! [*They both leave the table.*]

LAURENT. Listen, you're a coward to refuse your part in the crime. You want to make my guilt heavier, don't you? Since you've pushed me to the edge, I want to get it over with. As you can see, I am quite calm. [*He gets his hat.*] I'm going to tell the police everything.

THÉRÈSE. [*Mocking him.*] What a good idea!

LAURENT. We'll both be arrested. We'll see what the judge makes of your innocence.

THÉRÈSE. [*In a flash.*] Are you trying to scare me? I am more exhausted than you. If you don't go to the police, I will.

LAURENT. I don't need you to come with me; I know what to say.

THÉRÈSE. No, no! In every quarrel, when you run out of options, you threaten me. Today I want it to be serious. Well, I'm not a coward like you; I'm ready to follow you to the scaffold. Let's go; I'm coming with you. [*She goes with him to the little stairs.*]

LAURENT. [*Stuttering.*] As you wish, let's go to the police together. [*He starts down the stairs.* THÉRÈSE *remains leaning on the rail, immobile, listening. Little by little she is seized by a shiver of terror.* MME. RAQUIN *turns her face which is lit up by a savage smile.*]

THÉRÈSE. He's downstairs in the shop. Will he have the courage to free us? I don't want it, I'll run after him, take him by the arm, and bring him back. What if he shouts it out on the street, what if he tells everything to a passerby? I was wrong, My God, to push him to the edge. I should have been more sensible. [*Listening.*] He's still in the shop; the bell has stopped. What's he doing? He's coming back. I can hear his footsteps. I knew that he wasn't brave enough to do it! [*In a flash.*] Coward! Coward!

LAURENT. [*Entering, sitting at the work table, broken, holding his head in his hands.*] I couldn't do it. I couldn't do it!

THÉRÈSE. [*Approaching, in a mocking voice.*] Back so soon? What did you tell them? How I pity you because you don't have blood in your veins? [*She passes between the fireplace and* LAURENT, *then stands in front of him with her fists resting on the worktable.*]

LAURENT. [*In a low voice.*] I couldn't do it.

THÉRÈSE. You were supposed to help me carry this terrible memory, and you are weaker than I. How will we ever be able to forget it?

LAURENT. You accept, then, your part in the crime?

THÉRÈSE. Yes, if you wish, I am guilty, guiltier than you. I should have saved my husband from your hands. Camille was good.

LAURENT. Don't start again, please. When the madness comes over me, you toy with me. You don't look at me or smile at me. I will escape you when I want . . . [*He takes a little bottle from his pocket.*] I have here release, peaceful sleep. Two sips of prussic acid will cure me.

THÉRÈSE. Poison! You're too much of a coward; I dare you to drink it. Drink, Laurent, drink a little, to see . . .

LAURENT. Be quiet! Don't push me any further.

THÉRÈSE. I know that you won't drink it. Camille was good, do you hear? I wish you were in the ground instead of him. [*She goes to the left.*]

LAURENT. Be quiet!

THÉRÈSE. See here, you don't understand women. Why shouldn't I hate you now that you are covered with Camille's blood?

LAURENT. [*Pacing, as if hallucinating.*] You will be quiet! I can hear my head pounding. You'll shatter my skull! What an infernal torturer you are—being remorseful and then crying out for Camille! I am forever reminded of him. He did this, he did that, he was good, he was generous. I'm going mad! He lives with us. He sits in my chair, at the table, everywhere in the room. I have his wife, I have his blankets, I have his sheets. I am Camille, Camille, Camille.

THÉRÈSE. It was a cruel joke to sketch him.

LAURENT. So, you even know that! [*Lowering his voice.*] Lower your voice. What a terrible thing; my hands are no longer mine. I can't paint any more. He is always reborn through my hands. No, these hands, these two hands no longer belong to me. They will betray me if I don't cut them off first. They are his now, he has taken them from me.

THÉRÈSE. It's your punishment.

LAURENT. Tell me, is my mouth like Camille's? Listen, I'm going to say this sentence as Camille could have. "I have his mouth, I have his mouth." Eh? Isn't that good? I talk like him. I laugh like him. And he is there, always there in my head, pounding with his closed fists.

THÉRÈSE. It's your punishment.

LAURENT. [*In a fury.*] Get out of here, woman, you're driving me crazy. Get out or I'll . . . [*He forces her to her knees and raises his fist.*]

THÉRÈSE. [*Kneeling.*] Kill me as you killed him! Finish it! Camille never raised his hand against me. You are a monster. Kill me as you killed him! [LAURENT, *horrified, backs up; he sits near the bed alcove with his head in his hands. During this time,* MME. RAQUIN *has been able to slide a knife across the table. It falls in front of* THÉRÈSE. *At the sound,* THÉRÈSE, *whose eyes have been following* LAURENT, *turns her head. She looks at the knife and then at* MME. RAQUIN.] You did that! Your eyes are glowing like two hell holes. I know what you are trying to tell me. You are right, this man had made my life intolerable. If he weren't always here to remind me of what I want to forget, I'd be at peace. My life would be pleasant. [*To* MME. RAQUIN, *as she picks up the knife.*] You're looking at the knife, aren't you? Yes, I have it, and I don't want that man to torture me any more. He killed Camille because he was in the way. He's in my way now. [*She gets up, holding the knife in her fist.*]

LAURENT. [*Coming back, hiding the vial of poison in his hand.*] Let's make up; let's finish dinner, all right?

THÉRÈSE. As you wish. [*Aside.*] Never have I longed for night to come as I do now; the knife is burning in my hand.

LAURENT. What are you dreaming about? Sit down. Wait, I'll get you something to drink. [*He pours some water in a glass.*]

THÉRÈSE. [*Aside.*] I can't wait to end it. [*She approaches with the knife raised. She sees* LAURENT *pour the poison into the glass. She grabs his arm.*] What are you pouring into that glass, Laurent?

LAURENT. [*Seeing the knife.*] Why have you raised your arm? [*Silence.*] Coward, a knife!

THÉRÈSE. Coward, poison! [*They stare at each other, then drop the knife and vial.*]

LAURENT. [*Dropping into a chair.*] At the

same moment both of us had the same horrible thought.

THÉRÈSE. [*Same action.*] Do you remember, Laurent, the passionate kisses that we shared? And now, here we are, face to face, with poison and a knife. [*She glances at* MME. RAQUIN, *gets up and gasps.*] Look, Laurent!

LAURENT. [*Getting up, turning to* MME. RAQUIN *with horror.*] She's watching us kill each other.

THÉRÈSE. Look, she's moving her lips! She's smiling! What a horrible smile!

LAURENT. She's starting to shake!

THÉRÈSE. She's about to speak, I tell you, she's about to speak!

LAURENT. I know how to shut her up. [*He goes to* MME. RAQUIN, *who has slowly stood up. He backs off; he passes to the right, as he turns.*]

MME. RAQUIN. [*Standing, in a terrible low voice.*] Murderer! How dare you hit me!

THÉRÈSE. Oh! God! Don't hand us over to the police!

MME. RAQUIN. The police! No, no, I considered it for a while as my strength was returning to me. I started to write your act of murder on the table; but I stopped because I knew that human justice would be too swift. I decided to watch you pay for your crime here in this room where you stole my happiness.

THÉRÈSE. [*Sobbing, throwing herself at* MME. RAQUIN'*s feet.*] Forgive me. My tears are suffocating me; I'm a wretch. Just raise your foot, and I'll put my head under it so that you can crush it on the floor. Pity! Have pity!

MME. RAQUIN. [*Leaning on the table, slowly raising her voice.*] Pity? Where was your pity for my poor beloved child? Don't beg me. I have no pity. You have torn out my heart! [LAURENT *falls on his knees on the right.*] No, I won't save you from yourselves. I'll let you hurl accusations against each other like the horrible beasts that you are. No, I won't hand you over to justice. You are mine, mine alone; and I'm keeping you for myself.

THÉRÈSE. Your punishment is too cruel; you have forced us to be our own judge and jury! [*She takes the acid, drinks avidly and falls dead at* MME. RAQUIN'*s feet.* LAURENT *grabs the vial from her, drinks and falls to the right near the work table.*]

MME. RAQUIN. [*Sitting down slowly.*] They died too quickly!

Peer Gynt

Henrik Ibsen

Without question, the dominant figure in European drama after the seventeenth century was Henrik Johan Ibsen. Born in Norway, far to the north of the principal centers of European theatrical life and in a country that had no national drama of consequence (despite Holberg's pioneering work in neighboring Denmark), Ibsen established Scandinavia's claim to literary excellence. He also revolutionized world theater by bringing together several of the forces in nineteenth-century drama in bold new patterns destined to influence the work of every significant playwright who came after him. In a fifty-year writing career covering almost exactly the last half of the nineteenth century, Ibsen devoted his first twenty-five years to learning his craft and to writing in the earlier forms that were the basis of the European tradition. Then, at midcareer, Ibsen dramatically shifted focus to the naturalistic theater advocated by Zola and others of the avant-garde, making of realistic plays not just mundane slices of life, but genuine works of theatrical art. The standards set by Ibsen have dominated the realistic theater ever since.

Henrik Ibsen was born in Skien, Norway (then under the political domination of Sweden), on March 20, 1828. His father was a well-to-do businessman whose extravagant way of life led to bankruptcy in 1836; his mother, also from a wealthy family, was sensitive, pious, and ill-suited to the difficult life that bankruptcy suddenly forced upon the family. Henrik was the second of six children (five boys and a girl), but his elder brother died in infancy and the responsibilities of being the eldest child weighed heavily on Henrik. The family lived for several years in what Henrik perceived as severe social ostracism on the one piece of property remaining to them—a farm; they returned to Skien in 1843, but Henrik's schooling was curtailed as he had to help support the family. In 1844, he was apprenticed to an apothecary in Grimstadt; in this tiny town of eight hundred people, he fathered an illegitimate son by a servant girl ten years older than he. Ibsen supported the child for fourteen years, but did his best to conceal the entire matter from public gossip.

Having studied on his own in preparation for the entrance examinations, Ibsen went to Christiania (now Oslo) in 1850 with the intention of entering the university to become a physician. Failing parts of the examination, he matriculated for a time as a conditional student, and saw his first play produced at the Christiania Theater (another had been published earlier that year, but not produced). Through a friendship with Ole Bull, Ibsen was invited in 1851 to become stage director of the newly formed Norwegian National Theater in Bergen, where during the next six years he directed 145 plays (including 21 by Scribe), thus mastering the crafts that he was to serve as writer. Moving to the Norwegian Theater in Christiania in 1857, Ibsen continued his practical stage work until 1862, when the Norwegian Theater went bankrupt. Somehow he found time to write plays during these years as well, none of which is now regarded as among his better ones.

In 1858, Ibsen married Susannah Thoresen, and on December 23, 1859, his only legitimate child, Sigurd, was born. Sigurd was later to become an important government official and a leader in the establishment of an independent Norway early in the twentieth century. In 1863, Ibsen was awarded a travel grant, and in 1866 an annual stipend, by the Norwegian government (a not uncommon means of supporting promising writers in Europe); Ibsen moved to Rome with his family and did not return to Norway, except for two brief visits, for twenty-seven years. He preferred to live in southern Europe, sending his work back to Norway for publication and production, a procedure that in his case paid off handsomely. The quality of his playwriting improved markedly, and the major portion of his career was launched with the publication of *Brand* in 1866. *Peer Gynt* followed in 1867, and *The Emperor and the Galilean* in 1873. These romantic works mark the peak of Ibsen's accomplishment during the first half of his career.

Peer Gynt is regarded by many as Ibsen's finest achievement, and it is certainly his best play before he turned to realism. An epic work that resists (but does not preclude) confinement to a stage, it was published on November 14, 1867, but not produced until February 24, 1876, with stirring music by Edvard Grieg. Clearly related, both in form and in content, to Goethe's *Faust*, *Peer Gynt* might be described as the inverse of romantic philosophy rendered in romantic structure. If Faust devotes his life to seeking the fullest experience of living, ever striving and never content with the status quo, Peer devotes most of life to the way of the troll: "To yourself be enough." Although continually presented with new opportunities, Peer is smugly satisfied with whatever is at hand, until at the end of his life he finds that he has missed every opportunity that was offered him to create a genuine self. As does Goethe at the end of Part 2 of *Faust*, Ibsen finds salvation in the Eternal Feminine, though Peer is too spiritually dead to grasp the full significance of this even when it is presented to him.

If Faust was in many respects the embodiment of the Renaissance man, interested in everything and seeking the fullest experience and knowledge of every aspect of life, Peer Gynt may be said to represent modern man, creating his own essence with every choice he makes, but in fact unwilling to commit himself to any ideal. Peer is a man of great charm, energy and potential, of whom much is expected in life and who in a materialistic sense has the highest goals for himself. "I'll be a king, an emperor!" Peer insists in the opening scene, and this motif runs ironically through the play as Peer is by turns a troll prince, a plantation owner, a prophet, and an emperor among madmen, only to learn in the last act that "here's where my empire lay!"—with Solveig. Ibsen neatly contrasts Peer with the boy in the first scene of act 3 who cuts off his finger to avoid the draft. Although he does not appear in the play again, his life is movingly summarized in the funeral sermon in scene 3 of act 5. Little was expected of so timid and cowardly a man, yet he devoted his life to hard and fulfilling work, which, although making no great mark in world affairs, created a home and security for his wife and children. Quietly going about his daily tasks and doing his best with his limited resources, this nameless man realizes the full potential inherent in himself. Peer, however, has unthinkingly characterized himself just after the boy cuts off his finger: "Yes, think it; wish it; *will* it so— / But to *do* it! No, that's not for Peer." To the romanticist, Peer is an antihero, though that term has not been used until modern times. In a fundamental sense, the antihero is modern man, adrift in a world in which he no longer finds meaning or purpose, but creating for himself shallow, meaningless purposes to cover over that void.

Peer Gynt is as vivid and rich a character as any to be found in drama; obviously he totally dominates the play named after him, and his character is the key to the play's meanings. Other characters exist only as foils for the many aspects of Peer's personality, and naturalistic questions about why Solveig would wait a lifetime in a mountain cabin for Peer or who the Button-Molder represents are deeply misleading. Like the trolls and the Boyg, the Lean Person and the Strange Passenger, the Woman in Green and the Statue of Memnon, all the characters are in some degree projections of Peer's mind, not totally susceptible to scientific analysis because they are intended to be imagistic rather than scientific. If ideas such as Ibsen is probing could conveniently be presented in rational exposition, it would not be necessary to write the play. The totality of the play's symbols, acting together, forms a richly evocative montage of images that tellingly explores the meaning of human life. Few plays in western literature do so as compellingly. Peer's mother, Aase, might be something of an exception to these generalizations; she does live as an independent character of some stature, and her death scene is a magnificent piece of theater.

Structurally, *Peer Gynt* is pure romanticism. In five acts and thirty-eight scenes, it is a sprawling giant that is somewhat intimidating for its sheer size. Actually the first three acts are relatively compact and tell a straightforward, if fantastic, story. Act 1 establishes some of the more picaresque and attractive aspects of Peer's character and portrays the abduction of the bride. Act 2 is essentially Peer's encounter with the trolls. Act 3 offers him Solveig, but he is convinced that he must go "roundabout" to deserve her; he parts from sweetheart, mother, and home upon his life quest. Act 4 is perhaps the most perplexing, for one senses that it is too long and sprawling; yet any cuts would leave out vital thematic aspects of Peer's search. Acts 4 and 5 together consist of twenty-three scenes and constitute over half the playing time of the work, but they complete the phantasmagoria of Peer's worldwide quest and (in Act 5) his homecoming. Only with the cycle finished, as Peer nears the end of his life and returns to Solveig, can the completed figure of the whole work be seen—a man's total life pattern, incomplete if any part of it were removed.

Ibsen saw himself as a poet (even in his prose plays), and *Peer Gynt* offers poetry that soars magnificently in the theater. Fjelde has here done a remarkable job of finding, for Ibsen's original creation, English equivalents that are widely acknowledged to share more of Ibsen's spirit than have those of any previous translation of *Peer Gynt*. Not only in his language, but also in his total manipulation of the elements of the theater, Ibsen has here mastered the poetry that is at the heart of all romanticism and has given the world one of its finest examples of the romantic spirit at work in the theater.

N.B. All notes to this play are by the translator.

Peer Gynt

Translated by Rolf Fjelde

Characters
Aase, a farmer's widow
Peer Gynt, her son
Two Old Women with sacks of grain
Aslak, a blacksmith
Wedding guests, Master of Ceremonies, Fiddler, etc.
A Newcomer
His Wife
Solveig }
Little Helga } their daughters
The Farmer at Hegstad
Ingrid, his daughter
Mads Moen, the bridegroom
His Parents
Three Herd Girls from a mountain hut
A Woman in Green
The Troll King
A Troll Courtier, Others like him, Troll Girls and Troll Children, A Pair of Witches, Gnomes, Goblins, Elves, etc.
A Voice in the Darkness, Bird Cries
Kari, a cottar's wife
An Ugly Brat
Mr. Cotton }
M. Ballon }
Herr von Eberkopf } traveling gentlemen
Herr Trumpeterstraale }
A Thief and a Fence
Anitra, daughter of a Bedouin chief
Arabs, Female Slaves, Dancing Girls, etc.
The Statue of Memnon (singing), The Sphinx at Gizeh (mute)
Prof. Begriffenfeldt, Ph.D., director of the insane asylum at Cairo
Huhu, a language reformer from the Malabar coast
A Fellah with a royal mummy
Hussein, a Near Eastern cabinet minister
Other Inmates, along with their Keepers
A Norwegian Sea Captain and his Crew
A Strange Passenger
A Pastor, Mourners
A Sheriff
A Button-Molder
A Lean Person

The action opens in the early years of the nineteenth century and ends in the late 1860s. It takes place partly in Gudbrandsdal and the surrounding mountains, partly on the coast of Morocco, in the Sahara Desert, in a Cairo insane asylum, at sea, etc.

Act 1

Scene 1

A wooded hillside near AASE's *farm. A stream runs brawling through, past an old mill set on its farther side. It is a hot summer day.* PEER GYNT, *a powerfully built youth of twenty, comes down the path.* AASE, *his mother, small and frail, trails after him, angrily scolding.*

AASE. Peer, you're lying!
PEER GYNT. [*Without stopping.*] No, I'm not!
AASE. Well, go on then—swear it's true!
PEER GYNT. Swear? Why should I?
AASE. Hah! Know what?
You don't dare; they're lies right through!
PEER GYNT. [*Stops.*] It's truth I've told you, altogether!
AASE. [*Confronts him.*] And no shame before your mother?
First you run off to the mountains

In my hardest months, to go
Tracking reindeer through the snow;
Come back with your clothes in ribbons,
Lose your quarry—*and* your gun—
Then, to boot, with big wide eyes,
You scheme to see me taken in
By the worst of hunters' lies.
Well—where did you meet this buck?
PEER GYNT. West of Gjendin.
AASE. [*Laughs derisively.*] Oh, of course!
PEER GYNT. I'm stalking down a wind that roars
About me; hid up behind a grove
Of alders, he's pawing in a pack
Of snow for moss—
AASE. [*As before.*] Oh yes, of course!
PEER GYNT. My breath stops short; I freeze and listen,
Hear the scraping of his hoof,
See a glint of antler horns.
With that I'm flat between the stones,
Worming up so's not to miss him.
Then, screened by rocks, I feast my eyes on—
Such a buck, so sleek and fat,
You've never seen his equal yet!
AASE. I'm sure of that!
PEER GYNT. So bang! I shoot.
He hits the dirt whump, like a mallet.
But in that instant as the brute
Lies still, I'm there astride his back,
Seize him by the left ear tight,
And poise to drive my knife in right
Below the jawbone for his gullet—
When hi! the scum lets out a shriek,
Scrambles bolt up on his feet
And, with this one head-backward flip,
Knocks knife and scabbard out of reach
Clamps me neatly at the hip,
Rams his horns down on my legs
To pin me like a pair of tongs—
And then with dizzy leaps he springs
Along the brink of Gjendin ridge![1]
AASE. [*Involuntarily.*] Oh, my Jesus—!
PEER GYNT. Have you seen
The way the cliffs of Gjendin hang?
They run out nearly four miles long,
Lean as a scythe edge at the top.
Past glaciers, ledges, rockslides,
Herbs clinging to the gray-green slope,
You can look down either side
Straight into water, where in a slow
Black heavy sleep it lies one
Thousand yards, almost, below.
   He and I, on that blade of ground,
Cut a channel through the wind.
   I've never had me such a run!
Sometimes in the headlong pace
The air seemed full of flashing suns.
In the reeling gulfs of space
Eagles with brown backs would float
Midway between us and the water—
Then fall away behind, like motes.
   I could see ice floes crack and shatter
On the shore, without a sound to hear.
Only the imps of swimming senses
Came singing, swirling, weaving dances
In rings around my eyes and ears.
AASE. [*Giddy.*] Oh, God help me!
PEER GYNT. Suddenly,
At a spot where the cliff drops violently,
This great cock ptarmigan explodes
Into wings, squawking terrified
From some nook where he'd thought to hide
Till the hoofs came on too loud.
   The buck goes spinning half around
And takes off with a tremendous bound,
Plunging both of us straight for the deep. [AASE *sways and steadies herself against a tree.* PEER GYNT *continues.*]
Behind us, rock walls sheering up,
Beneath us, gaping nothingness—
And we two dropping, first through veils
Of mist, then through a flock of gulls
That wheel off, scattering their cries
To all the corners of the sky.
   Downward, endlessly, we go.
But in the depths something shows
Dim white, like reindeer's belly fleece.
Mother, it was *our* reflection
Shooting upward in the lake from
Silent darkness to the glassy calm
On top with the same breakneck
Speed as we were hurtling down.
AASE. [*Gasping for breath.*] Peer! Dear Lord, what happened? Quick!
PEER GYNT. My buck from above, the other
From below lock horns together
In one huge shower burst of foam.
   Well, there we lay and thrashed awhile—
Then at last, somehow, we struck
Out for the northern shore, the buck
He swam, and I hung on his tail—
So, here I am—
AASE. But the reindeer?

PEER GYNT. Oh, I guess he's out there
    somewhere— [*Snaps his fingers, turns
    on his heel, adding.*]
Finders keepers—you can have him!
AASE. And you didn't break your neck?
Or both your legs? What an escape!
You really didn't crack your spine?
Oh, great God—all thanks and praise
To Thee for delivering my son!
Your trousers got a little torn,
It's true; but that's of no concern
When you realize just how black
Things might have been after such a
    leap—! [*Stops abruptly, stares at him
    wide-eyed and open-mouthed, struggles
    for words until, at length, she bursts out.*]
Oh, you tricky little devil—
God in heaven, you can lie!
I remember all this drivel
Now; it happened to Gudbrand
Glesne, back when I was twenty.
This is his ride secondhand,
Not your own, you—!
PEER GYNT. His *and* mine.
Things like that can happen twice.
AASE. [*Angrily.*] Yes, give a lie a new
    disguise,
Twist it, turn it out so fine
The bony carcass can't be seen
Spruced up in the fancy dress.
That's the only thing you've done—
Run wild in your imagination,
Trotted out those eagles' backs
And all your other rotten tricks,
Lied the sun and moon away,
And stirred up such a misery
Of fright that one forgets old
Things one heard once as a child.
PEER GYNT. If anyone else talked like
    that
To me, I'd cripple him for life!
AASE. [*Weeping.*] Oh, God, please let me
    die; oh, let
Me sleep in the earth and rest!
Prayers and weeping leave him deaf—
Now and forever, Peer—you're lost!
PEER GYNT. You pretty little mother,
    you,
Every word you say is true;
So give us a happy smile—
AASE. Be still!
How can I be happy while
I have such a pig for a son?
Don't you think it's hard for me,
A helpless, struggling widow, to be
Always put to shame again? [*Once more
    weeping.*]
What have we got now from the days
When your grandfather's fortunes
    rose?
Those sacks of coin that Rasmus Gynt
Willed us—you know where they went?
Your father! Him, with his open hand,
And the money running through like
    sand,
Buying property right and left,
Driving his gilded carriages—
Where's it gone now, all the waste
Poured out for that winter feast
When the guests flung every glass
And bottle to the wall to smash?
PEER GYNT. Where are the snows of
    yesteryear?[2]
AASE. Don't talk back to your mother,
    Peer!
Look at the farm there! Nearly half
The windows plugged with rags and
    stuff.
Railings, fences, hedges down;
Cattle shifting to the wind and rain;
Fields and pastures gone to weeds;
And every month the sheriff takes—
PEER GYNT. That's enough of this old
    maid's
Talk! One's luck has losing streaks
Only to spring up good as new!
AASE. The ground is barren where it
    grew.
Lord, aren't you the country squire—
Just as haughty and cocksure
And impudent as when the preacher,
Newly come from Copenhagen,
Hearing you blab your name, at once
Swore the brain in your little noggin
Outclassed the mind of many a prince,
So that your father, true to nature,
Went and gave him a horse and sleigh
For talking in such a generous way.
Ah, but things looked rosy then!
Bishops, captains—how they all came
Flocking daily to drink and eat,
Stuffing themselves till they nearly
    split!
Who knows his friends in an easy time?
No one, not a soul, stopped in
The day "Jon Moneybags" took
To the road with a peddler's pack.
[*Drying her eyes with her apron.*]
Ah, Peer, you're big and strong;
You should be the mainstay now
That your mother's getting on—
Keep the farm in trim, and show

Some fight to save your nest egg. [*With a new burst of tears.*]
Oh, God help me if I owe
Any thanks to you, you lazy slug!
Loafing in the chimney-corner
Home,[3] and poking up the fire,
Or out at dances where you scare
The local girls with your crazy manner—
You make me a common laughingstock;
And now, brawling with the lowest pack—
PEER GYNT. [*Moves away from her.*] Leave me alone.
AASE. [*Following him.*] Go on, make
Believe you didn't lead that row
The other day at Lunde[4] when you
Boys all wound up swapping blows,
Mad as dogs. Oh, I suppose
It wasn't you that laid Aslak
The smith's arm up in a splint?
Or at least didn't you crack
One of his fingers out of joint?
PEER GYNT. Who fed you all that foolishness?
AASE. [*Hotly.*] Kari, downhill, heard the yelling!
PEER GYNT. [*Rubbing his elbow.*] Yes, but I made all the noise.
AASE. You?
PEER GYNT. That's right—*I* got the mauling.
AASE. What—?
PEER GYNT. He can raise a bruise.
AASE. Who can?
PEER GYNT. He, Aslak, can. Who else?
AASE. You—pah, you! I could spit!
You mean a blubber-bellied sot,
A walking sponge, a piece of tripe
Like that could ever beat you up?
[*Weeping again.*]
Shame and scandal, how it fills
My life—and now, worst of all, this
Has to happen, this disgrace.
Let him be brawny as an ox—
Why should you be the one he licks?
PEER GYNT. Win or lose, it doesn't matter—
You boil me in the same hot water.
[*Laughing.*]
Ah, cheer up—
AASE. What! Were you lying
Once again?
PEER GYNT. Just this once.
Dry your tears now; stop crying.
[*Clenches his left hand.*]
Look—in these tongs, what chance
Did he have, bent double, glowing
Under the hammer of my right—
AASE. Oh, you fire-eater! You'll put
Me in the grave, the way you act.
PEER GYNT. Oh no, what you can expect
Is twenty thousand times finer
Than that! Dearest, ugly, little
Mother, be patient with it all:
This whole parish'll do you honor;
You just wait till I come out
With something—something really great!
AASE. [*Snorting.*] You!
PEER GYNT. Who knows what's in the cards?
AASE. If only someday you'd have sense
Enough to make an effort toward
Sewing the holes up in your pants.
PEER GYNT. [*Hotly.*] I'll be a king, an emperor!
AASE. An emperor? God help me, there
He's losing the little mind he had!
PEER GYNT. But I will! Just give me time!
AASE. Yes, time brings all things to him
Who waits, or so I've heard it said.
PEER GYNT. You'll see, Mother!
AASE. Hold your tongue!
The madhouse, that's where you belong—
Still, you're not completely off—
Something is what you might have been
If you hadn't sunk yourself in
Lies and windy dreams and bluff.
The Hegstad girl was fond of you.
That plum was ripening to fall,
And would have, if you'd had the will—
PEER GYNT. Think so?
AASE. The old man hasn't got
The strength to tell his daughter "no."
He's strict with her, or tries to be,
But Ingrid always gets her way;
And where she goes, Old Stumble-shoe
Clumps after, angry as a beet. [*Starts crying again.*]
Ah, my Peer, a girl with land,
Clear property, an heiress! Think—
If you'd only had the will,
You could have married into rank—
You, in your tatters, black as coal.
PEER GYNT. [*Briskly.*] Well, let's go courting someone's hand.
AASE. Where?
PEER GYNT. At Hegstad!
AASE. You poor child,

Your hopes are locked out in the cold.
PEER GYNT. What do you mean?
AASE. Oh, it's too much!
The moment's flown, and so's the luck—
PEER GYNT. Why?
AASE. [*Sobbing.*] While you went riding your buck
Through the air over the western ridge,
Mads Moen proved the plum was ripe.
PEER GYNT. What—? You mean that scarecrow! Him!
AASE. Yes, he's going to be the groom.
PEER GYNT. Wait here till I harness up
The horse and cart— [*Starts off.*]
AASE. No use leaving.
The wedding's set now for tomorrow.
PEER GYNT. Ffft! I'll be there this evening!
AASE. For shame! Don't you think my sorrow's
Enough, without their ridicule?
PEER GYNT. Don't worry; it'll all go well.
Cheer up, Mother! Let the cart stay here; [*Shouting and laughing at once.*]
There isn't time to get the mare. [*Lifts her in his arms.*]
AASE. Put me down!
PEER GYNT. No, like this you'll
Arrive in style at the wedding farm. [*Wades out in the stream.*]
AASE. Help! Oh, God, be merciful! Peer! We'll drown!
PEER GYNT. I was born
To die a nobler death—
AASE. That's true,
Hanging's more in line for you! [*Pulls his hair.*]
Oh, you monster!
PEER GYNT. Now be calm;
The footing here is slippery-smooth.
AASE. Jackass!
PEER GYNT. Sure, just use your mouth;
Words do no one any harm.
There, you see, it's shelving up—
AASE. Don't let me drop!
PEER GYNT. Hi, giddap!
Time to play at Peer and the buck— [*Cavorting about.*]
I'm the reindeer, you be Peer!
AASE. I don't know who I am, I swear!
PEER GYNT. We're almost in the shallows, look— [*Wading ashore.*]
So be nice, give the buck a kiss
And thank him for the ride across—

AASE. [*Clouts him on the ear.*] There's my thanks for the ride!
PEER GYNT. Ow!
Your sense of gratitude is low.
AASE. Let me go!
PEER GYNT. To the wedding first.
Be my spokesman. You're clever;
Have a talk with the old crust;
Tell him Mads is a real loafer—
AASE. Let go!
PEER GYNT. Then give him a chance to hear
Something about *my* character.
AASE. Oh yes, you can bet I will!
You'll have a testimonial
And your portrait painted front and back;
I'll spill out every devil's trick
I've seen you do, till his ears are limp—
PEER GYNT. Oh?
AASE. [*Kicking furiously.*] This tongue of mine will wag
Until the old man sics his dogs
On you, as if you were a tramp!
PEER GYNT. Hm, then I'll have to go alone.
AASE. Yes, but I'll be right behind you!
PEER GYNT. Mother, you're not strong enough to—
AASE. Strong enough? I feel so violent
Inside that I could crumple stone!
Hoo, I could make a meal of flint!
Let go!
PEER GYNT. All right, if you'll promise—
AASE. Nothing! We're going, both of us.
They have to find out who you are!
PEER GYNT. No, you'd better stay right here.
AASE. Never! To the feast! Let's be off.
PEER GYNT. I can't allow it.
AASE. What will you do?
PEER GYNT. I'll set you up on the millhouse roof. [*Lifts her up there. AASE screams.*]
AASE. Lift me down!
PEER GYNT. Will you listen now—?
AASE. Rubbish!
PEER GYNT. I'm asking you, Mother dear—
AASE. [*Throws sod from the roof at him.*]
Get me down this instant, Peer!
PEER GYNT. If I dared, you know I would. [*Comes closer.*]
Now, see if you can't stay quiet, glued
To one spot. Try not to kick and flop
About, and don't pull the shingles up—

Or you might find out you've gone from bad
To worse with a nasty fall.
AASE. You beast!
PEER GYNT. Stop wiggling!
AASE. Oh, for a wind to blast
You like a changeling[5] off this earth!
PEER GYNT. Mother, shame!
AASE. Pah!
PEER GYNT. Aren't I worth
Your blessing in taking on this struggle?
Can't you give it?
AASE. I'll give a whipping
To you for all your size, that's what!
PEER GYNT. Then fare thee well, Mother, my sweet.
Just be patient; I won't be long. [*Starts off, then turns and shakes his finger at her.*]
Remember now: you mustn't wiggle!
AASE. Peer! God help me, there he goes!
Reindeer rider! Liar! Hi!
Will you listen—? No; now he's
Running—! [*Shouts.*] Help, I'm dizzy!
Hurry! [TWO OLD WOMEN, *with sacks on their backs, come down the path toward the mill.*]
FIRST OLD WOMAN. Mercy, who's that screaming?
AASE. Me!
SECOND OLD WOMAN. Aase! You've come up in life.
AASE. This won't give me much relief—
But soon I'll rise to eternity!
FIRST OLD WOMAN. God speed your journey!
AASE. Fetch a ladder;
Get me down! That devil Peer—
SECOND OLD WOMAN. Your son again?
AASE. Now consider
This for what he makes me endure.
FIRST OLD WOMAN. We're witnesses.
AASE. If you'd just
Help me, I could be at Hegstad fast—
SECOND OLD WOMAN. Is he there?
FIRST OLD WOMAN. You'll have your vengeance;
The smith's left, too, for the celebration.
AASE. [*Wringing her hands.*] Oh, God save me! The poor boy,
They'll kill him, if they have their way!
FIRST OLD WOMAN. It's time and again we've heard that talk;
Take heart: if it's going to be, it will!
SECOND OLD WOMAN. Her wits are scattering everywhere. [*Calling up the hill.*]
Eivind! Anders! Hey, come here!
A MAN'S VOICE. What's the matter?
SECOND OLD WOMAN. Peer Gynt's stuck
His mother up on top of the mill!

Scene 2

A small rise of ground covered with shrubs and heather. Upslope and behind a fence runs the high road. PEER GYNT *comes along a footpath, hurries up to the fence and stands gazing out over the landscape.*
PEER GYNT. There it lies, Hegstad. I'll be there soon. [*Climbs half over the fence, then hesitates.*]
Wonder if Ingrid's at home alone? [*Shades his eyes and looks off.*]
No, the guests are swarming in like flies—
It might be better just to return. [*Climbs down again.*]
They whisper behind your back, always
Sneering, and it sears you like a burn. [*Goes a few steps from the fence and begins aimlessly plucking leaves.*]
If I only had something strong to drink—
Or I could slip in without being seen—
Or just be unknown—For numbing the pain
Of their laughter, nothing beats getting drunk. [*Looks about him in a sudden fright, then hides among some bushes. Several* WEDDING GUESTS, *with presents, go by on the road toward the farm.*]
A MAN. [*In conversation.*] With his father a drunkard—and that mother's a case.
A WOMAN. Yes, it's not hard to see why the boy's such a mess. [*The* GUESTS *pass on. A moment later* PEER GYNT *emerges, blushing with shame, and stares after them.*]
PEER GYNT. [*Softly.*] Were they speaking of me? [*With a forced shrug.*] Well, let them speak.
They can't kill the life in my veins with talk! [*Throws himself down in the heather and lies on his back awhile, hands under his head, gazing up into the sky.*]
What an odd-shaped cloud! Like a

horse almost.
Someone's riding him—he's saddled
 and reined—
And there's an old witch on a broom
 behind. [*With a quiet little laugh.*]
It's Mother. She's scolding and yelling:
 "You beast!
Hi, wait for me, Peer!" [*Slowly closing his
 eyes.*]
She's frightened now—
Peer Gynt rides ahead, with an army in
 tow—
 His harness is silver, his mount is
 gold-shod.
He wears gauntlets, a scabbard, a fine
 saber blade,
 And a cape flowing-long and silken-
 lined.
They're the salt of the earth, the men
 of his band;
 Yet not one sits so bold in his saddle
 as Peer,
Or glitters like him in the sunlit air.
 Below by the road people gather in
 groups,
Tipping their hats, and everyone
 gapes.
 The women are curtsying, Who
 hasn't heard
Of the Emperor Peer Gynt and his
 thousand-man horde?
 Pieces of silver and new copper coins
He scatters like sand till his pathway
 shines,
 And every citizen's rich as a lord.
Then Peter makes the ocean his
 boulevard.
 On a far-off shore stands
 Engelland's[6] prince,
And all Engelland's maidens wait in
 suspense.
 And Engelland's nobles and
 Engelland's king,
As Peer canters up, rise from parleying.
 Their emperor takes off his crown
 and speaks—
ASLAK THE SMITH. [*To some others, passing
 on the road.*] Well, look; it's Peer Gynt,
 the drunken swine—!
PEER GYNT. [*Half rising with a start.*] My
 sovereign—?
ASLAK. [*Leaning over the fence and grin-
 ning.*] Get off your haunches, son!
PEER GYNT. What the devil! Aslak! What
 do you want?
ASLAK. [*To the others.*] He's still hung up
 from his Lunde jaunt.
PEER GYNT. [*Springing up.*] Get out of
 here!
ASLAK. Yes, I can do that.
But where have you been, lad? Out of
 sight
For six whole weeks. Trolls get you,
 what?
PEER GYNT. Aslak, I've done fantastic
 things!
ASLAK. [*Winks at the others.*] Give us the
 word, Peer!
PEER GYNT. Can't waste my lungs.
ASLAK. [*After a pause.*] You going to
 Hegstad?
PEER GYNT. No.
ASLAK. They say
That girl there used to give you the
 eye.
PEER GYNT. You filthy crow—!
ASLAK. [*Drawing back a little.*] Easy now,
 Peer!
If Ingrid's dropped you, there's plenty
 more—
Think—Jon Gynt's son! Join the ca-
 rouse;
There'll be tender lambs and bouncy
 widows—
PEER GYNT. Go to hell!
ASLAK. You'll find someone who'll have
 you.
Good day! I'll be giving the bride your
 love now. [*They move on, laughing and
 whispering.* PEER *stares after them briefly,
 then tosses his head and turns half
 around.*]
PEER GYNT. Anyone Ingrid wants to
 marry
She's welcome to. Who gives a damn!
 [*Inspecting himself.*]
Trousers torn. Ragged and grim—
I could use some new clothes in a
 hurry. [*Stamps on the ground.*]
If I could just take a butcher's knife
And cut the mockery out of their
 chests! [*Staring suddenly around.*]
What—! Who's that? Did somebody
 laugh?
Hm, I was sure—Nothing but ghosts—
I'll go home to Mother. [*Turns up the
 hill, stops again and stands, ears cocked
 toward the farm.*] The dancing's be-
 gun! [*Gazing and listening, then moving
 downslope step by step, his eyes kindling,
 his palms rubbing his thighs.*]
What a swarm of girls! Seven, eight to a

man!
Hell and blazes! To the wedding I'm off!
But Mother, perched on top of the roof— [*His eyes are drawn back to Hegstad; he kicks up his heels and laughs.*]
Ah, the halling![7] How it floats and swirls
For Guttorm; how sweetly his fiddle's stroked—!
It sparkles and dips like a cataract.
And that flock, that shimmering flock of girls!
Oh, hell and blazes! To the wedding, I'm off! [*Leaps the fence and heads down the road.*]

Scene 3

The grounds at Hegstad. Farthest to the rear, the farmhouse. A THRONG OF GUESTS. *Lively dancing on the grass. The* FIDDLER *is seated on a table. The* MASTER OF CEREMONIES[8] *stands in the doorway.* KITCHEN MAIDS *go back and forth between the buildings.* ELDERLY PEOPLE *sit here and there, conversing.*

A WOMAN. [*Joining a group seated on some logs.*] The bride? Oh yes, she's crying some,
For the usual reasons, mostly vague—
MASTER OF CEREMONIES. [*In another group.*] Now, folks, let's see you drain the keg.
A MAN. How—when you're filling it all the time?
A YOUTH. [*To the* FIDDLER, *as he flies past with a girl by the hand.*] Hi, Guttorm, don't spare the bow!
THE GIRL. Stroke till it rings through every meadow!
OTHER GIRLS. [*Around a young man dancing.*] That's kicking!
A GIRL. He's got legs like steel!
THE YOUNG MAN. [*As he dances.*] It's high to this ceiling[9] and wide to the wall! [*The* BRIDEGROOM, *whimpering, comes up to his* FATHER, *who is talking to several others, and tugs at his sleeve.*]
BRIDEGROOM. Father, she won't; she's just too proud!
FATHER. Won't what?
BRIDEGROOM. She's locked herself away.
FATHER. Well, it's up to you, then, to find the key.
BRIDEGROOM. I don't know how.
FATHER. You're a knucklehead! [*Turns back to the others. The* BRIDEGROOM *wanders off.*]
A BOY. [*Rounding the house.*] Hey, girls! The party's coming alive!
Peer Gynt—!
ASLAK. [*Newly arrived on the scene.*] Was he asked?
MASTER OF CEREMONIES. Not by my leave. [*Goes toward the house.*]
ASLAK. [*To the girls.*] If he talks to you, don't listen to him!
A GIRL. [*To the others.*] No. Pretend that we look right through him.
PEER GYNT. [*Hot and ardent, enters, stops in front of the group and claps his hands.*] Which one of you girls can really move?
A GIRL. [*As he approaches.*] Not me.
ANOTHER. Not me.
A THIRD. Nor me either.
PEER GYNT. [*To a fourth.*] All right, you— before I'm lured by another.
THE GIRL. [*Turning aside.*] Too busy.
PEER GYNT. [*To a fifth.*] Then you!
THE GIRL. [*As she leaves.*] I was just going home.
PEER GYNT. So early? You must be out of your mind!
ASLAK. [*After a moment, in a low voice.*] See, Peer, she'll dance with the first man around.
PEER GYNT. [*Turns quickly to an elderly man.*] Where are the unattached girls?
THE MAN. Find them. [*He walks away.* PEER, *suddenly subdued, glances shyly and furtively at the group. They all look at him, but nobody speaks. He approaches other groups. Wherever he goes, there is silence; as he moves on, looks follow him and smiles.*]
PEER GYNT. [*In an undertone.*] Glances, hard thoughts and mocking smiles— They grate, like a saw blade under a file! [*He slinks along the fence.* SOLVEIG, *leading* LITTLE HELGA *by the hand, comes into the yard with her parents.*]
A MAN. [*To another, close by* PEER GYNT.] Look, the new neighbors.
THE OTHER. From the west country, right?
FIRST MAN. I think, from Hedal.[10]
THE OTHER. Yes, that was it.

PEER GYNT. [*Steps in the newcomers' path and, pointing at* SOLVEIG, *asks her father.*]
Can I dance with your daughter?
THE FATHER. [*quietly.*]You may; but first
We'll go in and pay our respects to the host. [*They enter the house.*]
MASTER OF CEREMONIES. [*To* PEER GYNT, *offering him a drink.*] Since you're here, you'll want the bottle passed.
PEER GYNT. [*Staring fixedly after the newcomers.*] I'll be dancing, thanks. I have no thirst. [*The* MASTER OF CEREMONIES *moves away.* PEER GYNT *looks toward the house and laughs.*]
How fair! Who's ever seen one like this!
Eyes on her shoes and snow-white apron—!
And how she held onto her mother's dress,
And the kerchief she carried her prayer book in—![11]
I must see her again. [*Starts into the house, but is met by several young men coming out.*]
A YOUTH. You already the worse
For dancing?
PEER GYNT. No.
THE YOUTH. Then you're headed off course. [*Takes his shoulder to turn him about.*]
PEER GYNT. Let me pass!
THE YOUTH. Are you scared of the smith?
PEER GYNT. Me scared?
THE YOUTH. So, the memory of Lunde has teeth! [*The group laughs and goes on to the dancing.*]
SOLVEIG. [*Appears at the door.*] Aren't you the boy that wanted to dance?
PEER GYNT. Why, yes; didn't you know me at once? [*Taking her hand.*]
Come on!
SOLVEIG. Mother says, not too far.
PEER GYNT. Mother says? Mother says!
Were you born last year?
SOLVEIG. You're making fun—!
PEER GYNT. But you're nearly a child.
Are you grown?
SOLVEIG. I'm just confirmed[12]—that old.
PEER GYNT. Tell me your name, girl, and things'll go lighter.
SOLVEIG. My name is Solveig. And who are you?
PEER GYNT. Peer Gynt.

SOLVEIG. [*Draws back her hand.*] Oh, my goodness!
PEER GYNT. What's wrong now?
SOLVEIG. My garter's come loose; let me tie it tighter. [*Leaves him.*]
BRIDEGROOM. [*Pulling his mother's sleeve.*] Mother, she won't—!
MOTHER. She won't? Won't what?
BRIDEGROOM. Just won't, Mother!
MOTHER. What?
BRIDEGROOM. Unlock the door.
FATHER. [*In quiet fury.*] Uf! A stall—that's all you're good for.
MOTHER. Now don't scold. Poor boy, he'll be all right. [*They go off.*]
A YOUTH. [*Coming up with a crowd from the dancing.*] Little brandy, Peer?
PEER GYNT. No.
THE YOUTH. Ah, come on.
PEER GYNT. [*Looking somberly at him.*] You have some?
THE YOUTH. Oh, it just might be. [*Pulls out a pocket flask and drinks.*]
Ai, that burns—! Well?
PEER GYNT. Let me see. [*Drinks.*]
ANOTHER YOUTH. Now you can have a taste of mine.
PEER GYNT. No.
THE OTHER. Ah, rubbish! Don't be a mope.
Drink up, Peer!
PEER GYNT. Well, maybe a drop. [*Drinks again.*]
A GIRL. [*In an undertone.*] Come on, let's go.
PEER GYNT. You afraid of me, puss?
A THIRD YOUTH. Who isn't afraid of *you*?
A FOURTH. We saw
You in action at Lunde, you know.
PEER GYNT. You should see me when I really cut loose!
FIRST YOUTH. [*Whispering.*] Now he's started.
OTHERS. [*Thronging around in a circle.*]
Tell us! Say what
You can do!
PEER GYNT. Tomorrow—!
MORE VOICES. No, now; tonight!
A GIRL. Can you conjure, Peer?
PEER GYNT. I can call up the devil.
A MAN. My grandmother, before I was born, did that!
PEER GYNT. Liar! What *I* do, no one can equal.
Once I conjured him inside a nut.
Through a wormhole, that is.

SEVERAL. [*Laughing.*] Obviously!
PEER GYNT. He wept and swore and tried bribing me
With all kinds of things—
ONE OF THE CROWD. But he had to remain?
PEER GYNT. Oh yes. I'd closed up the hole with a pin.
You should've heard him buzzing and booming—
A GIRL. Imagine!
PEER GYNT. It was like a bumblebee humming.
THE GIRL. You still have him trapped in the nut?
PEER GYNT. Oh, no,
The devil's made off on his own by now.
It's *his* fault the smith has it in for me.
A YOUTH. How come?
PEER GYNT. I went to the smith and, "Say,"
I asked him, "could you crack this shell?"
"Sure"—and he laid it down on his anvil;
But that man's got a grip like a couple of hams
When he swings his sledge, so he just let fall—
VOICE FROM THE CROWD. Did he kill the devil?
PEER GYNT. He came down, wham!
But the devil was quicker and shot like a flame
Straight through the roof and split the walls.
SEVERAL VOICES. And the smith?
PEER GYNT. Just stood there with charred hands.
From that day on, we've never been friends. [*General laughter.*]
MORE VOICES. That's a good one!
OTHER VOICES. It's nearly his best!
PEER GYNT. You think I'm inventing it?
A MAN. No, I agree
With you there; my grandfather told me most
Of this—
PEER GYNT. Liar! It happened to me!
THE MAN. Yes, everything has.
PEER GYNT. [*Tossing his head.*] Why, I can ride
Through the air like the wind going past!
The things I can do, the things—Oh, God! [*Another roar of laughter.*]
ONE OF THE CROWD. Peer, ride in the air a bit!
MANY VOICES. Yes, Peer, do—
PEER GYNT. Don't be so anxious begging me to.
I can ride like a hurricane over your lot,
And you'll fall, all of you, fall at my feet!
AN OLDER MAN. Now he's raving mad.
ANOTHER. What audacity!
A THIRD. Loudmouth!
A FOURTH. Liar!
PEER GYNT. [*Threatening them.*] You wait and see!
A MAN. [*Half drunk.*] You wait, and you'll get your coat dusted, hey!
OTHERS. Your back gone over! A fat black eye! [*The crowd disperses, the older ones angry, the younger ones laughing and jeering.*]
THE BRIDGEGOOM. [*Close by* PEER.] Say, Peer, is it true you can ride in the air?
PEER GYNT. [*Brusquely.*] Anything, Mads! I'm a rare kind of man.
BRIDGEGROOM. Then you have the invisible cloak, I'm sure.
PEER GYNT. The hat, you mean? Yes, I have one. [*Turns from him,* SOLVEIG *comes across the yard, leading* HELGA *by the hand.*]
PEER GYNT. [*Goes toward them, his face lighting up.*] Solveig! Oh, it's good to see you again! [*Seizing her by the wrist.*] Now you're going to be swung and held!
SOLVEIG. Let go of me!
PEER GYNT. Why?
SOLVEIG. You're much too wild.
PEER GYNT. Wild like the reindeer when summer dawns.
Come on, lass; don't be contrary!
SOLVEIG. [*Pulls her arm free.*] I don't dare.
PEER GYNT. Why?
SOLVEIG. Because—you've been drinking. [*Moves away with* HELGA.]
PEER GYNT. Oh, to feel my knife blade sinking
Into the hearts of each and every
One of them!
BRIDGEGROOM. [*Nudging his elbow.*] Help me get in to the bride?
PEER GYNT. The bride? Where is she?

BRIDEGROOM. The storehouse.
PEER GYNT. So.
BRIDEGROOM. Oh, please, Peer Gynt, give it a try!
PEER GYNT. No, you can do it without my aid. [*A thought strikes him. In a low, hard voice.*]
Ingrid! The storehouse! [*Goes over to* SOLVEIG.] Now what do you say? [SOLVEIG *turns to leave; he bars the path.*]
You're ashamed; I look like a tramp to you.
SOLVEIG. [*Hastily*] No, you don't! That just isn't true!
PEER GYNT. Yes! And now I've gone a little askew.
But that was for spite, when you slighted me.
Come on!
SOLVEIG. If I wished to, I still wouldn't dare.
PEER GYNT. Who are you scared of?
SOLVEIG. Mostly my father.
PEER GYNT. Your father? I know; he's a living prayer!
The soul of piety,[13] eh? Well—answer!
SOLVEIG. What should I answer?
PEER GYNT. Is he one of the saints?
And you and your mother sing the same tune?
Well, will you answer?
SOLVEIG. Leave me alone.
PEER GYNT. No. [*In a low, bitter, intimidating voice.*] I can turn myself into a troll.
I'll come to your bed at midnight, I will.
If you hear something that hisses and grunts,
Don't try to pretend it's only the cat.
It's me, child! I'll drain off your blood in a cup;
And your little sister—I'll eat her up;
Because, you know—I'm a werewolf at night—
I'll bite you all over the loins and back—[*Suddenly changes his tone and begs, as if in anguish.*]
Dance with me, Solveig!
SOLVEIG. [*Looking darkly at him.*] That was ugly talk! [*Goes into the house.*]
BRIDEGROOM. [*Wanders up again.*] I'll give you an ox if you'll help me.
PEER GYNT. Come! [*They go behind the house. At the same time a crowd comes up from the dancing, most of them drunk.*

Noise and confusion. SOLVEIG *and* HELGA, *their parents, and a number of older people come out the door.*]
MASTER OF CEREMONIES. [*To the* SMITH, *leading the crowd.*] Calm down!
ASLAK. [*Pulling off his jacket.*] No, this is the reckoning time.
Peer Gynt or I will get laid out flat.
SEVERAL VOICES. Yes, let them fight!
OTHERS. No, argue it out!
ASLAK. We'll settle with fists; no more blather.
SOLVEIG'S FATHER. Control yourself, man!
HELGA. Will they hit him, Mother?
A YOUTH. Let's tease him instead with all his lies!
ANOTHER. Boot him out of here!
A THIRD. Spit in his eyes!
A FOURTH. [*To* ASLAK.] You backing down?
ASLAK. [*Throwing his jacket away.*] I'll murder the swill!
SOLVEIG'S MOTHER. [*To* SOLVEIG.] Now you see what they think of that fool.
AASE. [*Coming up with a stick in her hand.*] Where's my son? He'll be getting it, fore and aft!
Ah, the pleasure I'll have in walloping him!
ASLAK. [*Rolling up his short sleeves.*] For his kind of carcass, a stick is too soft.
SEVERAL VOICES. The smith's going to wring him!
OTHERS. Bung him!
ASLAK. [*Spitting on his hands and nodding at* AASE.] Hang him!
AASE. What! Hang my boy! Yes, try, if you dare—!
Me and myself, we've got claws that tear—!
Where is he? [*Calls across the yard.*] Peer!
BRIDEGROOM. [*Running up.*] Hell and damnation!
Come, Father and Mother—!
HIS FATHER. What, on my soul—?
BRIDEGROOM. It's Peer Gynt—
AASE. [*Screams.*] Have they killed my son?
BRIDEGROOM. No, he's—! Look, up there on the hill—
THE CROWD. With the bride!
AASE. [*Let's her staff sink.*] The beast!
ASLAK. It's a sheer drop;
But he climbs, God, like a goat on a crag!

BRIDEGROOM. [*Sobbing.*] Mother, how he carries her—just like a pig!
AASE. [*Shakes her fist at him.*] I hope you fall down and—! [*Shrieks in fright*] Hi, watch your step!
INGRID'S FATHER. [*Comes up, bareheaded, white with rage.*] I'll have his life for stealing the bride!
AASE. If I ever let you, God strike me dead!

Act 2

Scene 1

A narrow path, high in the mountains. It is early morning. PEER GYNT *comes hurrying sullenly along the path.* INGRID, *partly dressed in bridal costume, tries to hold him back.*

PEER GYNT. Just go away!
INGRID [*Weeping.*] After this! Where?
PEER GYNT. Anywhere away from me.
INGRID. [*Wringing her hands.*] Oh, you cheat!
PEER GYNT. Don't make a fuss. We'd each better go off separately.
INGRID. We're bound by sin—and sin again!
PEER GYNT. The devil take all memories!
The devil take all women; that is—
All but one—!
INGRID. Who is that one?
PEER GYNT. It isn't you.
INGRID. But what's her name?
PEER GYNT. Go away! Back where you came from!
To your father, quick!
INGRID. My dearest own—!
PEER GYNT. Don't!
INGRID. You can't possibly mean What you're saying.
PEER GYNT. I can and do.
INGRID. Ruin me first—then cast me off!
PEER GYNT. And what kind of future can you give?
INGRID. Hegstad farm, and a lot more too.
PEER GYNT. What do you wrap your prayer book in?
Does your hair fall golden at your throat?
Do you gaze down into your apron?
Your mother's skirt, do you hold it tight?
Answer!
INGRID. No; but—?
PEER GYNT. And were you just Now confirmed?
INGRID. No, but Peer—
PEER GYNT. Do I feel your shyness like a wound?
Can you refuse what I'm craving for?
INGRID. Oh, God, I think he's lost his mind—!
PEER GYNT. Does the very sight of you bless the air?
Well!
INGRID. No, but—
PEER GYNT. Then what's all the rest? [*Starts off.*]
INGRID. [*Blocking his way.*] Don't you know it's a hanging crime
If you run off now?
PEER GYNT. I don't care.
INGRID. You could have property and honor
If you'd take me—
PEER GYNT. Can't afford them.
INGRID. [*Bursting into tears.*] The way you coaxed—
PEER GYNT. You were willing!
INGRID. I was desperate!
PEER GYNT. And I was mad.
INGRID. [*Threatening.*] You won't escape till the price is paid!
PEER GYNT. The highest price would seem like nothing.
INGRID. You're really set on that?
PEER GYNT. Like stone.
INGRID. Good! We'll see who's going to win! [*Starts down the slope.*]
PEER GYNT. [*Silent a moment, then cries out.*] The devil take all memories!
The devil take all women—
INGRID. [*Turns her head and calls up mockingly.*] That is—
All but *one!*
PEER GYNT. Yes, all but *one.* [*They go off separately.*]

Scene 2

Soft marsh country near a mountain lake. A storm is gathering. AASE, *in despair, is peering in every direction and calling out.* SOLVEIG *finds it hard to keep up with her.* SOLVEIG'S PARENTS *and* HELGA *follow close behind.*

AASE. [*Flailing her arms and tearing her hair.*] Everything spites me with a vengeance—
Sky and water and these wicked mountains!
Fog pouring out of the sky to confound him,
The water luring him in to drown him,
The mountains poising their rocks to fall—
And those people! All of them out for the kill!
Oh Lord, not that! I mustn't lose him.
The lout! Why the devil has to tease him—? [*Turning to* SOLVEIG.]
It's hard enough to believe, God knows—
He who was nothing but dreams and lies.
He whose strength was all in his mouth,
Who'd never done work of any worth,
That he—! You want to both laugh and cry!
Oh, we've had to stick close in misery.
Because, you know, my man—he drank,
Roamed the parish with a line of bluff,
Scattered and trampled our goods to dust—
While back at home my Peer and I sat.
All we could do was try and forget;
I'm no good when something has to be faced.
It's so painful staring fate in the eyes;
You'd much rather shake your troubles off
And just do anything not to think.
Some turn to brandy, others to lies,
And we—well, we took to fairy tales
Of princes and trolls and strange animals.
Stolen brides too. But who'd have thought
Those infernal stories would be in him yet. [*Terrified again.*]
Hoo, what a scream! It's a draug[14] or a troll!
Peer! Peer! Up there on the hill—!
[*Runs to the top of a small rise and looks out over the lake.* SOLVEIG'S PARENTS *come up.*]
Not a trace!
THE FATHER. [*Quietly.*] The worse for him.
AASE. [*In tears.*] Oh, my Peer, my poor lost lamb!
THE FATHER. [*Nodding gently.*] Yes, he *is* lost.
AASE. Oh, forget his faults!
He's so fine. He's like no one else.
THE FATHER. You foolish woman!
AASE. Yes, that's it,
I'm a fool; but the boy's all right!
THE FATHER. [*Continues quietly, looking gently at her.*] His heart is hardened; his soul is lost.
AASE. [*Anguished.*] Not true! The Lord isn't so unjust!
THE FATHER. You think he can feel his weight of sin?
AASE. [*Hotly.*] No; but he and a buck have flown!
THE MOTHER. My stars, are you crazy?
THE FATHER. What was that?
AASE. There's nothing he can take on too great.
You'll find out, if he lives that long—
THE FATHER. You'd be better off to see him hang.
AASE. [*Shrieks.*] Oh my Jesus!
THE FATHER. A length of rope
Might turn him toward our eternal hope.
AASE. [*Dazed.*] Oh, you'll talk me into a fainting spell!
Let's find him!
THE FATHER. To save his soul!
AASE. And skin!
If he's stuck in the marsh, let's bring him in;
And ring the church bells to ward off trolls.
THE FATHER. Hm—! Here's a cow path—
AASE. God repay
You for helping me!
THE FATHER. It's Christian duty.
AASE. Then they're heathens, all the other
Ones! Not *any* of them would bother—
THE FATHER. They knew him too well.

AASE. He's above their like! [*Wringing her hands.*]
And to think—to think his life's at stake!
THE FATHER. Here's a man's footprints.
AASE. Better make sure!
THE FATHER. We'll scatter downhill across the pasture. [*He and his WIFE go ahead.*]
SOVEIG. [*To AASE.*] Tell me some more.
AASE. [*Drying her eyes.*] Of my son?
SOLVEIG. Yes—
Everything!
AASE. [*Smiles and throws back her head.*]
Everything—? You'll weary of this.
SOLVEIG. You'll grow tired of talking long
Before I'm done listening.

Scene 3

Low treeless knolls under a towering waste of mountain; high peaks farther off. The shadows are lengthening; it is late in the day. PPER GYNT *comes running full tilt and stops on the hillside.*

PEER GYNT. The whole parish is hot on my tracks
Armed to the teeth with rifles and sticks!
Old Hegstad's in front, you can hear him howl—
The news is out, Peer Gynt's on the prowl!
This is no row with a blacksmith here!
This is life! I feel strong as a bear.
   [*Leaping in the air and lashing out.*]
To crush, overthrow! Swim cataracts!
Smash! Rip fir trees up by the roots!
This is life! How it toughens and frees
The soul! To hell with those sickly lies!
   [THREE HERD GIRLS[15] *from a mountain but come running over the hill, shouting and singing.*]
HERD GIRLS. Trond of the Valfjeld! Kaare and Baard!
Trolls, come sleep with us, hold us hard!
PEER GYNT. Who're you shouting for?
HERD GIRLS. Trolls! For trolls!
FIRST GIRL. Trond, go easy!
SECOND GIRL. Baard, be rough!
THIRD GIRL. The beds are all lying empty at home!
FIRST GIRL. Rough is easy.
SECOND GIRL. And easy is rough!
THIRD GIRL. When there aren't any boys, a troll's good enough.
PEER GYNT. And where are your boys then?
ALL THREE. [*Roaring with laughter.*] They can't come!
FIRST GIRL. Mine called me near and dear as his shadow.
Now he's hitched to a middle-aged widow.
SECOND GIRL. Mine met a gypsy girl up north.
Now they're tramping the country earth.
THIRD GIRL. Mine put our bastard out of his pains.
Now his head sticks on a stake and grins.
ALL THREE. Trond of the Valfjeld! Kaare and Baard!
Trolls, come sleep with us, hold us hard!
PEER GYNT. [*Leaps in among them.*] I'm a three-headed troll[16] and a three-woman man!
THE GIRLS. Do you ride so well?
PEER GYNT. Find out if I can!
FIRST GIRL. Up to the cabin!
SECOND GIRL. We've mead!
PEER GYNT. Let it flow!
THIRD GIRL. We won't have a bed lying empty now![17]
SECOND GIRL. [*Kissing him.*] He sputters and glows like white-hot steel.
THIRD GIRL. [*Kissing him.*] With his baby eyes from a bottomless pool.
PEER GYNT. [*Dancing among them.*] Heart like a stone, blood like a goat,
Eyes full of laughter, tears in the throat!
THE GIRLS. [*Thumbing their noses at the mountaintops, shouting and singing.*]
Trond of the Valfjeld! Kaare and Baard!
Did you sleep with us once? Did you hold us hard? [*They dance away over the heights with* PEER GYNT *in their midst.*]

Scene 4

In the Ronde Mountains.[18] *Sunset. Snow-capped mountains gleaming on all sides.*
PEER GYNT. [*Enters, wild and distraught.*]

Castle on castle soaring!
See, what a glittering gate!
Stay! Will you stay! It's veering
Farther and farther about!
The cock on the weathervane's lifting
His golden wings into flight.
He fades in a blue mist, drifting;
The mountains freeze in for the night.
    What are those trees there, rooted
In crevasses of the rock?
They're warriors, heron-footed!
Now they're passing into the dark.
    The air, like a rainbow streaming,
Cuts into my eyes and soul.
What far-off bells are chiming?
What's pressing down on my skull?
My head swells bigger and bigger;
It's clamped in an iron band—!
I can't for the life of me figure
How that got wrapped around! [*Sinks down.*]
A race along Gjendin's ridges.
Dreams and damnable lies!
Straight over the sheerest ledges
With the bride—then a drunken daze;
Hunted by hawks and falcons,
Menaced by trolls and gnomes,
Wenching with crazy women—
Lies and damnable dreams! [*Gazing up for a long time.*]
Way up there, two brown eagles.
Southward, a flight of geese.
And here I wallow and straggle
Through mud and filth to the knees!
[*Springing up.*]
I'll join them! Wash myself clean in
A bath of the flurrying wind!
Fly to the heights, then dip down in
The waters and rise up christened!
I'll skim the mountain cabins
Glide till my spirits dance,
Soar out over rolling oceans,
And high over Engelland's prince!
Yes, you can look, young maidens,
My flight won't touch you at all;
Your waiting is quite unbidden—!
Well, I might drop down for a while.
    That's funny. Those two eagles—?
They've vanished, devil knows where—
    Wait! There's the peak of a gable,
And now the eaves coming clear,
Sprung up from the ruins—yes,
And look, the gate's open wide!
Why, I remember that house:
Grandfather's farm in its pride!
The rags are gone from the windows;
The fences are straight and tall.
Light blazes from every pane now;
They're feasting in the great hall.
    I can hear a chinking of metal;
It's the bishop's knife on his glass—
Now the captain's flinging his bottle,
And the mirror shivers to smash.
Let's squander! This is tremendous!
Hush, Mother; who says we can't!
The rich Jon Gynt's behind us—
Three cheers for the house of Gynt!
What's that? Pandemonium
Breaking out at the feast—?
The captain calls me to join him;
The bishop makes me a toast.
Go in, Peer, in where your fate is
Sung out in prophecy:
Peer Gynt, thou art born of greatness,
And greatness is coming to thee! [*Leaps forward, but bangs his nose against a rock and falls senseless.*]

Scene 5

A hillside with great sighing shade trees. Stars twinkle through the leaves; birds sing in the treetops. A WOMAN IN GREEN[19] *walks on the slope.* PEER GYNT *follows her, making all sorts of amorous gestures.*

WOMAN IN GREEN. [*Stops and turns.*] Is that true?
PEER GYNT. [*Drawing his finger across his throat.*[20]] True as my name is Peer,
And true as you're a beautiful woman!
Will you have me? You'll see the way I care;
You won't ever have to weave or spin—
Just eat; and the meals will be immense.
I'll never pull your hair, not once—
WOMAN IN GREEN. Nor beat me, either?
PEER GYNT. Am I the type?
We kings' sons don't beat our women up.
WOMAN IN GREEN. You're a king's son?
PEER GYNT. Yes.
WOMAN IN GREEN. I'm the Dovre King's daughter.
PEER GYNT. You are? Well, that's a coincidence.
WOMAN IN GREEN. Deep in the Ronde his castle stands.
PEER GYNT. My mother's is bigger, if it's any matter.

WOMAN IN GREEN. You know my father? His name's King Brose.
PEER GYNT. You know my mother? Her name's Queen Aase.
WOMAN IN GREEN. When my father's mad, the mountains blanch.
PEER GYNT. When my mother scolds, there's an avalanche.
WOMAN IN GREEN. My father can kick to the highest beams.
PEER GYNT. My mother rides through the swiftest streams.
WOMAN IN GREEN. Have you no other clothes than those tatters there?
PEER GYNT. Ah, you should see my Sunday gear!
WOMAN IN GREEN. Weekdays, I'm always in silks and gold.
PEER GYNT. It looks more to me like straw and mold.
WOMAN IN GREEN. Yes, but there's one thing to understand
About Ronde customs: here you'll find
Everything has to be seen two ways.
You could easily think, if you went on
To my father's court, that his royal house
Was nothing more than a bleak moraine.
PEER GYNT. Well, isn't it just the same with us?
Our gold would look to you like dross,
And every glittering pane might seem
Like clouts of stockings, rags and grime.
WOMAN IN GREEN. Black looks white, and vile looks fair.
PEER GYNT. Great looks small, and foul looks pure.
WOMAN IN GREEN. [*Embracing him.*]
Oh Peer, I can see, we're like one and the same!
PEER GYNT. Like a leg for a trouser; like hair for a comb.
WOMAN IN GREEN. [*Calls off across the hill.*]
My steed, my steed! Come, bridal steed! [*An enormous pig comes running in, with a rope end for a bridle and an old sack for a saddle.* PEER *swings up onto its back and sets the* WOMAN IN GREEN *in front of him.*]
PEER GYNT. Giddap! Straight for the Ronde gate, ride!
Gee-up! Gee-up there, my prancer! Up, boy!
WOMAN IN GREEN. [*Caressingly.*]
And just now my mood was so sad and grey—
How life provides, if you give it a chance!
PEER GYNT. [*Whips the pig to a trot.*]
You can tell great men by the style of their mounts.

Scene 6

The Royal Hall of the King of the Dovre Mountains.[21] *A great assembly of* TROLL COURTIERS, GOBLINS, *and* GNOMES. *The* TROLL KING *sits on his throne, sceptered and crowned. His* CHILDREN *and* CLOSE RELATIVES *are grouped around him.* PEER GYNT *stands before him. Wild uproar in the hall.*

TROLL COURTIERS. Kill him! A Christian's tried to lure
The Dovre King's most beautiful girl!
A TROLL CHILD. May I slash his finger?
ANOTHER. May I tear his hair?
A TROLL GIRL. Hei! Hoo, let me bite his rear!
TROLL WITCH. [*With a ladle.*] Shouldn't we boil him down for gruel?
ANOTHER WITCH. [*With a carving knife.*]
Turn him on a spit, or brown him for stew?
THE TROLL KING. Cool your blood! [*Beckons his counselors to him.*] It's no time to crow.
We've been slipping downhill these latter years—
Who knows if things'll go better or worse,
So let's not discourage a new recruit.
Besides, the boy looks perfectly fit,
And he's well set up, if I see him clear.
It's true, he hasn't a head to spare,
But my daughter's only a one-headed troll.
Three-headed trolls have gone out of style;
You scarcely see two-headers any more,
And the ones you do see are pretty poor.[*To* PEER GYNT.]
So—it's my daughter you want to have?
PEER GYNT. Yes, and your realm for the dowry too.
TROLL KING. You can have half while I still live,
And the other half right after I go.

PEER GYNT. That's fair enough.
TROLL KING. Just a minute, boy—
There are some promises you have to give.
Break only one, and the contract's clay,
And you'll never get out of here alive.
First, you must promise never to care
For the world beyond our own frontier;
Renounce day, deeds, the things of light.
PEER GYNT. If I can be king, there's nothing to that.
TROLL KING. Next—I'll put your wits to the test—[*Draws himself up on his throne.*]
THE OLDEST COURTIER TROLL. [*To* PEER GYNT.] Let's see if your wisdom tooth can
Crack the shell of our king's request!
TROLL KING. What difference is there between troll and man?
PEER GYNT. No difference at all, from what I can see.
Big trolls roast you, and little trolls claw—
Same as with us,[22] if our nerves are raw.
TROLL KING. Yes, there and in other points, we agree.
But morning is morning and night is night,
And there *is* a difference down at the root.
I'll tell you what it is. Outside,
Among men, under the shining sky,
They say: "Man, to yourself be true!"
While here, under our mountain roof,
We say: "Troll, to yourself be—enough!"[23]
THE COURTIER TROLL. [*To* PEER GYNT.] Can you fathom that?
PEER GYNT. Through a dark cloud.
TROLL KING. "Enough," my son—that severing term—
Must boldly stand on your coat of arms.
PEER GYNT. [*Scratching behind his ear.*] Well, but—
TROLL KING. It *must*, if you want to rule here!
PEER GYNT. Well, all right, I guess that's fair—
TROLL KING. Next, you must learn the value of
Our simple, domestic way of life.[24] [*He gestures; two* TROLLS *with pigs' heads and white nightcaps bring food and drink.*[25]]
Our cows give cake and our bulls give mead;
Don't ask if the flavor is sour or sweet;
The main thing that you must never forget
Is—that it's home-brewed.
PEER GYNT. [*Pushing the things away.*] To hell with all your homemade brews!
I'll never get used to this country's ways.
TROLL KING. The bowl belongs with the drink; it's gold.
Who owns this bowl, my daughter will hold.
PEER GYNT. [*Musing.*] It's written: Thy nature must be subdued—
In time the drink may seem less crude.
So, here goes! [*Drinks.*]
TROLL KING. Ah, wisely put.
Did you spit?
PEER GYNT. One obeys the force of habit.
TROLL KING. Now, throw off your Christian dress.
Everything's mountain-made with us;
From the valleys we get nothing else
But the silk bows that adorn our tails.[26]
PEER GYNT. [*Angrily.*] I have no tail!
TROLL KING. We'll get you one.
Steward, my Sunday best! Tie it on.
PEER GYNT. Lay off! You think I've lost my mind?
TROLL KING. You can't court my daughter with a smooth behind.
PEER GYNT. Turn man to a beast!
TROLL KING. You're wrong, my son;
I want you decked out like a proper swain.
You'll get a flame-yellow bow to wear,
And that rates the highest honors here.
PEER GYNT. [*Thoughtfully.*] Well, they say that man is only a mote,
So custom and fashion have to guide us a bit.
Tie away!
TROLL KING. What a responsive guest.
COURTIER TROLL. Show us how well you can wag your tail!
PEER GYNT. Ha, there's more you want of me still?
Would you also like my Christian faith?
TROLL KING. No, you can keep that under your breath.
Faith is free; we impose no tax;
A troll is known by the way he looks.

Once we're the same in manner and clothes,
You're free to believe in what a troll loathes.
PEER GYNT. You know, despite the conditions you make,
You're more sensible than I thought you'd be.
TROLL KING. Trolls aren't as bad, son, as people say;
It's one other point where we're unalike—
Well, that ends the party's serious side;
Now we'll enjoy what our senses bring—
Musician! Strike the Dovre harp-strings!
Dancer! Let the floor echo your tread! [*Music and dance.*]
COURTIER TROLL. How do you like it?
PEER GYNT. Hm—
TROLL KING. Speak out. What do you see?
PEER GYNT. A horrible sight.
A bell cow strumming a catgut lyre,
And a sow in stockings dancing to her.
COURTIERS. Eat him!
TROLL KING. He sees us with human senses,
Remember!
TROLL GIRLS. Tear out his eyes and ears!
WOMAN IN GREEN. [*Sobbing.*] Boo-hoo! What things our performance endures
When my sister and I put on our dances!
PEER GYNT. Oh no, was it you? Well, a little guying
At a banquet is hardly a sign of spite.
WOMAN IN GREEN. Do you swear to that?
PEER GYNT. Both dancing and playing—
May the cat claw my tongue—were pure delight.
TROLL KING. It's strange about this human nautre,
Just how remarkably deep it goes.
If it gets gashed in some battle with us,
It heals right up and wears its scar.
Now my son-in-law's lenient as any man;
He willingly dropped the garb of a Christian,
Willingly drank the bowl of mead,
Willingly let his tail be tied—
In fact, was so willing in all we made him

Do that I really thought the old Adam
Had at last been safely kicked out of doors;
But, look, in a wink he's back in force.
Ah yes, my son, you need a cure
To reform your accursed human nature.
PEER GYNT. What do you mean?
TROLL KING. I'll make a slit
In your left eye, till you see the worlds slant—
But all that you see will make you content.
Then I'll cut out the right windowpane—
PEER GYNT. Are you drunk?
TROLL KING. [*Puts some sharp implements on the table.*] Here you see a glazier's kit.
You'll be blinkered like an unruly bull.
Then you'll realize your bride is beautiful,
And your eyesight will never again confuse
Her charms with pigs or musical cows.
PEER GYNT. You're raving mad!
THE OLDEST COURTIER. You heard what he said;
It's he who's wise, and you that's mad.
TROLL KING. Think of the torments, the miseries
You'll save yourself in afterdays.
Vision, don't forget, is the source
Of tears, and the body's bitter light.
PEER GYNT. That's true; and there's the Bible verse:
"If thine eye offend thee, pluck it out."
Wait! But tell me, when would it mend
Back to human sight?
TROLL KING. Never, my friend.
PEER GYNT. Hm! Well, then I'll say thanks, but no.
TROLL KING. Where are you heading?
PEER GYNT. It's time to go.
TROLL KING. Hold on! Here it's easy to enter in,
But the gate isn't made to swing out again.
PEER GYNT. You're not going to keep me here forcibly?
TROLL KING. Now listen, be reasonable, Prince Peer!
You're gifted for trollhood. Doesn't he bear
Himself already quite trollishly?
And you want the job—?

PEER GYNT. Of course I do.
For a bride, and a well-run empire to boot,
There are losses I can accommodate.
Everything has its limits, though.
I've taken a tail, that I'll admit;
But what's been tied, my hands can unknot.
I've shed my trousers; they were old and thin,
But I surely can button them on again.
And I'm sure as well that I can slough off
All signs of your Dovre way of life.
I'll gladly swear that a cow is a woman;
An oath one can always whistle away—
But *this*—to know you can never be free,
Never die decently as a human,
To run as a hill troll till kingdom come—
It's this—the fact that you can't go home
The way the book says, *this* you're intent on;
But it's what I'll never put my consent in.
TROLL KING. Now, bless my sins, I'm getting cross;
And I'll have no more of this foolishness.
You know who I am, you whey-faced rotter?
First, you're fast and loose with my daughter—
PEER GYNT. You lie in your teeth!
TROLL KING. You must marry her.
PEER GYNT. You dare to accuse me—?
TROLL KING. What? Can you swear She hasn't gone flickering through your desire?
PEER GYNT. [*Snorting.*] Is that all? Who's going to make *that* stick?
TROLL KING. You human beings are all alike.
You serve the spirit with your lips
And settle for what your hands can keep.
So you think desire doesn't matter, either?
You'll soon have visible proof, just wait—
PEER GYNT. You won't catch me with your liar's bait!
TROLL KING. Peer, by the year's end, you'll be a father.

PEER GYNT. Open up; let me out.
TROLL KING. You'll get the brat Wrapped in a goatskin.
PEER GYNT. [*Mopping sweat from his brow.*] Oh, to wake up!
TROLL KING. Should he go to your palace?
PEER GYNT. To the poorhouse doorstep!
TROLL KING. Splendid, Prince Peer; you can manage that.
But *one* thing is certain: what's done is done,
And your offspring will sprout up like a weed;
These mongrels ripen remarkably soon.
PEER GYNT. Now don't be so stubborn-minded, dad.
Be sensible, girl. Let's compromise.
I'm neither a prince nor rich, God knows—
And no matter how you measure or weigh me
You're not going to gain much profit by me. [*The* WOMAN IN GREEN *faints and is carried out by the* TROLL GIRLS.]
TROLL KING. [*Gives him a look of utter contempt.*] Dash him to bits on the rocks, children!
TROLL CHILDREN. Can we play owls and eagles then?
The wolf game! Gray mouse and glow-eyed cat!
TROLL KING. Yes, quickly. I'm vexed and sleepy. Good night! [*He leaves.*]
PEER GYNT. [*Hunted by* TROLL CHILDREN.] Let go, you devils! [*Starts to squirm up the chimney.*]
TROLL CHILDREN. Come, goblins! Gnomes!
Bite his back!
PEER GYNT. Ow! [*Tries the cellar trapdoor.*]
TROLL CHILDREN. Plug up the seams!
COURTIER TROLL. What fun for the young!
PEER GYNT. [*Struggling with a tiny troll, who has bitten deep in his ear.*] Let go, you crud!
COURTIER TROLL. [*Raps his knuckles.*] Careful, you lowlife; that's royal blood.
PEER GYNT. A rathole—! [*Runs toward it.*]
TROLL CHILDREN. Goblins! Head him off course!
PEER GYNT. The old man was foul, but

the children are worse!
TROLL CHILDREN. Flay him!
PEER GYNT. Oh, to be small as a mouse! [*Runs aimlessly.*]
TROLL CHILDREN. [*Swarming about him.*] Close in! Pen him!
PEER GYNT. [*In tears.*] The size of a louse! [*He falls.*]
TROLL CHILDREN. Now, get his eyes!
PEER GYNT. [*Buried in a heap of trolls.*] Help, Mother, I'll die! [*Church bells ring far off.*]
TROLL CHILDREN. Bells in the mountains! Blackfrock's cows![27]
[*The* TROLLS *flee in a turmoil of howls and shrieks. The hall collapses; everything vanishes.*]

Scene 7

Pitch blackness. PEER GYNT *can be heard striking and flailing about with the branch of a tree.*
PEER GYNT. Speak out! Who are you?
A VOICE IN THE DARKNESS. Myself.
PEER GYNT. Move aside!
THE VOICE. Go roundabout, Peer! The heath is wide.
PEER GYNT. [*Starts to go through at another point, but is stopped by something.*] Who are you?
THE VOICE. Myself. Can you say the same?
PEER GYNT. I can say what I please; and my sword hits home!
Look out! Ahh! Now he feels his wounds!
King Saul killed hundreds;[28] Peer Gynt, thousands! [*Hewing and slashing.*]
Who are you?
THE VOICE. Myself.
PEER GYNT. That stupid answer
You can keep; it makes nothing clear.
What are you?
THE VOICE. The great Boyg.[29]
PEER GYNT. I see!
The riddle was black, and now it's gray.
Out of my way, Boyg!
THE VOICE. Go roundabout, Peer!
PEER GYNT. Straight through! [*Striking out.*] He's down! [*Tries to go on, but again is stopped.*] What? Still more?
THE VOICE. The Boyg, Peer Gynt! The one only one.
The Boyg that's unhurt, and the Boyg that's in pain.
The Boyg that's dead, and the Boyg that's alive.
PEER GYNT. [*Flinging the branch away.*]
The sword's bewitched, but fists are enough. [*Hammers his way ahead.*]
THE VOICE. Yes, trust to your fists, your body's hope.
Ho-ho, Peer Gynt, you'll reach the top.
PEER GYNT. [*Returning.*] Forward and back, it's just as far.
Out or in, it's a narrow door.
He's *there!* And *there!* and beyond the bend!
As soon as I'm out, he rings me around—
Your name? Let me see you! Say what you are!
THE VOICE. The Boyg.
PEER GYNT. [*Groping about.*] Not dead, nor alive. Slime; gray air,
Not even a form. It's like trading jabs
With a den of snarling, half-awake bear cubs. [*Shrieks.*]
Stand up to me!
THE VOICE. The Boyg's not insane.
PEER GYNT. Strike!
THE VOICE. The Boyg doesn't strike.
PEER GYNT. Fight! Come on!
THE VOICE. The great Boyg wins, though no fighting rages.
PEER GYNT. For a goblin raking my back with a knife!
Or only so much as a year-old troll!
Something to scrap with. But there's nothing at all—
Now he's snoring! Boyg!
THE VOICE. What?
PEER GYNT. Get rough!
THE VOICE. The great Boyg wins all by easy stages.
PEER GYNT. [*Bites his own hands and arms.*] Gashing teeth and claws in the flesh!
I've got to feel my own blood drop. [*A sound like the wingbeats of great birds[30] is heard.*]
BIRD CRIES. Boyg, is he coming?
THE VOICE. Yes, step by step.
BIRD CRIES. Sisters far off, fly here in a rush!
PEER GYNT. If you want to save me, girl, do it quick!
Don't lower your gaze, tender and shy—!

The prayer book! Fling it straight in his eye!
BIRD CRIES. He wavers!
THE VOICE. We've got him.
BIRD CRIES. Sisters, attack!
PEER GYNT. If the price of life is this agony,
Even one hour's too much to pay. [*Sinks down.*]
THE BIRDS. Boyg, he's fallen! Take him! End him! [*Church bells and hymns in the distance.*]
THE BOYG. [*Dwindles to nothing, his voice a gasp.*]
He was too strong. There were women behind him.

Scene 8

Sunrise. On the slope by AASE's *mountain hut. The door is bolted; everything is deserted and still.* PEER GYNT *lies asleep alongside one wall. He wakes, looks about with a dull, heavy stare, then spits.*

PEER GYNT. Oh, what I'd give for a pickled herring! [*Spits again, and at the same moment notices* HELGA *approaching with a food basket.*]
Well, what brings you up here, child? Exploring?
HELGA. It's Solveig—
PEER GYNT. [*Leaps up.*] Where is she?
HELGA. Back of your hut.
SOLVEIG. [*Hidden.*] Come any closer, and I'm going to run!
PEER GYNT. [*Stops.*] Afraid you'll wind up in the arms of a man?
SOLVEIG. Shame on you!
PEER GYNT. Know where I was last night?
The Troll Princess went after me like a bat.
SOLVEIG. It's a good thing, then, that we rang the bells.
PEER GYNT. Peer Gynt isn't one that her sort beguiles—
What'd you say?
HELGA. [*Bursting into tears.*] Oh, she's running! Wait!
Wait! [*Hurries after.*]
PEER GYNT. [*Seizing her arm.*] Look here, in my pocket, I had
This silver button. Take it! It's for you—
If you just speak well of me!

HELGA. Please, let me go!
PEER GYNT. It's yours.
HELGA. Please—in the basket, there's food!
PEER GYNT. If you don't, God help you—
HELGA. Oh, you upset me!
PEER GYNT. [*Gently, releasing her.*] No, I mean—ask her not to forget me!
[HELGA *runs off.*]

Act 3

Scene 1

Deep in a pine forest. Gray autumn weather, with snow falling. PEER GYNT *stands in his shirt sleeves, felling timber. He is hewing away at a great fir with crooked branches.*

PEER GYNT. Ah, you're tough, you old mountain man—
But it's no use; you're coming down.
[*Hewing away again.*]
I see you're wearing a coat of mail;
It's strong, but I'll stave it in for the kill—
Go on; shake your crooked arm;
Of course you're angry and out of form;
But still you're going to bow to me—!
[*Breaks off abruptly.*]
Lies! It's just a battered tree.
Lies! It's no armor maker's work;
Only a fir with peeling bark.
It's weary labor, chopping wood,
But to chop *and* dream is crazy mad.
I'm through with it—this life of mist
That weaves the living moment past.
You're an outlaw, Peer! A hunted beast.
[*Chopping hard for a time.*]
An outlaw, yes. No mother glad
To set your table and bring you food.
If you're hungry, boy, you're on your own;
Fetch it raw from woods or stream;
Split your kindling, build your fire,
Putter and mend and make secure.
If you want to dress warmly, kill a

buck;
If your house needs shoring, break the
  rock;
If you're short of timber, fell the logs
And haul them in on aching legs. [*The
  ax sinks; he gazes off.*]
Build it with splendor. A tower and
  vane
On the ridgepole, soaring high and
  clean.
And then I'll carve, for the end of the
  gable,
A mermaid, fish-shaped down from the
  navel.
The vane and the locks will be of
  brass—
And panes of glass, I can try for that.
Passing strangers will wonder what
It is that shines on this distant rise.
  [*Laughs angrily.*]
Infernal lies! I went off again.
You're an outlaw, Peer! [*Chopping
  fiercely.*] A plain bark roof
For the rain and frost is good enough.
  [*Looks up at the tree.*]
Now he's swaying. A kick, just one—
And there he falls to cut a swath
Across the shuddering undergrowth!
  [*Starts to trim off branches; suddenly he
  listens, motionless, ax in midair.*]
Someone's after me—! Are you that
  kind,
Old Hegstad—to come here, sneaking
  around? [*Crouches behind the tree and
  peeps out.*]
A boy! And alone. He looks afraid.
He's staring about. What is that, hid
By his jacket? A sickle. His eyes keep
  scanning—
Now he's spread his hand on the fence
  rail.
What now? Why does he stand there,
  leaning—?
Ugh, his finger, it's off! He's cut
The whole finger off! He bleeds like a
  bull—
He's running away with his fist in a
  clout. [*Rises.*]
The devil! An irreplaceable finger—
Lost! And through his, not another's
  anger.
Ah, now I know—! That's the price
For escaping his military service.
That's it. They want to send him to
  war;
And the boy, of course, doesn't want to
  go—
But to cut off—? For all time, never
  to—
Yes, think it; wish it; *will* it so—
But to *do* it! No, I can't follow him
  there. [*Shakes his head quietly, then re-
  turns to work.*]

Scene 2

A room in AASE's *house. Everything in
disorder, boxes standing open, clothing
strewn about, a cat lying on the bed.* AASE
and KARI *are hard at work, packing and
straightening up.*

AASE. [*Running to one side of the room.*]
  Kari, listen!
KARI. Now what?
AASE. [*Back to the other side.*] Tell me—!
Where's—? Where did I—? You know,
  where's the—?
What do I want? My mind's in a whirl!
Where's the key to the chest?
KARI. In the keyhole.
AASE. What's that's rumbling?
KARI. The last cartload
Going over to Hegstad.
AASE. [*Weeping.*] I'd be glad
To be going myself in a long black box.
Ah, what a person suffers in heart-
  breaks!
Merciful God! The house stripped
  clean!
What old Hegstad left, the sheriff
  held—
Even the clothes on my back were sold.
Shame on a justice that can be so mean!
  [*Sitting on the edge of the bed.*]
The farm and the land, lost to our
  name.
The old man was hard; but the law was
  a crime—
No one to help; no mercy given;
Peer far away; no counsel even—
KARI. But the house is yours till the day
  you die.
AASE. Yes, I and the cat can take
  charity!
KARI. God help you, Aase; you've paid
  for your son.
AASE. Peer? Now that's an odd opinion!
Ingrid got home safe, finally.
They ought to lay the blame on the
  devil—
He's the power in all that's evil;

The prince of hell seduced my boy!
KARI. Maybe I'd better send for the pastor?
You might have worsened without your knowing.
AASE. The pastor? I guess it would be best for— [*Starting up.*]
God no, I can't! What am I saying?
His mother must help him; it's the least I owe—
To be there when the others all turn away.
They left him this coat. I'll patch it up.
Ah, the fur rug's something I'd like to keep!
Where are the stockings?
KARI. There, in that muddle.
AASE. [*Rummaging around.*] What's this—? Look, it's the casting ladle
From the old days! With this he used to play
Button-molder—melt and pour and ply
The metal. At a party once, he came in
And asked his father for a lump of tin.
"Not tin," says Jon, "but coin of the mint—
Silver, because you're the son of Jon Gynt."
God save him, he was a little wild
From drink, and couldn't tell tin from gold.
There, the stockings. And full of holes!
They ought to be darned.
KARI. They really should.
AASE. When that's been done, I'll go to bed.
I feel so weak, so sick and depressed— [*Joyfully.*]
Two wool shirts, Kari—these they missed!
KARI. So they did.
AASE. It's something at least.
One of them's yours; we can settle with
That—or—no, we can take them both.
The ones he's got are wearing thin.
KARI. But, Mother Aase, stealing is sin!
AASE. Oh well, but you know the pastor brings
Forgiveness for that, and all our wrongs.

Scene 3

Outside a newly built hut in the forest. Reindeer antlers over the door. The snow lies deep. It is dusk. PEER GYNT *stands in front of the door, fixing a large wooden bar in place.*

PEER GYNT. There must be a bolt, one that can fasten
This door against trolls, and women and men.
There must be a bolt, one that can lock
The goblins out, all the merciless pack.
They come with the dark; they hammer and hit:
"Open up, Peer Gynt, we're as quick as thought!
We're under the bed, in the ash of the fire;
We stream down the chimney like dragons. Ah, Peer—
What made you think that nails and slats
Could shut out the merciless goblin thoughts?" [SOLVEIG *comes across the snowfield on skis; she has a kerchief on her head and a bundle in her hand.*]
SOLVEIG. God bless your work. Don't turn me away.
I've come to your call; now let me stay.
PEER GYNT. Solveig! It can't be—! Oh, but it is!
And you're not afraid to come so close!
SOLVEIG. Your call reached out in my sister's voice;
It came on the wind and in silences.
In your mother's words I felt it flame;
And it echoed out of my waking dreams.
The heavy nights, the empty days
Kept calling me, telling me, "Go where he goes."
My joy was gone, my life cut short;
I couldn't laugh or cry from my heart.
I couldn't be sure what your feelings were;
I only knew I had to come here.
PEER GYNT. But your father?
SOLVEIG. On this whole wide earth
I've no one for father or mother both.
I've left them forever.
PEER GYNT. Solveig, my own—
You did this for me?
SOLVEIG. Yes, for you alone;
You must be all to me—lover and friend. [*In tears.*]
The worst was leaving my sister behind—
No, leaving my father, *that* was the worst;

But still worse, to leave her whose
   breast
Had nourished me; oh, God, no, the
   real
Pain and sorrow was leaving them all!
PEER GYNT. You know the judgment
   read last spring?
I'm stripped of my farm, of everything.
SOLVEIG. You think I cast off the ones I
   love
Just for some property you might
   have?
PEER GYNT. You've heard the sentence?
   Outside this wood
I'm fair game for all, with a price on
   my head.
SOLVEIG. I asked my way here with each
   turn of the climb;
They said, "Why go there?" I said, "It's
   my home."
PEER GYNT. Then away, away with these
   nails and slats!
Who needs bars against merciless
   thoughts?
If you can dare live in my hunter's
   house,
This ground will become a holy place.
Solveig! Let me look at you! Not too
   near!
Only to look at you! Oh, how pure and
   fair!
Let me lift you! But you're slender and
   light!
I could carry you forever and feel no
   weight!
I won't ever soil you. These arms,
   Solveig,
Will hold your lovely, warm body from
   me!
Who would have thought I could win
   your love?
Oh, the nights, the days, and the
   longing I've—
Look, you can see how I've built my
   hut;
But it's coming down; it's mean and
   squat—
SOLVEIG. Mean or great—it suits my
   mind.
It's so easy to breathe against this wind.
Down there it was stifling, closed like a
   trap;
That was partly what drove me up.
But here, where the firs cut the sky like
   gems,
What stillness and song! Here I'm at
home.
PEER GYNT. Are you sure of that? For as
   long as you live?
SOLVEIG. The path I've chosen doesn't
   swerve.
PEER GYNT. Then you're mine! Go in!
   Let me hold the door.
Please! I'll get some roots for a fire.
In that bright warmth, that cozy glow,
You can rest content; you won't freeze
   now. [*He opens the door, and* SOLVEIG
   *enters. He stands silent a moment, then
   laughs with joy and leaps in the air.*]
My princess! At last, she's found and
   won!
Now my palace will rise on a true
   foundation! [*He picks up his ax and
   starts off; at the same moment, an* OLD-
   LOOKING WOMAN *in a tattered green
   dress comes out of the wood; an* UGLY
   BRAT *with a flask of beer in his hand
   limps after, holding onto her skirt.*]
THE WOMAN. Good evening, Peer
   Lightfoot!
PEER GYNT. Hello, who's there?
THE WOMAN. Old friends, Peer Gynt!
   Our place isn't far.
We're neighbors.
PEER GYNT. Oh? That's more than I
   knew.
THE WOMAN. As your hut built up, mine
   built itself too.
PEER GYNT. I'm in a rush—
THE WOMAN. You always were;
But I'll track you down and get you for
   sure.
PEER GYNT. You've made a mistake,
   woman!
THE WOMAN. Only once;
That time you promised me into a
   trance.
PEER GYNT. I promised—? What the
   hell kind of nonsense is that?
THE WOMAN. You've forgotten you
   drank at my father's one night?
You've forgotten—?
PEER GYNT. Yes; what I've never known.
What *is* this? When did we meet last?
   When?
THE WOMAN. We met last—the day we
   met first. [*To the* BRAT.]
Give Daddy a drink; he suffers from
   thirst.
PEER GYNT. Daddy? You're drunk! Do
   you call him—?
THE WOMAN. You know it's bacon when

you see the rind!
Where are your eyes? Don't you see,
    he's lame
In his leg as you're lame in your mind.
PEER GYNT. You mean to imply—?
THE WOMAN. You mean to protest—?
PEER GYNT. That gangling calf—!
THE WOMAN. He grew up fast.
PEER GYNT. You troll snout, how dare
    you invent—?
THE WOMAN. Listen, you're crude as an
    ox, Peer Gynt! [*Crying.*]
How can I help it if I'm less beautiful
Than when you lured me on that
    heathery hill?
Last fall in my labor, the fiend held my
    back,
So it's no surprise I've a twisted look.
If you want to see me as fair as before,
Turn that female away from your door,
Tear her out of your mind and sight—
Do that, my love, and I'll lose my snout!
PEER GYNT. Get away, you witch!
THE WOMAN. Just see if I do!
PEER GYNT. I'll split your skull!
THE WOMAN. I dare you to!
Ho-ho, Peer Gynt, I can take your
    blows!
I'll keep coming back till the end of
    your days.
I'll squint through the door and spy on
    you both;
And if you sit with your girl by the
    fire—
And start to caress—and put off your
    clothes—
I'll slip in between and take my share.
She and I, we'll have you by turns.
So marry her, Peer, while your pleasure
    burns!
PEER GYNT. You nightmare from hell!
THE WOMAN. Oh, I nearly forgot!
My light-footed love, you can raise the
    brat.
There, pet, run to your daddy?
THE BRAT. [*Spits at him.*] Pfft!
I'll take the ax to you—wait, just wait!
THE WOMAN. [*Kisses the* BRAT.] Oh, but
    there's a head on that pup!
You'll be like your father when you
    grow up.
PEER GYNT. [*Stamping.*] I could wish you
    as far—!
THE WOMAN. As now we're near?
PEER GYNT. [*Clenching his fists.*] And all
    this—!

THE WOMAN. Only for thoughts, for
    desire?
It's hard on you, Peer!
PEER GYNT. Worse for another—!
Solveig, my treasure, my pure delight!
THE WOMAN. "How the innocent
    suffer," said Old Nick to his mother,
When she whacked him because his
    father got tight! [*She plods off into the
    forest, followed by the* BRAT, *who hurls
    the flask back toward* PEER.]
PEER GYNT. [*After a long silence.*]
"Roundabout," said the Boyg. I have
    no choice—
My palace is ruined, shivered to bits!
There's a wall around her. We came so
    close—
Now everything's foul; my happiness
    rots.
Roundabout, lad! There's just no way
Straight through to her—no, not for
    you.
Straight through? Hm, there ought to
    be, still.
There's a text on repentance, I seem to
    recall.
But what? What is it? I forget what it
    said.
Don't have the book; and there's no
    one to guide
My footsteps here in this trackless
    wood.
    Repentance? It could run on for
        years
Till I fought my way through. That's a
    poor life.
To shatter what's holy and pure, what I
    love,
Just to bind it together in cracks and
    scars?
That can work for a fiddle, but not for
    a bell.
If you want a field green, keep it free
    of your heel.
    But that was a lie, that with the troll
        snout!
Now the corruption's all out of sight—
Yes, out of sight, but not out of mind.
Cringing thoughts would trail me
    around.
Ingrid! And the three who danced on
    that crest!
Would they appear too? Cry out, with
    storms
Of laughter, like her to be hotly
    embraced,

Or tenderly borne on outstretched
   arms?
Roundabout, boy. Were my arms as
   long
As the fir tree's root or the river's
   tongue,
I know I'd be holding her still too near
To set her down again holy and pure.
   Let me work around it, this way or
   that,
So I manage neither to win nor lose.
Just push it away and try to forget—
   [*Goes several steps toward the hut and
   stops.*]
   Go in after this? So foul and coarse?
Go in, with all this odor of troll?
Speak, but be silent; confess, but
   conceal? [*Throws the ax away.*]
   It's a holy-day evening. For me to
   approach
The way I am now, would be sacrilege.
SOLVEIG. [*In the doorway.*] Are you
   coming?
PEER GYNT. [*In an undertone.*]
   Roundabout!
SOLVEIG. What?
PEER GYNT. You must wait.
It's dark here, and I've something
   heavy to get.
SOLVEIG. Wait, I'll help you. We'll share
   to the full.
PEER GYNT. No, stay where you are! I'll
   bear it all.
SOLVEIG. Please, not too far!
PEER GYNT. Be patient, my sweet;
Far or near—you must wait.
SOLVEIG. [*Nods to him.*] Yes, I'll wait!
   [PEER GYNT *goes down the path to the
   forest.* SOLVEIG *remains standing in the
   open half-door.*]

Scene 4

AASE's *hut. Evening. A log fire throws its
   light on the walls. The cat is on a chair at
   the foot of the bed, where* AASE *lies,
   pulling restlessly at the sheets.*
AASE. Lord God, why doesn't he come?
The hours drag endlessly by.
I've no way of sending to him,
And so terribly much to say.
There isn't a moment to lose!
So soon! How little we know!
If I'd thought it would end like this,
I'd never have scolded him so!

PEER GYNT. [*Comes in.*] Good evening.
AASE. God bless you, dear!
Oh, my boy! So you did come then!
But what are you doing down here?
Your life's at stake near town.
PEER GYNT. My life? It's not worth a
   hang.
I just had to see your face.
AASE. This proves that Kari was wrong;
And I can go out in peace.
PEER GYNT. Go out? What are you say-
   ing?
Where do you plan to go?
AASE. Ah, Peer, there's no denying—
It's plain that my time is due.
PEER GYNT. [*Writhing and pacing the
   floor.*] I've run from one heavy
   weight;
I thought at least *here* I'd be free—!
Are you cold in your hands and feet?
AASE. Yes, Peer; but it soon goes away—
When my eyes begin to glaze,
You must carefully close each lid.
And see to my coffin, please;
Take care it's the finest wood—
Oh no, I forgot—
PEER GYNT. Be still!
There's plenty of time for that.
AASE. Yes, true. [*Looks restlessly about.*]
   You can see how little
They left. That's them, all right.
PEER GYNT. [*Wincing.*] Again! [*Sharply.*]
   I know I'm to blame.
But why must you hammer it in?
AASE. You? No, the demon rum;
That's what struck us down!
You know you'd been drinking, Peer;
And so your wits were dulled;
And then you'd been riding reindeer—
No wonder you acted wild!
PEER GYNT. All right, let that story drop.
Enough of that whole display.
Whatever is heavy we'll keep—
Till later—some other day. [*Sits on the
   edge of the bed.*]
Mother, let's talk, you and I—
But only of this and that.
Things that are twisted and wry,
That rankle and hurt, let's forget—
Ah, look! It's the old cat;
Is he really still alive?
AASE. He screeches so in the night;
You know what that's warning of!
PEER GYNT. [*Turning away.*] What's the
   news of the parish?
AASE. [*Smiling.*] They say there's a girl

who's bent
On the uplands with every wish—
PEER GYNT. [*Quickly.*] Mads Moen, is he
  content?
AASE. They say she's deafened her ears
To her father's and mother's pleas.
If you saw her a moment, Peer—
You might be the one to advise—
PEER GYNT. And Aslak, he's getting
  ahead?
AASE. Don't speak of that filthy smith.
Let me tell you the girl, instead;
Her name's on the tip of my breath—
PEER GYNT. No, let's talk now, you and
  I—
But only of this and that.
Things that are twisted and wry,
That rankle and hurt, let's forget.
You're thirsty? Do you want a drink?
Have you room? That bed's like a toy.
Let me see—but, yes, I think
It's the one I had as a boy!
Remember the evenings you sat
By my bedside when I was young
And tucked me under the coverlet
And sang me ballad and song?
AASE. Of course! And when your father
Was out, then we played sleighs.
The spread was a lap robe of fur,
And the floor was a sheet of ice.
PEER GYNT. Yes, but all else above—
You remember, Mother, too—?
The dashing horses we drove—
AASE. Yes, don't you think I know—?
Our cat, and that other one—
Kari's; we had her on loan.
PEER GYNT. To the Castle East of the
  Sun
And the Castle West of the Moon,
To Soria-Moria Castle[31]
The high and the low roads wound.
You had a whip with a tassel—
It was just a stick we'd found.
AASE. I drove like a real cavalier—
PEER GYNT. Yes, you reined the horses
  loose;
And you'd turn as the hoofs struck fire,
Always afraid I might freeze.
Bless you, you dear old relic,
You did have a loving soul—!
Why did you moan?
AASE. My back.
It's these hard boards I feel.
PEER GYNT. Here, take a better position.
There now; more comfortable?
AASE. [*Restlessly.*] No, I want to move on!
PEER GYNT. Move on?
AASE. Yes, move on for good, that's all.
PEER GYNT. Pah! Let me tuck in the
  coverlet.
Like so. If the night seems long,
We'll shorten it. There; I'll sit
And sing you ballad and song.
AASE. No, my Bible! I'll read the Apostle.
My thoughts are weighing me down.
PEER GYNT. In Soria-Moria Castle
There's a feast for the king and queen.
Lie back on the silken cushion;
We'll drive there over the snow.
AASE. But—have I an invitation?
PEER GYNT. Why, of course! Both of us
  do. [*He throws a cord round the chair
  where the cat lies, picks up a stick, and
  sits on the end of the bed.*]
Gee-up! Get along, Blackie!
Mother, you're not going to freeze?
Ho, but the ride goes quickly
When Grane[32] sets the pace!
AASE. Dear heart, what is it, that ringing—?
PEER GYNT. The silver sleighbells you
  heard!
AASE. But those hollow echoes thronging?
PEER GYNT. We're galloping over a
  fjord.
AASE. I'm frightened! What is that roaring
Like some great, hungry mouth?
PEER GYNT. Only the night wind tearing
Through the branches on the heath.
AASE. Far off there, something glimmers.
What makes that wavering blaze?
PEER GYNT. The castle's doors and windows.
Can you hear them dancing?
AASE. Yes.
PEER GYNT. Saint Peter stands at the
  main door;
He's motioning you to come in.
AASE. He greets me?
PEER GYNT. Yes, with honor,
And pours out the sweetest wine.
AASE. Wine! Are there cakes as well,
  Peer?
PEER GYNT. In droves! The finest sort.
And the bishop's wife, his helper,
Makes you coffee and dessert.
AASE. My Lord, will she and I meet?
PEER GYNT. As easy and free as you like.

AASE. You mean it? Peer, what a banquet
They're giving for my poor sake!
PEER GYNT. [*Cracking his whip.*] Hup!
Get along there, Blackie!
AASE. You're sure, dear, this is the way?
PEER GYNT. [*Cracks it again.*] Yes, the broad road.
AASE. I feel shaky
And weak from this racketing sleigh.
PEER GYNT. I can see the castle so close;
The race is just about run.
AASE. I'll lie back and rest my eyes
And trust it to you, my son.
PEER GYNT. Press on, Grane, my pacer!
The courtyard's filled to the brim;
They swarm to the portals and stare.
Peer Gynt and his mother have come!
Saint Peter, what did you say?
My mother may not come in?
You could look till the seas run dry
To find a worthier one!
Of myself, I won't say a word;
I can turn at the castle gate.
If you stand for drinks, I'd be flattered;
If not, I won't be put out.
I've made up more lies already
Then the devil trying to preach,
And called my mother "Old Biddy"
For the way she'd cackle and scratch.
But you give her love and honor.
Make her at home in your truth.
They don't come up now any finer
From the parishes of our faith.
Ho-ho, there's God the Father!
Saint Peter, you'll get yours today! [*In a deep voice.*]
"An end to this fuss and bother—
Mother Aase can come in free!" [*Laughs aloud and turns to* AASE.]
Isn't *that* how I said it would break?
Now they're singing a different tune!
[*Anxiously.*]
Mother! That faraway look!
It's as though your wits had flown!
[*Goes to the head of the bed.*]
Don't stare! Your eyes are like china.
Mother, speak! It's me, your son! [*Cautiously feels her forehead and hands, then throws the cord on the chair and says quietly.*]
So that's it. You can rest now, Grane.
The long haul is really done. [*Closes her eyes and bends over her.*]
Here's thanks for all of your days,
For the blows and the kisses I had—
But give back some little praise—
[*Presses his cheek to her mouth.*]
There—that was thanks for the ride.
KARI. [*Entering.*] What? Peer! So then we're beyond
Our heaviest sorrow and dread!
Dear Lord, but she's sleeping sound.
Or is she—?
PEER GYNT. Shh. She's dead. [KARI *weeps over the body;* PEER GYNT *walks slowly about the room, finally coming to a stop by the bed.*]
PEER GYNT. See that she's buried worthily.
It's time that I quit this soil.
KARI. Are you going far?
PEER GYNT. To the sea.
KARI. So far?
PEER GYNT. Yes; and farther still. [*He goes out.*]

Act 4

Scene 1

The southwest coast of Morocco. Under an awning in a palm grove, a table, on rush matting, set for dinner. Farther back, hammocks slung from the trees. A steam yacht, flying Norwegian and American flags, lies offshore. On the beach, a jolly boat. It is near sundown. PEER GYNT, *a handsome, middle-aged man in an elegant traveling suit, gold pince-nez dangling at his chest, presides at the head of the table.* MR. COTTON[33] *and* MONSIEUR BALLON,[34] *along with* HERR VON EBERKOPF[35] *and* HERR TRUMPETERSTRAALE,[36] *are finishing dinner.*

PEER GYNT. Gentlemen, drink! If man is made
For pleasure, then let his pleasure thrive.
As somebody wrote: the past is dead,
What's done is done—Now what'll you have?
TRUMPETERSTRAALE. As a host, brother Gynt, you're enormous!
PEER GYNT. I share that honor with my

ample purse,
My steward and my cook—
COTTON. Very well,
A toast to the four. Here's to them all!
BALLON. Monsieur, you have *un goût, un ton*
Nowadays one rarely finds
In gentlemen living *en garçon*—
A certain—how should I say—?
EBERKOPF. A taste
Of free self-consciousness, a grip
On world-historical-fellowship,[37]
A vision piercing veils of mist,
The most unprejudiced of minds
Stamped by the higher criticism,
An *Ur-natur,* whose empiricism
Is raised to a total synthesis.
That was, monsieur, your intention, yes?
BALLON. Yes, probably—but with a tinge
Of beauty it could never have in French.
EBERKOPF. *Ei was!* That language, much too stiff—
But if we wish to seek the ground
Of the phenomenon—
PEER GYNT. That's been found.
It's because I've forsaken married life.
Gentlemen, indeed, things are
Very clear. What should a man be?
I say *himself* and nothing more.
All for *himself* and *his!* I say
Why, like a camel, should he carry
Someone else's burden of worry?
EBERKOPF. But this In-and-for-your-selfness
Has cost you a struggle, I'm sure—
PEER GYNT. Oh yes, early in my career;
But my honor was never at a loss.
Once I nearly put my leg
Into a trap that Cupid laid.
I was a gay and salty dog,
And the lady that I coveted—
She was born of royal blood—
BALLON. Of royal—?
PEER GYNT. [*Carelessly.*] Of the real old stock,
You know—
TRUMPETERSTRAALE. [*Slaps the table.*] A damned aristocrat!
PEER GYNT. [*With a shrug.*] Thin-blooded snobs, the kind that take
Their pride in a family record book
Free of the least plebeian blot.
COTTON. You mean your courtship hit a snag?

BALLON. Her parents thwarted the alliance?
PEER GYNT. Quite the reverse.
BALLON. Ah!
PEER GYNT. [*Forbearingly.*] Well, you see,
There was a growing reason why
The marriage better be held at once.
But, to be frank, the whole business
Right from the start made me recoil.
In certain ways, I'm fastidious,
And I like an independent role.
And so, when her father came around
Insinuating his demand
That I shed my name and occupation
To dance in the puppet show of fashion,
Along with other requests as well,
Irksome, if not impossible—
Why then, gracefully, out I bowed,
Gave him his ultimatum back—
And renounced my budding bride.
[*Drumming on the table with a pious air.*]
Yes, there's a Fate behind our luck!
We mortals can rely on that—
And take some comfort in the thought.
BALLON. But—was the matter really closed?
PEER GYNT. Oh no; that I discovered next.
Some meddling relatives got mixed
Up in it and violently aroused.
The worst was the family's younger set.
With seven of them I fought a duel.
It's one time I never will forget,
Although I weathered the ordeal.
It cost me blood; but that same blood
Confirmed my birthright to be great,
And boldly pointed, as I said,
To the wise governance of Fate.
EBERKOPF. You have an outlook on life's course
That ranks you with the philosophers.
For, while the common-sense observer
Views the world in scattered scenes
And gropes his stumbling way forever,
Your mind orders and combines;
All things measure to your norm.
You point up every separate rule
Until it shines forth like a beam
Of light from one Life-Principle.
And you've had no formal education?
PEER GYNT. I am—I'm happy to repeat—
A man exclusively self-taught.
My studies have had no discipline;
But fed by thought and speculation

And random reading, my mind has
   grown.
I started rather late in life;
And then, as you know, it's heavy stuff
Plowing your way from page to page
And prodding your memory to gorge.
History I picked up in scraps;
Never had the time for more.
And then of course, for the evil days
One needs a faith in something sure—
So I took religion, in little sips;
It goes down easier that way.
Study should not be omnivorous,
But strictly with an eye to use—
COTTON. Now that's practical!
PEER GYNT. [*Lighting a cigar.*] Dear
   friends,
Consider the career I've traced.
What was I when I headed west?
A ragged boy with empty hands.
I had to grub hard for everything,
And, believe me, I came near despair.
But life, my friends, life is dear,
And death, as they say, has a sting.
Well! Luck, as you know, was kind to
   me;
And old Fate showed liberality.
Things moved. I took them flexibly
And, step by step, rose up the ladder.
Within ten years I bore the name
Of Croesus with the Charleston
   traders.
Port after port declared my fame,
And fortune rode in all my hulls—
COTTON. What was the trade?
PEER GYNT. I made my deals
Mainly in slaves for Carolina
And pagan images for China.
BALLON. *Fi donc!*
TRUMPETERSTRAALE. By thunder, Uncle
   Gynt!
PEER GYNT. No doubt you feel that,
   morally,
Traffic like that had a certain taint?
I know the feeling thoroughly.
I, too, found it odious.
But, as you know, a good investment
Isn't so easily shaken loose.
And then it's especially difficult
In such a prodigious operation,
Setting thousands of men in motion,
Once and for all, to call a halt.
That "once and for all" I could never
   stand;
But I will admit, on the other hand,
That I've always nourished a respect
For what they call the consequences;
Crossing the bounds of common sense
   is
Something that leaves me feeling
   spooked.
Then, besides, I was getting on—
The last of my forties running out,
And my hair shot through with graying
   streaks.
My health remained exceptional,
But a thought kept throbbing in my
   skull:
"Who knows how soon the hour may
   strike
When the great judgment's handed
   down
That forever parts the sheep and
   goats?"
What to do? To end the trade
With China was insupportable.
I saw the answer, pushed ahead
With something else exportable.
In the spring I sent out idols still—
But added missionaries in the fall,
Providing them with every need,
Like stockings, Bibles, rum, and rice—
COTTON. At a profit?
PEER GYNT. Why, naturally, yes.
Things moved. They worked like mad.
For every idol sale we closed,
They got a coolie's soul baptized;
The result—was equilibrium.
The missions' business never lacked;
For the idols came in a steady stream,
And the preachers kept them neatly
   checked.
COTTON. But what about the African
   wares?
PEER GYNT. Triumph again for my
   moral code.
I realized that the trade was bad
For a person of advancing age;
Death might suddenly give a nudge.
Then, too, there were the thousand
   snares
Of do-gooders obsessed by slaves,
As well as the hostile privateers,
The hazards of the winds and waves—
All these made me quite positive.
I thought: ah, Peter, reef your sails,
Mend your errors, prune your goals.
So I bought a piece of land down
   south,
Held back the last payload of meat,
Which turned out prime, a perfect lot.
They flourished well, fat and glossy,

Which tickled them as much as me.
Yes, I'll tell you the sober truth:
I was like a father to them—
And sure enough, the profits came.
I built them schools so their virtue
Could be pegged not to fall beneath
A certain general *niveau*,
And watched its temperature like a hawk
So it wouldn't waver from that mark.
Now, moreover, I've resigned
From that whole phase of my career—
I've sold off the plantation and
All the livestock, hide and hair.
On leaving, I rolled out the keg,
And young and old had gratis grog;
The men, the women, all got stiff—
And the widows reveled in my snuff.
So now I hope—provided that
It's not untrue what I've heard said:
"Do no evil, and you've done some good—"
That my mistakes will fade from sight,
And, more than most, I'll find a rinse
Of virtue will dissolve my sins.
EBERKOPF. [*Clinking glasses with him.*]
How inspiriting to hear
A master principle worked out,
Redeemed from theoretic doubt,
Unshaken by the world's uproar!
PEER GYNT. [*Who has, through the above, been steadily pulling at the bottle.*] We northmen, we know how to bear
A battle through! Yes, the key
To the art of living is simply that
Of keeping both your ears shut tight
Against an evil serpent's entry.
COTTON. And what sort of serpent, friend, is that?
PEER GYNT. A little one, one that can twist
A man to whatever is hard and fast. [*Drinks again.*]
What's the whole art of daring, of
Courage in action, what is it
But to move with uncommitted feet
Between the pitfalls dug by life—
To know for sure that all your days
Aren't over on the day you fight—
To know that behind you always lies
A bridge secured for your retreat?
This policy has built my name
And colored all I've consummated.
It's something I inherited.
From the people of my childhood home.

BALLON. You're Norwegian?
PEER GYNT. Born, yes! But a
Citizen of the world by creed.
For the good fortune I've enjoyed,
I have to thank America.
I've drawn my library of books
From the latest German scholars' works.
From France, I took my taste in dress,
My manners and my turn of wit—
From England, an enterprising spirit
And an eye for my own advantages.
The Jews have taught me how to wait.
From Italy, I gained a bit
Of a flair for *dolce far niente*—
And once, when I was in plenty
Of trouble, I stretched my years no small
Amount with the aid of Swedish steel.
TRUMPETERSTRAALE. [*Raising his glass.*]
Ah, Swedish steel—!
EBERKOPF. A toast instead
To the man of steel who swung the blade! [*They clink glasses and drink with* PEER, *who begins to show the wine.*]
COTTON. What you've said is awfully nice—
But now, sir, I'm most curious
About your plans for all your treasure.
PEER GYNT. [*Smiling.*] Hm—plans? What—?
ALL FOUR. [*Edging closer.*] Yes, let's hear!
PEER GYNT. Well, first of all, to take a cruise.
That's why I asked you gentlemen on
To keep me company at Gibraltar.
I needed friends to dance a tune
For the golden calf on his seagoing altar.
EBERKOPF. That's clever!
COTTON. But no one's going to raise
Canvas merely to take a sail.
You have some project, I can tell.
And that project is—
PEER GYNT. To become emperor.
ALL FOUR. What?
PEER GYNT. [*Nodding.*] Emperor!
ALL FOUR. Where?
PEER GYNT. Of the whole earth.
BALLON. But how, my friend—?
PEER GYNT. The power of money!
The idea hasn't just entered my head;
It's inspired me almost since birth.
As a boy in dreams I used to journey
Over the ocean on a cloud.
I floated with cape and golden scab-

bard—
Then fell down, barking my elbows hard.
But, friends, my will has never swayed—
It's been written or else been said
Someplace, I can't remember where,
That if you won the earth entire
And *lost your self*,[38] what would you gain
But a wreath on a grinning skeleton.
That's the text—approximately;
And it's a lot more truth than poetry.
EBERKOPF. But what, then, is this Gyntian self?
PEER GYNT. The world behind my brow that serves
To set me as far from anyone else
As God is from the devil's wiles.
TRUMPETERSTRAALE. Now I fathom what drives you to it!
BALLON. Sublime thinker!
EBERKOPF. Exalted poet!
PEER GYNT. [*With rising emotion.*] The Gyntian self—it's an army corps
Of wishes, appetites, desires.
The Gyntian self is a mighty sea
Of whim, demand, proclivity—
In short, whatever moves my soul
And makes me live to *my* own will.
But just as our Lord had need of clay
To be creator of the universe,
So I need gold if I'm to play
The emperor's part with any force.
BALLON. But you have the gold!
PEER GYNT. Poppycock!
Yes, maybe for three days, if I ruled
As emperor à la Lippe-Detmold.[39]
But I have to be *myself* en bloc,
A name in every country known—
Sir Peter Gynt from heel to crown.
BALLON. [*Enraptured.*] And possess the world's most ravishing beauties!
EBERKOPF. Johannisberger, cellars full!
TRUMPETERSTRAALE. And Charles the Twelfth's[40] whole arsenal!
COTTON. But first, the right opportunities
For profit—
PEER GYNT. All provided for.
It's the reason why we anchored here.
Tonight we set a course northeast.
Those papers brought on board were spiced
With news that's quickened my resolve.
[*Rises, lifting his glass.*]
It seems that Fortune finds it normal
To help the man who helps himself—
THE FOUR. Well? Tell us—!
PEER GYNT. Greece is in a turmoil.
ALL FOUR. [*Springing up.*] What! The Greeks—?
PEER GYNT. Are out to fight.
ALL FOUR. Hurray!
PEER GYNT. And the Turks are in a sweat! [*Drains his glass.*]
BALLON. To Hellas—and honor! I'll take the chance
And help them—with French armaments!
EBERKOPF. I'll do what I can—on long-term notes!
COTTON. And I too—at low interest rates!
TRUMPETERSTRAALE. Lead on! In Bender[41] let me find
Those buckles King Charles left behind!
BALLON. [*Embracing* PEER GYNT.] My friend, forgive me; for a while
I misjudged you!
EBERKOPF. [*Pressing his hands.*] And I'm a fool;
I'd found you almost contemptible!
COTTON. That's too strong. Just rather simple—
TRUMPETERSTRAALE. [*Trying to kiss him.*] And I, Uncle, for an example
Of the lowest kind of Yankee rabble.
Forgive me—!
EBERKOPF. We've all been led astray—
PEER GYNT. What do you mean?
EBERKOPF. Now we can see
The thronging splendor of that army corps
Of Gyntian wishes and desires—!
BALLON. [*Admiringly.*] So *that's* what it means to be Monsieur Gynt!
EBERKOPF. [*In the same tone.*] A Gynt of honor and accomplishment!
PEER GYNT. What *is* this—?
BALLON. You don't comprehend?
PEER GYNT. If I do, you're welcome to string me up!
BALLON. Why so? Aren't you off to lend
The Greeks your money and your ship?
PEER GYNT. [*Snorting.*] Oh, no thanks! My money works
For power; I'm lending to the Turks.
BALLON. Absurd!
EBERKOPF. Amusing, for a joke!

PEER GYNT. [*Is briefly silent, then leans against a chair and assumes a superior look.*] Listen, gentlemen, it's best
We separate before the rest
Of our friendship blows away like smoke.
A man with next to nothing favors
Risk; if he owns no more of earth
Than the strip of ground his shadow covers,
He'll fling his life in the cannon's mouth.
But when your fat's well out of the fire,
As mine is, then the stakes are higher.
Go on to Greece. I'll gladly arm
You gratis and put you safe ashore.
The more you fan the flames of war,
The more propitious for my terms.
Strike for freedom and for right!
Smite the Turk! Pour on the heat—
Till all your blood and glory drenches
Down the janissary lances—
But excuse *me* out. [*Slaps his pocket.*]
That's all I want—
Money! And myself, Sir Peter Gynt!
[*Puts up his sunshade and goes into the grove where the hammocks can be seen.*]
TRUMPETERSTRAALE. The swine!
BALLON. No respect for honor—!
COTTON. Oh, honor rot! The profits—! When or
Where can we find another chance
Like this, if they win independence—
BALLON. I saw myself in triumph, hidden
By wreaths of beautiful Greek maidens!
TRUMPETERSTRAALE. There, in my Swedish hands, I saw
Those great, heroic buckles glow!
EBERKOPF. And I saw my great fatherland's *Kultur*
Expanding on every foreign shore!
COTTON. We've lost the most financially.
Goddam![42] So help me, I could cry!
I saw Olympus all my own;
And if that mountain's what they say,
There ought to be some copper mines
Still reworkable today.
And the Castalia,[43] that stream
That's talked about so much, with all
Its falls— an engineer could pull
Some thousand horsepower out of them—
TRUMPETERSTRALLE. I'm going anyway!
My Swedish
Sword's worth more than Yankee cash!

COTTON. Perhaps. But fighting in the line,
Lost in those multitudes, we'd drown;
And then what profits would we have?
BALLON. *Dommage!* So near to Fortune's lap—
Now to be stranded on her grave!
COTTON. [*Shaking his fist at the yacht.*]
And locked up in that coffin ship,
The gold he sweated from his blacks—!
EBERKOPF. A master stroke! Come on—! Quick!
His empire's in its final hour!
BALLON. What are you doing?
EBERKOPF. Seizing power!
The crew can easily be bought.
On board! I hereby annex the yacht!
COTTON. You—what—?
EBERKOPF. Give it my protection! [*Goes to the jolly boat.*]
COTTON. Self-interest tells me I ought to give
My share of that. [*Follows* EBERKOPF.]
TRUMPETERSTRAALE. Just like a thief!
BALLON. A shameful business—! But— *enfin!* [*Follows after.*]
TRUMPETERSTRAALE. I'll have to go— but, you understand,
I protest this act to all mankind—!
[*Joins the others.*]

Scene 2

Another part of the coast. Moonlight and driving clouds. In the far distance, the yacht sails under full steam. PEER GYNT *comes running along the beach. He pinches himself on the arm, then stares out over the sea.*
PEER GYNT. Nightmares—! Phantoms—!
I have to wake up!
She's put out to sea! At a furious clip—!
Just phantoms! I'm sleeping! Drunk!
Or mad! [*Wringing his hands.*]
Impossible that I could wind up dead!
[*Tearing his hair.*]
A dream! I will it to be a dream!
It's terrible! Oh, but it's true. I'm afraid!
My jackass friends—! Hear me, oh God!
Thou righteous and wise—judgment on them—! [*Reaching up his arms.*] It's *me*, Peer Gynt! Are you listening, Lord?

Look after me, Father; let me be
  spared!
Make them turn back! Or lower the
  gig!
Stop thief! Oh, let the sails unrig!
Please—! Don't fuss with the world's
  affairs!
It'll manage itself for a while—
Damned if he's listening! Deaf! That's
  his style.
What a mess! A God unable to answer
  prayers! [*Beckoning upward.*]
Hsst! I'm rid of the slave plantation!
Look what I did for the China mis-
  sions!
One good turn, now isn't it worth
Another? Help me—! [*A sheet of flame
  leaps up from the yacht, followed by thick,
  billowing smoke, then the dull boom of an
  explosion.* PEER GYNT *lets out a shriek
  and drops to the sand. Gradually the
  smoke clears. The yacht has vanished.*
  PEER *is hushed and pale.*] The sword of
  wrath!
To the bottom, sunk—every man and
  mouse!
What a lucky chance! Oh, infinite
  praise— [*With emotion.*]
To chance? No, it was more than that.
I was fated to live, and they were not.
All thanks to Thee, who steadfastly
  loved
And shielded me, in spite of my sins—
  [*Draws a deep breath.*]
What a feeling of peace and confidence
To know I was singled out to be saved.
But the desert! What will I drink and
  eat?
Oh, I'll find something. He'll provide.
Nothing to fear—[*In a loud, wheedling
  tone.*] He wouldn't let
A poor little sparrow like me go unfed!
Be humble in spirit. And learn to wait.
Trust in the Lord with a will of iron—
  [*Springs to his feet in terror.*]
That noise in the brush, was that a lion?
  [*His teeth chattering.*]
No, that was no lion. [*Mustering cour-
  age.*] A lion, all right!
Those animals, they go their own way.
They don't bite their betters. They rely
On instinct; they can feel, for instance,
That it's dangerous playing with ele-
  phants.
All the same—I could do with a tree.
Over there, those acacias and palms;

If I climbed up, how secure I could
  be—
Especially if I could sing a few
  psalms—[*Clambers up.*]
"Morning and evening are not
  alike—"⁴⁴
Now that verse has often been
  analyzed. [*Settles himself comfortably.*]
How delightful to feel one's soul
  upraised.
Thinking noble is more than getting
  rich quick.
Trust all to Him. He knows just how
  full
He can portion my cup with
  wormwood and gall.
He does keep a fatherly eye on my
  fate—[*Glances out to sea and breathes
  with a sigh.*]
But economical—that He's not!

Scene 3

*Night. A Moroccan camp on the edge of the
desert. Watch fires and lounging soldiers.*
A SLAVE. [*Runs in and tears his hair.*]
  Gone! The Emperor's white charger,
  gone!
ANOTHER SLAVE. [*Runs in and rends his
  garments.*] The Emperor's sacred
  robes have been stolen!
MOORISH CAPTAIN. [*Coming up.*] Find
  them, or a hundred lashes will fall on
The bare feet of all you excuses for
  men! [*The soldiers mount horse and gallop off in all directions.*]

Scene 4

*Daybreak. The grove of acacias and palms.
Up in his tree,* PEER GYNT, *with a broken
branch in his hand, is beating off a pack
of monkeys.*
PEER GYNT. Wretched! A most dis-
  agreeable night. [*Striking about him.*]
Are you back again? Oh, hell's bells,
They're throwing fruit! No, it's some-
  thing else—
The monkey is such a disgusting brute!
"Watch and fight," as the Scripture says,
But I can't do that, when I'm dull and
  weary. [*Freshly attacked; loses patience.*]
I'll put a spike in their repertory!
Let me get hold of one of those boys,
Hang him, skin him, and worm inside

Whatever's left of his shaggy hide,
So the others honor the family ties—
What is man anyway? Only a mote.
Fashion and custom can guide us a bit—
Still they come on! Swarming like locusts.
Get away! Shoo! The gibbering fools.
Oh, if I only had a false tail—
Something so I'd resemble the beasts—
Now what? That pattering overhead—!
[*Looking up.*]
An old one—brandishing filth in his paws—! [*Crouches apprehensively and remains still for a time. The ape makes a gesture;* PEER GYNT *stairs coaxing him, as if he were a dog.*]
Ah—there's a boy, good old Bus!
He's reasonable. And perfectly bred.
Would he throw—? No, not on your life—
It's me! Pip-pip! We're the best of friends!
Ai-ai! There now, he understands.
Bus and I, why, we're relatives—
But can have sugar tomorrow—! The beast!
The whole load on top of me! Ugh, horrible—!
Or could it be food? It tastes—equivocal;
But then, it's habit that forms our taste.
Who was that thinker, the one who wrote:
"Spit, and trust to the force of habit"—?
Hi, now the young! [*Striking about.*] But this is crazy,
That man, who's lord of this universe,
Should have to put up with—! Help! Mercy!
The old one's foul, but the children are worse!

Scene 5

Early morning. A rocky ground overlooking the desert. On one side, a cleft in the rocks and a cave. A THIEF *and a* FENCE *in the cleft with the Emperor's horse and robes. The horse, richly caparisoned, stands tied to a stone. Riders can be seen far off.*

THE THIEF. The tongues of the lances
Flicker and flash—
See, see!
THE FENCE. They lick at my head—
I feel them slash!
Woe, woe!
THE THIEF. [*Folding his arms across his chest.*] My father stole;
His son must steal.
THE FENCE. My father's a fence;
I'm a fence as well.
THE THIEF. You must bear your lot;
Be the self you were taught.
THE FENCE. [*Listening.*] Steps in the thicket!
Away! But where?
THE THIEF. The cavern is deep,
And the Prophet near! [*They flee, leaving their stolen goods. The riders vanish in the distance.* PEER *comes in, cutting himself a reed pipe.*]
PEER GYNT. What a delicious morning! How mild!
The scarab's rolling his ball in the dust;
The snail pokes out of his shell to feast.
Morning! Yes, it's the purest gold—
Just think what marvelous potency
Nature gave to the light of day.
You feel so safe—your courage swells—
You could easily wrestle a couple of bulls—
How peaceful! Oh, the country joys—
Strange I never felt them before;
Why be penned in some crowded place,
Victim to every knock at the door—?
Ah, look at the lizards whisking their tails,
Snapping and thinking of nothing at all.
What innocence the animals have!
They each obey the Creator's will,
Hold their own features immutable,
Are themselves, themselves through joy and strife
Just as they were when He first said,
"Live!" [*Puts on his pince-nez.*]
A toad—in a sandstone block. The rough
Stone frames him in. Only his face is
Showing. The way he sits and gazes
At the world and is to himself—
enough—[*Reflectively.*]
Enough! Himself—? Now where's that from?
It must be some classic I read it in.
The prayer book was it? Or Proverbs then?
Maddening, how with passing time
My memory for dates and places dims.

[*Sits down in the shade.*]
Here's a cool spot for tired feet.
And look, ferns growing. Edible roots.
[*Eats a little.*]
This food's better fit for an animal—
But it's written, "Our nature must be molded."
And elsewhere, "Pride must have a fall."
And, "He who's humbled shall be exalted." [*Uneasily.*]
Exalted? For me it will happen too—
There's just no other possible end.
Fate will guide me out of this land
And arrange it so that I come through.
This all is a trial, but I'll be spared
If only, God grant, my health's not impaired. [*Shakes off such thoughts, lights a cigar, stretches out, and surveys the desert.*]
What an immense, unbounded waste—
There in the distance, an ostrich strides—
What can one think was really God's
Meaning in these endless miles of dust?
This desert, lacking all sources of life;
This burnt-out cinder on the world's roof—
This patch on the map, forever blank;
This corpse since the dawn of time, that can't
Give its Maker so much as thanks—
Why was it formed—? Nature's extravagant.
Is that the sea eastward, that shimmering streak?
No, it can't be. That's a mirage.
The sea's to the west behind my back,
Dammed out from the plain by a sloping ridge. [*A thought flashes through him.*]
Dammed out? Then I could—! The hills are small.
Dammed out! A cut, that's it; a canal—
Like a river of life, the waters would run
In through the channel and flood the plain
Soon all this furnace of sand and rock
Would be as fresh as a rippling lake.
Oases would rise like desert isles,
Atlas turn green like our mountain coast;
White sails would skim, like wind-blown gulls,
Southward where once the caravans passed.
Quickening breezes would scatter the fumes
Of decay, and dew would drop from the sky;
Men will come building city on city,
And grass will grow round the swaying palms.
Beyond the Sahara the country south
Will be the new cradle of human growth.
Factories will hum in Timbuktu;
Bornu[46] will soon be colonized, while
Up through Habes[47] explorers will go
By sleeping car to the Upper Nile.
In the midst of my sea, on a rich oasis,
I'll reproduce the Nordic races.
The dalesman's blood is royal almost;
Arabian crossings will do the rest.
Within a cove, on a shelving strand,
I'll found Peeropolis, my capital.
The world's obsolete! Now the ages call.
For Gyntiana,[48] my virgin land!
[*Springs up*]
Only the funding; then it's set—
A key of gold for the ocean's gate!
A crusade against Death! Let the grim miser
Spill the sack where he hoards his treasure.
In every country, freedom burns—
Like the ass in the ark,[49] I'll send a cry
Round the world and baptize in liberty
The bright shores, dreaming in their chains.
Capital! Raise it! Find a source—!
My kingdom—no, half of it—for a horse![50] [*The horse whinnies among the rocks.*] A horse! Clothing—! Jewels—!
And a sword! [*Going closer.*]
It can't be! But, yes—! Faith is a force,
A mover of mountains, that I've heard—
But, that it also can move a horse—?
Pah! The fact is, the horse is real—
Ab esse ad posse et cetera,[51] as well— [*Puts on the robes and regards himself.*]
Sir Peter—and Turk from head to toe!
How life provides if you give it a chance—
Come on, Grane, up we go! [*Climbs into the saddle.*]
And under my feet, gold stirrups now—!
You can tell great men by the style of

their mounts! [*Gallops off into the desert.*]

Scene 6

The tent of an Arab chief in an oasis. PEER GYNT, *in his eastern dress, reclines on cushions. He is drinking coffee and smoking a long pipe.* ANITRA *and a company of girls are dancing and singing to him.*
CHORUS OF GIRLS. The prophet has come!
The Prophet, the Lord, the All-knowing Mind,
Has come to us riding, to us has come
Over the ocean of sand!
The Prophet, the Lord, the Unfailing One,
Has come to us sailing, to us has come
Over the ocean of dunes!
   Sound the flute and the drum;
The Prophet, the Prophet has come!
ANITRA. His steed is like milk, the purest white
That streams in the rivers of Paradise.
Bend your knee! Cover your face!
His eyes are stars, tender and bright.
No child of clay can endure
The rays of their heavenly fire.
   Out of the desert he came.
Gold and pearls blazed on his chest.
Where he rode, the sun passed.
Behind him was night,
Simoon and drought.
He, the All-glorious, came!
Out of the desert he came,
Dressed like a son of man.
Kaaba,[52] Kaabe's a tomb—
He has enlightened his own!
CHORUS OF GIRLS. Sound the flute and the drum;
The Prophet, the Prophet has come!
[*They dance on to quiet music.*]
PEER GYNT. I've read it in print—and I'll be bound,
"No man's a prophet in his native land."
All this pleases me so much better
Than life among the Charleston traders.
There was something hollow in that affair,
Something bogus and alien there—
I never could feel myself at home,
Never really fit in with them.

What did I ever want in that crew,[53]
Rooting around in the bins of trade?
When I think it over, I hardly know—
It happened, that's all; so let it ride.
   To be yourself on a base of gold
Is the same as building your house on sand.
For a watch and a ring, the wealth you wield,
The people grovel and lick your hand;
They tip their hats to a diamond pin,
But the ring and stickpin aren't the man—
A prophet! That has a lot more point.
There, at least, you know your place.
If you're taken up, it's *yourself* they praise,
Yourself, and not your bank account.
You are what you are, and no mistake;
You owe no credit to chance or luck,
Or the support of some patent or grant—
A prophet! It's really the thing for me.
And to think it took me so unaware—
I was simply crossing the desert here
And these children of nature barred the way.
They made it plain that their prophet had come.
I really didn't try to deceive—
A lie and a prophet's reply aren't the same;
Besides, you know, I can always leave.
I'm not tied down; no cause for depression—
The deal, so to say, is thoroughly private;
I can go as I came; my horse is all set;
In short, I'm on top of the situation.
ANITRA. [*Approaching.*] Prophet and Lord!
PEER GYNT. Yes, my slave?
ANITRA. The sons of the desert are nearing thy tent;
They ask a glimpse of thy features—
PEER GYNT. Stop!
At a distance, tell them to muster up.
At a distance, let them be reverent.
And add, no man may enter this grove!
   Men, my child, are a slippery batch—
Low-minded, itchy-fingered, wild—!
Anitra, you couldn't guess how much
They've swind—I mean, have sinned, my child—
Enough of that! Dance, my maidens!
Let the Prophet forget his heavy

burdens.
THE GIRLS. [*Dancing.*] The Prophet is
   good; his heart is grieved
By the evil the sons of dust have loved!
The Prophet is gentle; for this, all
   praise;
He raises sinners to Paradise!
PEER GYNT. [*His eyes following* ANITRA *in
   her dance.*] Her legs go like
   drumsticks; faster still.
Ai! She's a succulent dish, that quail.
Her figure has some extravagant
   forms—
Hardly in line with beauty's norms;
But then, what's beauty? Convention's
   choice—
A coin made current by time and place.
It's such extravagances that enchant
When you've had it to here with the
   normal run.
Keep the legal limit, and you cheat
   your fun.
They're either too stout, or else too
   gaunt,
Disturbingly young, or grimly
   antique—
The ones in between make you sick—
   Her feet, they're not entirely clean;
Same with the arms; especially the one.
But that's no cause to be critical.
In fact, it's one morsel of her appeal—
   Anitra, hear me!
ANITRA. [*Approaching.*] Thy hand-
   maiden hears!
PEER GYNT. Child, you're bewitching!
   Lo, you inspire
The Prophet. If you doubt me, con-
   sider this:
I'll make you a houri in Paradise!
ANITRA. Impossible, Lord!
PEER GYNT. Would I deceive?
I'm dead serious, sure as I live!
ANITRA. But I have no soul.
PEER GYNT. It's what you'll get!
ANITRA. But how my Lord?
PEER GYNT. I'll see to that—
I'm taking over your education.
No soul? Yes, you are rather dumb;
It's struck me, with a certain vexation.
But, for a soul, there's always room.
Come here! Let me measure your
   braincase—
There's room, room enough; I *knew*
   there was.
It's true—you aren't ever going to go
Very deep; a *large* soul isn't for you—
But, after all, what's the difference—
You'll have enough for all your wants—
ANITRA. The Prophet is kind—
PEER GYNT. You hesitate? Well!
ANITRA. But I'd rather have—
PEER GYNT. Come on, speak out!
ANITRA. When it comes to a soul, I
   think I can wait
But give me—
PEER GYNT. What?
ANITRA. [*Points at his turban.*] That
   pretty opal!
PEER GYNT. [*Enraptured, giving her the
   jewel.*] Anitra! Child! Eve's own
   daughter!
Like a magnet drawing me—for I'm a
   man;
And just as he said, that well-known
   writer:
"*Das Ewig-Weibliche zieht uns an!*"[54]

Scene 7

*A moonlit night. The palm grove outside
   ANITRA's tent.* PEER GYNT, *with an Ara-
   bian lute in hand, sits under a tree. His
   beard and hair have been trimmed; he
   looks noticeably younger.*
PEER GYNT. [*Plays and sings.*] I locked
   away my paradise
And carried off the key,
Sailed out before the northern breeze,
While lovely ladies spent their cries
Forlornly by the sea.

Southward, southward raced the keel
Across the ocean stream.
Where palm trees swaying proud and
   tall
Around a bay stood sentinel,
I put my ship to flame.

I climbed aboard the desert ship,
A ship on four swift legs.
It foamed beneath the lashing whip;
Oh, catch me on the wing! I slip,
A songbird, through the twigs!

Anitra! Nectar of the palm
Is how I see thee now!
Angora goat cheese in its prime
Gives hardly half so sweet a balm,
Anitra, dear, as thou! [*Hangs the lute
   over his shoulder and approaches the
   tent.*]
Silence! Did my beauty listen?
What did she think of my little song?

Is she spying behind the curtain,
Stripped of veils and everything?
What's that? Sounds like someone tore
A cork from a bottle violently!
Again? And again! What could it be?
Sighs, perhaps? Love's melody—
No, that was a definite snore—
Sweetest music! Anitra sleeps.
Nightingale, be muted now!
Ten thousand plagues will lay you low
If you dare to match your chirps and
   peeps—
Oh well, as the book says, let it go!
The nightingale is a troubadour;
And, for all that, so am I.
Both of us with our music snare
Hearts that are tender, mild, and shy.
The cool of night is made for singing;
Song defines our common role.
Song is our way of remaining
Us, Peer Gynt and the nightingale.
And just that, my beauty's there asleep
Is the crowning bliss of love—
No more; only to touch my lip
To the cup, and leave the nectar safe—
But look, she's coming out at last!
Well, after all, that is the best.
ANITRA. [*From the tent.*] Lord, were you
   calling in the night?
PEER GYNT. Yes, I was; the Prophet's
   calling.
I was awakened by the cat
Out hunting, with a frightful yowling.
ANITRA. Those weren't sounds of hunt-
   ing, Lord;
It was something worse you heard.
PEER GYNT. What was it, then?
ANITRA. Oh, spare me!
PEER GYNT. Tell!
ANITRA. Oh, I'm blushing—
PEER GYNT. [*Coming closer.*] Could it
   have been
That feeling that suffused me when
I made you a present of my opal?
ANITRA. [*Horrified.*] You compare your-
   self, oh earth's delight,
With an old disgusting alley cat!
PEER GYNT. Child, in love's delirium,
A prophet and a tomcat come
Out to very much the same.
ANITRA. Lord, from your lips diversion
   flows
Like beads of honey.
PEER GYNT. Little one—
You, like other girls, appraise
Only the surfaces of great men.

Inside me, comedy runs wild,
The more when we're alone like this.
In my position, I'm compelled
To mask it under seriousness.
The day's routine is a heavy weight;
All the worry and distress
That comes to me on every face
Makes me prophetically morose;
But only from the surface out—
No more! Away! In a tête-à-tête,
I'm what I've always been—I'm Peer.
Hi, the prophet gets his hat;
He's gone! Myself, you have me here!
   [*Sits under a tree and draws her to him.*]
Come, Anitra, rest a while
Beneath the palm tree's emerald fan.
Let me whisper to your smile;
Later we'll change roles, and then
I'll lie and smilingly approve
Your fresh, young lips that whisper
   love.
ANITRA. [*Stretching out at his feet.*] The
   words you speak like music fall;
I wish I followed the meaning better.
Master, tell me, can your daughter,
Just by listening, gain a soul?
PEER GYNT. The spirit's light and truth,
   a soul—Yes, you'll gain one after a
   spell.
When the rose-streaked east horizon
Reads, in gold print—"Now it's day"—
Then, my puss, you'll have your lesson;
You'll be tutored properly.
But in the night's enchanted calm
It would be stupid if my aim
Were only, with some worn-out tags
Of learning, to play pedagogue.
In our lives, the soul is—once
You see it rightly—not the key.
It's the heart that really counts.
ANITRA. Speak, oh Master! In your
   meaning
Now I see light, like opals shining!
PEER GYNT. Too much cunning ends in
   folly;
The fruit of fear is cruelty;
Truth, exaggerated, can
Be wisdom written upside down.
Yes, my child—I'd take my oath
And swear that there's a certain class
Of soul-inflated folk on earth
Who won't reach clarity with ease.
I knew a fellow just like that,[55]
The pearl he was of all the lot;
Yet even he mistook the point
And lost his meaning, spouting rant.

Around this grove, you see the wastes?
If I swung my turban to the skies,
I could make the seven seas
Pour in and drown these miles of dust.
But I'd be simply out of mind
To go creating seas and lands.
Do you know what it means to live?[56]
ANITRA. Teach me that!
PEER GYNT. It's just to move
Dryshod down the stream of time,
Oneself, intact, beyond all claim.
Only in full manhood can I
Be what I am, my dearest joy!
Old eagles shed their feathers,
Old beggars lag their paths,
Old fishwives lose their teeth,
Old hands of dotards wither;
All of them wither in their souls—
Youth! Oh, youth! I want to reign
Like a sultan, fiery in my pulse—
Not on Gyntiana's shores
Under vine and palm-tree arbors—
But grounded in the fresher green,
Of a maiden's pure desires.
   Now do you see, my little one,
Why I've paid you gracious court—
Why I singled out your heart
To be, as it were, the cornerstone
Of all my being's caliphate?
Over your longings, I'll be lord.
In passion, I'm an autocrat!
You must be mine, and mine alone.
I'll be always there to guard
Your charms like a jeweled cameo.
If we should part, then life is over—
Nota bene, that is, for *you!*
I want your every inch and fiber
Drained of will and, utterly
Past resistance, filled with me.
Your nest of midnight hair, your skin,
Everything lovely one could name,
Will, like the gardens of Babylon,
Beckon me to my sultan's realm.
   So it's lucky, after all,
You've kept your head so vacuous.
Those who entertain a soul
Get swallowed in self-consciousness.
Listen, while we're on this thing—
My truelove, if you like, I'll do
Your beauty proud with an ankle
   ring—
It's best, as well, for me and you
If *I'm* installed where your soul is
   hiding—
As for the rest—it's status quo. [ANITRA
   snores.]

What? Asleep! Has it gone gliding
Past her, everything I've said?
No; it shows the mark I've made,
That, borne on my passionate stream
Of speech, she's wafted into dreams.
   [*Rises and lays jewels in her lap.*]
Take these jewels! And here, some
   more!
Sleep, Anitra! Dream of Peer—
Sleep on! Your slumber is a crown
Upon your emperor's flow of wit!
Character is the cornerstone
Of the victory Peer Gynt won tonight.

Scene 8

A caravan route. The oasis far off in the distance. PEER GYNT, *on his white horse, comes galloping across the desert, with* ANITRA *in front on his saddle-bow.*

ANITRA. Let go; I'll bite!
PEER GYNT. Now, puss, behave!
ANITRA. What are you up to?
PEER GYNT. Playing hawk and dove.
I abduct you! And do mad tricks!
ANITRA. Shame! An old prophet—!
PEER GYNT. What foolishness!
The prophet isn't old, you goose!
Is this a role that old age picks?
ANITRA. Let go! You take me home!
PEER GYNT. Coquette!
Home? To father-in-law? How neat!
We mad birds that fly our cages
Can't ever go back where *he* can watch
   us.
Besides, my child, it never pays
To stay too long in any one place.
What's won in friendship is lost in esteem—
That's where prophets and such get
   caught.
You must flash in view, then fade like a
   dream.
It was time to close the visit out.
The sons of the desert are fickle at
   heart—
The prayers and incense were running
   short.
ANITRA. But *are* you a prophet?
PEER GYNT. I'm your emperor! [*Tries to
   kiss her.*]
My, how ruffled our feathers are!
ANITRA. Give me that ring there on
   your finger.
PEER GYNT. Anitra dear, you can have

them all!
ANITRA. Your words are songs! Sweetly they linger.
PEER GYNT. Bliss, to know that one's loved so well!
Wait! I'll lead the horse, as your slave! [*Hands her the riding whip and gets off.*]
There, my rosebud, my dainty flower;
I'll push on over the desert, move
Till I'm felled by sunstroke and expire.
I'm young, Anitra; remember that!
Don't give my highjinks too much weight.
Jokes and games are youth's own splendor!
If your mind wasn't such a languid thing,
You'd know, my fetching oleander—
That your lover jokes—*ergo*, he's young!
ANITRA. Yes, you're young. The rings, have you more?
PEER GYNT. Aren't I? Here, catch! I can leap like a deer!
If I had vineleaves, I'd crown my brow.
Hi, but I'm young! I'm dancing now! [*Dances and sings.*]
  Oh, I'm a happy rooster!
  Peck me, my little chick!
  Hi! See the footwork, look—
  Oh, I'm a happy rooster!
ANITRA. You're sweating, prophet; I'm afraid you'll melt—
Throw me that heavy bag at your belt.
PEER GYNT. What thoughtfulness! Keep it, child—
Hearts full of love can live without gold! [*Dances and sings again.*]
  Young Peer Gynt is a zany—
  He doesn't know what foot he's standing on.
    Ffft, says Peer—ffft, be gone—
  Young Peer Gynt is a zany!
ANITRA. The dance of the prophet charms and soothes.
PEER GYNT. Stuff the prophet! Let's switch clothes!
Here! Undress!
ANITRA. Your caftan's too long;
Your waistband's too wide; your stockings, all wrong—
PEER GYNT. *Eh bien!* [*Kneels.*] But give me a piercing sorrow—
Hearts full of love find suffering sweet!
And when you enter my castle door, you—
ANITRA. Your paradise—is it much farther yet?
PEER GYNT. Oh, a thousand miles—
ANITRA. Too far!
PEER GYNT. I swear—
You'll get the soul I promised before.
ANITRA. Thanks—I'll make it without a soul.
But you asked for a sorrow—
PEER GYNT. [*Rising.*] By heaven, yes!
Racking, but brief—for two or three days.
ANITRA. Anitra obeys the Prophet! Farewell! [*She cuts him sharply across the knuckles and gallops away full tilt across the desert.*]
PEER GYNT. [*Dumbfounded.*] Well, I'll be a—

Scene 9

The same, an hour later. PEER GYNT, *solemn and thoughtful, is stripping his Turkish costume off piece by piece. Finally he takes his little traveling cap out of his coat pocket, puts it on, and stands once more in European dress.*

PEER GYNT. [*Hurling the turban far away.*]
There lies the Turk, and here am I—!
Heathen existence just isn't for me.
Lucky it's only the clothes I wore,
And not burned into me like a scar—
What did I ever want in that crew?
It's best as a Christian to live in
This world, to stifle your peacock pride,
Take law and morality for your guide,
And be yourself, till at last you're given
Praise at your grave and wreaths on your coffin. [*Pacing a few steps.*]
That wench—she came within a hair
Of managing to turn my head.
I'll be a troll if I can figure
What it was that made me crazy mad.
Ah well, it's done! If I'd let things progress,
I could have appeared ridiculous.
I made a mistake. But it's consolation
That what I mistook was the situation.
It wasn't my inner self that fell.
It was that prophetical way of life,
So removed from the salt of honest toil,
That took revenge in a cheap rebuff.
The prophet's role is a sorry show!

The gist of the art is to grope in mist;
And if the prophet attempts to go
Straight and act sober, the game is lost.
In that sense, I really ran true to form
To fall when that goose turned on the
   charm.
Still, all the same—
[*Bursts out laughing.*] It piques your
   fancy!
To try to stop time by skipping and
   dancing;
To fight the current by preening and
   mincing!
To strum the lute, take love for a fact,
Then end like a hen—by getting
   plucked.
That's conduct to call prophetic
   frenzy—
Plucked! Oh Lord, I've been plucked
   all right!
Well, it's good that I kept a little out—
Some in America, and some in my
   pocket;
So I'll not be a beggar housed in a
   thicket.
And the happy medium is really best.
A coach-and-four isn't worth the cost—
Why should I travel like a patrician?
In short, I'm on top of the situation—
Now what should I choose? Such vistas
   call;
And choice marks the master from the
   fool.
My business life is a closed book;
My love game is a ragged cloak.
I'm not going crabwise, back again.
"Forward and back, it's just as far;
Out or in, it's a narrow door,"
Was written, I think, by some brilliant
   man.
For something new; some flight of
   valor;
Some end worth every effort and dol-
   lar
Spent! If I set my life story down
Complete, for guidance and imita-
   tion—?
Or, wait—! I've plenty of time on
   hand—
What if I went as a wandering scholar
To trace the past ages, the greed of
   mankind?
Yes, that's it! *There's* my place!
I always read legends as a child;
And now, with the sciences I've dis-
   tilled—

I'll follow the course of the human
   race!
I'll float like a feather on history's
   stream,
Relive it all, as if in a dream—
See the heroes battle for truth and
   right,
But as an onlooker, safe in thought—
See thinkers perish and martyrs bleed,
See empires rise and sweep to doom,
See the world epochs sprout from
   seed—
In short, I'll skim off history's cream.
I must get hold of a volume of
   Becker[57]
And become a strict chronological
   seeker.
It's true—my groundwork's not very
   deep.
And history's mazes can be a trap—
But then sometimes the wildest notions
Can lead to the most original con-
   clusions—
How exalting, to set up a goal
And drive right to it, like flint and
   steel! [*With quiet feeling.*]
To break off every tie that binds
One to homeland and to friends—
To blow one's treasured goods to bits—
Give all to love, then call it quits—
For truth, for light from the ultimate
   torch—[*Brushing a tear from his eye.*]
That's in the spirit of pure research!
I feel so happy, beyond compare.
Now I've unriddled my destiny here.
Now to hold out, through wealth and
   want!
I shouldn't be blamed for vanity if
I savor being the man Peer Gynt,
Called also the Emperor of Human
   Life—
The sum of the past I want to own;
Never come near the living again—
This age isn't worth the heel of my
   shoe.
Men have no faith, no substance now:
Souls without wings, deeds without
   weight—[*Shrugging his shoulders.*]
And the women—pah, they're a
   scrubby lot! [*Goes off.*]

Scene 10

*A summer day in the far north. A hut in the
forest. The door, with its large wooden*

bar, stands open. A reindeer horn over the doorway. A flock of goats by one wall. A MIDDLE-AGED WOMAN, *fair and still lovely, sits out in the sunlight, spinning.*

THE WOMAN. [*Glances down the path and sings.*] The winter may pass, and the spring disappear,
And next summer too, and the whole of the year—
But one day you'll come, I know that you will;
Then, as I promised, I'll wait for you still. [*Calls to the goats, spins, and sings again.*]
God give you strength if you wander alone!
God give you joy if you stand at His throne!
I'll wait for you here till you're home again, love;
And if heaven has you, we'll meet up above!

Scene 11

Egypt. The statue of Memnon,[58] *in the first light of dawn, surrounded by desert.* PEER GYNT *approaches on foot and studies the scene for a while.*

PEER GYNT. Here's a good spot for the trip to begin—
Now, for a change, I'll be an Egyptian,
Founded, that is, on a Gyntian core.
Then Assyria—I'll go there.
To start right back at the world's creation
Would only lead me into confusion—
I'll skip over Biblical fact and belief;
Their secular traces will give me enough;
And to put them under hard scrutiny
Lies beyond both my plan and ability.
[*Sitting on a rock.*]
Now let me rest and quietly wait
Till the statue's morning song floats out.
After breakfast, a climb up the pyramid;
Then, if there's time, I'll explore it inside.
Next, round the top of the Red Sea shore;
I might find the grave of King Potiphar—
Now I'm Asian. I'm searching for Babylon's
Famed hanging gardens and concubines—
In short, for the cultural spoor of mankind.
Next, to the walls of Troy in one bound.
From Troy there's a sea route goes direct
To Athens, queen city of monuments—
There I'll explore the pass that once
Leonidas fought and died to protect—
I'll study the leading philosophers,
Find Socrates' cell, where he ended his years—
Damn! I forgot—there's a war going on—!
Well, Hellenism I'll have to postpone.
[*Looks at his watch.*]
It's really absurd how long it takes
For the sun to rise. I'm wasting time.
So, after Troy—that's as far as I'd come—[*Gets up and listens.*]
What is it, that curious murmur that breaks—? [*Sunrise.*]

MEMNON'S STATUE. [*Sings.*] From the demigod's ashes rise youth-renewing birds brightly singing.
Zeus, the All-knowing,
made struggle their longing.
Wise Owl, among
birds, is sleep so much safer?
You must die or decipher
this riddle in song!

PEER GYNT. Fantastic—I do think the statue expressed
Those sounds! Music, it was, of the past.[59]
I heard the stone voice rise and then fall—
I'll write it up for the scholars to mull.
[*Writes in his notebook.*]
"The statue sang. Heard definite tones,
But can't quite figure what it all means.
A hallucination, obviously.
Nothing else worthy of note today."
[*Moves on.*]

Scene 12

Near the village of Gizeh. The Great Sphinx, carved out of rock. Far off, the spires and minarets of Ciaro. PEER GYNT *enters; he observes the Sphinx with some care, by turns first through his pince-nez*

and then through his hollowed hand.
PEER GYNT. Where in the world did I meet up before
With this thing, this nightmare from long ago?
I know we've met—up north, or here.
Was it a person? And, if so, who?
Memnon, it came to me afterward,
Looked like the King of the Dovre Trolls,
The way he was sitting, stiff as a board,
With pillars propping his bottom like stools—
But this wonder that's neither fish nor fowl,
This break, this lion and woman joined—
Is it also out of some fairy tale?
Or something real that I've held in mind—?
From a fairy tale? Ho, I remember the brute!
It's the Boyg, of course, whose skull I split—
Or dreamed I did—I was ill of fever—
[*Going closer.*]
The selfsame eyes; the lips, same as ever—
Not quite so listless, a bit more sly;
But otherwise, one and the same to a tee.
So that's it, Boyg; you look like a lion,
Seen from behind by the light of day.
You still make riddles? We can try one
And see if you answer the same in this too—! [*Calls to the Sphinx.*]
Hi, Boyg, who are you?
A VOICE. [*Behind the Sphinx.*] Ach, Sphinx, *wer bist du?*
PEER GYNT. What? An echo in German? How odd!
THE VOICE. *Wer bist du?*
PEER GYNT. The accent, it's very good!
This observation is new, and mine.
[*Writes in his notebook.*]
"Echo speaks German. Dialect—Berlin." [BEGRIFFENFELDT *comes out from behind the Sphinx.*]
BEGRIFFENFELDT. A man!
PEER GYNT. So *he's* the explanation.
[*Notes again.*]
"Later came to another conclusion."
BEGRIFFENFELDT. [*With agitated gestures.*] Pardon, *mein Herr*—! *Eine Lebensfrage*—!
What brought you here at just this second?
PEER GYNT. A visit. I'm greeting a childhood friend.
BEGRIFFENFELDT. The Sphinx—?
PEER GYNT. [*Nods.*] An early page in my saga.
BEGRIFFENFELDT. Splendid! And this after, ah, what a night!
My head is throbbing. It's ready to burst!
You know him? Speak, man! Tell me first
What is he?
PEER GYNT. What is he? Nothing to that. He's *himself.*
BEGRIFFENFELDT. [*With a bound.*] The riddle of life, in a blaze
Of light, is clear? You're sure that he *is* Himself?
PEER GYNT. Yes; or that's what he says.
BEGRIFFENFELDT. Himself? Revolution's hour is close! [*Takes off his hat.*]
Your name, *mein Herr?*
PEER GYNT. I was christened Peer Gynt.
BEGRIFFENFELDT. [*With quiet admiration.*] Peer Gynt! Allegorical! The One foreseen—
Peer Gynt? Which is to say: the Unknown—
He whose coming came to me as a portent—
PEER GYNT. No, really! So now you're here to bring in—?
BEGRIFFENFELDT. Peer Gynt! Profound! Mystical! Robust!
Each word is like a fathomless sea!
What are you?
PEER GYNT. [*Modestly.*] I've always attempted to be
Myself. My passport covers the rest.
BEGRIFFENFELDT. Again the mysterious phase intoned! [*Seizes his wrist.*]
To Cairo! The Interpreters' Emperor is found!
PEER GYNT. Emperor?
BEGRIFFENFELDT. Come!
PEER GYNT. Have they heard of me?
BEGRIFFENFELDT. [*Pulling him along.*]
The Interpreters' Emperor—by self's decree!

Scene 13

In Cairo. A large courtyard enclosed by high walls and buildings. Barred windows;

iron cages. THREE KEEPERS *in the yard. A* FOURTH *enters.*
FOURTH KEEPER. Say, Schafmann, where's the director gone?
FIRST KEEPER. Went out this morning before it was light.
FOURTH KEEPER. Something's gotten him all upset;
Last night—
SECOND KEEPER. Hsst, quiet; he's coming in! [BEGRIFFENFELDT *enters, leading* PEER GYNT, *locks the gate and puts the key in his pocket.*]
PEER GYNT. [*To himself.*] This man is incredibly talented;
Nearly all he says goes over my head. [*Looking about.*]
So here we are, in the Scholars' Club?
BEGRIFFENFELDT. Here's where you'll find them, all that mob—
The threescore and ten Interpreters;[60]
Now raised by a hundred and sixty more—[*Shouts at the* KEEPERS.]
Mikkel, Schlingelberg, Schafmann, Fuchs—
Into the cages, in just two shakes!
KEEPERS. Us?
BEGRIFFENFELDT. Who else? Come on! Get in!
When the world goes spinning, we have to spin. [*Forces them into a cage.*]
He came this morning, Peer the Great—
You can guess the rest—I'll leave it at that. [*Locks the cage and throws the key down a well.*]
PEER GYNT. But Doctor—my dear Herr Director, please—
BEGRIFFENFELDT. Not anymore! That's what I *was*—
Can you keep a secret? I have a confession—
PEER GYNT. [*Increasingly uneasy.*] What's that?
BEGRIFFENFELDT. You think you can stand the shock?
PEER GYNT. Well, I'll try—
BEGRIFFENFELDT. [*Draws him into a corner and whispers.*] Absolute Reason
Died last night at eleven o'clock.
PEER GYNT. Good God—!
BEGRIFFENFELDT. Yes, it's really deplorable.
And in *my* position, doubly horrible,
For these grounds have been, up to this time,
An insane asylum.[61]
PEER GYNT. An insane asylum!
BEGRIFFENFELDT. But not now!
PEER GYNT. [*Pale and subdued.*] This place, now I recognize it.
The man's gone mad—and nobody knows it! [*Moves away.*]
BEGRIFFENFELDT. [*Following him.*] I wouldn't want you to misunderstand.
When I say He's dead—I'm making jokes.
He's escaped himself. He's come unskinned
Just like my countryman Munchausen's fox.[62]
PEER GYNT. Excuse me—
BEGRIFFENFELDT. [*Catching hold of him.*] He was more like an eel than
A fox. That's it! Through the eye, a pin—
He writhed on the wall—
PEER GYNT. Who can rescue me—!
BEGRIFFENFELDT. Round the neck, a slit—and whip! it's free
Of its skin!
PEER GYNT. Crazy! He's lost his mind!
BEGRIFFENFELDT. You can't get away from it; it's clear—
This escape-from-selfing has to inspire
Complete revolution in every land.
Those persons who before were called crackbrain
At eleven last night became quite sane,
Conforming to Reason's latest phase.
And from this standpoint, it's even more
Clear that, at that identical hour,
The so-called sane lost their faculties.
PEER GYNT. You mentioned the hour; my time is short—
BEGRIFFENFELDT. Your time? That gives my thinking a spurt! [*Opens a door and calls out.*]
Come forth! The veil of the future is rent!
Reason is dead. Long live Peer Gynt!
PEER GYNT. My man, you're too kind—!
[*The lunatics come, one after another, into the courtyard.*]
BEGRIFFENFELDT. Good morning! Come in.
Greet the dawning age of liberation!
Your emperor's here!
PEER GYNT. Emperor?
BEGRIFFENFELDT. Yes!
PEER GYNT. But the honor's too much;

it's way beyond—
BEGRIFFENFELDT. Ah, false modesty—
  don't let it bind
This moment.
PEER GYNT. Give me some peace—!
No, I'm not worthy! What can I say?
BEGRIFFENFELDT. A man who brought
  the Sphinx to bay?
A man who's himself?
PEER GYNT. But that's just it.
I'm myself in everything I do;
But as far as I can see, here you
Have to be beside yourself to rate.
BEGRIFFENFELDT. Beside yourself? What
  a huge mistake!
Everyone here is himself to the gills,
Completely himself and nothing else—
So far in himself he can't come back.
Everyone's shut in his cask of skin;
He dives in the self's fermenting murk,
Hermetically sealed by a self-made
  cork—
Shrinking his staves down a well of
  brine.
No one has tears for the others' griefs,
Or feels at all for the others' beliefs.
We're ourselves in every thought and
  tone,
Ourselves to the farthest margin out—
And so, if an emperor on a throne
Is what we need, you're exactly right.
PEER GYNT. Oh, how the devil—!
BEGRIFFENFELDT. Don't feel blue;
Nearly all that is once had to be new.
"Oneself"—here, look, I'll show you a
  case;
I'll pick at random the first that
  passes—[*To a dark figure.*]
Good day, Huhu![63] Why's there a crisis
Always written across your face?
HUHU. Can I help it when my nation
Dies without interpretation? [*To* PEER
  GYNT.]
You're a stranger; want to hear?
PEER GYNT. [*Bows.*] Why, of course!
HUHU. Then lend an ear—
Strung like garlands, eastward far,
Lie the coasts of Malabar.
Dutch and Portuguese have seeded
Culture with the goods they traded,
While the jungle hid their quarries—
Droves of native Malabaris.
These get by on hybrid words—
In that country they're the lords—
But the ages past belong
To the fierce orangoutang.

He, the forest's lord and master,
Free to fight or merely bluster—
Shaped direct from nature's hand,
How he gaped and how he whined.
Unrestrained he shrieked his fill;
He was monarch over all—
But then foreign sirens sang,
Muddling our primeval tongue,
While four centuries of sleep
Quelled the vigor of the ape—
For, you know, a night like that
Snuffs a people's spirit out.
No more forest cries are heard;
Growls and grunts now go ignored—
If we want to share our views,
Language is the crutch we use.
What a curse on every race!
Hollanders and Portuguese,
Malabaris, octaroons—
All are punished for their pains.
I have tried to keep in touch
With the old, authentic speech—
Tried to raise its corpse and strike
For the people's right to shriek—
Shriek myself and bring new fire
To the folk songs we admire.
Still, my efforts win no favor—
Now you see the way I suffer.
Thanks for lending me your ear—
How would you advise me, sir?
PEER GYNT. [*To himself.*] It's been said:
  when wolves are howling,
Then it's wise to do some growling.
  [*Aloud.*]
Friend, if I remember right,
In Morocco there's a spot
Where the apes are pining for
Poets and interpreters.
Their tongue sounded Malabaric,
Folkloristic, prehistoric!
Why don't you, like other gentry,
Emigrate to serve your country?
HUHU. Thanks for lending me your
  ear—
You have counseled; I concur. [*With a
  sweeping gesture.*]
East! Thy bard has suffered wrongs!
West! Thou has orangoutangs! [*He
  goes.*]
BEGRIFFENFELDT. Well, was he himself?
I think he was.
Completely filled with his own distress.
Himself in all that his thoughts in-
  volve—
Himself by being beside himself.
Come here! I'll show you another one

Who found last night he was truly sane.
[*To a* FELLAH *carrying a mummy on his back.*]⁶⁴
King Apis, how goes my noble lord?
FELLAH. [*Wildly, to* PEER GYNT.] Am I King Apis?
PEER GYNT. [*Shrinking behind the doctor.*] Well, it's hard
To say; I don't know the situation.
But if I were judging by your passion—
FELLAH. Now you're lying too.
BEGRIFFENFELDT. Your Highness should tell
How matters stand.
FELLAH. As you will. [*Turning to* PEER GYNT.]
You see him, there on my shoulders?
His name was Apis, the King.
Now he goes by the name of a mummy,
And he's dead to everything.
   He built the pyramids skyward
And carved out the mighty Sphinx,
And fought, as the Doctor puts it,
With the Turk both *rechts* and *links*.
   For this the people of Egypt
Hailed him a god over all,
And raised him up in the temples
In the likeness of a bull.⁶⁵
   But *I* am this same King Apis,
I see that as plain as day;
And if you can't understand me,
I'll clear it up right away.
   King Apis, you see, was out hunting
When he suddenly started to squirm,
And he got off his horse and retired
To part of my ancestor's farm.
   But the field that King Apis manured
Has nourished *me* with its corn;
And if more proof is required,
Well—I have an invisible horn.
   Now isn't it quite outrageous
That no one bows down to my might!
By birth, I'm Apis, the pharaoh,
But a fellah in other men's sight.
   If you see my course of action,
Please put it to me straight—
The thing is, what can I do now
To be like King Apis the Great?
PEER GYNT. Build pyramids, your Highness,
And carve out a mightier Sphinx,
And fight, as the Doctor puts it,
With the Turk both *rechts* and *links*.
FELLAH. Yes, that's very high-spoken!
A fellah! A hungry louse!
It's enough just keeping my hovel
Empty of rats and mice.
   Quick, man—find something better,
A greatness firm as a rock
To make me the spitting image
Of Apis here on my back!
PEER GYNT. What if you hanged your Highness
And then, in the earth's deep bed
And the coffin's natural confines,
Behaved like one totally dead?
FELLAH. I'll do it! My life for a gallows!
A rope to hold my weight!
At first there'll be some difference,
But time will even that out. [*Goes off and prepares to hang himself.*]
BEGRIFFENFELDT. Now that's personality, *mein Herr*—
A man of method—
PEER GYNT. Oh yes, I'm sure—
But he's really hanging himself! God in heaven!
I feel sick—! My brain's like an oven!
BEGRIFFENFELDT. A state of transition; it won't last long.
PEER GYNT. Transition? To what?
Sorry—I'm going—
BEGRIFFENFELDT. [*Holding him.*] Are you mad?
PEER GYNT. Not yet. Mad? Good Lord!
[*Commotion.* HUSSEIN, *a cabinet minister,*⁶⁶ *pushes his way through the crowd.*]
HUSSEIN. They tell me an emperor came today. [*To* PEER GYNT.]
Is it you?
PEER GYNT. [*In despair.*] It's turning out that way!
HUSSEIN. Good. You have dispatches to be answered?
PEER GYNT. [*Tearing his hair.*] Yes! Why not? The madder, the better!
HUSSEIN. Would you honor me, sire, with a dip for your letter? [*Bowing low.*]
I am a pen.
PEER GYNT. [*Bows lower still.*] And I'm a sorry
Scrap of imperial stationery.
HUSSEIN. My story, sire, I can put in one line:
They call me a blotter, but I'm a pen.
PEER GYNT. My story, Sir Pen, is quickly spun:
I'm a blank sheet of paper, unwritten on.
HUSSEIN. Nobody knows my true

potential—
They want me to soak up ink, that's all!
PEER GYNT. For a woman, I was a silver-clasped book;
Either mad or sane is a printer's mistake.
HUSSEIN. Imagine—what a meaningless life—
For a pen not to taste the edge of a knife!
PEER GYNT. [*With a high leap.*] Imagine—a reindeer, falling free—
With never the hard earth under me!
HUSSEIN. A knife! Cut me! Carve me! I'm blunt!
The world will end if I lose my point!
PEER GYNT. How sad for the world, when all that's self-made
Was found by our Lord to be so well made.
BEGRIFFENFELDT. Here's a knife!
HUSSEIN. [*Seizing it.*] Ah! To lap ink the better,
What pleasure to slash oneself!
BEGRIFFENFELDT. [*Jumping aside.*] Don't spatter.
PEER GYNT. [*In mounting terror.*] Hold him!
HUSSEIN. Yes, hold me! Do what's proper!
Hold! Hold the pen! Set me to paper! [*Falls.*]
I'm worn out. The postscript—bear it in mind:
He lived and died in other men's hands!
PEER GYNT. [*Reeling.*] What should I—! What am I? Oh Thou—take hold!
I'm whatever you want—a Turk, a sinner,
A hill troll—but help—somewhere it's failed—! [*Cries out.*]
I can't remember your name for the world,
Thou—comfort of madmen, sustainer! [*Falls in a faint.* BEGRIFFENFELDT, *a wreath of straw in his hand, leaps to sit astride him.*]
BEGRIFFENFELDT. Hah! Look at him, enthroned in the filth—
Out of himself—! Crown him there! [*Presses the wreath down on* PEER'S *head and shouts.*]
Hail, all hail the Emperor of Self!
SCHAFMANN. [*In the cage.*] *Es lebe hoch der grosse Peer!*

Act 5

Scene 1

On board a ship in the North Sea, off the Norwegian coast. Sunset. Stormy weather.
PEER GYNT, *a rugged old man with grizzled hair and beard, stands on the poop. He is partly dressed as a seaman, with pea jacket and high boots. His clothes are rather worn; he himself is weather-beaten, and his face appears harder. The* CAPTAIN *and the helmsman are at the wheel. The crew is forward.* PEER *leans on the ship's rail and gazes toward land.*
PEER GYNT. That's Hallingskarv in his winter coat,
Lording it there in the evening light,
And Jøkel,[67] his brother, next in line;
He still has his ice-green mantle on.
And there, how lovely! It's Folgefonnen,[68]
Dressed like a maid in the whitest linen.
No cutting up, you old characters!
Stand where you are, like granite spires.
CAPTAIN. [*Calling forward.*] Two hands to the wheel—and the lantern set!
PEER GYNT. It's blowing up.
CAPTAIN. Aye. Storm tonight.
PEER GYNT. Can we see the Ronde peaks from here?
CAPTAIN. Not likely—they're back beyond the glacier.
PEER GYNT. Or Blaahø?[69]
CAPTAIN. No; but from up the rigging
You can see on a clear day to Galdhøpiggen.[70]
PEER GYNT. Which way is Haarteigen?[71]
CAPTAIN. [*Pointing.*] Thereabouts.
PEER GYNT. Ah, yes.
CAPTAIN. You seem to know these parts.
PEER GYNT. When I shipped out, it was down this coast;
And the dregs, they say, leave the bottle last. [*Spits and gazes toward shore.*]
Up in those blue ravines and notches,
Those narrow valleys, dark as ditches—
And below, along the open fjord—
These people live *there*, of their own accord. [*Looks at the* CAPTAIN.]
They build wide apart up here.

CAPTAIN. Aye,
Far between and long away.[72]
PEER GYNT. Will we land by morning?
CAPTAIN. About that,
If it doesn't get too rough tonight.
PEER GYNT. It's threatening westward.
CAPTAIN. It is.
PEER GYNT. I hope
You'll remind me when we settle up—
I want to do a good turn for each
Of the crew—
CAPTAIN. Thanks!
PEER GYNT. It won't be much.
I've grubbed for gold and lost the lot—
Fate and I had a falling out.
You know what I have in the safe below;
That's it—the rest was the devil's due.
CAPTAIN. It's more than enough to raise your stock
With the home folk.
PEER GYNT. I have no relatives.
No one waiting till the old boy arrives—
At least you miss the scene on the dock!
CAPTAIN. Here comes the storm.
PEER GYNT. So remember then—
If anyone here is really pressed,
I won't be niggling about the cost—
CAPTAIN. That's fair. They're mostly hard-up men.
They all have wives and children home,
And the wages barely get them by—
But if they brought in some extra pay,
They'd praise that day for a good long time.
PEER GYNT. What's that? They have wives and families?
Are they married?
CAPTAIN. Married? Aye, the whole flock.
But the one who's hardest pressed is the cook;
There's always black famine at his house.
PEER GYNT. Married? With someone there to wait,
Who's glad when they come?
CAPTAIN. Aye, as the poor
Do things.
PEER GYNT. So one evening they appear—
What then?
CAPTAIN. Oh, I guess the wife'd set
Out a special treat—
PEET GYNT. A lamp on the table?

CAPTAIN. Maybe two—and a brandy, double.
PEER GYNT. And so they sit, snug and warm by the fire—?
Children around them—the whole room astir—
And nobody's words are heard to the end
For the joy they feel—
CAPTAIN. You understand;
And that's why it's fair that you offered to fill
Their pockets a bit.
PEER GYNT. [*Pounds the railing.*] Damned if I will!
You think I'm mad? That I'll fork out
To provide for somebody else's brats?
I've slaved like a dog to make my mint!
No one's waiting for old Peer Gynt.
CAPTAIN. Do as you please; your money's your own.
PEER GYNT. Right! It's nobody's at all but mine.
We'll settle as soon as the anchor's struck.
My cabin passage from Panama here;
A round of drinks for the crew. No more.
If I add one cent, you give me a smack!
CAPTAIN. You'll have my receipt, and not a brawl—
Excuse me; we're heading into a gale.
[*He crosses the deck forward. It has now grown dark; lights are lit in the cabin. The sea runs higher. Fog and thick clouds.*]
PEER GYNT. To leave a whole tribe of children behind—
To sow delight in their growing minds—
To be borne by others' thoughts on your way—!
There's no one ever who thinks of me—
A lamp on the table? I'll put it out.
Just let me think—! I'll get them tight—
Not one of the clods'll go sober ashore.
They'll break in drunk on those family groups!
They'll curse and hammer the table tops—
And stiffen their own with the breath of fear!
The wives'll scream and bolt from the house—

And the children too! Now let 'em
  rejoice! [*The ship heels over; he staggers
  and holds his balance with difficulty.*]
Well, that was a lively roll. The ocean
Works as if it were paid on commission.
It's still its old self by the northern
  skerries;
The riptide plotting its treacheries—
  [*Listens.*]
What were those shouts?
THE WATCH. [*Forward.*] A wreck on the
  lee!
CAPTAIN. [*Amidships.*] Wheel hard starboard! Close to the wind!
THE MATE. Are there men aboard?
THE WATCH. I make out three!
PEER GYNT. Lower a boat—
CAPTAIN. She'd be swamped and
  drowned! [*Goes forward.*]
PEER GYNT. Who thinks of that? [*To
  several of the crew.*] You'll try, if you're
  men!
What the hell if you wet your skin—
THE BOATSWAIN. It can't be done in
  waves like those.
PEER GYNT. They're screaming again!
  And the wind is dying—
Cook, will you try? Quick! I'm paying—
THE COOK. For twenty pounds sterling,
  I'd refuse—
PEER GYNT. You curs! Cowards! Are you
  forgetting,
Those men have wives and children
  waiting
At home for them—
THE BOATSWAIN. Patience works wonders.
CAPTAIN. Bear off the breakers!
THE MATE. The wreck's gone under.
PEER GYNT. And in silence—
THE BOATSWAIN. If they *were* married,
  right this minute
The world's got three fresh-baked widows in it. [*The storm increases.* PEER
  GYNT *moves aft.*]
PEER GYNT. There's no faith left among
  men anymore—
No Christian love, as it's written and
  taught—
Few good deeds, and still less prayer—
And no respect for the Deity's might.
In a storm like this, the Lord God
  rages.
Those beasts should remember, they
  take a chance,
That it's dangerous playing with elephants—
But instead, they're openly sacrilegious!
But *I* have no guilt, when I can prove
I was there with my money, ready to
  give.
And what do I get for it—? It's been
  said:
"A conscience at ease is a downy pillow."[73]
Oh yes, on land that can't be denied;
But on board ship, it's not worth mud
To be honest among that rabble below.
At sea, you can't be yourself at all;
You follow the crowd from deck to
  keel.
Let judgment strike for the bo'sun or
  cook,
And I go plunging down with the
  pack—
Personal values don't have any place—
You rate like a hog in a slaughterhouse—
  It's my mistake that I've been too
    soft,
With nothing to show for it, only
  reproach.
If I were younger, my ways would shift
And I'd try playing the boss for a
  stretch.
There's time for it still! The parish'll
  hear
How Peer came swaggering home from
  afar!
I'll win back the farm by hook or crook,
Rebuild it, give it a regal look
Like a castle. Ah, but they can't come
  in!
They can stand at the gate, cap in
  hand,
Begging and pleading—*that* I don't
  mind;
But they won't get a penny of mine, not
  one—
If *I've* howled under the whips of Fate,
Trust me to find people I can beat—[*A
  STRANGE PASSENGER*[74] *appears in the
  dark at* PEER GYNT'*s side and greets him
  amiably.*]
THE PASSENGER. Good evening!
PEER GYNT. Good evening! What—?
  Who are you?
THE PASSENGER. Your servant—and
  fellow passenger.
PEER GYNT. Odd? I thought I was all
  alone here.
THE PASSENGER. A false impression. It's
  over now.
PEER GYNT. But it's certainly strange

that I see you tonight
For the very first time—
THE PASSENGER. I don't go out days.
PEER GYNT. Have you been sick? You're white as a sheet—
THE PASSENGER. Not at all. I'm in perfect health, otherwise.
PEER GYNT. What a storm!
THE PASSENGER. Yes, what a blessing, man!
PEER GYNT. Blessing?
THE PASSENGER. The waves are as big as houses.
It's simply mouth-watering! Ah, can
You imagine, on a night like this, the losses
In shipwrecks, and the men that go down!
PEER GYNT. My God!
THE PASSENGER. Ever seen a man who's choked—
Or been hanged—or drowned?
PEER GYNT. What a subject!
THE PASSENGER. The corpses laugh. But that laughter's wrung
From them; most have bit off a tongue.
PEER GYNT. Get away from me—!
THE PASSENGER. One question. Wait!
Suppose, for example, we struck a reef
And went down in the dark—
PEER GYNT. Do you think we might?
THE PASSENGER. I hardly know what answer to give.
But let's say I float, and you sink like a stone—
PEER GYNT. Oh, rubbish—
THE PASSENGER. Just something to speculate on.
But when a man has one foot in the grave,
He's more disposed to do a small favor—
PEER GYNT. [*Reaching in his pocket.*] Ho, money!
THE PASSENGER. No; I'd be satisfied if
You'd make me a gift of your cadaver—?
PEER GYNT. Now this is too much!
THE PASSENGER. Just the corpse, you know!
For my scientific research—
PEER GYNT. Will you go!
THE PASSENGER. But, my dear sir, think—how you'll benefit!
You'll be opened up and brought to light.
I'm investigating the source of dreams,
But I'll also go into your joints and seams—
PEER GYNT. Get away!
THE PASSENGER. But, friend—a dripping stiff—!
PEER GYNT. Blasphemer! You've helped the storm enough!
It's madness! In all this wind and rain
And roaring sea, with every sign
That terrible things are due for this ship—
You have to tempt them to hurry up!
THE PASSENGER. I see you're not in a mood for discussion;
But time may force another conclusion—[*With a friendly nod.*]
We'll meet when you're sinking, if not before;
Perhaps then you'll be in better humor. [*Goes into the cabin.*]
PEER GYNT. Bizarre companions, these scientists!
Damned freethinkers—[*To the* BOATSWAIN, *passing by.*] A word, mine host!
That passenger? Who is that lunatic?
THE BOATSWAIN. There's nobody else but you coming back.
PEER GYNT. Nobody else? That's certainly queer. [*To a* YOUNG SAILOR, *leaving the cabin.*]
Who just went inside?
THE SAILOR. The ship's dog, sir! [*Passes on.*]
THE WATCH. [*Crying out*] Land dead ahead!
PEER GYNT. My box! My trunk!
All baggage on deck!
THE BOATSWAIN. You want us to sink? We're busy.
PEER GYNT. Captain! I was carrying on—
Joking; but by God, now I'll help the cook—!
CAPTAIN. The jib has sprung!
THE MATE. The foresail's gone!
THE BOATSWAIN. [*Screaming from the bow.*] Breakers under us!
THE CAPTAIN. She's going to strike! [*The ship grounds. Noise and confusion.*]

Scene 2

Close to land, among surf and skerries. The ship is sinking. Through the fog, glimpses of a boat with two men. A heavy sea breaks over it; it overturns; a shriek is heard, then silence. After a moment the boat reappears, bottom up. PEER GYNT *comes to the surface nearby.*

PEER GYNT. Help! A boat! Help me! I'll die!
God have mercy—as the Scriptures say! [*Clutches the keel.*]
THE COOK. [*Comes up on the other side.*] Lord! Oh, God! For my babies' sake—
Be merciful! To my rescue! Quick! [*Clings to the keel.*]
PEER GYNT. Let go!
THE COOK. Lay off!
PEER GYNT. I'll smack you!
THE COOK. Try!
PEER GYNT. I'll smash you to pieces, wait and see!
Let go! She'll carry one; no more!
THE COOK. I know that! Swim for it!
PEER GYNT. *You* swim!
THE COOK. Sure! [*They fight; one of the* COOK'*s hands is injured; he hangs on tight with the other.*]
PEER GYNT. Let go that hand!
THE COOK. Spare me, please!
Think of my children, what they'll lose!
PEER GYNT. I'm more in need of life than you;
I haven't had children up till now.
THE COOK. Let go! You've lived, and I'm still young!
PEER GYNT. Hurry up, sink—we're foundering.
THE COOK. Have mercy! Swim it, in heaven's name!
You break no hearts if you don't get home—[*He screams and slips under.*]
I'm drowning—!
PEER GYNT. [*Seizing him.*] I've got you by the hair
Of your head; say a "Lord's Prayer"!
THE COOK. I can't remember—it's turning black—
PEER GYNT. Just the essentials! Say it, quick!
THE COOK. Give us this day—!
PEER GYNT. The same old song!
It's obvious you've been a cook too long—[*His hold loosens.*]
THE COOK. [*Sinking.*] Give us this day our—[*Goes under.*]
PEER GYNT. Amen, friend!
You were yourself, right to the end—[*Draws himself up on the keel.*]
Where there's life, there's always hope—
THE STRANGE PASSENGER. [*Takes hold of the boat.*] Good morning!
PEER GYNT. Ai!
THE PASSENGER. I heard a whoop—
Funny I should be meeting you.
Well? Did my prophecy come true?
PEER GYNT. Let go! There's hardly room for one!
THE PASSENGER. I'll swim with my left leg and hang on
By my fingertips over this cleat
On the keel of the boat. How's that?
But, apropos your corpse—
PEER GYNT. Shh!
THE PASSENGER. The rest of you reeks like a rotten fish.
PEER GYNT. Shut your mouth!
THE PASSENGER. If you prefer that. [*Silence.*]
PEER GYNT. Well?
THE PASSENGER. I'm speechless.
PEER GYNT. Satan's bait—
What now?
THE PASSENGER. I'm waiting.
PEER GYNT. [*Tearing his hair.*] I'll go mad!
Who are you?
THE PASSENGER. [*With a nod.*] Friendly.
PEER GYNT. What, beside?
THE PASSENGER. What do *you* think?
Know any other who's
Akin to me?
PEER GYNT. The devil is—!
THE PASSENGER. [*Softly.*] But is it his way to illuminate
Life's dark journey by means of fright?
PEER GYNT. Oh, I see! I suppose it's your claim
That a messenger of light has come?
THE PASSENGER. Even *once* in a half year, can it be said
You've been shaken to the roots by dread?
PEER GYNT. Sure, anyone's frightened when danger lunges.
But all your words are set on hinges—
THE PASSENGER. My friend, have you even *once* in your life
Known the victory only dread can give?
PEER GYNT. [*Looking at him.*] If you came to open me a door
It's stupid you didn't come before.
This is absurd, to choose a time
When the ocean's swallowing me like

foam.

THE PASSENGER. Would the victory be more likely, then,
By the fireside in your drowsy den?

PEER GYNT. All right—but your words were laughable.
How could you think they'd stir my soul?

THE PASSENGER. Where I come from they value smiles
As high as all the pathetic styles.

PEER GYNT. Each in its time; the barber thrives
On what puts bishops into their graves.

THE PASSENGER. The souls in funeral urns don't try
On weekdays to dress for tragedy.

PEER GYNT. Clear off, you monster! Get away!
I won't die! It's the land for me!

THE PASSENGER. You needn't worry in *that* respect—
No one dies halfway through the last act. [*Glides away.*]

PEER GYNT. There, he got it out at last—
He was a tedious moralist.

Scene 3

A churchyard high in the mountains. A funeral in progress. The PASTOR *and the mourners are just singing the final verse of a hymn.* PEER GYNT *is passing by on the road.*

PEER GYNT. Here's another who's gone our mortal way.
Thanks be to God, it isn't me. [*Enters the churchyard.*]

THE PASTOR. [*Over the grave.*]
  Now, as the soul goes out to meet its doom
And leaves the dust here, hollow as a drum—
Now, dear friends, we must set a few things forth
About this dead man's pilgrimage on earth.
  He wasn't rich, nor could you call him wise;
His voice lacked force; his bearing, manliness;
What thoughts he spoke were hesitant and tame;
He scarcely seemed the master of his home;
And when he entered church, he'd sidle in
As if he begged his place with other men.
  From Gudbrandsdal he came, over the wicked
Winding roads, as a boy; and he remained.
And you remember how, to the very end,
He always hid his right hand in his pocket.
  That hand thrust in his pocket is the thing
That, in one's memory, stands pre-eminent—
That and a certain diffidence, a shrinking
Look, that marked him everywhere he went.
  But, though his chosen path in life was lonely,
And he kept himself a stranger to our breed,
We all knew what he struggled so to hide—
The hand he covered had four fingers only—
  I well remember, many years ago,
A morning down at Lunde. Conscripts had
Been called; a war was on; all talk was stayed
On Norway's griefs and the fate of those we knew.
  I watched the drafting. At a table sat
A captain, flanked by sergeants, and the mayor.[75]
Boy after boy was summoned to their fire,
Measured, questioned, signed as a new recruit.
  The room was full; and outside on the square,
Loud laughter rang from the young folk gathered there.
  Another name was called. We saw approach
One who was pale as snow on the glacier's edge.
They told him to step up; and as he neared,
We saw his right hand bandaged in a clout.
  He gulped and swallowed hard; he groped for words,

And yet, despite their bidding, stood
  there mute.
Ah, yes, at last! With burning cheeks, in
  a voice
That failed at times, then caught up
  with his breath,
He mumbled of some accident, a scythe
That cut his finger right off at the base.
  Then suddenly the room was deathly
    still.
Glances were exchanged; men set their
  jaws;
They stoned the boy with silence in
  their eyes.
He felt the hailstorm, though he never
  saw it fall.
And then the captain rose and,
  pointing to
The door, spat and rapped out one
  word, "Go!"
  And so he went. On both sides men
    drew back
And made a kind of gantlet to be run.
He reached the door; and then his
  courage broke—
He fled—up and up the wooded slope
Past the rockslides, treacherous and
  steep.
He had his home high in the
  mountains then—
  Some six months later, he came here
    to us
With mother and betrothed and baby
  child.
He rented land beyond the ridge, a
  field
Toward Lom where the tracts of
  wasteland rise.
He married just as soon as possible.
He built a house; he fought the
  stubborn soil
And made it yield, his efforts bravely
  shown,
Between the rocks, in the sway of
  yellow grain.
In church he kept his right hand in his
  pocket—
But at home, I'd say his fingers, though
  but nine,
Slaved just as hard as other people's
  ten.
One spring the torrent struck his farm
  and took it.
  They got out with their skins. A
    ruined man,
He started in anew to clear the land;
And by that fall, the smoke rose up
  again
Over a farmhouse built on safer
  ground.
Safer? Yes, from flood—but not from
  glaciers.
Within two years, a snow-slide crushed
  his labors.
  And yet no avalanche could crush his
    spirit.
He dug, he raked, he swept, he carted
  trash—
Till he could see, as winter's first snow
  flurried,
His house raised up a third time, clean
  and fresh.
  Three sons he had, three clever,
    active boys;
Time came for school, which lay a long
  way off—
To reach the parish road, they'd have to
  squeeze
Down snow-banked ledges clinging to
  the cliffs.
What did he do? He let the eldest shift
As best he could; but where no man
  would walk,
He'd lead the boy, tied by a line, and
  lift
The others in his arms and on his back.
  So year by year he toiled, and they
    grew up.
Some help from them now seemed a
  decent hope.
In the New World, three wealthy
  businessmen
Forgot their father here and all he'd
  done.
  Shortsighted, he was that. He had no
    eyes
For anything beyond his family's call.
He found as meaningless as sounding
  brass
Words that ought to pierce the heart
  like steel.
This land, our people, all the shining
  dreams,
Weighed less to him than mist on
  mountain streams.
  Yet he was humble, humble as men
    come;
That day in Lunde stripped his
  conscience naked—
As certain as his cheeks that burned
  with shame
And those four fingers hiding in his

pocket.
Lost to his country's laws? Yes, if you want.
But one true light above the law prevails,
As sure as over Glittertind's[76] white tent
The piling clouds build higher mountains still.
No patriot, this man. For church as well as state,
A barren tree. But up where the wasteland shelves,
In his family circle where he saw his lot,
There he was great, because he was himself.
His inborn note was steadfast as a star.
His life was music, like a muted bell.
So, peace be with you, silent warrior,
Who fought the peasant's little fight, and fell.
  It's not our place to sift the heart and soul—
That's not for dust, but for the Judge of all—
Still I believe—and here it must be said:
This man stands now no cripple to his God! [*The mourners scatter and depart.* PEER GYNT *remains behind alone.*]
PEER GYNT. Now *that's* what I call Christianity!
Nothing unpleasant to jar the mind—
And the subject—being oneself to the end—
Brought out in the pastor's eulogy,
Has everything in it to recommend.
  [*Looks down into the grave.*]
Was it him, I wonder, that boy who cut
Off his finger one day not far from my hut?
Who knows? If I didn't stand with my staff
By the edge of this kindred spirit's grave,
I could almost believe it was *me* that slept
And heard in dreams my character wept.
It's really a beautiful Christian trait,
This casting of retrospective thought
In charity over the days gone by.
I wouldn't mind facing my destiny
At the hands of this excellent parish priest.
Well, I have a while, undoubtedly,
Before I'm called as the gravedigger's guest—
And as Scripture says: "It's all for the best—"
And: "Sufficient unto the day, its evil—"
And: "Don't borrow to buy the sexton a shovel—"
Ah, the church is the true consoler. Up
Till now, I've really not given it credit—
But how good it is to hear restated,
From the highest and surest authorship:
"Whatever ye sow, ye shall also reap."
We should be ourselves, that's the key;
All for yourself and your own, I say.
If your luck runs out, at least there's honor
In having lived in a principled manner.
Now homewards! What if Fortune frowns,
And the road ahead is hard and tortuous—
Old Peer Gynt will go it alone,
True to his nature: poor, but virtuous.
  [*Moves on.*]

Scene 4

A hillside with a dried-out river bed and, beside it a ruined mill. The ground is torn up; everything is desolate. Higher up-slope, a large farm, where an auction is taking place. A noisy crowd has gathered; many are drinking. PEER GYNT *is seated on a rubbish heap by the mill.*
PEER GYNT. Forward or back, it's just as far;
Out or in, it's a narrow door.
Time corrodes, and the stream wears out.
Remember the Boyg—and go round-about.
A MAN IN MOURNING. Now there's only the rubbish here.[77] [*Catches sight of* PEER GYNT.]
And strangers too? God save you, sir!
PEER GYNT. And you! This crowd looks well amused.
A christening, or a wedding feast?
THE MAN IN MOURNING. A housewarming, I'd call it instead—
Except it's a bed of worms for the bride.

PEER GYNT. And the worms are fighting for rags and scraps.
THE MAN IN MOURNING. It's the end of the song; so there it stops.
PEER GYNT. They all end alike, every song;
They're old; I sang them when I was young.
A YOUTH OF TWENTY. [*With a casting ladle.*] Look what I bought! An antique piece!
Peer Gynt poured silver buttons from this.
ANOTHER. See mine! Two cents for a money sack!
A THIRD. That's nothing! Five for a peddler's pack!
PEER GYNT. Peer Gynt? Who was he?
THE MAN IN MOURNING. I only know Death
Was his brother-in-law. And Aslak the smith.
A MAN IN GRAY. You're forgetting me! Had too much beer?
THE MAN IN MOURNING. You're forgetting Hegstad, a storehouse door!
THE MAN IN GRAY. True; but when have you been that delicate?
THE MAN IN MOURNING. Let's see if she finds Death easy to cheat—
THE MAN IN GRAY. Come, brother! A drink, for brotherhood's sake!
THE MAN IN MOURNING. Brotherhood, hell! You've had a crock—
THE MAN IN GRAY. Nonsense! Our bloodlines don't run so faint;
We're all brothers in old Peer Gynt.
[*They go off together.*]
PEER GYNT. [*Softly.*] One meets acquaintances.
A BOY. [*Calls after* THE MAN IN MOURNING.] My dead mother
Will haunt you, Aslak, if you drink your meal.
PEER GYNT. [*Getting up.*] What the farmers say doesn't hold altogether:
"The deeper you dig, the better the smell."
A YOUTH. [*With a bearskin.*] The Dovre-cat, look! Ready to stuff.
He routed the trolls on Christmas Eve.
A SECOND. [*With reindeer horns.*] Here's that marvelous buck whose fleece
Carried Peer Gynt down Gjendin ridge.
A THIRD. [*With a hammer, calls to* THE MAN IN MOURNING.] Hi, Aslak, you remember this sledge?
Is that what you used when the devil cut loose?
A FOURTH. [*Empty-handed.*] Mads Moen, here's the invisible cloak
That Peer Gynt and Ingrid flew with, look!
PEER GYNT. Some brandy, boys! I'm feeling old—
Let's have a beggar's auction held!
A YOUTH. What have you to sell?
PEER GYNT. I have a castle—
It lies in the Ronde, tough as your muscle.
THE YOUTH. I bid a button.
PEER GYNT. Make it a pint.
To bid any less would gall a saint.
ANOTHER YOUTH. He's fun, the old boy!
[*A crowd flocks around.*]
PEER GYNT. Grane, my horse— Who bids?
ONE OF THE CROWD. Where is he?
PEER GYNT. [*Cries out.*] Far to the west!
In the sunset, lads! He can fly as fast—
As fast as Peer Gynt could lie for a purse.
VOICES. What else do you have?
PEER GYNT. Both gold and dross!
I bought them cheap; I'll sell at a loss.
A YOUTH. Put up!
PEER GYNT. One dream of a silver-clasped book.
That you can have for a buttonhook.
THE YOUTH. To hell with dreams!
PEER GYNT. My empire, then!
I'll throw it among you; catch as you can!
THE YOUTH. Does a crown come with it?
PEER GYNT. Of the finest straw.
It'll fit the first man that gives it a try.
And wait, here's more! The Prophet's beard!
A rotten egg![78] A gray hair, snared
From a madman! All for him who can show
Me a sign in the hills saying, "Here lies the way!"
THE SHERIFF. [*Just arrived.*] Run on like that, my man, and you'll
Find your way takes you straight to jail.
PEER GYNT. [*Hat in hand.*] Most likely.
But, tell me, who was Peer Gynt?
THE SHERIFF. What trash—
PEER GYNT. Please! Just some account—!
THE SHERIFF. Oh, they say he was such a

crass romancer—
PEER GYNT. Romancer—?
THE SHERIFF. Yes, anything brave and fine
He could weave into something *he* must have done.
Excuse me—I have to be law-dispenser— [*Goes.*]
PEER GYNT. And where's this amazing fellow now?
AN ELDERLY MAN. Shipped out, he did—and went askew
In some foreign land where he never belonged.
Been a good many years since he was hanged.
PEER GYNT. Hanged? I see! Well, I'm not surprised.
Old Peer Gynt was himself to the last. [*Bows.*]
Good-bye—and thanks for all your trouble! [*Goes a few steps, then pauses.*]
You lovely ladies and gay young blades—
Could I repay you with a fable?[79]
SEVERAL VOICES. Yes, you know one?
PEER GYNT. I know hundreds— [*Comes closer; a strange look passes over him.*]
In San Francisco, I once panned for gold.
The town had more acrobats than it could hold.
One played the fiddle, using his toes;
Another fandangoed down on his knees;
A third one, I heard, wrote verse that he read
While a hole was bored in the top of his head.
For the acrobat fair, the devil came west
To try out his luck with all the rest.
His talent was this: he'd come on big,
Uttering grunts like an actual pig.
He was quite unknown, but he had a style.
Suspense ran high; the house was full.
He strode out in a cape cut sweepingly;
Man muss sich drapieren, as the Germans say.
But under his cape—which nobody guessed—
He had a live pig stowed up by his chest.
And now the representation began—
The devil, he pinched, and the pig struck a tune.

The work took the form of a fantasy
Of life through a pig's eye, from A to Z—
Till the grand crescendo, a slaughterhouse squeal;
Then the artist bowed low, and the curtain fell.
The critics weighed and discussed the results,
Defined the merits and labeled the faults—
Some found the vocal development scant;
The death-cry, for others, was mere technique—
But all were agreed in this: *qua* grunt,
The performer had laid it on much too thick.
So the devil got it; he had no sense,
Not to take stock of his audience. [*Bows and departs. An uneasy silence settles over the crowd.*]

Scene 5

The eve of Pentecost.[80] *Deep in the forest. At a distance, in a clearing, a hut with reindeer antlers over the door.* PEER GYNT, *on his hands and knees, picking wild onions.*
PEER GYNT. Here's one point of view. I hope, not the last—
One tries all things and chooses the best.
That's what I've done—up from Caesar
And now almost down to Nebuchadnezzar.
So I did have to go through Bible history—
The old boy's back in his mother's custody.
"Of earth thou art come,"[81] says Holy Writ—
The main thing in life is to fill your gut.
But fill it with onions? Much too coarse;
I'll have to be clever and set some snares.
Here's good brook water; I won't parch—
And among the wild beasts, I'll have no match.
When I come to die—as it has to be—
I'll crawl in under a windfallen tree;

Like a bear, I'll heap leaves over my tatters
And carve in the bark, in ample letters:
"Here lies Peer Gynt, a decent soul,
Emperor of all the animals—"
Emperor? [*Laughs silently.*] You prophet's false companion!
You're no emperor; you're an onion.
And I'm going to skin you, Peer, old top!
No blubbering now; you can't escape. [*Starts peeling an onion layer by layer.*]
This outer layer, like a torn coat—
It's the shipwrecked man on the drifting boat.
Here's the passenger layer, thin as paint—
But the taste has a dash of the real Peer Gynt.
The prospector life was a run for the money;
The juice is gone—if it ever had any.
And now this rough-skinned layer—why,
That's the fur trader up at Hudson's Bay.
The next resembles a crown—no, thanks!
That we'll throw away—it's a jinx.
Here's the archaeologist, brief and brassy.
And here's the prophet, green and juicy.
He stinks, as the Scripture says, of lies,
Enough to bring tears to an honest man's eyes.
This layer that curls in softly together
Is the man of the world, living for pleasure.
The next looks sick. It has streaks of black—
Meaning priests—and slaves on the auction block. [*Pulls off several layers at once.*]
These layers just go endlessly on!
Shouldn't it give up its kernel soon? [*Pulls the whole onion apart.*]
Damned if it does! To the innermost filler,
It's nothing but layers—smaller and smaller—
Nature is witty! [*Throws the pieces away.*]
To hell with brooding!
Go lost in thought, and you stumble for sure.
Well, *I* can make light of that foreboding,
Planted solid on all fours here. [*Scratches his neck.*]
How strange it is, this business—life,
As it's called! It has cards up its sleeve;
But try to play them, they disappear,
And you hold something else—or empty air. [*He has approached close to the hut, catches sight of it and starts.*]
That hut? On the moor—! Hm! [*Rubs his eyes.*] It's as though
This building is one that I used to know—
The reindeer horns under the gable—!
A mermaid, fish-shaped down from the navel—!
Lies! No mermaid—! Nails—slats—
Bars for shutting out goblin thoughts—!

SOLVEIG. [*Singing in the hut.*] Now the room's ready for Pentecost.
My dearest boy, in some far land—
  Will you come at last?
If your burden is heavy,
  Then rest for a while—
As I promised to be,
  I'll be waiting still.

PEER GYNT. [*Rises, hushed and deathly pale.*] One who remembered—and one who forgot.
One who squandered—and one who could wait—
Oh, life—! No second chance to play!
Oh, dread—! *Here's* where my empire lay! [*Runs down the forest path.*]

Scene 6

Night. A moor with fir trees burnt out by forest fire. Charred tree trunks can be seen for miles around. Here and there patches of mist clinging to the earth. PEER GYNT *comes running.*

PEER GYNT. Ashes, fog, and dust, wind-driven—
There's enough to build with here!
Stench and rottenness within;
Only a white sepulcher.
Dreams, romances, stillborn visions
Laid the pyramid's foundations;
Up from these a stonework rose
With the stairways made of lies.
"Spurn the truth; nothing's sacred."
Fly that from the highest banner;
Let the trump of judgment clamor:

Petrus Gyntus Caesar fecit. [*Listens.*]
What sound is that, like children weeping?
Weeping halfway into song—
And by my feet, threadballs creeping—! [*Kicks at them.*]
Out of my way! You don't belong—!
THREADBALLS. [*On the ground.*] We are thoughts;
You should have thought us—
Legs to walk on
You should have brought us!
PEER GYNT. [*Going around them.*] I brought life to *one*, in rags—
And it had twisted, bandy legs!
THREADBALLS. We should have soared
In a blending choir—
Instead we roll
Like threadballs here.
PEER GYNT. [*Stumbling.*] Threadballs!
Drones, you mean—! Stop!
You want to trip your father up? [*Flees.*]
WITHERED LEAVES. [*Flying before the wind.*] We are watchwords
You should have spoken!
See, while you dozed,
We were stripped and broken.
The worm has eaten us
Down to the root;
We'll never spread out
To garland fruit.
PEER GYNT. You've lived in vain, is that your fear?
Lie still; you'll make a good manure.
A SIGHING IN THE AIR. We are songs
You should have sung!
A thousand times
You bit your tongue.
Deep in your heart
We waited for you—
You never called.
We're poison now!
PEER GYNT. Then poison yourselves, right at the source!
What time did I have to waste on verse? [*Tries a shortcut.*]
DEWDROPS. [*Dripping from the branches.*]
We are tears
That were never shed.
Barbed ice that wounds
We could have thawed.
Now the barb is fixed
In the marrowbone;
The wound is closed;
Our strength is gone.
PEER GYNT. Thanks—I wept in the Ronde hall
And still I got it in the tail!
BROKEN STRAW. We are deeds
That you should have done!
The strangler, Doubt,
Has struck us down.
In the crack of doom,
We'll arrive like chaff
And state your case—
Till you cry, "Enough!"
PEER GYNT. Filthy tricks! You can't believe
I ought to be blamed for what's *negative*?[82] [*Hurries away.*]
AASE'S VOICE. [*Far off.*] Ai, what a driver!
Hoo, I'm upset
In the new-fallen snow—
I'm chilled and wet—
Peer, where's the castle?
You've turned the wrong way.
The devil misled you;
He's guided the sleigh!
PEER GYNT. It's time a poor fellow picks up and runs.
If I had to carry the devil's sins,
I'd soon be flat on the ground for sure—
One's own are heavy enough to bear.
[*Runs off.*]

Scene 7

Another part of the moor.
PEER GYNT. [*Singing.*] A sexton, a sexton! Where's the throng?
Open your bleating mouths and sing;
To rim your hats, a mourning band—
I've many dead to walk behind! [*The* BUTTON-MOLDER, *with a box of tools and a large casting ladle, comes from a side path.*]
THE BUTTON-MOLDER. Greetings, old man!
PEER GYNT. Good evening, friend!
BUTTON-MOLDER. You're in a hurry. Where are you bound?
PEER GYNT. A funeral.
BUTTON-MOLDER. Really? My eyesight's poor—
Excuse me—but is your name Peer?
PEER GYNT. I'm called Peer Gynt.
BUTTON-MOLDER. What a stroke of luck!
It's precisely Peer Gynt I've come to take.
PEER GYNT. To take? What for?

BUTTON-MOLDER. That's an easy guess.
I'm a button-molder; you go in this.
PEER GYNT. Why should I go?
BUTTON-MOLDER. To be melted down.
PEER GYNT. Melted—?
BUTTON-MOLDER. The ladle's empty and clean.
Your grave is dug; your coffin's made;
The worms in your body'll be well fed—
But the Master has instructed me
To bring in your soul without delay.
PEER GYNT. You can't—! Like this? Without a warning—!
BUTTON-MOLDER. It's a well-known ancient custom, concerning
Wakes and christenings, to keep the banner
Day a secret from the guest of honor.
PEER GYNT. Yes, that's so. These thoughts—they bewilder
Me. Are you—?
BUTTON-MOLDER. You heard. A button-molder.
PEER GYNT. I see! A pet child has many nicknames.
So, Peer, *that's* where you land, it seems.
But, listen, this is a rotten trick!
I know I deserve a better shake—
I'm not as bad as maybe you think—
I've done lots of good on earth; to be frank,
My offenses, at worst, have all been minor—
I could never be called a major sinner.
BUTTON-MOLDER. But, my friend, that precisely *is* your offense.
You aren't a sinner in the larger sense;
That's why you're let off the fiery griddle
And go, like the rest, in the casting ladle.
PEER GYNT. Oh, ladle or pit—what do I care?
Lager and bock are, both of them, beer.
Behind me, Satan!
BUTTON-MOLDER. You're not such an oaf
As to think I trot on a cloven hoof?
PEER GYNT. Be it horse's hoof or fox's claw—
Pack out! And mind you obey the law!
BUTTON-MOLDER. My friend, you're making a big mistake.
We're both in a hurry; so for clarity's sake,
I'll explain your case as quick as I can.
As you said yourself, you're scarcely one
Who's made a name for exceptional sinning—
You barely break even—
PEER GYNT. Now you're beginning
To talk some sense—
BUTTON-MOLDER. Not so fast there—
But to call you virtuous wouldn't be right—
PEER GYNT. I never laid any claim to that.
BUTTON-MOLDER. You're average then, just middling fair.
A sinner in the old flamboyant style
One meets with nowadays hardly at all.
There's more to sin than making a mess;
A sin calls for vigor and seriousness.
PEER GYNT. That's true enough; you can't be a piker.
You have to plunge in like an old berserker.[83]
BUTTON-MOLDER. But you, my friend, you took sin lightly.
PEER GYNT. Like a splash of mud; something unsightly.
BUTTON-MOLDER. Now we're agreeing. The sulfur pit
Is hardly for those who dabble in smut—
PEER GYNT. And, therefore, friend, I can go as I came?
BUTTON-MOLDER. No, therefore, friend, it's melting time.
PEER GYNT. What are these tricks you've hit upon
Back here at home while I've been gone?
BUTTON-MOLDER. The custom's as old as the serpent's creation;
It follows the laws of conservation.
You've worked at the craft—so you know how
A casting often turns out with a flaw.
Suppose, say, a button was missing a loop;
What did you do?
PEER GYNT. I threw it out.
BUTTON-MOLDER. Ah yes, Jon Gynt was a waster all right,
As long as his wallet was well filled up.
But the Master, you see, is thrifty, he is;
And that's why he's grown so pros-

perous.
He throws out nothing as unrepairable
That still can be used for raw material.
Now *you* were planned as a shining button
On the vest of the world, but your loop gave way;
So you'll have to go into the rubbish carton
And merge with the masses, as people say.

PEER GYNT. But you can't mean to melt me together now
With Tom, Dick, and Harry into something new?

BUTTON-MOLDER. Yes, so help me, it's just what I mean.
We've done it to others, time and again.
It's what they do with coins at the mint
When the image has worn away too faint.

PEER GYNT. But why be so wretched miserly!
My dear good friend, let me go free—
A loopless button, a worn-out coin—
What's that to your Master, so great a man!

BUTTON-MOLDER. Oh, as long as there's spirit in you, it'll
Lend you some value as casting metal.

PEER GYNT. No, I say! No! Tooth and nail,
I'll fight against it! I won't, that's all!

BUTTON-MOLDER. But what else? Use the brain you were given.
You're hardly buoyant enough for heaven—

PEER GYNT. I'm easily pleased. I don't aim so high—
But I won't give one jot of myself away.
Let the old-time judgment settle my life!
Send me a while to Him with the Hoof—
Say a hundred years, if it comes to that;
I know I could manage to bear it out—
The torture is moral, so it must be gentle;
At least it could hardly be monumental.
It's a transition, as the adage goes,
And as the fox said.[84] One waits; the news
Of deliverance will come; one can pull back
And hope, in the meantime, for better luck.
But this other—simply to disappear
Like a mote in a stranger's blood, to forswear
Being Gynt for a ladle-existence, to melt—
It makes my innermost soul revolt!

BUTTON-MOLDER. But, my dear Peer, why all the fuss
Over a technical point like this?
Yourself is just what you've never been—
So what difference to you to get melted down?

PEER GYNT. I've never been—? That's a funny thought!
Peer Gynt's been somebody else, no doubt!
No, button-molder, you judge in the dark.
If you could see into me, straight to the mark,
You'd discover then that I'm solid Peer,
And nothing but Peer, to the very core.

BUTTON-MOLDER. Not so. Here in my orders, you're named.
See, where it's written: "Peer Gynt; to be claimed
For setting his life's definition at odds;
Consigned to the ladle as damaged goods."

PEER GYNT. What rot! It's some other person they mean.
Does it really say Peer? Not Rasmus or Jon?

BUTTON-MOLDER. I melted them down a long while back.
Come quietly now, and no more talk!

PEER GYNT. Damned if I will! Oh, that'd be nice
If you heard tomorrow you'd made a wrong choice.
Better be careful, my excellent man!
Consider the burden you're taking on—

BUTTON-MOLDER. I have it in writing—

PEER GYNT. Just a little more time!

BUTTON-MOLDER. What would you do then?

PEER GYNT. Get some proof
That I've been myself all of my life—
Since it's there that we're at odds, it would seem.

BUTTON-MOLDER. Proof? Of what sort?

PEER GYNT. Statements sworn—
Witnesses—

BUTTON-MOLDER. The Master, I fear,

would decline.
PEER GYNT. Impossible! Well, sufficient unto the day—
My friend, allow me the loan of myself;
I'll come back soon. We're born only once;
And it's hard for creatures like us to dissolve.
Yes; you agree?
BUTTON-MOLDER. All right; one chance—
But at the next crossroads, there we'll see. [PEER GYNT *runs off.*]

Scene 8

Farther along on the moor.
PEER GYNT. [*Running full tilt.*] Time is money, as the Gospel says.
If only I knew where the crossroad lies!
It could be far, or it could be near—
The earth's like a red-hot iron floor.
A witness! A witness! Wherever one is!
It looks hopeless, almost, in this wilderness.
The world's botched up. It stuns your wits
That a man has to prove his obvious rights! [*A bent* OLD MAN, *with a staff in his hand and a bag on his back, trudges in front of him.*]
THE OLD MAN. [*Stopping.*] Good sir—a few coins for a homeless man?
PEER GYNT. Sorry—but I'm terribly short of funds.
THE OLD MAN. Prince Peer! Ah no; so we meet again—?
PEER GYNT. But who—?
THE OLD MAN. He's forgotten his Ronde friends?
PEER GYNT. But you can't be—?
THE OLD MAN. The Troll King, yes!
PEER GYNT. The Troll King? Really? The Troll King! Speak!
TROLL KING. Oh, but I'm miserably down on my luck—!
PEER GYNT. Ruined?
TROLL KING. Stripped to my very self.
A tramp on the highway, starved as a wolf.
PEER GYNT. Hurrah! Such witnesses don't grow on trees!
TROLL KING. But your Lordship's also gray as a squirrel.
PEER GYNT. Dear father-in-law, the years leave scars.
Ah, well; let's pass over our private affairs—
And please, above all, no family quarrels.
I was headstrong then—
TROLL KING. Yes; ah, yes—
The Prince was young. And the things youth does!
But your Lordship was wise in leaving his bride;
She'd only have brought him shame and bother;
For later, she went completely bad—
PEER GYNT. She did!
TROLL KING. It's wretched, the life she's had.
Just think—she and Trond are living together.
PEER GYNT. Trond who?
TROLL KING. Of the Valfjeld.
PEER GYNT. Oh, yes, him!
The one I took those herd girls from.
TROLL KING. But my grandson's grown up fat and strong,
With strapping children all over the land—
PEER GYNT. Yes, my dear man, but we can't talk long—
There's something quite different on my mind—
I'm caught in a rather awkward spot
Where I need a character affidavit—
You'd help me greatly if you could give it.
I'll dig up some change, and we'll down a shot—
TROLL KING. Oh, really; could I help the Prince?
Then maybe you'd give me a reference?
PEER GYNT. Gladly. It's just that I'm pinched for cash
And have to be careful more than I'd wish.
But now, here's the thing. You must recall
The night I courted your daughter well—
TROLL KING. Of course, your Lordship!
PEER GYNT. You can drop the title!
All right. By force, you were going to drill
My eyes and adjust my vision a little
And turn me from Peer Gynt into a troll.

But what did I do? I put up a fight—
Swore I'd stand on my own two feet;
I gave up love and power and glory
Since being myself was more necessary.
I want you to swear to that in court—
TROLL KING. No, but I can't!
PEER GYNT. What do you mean?
TROLL KING. You want me to play the
  liar's part?
Remember, you put our troll gear on,
And tasted the mead—?
PEER GYNT. You set the trap;
But I never took the ultimate step.
And a man's made of just that kind of
  thing.
It's the final verse that makes the song.
TROLL KING. But, Peer, it's closing quite
  differently.
PEER GYNT. What rot is that?
TROLL KING. When you went away,
You'd cut our motto in your coat of
  arms.
PEER GYNT. Motto?
TROLL KING. That shrewd and severing
  term.
PEER GYNT. What term?
TROLL KING. The one that parts human
  life
From trolldom: Troll, to yourself be
  enough!
PEER GYNT. [*Recoils a step.*] Enough!
TROLL KING. Since then you've lived to
  serve
Our realm with every straining nerve.
PEER GYNT. I! Peer Gynt!
TROLL KING. [*Weeping.*] It's so un-
  grateful!
You've lived as a troll, secret, deceit-
  ful—
You used the word I taught you to win
Your place as a well-established man—
And now you come back to me and
  sneer
At the motto you ought to be thankful
  for.
PEER GYNT. *Enough!* A hill troll! An
  egoist!
It must be nonsense; I know it must!
TROLL KING. [*Pulls out a bundle of old
  newspapers.*] Aren't you aware that we
  read our papers?
Here, look; you can see it in black and
  red,
How the *Bloksberg Post* accords you all
  proper
Praise; and the *Heklefjeld Times*[85] has
  played
Up your story from the winter you
  went abroad—
Want to read them, Peer? I'll give you
  leave.
Here's an article, signed by "Stallion-
  hoof."
And another, "On Troll Nationalism."
The writer demonstrates that a simple
And natural trollish enthusiasm
Is worth far more than horns and a
  tail.
"Our *enough*," he says, "gives the mark
  of the troll
To man"—and you're his conclusive ex-
  ample.
PEER GYNT. A hill troll? Me?
TROLL KING. It's perfectly clear.
PEER GYNT. I might just as well have
  stayed on here,
Snug in the Ronde mountains, right?
Spared toil and trouble and tired feet!
Peer Gynt—a troll? You lunatic, you!
Good-bye! Here's something to buy to-
  bacco.
TROLL KING. No, Prince!
PEER GYNT. Let go! You're out of your
  skull,
Or senile. Be off! Find a hospital!
TROLL KING. Ah, just the cure for my
  pains and aches.
But, as I told you, my grandson's brats
Have been taking over hereabouts;
And they're saying I only exist in
  books.
Your relatives always treat you worst:
I've heard that said, and I've learned
  it's true.
It's hard being only a legend now—
PEER GYNT. So many have been in that
  way cursed.
TROLL KING. And we trolls, we have no
  pension plan,
No mutual savings, or home relief—
In the Ronde they'd hardly be in line.
PEER GYNT. Thanks to that damned,
  "To yourself be enough"!
TROLL KING. Oh, the Prince doesn't
  have any cause for complaint.
And now, if somehow or other you
  could—
PEER GYNT. My man, you're sniffing on
  the wrong scent;
As it stands with me, I haven't a
  shred—
TROLL KING. Is it really true? His High-

ness, a beggar?
PEER GYNT. To the core. My princely ego spoils
In hock. It's your fault, you hellish trolls!
That shows what low company can augur.
TROLL KING. There goes another one of my hopes!
Farewell! It's not far to town, I'd judge—
PEER GYNT. What will you do there?
TROLL KING. Go on the stage.
The papers are calling for national types—
PEER GYNT. Good luck on your journey, Greet them from me.
If I can break loose, I'll go the same way.
I'll write them a farce, half gall, half candy,
And call it, *"Sic transit gloria mundi."*
[*Runs off down the road, as the* TROLL KING *shouts after him.*]

Scene 9

At a crossroads.
PEER GYNT. Now you're in for it, Peer—and then some!
The trolls' *enough* has sealed your doom.
The ship is wrecked. Cling to the spars!
Try anything; melting has to be worse!
BUTTON-MOLDER. [*At the crossroads.*]
Well, where's your affidavit, Peer?
PEER GYNT. Is this the crossroads? Here, so soon?
BUTTON-MOLDER. I can see spelled out on your face like a sign
How the message goes; I've read it before.
PEER GYNT. I'm tired of running—it does no good—
BUTTON-MOLDER. Yes; and besides, where does it lead?
PEER GYNT. True. To a forest, in the dead of night—
BUTTON-MOLDER. But there's an old tramp. Shall we have him wait?
PEER GYNT. No, let him go. He's been drinking, man!
BUTTON-MOLDER. But perhaps—
PEER GYNT. Shh; no—leave him alone!
BUTTON-MOLDER. Then, shall we start?
PEER GYNT. One question only.
What is it, "to be yourself," in truth?
BUTTON-MOLDER. A curious question out of the mouth
Of someone who recently—
PEER GYNT. Answer me plainly.
BUTTON-MOLDER. To be yourself is to slay yourself.[86]
But on you, that answer's sure to fail;
So let's say: to make your life evolve
From the Master's meaning to the last detail.
PEER GYNT. But suppose a man never gets to know
What the Master meant with him?
BUTTON-MOLDER. He must use intuition.
PEER GYNT. Intuitions can often be wrong and draw
A man *ad undas* in his profession.
BUTTON-MOLDER. Of course, Peer Gynt; but closing them out
Gives Him with the Hoof the choicest bait.
PEER GYNT. This affair is complicated at best—
All right; that I've been myself, I'll waive—
It's maybe too difficult to prove.
I'll accept that part of the case as lost.
But just now, walking the dew and drench,
I felt the shoes of my conscience pinch,
And I said to myself: yes, you have sins—
BUTTON-MOLDER. You're not going to start all over again—
PEER GYNT. No, not at all; great ones, I mean.
Not only in deeds, but thoughts and plans.
Abroad, I lived in dissipation—
BUTTON-MOLDER. Perhaps; but I have to see the list.
PEER GYNT. Well, give me time; I'll find a priest,
Confess, and bring you a declaration.
BUTTON-MOLDER. Yes, bring me that, and I can promise
You won't have the casting ladle to face.
But my orders, Peer—
PEER GYNT. That paper's old;
I'm sure it's already obsolete—
I played the prophet and trusted in Fate.
Well, may I try?

BUTTON-MOLDER. But—!
PEER GYNT. My dear, good man—
You can't have so much that needs to be done.
Here in this district, the air's so sweet,
It makes the people age more slowly.
You know what the Justedal pastor[87] wrote:
"It's rare that anyone dies in this valley."
BUTTON-MOLDER. To the next crossroads; not a step beyond.
PEER GYNT. A priest, if he has to be tied and bound! [*Runs off.*]

Scene 10

A hillside with heather, and a path winding over the ridge.

PEER GYNT. "This could be useful for many a thing,"
Said Espen, finding the magpie's wing.[88]
Who would have thought the sins I've done
Would save me when the night came on.
Well, it's a ticklish matter, I'm sure,
To go from the frying pan into the fire—
Still there's a precept you can't escape—
Namely, that as long as there's life, there's hope. [*A* LEAN PERSON, *dressed in a priest's cassock kilted up high and carrying a fowling net over his shoulder, comes hurrying along the slope.*]
Who's that? A priest with a fowling net!
Hi! I'm Fortune's child, all right!
Good evening, Pastor! This path is foul—
THE LEAN ONE. It is; the things one does for a soul.
PEER GYNT. Ah, someone's soon for heaven?
THE LEAN ONE. No; There's another route I hope he'll go.
PEER GYNT. Could I walk with you, Pastor, a little way?
THE LEAN ONE. With pleasure; I'm fond of company.
PEER GYNT. I'm quite disturbed—
THE LEAN ONE. *Heraus!* Explain!
PEER GYNT. You see here before you a decent man.
I've always obeyed our country's laws;
Never been booked in a station house—
But a man can sometimes lose his foothold
And stumble—
THE LEAN ONE. Yes, even the best have failed.
PEER GYNT. You know, small things—
THE LEAN ONE. Just trifles?
PEER GYNT. Yes;
When it comes to sinning in bulk, I pass.
THE LEAN ONE. Then, my dear man, find someone else;
I'm not what you seem to think I am—
You stare at my fingers; what about them?
PEER GYNT. You have such developed fingernails.
THE LEAN ONE. And now at my feet? Do you disapprove?
PEER GYNT. [*Pointing.*] Is that hoof natural?[89]
THE LEAN ONE. So I believe.
PEER GYNT. [*Raising his hat.*] I could have sworn that you were a priest;
And now I've the honor—Well, all for the best.
When the front door's open, avoid the back way;
When the king appears, bid the help good-by.
THE LEAN ONE. Shake hands! You seem unprejudiced.
Well, friend, what can I do to assist?
Now please, don't ask for money or power;
I haven't got them to give any more.
It's shameful how business has fallen off;
There's not enough market to feed a dwarf—
Souls aren't moving; just now and again,
A stray—
PEER GYNT. Has the race advanced so far?
THE LEAN ONE. On the contrary; no, it's slipping lower.
The majority end in a melting spoon.
PEER GYNT. Oh yes—I heard about that one time.
In fact, it's the reason why I've come.
THE LEAN ONE. Speak out!
PEER GYNT. If it wouldn't be immodest,
I'd be so glad—
THE LEAN ONE. For a lodging place?

PEER GYNT. You guessed what I need exactly, yes.
Business, you say, is declining fast;
So maybe you might relax a rule—
THE LEAN ONE. But, friend—
PEER GYNT. My demands are very small.
A salary is hardly necessary;
Just pleasant companions, if that's the story—
THE LEAN ONE. A heated room?
PEER GYNT. Not *overly* warmed—
Mainly the chance to leave unharmed—
The right, as they say, to transfer out
If a better position comes to light.
THE LEAN ONE. This makes me truly sorry, friend—
But you can't imagine how many requests
Of a similar type I've heard expressed
By those departing their mortal round.
PEER GYNT. But when I think over my former life,
I know that I'm highly qualified—
THE LEAN ONE. They were only trifles—
PEER GYNT. That's what I said;
But now I remember, I traded in slaves—
THE LEAN ONE. There are men who've traded in minds and wills,
But done it badly, and lost their appeals.
PEER GYNT. I've packed out idols to the Orient.
THE LEAN ONE. Mere quibbles! Pure divertissement.
People pack idols of a viler sort
Into sermons, literature, and art—
And they stay outside—
PEER GYNT. But the worst of it
You couldn't guess—I played a prophet!
THE LEAN ONE. Abroad? Humbug! The end of most subtle
Sehen ins Blaue is the casting ladle.
If that's all you have to support your case,
With the best good will, I'll have to refuse.
PEER GYNT. But wait; in a shipwreck—I clung to a boat—
"Drowning men clutch at straws"—there's proof;
And, "it's every man for himself"—I quote—
Well, I halfway robbed a cook of his life.
THE LEAN ONE. I couldn't care if you'd half-robbed a pretty
Kitchenmaid of her virginity.
What kind of stuff is this "halfway" talk?
Begging your pardon, but I wish you'd tell
Me who's going to waste expensive fuel,
In times likes these, on such poppycock?
Now don't get mad; it's your sins I'm attacking,
Not you; forgive this bold way of speaking.
Listen, my friend, don't be absurd;
Resign yourself to the melting spoon.
What would you gain by my bed and board?
Consider; you're a sensible man.
Well, you'd have memory, that's for certain—
But in the country of memory, the scene
Would offer both your mind and your brain,
As the Swedes would put it, "Mighty poor sport."
You'd have nothing to rouse a moan or a laugh;
Nothing to fill you with joy or grief;
Nothing to make you run cold or hot;[90]
Just barely enough to irritate.
PEER GYNT. As they say: it isn't that easy to know
Where the shoe hurts when it's not on you.
THE LEAN ONE. That's the truth. Thanks to so-and-so
I've no need for more than a single shoe.
But it's fortunate one of us brought up shoes;
It reminds me I have to be hurrying on—
I'm fetching a roast that's far from lean;
And I can't stand around, shooting the breeze—
PEER GYNT. May I ask what fodder of sin you used
To fatten the man?
THE LEAN ONE. I was advised
That he'd been himself in every respect;
And that, after all, is the crucial fact.

PEER GYNT. Himself! Tell me, is *that* group yours?
THE LEAN ONE. It depends. Some find their way in downstairs.
Remember, there are two ways that a man
Is himself; two sides, right and wrong, to a coat.
You know they've discovered in Paris of late,
How to make portraits by means of the sun.
The picture comes either direct and alive,
Or else in the form of a negative.
In the latter the lights and shadows reverse;
The casual eye will find it coarse—
But the likeness is there for all of that,
And it only remains to bring it out.
Now if, in the path of its life, a soul
Records itself in the negative way,
The plate doesn't go in the rubbish pile—
Rather, it's simply turned over to me.
I take it and treat it in suitable fashion
And gradually work a transformation.
I steam and I dip, I burn and rinse
With sulfur and other ingredients,
Till it has the image it ought to have—
Or as people call it, the positive.
But with someone like you that's half erased,
Sulfur and lye just go to waste.
PEER GYNT. So one has to come to you black as a crow
To become a white grouse? May I ask you now
What name is under this negative portrait
That you're going to change to the positive state?
THE LEAN ONE. The name's Peter Gynt.
PEER GYNT. Peter Gynt? Ah, yes! Is he himself?
THE LEAN ONE. He swears that he is.
PEER GYNT. Well, he can be trusted, this same Herr Peter.
THE LEAN ONE. You know him perhaps?
PEER GYNT. Oh, just a smatter—
One knows so many—
THE LEAN ONE. I've got to skip; Where'd you see him last?
PEER GYNT. Down by the Cape.
THE LEAN ONE. *Di buona speranza?*
PEER GYNT. Yes, but I'd guess
He'd be sailing soon, if I'm not amiss.
THE LEAN ONE. Then I'd better be heading down there quick.
If I only can catch him now in a hurry!
That Cape of Good Hope, it makes me sick—
It's been ruined by Stavanger[91] missionaries. [*Rushes off southward.*]
PEER GYNT. The stupid dog! There he's racing off
With his tongue hanging out. That's a laugh.
What a pleasure it is to fool such an ass
With his precious airs and his solemn face!
He thinks he has something to swagger about!
His job's not likely to make him fat—
He'll fall from his perch, with all that's his.
Hm! I'm not that secure in *my* own nest,
Expelled, as it were, from the *self*-possessed. [*A falling star is seen. He nods after it.*]
Here's from Peer Gynt, Brother Shooting-Star!
Shine, flash down, and disappear—
[*Pulls himself together apprehensively and goes deeper into the mists; silence for a moment; then he cries.*]
Is there no one, no one to hear me even—
No one in darkness, no one in heaven—!
[*Re-emerges farther down, throws his hat on the path and tears at his hair. Gradually a stillness comes over him.*]
So unspeakably poor, then, a soul can go
Back to nothingness, in the misty gray.
You beautiful earth, don't be annoyed
That I've left no sign I walked your grass.
You beautiful sun, in vain you've shed
Your glorious light on an empty house.
There was no one within to cheer and warm—
The owner, they tell me, was never at home.
Beautiful sun and beautiful earth,
All you gave to my mother went to beg.
Nature is lavish; the spirit is mean.
How costly to pay with your life for your birth!
I want to climb up on the highest crag

And see the sunrise once again
And stare myself blind at the promised land;
Then let me be covered by drifting snows;
Scratch on a rock, "Here No One lies."
And afterward—then—! Ah, never mind.
CHURCHGOERS. [*Singing on the forest path.*] O blessed morn,
When the tongues of God
Struck the earth like flaming steel!
From the earth reborn
Now the sons of God
Raise songs to praise His will.
PEER GYNT. [*Shrinking in fright.*] Don't look! It's desert there inside—
I fear I was dead long before I died. [*Tries to creep into the bushes, but stumbles out onto the crossroads.*]
BUTTON-MOLDER. Good morning, Peer! Where's your list of sins?
PEER GYNT. Don't you think I've been turning stones
For all I'm worth?
BUTTON-MOLDER. You met no one here?
PEER GYNT. Only a traveling photographer.
BUTTON-MOLDER. Well, your time is up.
PEER GYNT. Everything's up.
The owl smells a rat. He hoots in his sleep.
BUTTON-MOLDER. That's the matin's bell—
PEER GYNT. [*Pointing.*] What's that shining?
BUTTON-MOLDER. Just light in a hut.
PEER GYNT. That sound growing louder?
BUTTON-MOLDER. Just a woman's song.
PEER GYNT. Yes, *there's* the meaning
To all my sins.
BUTTON-MOLDER. [*Seizing him.*] Put your house in order![92] [*They have come out of the wood and stand near the hut.*]
PEER GYNT. Put my house in order? That's it! Go on!
Pack out! If your ladle was big as a chest—
It still couldn't hold both me and my list!
BUTTON-MOLDER. To the third crossroads, Peer; but *then*—! [*Turns aside and goes.*]
PEER GYNT. [*Approaching the hut.*] Forward and back, it's just as far.

Out or in, it's a narrow door. [*Stops.*]
No! Like an endless, wild lament,
It tells me: return, go in where you went. [*Takes several steps, but stops again.*]
Roundabout, said the Boyg! [*Hears singing in the hut.*] No! This time
Straight through, no matter how steep the climb! [*He runs toward the hut. At the same moment,* SOLVEIG *appears in the doorway, dressed for church, with a hymnbook wrapped in a kerchief and a staff in her hand. She stands there, erect and mild.* PEER GYNT *throws himself down on the threshold.*]
Lay judgment on a sinner's head!
SOLVEIG. It's him! It's him! Praise be to God! [*Gropes toward him.*]
PEER GYNT. Cry out how sinfully I've gone astray!
SOLVEIG. You've sinned in nothing, my only boy! [*Groping again and finding him.*]
BUTTON-MOLDER. [*Behind the hut.*]
The list, Peer Gynt?
PEER GYNT. Cry out my wrongs!
SOLVEIG. [*Sitting down beside him.*] You've made my whole life a beautiful song.
Bless you now that you've come at last!
And bless our meeting this Pentecost!
PEER GYNT. So then I'm lost!
SOLVEIG. That's for One to settle.
PEER GYNT. [*With a laugh.*] Lost! Unless you can solve a riddle!
SOLVEIG. Ask me.
PEER GYNT. Ask you? Yes! Tell me where Peer Gynt has been this many a year?
SOLVEIG. Been?
PEER GYNT. With his destiny on him, just
As when he first sprang from the mind of God!
Can you tell me that? If not, I'm afraid
I'll go down forever in the land of mist.[93]
SOLVEIG. [*Smiling.*] O that riddle's easy.
PEER GYNT. What reply can you give!
Where have I been myself, whole and true?
Where have I been, with God's mark on my brow?
SOLVEIG. In my faith, in my hope, and in my love.
PEER GYNT. [*Starting back.*] What are you saying—? Don't play with words!

To the boy inside you're mother and nurse.
SOLVEIG. I am, yes—but who is his father?
It's He who grants the prayers of the mother.
PEER GYNT. [*A light breaks over him; he cries out.*] My mother; my wife! You innocent woman—!
O, hide me, hide me within!⁹⁴ [*Clings to her, covering his face in her lap. A long silence. The sun rises.*]⁹⁵
SOLVEIG. [*Singing softly.*] Sleep, my dear, my dearest boy,
Here in my arms! I'll watch over thee—

The boy has sat on his mother's lap.
In play, they've used their life's day up.

The boy's been safe in his mother's breast
His whole life's day. May his life be blessed!

The boy has lain so near to my heart
His whole life's day. Now he's tired out.

Sleep, my dear, my dearest boy,
Here in my arms! I'll watch over thee!
BUTTON-MOLDER'S VOICE. [*From behind the hut.*] We'll meet at the final crossroads, Peer;
And *then* we'll see—I won't say more.
SOLVEIG. [*Her voice rising in the early light.*] Sleep in my arms; I'll watch over thee—
Sleep and dream, my dearest boy!

With proper names and place-names, I have followed as far as possible the spellings of Ibsen's nineteenth-century Dano-Norwegian, rather than the later revisions of the language reformers he regarded with such suspicious concern. In a few cases I have made or kept transliterations where euphony in English or precedents of usage seemed to recommend them: Boyg, for instance, for Bøyg in the original.

For a number of other instances, in which the original forms have been retained, some guide to Norwegian pronunciation might be useful. The phoneme *aa* (the modern *å* recommended by the Nordic Orthographic Congress, Stockholm, 1869, to which Ibsen was a delegate) is sounded like the *aw* in "flaw"; and the final *e* is pronounced: thus *Aase* is "AW-suh." The double *ee* has the *ai* sound in "chair"; and *y* is equivalent to German *ü*: thus *Peer Gynt* is "PAIR GÜNT." The *a* has its full sound as in "fall"; and *j* is pronounced as *y*: thus *Valfjeld* is "VOL-f(yell)d." *Ei* has the sound of *ay* in "play"; final *g* is mute: thus *Solveig* is "SOHL-vay." Among the vowels, *i* is pronounced *ee* (*Kari*, "KAHR-ee"), and *ø* has the sound of German *ö*. As in Danish, the letter *d* within a word is often not pronounced: *Mads Moen* is "MAHSS MOAN." The above are only approximations, but they should allow an actor or reader to find intonations that have some flavor of the original. [R. F.]

1. *Gjendin ridge:* A precipitous mountain edge between Lake Bygdin and Lake Gjendin in Jotunheimen, Norway.

2. *Where are the snows of yesteryear:* This expression, though originating in Villon's "*Où sont les neiges d'antan?*" had become assimilated in Norwegian and Danish.

3. *loafing in the chimney-corner home:* The hero of Norse fairy tales from at least as far back as the Middle Ages is the Askeladd, the male counterpart of Cinderella. Usually the youngest of three brothers, he holds the most menial position in the household and is assumed to be lazy, stupid, and incompetent. When he escapes from the narrow and humiliating conditions at home, however, he proves that, without difficulty, he can master any task set before him. He vaniquishes trolls, confounds the king, and wins the princess and half the kingdom. Aase's denunciation is in part her hope that Peer will live out the Askeladd's destiny.

4. *Lunde:* A common name for a farm throughout Norway; so probably a large farm, consisting of as many as twenty-five to thirty buildings, virtually on the scale of a small village.

5. *changeling:* An ugly, malformed, or imbecilic child, thought to be the offspring of gnomes or evil spirits and substituted by them for a normal human child. One way that the mother could recover her own was to beat the changeling soundly, whereupon it would vanish through the air and the true child would reappear in the cradle.

6. *Engelland:* An old form, found in ballads and nursery rhymes, for England. Logeman observes that the name connotes the country of angels (Engel-land), suggesting that it must be taken as a vague, cloud-borne realm of chivalry and high romance.

7. *the halling:* The most acrobatic of the Norwegian folk dances, performed only by men, who dance alone, frequently to show off their agility before a girl.

8. *Master of Ceremonies:* Literally, the chief cook, but in function a kind of master of ceremonies at a country wedding feast.

9. *It's high to this ceiling:* In the halling, it is considered a great feat for the dancer to kick the rafters. Here, in the open air, the young man is saying, his leaps will be even more spectacular.

10. *Hedal:* Near the Sperillen lake in Valdres.

11. *the kerchief she carried her prayer book in:* Peasant women had the custom, when going to church, of carrying their hymnbooks wrapped in their kerchiefs. Solveig's parents thus show their expec-

tation that the wedding will be a solemn and religious one.

12. *I'm just confirmed:* About fifteen or sixteen years old.

13. *The soul of piety:* Solveig's father belongs to a sect of pietists, possibly that begun in the early nineteenth century by H. N. Hauge, whose followers were known as "the awakened ones"; therefore he would regard most forms of pleasure as sinful and to be avoided.

14. *draug:* "an apparition of a headless man (often in a half-boat), which appears to somebody destined to die soon, especially by drowning." Haugen, *Norwegian-English Dictionary.* Exactly how a headless apparition screams is a fine point for pneumatologists; but Aase, in her distraction, is clearly beyond such considerations.

15. *Three Herd Girls:* Literally, three *seter* girls, the *seter* being the alpine meadows where the cattle were driven to pasture for the summer months, watched over by dairy maids, who lived an isolated life in the outfarms, or *seter*-huts.

16. *a three-headed troll:* Trolls came not only in the two- and three-headed varieties, but also with four, five, six, eight, nine, and twelve heads. But these hardly bore comparison with the Devil's grandmother, who, according to report, had three hundred.

17. *We won't have a bed lying empty now:* "Now," in the original, reads "this Saturday night." On Saturday evening, when the week's farmwork was done, the unmarried girls would retire, usually to the *stabbur* or storehouse, and the young men would meet them in bed, although decorum dictated that the strict rules of bundling must be observed. This was often the only way for young people to get to know one another, since it was considered effeminate for a young man openly to seek a girl's company.

18. *The Ronde Mountains:* A mountain group on the southeastern edge of the Dovre range.

19. *A Woman in Green:* Cf. Asbjørnsen, "Reindeer Hunt at Ronde," in which a hunter named Klomsrud falls in with fourteen green-clad women, green because they belong to the race of the *underjordiske,* those who live under the green sod and are thought to incorporate the souls of the dead.

20. *drawing his finger across his throat:* Probably with the implication of Polonius (*Hamlet*, 2.2), who points to his head and shoulders, saying, "Take this from this, if this be otherwise."

21. *The Royal Hall of the King of the Dovre Mountains:* Much of the basic material for this scene has been freely adapted from H. C. Andersen's charming tale, "Elf Hill" ("Elverhøj").

22. *Same as with us:* cf. Holberg, *Ulysses von Ithacia*, 2.2. Ulysses' servant Chilian, encountering a Trojan, questions him about life on the other side of the lines and, to every disclosure of folly and corruption, can rightly reply, with a score of minor variations of the phrase, "Same as with us."

Ibsen puts the quotation to ironic use: Whereas Chilian realistically perceives the universality of human nature everywhere and thus the supreme folly of misunderstanding and war, Peer is spiritually blind to the very real difference between the complacent self-satisfaction of the trolls and the striving toward self-realization of the truly human being.

23. *to yourself be—enough:* Herman Weigand finds the conceptual equivalent of this phrase in Augustine's *De Civitate Dei*, Book 14, chap. 13. In discussing the fall of man, Augustine states that man's fundamental sin consists in *"sibi sufficere,"* i.e., falling away from God, the source of all being. *"Sibi sufficere,"* Weigand suggests, may have filtered down to the theological language of Ibsen's time in sermons or the catechism, to be exactly rendered, then, in the phrasing of the troll's motto.

24. *Our simple, domestic way of life:* "Under the figure of the trolls, the party in Norway which demands commercial isolation and monopoly for home products is most acutely satirized." Edmund Gosse, *Northern Studies*.

25. *food and drink.* The act of eating or joining with others in a common meal has a sacramental and binding character in many myths and rituals, e.g., the seven pomegranate seeds that condemned Persephone to three months each year in the Underworld.

26. *our tails:* Trolls are most easily recognized by their tails, which link them both to prehuman existence and to the family and domain of Satan. The outward symbol of certain inward traits, the tail falls off of itself when the *huldre* (literally, one of the "hidden people," from Germanic *haljō*, "concealed place," whence also Old Norse *Hel*, "the underworld"), through marriage with a human being, is consecrated by the priest.

27. *Blackfrock's cows:* A reference to the cassock of the priest. The trolls identify the church bells, which they cannot abide, with cow bells.

28. *King Saul killed hundreds:* Cf. 1 Samuel 18:7. "Saul has slain his thousands, And David his ten thousands." Peer might be identifying with David in another context as well, casting the Boyg as his Goliath.

29. *The great Boyg:* The enigma of this symbolic presence has called forth a wide spectrum of interpretations. In Asbjørnsen's original folk tale, it is an invisible, apparently enormous troll. The word *bøyg* is related to the German *beugen:* to curve, meander, bend. Thus, some have identified the Boyg with the Midgardsorm of the Eddas, the world serpent coiled, like Okeanos, about the earth. Others have suggested that this voice speaking out of the darkness may be taken to be a voice out of the depth of Peer's own being. Groddeck describes it as "the self, the objective self, the opposite to the ego." On this point, as with everything else in the poem, readers had best follow the Button-Molder's advice and subordinate the commentators to what, intuitively, they feel is mean-

ingful to them.

30. *the wingbeats of great birds:* Probably the sound of witches in flight, cf. Asbjørnsen, "Tales of a Sexton." Or possibly, the spirits of the dead, which also are often reincarnated in birds (cf. *New Golden Bough,* 2: "Taboo and the Perils of the Soul," 151, and Add. Note). When the saga hero Sigurd killed the dragon Fafnir and tasted his heart's blood, he acquired a knowledge of the language of birds. But Peer, already partly in the trolls' power, by closing out the hero's mission he was born for, makes the birds his enemies.

31. *Soria-Moria Castle:* The name "Soria-Moria" comes from the Arabic and refers to a group of small islands outside the Red Sea which the Arabs believe to be the Isles of the Blessed.

32. *Grane:* The legendary horse belonging to Sigurd Fafnirsbane.

33. *Mr. Cotton:* In his poem "Abraham Lincoln's Death" Ibsen designates John Bull as "the cotton magnate." And elsewhere, in an early piece of drama criticism, he comments on "a complete Englishman, who is willing enough to help his friend, but by no means loses sight of his cotton interests."

34. *Ballon:* The surname "balloon" evokes the airiness of French politesse, with possibly an allusion to vacillating policies of the Emperor Napoleon III.

35. *Eberkopf:* In German, "boar's head," an image suggesting recent Prussian aggressions against Austria and Denmark.

36. *Trumpeterstraale:* Literally, "trumpet blast," a barbed thrust at Swedish nonintervention in the Prusso-Danish War.

37. *world-historical-fellowship:* In the original, *verdenborgerdomsforpagtning*—a far-fetched example of German agglutinated words.

38. *if you won the earth entire, and lost your self:* Cf. Luke 9:25; Matthew 16:26; Mark 8:36.

39. *Lippe-Detmold:* A small Westphalian principality, later incorporated in 1870 in the German Empire.

40. *Charles the Twelfth:* The Swedish warrior-king (1682–1718) who led campaigns against Denmark, Norway, Poland, Russia, and Turkey.

41. *Bender:* The town in which Charles XII is said to have torn the caftan of the Turkish vizier with his spurs for betraying his ambitions by concluding a truce with Russia.

42. *Goddam:* Ibsen inserts this old form of the oath, in English, in his Norwegian text. As far back as the fifteenth century, Joan of Arc had called the English soldiers in France "the Goddams" for their effusive swearing.

43. *Castalia:* Not a stream, but the celebrated fountain sacred in antiquity to Apollo and the Muses. It is situated on Mount Parnassus, not Olympus, as Cotton seems to believe.

44. *Morning and evening are not alike:* Probably an allusion to Psalms 90:6, although there is also a recall of the Troll King's words in act 2.

45. *Bus and I, why, we're relatives:* Darwin's theories had been introduced into Norway by way of thorough and intelligent expositions appearing in the magazine *Budstikken* for February and March 1861.

46. *Bornu:* A region in the Sudan, south of the desert.

47. *Habes:* Or Habesch, the Arabic word for Abyssinia.

48. *Gyntiana:* In 1852, Ole Bull, the celebrated violinist, had founded a Norwegian colony in America, modeled after those of the French socialists, which he named "Oleana." The name and the fantastic claims advanced by the founder—here echoed by Peer—survive today in the well-known folk song.

49. *The ass in the ark:* probably alludes to a venerable conundrum: Q. What ass brayed so loud that everyone in the world could hear it? A. The ass on Noah's ark.

50. *My kingdom . . . for a horse:* Cf. Shakespeare, *Richard III,* 5.4.

51. *Ab esse ad posse:* The axiom in logic, *ab esse ad posse valet, ab posse ad esse non valet consequentia.* It is permissible to argue from fact to possibility, but not the reverse.

52. *Kaaba:* A small, cubical building in the court of the Great Mosque in Mecca, which contains the famous Black Stone, believed to have been given the prophet Abraham by the angel Gabriel.

53. *What did I ever want in that crew:* Cf. Molière, *Les Fourberies de Scapin,* 2.7, "*Que diable allait-il faire dans cette galère?*" Ibsen had staged *Scapins skalkestykker* at Det Norske Theater in Christiania in March 1859. {See *Our Dramatic Heritage,* 2:579.}

54. *Das Ewig-Weibliche zieht uns an.* An intentional misquotation of the concluding lines of *Faust:* "*Das Ewig-Weibliche zieht uns hinan.*" Goethe's "The Eternal Feminine draws us upward," filtered through the Gyntian soul, becomes "The Eternal Feminine lures us on."

Ibsen's series of pointed references to Shakespeare, Molière, Holberg, and Goethe may be taken both as an *hommage* to his great predecessors, their influence and inspiration, and as a discreet bid to be considered in their company.

55. *I knew a fellow just like that:* Frances Bull makes the interesting suggestion about this otherwise obscure passage that the soul-inflated man who lost his meaning, spouting rant, was Brand. If so, Peer sees his antithesis through a degree of self-projection.

56. *do you know what it means to live:* Peer's reply to his rhetorical question should be compared with Ibsen's own answer, phrased in a famous quatrain:

> What is life—but to fight
> In heart and mind with trolls?
> And poetry? That's to write
> The last judgment of our souls.

57. *Becker:* K. F. Becker's *Weltgeschichte,* a popular textbook published 1801–9, and translated into

Danish in 1851.

58. *The statue of Memnon:* Memnon was the son of the dawn, king of the Ethiopians, and lived in the extreme east, on the shore of Ocean. He and his warriors fought for Troy, where he was slain by Achilles. On his death, his mother Eos (Dawn) begged Zeus to grant him honor and immortality. Zeus did so by turning the sparks of his funeral pyre into birds, which rose, divided into two flocks, and fought until they turned back into ashes. Every year the battle of these birds, called Memnonides, is re-enacted. The enormous stone seated figure by the Nile at Thebes is said to give forth a sound like the breaking of a lyre string each morning at sunrise, which supposedly is Memnon greeting Eos. Ovid relates the story in Book 13 of the *Metamorphoses*.

The owl of wisdom was the emblem of the University of Christiania; so that, in the midst of Peer's historical phase, in a land burdened by a dead past, Ibsen would seem to be accusing the academics in his own country of doting on the dead past, rather than perpetuating and renewing their culture through song (poetry) and struggle (healthy controversy).

59. *Music of the past:* An allusion to the *Zukunftsmusik* of Richard Wagner, whose book, *The Art Work of the Future*, had appeared in 1849.

60. *threescore and ten Interpreters:* The authors of the Greek version of the New Testament known as the Septuagint. No satisfactory explanation has been offered for the 160 more.

61. *An insane asylum:* Ibsen follows the tradition of Dante in the Inferno of *The Divine Comedy* and Goethe in the Walpurgisnacht scenes of *Faust*, by elaborating a symbolic setting that will fitly contain, characterize, and condemn the definitive evils of the time. The dawning age of a deranged future over which Peer Gynt is to reign would appear to be a complete and self-centered transvaluation of values of the sort that the later Ibsen was often, if falsely, accused of abetting.

62. *my countryman Munchausen's fox:* Cf. Chap. 2, *The Adventures of Baron Munchausen*. The Baron, out hunting in a Russian forest, encounters a black fox whose skin is too fine to spoil by gunshot. He skewers the fox's tail to a tree with a spike nail, and flogs him with his whip till he leaps out of his skin.

63. *Huhu:* A caricature of the *Maalstrevere*, the ultranationalist group of language reformers, and particularly, Logeman notes, an attack on A. O. Vinje. As a result of Ivar Aasen's publications, beginning in 1848, demonstrating the continuity of local Norwegian dialects with Old Norse, and led by him and Vinje, the *maalstrevere* faction agitated against Dano-Norwegian in favor of return to the old language, the *Landsmål* which Aasen codified, eventually renamed *Nynorsk* or "New Norwegian" in 1929. Foreign sirens refers to the cultural domination of the Danes, who had ruled the country from the end of the fourteenth to the beginning of the nineteenth centuries. The *orangoutangs* are the Norse vikings, whose "growls and grunts" must be fostered in the latter-day, peasant Malabaris.

64. *a Fellah carrying a mummy on his back:* A satire on the cult of the heroic Charles XII among the Swedes, who had proved themselves like their venerated "royal mummy," during the events in 1864, only in the lifelessness of their responses.

Of more general importance here is the fact that Ibsen is showing two forms of the self-preoccupied withdrawal from and distortion of reality that arises out of living in and for an irrecoverable past, first as it affects words, then as it affects deeds.

65. *In the likeness of a bull:* The sacred bull worshiped in Ptolemaic times as the earthly incarnation of the Egyptian god of the underworld, Serapis (Osiris-Apis).

66. *Hussein, a cabinet minister:* An allusion to the Swedish Foreign Secretary, Count Manderström, who had thought to deter Prussian aggression with a flurry of diplomatic notes. F. L. Lucas aptly compares him to Neville Chamberlain.

67. *Hallingskarv, Jøkel:* A mountain and a glacier, respectively, in the Hardanger district, along which the ship is coasting.

68. *Folgefonnen:* An immense glacier between the Hardanger Fjord and its branch, the Sør Fjord.

69. *Blaahø:* Literally, in Norwegian dialect, "bluetop," the name of several peaks in Jotunheim.

70. *Galdhøpiggen:* The highest mountain (8,097 ft.) in Scandinavia, near the end of the Sogne Fjord in Jotunheim.

71. *Haarteigen:* A mountain east of Odda in Hardanger.

72. *Far between and long away:* In 1886, Ibsen wrote to a German friend: ". . . he who would know me fully must know Norway. The grand but austere nature with which people are surrounded in the North, the lonely, isolated life—their homes often lie many miles apart—compel them to be indifferent to other people and to care only about their own concerns; therefore they become ruminative and serious-minded; they ponder and doubt; and they often despair. With us every other man is a philosopher. Then there are the long dark winters, with the thick fog about the houses—oh, they long for the sun!"

73. *A conscience at ease is a downy pillow:* The proverb appears both in Norwegian and German: *Ein gutes Gewissen ist ein sanftes Ruhekissen*.

74. *The Strange Passenger:* This personification of Peer's destiny as guide has been variously interpreted—as Peer's double, as an emissary from the supernatural world, as the Devil, as Lord Byron, and as a projection of Kierkegaardian dread.

75. *mayor:* i.e., *lensmann*, rural mayor (Brynildsen, *Norsk-Engelsk Ordbok*), that is, the chief civil authority in a district. The titles of functionaries, being intrinsically bound up with the par-

ticular social system of a country, are the translator's despair.

76. *Glittertind:* A peak almost as high as its close neighbor, Galdhøpiggen. Its summit is covered by a snow mantle nearly one hundred feet thick.

77. *Now there's only the rubbish here:* In this scene, relationships that have developed during Peer's long absence are made to surface and disappear in such obscurity that some explanation seems called for. Both Hegstad and Ingrid have apparently gone downhill since Peer's bride-rape. Aslak (The Man in Mourning) has married her; he shows, however, no great love for her, perhaps because her ways have become too free and easy even for him, though Mads Moen (The Man in Gray) observes that Aslak has never been overly delicate. Their conversation degenerates into a coarse joke that Ingrid may yet cheat Death: i.e., Death has been the last of her several lovers. Considering the time lapse, the boy is hardly Peer's child, as some have conjectured, but Aslak's or, perhaps, Mads Moen's.

78. *A rotten egg:* In the original, a wind egg, i.e., one which has lost power of development and become putrid.

79. *a fable:* Peer's adventure in San Francisco is adapted directly out of Phaedrus, *Fabulae*, 5.5, "Scurra et Rusticus." In the original fable, after the buffoon has won the prize for the realism of his grunts, the countryman produces the real pig from under his cloak, rebuking his audience with the words: "Look, this shows what sort of judges you are."

80. *The eve of Pentecost:* The feast of Pentecost, being the ceremony of the descent of the Spirit, is central to the emphases Ibsen wishes to develop, as against the more familiar and orthodox Christian Easter symbolism in such works as *The Divine Comedy* and *Faust*.

81. *Of earth thou art come:* Cf. Genesis 3:19 (or Eccles. 12:7), characteristically misquoted by Peer.

82. *What's negative:* A play upon Hegelian terminology, in which "the negative"—that which opposes the primary thesis—creates the opportunity in turn for the higher concept, the synthesis.

83. *an old berserker:* One of a class of legendary warriors, who, in battle, fought in a frenzied rage, howled, bit their shields, foamed at the mouth, and were generally thought invulnerable. Peer briefly imitates their spirit in the Boyg scene when he bites his own arm.

84. *as the fox said:* A reference to the proverb: "This is a change," said the fox as they flayed him.

85. *Bloksberg ... Heklefjeld:* The Blocksberg, where German as well as Norwegian witches gathered for their great sabbaths on the Eve of May Day (Walpurgis Night) and Midsummer Eve, is commonly identified with the Brocken, the highest peak of the Harz Mountains. The Hekla Mountain in Iceland is another similar trysting place.

86. *To be yourself is to slay yourself:* This prescription has overtones of Matthew 16:25–26, but more directly concerns the choice first stated and now recently revived by the Troll King, namely, to kill one's self-sufficiency in order to become the open, full, and true self. The nature of the latter is eloquently indicated by Ibsen's French translator, Count Prozor, as follows: "*Être soi-même, ce n'est pas être Peer Gynt ou un autre, c'est être homme, c'est tuer en soi ce que Peer appelle orgueilleusement le moi Gyntien pour y faire vivre le moi humain.*"

87. *the Justedal pastor:* Matthias Foss (1714–92) became the parish priest of Justedal in 1742 and, eight years later, wrote a "short description of Justedal" in which this claim is advanced.

88. *Espen, finding the magpie's wing:* Refers to the folk tale "The Princess That No One Could Silence," in which Espen Askeladd finds a cringle, then a potsherd, and finally a dead magpie, and these apparently worthless things enable him to win "the princess and half the kingdom."

89. *Is that hoof natural:* The Devil in Norwegian folklore is represented as having a single hoof.

90. *Nothing to make you run cold or hot:* Cf. Revelation 3:15–16.

91. *Stavanger:* The Norwegian Missionary Society, founded in 1842, had its headquarters in Stavanger.

92. *Put your house in order:* Cf. Isaiah 38:1.

93. *the land of mist:* According to the Eddas, there was once no heaven above nor earth beneath, but only a bottomless deep, and a world of mist in which flowed a fountain that froze into rivers of ice. The world of mist was contrasted with the world of light lying to the south.

94. *hide me within:* Cf. John 3:3–7.

95. *The sun rises:* Ibsen may have been thinking of the belief, in folk tales, that the troll monster can only remain abroad until dawn, whereupon this primeval mountain spirit is changed back ("stone thou wast, to stone returnest") into its element, symbolically vanquished, as when the first rays of the Light of the World were shed on it. The hope of the ending is that the troll within Peer Gynt is immobilized at last.

Hedda Gabler

Henrik Ibsen

Having achieved excellence in romantic drama during the first half of his career, Ibsen in his late forties abruptly changed his approach to theater. Despite extensive critical investigation, there is no consensus as to precisely what caused Ibsen to strike out in such a markedly new direction, but the fact is that, in the middle 1870s, Ibsen dropped romanticism completely and turned instead to photographic realism. Ibsen, who had seriously considered in his younger days becoming a painter, now described himself metaphorically as a "photographer," but the slice-of-life technique pioneered by Zola was markedly transformed in Ibsen's hands. He also took up the well-made play form that had been so efficiently exploited by Scribe, turning the exciting but mechanical twists of plotting that Scribe's successors had reduced to formula into a meticulously crafted and beautifully articulated structure that brought realism to theatrical life as never before.

The Pillars of Society (1877) was Ibsen's first play in the new genre; it immediately broadened his fame across Europe, but his next work, *A Doll House* (1879), caused an outcry of incredible proportions. Depicting a marriage between a father-figure husband and a doll-like wife unused to dealing with the real world, *A Doll House* ends with the wife walking out on her husband; the door slam was "heard round the world." Victorian Europe was outraged at this attack upon the sanctity of marriage, and Ibsen's plays became both increasingly popular and increasingly the subject of violent controversy. As though in response to this controversy, Ibsen next wrote *Ghosts* (published in 1881) in which a wife, against her deepest instincts, has stuck with her husband through his debauchery and death, only to see her son die of inherited syphilis; the outcry against *A Doll House* was as nothing compared with that greeting *Ghosts:* "An open drain," wrote a British critic, "a loathsome sore unbandaged; a dirty act done publicly." For decades, even into the twentieth century, no "respectable" home contained a volume of Ibsen's plays. Of course a modern perspective reveals that their alleged violations of good taste were mild indeed, and that their true excellence lies altogether elsewhere.

The rise of the more important experimental European theaters devoted to the production of realistic plays, such as the Théâtre Libre in Paris, the Freie Bühne in Berlin and the Independent Theatre in London, is closely associated with Ibsen's important plays of this period. The production of his works was one of the major reasons for creating such theaters, and often his plays sustained them. All three of the theaters mentioned above produced *Ghosts* as their initial offering. Some critics, most notably George Bernard Shaw in London, championed Ibsen and proclaimed that the theatrical future had arrived. In retrospect, it has become clear that they were right: the theatrical movement pioneered by these experimental theaters has dominated world theater ever since. Others of Ibsen's major plays in this mode include *An Enemy of the People* (1883), *The Wild Duck* (1885), *Rosmersholm* (1887), *Hedda Gabler* (1891), and *The Master Builder* (1892). (All dates are those of first productions; some were published a year or so earlier.)

Ibsen, who had been living abroad for many years, returned to Norway in 1891, where he was virtually a hero. He made his home in Christiania, and devoted his last years to writing several plays that experimented with new techniques beyond realism; symbolism pervaded such works as *John Gabriel Borkman* (1896) and *When We Dead Awaken* (1900). Ibsen suffered an incapacitating stroke in 1900 and another in 1903; bedridden, he lingered until 1906, when he died on May 23 at the age of seventy-eight.

Hedda Gabler was published on December 16, 1890, and was first performed in Munich on January 31, 1891, with Ibsen in the audience. He did not like the performance, believing that the actress playing Hedda was too flamboyantly romantic in her acting style and unaccustomed to the naturalism that the new drama required. The play represents Ibsen at the mature peak of his dramatic powers, creating psychologically complex and yet consistent characters, a plot convincingly logical and yet carefully crafted to hold theatrical interest, and intellectually challenging thematic issues of social consequence—all in an environment scientifically and observably accurate and at the same time of immense significance in its impact on the lives of those within it. It was Ibsen's genius to bring these factors together in so carefully controlled a fashion as to create a kind of theatrical poetry; although the dialogue is prose, the several theatrical elements work together as do the elements of a poem to create both an emotional and an intellectual impact more profound than the sum of their parts. The poet that Ibsen had been earlier in his career was not dead; rather, he was creating poetry of a new type—"poetry of the theater," long before that phrase was coined by Cocteau.

Hedda dominates her play in spellbinding fashion. The title emphasizes that she is the General's daughter more than she is Tesman's wife, but she is a product of an environment in which she has never been able to find herself. Afraid to defy society by yielding to the more Dionysian impulses she feels within herself, and yet unable to find fulfillment in the domestic pursuits that society would assign her, Hedda is restless, bored, intelligent, and dangerous. Frigid herself, she is fascinated by the sex lives of others. Unable to create her own destiny, she yearns to control someone else's. Trapped and unhappy in a domestic situation of her own making, she yearns to break out but lacks the nerve to do so. Judge Brack brazenly offers Hedda a discrete sexual fling, but although he fascinates her, she is unwilling to make that commitment. Løvborg had once offered her the emancipated life for which a part of her evidently yearns, but Hedda hadn't the nerve to accept that alternative either. Most obviously, her pregnancy offers her a socially acceptable way to control a human destiny, but the responsibilities and the untidiness of motherhood are equally repugnant to Hedda. All her energy, therefore, is channeled into meddling in Løvborg's life; having rejected him as a lover, she still wants the satisfaction of molding him to fit her whims, and she is bitterly jealous of Thea who, through passive femininity, has shaped Løvborg's life as Hedda never can. Frustrated at every turn in this obsession, each manipulative ploy leading to disgrace and embarrassment rather than to the "beautiful destiny" that she envisions, Hedda finally takes the one definitive step left open to her—suicide—rather than submit her own life to Brack's control. But like most such desperate acts in real life, Hedda's suicide is caused by an accumulation of all the frustrations in her life; it is not the simple consequence of Brack's maneuvering, of a loveless marriage, of her unwanted pregnancy, or of her failure with respect to Løvborg.

In Hedda's eyes, Tesman is virtually a nonentity. She rarely thinks about him one way or another in contemplating her course of action. The wonder is that he had opportunity to get her pregnant at all, but it would be a mistake to think of Tesman as either stupid or uncaring. Sheltered and naïve, Tesman is, as Hedda says, a specialist, and he simply pays little attention to aspects of life outside that specialty. Narrow in that specialty, Tesman lacks the vision to create anything so original as Løvborg's book, but he does not lack either the honesty to appreciate Løvborg's genius or the integrity to devote himself to preserving that genius when he is suddenly thrust into a position to do so. Thea is essentially a selfless individual who takes warm satisfaction in helping the man she loves and who has had the courage that Hedda lacks to walk out of a loveless marriage. Clearly Tesman and Thea belong together, but Hedda projects no sexual jealousy—only frustration regarding her own goals—when, at the end of the play, it becomes clear that Thea will be the helpmeet that Tesman needs. There is no space here for detailed analysis of all the characters, but clearly Ibsen has found effective, natural, psychologically consistent ways to create all of them, and actors trained in the methods of inner truth that Ibsen foresaw can play his characters with stunning impact.

Structurally, Ibsen has used the well-made play form without the hurly-burly or sensationalism that the form often takes on in lesser hands. The central action is to control a human destiny. Ibsen employs the late point of attack, in which most of the story has already taken place before the opening curtain and must be told in artfully inserted exposition. The arrival of Thea gets the central action under way, and the burning of the manuscript is the turning point which eventually determines the outcome. The climax, of course, is Hedda's suicide. Along the way, each new complication is skillfully introduced as the logical outcome of that which has gone before, and the eventual disposition of every problem seems logically to result from the situation itself and from the nature of the people involved in it. A climax of sorts is reached at the end of each act, exciting further interest in what is to come and encouraging an audience back to its seats following intermission.

Because Ibsen dared to introduce subject matter previously not acceptable on the stage, and because he found his subjects in the real world about him, he has often been thought of as a playwright of social issues, and his plays as social problem plays. Ibsen insisted, however, that he was not a crusader, not attempting to solve any of society's problems through the theater, but was simply portraying real people in their real environments. *Hedda Gabler* demonstrates the way in which this approach both does and does not lead to social problems. The play is certainly not a "social problem play" in any narrow propagandistic sense of proposing political solutions to issues of the day. Attempts have been made, without success, to find arguments both for and against the "emancipated woman" in Hedda's search for some meaning in her rootless life. On the other hand, the problems of the characters are certainly shaped in part by their environments, and the social forces that have influenced Hedda, Thea, Løvborg and the others raise serious thematic questions about whether changes in society might not be both possible and desirable. Ibsen, more than any other writer, has helped to shape a kind of modern tragedy in which social and economic forces replace the sense of fate inherent in classical tragedy. The thematic questions thus raised are of the deepest and most serious kind, but they do change somewhat with the times, as social problems always do, whereas the more philosophical problems of the classical tragedy are eternal.

As a master of the theater, and not just of writing, Ibsen uses properties, scenery, costumes, and every element of production to create the total, scientifically accurate environment that not only influences the characters' lives so profoundly, but also takes on symbolic significance in the manner of the best poetry. Thea's hair (as contrasted to Hedda's) and General Gabler's pistols are significant symbols without being obtrusive. In the best well-made play tradition, a manuscript, a letter, a pistol are fulcrums on which plot matters turn without becoming trivial or banal as they sometimes did with Scribe. Even Ibsen's meticulous descriptions of the set can be ignored only at one's peril. The portrait of General Gabler, for example, although never mentioned in the dialogue, is of vital significance not only in brooding over all Hedda's actions, but also in being immediately above her at the moment she dies. The exact disposition of Aunt Juliana's hat is critically important in act 1, for it must reveal not only her confusion at apparently committing a social faux pas, and Tesman's absent-mindedness in being responsible for it, but also Hedda's degree of culpability at the calculated insult. Does she know from the beginning that the hat is Juliana's, or is she rationalizing her own cruelty when she tells Brack that she did?

Ibsen's achievement moves far beyond the "slice-of-life" technique in which it is rooted to create a benchmark by which all modern realistic drama has since been measured.

Because of the difficulties of translation, Ibsen's plays have sometimes been dismissed as stilted, and changing social values have sometimes suggested they were dated. As greater passage of time has allowed a more accurate perspective, however, and as such excellent translations as Fjelde's have appeared, it has become clear that Ibsen's plays are for all time and that his influence has been overwhelming. In the entire history of European drama, only a handful of playwrights can be counted his peers.

Hedda Gabler

Translated by Rolf Fjelde

Characters
George Tesman, *research fellow in cultural history*
Hedda Tesman, *his wife*
Miss Juliana Tesman, *his aunt*
Mrs. Elvsted
Judge Brack
Eilert Løvborg
Berta, *the Tesmans' maid*

The action takes place in TESMAN's *residence in the fashionable part of town.*

Act 1

A large, attractively furnished drawing room, decorated in dark colors. In the rear wall, a wide doorway with curtains drawn back. The doorway opens into a smaller room in the same style as the drawing room. In the right wall of the front room, a folding door that leads to the hall. In the left wall opposite, a glass door, with curtains similarly drawn back. Through the panes one can see part of an overhanging veranda and trees in autumn colors. In the foreground is an oval table with tablecloth and chairs around it. By the right wall, a wide, dark porcelain stove, a high-backed armchair, a cushioned footstool, and two taborets. In the right-hand corner, a settee with a small round table in front. Nearer, on the left and slightly out from the wall, a piano. On either side of the doorway in back, étagères with terra-cotta and majolica ornaments. Against the back wall of the inner room, a sofa, a table, and a couple of chairs can be seen. Above this sofa hangs a portrait of a handsome, elderly man in a general's uniform. Over the table, a hanging lamp with an opalescent glass shade. A number of bouquets of flowers are placed about the drawing room in vases and glasses. Others lie on the tables. The floors in both rooms are covered with thick carpets. Morning light. The sun shines in through the glass door.

MISS JULIANA TESMAN, *wearing a hat and carrying a parasol, comes in from the hall, followed by* BERTA, *who holds a bouquet wrapped in paper.* MISS TESMAN *is a lady around sixty-five with a kind and good-natured look, nicely but simply dressed in a gray tailored suit.* BERTA *is a maid somewhat past middle age, with a plain and rather provincial appearance.*

MISS TESMAN. [*Stops close by the door, listens, and says softly.*] Goodness. I don't think they're even up yet!

BERTA. [*Also softly.*] That's just what I said, Miss Juliana. Remember how late the steamer got in last night. Yes, and afterward! My gracious, how much the young bride had to unpack before she could get to bed.

MISS TESMAN. Well, then—let them enjoy a good rest. But they must have some of this fresh morning air when they do come down. [*She goes to the glass door and opens it wide.*]

BERTA. [*By the table, perplexed, with the bouquet in her hand.*] I swear there isn't a bit of space left. I think I'll have to put it here, miss. [*Places the bouquet on the piano.*]

MISS TESMAN. So now you have a new mistress, Berta dear. Lord knows it was misery for me to give you up.

BERTA. [*On the verge of tears.*] And for me, miss! What can I say? All those many blessed years I've been in your

service, you and Miss Rina.
MISS TESMAN. We must take it calmly, Berta. There's really nothing else to do. George needs you here in this house, you know that. You've looked after him since he was a little boy.
BERTA. Yes, but miss, I'm all the time thinking of her, lying at home. Poor thing—completely helpless. And with that new maid! She's never take proper care of an invalid, that one.
MISS TESMAN. Oh, I'll manage to teach her. And most of it, you know, I'll do myself. So you mustn't be worrying over my poor sister.
BERTA. Well, but there's something else too, miss. I'm really so afraid I won't please the young mistress.
MISS TESMAN. Oh, well—there might be something or other at first—
BERTA. Because she's so very particular.
MISS TESMAN. Well, of course. General Gabler's daughter. What a life she had in the general's day! Remember seeing her out with her father—how she'd go galloping past in that long black riding outfit, with a feather in her hat?
BERTA. Oh yes—I remember! But I never would have dreamed then that she and George Tesman would make a match of it.
MISS TESMAN. Nor I either. But now, Berta—before I forget: from now on, you mustn't say George Tesman. You must call him Doctor Tesman.
BERTA. Yes, the young mistress said the came thing—last night, right after they same in the door. Is that true, then, miss?
MISS TESMAN. Yes, absolutely. Think of it, Berta—they gave him his doctor's degree. Abroad, that is—on this trip, you know. I hadn't heard one word about it, till he told me down on the pier.
BERTA. Well, he's clever enough to be anything. But I never thought he'd go in for curing people.
MISS TESMAN. No, he wasn't made that kind of doctor. [*Nods significantly.*] But as a matter of fact, you may soon now have something still greater to call him.
BERTA. Oh, really! What's that, miss?
MISS TESMAN. [*Smiling.*] Hm, wouldn't you like to know! [*Moved.*] Ah, dear God—if only my poor brother could look up from his grave and see what his little boy has become! [*Glancing about.*] But what's this, Berta? Why, you've taken all the slipcovers off the furniture—?
BERTA. Madam told me to. She doesn't like covers on chairs, she said.
MISS TESMAN. Are they going to make this their regular living room, then?
BERTA. It seems so—with her. For his part—the doctor—he said nothing.
[GEORGE TESMAN *enters the inner room from the right, singing to himself and carrying an empty, unstrapped suitcase. He is a youngish-looking man of thirty-three, medium sized, with an open, round, cheerful face, blond hair and beard. He is somewhat carelessly dressed in comfortable lounging clothes.*]
MISS TESMAN. Good morning, good morning, George!
TESMAN. [*In the doorway.*] Aunt Julie! Dear Aunt Julie! [*Goes over and warmly shakes her hand.*] Way out here—so early in the day—uh?
MISS TESMAN. Yes, you know I simply had to look in on you a moment.
TESMAN. And that without a decent night's sleep.
MISS TESMAN. Oh, that's nothing at all to me.
TESMAN. Well, then you did get home all right from the pier? Uh?
MISS TESMAN. Why, of course I did—thank goodness. Judge Brack was good enough to see me right to my door.
TESMAN. We were sorry we couldn't drive you up. But you saw for yourself—Hedda had all those boxes to bring along.
MISS TESMAN. Yes, that was quite something, the number of boxes she had.
BERTA. [*To* TESMAN.] Should I go in and ask Mrs. Tesman if there's anything I can help her with?
TESMAN. No, thanks, Berta—don't bother. She said she'd ring if she needed anything.
BERTA. [*Going off toward the right.*] All right.
TESMAN. But wait now—you can take this suitcase with you.
BERTA. [*Taking it.*] I'll put it away in the

attic. [*She goes out by the hall door.*]

TESMAN. Just think, Aunt Julie—I had that whole suitcase stuffed full of notes. You just can't imagine all I've managed to find, rummaging through archives. Marvelous old documents that nobody knew existed—

MISS TESMAN. Yes, you've really not wasted any time on your wedding trip, George.

TESMAN. I certainly haven't. But do take your hat off, Auntie. Here—let me help you—uh?

MISS TESMAN. [*As he does so.*] Goodness—this is exactly as if you were still back at home with us.

TESMAN. [*Turning the hat in his hand and studying it from all sides.*] My—what elegant hats you go in for!

MISS TESMAN. I bought that for Hedda's sake.

TESMAN. For Hedda's sake? Uh?

MISS TESMAN. Yes, so Hedda wouldn't feel ashamed of me if we walked down the street together.

TESMAN. [*Patting her cheek.*] You think of everything, Aunt Julie! [*Laying the hat on a chair by the table.*] So—look, suppose we sit down on the sofa and have a little chat till Hedda comes. [*They settle themselves. She puts her parasol on the corner of the sofa.*]

MISS TESMAN. [*Takes both of his hands and gazes at him.*] How wonderful it is having you here, right before my eyes again, George! You—dear Jochum's own boy!

TESMAN. And for me too, to see you again, Aunt Julie! You, who've been father and mother to me both.

MISS TESMAN. Yes, I'm sure you'll always keep a place in your heart for your old aunts.

TESMAN. But Auntie Rina—hm? Isn't she any better?

MISS TESMAN. Oh no—we can hardly expect that she'll ever be better, poor thing. She lies there, just as she has all these years. May God let me keep her a little while longer! Because otherwise, George, I don't know what I'd do with my life. The more so now, when I don't have you to look after.

TESMAN. [*Patting her on the back.*] There, there—

MISS TESMAN. [*Suddenly changing her tone.*] No, but to think of it, that now you're a married man! And that it was *you* who carried off Hedda Gabler. The beautiful Hedda Gabler! Imagine! She, who always had so many admirers!

TESMAN. [*Hums a little and smiles complacently.*] Yes, I rather suspect I have several friends who'd like to trade places with me.

MISS TESMAN. And then to have such a wedding trip! Five—almost six months—

TESMAN. Well, remember, I used it for research, too. All those libraries I had to check—and so many books to read!

MISS TESMAN. Yes, no doubt. [*More confidentially; lowering her voice.*] But now listen, George—isn't there something—something special you have to tell me?

TESMAN. From the trip?

MISS TESMAN. Yes.

TESMAN. No, I can't think of anything beyond what I wrote in my letters. I got my doctor's degree down there—but I told you that yesterday.

MISS TESMAN. Yes, of course. But I mean—whether you have any kind of—expectations—?

TESMAN. Expectations?

MISS TESMAN. My goodness, George—I'm your old aunt!

TESMAN. Why, naturally I have expectations.

MISS TESMAN. Ah!

TESMAN. I have every expectation in the world of becoming a professor shortly.

MISS TESMAN. Oh, a professor, yes—

TESMAN. Or I might as well say, I'm sure of it. But, Aunt Julie—you know that perfectly well yourself.

MISS TESMAN. [*With a little laugh.*] That's right, so I do. [*Changing the subject.*] But we were talking about your trip. It must have cost a terrible amount of money.

TESMAN. Well, that big fellowship, you know—it took us a good part of the way.

MISS TESMAN. But I don't see how you could stretch it enough for two.

TESMAN. No, that's not so easy to see—uh?

MISS TESMAN. And especially traveling with a lady. For I hear tell that's much more expensive.

TESMAN. Yes, of course—it's a bit more expensive. But Hedda just had to have that trip. She *had* to. There was nothing else to be done.

MISS TESMAN. No, no, I guess not. A honeymoon abroad seems to be the thing nowadays. But tell me—have you had a good look around your house?

TESMAN. You can bet I have! I've been up since daybreak.

MISS TESMAN. And how does it strike you, all in all?

TESMAN. First-rate! Absolutely first-rate! Only I don't know what we'll do with the two empty rooms between the back parlor and Hedda's bedroom.

MISS TESMAN. [*Laughing again.*] Oh, my dear George, I think you can use them—as time goes on.

TESMAN. Yes, you're quite right about that, Aunt Julie! In time, as I build up my library—uh?

MISS TESMAN. Of course, my dear boy. It was your library I meant.

TESMAN. I'm happiest now for Hedda's sake. Before we were engaged, she used to say so many times there was no place she'd rather live than here, in Secretary Falk's town house.

MISS TESMAN. Yes, and then to have it come on the market just after you'd sailed.

TESMAN. We really have had luck, haven't we?

MISS TESMAN. But expensive, George dear! You'll find it expensive, all this here.

TESMAN. [*Looks at her, somewhat crestfallen.*] Yes, I suppose I will.

MISS TESMAN. Oh, Lord, yes!

TESMAN. How much do you think? Approximately? Hm?

MISS TESMAN. It's impossible to say till the bills are all in.

TESMAN. Well, fortunately Judge Brack has gotten me quite easy terms. That's what he wrote Hedda.

MISS TESMAN. Don't worry yourself about that, dear. I've also put up security to cover the carpets and furniture.

TESMAN. Security? Aunt Julie, dear—you? What kind of security could *you* give?

MISS TESMAN. I took out a mortgage on our pension.

TESMAN. [*Jumping up.*] What! On your—and Auntie Rina's pension!

MISS TESMAN. I saw nothing else to do.

TESMAN. [*Standing in front of her.*] But you're out of your mind, Aunt Julie! That pension—it's all Aunt Rina and you have to live on.

MISS TESMAN. Now, now—don't make so much of it. It's only a formality; Judge Brack said so. He was good enough to arrange the whole thing for me. Just a formality, he said.

TESMAN. That's all well enough. But still—

MISS TESMAN. You'll be drawing your own salary now. And, good gracious, if we have to lay out a bit, just now at the start—why, it's no more than a pleasure for us.

TESMAN. Oh, Aunt Julie—you hever get tired of making sacrifices for me!

MISS TESMAN. [*Rises and places her hands on his shoulders.*] What other joy do I have in this world than smoothing the path for you, my dear boy? You, without father or mother to turn to. And now we've come to the goal, George! Things may have looked black at times; but now, thank heaven, you've made it.

TESMAN. Yes, it's remarkable, really, how everything's turned out for the best.

MISS TESMAN. Yes—and those who stood against you—who wanted to bar your way—they've gone down. They've fallen, George. The one most dangerous to you—he fell farthest. And he's lying there now, in the bed he made—poor, misguided creature.

TESMAN. Have you heard any news of Eilert? I mean, since I went away.

MISS TESMAN. Only that he's supposed to have brought out a new book.

TESMAN. What's that? Eilert Løvborg? Just recently, uh?

MISS TESMAN. So they say. But considering everything, it can hardly amount to much. Ah, but when *your* new book comes out—it'll be a different story, George! What will it be about?

TESMAN. It's going to treat the domestic handicrafts of Brabant in the Middle Ages.

MISS TESMAN. Just imagine—that you can write about things like that!

TESMAN. Actually, the book may take quite a while yet. I have this tremendous collection of material to put in order, you know.

MISS TESMAN. Yes, collecting and ordering—you do that so well. You're not my brother's son for nothing.

TESMAN. I look forward so much to getting started. Especially now, with a comfortable home of my own to work in.

MISS TESMAN. And most of all, dear, now that you've won her, the wife of your heart.

TESMAN. [*Embracing her.*] Yes, Yes, Aunt Julie! Hedda—that's the most beautiful part of it all! [*Glancing toward the doorway.*] But I think she's coming—uh? [HEDDA *enters from the left through the inner room. She is a woman of twenty-nine. Her face and figure show breeding and distinction; her complexion is pallid and opaque. Her steel gray eyes express a cool, unruffled calm. Her hair is an attractive medium brown, but not particularly abundant. She wears a tasteful, rather loose-fitting gown.*]

MISS TESMAN. [*Going to meet* HEDDA.] Good morning, Hedda dear—how good to see you!

HEDDA. [*Holding out her hand.*] Good morning, my dear Miss Tesman! Calling so early? This *is* kind of you.

MISS TESMAN. [*Slightly embarrassed.*] Well—did the bride sleep well in her new home?

HEDDA. Oh yes, thanks. Quite adequately.

TESMAN. Adequately! Oh, I like that, Hedda! You were sleeping like a stone when I got up.

HEDDA. Fortunately. But of course one has to grow accustomed to anything new, Miss Tesman—little by little. [*Looking toward the left.*] Oh! That maid has left the door open—and the sunlight's just flooding in.

MISS TESMAN. [*Going toward the door.*] Well, we can close it.

HEDDA. No, no—don't! [*To* TESMAN.] There, dear, draw the curtains. It gives a softer light.

TESMAN. [*By the glass door.*] All right—all right. Look, Hedda—now you have shade and fresh air both.

HEDDA. Yes, we really need some fresh air here, with all these piles of flowers— But—won't you sit down, Miss Tesman?

MISS TESMAN. Oh no, thank you. Now that I know that everything's fine—thank goodness—I will have to run along home. My sister's lying there waiting, poor thing.

TESMAN. Give her my very, very best, won't you? And say I'll be looking in on her later today.

MISS TESMAN. Oh, you can be sure I will. But what do you know, George—[*Searching in her bag.*]—I nearly forgot. I have something here for you.

TESMAN. What's that, Aunt Julie? Hm?

MISS TESMAN. [*Brings out a flat package wrapped in newspaper and hands it to him.*] There, dear. Look.

TESMAN. [*Opening it.*] Oh, my—you kept them for me, Aunt Julie! Hedda! That's really touching! Uh!

HEDDA. [*By the* étagère *on the right.*] Yes, dear, what is it?

TESMAN. My old bedroom slippers! My slippers!

HEDDA. Oh yes. I remember how often you spoke of them during the trip.

TESMAN. Yes, I missed them terribly. [*Going over to her.*] Now you can see them, Hedda!

HEDDA. [*Moves toward the stove.*] Thanks, but I really don't care to.

TESMAN. [*Following her.*] Imagine—Auntie Rina lay and embroidered them, sick as she was. Oh, you couldn't believe how many memories are bound up in them.

HEDDA. [*At the table.*] But not for me.

MISS TESMAN. I think Hedda is right, George.

TESMAN. Yes, but I only thought, now that she's part of the family—

HEDDA. [*Interrupting.*] We're never going to manage with this maid, Tesman.

MISS TESMAN. Not manage with Berta?

TESMAN. But dear—why do you say that? Uh?

HEDDA. [*Pointing.*] See there! She's left

her old hat lying out on a chair.
TESMAN. [*Shocked; dropping the slippers.*] But Hedda—!
HEDDA. Suppose someone came in and saw it.
TESMAN. Hedda—that's Aunt Julie's hat!
HEDDA. Really?
MISS TESMAN. [*Picking it up.*] That's right, it's mine. And what's more, it certainly is not old—Mrs. Tesman.
HEDDA. I really hadn't looked closely at it, Miss Tesman.
MISS TESMAN. [*Putting on the hat.*] It's actually the first time I've had it on. The very first time.
TESMAN. And it's lovely, too. Most attractive!
MISS TESMAN. Oh, it's hardly all that, George. [*Looks about.*] My parasol—? Ah, here. [*Takes it.*] For that's mine too. [*Murmurs.*] Not Berta's.
TESMAN. New hat and new parasol! Just imagine, Hedda!
HEDDA. Quite charming, really.
TESMAN. Yes, aren't they, uh? But Auntie, take a good look at Hedda before you leave. See how charming *she* is!
MISS TESMAN. But George dear, there's nothing new in that. Hedda's been lovely all her life. [*She nods and starts out, right.*]
TESMAN. [*Following her.*] But have you noticed how plump and buxom she's grown? How much she's filled out on the trip?
HEDDA. [*Crossing the room.*] Oh, do be quiet—!
MISS TESMAN. [*Who has stopped and turned.*] Filled out?
TESMAN. Of course, you can't see it so well when she has that dressing gown on. But I, who have the opportunity to—
HEDDA. [*By the glass door, impatiently.*] Oh, you have no opportunity for anything!
TESMAN. It must have been the mountain air, down in the Tyrol—
HEDDA. [*Brusquely interrupting.*] I'm exactly as I was when I left.
TESMAN. Yes, that's your claim. But you certainly are not. Auntie, don't you agree?
MISS TESMAN. [*Gazing at her with folded hands.*] Hedda is lovely—lovely—lovely. [*Goes up to her, takes her head in both hands, bends it down and kisses her hair.*] God bless and keep Hedda Tesman—for George's sake.
HEDDA. [*Gently freeing herself.*] Oh—! Let me go.
MISS TESMAN. [*With quiet feeling.*] I won't let a day go by without looking in on you two.
TESMAN. Yes, please do that, Aunt Julie! Uh?
MISS TESMAN. Good-bye—good-bye!
[*She goes out by the hall door.* TESMAN *accompanies her, leaving the door half open. He can be heard reiterating his greetings to Aunt Rina and his thanks for the slippers. At the same time,* HEDDA *moves about the room, raising her arms and clenching her fists as if in a frenzy. Then she flings back the curtains from the glass door and stands there, looking out. A moment later* TESMAN *comes back, closing the door after him.*]
TESMAN. [*Retrieving the slippers from the floor.*] What are you standing and looking at, Hedda?
HEDDA. [*Again calm and controlled.*] I'm just looking at the leaves—they're so yellow—and so withered.
TESMAN. [*Wraps up the slippers and puts them on the table.*] Yes, well, we're into September now.
HEDDA. [*Once more restless.*] Yes, to think—that already we're in—in September.
TESMAN. Didn't Aunt Julie seem a bit strange? A little—almost formal? What do you suppose was bothering her? Hm?
HEDDA. I hardly know her at all. Isn't that how she usually is?
TESMAN. No, not like this, today.
HEDDA. [*Leaving the glass door.*] Do you think this thing with the hat upset her?
TESMAN. Oh, not very much. A little, just at the moment, perhaps—
HEDDA. But really, what kind of manners has she—to go throwing her hat about in a drawing room! It's just not proper.
TESMAN. Well, you can be sure Aunt Julie won't do it again.
HEDDA. Anyhow, I'll manage to smooth it over with her.
TESMAN. Yes, Hedda dear, I wish you would!

HEDDA. When you go in to see them later on, you might ask her out for the evening.

TESMAN. Yes, I'll do that. And there's something else you could do that would make her terribly happy.

HEDDA. Oh?

TESMAN. If only you could bring yourself to speak to her warmly, by her first name. For my sake, Hedda? Uh?

HEDDA. No, no—don't ask me to do that. I told you this once before. I'll try to call her "Aunt." That should be enough.

TESMAN. Oh, all right. I was only thinking, now that you belong to the family—

HEDDA. Hm—I really don't know— [*She crosses the room to the doorway.*]

TESMAN. [*After a pause.*] Is something the matter, Hedda? Uh?

HEDDA. I'm just looking at my old piano. It doesn't really fit in with all these other things.

TESMAN. With the first salary I draw, we can see about trading it on a new one.

HEDDA. No, not traded in. I don't want to part with it. We can put it there, in the inner room, and get another here in its place. When there's a chance, I mean.

TESMAN. [*Slightly cast down.*] Yes, we could do that, of course.

HEDDA. [*Picks up the bouquet from the piano.*] These flowers weren't here when we got in last night.

TESMAN. Aunt Julie must have brought them for you.

HEDDA. [*Examining the bouquet.*] A visiting card. [*Takes it out and reads it.*] "Will stop back later today." Can you guess who this is from?

TESMAN. No. Who? Hm?

HEDDA. It says "Mrs. Elvsted."

TESMAN. No, really? Sheriff Elvsted's wife. Miss Rysing, she used to be.

HEDDA. Exactly. The one with the irritating hair that she was always showing off. An old flame of yours, I've heard.

TESMAN. [*Laughing.*] Oh, that wasn't for long. And it was before I knew you, Hedda. But imagine—that she's here in town.

HEDDA. It's odd that she calls on us. I've hardly seen her since we were in school.

TESMAN. Yes, I haven't seen her either—since God knows when. I wonder how she can stand living in such an out-of-the-way place. Hm?

HEDDA. [*Thinks a moment, then bursts out.*] But wait—isn't it somewhere up in those parts that he—that Eilert Løvborg lives?

TESMAN. Yes, it's someplace right around there. [BERTA *enters by the hall door.*]

BERTA. She's back again, ma'am—that lady who stopped by and left the flowers an hour ago. [*Pointing.*] The ones you have in your hand, ma'am.

HEDDA. Oh, is she? Good. Would you ask her to come in? [BERTA *opens the door for* MRS. ELVSTED *and goes out.* MRS. ELVSTED *is a slender woman with soft, pretty features. Her eyes are light blue, large, round, and somewhat prominent, with a startled, questioning look. Her hair is remarkably light, almost a white-gold, and unusually abundant and wavy. She is a couple of years younger than* HEDDA. *She wears a dark visiting dress, tasteful, but not quite in the latest fashion.*]

HEDDA. [*Going to greet her warmly.*] Good morning, my dear Mrs. Elvsted. How delightful to see you again!

MRS. ELVSTED. [*Nervously; struggling to control herself.*] Yes, it's a very long time since we last met.

TESMAN. [*Gives her his hand.*] Or since *we* met, uh?

HEDDA. Thank you for your beautiful flowers—

MRS. ELVSTED. Oh, that's nothing—I would have come straight out here yesterday afternoon, but then I heard you weren't at home—

TESMAN. Have you just now come to town? Uh?

MRS. ELVSTED. I got in yesterday toward noon. Oh, I was in desperation when I heard that you weren't at home.

HEDDA. Desperation! Why?

TESMAN. But my dear Mrs. Rysing— Mrs. Elvsted, I mean—

HEDDA. You're not in some kind of trouble?

MRS. ELVSTED. Yes, I am. And I don't know another living soul down here

I can turn to.

HEDDA. [*Putting the bouquet down on the table.*] Come, then—let's sit here on the sofa—

MRS. ELVSTED. Oh, I can't sit down. I'm really too much on edge!

HEDDA. Why, of course you can. Come here. [*She draws* MRS. ELVSTED *down on the sofa and sits beside her.*]

TESMAN. Well? What is it, Mrs. Elvsted?

HEDDA. Has anything particular happened at home?

MRS. ELVSTED. Yes, that's both it—and not it. Oh, I do want so much that you don't misunderstand me—

HEDDA. But then the best thing, Mrs. Elvsted, is simply to speak your mind.

TESMAN. Because I suppose that's why you've come. Hm?

MRS. ELVSTED. Oh yes, that's why. Well, then I have to tell you—if you don't already know—that Eilert Løvborg's also in town.

HEDDA. Løvborg—!

TESMAN. What! Is Eilert Løvborg back! Just think, Hedda!

HEDDA. Good Lord, I can hear.

MRS. ELVSTED. He's been back all of a week's time now. A whole week—in this dangerous town! Alone! With all the bad company that's around.

HEDDA. But my dear Mrs. Elvsted, what does *he* have to do with you?

MRS. ELVSTED. [*Glances anxiously at her and says quickly.*] He was the children's tutor.

HEDDA. Your children's?

MRS. ELVSTED. My husband's. I have none.

HEDDA. Your stepchildren's, then.

MRS. ELVSTED. Yes.

TESMAN. [*Somewhat hesitantly.*] But was he—I don't know quite how to put it—was he sufficiently—responsible in his habits for such a job? Uh?

MRS. ELVSTED. In these last two years, there wasn't a word to be said against him.

TESMAN. Not a word? Just think of that, Hedda!

HEDDA. I heard it.

MRS. ELVSTED. Not even a murmur. I can assure you! Nothing. But anyway—now that I know he's here—in this big city—and with so much money in his hands—then I'm just frightened to death for him.

TESMAN. But why didn't he stay up there where he was? With you and your husband? Uh?

MRS. ELVSTED. After the book came out, he just couldn't rest content with us.

TESMAN. Yes, that's right—Aunt Julie was saying he'd published a new book.

MRS. ELVSTED. Yes, a great new book, on the course of civilization—in all its stages. It's been out two weeks. And now it's been bought and read so much—and it's made a tremendous stir—

TESMAN. Has it really? It must be something he's had lying around from his better days.

MRS. ELVSTED. Years back, you mean?

TESMAN. I suppose.

MRS. ELVSTED. No, he's written it all up there with us. Now—in this last year.

TESMAN. That's marvelous to hear. Hedda! Just imagine!

MRS. ELVSTED. Yes, if only it can go on like this!

HEDDA. Have you seen him here in town?

MRS. ELVSTED. No, not yet. I had such trouble finding out his address. But this morning I got it at last.

HEDDA. [*Looks searchingly at her.*] I must say it seems rather odd of your husband—

MRS. ELVSTED. [*With a nervous start.*] Of my husband—! What?

HEDDA. To send you to town on this sort of errand. Not to come and look after his friend himself.

MRS. ELVSTED. No, no, my husband hasn't the time for that. And then I had—some shopping to do.

HEDDA. [*With a slight smile.*] Oh, that's different.

MRS. ELVSTED. [*Getting up quickly and uneasily.*] I beg you, please, Mr. Tesman—be good to Eilert Løvborg if he comes to you. And he will, I'm sure. You know—you were such good friends in the old days. And you're both doing the same kind of work. The same type of research—from what I can gather.

TESMAN. We were once, at any rate.

MRS. ELVSTED. Yes, and that's why I'm

asking you, please—you too—to keep an eye on him. Oh, you will do that, Mr. Tesman—promise me that?

TESMAN. I'll be only too glad to, Mrs. Rysing—

HEDDA. Elvsted.

TESMAN. I'll certainly do everything in my power for Eilert. You can depend on that.

MRS. ELVSTED. Oh, how terribly kind of you! [*Pressing his hands.*] Many, many thanks! [*Frightened.*] He means so much to my husband, you know.

HEDDA. [*Rising.*] You ought to write him, dear. He might not come by on his own.

TESMAN. Yes, that probably would be the best, Hedda? Hm?

HEDDA. And the sooner the better. Right now, I'd say.

MRS. ELVSTED. [*Imploringly.*] Oh yes, if you could!

TESMAN. I'll write him this very moment. Have you got his address, Mrs.—Mrs. Elvsted?

MRS. ELVSTED. Yes. [*Takes a slip of paper from her pocket and hands it to him.*] Here it is.

TESMAN. Good, good. Then I'll go in— [*Looking about.*] But wait—my slippers? Ah! Here. [*Takes the package and starts to leave.*]

HEDDA. Write him a really warm, friendly letter. Nice and long, too.

TESMAN. Don't worry, I will.

MRS. ELVSTED. But please, not a word that I asked you to!

TESMAN. No, that goes without saying. Uh? [*Leaves by the inner room, to the right.*]

HEDDA. [*Goes over to* MRS. ELVSTED, *smiles, and speaks softly.*] How's that! Now we've killed two birds with one stone.

MRS. ELVSTED. What do you mean?

HEDDA. Didn't you see that I wanted him out of the room?

MRS. ELVSTED. Yes, to write the letter—

HEDDA. But also to talk with you alone.

MRS. ELVSTED. [*Confused.*] About this same thing?

HEDDA. Precisely.

MRS. ELVSTED. [*Upset.*] But Mrs. Tesman, there's nothing more to say! Nothing!

HEDDA. Oh yes, but there is. There's a great deal more—I can see that. Come, sit here—and let's speak openly now, the two of us. [*She forces* MRS. ELVSTED *down into the armchair by the stove and sits on one of the taborets.*]

MRS. ELVSTED. [*Anxiously glancing at her watch.*] But Mrs. Tesman, dear—I was just planning to leave.

HEDDA. Oh, you can't be in such a rush— Now! Tell me a little about how things are going at home.

MRS. ELVSTED. Oh, that's the last thing I'd ever want to discuss.

HEDDA. But with me, dear—? After all, we were in school together.

MRS. ELVSTED. Yes, but you were a class ahead of me. Oh, I was terribly afraid of you then!

HEDDA. Afraid of me?

MRS. ELVSTED. Yes, terribly. Because whenever we met on the stairs, you'd always pull my hair.

HEDDA. Did I really?

MRS. ELVSTED. Yes, and once you said you would burn it off.

HEDDA. Oh, that was just foolish talk, you know.

MRS. ELVSTED. Yes, but I was so stupid then. And, anyway, since then—we've drifted so far—far apart from each other. We've moved in such different circles.

HEDDA. Well, let's try now to come closer again. Listen, at school we were quite good friends, and we called each other by our first names—

MRS. ELVSTED. No, I'm sure you're mistaken.

HEDDA. Oh, I couldn't be! I remember it clearly. And that's why we have to be perfectly open, just as we were. [*Moves the stool nearer* MRS. ELVSTED.] There now! [*Kissing her cheek.*] You have to call me Hedda.

MRS. ELVSTED. [*Pressing and patting her hands.*] Oh, you're so good and kind—! It's not at all what I'm used to.

HEDDA. There, there! And I'm going to call you my own dear Thora.

MRS. ELVSTED. My name is Thea.

HEDDA. Oh yes, of course. I meant Thea. [*Looks at her compassionately.*] So you're not much used to goodness or kindness, Thea? In your own home?

MRS. ELVSTED. If only I had a home! But I don't. I never have.

HEDDA. [*Glances quickly at her.*] I thought it had to be something like that.

MRS. ELVSTED. [*Gazing helplessly into space.*] Yes—yes—yes.

HEDDA. I can't quite remember now—but wasn't it as a housekeeper that you first came up to the Elvsteds?

MRS. ELVSTED. Actually as a governess. But his wife—his first wife—she was an invalid and mostly kept to her bed. So I had to take care of the house too.

HEDDA. But finally you became mistress of the house yourself.

MRS. ELVSTED. [*Heavily.*] Yes, I did.

HEDDA. Let me see—about how long ago was that?

MRS. ELVSTED. That I was married?

HEDDA. Yes.

MRS. ELVSTED. It's five years now.

HEDDA. That's right. It must be.

MRS. ELVSTED. Oh, these five years—! Or the last two or three anyway. Oh, if you only knew, Mrs. Tesman—

HEDDA. [*Gives her hand a little slap.*] Mrs. Tesman! Now, Thea!

MRS. ELVSTED. I'm sorry; I'll try— Yes, if you could only understand—Hedda—

HEDDA. [*Casually.*] Eilert Løvborg has lived up there about three years too, hasn't he?

MRS. ELVSTED. [*Looks at her doubtfully.*] Eilert Løvborg? Yes—he has.

HEDDA. Had you already known him here in town?

MRS. ELVSTED. Hardly at all. Well, I mean—by name, of course.

HEDDA. But up there—I suppose he'd visit you both?

MRS. ELVSTED. Yes, he came to see us every day. He was tutoring the children, you know. Because, in the long run, I couldn't do it all myself.

HEDDA. No, that's obvious. And your husband—? I suppose he often has to be away?

MRS. ELVSTED. Yes, you can imagine, as sheriff, how much traveling he does around in the district.

HEDDA. [*Leaning against the chair arm.*] Thea—my poor, sweet Thea—now you must tell me everything—just as it is.

MRS. ELVSTED. Well, then you have to ask the questions.

HEDDA. What sort of man is your husband, Thea? I mean—you know—to be with. Is he good to you?

MRS. ELVSTED. [*Evasively.*] He believes he does everything for the best.

HEDDA. I only think he must be much too old for you. More than twenty years older, isn't he?

MRS. ELVSTED. [*Irritated.*] That's true. Along with everything else. I just can't stand him! We haven't a single thought in common. Nothing at all—he and I.

HEDDA. But doesn't he care for you all the same—in his own way?

MRS. ELVSTED. Oh, I don't know what he feels. I'm no more than useful to him. And then it doesn't cost much to keep me. I'm inexpensive.

HEDDA. That's stupid of you.

MRS. ELVSTED. [*Shaking her head.*] It can't be otherwise. Not with him. He really doesn't care for anyone but himself—and maybe a little for the children.

HEDDA. And for Eilert Løvborg, Thea.

MRS. ELVSTED. [*Looking at her.*] Eilert Løvborg! Why do you think so?

HEDDA. But my dear—it seems to me, when he sends you all the way into town to look after him— [*Smiles almost imperceptibly.*] Besides, it's what you told my husband.

MRS. ELVSTED. [*With a little nervous shudder.*] Really? Yes, I suppose I did. [*In a quiet outburst.*] No—I might as well tell you here and now! It's bound to come out in time.

HEDDA. But my dear Thea—?

MRS. ELVSTED. All right, then! My husband never knew I was coming here.

HEDDA. What! You husband never knew—

MRS. ELVSTED. Of course not. Anyway, he wasn't at home. Off traveling somewhere. Oh, I couldn't bear it any longer. Hedda. It was impossible! I would have been so alone up there now.

HEDDA. Well? What then?

MRS. ELVSTED. So I packed a few of my things together—the barest necessities—without saying a word. And I slipped away from the house.

HEDDA. Right then and there?
MRS. ELVSTED. Yes, and took the train straight into town.
HEDDA. But my dearest girl—that you could dare to do such a thing!
MRS. ELVSTED. [*Rising and walking about the room.*] What else could I possibly do!
HEDDA. But what do you think your husband will say when you go back home?
MRS. ELVSTED. [*By the table, looking at her.*] Back to *him*?
HEDDA. Yes, of course.
MRS. ELVSTED. I'll never go back to him.
HEDDA. [*Rising and approaching her.*] You mean you've left, in dead earnest, for good?
MRS. ELVSTED. Yes. There didn't seem anything else to do.
HEDDA. But—to go away so openly.
MRS. ELVSTED. Oh, you can't keep a thing like that secret.
HEDDA. But what do you think people will say about you, Thea?
MRS. ELVSTED. God knows they'll say what they please. [*Sitting wearily and sadly on the sofa.*] I only did what I had to do.
HEDDA. [*After a short silence.*] What do you plan on now? What kind of work?
MRS. ELVSTED. I don't know yet. I only know I have to live here, where Eilert Løvborg is—if I'm going to live at all.
HEDDA. [*Moves a chair over from the table, sits beside her, and strokes her hands.*] Thea dear—how did this—this friendship—between you and Eilert Løvborg come about?
MRS. ELVSTED. Oh, it happened little by little. I got some kind of power, almost, over him.
HEDDA. Really?
MRS. ELVSTED. He gave up his old habits. Not because I'd asked him to. I never dared do that. But he could tell they upset me, and so he dropped them.
HEDDA. [*Hiding an involuntary, scornful smile.*] My dear little Thea—just as they say—you rehabilitated him.
MRS. ELVSTED. Well, he says so, at any rate. And he—on his part—he's made a real human being out of me. Taught me to think—and understand so many things.
HEDDA. You mean he tutored you also?
MRS. ELVSTED. No, not exactly. But he'd talk to me—talk endlessly on about one thing after another. And then came the wonderful, happy time when I could share in his work! When I could help him!
HEDDA. Could you really?
MRS. ELVSTED. Yes! Whenever he wrote anything, we'd always work on it together.
HEDDA. Like two true companions.
MRS. ELVSTED. [*Eagerly.*] Companions! You know, Hedda—that's what he said too! Oh, I ought to feel so happy—but I can't. I just don't know if it's going to last.
HEDDA. You're no more sure of him than that?
MRS. ELVSTED. [*Despondently.*] There's a woman's shadow between Eilert Løvborg and me.
HEDDA. [*Looks at her intently.*] Who could that be?
MRS. ELVSTED. I don't know. Someone out of his—his past. Someone he's really never forgotten.
HEDDA. What has he said—about this!
MRS. ELVSTED. It's only once—and just vaguely—that he touched on it.
HEDDA. Well! And what did he say!
MRS. ELVSTED. He said that when they broke off she was going to shoot him with a pistol.
HEDDA. [*With cold constraint.*] That's nonsense! Nobody behaves that way around here.
MRS. ELVSTED. No. And that's why I think it must have been that red-headed singer that at one time he—
HEDDA. Yes, quite likely.
MRS. ELVSTED. I remember they used to say about her that she carried loaded weapons.
HEDDA. Ah—then of course it must have been her.
MRS. ELVSTED. [*Wringing her hands.*] But you know what, Hedda—I've heard that this singer—that she's in town again! Oh, it has me out of my mind—
HEDDA. [*Glancing toward the inner room.*] Shh! Tesman's coming. [*Gets up and whispers.*] Thea—keep all this just between us.

MRS. ELVSTED. [*Jumping up.*] Oh yes! In heaven's name—! [GEORGE TESMAN, *with a letter in his hand, enters from the right through the inner room.*]

TESMAN. There, now—the letter's signed and sealed.

HEDDA. That's fine. I think Mrs. Elvsted was just leaving. Wait a minute. I'll go with you to the garden gate.

TESMAN. Hedda, dear—could Berta maybe look after this?

HEDDA. [*Taking the letter.*] I'll tell her to. [BERTA *enters from the hall.*]

BERTA. Judge Brack is here and says he'd like to greet you and the Doctor, ma'am.

HEDDA. Yes, ask Judge Brack to come in. And, here, put this letter in the mail.

BERTA. [*Takes the letter.*] Yes, ma'am. [*She opens the door for* JUDGE BRACK *and goes out.* BRACK *is a man of forty-five, thickset, yet well-built, with supple movements. His face is roundish, with a distinguished profile. His hair is short, still mostly black, and carefully groomed. His eyes are bright and lively. Thick eyebrows; a moustache to match, with neatly clipped ends. He wears a trimly tailored walking suit, a bit too youthful for his age. Uses a monocle, which he now and then lets fall.*]

JUDGE BRACK. [*Hat in hand, bowing.*] May one dare to call so early?

HEDDA. Of course one may.

TESMAN. [*Shakes his hand.*] You're always welcome here. [*Introducing him.*] Judge Brack—Miss Rysing—

HEDDA. Ah—!

BRACK. [*Bowing.*] I'm delighted.

HEDDA. [*Looks at him and laughs.*] It's really a treat to see you by daylight, Judge!

BRACK. You find me—changed?

HEDDA. Yes. A bit younger, I think.

BRACK. Thank you, most kindly.

TESMAN. But what do you say for Hedda, uh? Doesn't she look flourishing? She's actually—

HEDDA. Oh, leave me out of it! You might thank Judge Brack for all the trouble he's gone to—

BRACK. Nonsense—it was a pleasure—

HEDDA. Yes, you're a true friend. But here's Thea, standing here, aching to get away. Excuse me, Judge; I'll be right back. [*Mutual good-byes.* MRS. ELVSTED *and* HEDDA *go out by the hall door.*]

BRACK. So—is your wife fairly well satisfied, then—?

TESMAN. Yes, we can't thank you enough. Of course—I gather there's some rearrangement called for here and there. And one or two things are lacking. We still have to buy a few minor items.

BRACK. Really?

TESMAN. But that's nothing for you to worry about. Hedda said she'd pick up those things herself. Why don't we sit down, hm?

BRACK. Thanks. Just for a moment. [*Sits by the table.*] There's something I'd like to discuss with you, Tesman.

TESMAN. What? Oh, I understand! [*Sitting.*] It's the serious part of the banquet we're coming to, uh?

BRACK. Oh, as far as monetary matters go, there's no great rush—though I must say I wish we'd managed things a bit more economically.

TESMAN. But that was completely impossible! Think about Hedda, Judge! You, who know her so well— I simply couldn't have her live like a grocer's wife.

BRACK. No, no—that's not the trouble, exactly.

TESMAN. And then—fortunately—it can't be long before I get my appointment.

BRACK. Well, you know—these things can often hang fire.

TESMAN. Have you heard something further? Hm?

BRACK. Nothing really definite—[*Changing the subject.*] But incidentally—I do have one piece of news for you.

TESMAN. Well?

BRACK. Your old friend Eilert Løvborg is back in town.

TESMAN. I already know.

BRACK. Oh? How did you hear?

TESMAN. She told me. The lady that left with Hedda.

BRACK. I see. What was her name again? I didn't quite catch it—

TESMAN. Mrs. Elvsted.

BRACK. Aha—Sheriff Elvsted's wife. Yes—it's up near them he's been staying.

TESMAN. And, just think—what a pleasure to hear that he's completely stable again!

BRACK. Yes, that's what they claim.

TESMAN. And that he's published a new book, uh?

BRACK. Oh yes!

TESMAN. And it's created quite a sensation.

BRACK. An extraordinary sensation.

TESMAN. Just imagine—isn't that marvelous? He, with his remarkable talents—I was so very afraid that he'd really gone down for good.

BRACK. That's what everyone thought.

TESMAN. But I've no idea what he'll find to do now. How on earth can he ever make a living? Hm? [*During the last words,* HEDDA *comes in by the hall door.*]

HEDDA. [*To* BRACK, *laughing, with a touch of scorn.*] Tesman always goes around worrying about how people are going to make a living.

TESMAN. My Lord—it's poor Eilert Løvborg we're talking of, dear.

HEDDA. [*Glancing quickly at him.*] Oh, really? [*Sits in the armchair by the stove and asks casually.*] What's the matter with him?

TESMAN. Well—he must have run through his inheritance long ago. And he can't write a new book every year. Uh? So I was asking, really, what's going to become of him.

BRACK. Perhaps I can shed some light on that.

TESMAN. Oh?

BRACK. You must remember that he does have relatives with a great deal of influence.

TESMAN. Yes, but they've washed their hands of him altogether.

BRACK. They used to call him the family's white hope.

TESMAN. They used to, yes! But he spoiled all that himself.

HEDDA. Who knows? [*With a slight smile.*] He's been rehabilitated up at the Elvsteds—

BRACK. And then this book that he's published—

TESMAN. Oh, well, let's hope they really help him some way or other. I just now wrote to him. Hedda dear, I asked him out here this evening.

BRACK. But my dear fellow, you're coming to my stag party this evening. You promised down on the pier last night.

HEDDA. Had you forgotten, Tesman?

TESMAN. Yes, I absolutely had.

BRACK. For that matter, you can rest assured that he'd never come.

TESMAN. What makes you say that, hm?

BRACK. [*Hesitating, rising and leaning on the back of the chair.*] My dear Tesman—and you too, Mrs. Tesman—I can't, in all conscience, let you go on without knowing something that—that—

TESMAN. Something involving Eilert—?

BRACK. Both you and him.

TESMAN. But my dear Judge, then tell us!

BRACK. You must be prepared that your appointment may not come through as quickly as you've wished or expected.

TESMAN. [*Jumping up nervously.*] Has something gone wrong? Uh?

BRACK. It may turn out that there'll have to be a competition for the post—

TESMAN. A competition! Imagine, Hedda!

HEDDA. [*Leaning further back in the chair.*] Ah, there—you see!

TESMAN. But with whom! You can't mean—?

BRACK. Yes, exactly. With Eilert Løborg.

TESMAN. [*Striking his hands together.*] No, no—that's completely unthinkable! It's impossible! Uh?

BRACK. Hm—but it may come about, all the same.

TESMAN. No, but, Judge Brack—that would just be incredibly inconsiderate toward me! [*Waving his arms.*] Yes, because—you know—I'm a married man! We married on my prospects, Hedda and I. We went into debt. And even borrowed money from Aunt Julie. Because that job—my Lord, it was as good as promised to me, uh?

BRACK. Easy now—I'm sure you'll get the appointment. But you will have to compete for it.

HEDDA. [*Motionless in the armchair.*] Just think, Tesman—it will be like a kind of championship match.

TESMAN. But Hedda dearest, how can you take it so calmly!

HEDDA. [*As before.*] I'm not the least bit calm. I can't wait to see how it turns out.
BRACK. In any case, Mrs. Tesman, it's well that you know now how things stand. I mean—with respect to those little purchases I hear you've been threatening to make.
HEDDA. This business can't change anything.
BRACK. I see! Well, that's another matter. Good-bye. [*To* TESMAN.] When I take my afternoon walk, I'll stop by and fetch you.
TESMAN. Oh yes, please do—I don't know where I'm at.
HEDDA. [*Leaning back and reaching out her hand.*] Good-bye, Judge. And come again soon.
BRACK. Many thanks. Good-bye now.
TESMAN. [*Accompanying him to the door.*] Good-bye, Judge! You really must excuse me—[BRACK *goes out by the hall door.*]
TESMAN. [*Pacing about the room.*] Oh, Hedda—one should never go off and lose oneself in dreams, uh?
HEDDA. [*Looks at him and smiles.*] Do *you* do that?
TESMAN. No use denying it. It was living in dreams to go and get married and set up house on nothing but expectations.
HEDDA. Perhaps you're right about that.
TESMAN. Well, at least we have our comfortable home, Hedda! The home that we always wanted. That we both fell in love with, I could almost say. Hm?
HEDDA. [*Rising slowly and wearily.*] It was part of our bargain that we'd live in society—that we'd keep a great house—
TESMAN. Yes, of course—how I'd looked forward to that! Imagine—seeing you as a hostess—in our own select circle of friends! Yes, yes—well, for a while, we two will just have to get on by ourselves, Hedda. Perhaps have Aunt Julie here now and then. Oh, you—for you I wanted to have things so—so utterly different—!
HEDDA. Naturally this means I can't have a butler now.
TESMAN. Oh no—I'm sorry, a butler—we can't even talk about that, you know.
HEDDA. And the riding horse I was going to have—
TESMAN. [*Appalled.*] Riding horse!
HEDDA. I suppose I can't think of that anymore.
TESMAN. Good Lord, no—that's obvious!
HEDDA. [*Crossing the room.*] Well, at least I have one thing left to amuse myself with.
TESMAN. [*Beaming.*] Ah, thank heaven for that! What is it, Hedda? Uh?
HEDDA. [*In the center doorway, looking at him with veiled scorn.*] My pistols, George.
TESMAN. [*In fright.*] Your pistols?
HEDDA. [*Her eyes cold.*] General Gabler's pistols. [*She goes through the inner room and out to the left.*]
TESMAN. [*Runs to the center doorway and calls after her.*] No, for heaven's sake, Hedda darling—don't touch those dangerous things! For my sake, Hedda! Uh?

Act 2

The rooms at the TESMANS', *same as in the first act, except that the piano has been moved out, and an elegant little writing table with a bookcase put in its place. A smaller table stands by the sofa to the left. Most of the flowers have been removed.* MRS. ELVSTED's *bouquet stands on the large table in the foreground. It is afternoon.*

HEDDA, *dressed to receive callers, is alone in the room. She stands by the open glass door, loading a revolver. The match to it lies in an open pistol case on the writing table.*

HEDDA. [*Looking down into the garden and calling.*] Good to see you again, Judge!
BRACK. [*Heard from below, at a distance.*] Likewise, Mrs. Tesman!
HEDDA. [*Raises the pistol and aims.*] And now, Judge, I'm going to shoot you!
BRACK. [*Shouting from below.*] No-no-no!

Don't point that thing at me!

HEDDA. That's what comes of sneaking in the back way. [*She fires.*]

BRACK. [*Nearer.*] Are you out of your mind—!

HEDDA. Oh, dear—I didn't hit you, did I?

BRACK. [*Still outside.*] Just stop this nonsense!

HEDDA. All right, you can come in, Judge. [JUDGE BRACK, *dressed for a stag party, enters through the glass door. He carries a light overcoat on his arm.*]

BRACK. Good God! Are you still playing such games? What are you shooting at?

HEDDA. Oh, I was just shooting into the sky.

BRACK. [*Gently taking the pistol out of her hand.*] Permit me. [*Looks at it.*] Ah, this one—I know it well. [*Glancing around.*] Where's the case? Ah, here. [*Puts the pistol away and shuts the case.*] We'll have no more of that kind of fun today.

HEDDA. Well, what in heaven's name do you want me to do with myself?

BRACK. You haven't had any visitors?

HEDDA. [*Closing the glass door.*] Not a single one. All of our set are still in the country, I guess.

BRACK. And Tesman isn't home either?

HEDDA. [*At the writing table, putting the pistol case away in a drawer.*] No. Right after lunch he ran over to his aunts. He didn't expect you so soon.

BRACK. Hm—I should have realized. That was stupid of me.

HEDDA. [*Turning her head and looking at him.*] Why stupid?

BRACK. Because in that case I would have stopped by a little bit—earlier.

HEDDA. [*Crossing the room.*] Well, you'd have found no one here then at all. I've been up in my room dressing since lunch.

BRACK. And there's not the least little crack in the door we could have conferred through?

HEDDA. You forgot to arrange it.

BRACK. Also stupid of me.

HEDDA. Well, we'll just have to settle down here—and wait. Tesman won't be back for a while.

BRACK. Don't worry, I can be patient.

[HEDDA *sits in the corner of the sofa.* BRACK *lays his coat over the back of the nearest chair and sits down, keeping his hat in his hand. A short pause. They look at each other.*]

HEDDA. Well?

BRACK. [*In the same tone.*] Well?

HEDDA. I spoke first.

BRACK. [*Leaning slightly forward.*] Then let's have a nice little cozy chat, Mrs. Hedda.

HEDDA. [*Leaning further back on the sofa.*] Doesn't it seem like a whole eternity since the last time we talked together? Oh, a few words last night and this morning—but they don't count.

BRACK. You mean, like this—between ourselves? Just the two of us?

HEDDA. Well, more or less.

BRACK. There wasn't a day that I didn't wish you were home again.

HEDDA. And I was wishing exactly the same.

BRACK. You? Really, Mrs. Hedda? And I thought you were having such a marvelous time on this trip.

HEDDA. Oh, you can imagine!

BRACK. But that's what Tesman always wrote.

HEDDA. Oh, him! There's nothing he likes better than grubbing around in libraries and copying out old parchments, or whatever you call them.

BRACK. [*With a touch of malice.*] But after all, it's his calling in life. In good part, anyway.

HEDDA. Yes, that's true. So there's nothing wrong with it—But what about *me!* Oh, Judge, you don't know—I've been so dreadfully bored.

BRACK. [*Sympathetically.*] You really mean that? In all seriousness?

HEDDA. Well, you can understand—! To go for a whole six months without meeting a soul who knew the least bit about our circle. No one that one could talk to about our kind of things.

BRACK. Ah, yes—I think that would bother me too.

HEDDA. But then the most unbearable thing of all—

BRACK. What?

HEDDA. To be everlastingly together with—with one and the same person—

BRACK. [*Nodding in agreement.*] Morning, noon, and night—yes. At every conceivable hour.

HEDDA. I said "everlastingly."

BRACK. All right. But with our good friend Tesman, I really should have thought—

HEDDA. My dear Judge, Tesman is—a specialist.

BRACK. Undeniably.

HEDDA. And specialists aren't at all amusing to travel with. Not in the long run, anyway.

BRACK. Not even—the specialist that one *loves*.

HEDDA. Ugh—don't use that syrupy word!

BRACK. [*Startled.*] What's that, Mrs. Hedda!

HEDDA. [*Half laughing, half annoyed.*] Well, just try it yourself! Try listening to the history of civilization morning, noon, and—

BRACK. Everlastingly.

HEDDA. Yes! Yes! And then all this business about domestic crafts in the Middle Ages—! That really is just too revolting!

BRACK. [*Looks searchingly at her.*] But tell me—I can't see how it ever came about that—? Hm—

HEDDA. That George Tesman and I could make a match?

BRACK. All right, let's put it that way.

HEDDA. Good Lord, does it seem so remarkable?

BRACK. Well, yes—and no, Mrs. Hedda.

HEDDA. I really had danced myself out, Judge. My time was up. [*With a slight shudder.*] Ugh! No, I don't want to say that. Or think it, either.

BRACK. You certainly have no reason to.

HEDDA. Oh—reasons—[*Watching him carefully.*] And George Tesman—he is, after all, a thoroughly acceptable choice.

BRACK. Acceptable and dependable, beyond a doubt.

HEDDA. And I don't find anything especially ridiculous about him. Do you?

BRACK. Ridiculous? No-o-o, I wouldn't say that.

HEDDA. Hm. Anyway, he works incredibly hard on his research! There's every chance that, in time, he could still make a name for himself.

BRACK. [*Looking at her with some uncertainty.*] I thought you believed, like everyone else, that he was going to be quite famous some day.

HEDDA. [*Wearily.*] Yes, so I did. And then when he kept pressing and pleading to be allowed to take care of me—I didn't see why I ought to resist.

BRACK. No. From that point of view, of course not—

HEDDA. It was certainly more than my other admirers were willing to do for me, Judge.

BRACK. [*Laughing.*] Well, I can't exactly answer for all the others. But as far as I'm concerned, you know that I've always cherished a—a certain respect for the marriage bond. Generally speaking, that is.

HEDDA. [*Bantering.*] Oh, I never really held out any hopes for *you*.

BRACK. All I want is to have a warm circle of intimate friends, where I can be of use one way or another, with the freedom to come and go as—as a trusted friend—

HEDDA. Of the man of the house, you mean?

BRACK. [*With a bow.*] Frankly—I prefer the lady. But the man, too, of course, in his place. That kind of—let's say, triangular arrangement—you can't imagine how satisfying it can be all around.

HEDDA. Yes, I must say I longed for some third person so many times on that trip. Oh—those endless tête-à-têtes in railway compartments—!

BRACK. Fortunately the wedding trip's over now.

HEDDA. [*Shaking her head.*] The trip will go on—and on. I've only come to one stop on the line.

BRACK. Well, then what you do is jump out—and stretch yourself a little, Mrs. Hedda.

HEDDA. I'll never jump out.

BRACK. Never?

HEDDA. No. Because there's always someone on the platform who—

BRACK. [*With a laugh.*] Who looks at your legs, is that it?

HEDDA. Precisely.

BRACK. Yes, but after all—

HEDDA. [*With a disdainful gesture.*] I'm not interested. I'd rather keep my seat—right here, where I am. Tête-à-tête.

BRACK. Well, but suppose a third person came on board and joined the couple.

HEDDA. Ah! That's entirely different.

BRACK. A trusted friend, who understands—

HEDDA. And can talk about all kinds of lively things—

BRACK. Who's not in the least a specialist.

HEDDA. [*With an audible sigh.*] Yes, that would be a relief.

BRACK. [*Hearing the front door open and glancing toward it.*] The triangle is complete.

HEDDA. [*Lowering her voice.*] And the train goes on. [GEORGE TESMAN, *in a gray walking suit and a soft felt hat, enters from the hall. He has a good number of unbound books under his arm and in his pockets.*]

TESMAN. [*Going up to the table by the corner settee.*] Phew! Let me tell you, that's hot work—carrying all these. [*Setting the books down.*] I'm actually sweating, Hedda. And what's this—you're already here, Judge? Hm? Berta didn't tell me.

BRACK. [*Rising.*] I came in through the garden.

HEDDA. What are all these books you've gotten?

TESMAN. [*Stands leafing through them.*] They're new publications in my special field. I absolutely need them.

HEDDA. Your special field?

BRACK. Of course. Books in his special field, Mrs. Tesman. [BRACK *and* HEDDA *exchange a knowing smile.*]

HEDDA. You need still more books in your special field?

TESMAN. Hedda, my dear, it's impossible ever to have too many. You have to keep up with what's written and published.

HEDDA. Oh, I suppose so.

TESMAN. [*Searching among the books.*] And look—I picked up Eilert Løvborg's new book too. [*Offering it to her.*] Maybe you'd like to have a look at it? Uh?

HEDDA. No, thank you. Or—well, perhaps later.

TESMAN. I skimmed through some of it on the way home.

HEDDA. Well, what do you think of it—as a specialist?

TESMAN. I think it's amazing how well it holds up. He's never written like this before. [*Gathers up the books.*] But I'll take these into the study now. I can't wait to cut the pages—! And then I better dress up a bit. [*To* BRACK.] We don't have to rush right off, do we? Hm?

BRACK. No, not at all. There's ample time.

TESMAN. Ah, then I'll be at my leisure. [*Starts out with the books, but pauses and turns in the doorway.*] Oh, incidentally, Hedda—Aunt Julie won't be by to see you this evening.

HEDDA. She won't? I suppose it's that business with the hat?

TESMAN. Don't be silly. How can you think that of Aunt Julie? Imagine—! No, it's Auntie Rina—she's very ill.

HEDDA. She always is.

TESMAN. Yes, but today she really took a turn for the worse.

HEDDA. Well, then it's only right for her sister to stay with her. I'll have to bear with it.

TESMAN. But you can't imagine how delighted Aunt Julie was all the same—because you'd filled out so nicely on the trip!

HEDDA. [*Under her breath; rising.*] Oh, these eternal aunts!

TESMAN. What?

HEDDA. [*Going over to the glass door.*] Nothing.

TESMAN. All right, then. [*He goes through the inner room and out, right.*]

BRACK. What were you saying about a hat?

HEDDA. Oh, it's something that happened with Miss Tesman this morning. She'd put her hat down over there on the chair. [*Looks at him and smiles.*] And I pretended I thought it was the maid's.

BRACK. [*Shaking his head.*] But my dear Mrs. Hedda, how could you do that! Hurt that fine old lady!

HEDDA. [*Nervously, pacing the room.*] Well, it's—these things come over me, just

like that, suddenly. And I can't hold back. [*Throws herself down in the armchair by the stove.*] Oh, I don't know myself how to explain it.
BRACK. [*Behind the armchair.*] You're not really happy—that's the heart of it.
HEDDA. [*Gazing straight ahead.*] And I don't know why I ought to be—happy. Or maybe you can tell me why?
BRACK. Yes—among other things, because you've gotten just the home you've always wanted.
HEDDA. [*Looks up at him and laughs.*] You believe that story too?
BRACK. You mean there's nothing to it?
HEDDA. Oh yes—there's something to it.
BRACK. Well?
HEDDA. There's this much to it, that I used Tesman as my escort home from parties last summer—
BRACK. Unfortunately—I was going in another direction then.
HEDDA. How true. Yes, you had other directions to go last summer.
BRACK. [*Laughing.*] For shame, Mrs. Hedda! Well—so you and Tesman—?
HEDDA. Yes, so one evening we walked by this place. And Tesman, poor thing, was writhing in torment, because he couldn't find anything to say. And I felt sorry for a man of such learning—
BRACK. [*Smiling skeptically.*] Did you? Hm—
HEDDA. No, I honestly did. And so—just to help him off the hook—I came out with some rash remark about this lovely house being where I'd always wanted to live.
BRACK. No more than that?
HEDDA. No more that evening.
BRACK. But afterward?
HEDDA. Yes, my rashness had its consequences, Judge.
BRACK. I'm afraid our rashness all too often does, Mrs. Hedda.
HEDDA. Thanks! But don't you see, it was this passion for the old Falk mansion that drew George Tesman and me together! It was nothing more than that, that brought on our engagement and the marriage and the wedding trip and everything else. Oh yes, Judge—I was going to say, you make your bed and then you lie in it.

BRACK. But that's priceless! So actually you couldn't care less about all this?
HEDDA. God knows, not in the least.
BRACK. But even now? Now that we've made it somewhat comfortable for you here?
HEDDA. Ugh—all the rooms seem to smell of lavender and dried roses. But maybe that scent was brought in by Aunt Julie.
BRACK. [*Laughing.*] No, I think it's a bequest from the late Mrs. Falk.
HEDDA. Yes, there's something in it of the odor of death. It's like a corsage—the day after the dance. [*Folds her hands behind her neck, leans back in her chair, and looks at him.*] Oh, my dear Judge—you can't imagine how horribly I'm going to bore myself here.
BRACK. But couldn't you find some goal in life to work toward? Others do, Mrs. Hedda.
HEDDA. A goal—that would really absorb me?
BRACK. Yes, preferably.
HEDDA. God only knows what that could be. I often wonder if—[*Breaks off.*] But that's impossible too.
BRACK. Who knows? Tell me.
HEDDA. I was thinking—if I could get Tesman to go into politics.
BRACK. [*Laughing.*] Tesman! No, I can promise you—politics is absolutely out of his line.
HEDDA. No, I can believe you. But even so, I wonder if I could get him into it?
BRACK. Well, what satisfaction would you have in that, if he can't succeed? Why push him in that direction?
HEDDA. Because, I've told you, I'm bored! [*After a pause.*] Then you think it's really out of the question that he could ever be a cabinet minister?
BRACK. Hm—you see, Mrs. Hedda—to be anything like that, he'd have to be fairly wealthy to start with.
HEDDA. [*Rising impatiently.*] Yes, there it is! It's this tight little world I've stumbled into—[*Crossing the room.*] That's what makes life so miserable! So utterly ludicrous! Because that's what it *is*.
BRACK. I'd say the fault lies elsewhere.

HEDDA. Where?

BRACK. You've never experienced anything that's really stirred you.

HEDDA. Anything serious, you mean.

BRACK. Well, you can call it that, if you like. But now perhaps it's on the way.

HEDDA. [*Tossing her head.*] Oh, you mean all the fuss over that wretched professorship! But that's Tesman's problem. I'm not going to give it a single thought.

BRACK. No, that isn't—ah, never mind. But suppose you were to be confronted now by what—in rather elegant language—is called your most solemn responsibility. [*Smiling.*] A new responsibility, Mrs. Hedda.

HEDDA. [*Angrily.*] Be quiet! You'll never see me like that!

BRACK. [*Delicately.*] We'll discuss it again in a year's time—at the latest.

HEDDA. [*Curtly.*] I have no talent for such things, Judge, I won't have responsibilities!

BRACK. Don't you think you've a talent for what almost every woman finds the most meaningful—

HEDDA. [*Over by the glass door.*] Oh, I told you, be quiet! I often think I have talent for only one thing in life.

BRACK. [*Moving closer.*] And what, may I ask, is that?

HEDDA. [*Stands looking out.*] Boring myself to death. And that's the truth. [*Turns, looks toward the inner room, and laughs.*] See what I mean! Here comes the professor.

BRACK. [*In a low tone of warning.*] Ah-ah-ah, Mrs. Hedda! [GEORGE TESMAN, *dressed for the party, with hat and gloves in hand, enters from the right through the inner room.*]

TESMAN. Hedda—there's been no word from Eilert Løvborg, has there? Hm?

HEDDA. No.

TESMAN. Well, he's bound to be here soon then. You'll see.

BRACK. You really believe he'll come?

TESMAN. Yes, I'm almost positive of it. Because I'm sure they're nothing but rumors, what you told us this morning.

BRACK. Oh?

TESMAN. Yes. At least Aunt Julie said she couldn't for the world believe that he'd stand in my way again. Can you imagine that!

BRACK. So, then everything's well and good.

TESMAN. [*Putting his hat with the gloves inside on a chair to the right.*] Yes, but I really would like to wait for him as long as possible.

BRACK. We have plenty of time for that. There's no one due at my place till seven or half past.

TESMAN. Why, then we can keep Hedda company for a while. And see what turns up. Uh?

HEDDA. [*Taking* BRACK'*s hat and coat over to the settee.*] And if worst comes to worst, Mr. Løvborg can sit and talk with me.

BRACK. [*Trying to take his things himself.*] Ah, please, Mrs. Tesman—! What do you mean by "worst," in this case?

HEDDA. If he won't go with you and Tesman.

TESMAN. [*Looks doubtfully at her.*] But Hedda dear—is it quite right that he stays with you here? Uh? Remember that Aunt Julie isn't coming.

HEDDA. No, but Mrs. Elvsted is. The three of us can have tea together.

TESMAN. Oh, well, that's all right.

BRACK. [*Smiling.*] And that might be the soundest plan for him too.

HEDDA. Why?

BRACK. Well, really, Mrs. Tesman, you've made enough pointed remarks about my little bachelor parties. You've always said they're only fit for men of the strictest principles.

HEDDA. But Mr. Løvborg is surely a man of principle now. After all, a reformed sinner—[BERTA *appears at the hall door.*]

BERTA. Ma'am, there's a gentleman here who'd like to see you—

HEDDA. Yes, show him in.

TESMAN. [*Softly.*] I'm sure it's him! Just think! [EILBERT LØVBORG *enters from the hall. He is lean and gaunt, the same age as* TESMAN, *but looks older and rather exhausted. His hair and beard are dark brown, his face long and pale, but with reddish patches over the cheekbones. He is dressed in a trim black suit, quite new, and holds dark gloves and a top hat in his hand. He hesitates by the door and bows abruptly. He seems somewhat embar-*

rassed.]
TESMAN. [*Crosses over and shakes his hand.*] Ah, my dear Eilert—so at last we meet again!
EILERT LØVBORG. [*Speaking in a hushed voice.*] Thanks for your letter, George! [*Approaching* HEDDA.] May I shake hands with you too, Mrs. Tesman?
HEDDA. [*Taking his hand.*] So glad to see you, Mr. Løvborg. [*Gesturing with her hand.*] I don't know if you two gentlemen—?
LØVBORG. [*Bowing slightly.*] Judge Brack, I believe.
BRACK. [*Reciprocating.*] Of course. It's been some years—
TESMAN. [*To* LØVBORG, *with his hands on his shoulders.*] And now, Eilert, make yourself at home, completely! Right, Hedda? I hear you'll be settling down here in town again? Uh?
LØVBORG. I plan to.
TESMAN. Well, that makes sense. Listen—I just got hold of your new book. But I really haven't had time to read it yet.
LØVBORG. You can save yourself the bother.
TESMAN. Why? What do you mean?
LØVBORG. There's very little to it.
TESMAN. Imagine—you can say that!
BRACK. But it's won such high praise, I hear.
LØVBORG. That's exactly what I wanted. So I wrote a book that everyone could agree with.
BRACK. Very sound.
TESMAN. Yes, but my dear Eilert——!
LØVBORG. Because now I want to build up my position again—and try to make a fresh start.
TESMAN. [*Somewhat distressed.*] Yes, that is what you want, I supposed. Uh?
LØVBORG. [*Smiling, puts down his hat and takes a thick manila envelope out of his pocket.*] But when this comes out—George Tesman—you'll have to read it. Because this is the real book—the one that speaks for my true self.
TESMAN. Oh, really? What sort of book is that?
LØVBORG. It's the sequel.
TESMAN. Sequel? To what?
LØVBORG. To the book.
TESMAN. The one just out?

LØVBORG. Of course.
TESMAN. Yes, but my dear Eilert—that comes right down to our own time!
LØVBORG. Yes, it does. And this one deals with the future.
TESMAN. The future! But good Lord, there's nothing we know about that!
LØVBORG. True. But there are one or two things worth saying about it all the same. [*Opens the envelope.*] Here, take a look—
TESMAN. But that's not your handwriting.
LØVBORG. I dictated it. [*Paging through the manuscript.*] It's divided into two sections. The first is about the forces shaping the civilization of the future. And the second part, here—[*Paging further on.*] suggests what lines of development it's likely to take.
TESMAN. How extraordinary! It never would have occurred to me to write about anything like that.
HEDDA. [*At the glass door, drumming on the pane.*] Hm—no, of course not.
LØVBORG. [*Puts the manuscript back in the envelope and lays it on the table.*] I brought it along because I thought I might read you a bit of it this evening.
TESMAN. Ah, that's very good of you, Eilert; but this evening—[*Glancing at* BRACK.] I'm really not sure that's possible—
LØVBORG. Well, some other time, then. There's no hurry.
BRACK. I should explain, Mr. Løvborg—there's a little party at my place tonight. Mostly for Tesman, you understand.
LØVBORG. [*Looking for his hat.*] Ah—then I won't stay—
BRACK. No, listen—won't you give me the pleasure of having you join us?
LØVBORG. [*Sharply and decisively.*] No, I can't. Thanks very much.
BRACK. Oh, nonsense! Do that. We'll be a small, select group. And you can bet we'll have it "lively," as Mrs. Hed—Mrs. Tesman says.
LØVBORG. I don't doubt it. But nevertheless—
BRACK. You could bring your manuscript with you and read it to Tesman there, at my place. I have a spare room you could use.

TESMAN. Why, of course, Eilert—you could do that, couldn't you? Uh?

HEDDA. [*Intervening.*] But dear, if Mr. Løvborg simply doesn't want to! I'm sure Mr. Løvborg would much prefer to settle down here and have supper with me.

LØVBORG. [*Looking at her.*] With you, Mrs. Tesman!

HEDDA. And with Mrs. Elvsted.

LØVBORG. Ah. [*Casually.*] I saw her a moment this afternoon.

HEDDA. Oh, did you? Well, she'll be here soon. So it's almost essential for you to stay, Mr. Løvborg. Otherwise, she'll have no one to see her home.

LØVBORG. That's true. Yes, thank you, Mrs. Tesman—I'll be staying, then.

HEDDA. Then let me just tell the maid— [*She goes to the hall door and rings.* BERTA *enters.* HEDDA *talks to her quietly and points toward the inner room.* BERTA *nods and goes out again.*]

TESMAN. [*At the same time, to* LØVBORG.] Tell me, Eilert—is it this new material—about the future—that you're going to be lecturing on?

LØVBORG. Yes.

TESMAN. Because I heard at the bookstore that you'll be giving a lecture series here this autumn.

LØVBORG. I intend to. I hope you won't be offended, Tesman.

TESMAN. Why, of course not! But—?

LØVBORG. I can easily understand that it makes things rather difficult for you.

TESMAN. [*Dispiritedly.*] Oh, I could hardly expect that for my sake you'd—

LØVBORG. But I'm going to wait till you have your appointment.

TESMAN. You'll wait! Yes, but—but—you're not competing for it, then? Uh?

LØVBORG. No. I only want to win in the eyes of the world.

TESMAN. But, my Lord—then Aunt Julie was right after all! Oh yes—I knew it all along! Hedda! Can you imagine—Eilert Løvborg won't stand in our way!

HEDDA. [*Brusquely.*] Our way? Leave me out of it. [*She goes up toward the inner room where* BERTA *is putting a tray with decanters and glasses on the table.* HEDDA *nods her approval and comes back again.* BERTA *goes out.*]

TESMAN. [*At the same time.*] But you, Judge—what do you say to all this? Uh?

BRACK. Well, I'd say that victory and honor—hm—after all, they're very sweet—

TESMAN. Yes, of course. But still—

HEDDA. [*Regarding* TESMAN *with a cold smile.*] You look as if you'd been struck by lightning.

TESMAN. Yes—something like it—I guess—

BRACK. That's because a thunderstorm just passed over us, Mrs. Tesman.

HEDDA. [*Pointing toward the inner room.*] Won't you gentlemen please help yourselves to a glass of cold punch?

BRACK. [*Looking at his watch.*] A parting cup? That's not such a bad idea.

TESMAN. Marvelous, Hedda! Simply marvelous! The way I feel now, with this weight off my mind—

HEDDA. Please, Mr. Løvborg, you too.

LØVBORG. [*With a gesture of refusal.*] No, thank you. Not for me.

BRACK. Good Lord, cold punch—it isn't poison, you know.

LØVBORG. Perhaps not for everyone.

HEDDA. I'll keep Mr. Løvborg company a while.

TESMAN. All right, Hedda dear, you do that. [*He and* BRACK *go into the inner room, sit down, drink punch, smoke cigarettes, and talk animatedly during the following.* LØVBORG *remains standing by the stove,* HEDDA *goes to the writing table.*]

HEDDA. [*Slightly raising her voice.*] I can show you some photographs, if you like. Tesman and I traveled through the Tyrol on our way home. [*She brings over an album and lays it on the table by the sofa, seating herself in the farthest corner.* EILERT LØVBORG *comes closer, stops and looks at her. Then he takes a chair and sits down on her left, his back toward the inner room.*]

HEDDA. [*Opening the album.*] You see this view of the mountains, Mr. Løvborg. That's the Ortler group. Tesman's labeled them underneath. Here it is: "The Ortler group, near Meran."

LØVBORG. [*Whose eyes have never left her, speaking in a low, soft voice.*] Hedda—Gabler!

HEDDA. [*With a quick glance at him.*] Ah! Shh!
LØVBORG. [*Repeating softly.*] Hedda Gabler!
HEDDA. [*Looks at the album.*] Yes, I used to be called that. In those days—when we two knew each other.
LØVBORG. And from now on—for the rest of my life—I have to teach myself not to say Hedda Gabler.
HEDDA. [*Turning the page.*] Yes, you have to. And I think you ought to start practicing it. The sooner the better, I'd say.
LØVBORG. [*Resentment in his voice.*] Hedda Gabler married? And to George Tesman!
HEDDA. Yes—that's how it goes.
LØVBORG. Oh, Hedda, Hedda—how could you throw yourself away like that!
HEDDA. [*Looks at him sharply.*] All right—no more of that!
LØVBORG. What do you mean? [TESMAN *comes in and over to the sofa.*]
HEDDA. [*Hears him coming and says casually.*] And this one, Mr. Løvborg, was taken from the Val d'Ampezzo. Just look at the peaks of those mountains. [*Looks warmly up at* TESMAN.] Now what were those marvelous mountains called, dear?
TESMAN. Let me see. Oh, those are the Dolomites.
HEDDA. Why, of course! Those are the Dolomites, Mr. Løvborg.
TESMAN. Hedda dear—I only wanted to ask if we shouldn't bring in some punch anyway. At least for you, hm?
HEDDA. Yes, thank you. And a couple of *petis fours*, please.
TESMAN. No cigarettes?
HEDDA. No.
TESMAN. Right. [*He goes through the inner room and out to the right.* BRACK *remains sitting inside, keeping his eye from time to time on* HEDDA *and* LØVBORG.]
LØVBORG. [*Softly, as before.*] Answer me, Hedda—how could you go and do such a thing?
HEDDA. [*Apparently immersed in the album.*] If you keep on saying Hedda like that to me, I won't talk to you.
LØVBORG. Can't I say Hedda even when we're alone?
HEDDA. No. You can think it, but you mustn't say it like that.
LØVBORG. Ah, I understand. It offends your—love for George Tesman.
HEDDA. [*Glances at him and smiles.*] Love? You *are* absurd!
LØVBORG. Then you don't love him!
HEDDA. I don't expect to be unfaithful, either. I'm not having any of that!
LØVBORG. Hedda, just answer me one thing—
HEDDA. Shh! [TESMAN, *carrying a tray, enters from the inner room.*]
TESMAN. Look out! Here come the goodies. [*He sets the tray on the table.*]
HEDDA. Why do you do the serving?
TESMAN. [*Filling the glasses.*] Because I think it's such fun to wait on you, Hedda.
HEDDA. But now you've poured out two glasses. And you know Mr. Løvborg doesn't want—
TESMAN. Well, but Mrs. Elvsted will be along soon.
HEDDA. Yes, that's right—Mrs. Elvsted—
TESMAN. Had you forgotten her? Uh?
HEDDA. We've been so caught up in these. [*Showing him a picture.*] Do you remember this little village?
TESMAN. Oh, that's the one just below the Brenner Pass! It was there and we stayed overnight—
HEDDA. And met all those lively summer people.
TESMAN. Yes, that's the place. Just think—if we could have had *you* with us, Eilert! My! [*He goes back and sits beside* BRACK.]
LØVBORG. Answer me just one thing, Hedda—
HEDDA. Yes?
LØVBORG. Was there no love with respect to me, either? Not a spark—not one glimmer of love at all?
HEDDA. I wonder, really, was there? To me it was as if we were two true companions—two very close friends. [*Smiling.*] You, especially, were so open with me.
LØVBORG. You wanted it that way.
HEDDA. When I look back on it now, there was really something beautiful and fascinating—and daring, it seems to me, about—about our secret closeness—our companionship that no one, not a soul, suspected.
LØVBORG. Yes, Hedda, that's true!

Wasn't there? When I'd come over to your father's in the afternoon—and the general sat by the window reading his papers—with his back to us—
HEDDA. And we'd sit on the corner sofa—
LØVBORG. Always with the same illustrated magazine in front of us—
HEDDA. Yes, for the lack of an album.
LØVBORG. Yes, Hedda—and the confessions I used to make—telling you things about myself that no one else knew of then. About the way I'd go out, the drinking, the madness that went on day and night, for days at a time. Ah, what power was it in you, Hedda, that made me tell you such things?
HEDDA. You think it was some kind of power in me?
LØVBORG. How else can I explain it? And all those—those devious questions you asked me—
HEDDA. That you understood so remarkably well—
LØVBORG. To think you could sit there and ask such questions! So boldly.
HEDDA. Deviously, please.
LØVBORG. Yes, but boldly, all the same. Interrogating me about—all that kind of thing!
HEDDA. And to think you could answer, Mr. Løvborg.
LØVBORG. Yes, that's exactly what I don't understand—now, looking back. But tell me, Hedda—the root of that bond between us, wasn't it love? Didn't you feel, on your part, as if you wanted to cleanse and absolve me—when I brought those confessions to you? Wasn't that it?
HEDDA. No, not quite.
LØVBORG. What was your power, then?
HEDDA. Do you find it so very surprising that a young girl—if there's no chance of anyone knowing—
LØVBORG. Yes?
HEDDA. That she'd like some glimpse of a world that—
LØVBORG. That—?
HEDDA. That she's forbidden to know anything about.
LØVBORG. So that was it?
HEDDA. Partly. Partly that, I guess.
LØVBORG. Companionship in a thirst for life. But why, then, couldn't it have gone on?
HEDDA. But that was your fault.
LØVBORG. You broke it off.
HEDDA. Yes, when that closeness of ours threatened to grow more serious. Shame on you, Eilert Løvborg! How could you violate my trust when I'd been so—so bold with my friendship?
LØVBORG. [*Clenching his fists.*] Oh, why didn't you do what you said! Why didn't you shoot me down!
HEDDA. I'm—much too afraid of scandal.
LØVBORG. Yes, Hedda, you're a coward at heart.
HEDDA. A terrible coward. [*Changing her tone.*] But that was lucky for you. And now you're so nicely consoled at the Elvsteds'.
LØVBORG. I know what Thea's been telling you.
HEDDA. And perhaps you've been telling her all about us?
LØVBORG. Not a word. She's too stupid for that sort of thing.
HEDDA. Stupid?
LØVBORG. When it comes to those things, she's stupid.
HEDDA. And I'm a coward. [*Leans closer, without looking him in the eyes, and speaks softly.*] But there *is* something now that I can tell you.
LØVBORG. [*Intently.*] What?
HEDDA. When I didn't dare shoot you—
LØVBORG. Yes?
HEDDA. That wasn't my worst cowardice—that night.
LØVBORG. [*Looks at her a moment, understands, and whispers passionately.*] Oh, Hedda! Hedda Gabler! Now I begin to see it, the hidden reason why we've been so close! You and I—! So it *was* your hunger for life—
HEDDA. [*Quietly, with a sharp glance.*] Careful! That's no way to think! [*It has begun to grow dark. The hall door is opened from without by* BERTA.]
HEDDA. [*Clapping the album shut and calling out with a smile.*] Well, at last! Thea dear—please come in! [MRS. ELVSTED *enters from the hall. She is in evening dress. The door is closed behind her.*]
HEDDA. [*On the sofa, stretching her arms out toward her.*] Thea, my sweet—I thought you were never coming! [*In passing,* MRS. ELVSTED *exchanges light*

greetings with the gentlemen in the inner room, then comes over to the table and extends her hand to HEDDA. LØVBORG *has gotten up. He and* MRS. ELVSTED *greet each other with a silent nod.*]

MRS. ELVSTED. Perhaps I ought to go in and talk a bit with your husband?

HEDDA. Oh, nonsense. Let them be. They're leaving soon.

MRS. ELVSTED. They're leaving?

HEDDA. Yes, for a drinking party.

MRS. ELVSTED. [*Quickly, to* LØVBORG.] But you're not?

LØVBORG. No.

HEDDA. Mr. Løvborg—is staying with us.

MRS. ELVSTED. [*Taking a chair, about to sit down beside him.*] Oh, it's so good to be here!

HEDDA. No, no, Thea dear! Not there! You have to come over here by me. I want to be in the middle.

MRS. ELVSTED. Any way you please. [*She goes around the table and sits on the soft to* HEDDA'*s right.* LØVBORG *resumes his seat.*]

LØVBORG. [*After a brief pause, to* HEDDA.] Isn't she lovely to look at?

HEDDA. [*Lightly stroking her hair.*] Only to look at?

LØVBORG. Yes. Because we two—she and I—we really *are* true companions. We trust each other completely. We can talk things out together without any reservations—

HEDDA. Never anything devious, Mr. Løvborg?

LØVBORG. Well—

MRS. ELVSTED. [*Quietly, leaning close to* HEDDA.] Oh, Hedda, you don't know how happy I am! Just think—he says that I've inspired him.

HEDDA. [*Regarding her with a smile.*] Really, dear; did he say that?

LØVBORG. And then the courage she has, Mrs. Tesman, when it's put to the test.

MRS. ELVSTED. Good heavens, me! Courage!

LØVBORG. Enormous courage—where I'm concerned.

HEDDA. Yes, courage—yes! If one only had that.

LØVBORG. Then what?

HEDDA. Then life might still be bearable. [*Suddenly changing her tone.*] But now, Thea dearest—you really must have a nice cold glass of punch.

MRS. ELVSTED. No, thank you. I never drink that sort of thing.

HEDDA. Well, then you, Mr. Løvborg.

LØVBORG. Thanks, not for me either.

MRS. ELVSTED. No, not for him either!

HEDDA. [*Looking intently at him.*] But if I insist?

LØVBORG. Makes no difference.

HEDDA. [*With a laugh.*] Poor me, then I have no power over you at all?

LØVBORG. Not in that area.

HEDDA. But seriously, I think you ought to, all the same. For your own sake.

MRS. ELVSTED. But Hedda—!

LØVBORG. Why do you think so?

HEDDA. Or, to be more exact, for others' sakes.

LØVBORG. Oh?

HEDDA. Otherwise, people might get the idea that you're not very bold at heart. That you're not really sure of yourself at all.

MRS. ELVSTED. [*Softly.*] Oh, Hedda, don't—!

LØVBORG. People can think whatever they like, for all I care.

MRS. ELVSTED. [*Happily.*] Yes, that's right!

HEDDA. I saw it so clearly in Judge Brack a moment ago.

LØVBORG. What did you see?

HEDDA. The contempt in his smile when you didn't dare join them for a drink.

LØVBORG. Didn't dare! Obviously I'd rather stay here and talk with you.

MRS. ELVSTED. That's only reasonable, Hedda.

HEDDA. But how could the judge know that? And besides, I noticed him smile and glance at Tesman when you couldn't bring yourself to go to their wretched little party.

LØVBORG. Couldn't! Are you saying I couldn't?

HEDDA. *I'm* not. But that's the way Judge Brack sees it.

LØVBORG. All right, let him.

HEDDA. Then you won't go along?

LØVBORG. I'm staying here with you and Thea.

MRS. ELVSTED. Yes, Hedda—you can be sure he is!

HEDDA. [*Smiles and nods approvingly at*

LØVBORG.] I see. Firm as a rock. True to principle, to the end of time. There, that's what a man ought to be! [*Turning to* MRS. ELVSTED *and patting her.*] Well, now, didn't I tell you that, when you came here so distraught this morning—

LØVBORG. [*Surprised.*] Distraught?

MRS. ELVSTED. [*Terrified.*] Hedda—! But Hedda—!

HEDDA. Can't you see for yourself? There's no need at all for your going around so deathly afraid that—[*Changing her tone.*] There! Now we can all enjoy ourselves!

LØVBORG. [*Shaken.*] What is all this, Mrs. Tesman?

MRS. ELVSTED. Oh, God, oh, God, Hedda! What are you saying! What are you doing!

HEDDA. Not so loud. That disgusting judge is watching you.

LØVBORG. So deathly afraid? For my sake?

MRS. ELVSTED. [*In a low moan.*] Oh, Hedda, you've made me so miserable!

LØVBORG. [*Looks intently at her a moment, his face drawn.*] So that's how completely you trusted me.

MRS. ELVSTED. [*Imploringly.*] Oh, my dearest—if you'll only listen—!

LØVBORG. [*Takes one of the glasses of punch, raises it, and says in a low, hoarse voice.*] Your health, Thea! [*He empties the glass, puts it down, and takes the other.*]

MRS. ELVSTED. [*Softly.*] Oh, Hedda, Hedda—how could you want such a thing!

HEDDA. Want it? I? Are you crazy?

LØVBORG. And your health too, Mrs. Tesman. Thanks for the truth. Long live truth! [*Drains the glass and starts to refill it.*]

HEDDA. [*Laying her hand on his arm.*] All right—no more for now. Remember, you're going to a party.

MRS. ELVSTED. No, no, no!

HEDDA. Shh! They're watching you.

LØVBORG. [*Putting down his glass.*] Now, Thea—tell me honestly—

MRS. ELVSTED. Yes!

LØVBORG. Did your husband know that you followed me?

MRS. ELVSTED. [*Wringing her hands.*] Oh, Hedda—listen to him!

LØVBORG. Did you have it arranged, you and he, that you should come down into town and spy on me? Or maybe he got you to do it himself? Ah, yes—I'm sure he needed me back in the office! Or maybe he missed my hand at cards?

MRS. ELVSTED. [*Softly, in anguish.*] Oh, Eilert, Eilert—!

LØVBORG. [*Seizing his glass to fill it.*] Skoal to the old sheriff, too!

HEDDA. [*Stopping him.*] That's enough. Don't forget, you're giving a reading for Tesman.

LØVBORG. [*Calmly, setting down his glass.*] That was stupid of me, Thea. I mean, taking it like this. Don't be angry at me, my dearest. You'll see—you and all the others—that if I stumbled and fell—I'm back on my feet again now! With your help, Thea.

MRS. ELVSTED. [*Radiant with joy.*] Oh, thank God—! [BRACK, *in the meantime, has looked at his watch. He and* TESMAN *stand up and enter the drawing room.*]

BRACK. [*Takes his hat and overcoat.*] Well, Mrs. Tesman, our time is up.

HEDDA. I suppose it is.

LØVBORG. [*Rising.*] Mine too, Judge.

MRS. ELVSTSED. [*Softly pleading.*] Oh, Eilert—don't!

HEDDA. [*Pinching her arm.*] They can hear you!

MRS. ELVSTED. [*With a small cry.*] Ow!

LØVBORG. [*To* BRACK.] You were kind enough to ask me along.

BRACK. Oh, then you *are* coming, after all?

LØVBORG. Yes, thank you.

BRACK. I'm delighted—

LØVBORG. [*Putting the manila envelope in his pocket, to* TESMAN.] I'd like to show you one or two things before I turn this in.

TESMAN. Just think—how exciting! But Hedda dear, how will Mrs. Elvsted get home? Uh?

HEDDA. Oh, we'll hit on something.

LØVBORG. [*Glancing toward the ladies.*] Mrs. Elvsted? Don't worry, I'll stop back and fetch her. [*Coming nearer.*] Say about ten o'clock, Mrs. Tesman? Will that do?

HEDDA. Yes. That will do very nicely.

TESMAN. Well, then everything's all set. But you mustn't expect *me* that early, Hedda.

HEDDA. Dear, you stay as long—just as long as you like.

MRS. ELVSTED. [*With suppressed anxiety.*] Mr. Løvborg—I'll be waiting here till you come.

LØVBORG. [*His hat in his hand.*] Yes, I understand.

BRACK. So, gentlemen—the excursion train is leaving! I hope it's going to be lively, as a certain fair lady puts it.

HEDDA. Ah, if only that fair lady could be there, invisible—!

BRACK. Why invisible?

HEDDA. To hear a little of your unadulterated liveliness, Judge.

BRACK. [*Laughs.*] I wouldn't advise the fair lady to try.

TESMAN. [*Also laughing.*] Hedda, you are the limit! What an idea!

BRACK. Well, good night. Good night, ladies.

LØVBORG. [*Bowing.*] About ten o'clock, then. [BRACK, LØVBORG, *and* TESMAN *go out the hall door. At the same time,* BERTA *enters from the inner room with a lighted lamp, which she sets on the drawing room table, then goes out the same way.*]

MRS. ELVSTED. [*Having risen, moving restlessly about the room.*] Hedda—Hedda—what's going to come of all this?

HEDDA. At ten o'clock—he'll be here. I can see him now—with vine leaves in his hair—fiery and bold—

MRS. ELVSTED. Oh, how good that would be!

HEDDA. And then, you'll see—he'll be back in control of himself. He'll be a free man, then, for the rest of his days.

MRS. ELVSTED. Oh, God—if only he comes as you see him now!

HEDDA. He'll come back like that, and no other way! [*Gets up and goes closer.*] Go on and doubt him as much as you like. *I* believe in him. And now we'll find out—

MRS. ELVSTED. There's something behind what you're doing, Hedda.

HEDDA. Yes, there is. For once in my life, I want to have power over a human being.

MRS. ELVSTED. But don't you have that?

HEDDA. I don't have it. I've never had it.

MRS. ELVSTED. Not with your husband?

HEDDA. Yes, what a bargain *that* was! Oh, if you only could understand how poor I am. And you're allowed to be so rich! [*Passionately throws her arms about her.*] I think I'll burn your hair off, after all!

MRS. ELVSTED. Let go! Let me go! I'm afraid of you, Hedda!

BERTA. [*In the doorway to the inner room.*] Supper's waiting in the dining room, ma'am.

HEDDA. All right, we're coming.

MRS. ELVSTED. No, no, no! I'd rather go home alone! Right away—now!

HEDDA. Nonsense! First you're going to have tea, you little fool. And then—ten o'clock—Eilert Løvborg comes—with vine leaves in his hair. [*She drags* MRS. ELVSTED, *almost by force, toward the doorway.*]

Act 3

The same rooms at the TESMANS'. *The curtains are down across the doorway to the inner room, and also across the glass door. The lamp, shaded and turned down low, is burning on the table. The door to the stove stands open; the fire has nearly gone out.*

MRS. ELVSTED, *wrapped in a large shawl, with her feet up on a footstool, lies back in the armchair close by the stove.* HEDDA, *fully dressed, is asleep on the sofa, with a blanket over her. After a pause,* MRS. ELVSTED *suddenly sits straight up in the chair, listening tensely. Then she sinks wearily back again.*

MRS. ELVSTED. [*In a low moan.*] Not yet—oh, God—oh, God—not yet! [BERTA *slips in cautiously by the hall door. She holds a letter in her hand.*]

MRS. ELVSTED. [*Turns and whispers anxiously.*] Yes? Has anyone come?

BERTA. [*Softly.*] Yes, a girl just now stopped by with this letter.

MRS. ELVSTED. [*Quickly, reaching out her hand.*] A letter! Give it to me!
BERTA. No, it's for the Doctor, ma'am.
MRS. ELVSTED. Oh.
BERTA. It was Miss Tesman's maid that brought it. I'll leave it here on the table.
MRS. ELVSTED. Yes, do.
BERTA. [*Putting the letter down.*] I think I'd best put out the lamp. It's smoking.
MRS. ELVSTED. Yes, put it out. It'll be daylight soon.
BERTA. [*Does so.*] It's broad daylight already, ma'am.
MRS. ELVSTED. It's daylight! And still no one's come—!
BERTA. Oh, mercy—I knew it would go like this.
MRS. ELVSTED. You knew?
BERTA. Yes, when I saw that a certain gentleman was back here in town—and that he went off with them. We've heard plenty about that gentleman over the years.
MRS. ELVSTED. Don't talk so loud. You'll wake Mrs. Tesman.
BERTA. [*Looks toward the sofa and sighs.*] Goodness me—yes, let her sleep, poor thing. Should I put a bit more on the fire?
MRS. ELVSTED. Thanks, not for me.
BERTA. All right. [*She goes quietly out the hall door.*]
HEDDA. [*Wakes as the door shuts and looks up.*] What's that?
MRS. ELVSTED. It was just the maid—
HEDDA. [*Glancing about.*] In here—? Oh yes, I remember now. [*Sits up on the sofa, stretches, and rubs her eyes.*] What time is it, Thea?
MRS. ELVSTED. [*Looking at her watch.*] It's after seven.
HEDDA. When did Tesman get in?
MRS. ELVSTED. He isn't back.
HEDDA. Not back yet?
MRS. ELVSTED. [*Getting up.*] No one's come in.
HEDDA. And we sat here and waited up for them till four o'clock—
MRS. ELVSTED. [*Wringing her hands.*] And how I've waited for him!
HEDDA. [*Yawns, and speaks with her hand in front of her mouth.*] Oh, dear—we could have saved ourselves the trouble.
MRS. ELVSTED. Did you get any sleep?
HEDDA. Oh yes. I slept quite well, I think. Didn't you?
MRS. ELVSTED. No, not at all. I couldn't, Hedda! It was just impossible.
HEDDA. [*Rising and going toward her.*] There, there, now! There's nothing to worry about. It's not hard to guess what happened.
MRS. ELVSTED. Oh, what? Tell me!
HEDDA. Well, it's clear that the party must have gone on till all hours—
MRS. ELVSTED. Oh, Lord, yes—it must have. But even so—
HEDDA. And then, of course, Tesman didn't want to come home and make a commotion in the middle of the night. [*Laughs.*] Probably didn't care to show himself, either—so full of his party spirits.
MRS. ELVSTED. But where else could he have gone?
HEDDA. He must have gone up to his aunts' to sleep. They keep his old room ready.
MRS. ELVSTED. No, he can't be with them. Because he just now got a letter from Miss Tesman. It's over there.
HEDDA. Oh? [*Looking at the address.*] Yes, that's Aunt Julie's handwriting, all right. Well, then he must have stayed over at Judge Brack's. And Eilert Løvborg—he's sitting with vine leaves in his hair, reading away.
MRS. ELVSTED. Oh, Hedda, you say these things, and you really don't believe them at all.
HEDDA. You're such a little fool, Thea.
MRS. ELVSTED. That's true; I guess I am.
HEDDA. And you really look dead tired.
MRS. ELVSTED. Yes, I feel dead tired.
HEDDA. Well, you just do as I say, then. Go in my room and stretch out on the bed for a while.
MRS. ELVSTED. No, no—I still wouldn't get any sleep.
HEDDA. Why, of course you would.
MRS. ELVSTED. Well, but your husband's sure to be home now soon. And I've got to know right away—
HEDDA. I'll call you the moment he comes.
MRS. ELVSTED. Yes? Promise me, Hedda?
HEDDA. You can count on it. Just go

and get some sleep.
MRS. ELVSTED. Thanks. I'll try. [*She goes out through the inner room.*]
HEDDA *goes over to the glass door and draws the curtains back. Bright daylight streams into the room. She goes over to the writing table, takes out a small hand mirror, regards herself and arranges her hair. She then goes to the hall door and presses the bell. After a moment,* BERTA *enters.*]
BERTA. Did you want something, ma'am?
HEDDA. Yes, you can build up the fire. I'm freezing in here.
BERTA. Why, my goodness—we'll have it warm in no time. [*She rakes the embers together and puts some wood on, then stops and listens.*] There's the front doorbell, ma'am.
HEDDA. Go and see who it is. I'll take care of the stove.
BERTA. It'll be burning soon. [*She goes to the hall door.* HEDDA *kneels on the footstool and lays more wood on the fire. After a moment,* GEORGE TESMAN *comes in from the hall. He looks tired and rather serious. He tiptoes toward the doorway to the inner room and is about to slip through the curtains.*]
HEDDA. [*At the stove, without looking up.*] Good morning.
TESMAN. [*Turns.*] Hedda! [*Approaching her.*] But what on earth—! You're up so early? Uh?
HEDDA. Yes, I'm up quite early today.
TESMAN. And I was sure you were still in bed sleeping. Isn't that something, Hedda!
HEDDA. Not so loud. Mrs. Elvsted's resting in my room.
TESMAN. Was Mrs. Elvsted here all night?
HEDDA. Well, no one returned to take her home.
TESMAN. No, I guess that's right.
HEDDA. [*Shuts the door to the stove and gets up.*] So—did you enjoy your party?
TESMAN. Were you worried about me? Hm?
HEDDA. No, that never occurred to me. I just asked if you'd had a good time.
TESMAN. Oh yes, I really did, for once. But more at the beginning, I'd say—when Eilert read to me out of his book. We got there more than an hour too soon—imagine! And Brack had so much to get ready. But then Eilert read to me.
HEDDA. [*Sitting at the right-hand side of the table.*] Well? Tell me about it—
TESMAN. [*Sitting on a footstool by the stove.*] Really, Hedda—you can't imagine what a book that's going to be! I do believe it's one of the most remarkable things ever written. Just think!
HEDDA. Yes, I don't mean the book—
TESMAN. But I have to make a confession, Hedda. When he'd finished reading—I had such a nasty feeling—
HEDDA. Nasty?
TESMAN. I found myself envying Eilert, that he was able to write such a book. Can you imagine, Hedda!
HEDDA. Oh yes, I can imagine!
TESMAN. And then how sad to see—that with all his gifts—he's still quite irreclaimable.
HEDDA. Don't you mean that he has more courage to live than the others?
TESMAN. Good Lord, no—I mean, he simply can't take his pleasures in moderation.
HEDDA. Well, what happened then—at the end?
TESMAN. I suppose I'd have to say it turned into an orgy, Hedda.
HEDDA. Were there vine leaves in his hair?
TESMAN. Vine leaves? Not that I noticed. But he gave a long, muddled speech in honor of the woman who'd inspired his work. Yes, that was his phrase for it.
HEDDA. Did he give her name?
TESMAN. No, he didn't. But it seems to me it has to be Mrs. Elvsted. Wait and see!
HEDDA. Oh? Where did you leave him?
TESMAN. On the way here. We broke up—the last of us—all together. And Brack came along with us too, to get a little fresh air. And then we did want to make sure that Eilert got home safe. Because he really had a load on, you know.
HEDDA. He must have.
TESMAN. But here's the curious part of it, Hedda. Or perhaps I should say, the distressing part. Oh, I'm almost

ashamed to say it—for Eilert's sake—

HEDDA. Yes, go on—

TESMAN. Well, as we were walking toward town, you see, I happened to drop back a little behind the others. Only for a minute or two—you follow me?

HEDDA. Yes, yes, so—?

TESMAN. And then when I was catching up with the rest of them, what do you think I found on the sidewalk? Uh?

HEDDA. Oh, how should I now!

TESMAN. You mustn't breathe a word to anyone, Hedda—you hear me? Promise me that, for Eilert's sake. [*Takes a manila envelope out of his coat pocket.*] Just think—I found this.

HEDDA. Isn't that what he had with him yesterday?

TESMAN. That's right. It's the whole of his precious irreplaceable manuscript. And he went and lost it—without even noticing. Can you imagine, Hedda! How distressing—

HEDDA. But why didn't you give it right back to him?

TESMAN. No, I didn't dare do that—in the state he was in—

HEDDA. And you didn't tell any of the others you'd found it?

TESMAN. Of course not. I'd never do that, you know—for Eilert's sake.

HEDDA. Then there's no one who knows you have Eilert Løvborg's manuscript?

TESMAN. No. And no one must ever know, either.

HEDDA. What did you say to him afterward?

TESMAN. I had no chance at all to speak with him. As soon as we reached the edge of town, he and a couple of others got away from us and disappeared. Imagine!

HEDDA. Oh? I expect they saw him home.

TESMAN. Yes, they probably did, I suppose. And also Brack went home.

HEDDA. And where've you been carrying on since then?

TESMAN. Well, I and some of the others—we were invited up by one of the fellows and had morning coffee at his place. Or a post-midnight snack, maybe—uh? But as soon as I've had a little rest—and given poor Eilert time to sleep it off, then I've got to take this back to him.

HEDDA. [*Reaching out for the envelope.*] No—don't give it back! Not yet, I mean. Let me read it first.

TESMAN. Hedda dearest, no. My Lord, I can't do that.

HEDDA. You can't?

TESMAN. No. Why, you can just imagine the anguish he'll feel when he wakes up and misses the manuscript. He hasn't any copy of it, you know. He told me that himself.

HEDDA. [*Looks searchingly at him.*] Can't such a work be rewritten? I mean, over again?

TESMAN. Oh, I don't see how it could. Because the inspiration, you know—

HEDDA. Yes, yes—that's the thing, I suppose. [*Casually.*] Oh, by the way—there's a letter for you.

TESMAN. No, really—?

HEDDA. [*Handing it to him.*] It came early this morning.

TESMAN. Dear, from Aunt Julie! What could that be? [*Sets the envelope on the other taboret, opens the letter, skims through it, and springs to his feet.*] Oh, Hedda—she says poor Auntie Rina's dying!

HEDDA. It's no more than we've been expecting.

TESMAN. And if I want to see her one last time, I've got to hurry. I'll have to hop right over.

HEDDA. [*Suppressing a smile.*] Hop?

TESMAN. Oh, Hedda dearest, if you could only bring yourself to come with me! Think of it!

HEDDA. [*Rises and dismisses the thought wearily.*] No, no, don't ask me to do such things. I don't want to look on sickness and death. I want to be free of everything ugly.

TESMAN. Yes, all right, then— [*Dashing about.*] My hat—? My overcoat—? Oh, in the hall— I do hope I'm not there too late, Hedda! Hm?

HEDDA. Oh, if you hurry— [BERTA *appears at the hall door.*]

BERTA. Judge Brack's outside, asking if he might stop in.

TESMAN. At a time like this! No, I can't possibly see him now.

HEDDA. But I can. [*To* BERTA.] Ask the

judge to come in. [BERTA *goes out.*]

HEDDA. [*Quickly, in a whisper.*] Tesman, the manuscript! [*She snatches it from the taboret.*]

TESMAN. Yes, give it here!

HEDDA. No, no, I'll keep it till you're back. [*She moves over to the writing table and slips it in the bookcase.* TESMAN *stands flustered, unable to get his gloves on.* BRACK *enters from the hall.*]

HEDDA. Well, aren't you the early bird.

BRACK. Yes, wouldn't you say so? [*To* TESMAN.] Are you off and away too?

TESMAN. Yes, I absolutely have to get over to my aunts'. Just think—the invalid one, she's dying.

BRACK. Good Lord, she is? But then you mustn't let me detain you. Not at a moment like this—

TESMAN. Yes, I really must run— Good-bye! Good-bye! [*He goes hurriedly out the hall door.*]

HEDDA. It would seem you had quite a time of it last night, Judge.

BRACK. I've not been out of my clothes yet, Mrs. Hedda.

HEDDA. Not you, either?

BRACK. No, as you can see. But what's Tesman been telling you about our night's adventures?

HEDDA. Oh, some tedious tale. Something about stopping up somewhere for coffee.

BRACK. Yes, I know all about the coffee party. Eilert Løvborg wasn't with them, I expect?

HEDDA. No, they'd already taken him home.

BRACK. Tesman, as well.

HEDDA. No, but he said some others had.

BRACK. [*Smiles.*] George Tesman is really a simple soul, Mrs. Hedda.

HEDDA. God knows he's that. But was there something else that went on?

BRACK. Oh, you might say so.

HEDDA. Well, now! Let's sit down, Judge; you'll talk more easily then. [*She sits at the left-hand side of the table, with* BRACK *at the long side, near her.*] So?

BRACK. I had particular reasons for keeping track of my guests—or, I should say, certain of my guests, last night.

HEDDA. And among them Eilert Løvborg, perhaps?

BRACK. To be frank—yes.

HEDDA. Now you really have me curious—

BRACK. You know where he and a couple of the others spent the rest of the night, Mrs. Hedda?

HEDDA. Tell me—if it's fit to be told.

BRACK. Oh, it's very much fit to be told. Well, it seems they showed up at a quite animated soiree.

HEDDA. Of the lively sort.

BRACK. Of the liveliest.

HEDDA. Do go on, Judge—

BRACK. Løvborg, and the others also, had advance invitations. I knew all about it. But Løvborg had begged off, because now, of course, he was supposed to have become a new man, as you know.

HEDDA. Up at the Elvsteds', yes. But he went anyway?

BRACK. Well, you see, Mrs. Hedda—unfortunately the spirit moved him up at my place last evening—

HEDDA. Yes, I hear that he *was* inspired there.

BRACK. To a very powerful degree, I'd say. Well, so his mind turned to other things, that's clear. We males, sad to say—we're not always so true to principle as we ought to be.

HEDDA. Oh, I'm sure you're an exception, Judge. But what about Løvborg—?

BRACK. Well, to cut it short—the result was that he wound up in Mademoiselle Diana's parlors.

HEDDA. Mademoiselle Diana's?

BRACK. It was Mademoiselle Diana who was holding the soiree. For a select circle of lady friends and admirers.

HEDDA. Is she a redhaired woman?

BRACK. Precisely.

HEDDA. Sort of a—singer?

BRACK. Oh yes—she's that too. And also a mighty huntress—of men, Mrs. Hedda. You've undoubtedly heard about her. Løvborg was one of her ruling favorites—back there in his palmy days.

HEDDA. And how did all this end?

BRACK. Less amicably, it seems. She gave him a most tender welcoming, with open arms, but before long she'd taken to fists.

HEDDA. Against Løvborg?
BRACK. That's right. He accused her or her friends of having robbed him. He claimed that his wallet was missing—along with some other things. In short, he must have made a frightful scene.
HEDDA. And what did it come to?
BRACK. It came to a regular free-for-all, the men and the women both. Luckily the police finally got there.
HEDDA. The police too?
BRACK. Yes. But it's likely to prove an expensive little romp for Eilert Løvborg. That crazy fool.
HEDDA. So?
BRACK. He apparently made violent resistance. Struck one of the officers on the side of the head and ripped his coat. So they took him along to the station house.
HEDDA. Where did you hear all this?
BRACK. From the police themselves.
HEDDA. [*Gazing straight ahead.*] So that's how it went. Then he had no vine leaves in his hair.
BRACK. Vine leaves, Mrs. Hedda?
HEDDA. [*Changing her tone.*] But tell me, Judge—just why do you go around like this, spying on Eilert Løvborg?
BRACK. In the first place, it's hardly a matter of no concern to me, if it's brought out during the investigation that he'd come direct from my house.
HEDDA. There'll be an investigation—?
BRACK. Naturally. Anyway, that takes care of itself. But I felt that as a friend of the family I owed you and Tesman a full account of his nocturnal exploits.
HEDDA. Why, exactly?
BRACK. Well, because I have a strong suspicion that he'll try to use you as a kind of screen.
HEDDA. Oh, how could you ever think such a thing!
BRACK. Good Lord—we're really not blind, Mrs. Hedda. You'll see! This Mrs. Elvsted, she won't be going home now so quickly.
HEDDA. Well, even supposing there were something between them, there are plenty of other places where they could meet.
BRACK. Not one single home. From now on, every decent house will be closed to Eilert Løvborg.
HEDDA. So mine ought to be too, is that what you mean?
BRACK. Yes. I'll admit I'd find it more than annoying if the gentleman were to have free access here. If he came like an intruder, an irrelevancy, forcing his way into—
HEDDA. Into the triangle?
BRACK. Precisely. It would almost be like turning me out of my home.
HEDDA. [*Looks at him with a smile.*] I see. The one cock of the walk—that's what you want to be.
BRACK. [*Nodding slowly and lowering his voice.*] Yes, that's what I want to be. And that's what I'll fight for—with every means at my disposal.
HEDDA. [*Her smile vanishing.*] You can be a dangerous person, can't you—in a tight corner.
BRACK. Do you think so?
HEDDA. Yes, now I'm beginning to think so. And I'm thoroughly grateful—that you have no kind of hold over me.
BRACK. [*With an ambiguous laugh.*] Ah, yes, Mrs. Hedda—perhaps you're right about that. If I had, then who knows just what I might do?
HEDDA. Now you listen here, Judge! That sounds too much like a threat.
BRACK. [*Rising.*] Oh, nothing of the kind! A triangle, after all—is best fortified and defended by volunteers.
HEDDA. There we're agreed.
BRACK. Well, now that I've said all I have to say, I'd better get back to town. Good-bye, Mrs. Hedda. [*He goes toward the glass door.*]
HEDDA. [*Rising.*] Are you going through the garden?
BRACK. Yes, I find it's shorter.
HEDDA. Yes, and then it's the back way, too.
BRACK. How true. I have nothing against back ways. At certain times they can be rather piquant.
HEDDA. You mean, when somebody's sharpshooting?
BRACK. [*In the doorway, laughing.*] Oh, people don't shoot their tame roosters!
HEDDA. [*Also laughing.*] I guess not. Not when there's only one— [*Still laughing, they nod good-bye to each other. He*

goes. *She shuts the door after him, then stands for a moment, quite serious, looking out. She then goes over and glances through the curtains to the inner rooms. Moves to the writing table, takes Løvborg's envelope from the bookcase, and is about to page through it, when* BERTA's *voice is heard loudly in the hall.* HEDDA *turns and listens. She hurriedly locks the envelope in the drawer and lays the key on the inkstand.* EILERT LØVBORG, *with his overcoat on and his hat in his hand, throws open the hall door. He looks confused and excited.*]

BRACK. [*Turned toward the hall.*] And I'm telling you, I have to go in! I will, you hear me! [*He shuts the door, turns, sees* HEDDA, *immediately gains control of himself and bows.*]

HEDDA. [*At the writing table.*] Well, Mr. Løvborg, it's late to call for Thea.

LØVBORG. Or rather early to call on you. You must forgive me.

HEDDA. How did you know she was still with me?

LØVBORG. They said at her lodgings that she'd been out all night.

HEDDA. [*Goes to the center table.*] Did you notice anything in their faces when they said that?

LØVBORG. [*Looking at her inquiringly.*] Notice anything?

HEDDA. I mean, did it look like they had their own thoughts on the matter?

LØVBORG. [*Suddenly understanding.*] Oh yes, that's true! I'm dragging her down with me! Actually, I didn't notice anything. Tesman—I don't suppose he's up yet?

HEDDA. No, I don't think so.

LØVBORG. When did he get in?

HEDDA. Very late.

LØVBORG. Did he tell you anything?

HEDDA. Well, I heard you'd had a high time of it out at Judge Brack's.

LØVBORG. Anything else?

HEDDA. No, I don't think so. As a matter of fact, I was terribly sleepy—
[MRS. ELVSTED *comes in through the curtains to the inner room.*]

MRS. ELVSTED. [*Running toward him.*] Oh, Eilert! At last—!

LØVBORG. Yes, at last. And too late.

MRS. ELVSTED. [*Looking anxiously at him.*] What's too late?

LØVBORG. Everything's too late now. It's over with me.

MRS. ELVSTED. Oh no, no—don't say that!

LØVBORG. You'll say the same thing when you've heard—

MRS. ELVSTED. I won't hear anything!

HEDDA. Maybe you'd prefer to talk with her alone. I can leave.

LØVBORG. No, stay—you too. Please.

MRS. ELVSTED. But I can tell you, I don't want to hear anything!

LØVBORG. It's nothing about last night.

MRS. ELVSTED. What is it, then—?

LØVBORG. It's simply this, that from now on, we separate.

MRS. ELVSTED. Separate!

HEDDA. [*Involuntarily.*] I knew it!

LØVBORG. Because I have no more use for you, Thea.

MRS. ELVSTED. And you can stand there and say that! No more use for me! Then I'm not going to help you now, as I have? We're not going to go on working together?

LØVBORG. I have no plans for any more work.

MRS. ELVSTED. [*In desperation.*] Then what will I do with my life?

LØVBORG. You must try to go on living as if you'd never known me.

MRS. ELVSTED. But I can't do that!

LØVBORG. You must try to, Thea. You'll have to go home again—

MRS. ELVSTED. [*In a fury of protest.*] Never! No! Where you are, that's where I want to be! I won't be driven away like this! I'm going to stay right here—and be together with you when the book comes out.

HEDDA. [*In a tense whisper.*] Ah, yes—the book!

LØVBORG. [*Looks at her.*] My book and Thea's—for that's what it is.

MRS. ELVSTED. Yes, that's what I feel it is. And that's why I have the right, as well, to be with you when it comes out. I want to see you covered with honor and respect again. And the joy—I want to share the joy of it with you too.

LØVBORG. Thea—our book's never coming out.

HEDDA. Ah!

MRS. ELVSTED. Never coming out!

LØVBORG. *Can* never come out.

MRS. ELVSTED. [*With anguished forebod-*

ing.] Eilert—what have you done with the manuscript?

HEDDA. [*Watching him intently.*] Yes, the manuscript—?

MRS. ELVSTED. Where is it!

LØVBORG. Oh, Thea—don't ask me that.

MRS. ELVSTED. Yes, yes, I have to know. I've got a right to know, this minute!

LØVBORG. The manuscript—well, you see—I tore the manuscript into a thousand pieces.

MRS. ELVSTED. [*Screams.*] Oh no, no—!

HEDDA. [*Involuntarily.*] But that just isn't—!

LØVBORG. [*Looks at her.*] Isn't so, you think?

HEDDA. [*Composing herself.*] All right. Of course; if you say it yourself. But it sounds so incredible—

LØVBORG. It's true, all the same.

MRS. ELVSTED. [*Wringing her hands.*] Oh, God—oh, God, Hedda—to tear his own work to bits!

LØVBORG. I've torn my own life to bits. So why not tear up my life's work as well—

MRS. ELVSTED. And you did this thing last night!

LØVBORG. Yes, you heard me. In a thousand pieces. And scattered them into the fjord. Far out. At least there, there's clean salt water. Let them drift out to sea—drift with the tide and the wind. And after a while, they'll sink. Deeper and deeper. As I will, Thea.

MRS. ELVSTED. Do you know, Eilert, this thing you've done with the book—for the rest of my life it will seem to me as if you'd killed a little child.

LØVBORG. You're right. It was like murdering a child.

MRS. ELVSTED. But how could you do it—! It was my child too.

HEDDA. [*Almost inaudible.*] Ah, the child—

MRS. ELVSTED. [*Breathes heavily.*] Then it *is* all over. Yes, yes, I'm going now, Hedda.

HEDDA. But you're not leaving town, are you?

MRS. ELVSTED. Oh, I don't know myself what I'll do. There's only darkness ahead. [*She goes out the hall door.*]

HEDDA. [*Stands waiting a moment.*] You're not going to take her home, then, Mr. Løvborg?

LØVBORG. I? Through the streets? So people could see that she'd been with me?

HEDDA. I don't know what else may have happened last night. But is it so completely irredeemable?

LØVBORG. It won't just end with last night—I know that well enough. But the thing is, I've lost all desire for that kind of life. I don't want to start it again, not now. It's the courage and daring for life—that's what she's broken in me.

HEDDA. [*Staring straight ahead.*] To think that pretty little fool could have a man's fate in her hands. [*Looks at him.*] But still, how could you treat her so heartlessly?

LØVBORG. Oh, don't say it was heartless!

HEDDA. To go ahead and destroy what's filled her whole being for months and years! That's not heartless?

LØVBORG. To you, Hedda—I can tell the truth.

HEDDA. The truth?

LØVBORG. Promise me first—give me your word that what I tell you now, you'll never let Thea know.

HEDDA. You have my word.

LØVBORG. Good. I can tell you, then, that what I said here just now isn't true.

HEDDA. About the manuscript?

LØVBORG. Yes. I didn't tear it up—or throw it in the fjord.

HEDDA. No, but—where is it, then?

LØVBORG. I've destroyed it all the same, Hedda. Utterly destroyed it.

HEDDA. I don't understand.

LØVBORG. Thea said that what I've done, for her was like killing a child.

HEDDA. Yes—that's what she said.

LØVBORG. But killing his child—that's not the worst thing a father can do.

HEDDA. *That's* not the worst?

LØVBORG. No. I wanted to spare Thea the worst.

HEDDA. And what's that—the worst?

LØVBORG. Suppose now, Hedda, that a man—in the early morning hours, say—after a wild, drunken night, comes home to his child's mother and says: "Listen—I've been out to this place and that—here and there. And I had our child with me. In this place and that. And I lost the child. Just lost it. God only knows what hands it's come into. Or who's got hold of it."

HEDDA. Well—but when all's said and done—it was only a book—

LØVBORG. Thea's pure soul was in that book.

HEDDA. Yes, I understand.

LØVBORG. Well, then you can understand that for her and me there's no future possible any more.

HEDDA. What do you intend to do?

LØVBORG. Nothing. Just put an end to it all. The sooner the better.

HEDDA. [*Coming a step closer.*] Eilert Løvborg—listen to me. Couldn't you arrange that—that it's done beautifully?

LØVBORG. Beautifully? [*Smiles.*] With vine leaves in my hair, as you used to dream in the old days—

HEDDA. No. I don't believe in vine leaves any more. But beautifully, all the same. For this once—! Good-bye! You must go now—and never come here again.

LØVBORG. Good-bye, then. And give my best to George Tesman. [*He turns to leave.*]

HEDDA. No, wait. I want you to have a souvenir from me. [*She goes to the writing desk and opens the drawer and the pistol case, then comes back to* LØVBORG *with one of the pistols.*]

LØVBORG. [*Looks at her.*] That? Is that the souvenir?

HEDDA. [*Nods slowly.*] Do you recognize it? It was aimed at you once.

LØVBORG. You should have used it then.

HEDDA. Here! Use it now.

LØVBORG. [*Puts the pistol in his breast pocket.*] Thanks.

HEDDA. And beautifully, Eilert Løvborg. Promise me that!

LØVBORG. Good-bye, Hedda Gabler.

[*He goes out the hall door.* HEDDA *listens a moment at the door. Then she goes over to the writing table, takes out the envelope with the manuscript, glances inside, pulls some of the sheets half out and looks at them. She then goes over to the armchair by the stove and sits, with the envelope in her lap. After a moment, she opens the stove door, then brings out the manuscript.*]

HEDDA. [*Throwing some of the sheets into the fire and whispering to herself.*] Now I'm burning your child, Thea! You, with your curly hair! [*Throwing another sheaf in the stove.*] Your child and Eilert Løvborg's. [*Throwing in the rest.*] Now I'm burning—I'm burning the child.

Act 4

The same rooms at the TESMANS'. *It is evening. The drawing room is in darkness. The inner room is lit by the hanging lamp over the table. The curtains are drawn across the glass door.* HEDDA, *dressed in black, is pacing back and forth in the dark room. She then enters the inner room, moving out of sight toward the left. Several chords are heard on the piano. She comes in view again, returning into the drawing room.* BERTA *enters from the right through the inner room with a lighted lamp, which she puts on the table in front of the settee in the drawing room. Her eyes are red from crying, and she has black ribbons on her cap. She goes quietly and discreetly out to the right.*

HEDDA *moves to the glass door, lifts the curtains aside slightly, and gazes out into the darkness.*

Shortly after, MISS TESMAN, *in mourning, with a hat and veil, comes in from the hall.* HEDDA *goes toward her, extending her hand.*

MISS TESMAN. Well, Hedda, here I am, all dressed in mourning. My poor sister's ordeal is finally over.

HEDDA. As you see, I've already heard. Tesman sent me a note.

MISS TESMAN. Yes, he promised he would. But all the same I thought that, to Hedda—here in the house of life—I ought to bear the news of death myself.

HEDDA. That was very kind of you.

MISS TESMAN. Ah, Rina ought not to have passed on just now. This is no time for grief in Hedda's house.

HEDDA. [*Changing the subject.*] She had a

peaceful death, then, Miss Tesman?
MISS TESMAN. Oh, she went so calmly, so beautifully. And so inexpressibly happy that she could see George once again. And say good-bye to him properly. Is it possible that he's still not home?
HEDDA. No, he wrote that I shouldn't expect him too early. But won't you sit down?
MISS TESMAN. No, thank you, my dear—blessed Hedda. I'd love to, but I have so little time. I want to see her dressed and made ready as best as I can. She should go to her grave looking her finest.
HEDDA. Can't I help you with something?
MISS TESMAN. Oh, you mustn't think of it. This is nothing for Hedda Tesman to put her hands to. Or let her thoughts dwell on, either. Not at a time like this, no.
HEDDA. Ah, thoughts—they're not so easy to control—
MISS TESMAN. [*Continuing.*] Well, there's life for you. At my house now we'll be sewing a shroud for Rina. And here, too, there'll be sewing soon, I imagine. But a far different kind, praise God![GEORGE TESMAN *enters from the hall.*]
HEDDA. Well, at last! It's about time.
TESMAN. Are you here, Aunt Julie? With Hedda? Think of that!
MISS TESMAN. I was just this minute leaving, dear boy. Well, did you get done all you promised you would?
TESMAN. No, I'm really afraid I've forgotten half. I'll have to run over and see you tomorrow. My brain's completely in a whirl today. I can't keep my thoughts together.
MISS TESMAN. But George dear, you mustn't take it that way.
TESMAN. Oh? Well, how should I, then?
MISS TESMAN. You should rejoice in your grief. Rejoice in everything that's happened, as I do.
TESMAN. Oh yes, of course. You're thinking of Auntie Rina.
HEDDA. It's going to be lonely for you, Miss Tesman.
MISS TESMAN. For the first few days, yes. But it won't be for long, I hope. I won't let dear Rina's little room stand empty.
TESMAN. No? Who would you want to have in it? Hm?
MISS TESMAN. Oh, there's always some poor invalid in need of care and attention.
HEDDA. Would you really take another burden like that on yourself?
MISS TESMAN. Burden! Mercy on you, child—it's been no burden for me.
HEDDA. But now, with a stranger—
MISS TESMAN. Oh, you soon make friends with an invalid. And I do so much need someone to live for—I, too. Well, thank God, in this house as well, there soon ought to be work that an old aunt can turn her hand to.
HEDDA. Oh, forget about us—
TESMAN. Yes, think how pleasant it could be for the three of us if—
HEDDA. If—?
TESMAN. [*Uneasily.*] Oh, nothing. It'll all take care of itself. Let's hope so. Uh?
MISS TESMAN. Ah, yes. Well, I expect you two have things to talk about. [*Smiles.*] And perhaps Hedda has something to tell you, George. Goodbye. I'll have to get home now to Rina. [*Turning at the door.*] Goodness me, how strange! Now Rina's both with me and with poor dear Jochum as well.
TESMAN. Yes, imagine that, Aunt Julie! Hm? [MISS TESMAN *goes out the hall door.*]
HEDDA. [*Follows* TESMAN *with a cold, probing look.*] I almost think you feel this death more than she.
TESMAN. Oh, it's not just Auntie Rina's death. It's Eilert who has me worried.
HEDDA. [*Quickly.*] Any news about him?
TESMAN. I stopped up at his place this afternoon, thinking to tell him that the manuscript was safe.
HEDDA. Well? Didn't you see him then?
TESMAN. No, he wasn't home. But afterward I met Mrs. Elvsted, and she said he'd been here early this morning.
HEDDA. Yes, right after you left.
TESMAN. And apparently he said he'd torn his manuscript up. Uh?
HEDDA. Yes, he claimed that he had.
TESMAN. But good Lord, then he must have been completely demented!

Well, then I guess you didn't dare give it back to him, Hedda, did you?
HEDDA. No, he didn't get it.
TESMAN. But you did tell him we had it, I suppose?
HEDDA. No. [*Quickly.*] Did you tell Mrs. Elvsted anything?
TESMAN. No, I thought I'd better not. But you should have said something to him. Just think, if he goes off in desperation and does himself some harm! Give me the manuscript, Hedda! I'm taking it back to him right away. Where do you have it?
HEDDA. [*Cold and impassive, leaning against the armchair.*] I don't have it anymore.
TESMAN. You don't have it! What on earth do you mean by that?
HEDDA. I burned it—the whole thing.
TESMAN. [*With a start of terror.*] Burned it! Burned Eilert Løvborg's manuscript!
HEDDA. Stop shouting. The maid could hear you.
TESMAN. Burned it! But my God in heaven—! No, no, no—that's impossible!
HEDDA. Yes, but it's true, all the same.
TESMAN. But do you realize what you've done, Hedda! It's illegal disposition of lost property. Just think! Yes, you can ask Judge Brack; he'll tell you.
HEDDA. It would be wiser not mentioning this—either to the judge or to anyone else.
TESMAN. But how could you go and do such an incredible thing! Whatever put it into your head? What got into you, anyway? Answer me! Well?
HEDDA. [*Suppressing an almost imperceptible smile.*] I did it for your sake, George.
TESMAN. For my sake!
HEDDA. When you came home this morning and told about how he'd read to you—
TESMAN. Yes, yes, then what?
HEDDA. Then you confessed that you envied him this book.
TESMAN. Good Lord, I didn't mean it literally.
HEDDA. Never mind. I still couldn't bear the thought that anyone should eclipse you.
TESMAN. [*In an outburst of mingled doubt and joy.*] Hedda—is this true, what you say! Yes, but—but—I never dreamed you could show your love like this. Imagine!
HEDDA. Well, then it's best you know that—that I'm going to—[*Impatiently, breaking off.*] No, no—you ask your Aunt Julie. She's the one who can tell you.
TESMAN. Oh, I'm beginning to understand you, Hedda! [*Claps his hands together.*] Good heavens, no! Is it actually *that*! Can it be? Uh?
HEDDA. Don't shout so. The maid can hear you.
TESMAN. The maid! Oh, Hedda, you're priceless, really! The maid—but that's Berta! Why, I'll go out and tell her myself.
HEDDA. [*Clenching her fists in despair.*] Oh, I'll die—I'll die of all this!
TESMAN. Of what, Hedda? Oh?
HEDDA. Of all these—absurdities—George.
TESMAN. Absurdities? What's absurd about my being so happy? Well, all right—I guess there's no point in my saying anything to Berta.
HEDDA. Oh, go ahead—why not that, too?
TESMAN. No, no, not yet. But Aunt Julie will have to hear. And then, that you've started to call me George, too! Imagine! Oh, Aunt Julie will be so glad—so glad!
HEDDA. When she hears that I burned Eilert Løvborg's book—for your sake?
TESMAN. Well, as far as that goes—this thing with the book—of course, no one's to know about that. But that you have a love that burns for me, Hedda—Aunt Julie can certainly share in that! You know, I wonder, really, if things such as this are common among young wives? Hm?
HEDDA. I think you should ask Aunt Julie about that, too.
TESMAN. Yes, I definitely will, when I have the chance. [MRS. ELVSTED, *dressed as on her first visit, with hat and coat, comes in the hall door.*]
MRS. ELVSTED. [*Greets them hurriedly and speaks in agitation.*] Oh, Hedda dear, don't be annoyed that I'm back again.

HEDDA. Has something happened, Thea?

TESMAN. Something with Eilert Løvborg? Uh?

MRS. ELVSTED. Yes, I'm so terribly afraid he's met with an accident.

HEDDA. [*Seizing her arms.*] Ah—you think so!

TESMAN. But, Mrs. Elvsted, where did you get that idea?

MRS. ELVSTED. Well, because I heard them speaking of him at the boardinghouse, just as I came in. Oh, there are the most incredible rumors about him in town today.

TESMAN. Yes, you know, I heard them too! And yet I could swear that he went right home to bed last night. Imagine!

HEDDA. Well—what did they say at the boardinghouse?

MRS. ELVSTED. Oh, I couldn't get anything clearly. They either didn't know much themselves, or else— They stopped talking when they saw me. And I didn't dare to ask.

TESMAN. [*Restlessly moving about.*] Let's hope—let's hope you misunderstood them, Mrs. Elvsted!

MRS. ELVSTED. No, no, I'm sure they were talking of him. And then I heard them say something or other about the hospital, or—

TESMAN. The hospital!

HEDDA. No—but that's impossible!

MRS. ELVSTED. Oh, I'm so deathly afraid for him now. And later I went up to his lodging to ask about him.

HEDDA. But was that very wise to do, Thea?

MRS. ELVSTED. What else could I do? I couldn't bear the uncertainty any longer.

TESMAN. But didn't you find him there either? Hm?

MRS. ELVSTED. No. And no one had any word of him. He hadn't been in since yesterday afternoon, they said.

TESMAN. Yesterday! Imagine them saying that!

MRS. ELVSTED. I think there can only be one reason—something terrible must have happened to him!

TESMAN. Hedda dear—suppose I went over and made a few inquiries—?

HEDDA. No, no—don't you get mixed up in his business. [JUDGE BRACK, *with hat in hand, enters from the hall,* BERTA *letting him in and shutting the door after him. He looks grave and bows silently.*]

TESMAN. Oh, is that you, Judge? Uh?

BRACK. Yes, it's imperative that I see you this evening.

TESMAN. I can see that you've heard the news from Aunt Julie.

BRACK. Among other things, yes.

TESMAN. It's sad, isn't it? Uh?

BRACK. Well, my dear Tesman, that depends on how you look at it.

TESMAN. [*Eyes him doubtfully.*] Has anything else happened?

BRACK. Yes, as a matter of fact.

HEDDA. [*Intently.*] Something distressing, Judge?

BRACK. Again, that depends on how you look at it, Mrs. Tesman.

MRS. ELVSTED. [*In an uncontrollable outburst.*] Oh, it's something about Eilert Løvborg!

BRACK. [*Glancing at her.*] Now how did you hit upon that, Mrs. Elvsted? Have you, perhaps, heard something already—?

MRS. ELVSTED. [*In confusion.*] No, no, nothing like that—but—

TESMAN. Oh, for heaven's sake, tell us!

BRACK. [*With a shrug.*] Well—I'm sorry, but—Eilert Løvborg's been taken to the hospital. He's dying.

MRS. ELVSTED. [*Crying out.*] Oh, God, oh, God—!

TESMAN. To the hospital! And dying!

HEDDA. [*Involuntarily.*] All so soon—!

MRS. ELVSTED. [*Wailing.*] And we parted in anger, Hedda!

HEDDA. [*In a whisper.*] Thea—be careful, Thea!

MRS. ELVSTED. [*Ignoring her.*] I have to see him! I have to see him alive!

BRACK. No use, Mrs. Elvsted. No one's allowed in to see him.

MRS. ELVSTED. Oh, but tell me, at least, what happened to him! What is it?

TESMAN. Don't tell me he tried to—! Uh?

HEDDA. Yes, he did, I'm sure of it.

TESMAN. Hedda—how can you say—!

BRACK. [*His eyes steadily on her.*] Unhappily, you've guessed exactly right, Mrs. Tesman.

MRS. ELVSTED. Oh, how horrible!

TESMAN. Did it himself! Imagine!

HEDDA. Shot himself!
BRACK. Again, exactly right, Mrs. Tesman.
MRS. ELVSTED. [*Trying to control herself.*] When did it happen, Mr. Brack?
BRACK. This afternoon. Between three and four.
TESMAN. But good Lord—where did he do it, then? Hm?
BRACK. [*Hesitating slightly.*] Where? Why—in his room, I suppose.
MRS. ELVSTED. No, that can't be right. I was there between six and seven.
BRACK. Well, somewhere else, then. I don't know exactly. I only know he was found like that. Shot—in the chest.
MRS. ELVSTED. What a horrible thought! That he should end that way!
HEDDA. [*To* BRACK.] In the chest, you say.
BRACK. Yes—I told you.
HEDDA. Not the temple?
BRACK. In the chest, Mrs. Tesman.
HEDDA. Well—well, the chest is just as good.
BRACK. Why, Mrs. Tesman?
HEDDA. [*Evasively.*] Oh, nothing—never mind.
TESMAN. And the wound is critical, you say? Uh?
BRACK. The wound is absolutely fatal. Most likely, it's over already.
MRS. ELVSTED. Yes, yes, I can feel that it is! It's over! All over! Oh, Hedda—!
TESMAN. But tell me now—how did you learn about this?
BRACK. [*Brusquely.*] One of the police. Someone I talked to.
HEDDA. [*In a clear, bold voice.*] At last, something truly done!
TESMAN. [*Shocked.*] My God, what are you saying, Hedda!
HEDDA. I'm saying there's beauty in all this.
BRACK. Hm, Mrs. Tesman—
TESMAN. Beauty! What an idea!
MRS. ELVSTED. Oh, Hedda, how can you talk about beauty in such a thing?
HEDDA. Eilert Løvborg's settled accounts with himself. He's had the courage to do what—what had to be done.
MRS. ELVSTED. Don't you believe it! It never happened like that. When he did this, he was in a delirium!

TESMAN. In despair, you mean.
HEDDA. No, he wasn't. I'm certain of that.
MRS. ELVSTED. But he was! In delirium! The way he was when he tore up our book.
BRACK. [*Startled.*] The book? His manuscript, you mean? He tore it up?
MRS. ELVSTED. Yes. Last night.
TESMAN. [*In a low whisper.*] Oh, Hedda, we'll never come clear of all this.
BRACK. Hm, that's very strange.
TESMAN. [*Walking about the room.*] To think Eilert could be gone like that? And then not to have left behind the one thing that could have made his name live on.
MRS. ELVSTED. Oh, if it could only be put together again!
TESMAN. Yes, imagine if that were possible! I don't know what I wouldn't give—
MRS. ELVSTED. Perhaps it can, Mr. Tesman.
TESMAN. What do you mean?
MRS. ELVSTED. [*Searching in the pockets of her dress.*] Look here. I've kept all these notes that he used to dictate from.
HEDDA. [*Coming a step closer.*] Ah—!
TESMAN. You've kept them, Mrs. Elvsted! Uh?
MRS. ELVSTED. Yes, here they are. I took them along when I left home. And they've stayed right here in my pocket—
TESMAN. Oh, let me look!
MRS. ELVSTED. [*Hands him a sheaf of small papers.*] But they're in such a mess. All mixed up.
TESMAN. But just think, if we could decipher them, even so! Maybe the two of us could help each other—
MRS. ELVSTED. Oh yes! At least, we could try—
TESMAN. We can do it! We *must*! I'll give my whole life to this!
HEDDA. You, George. Your life?
TESMAN. Yes, Or, let's say, all the time I can spare. My own research will have to wait. You can understand, Hedda. Hm! It's something I owe to Eilert's memory.
HEDDA. Perhaps.
TESMAN. And so, my dear Mrs. Elvsted, let's see if we can't join forces. Good

Lord, there's no use brooding over what's gone by. Uh? We must try to compose our thoughts as much as we can, in order that—

MRS. ELVSTED. Yes, yes, Mr. Tesman, I'll do the best I can.

TESMAN. Come on, then. Let's look over these notes right away. Where shall we sit? Here? No, in there, in the back room. Excuse us, Judge. You come with me, Mrs. Elvsted.

MRS. ELVSTED. Dear God—if only we can do this! [TESMAN *and* MRS. ELVSTED *go into the inner room. She takes off her hat and coat. They both sit at the table under the hanging lamp and become totally immersed in examining the papers.* HEDDA *goes toward the stove and sits in the armchair. After a moment,* BRACK *goes over by her.*]

HEDDA. [*Her voice lowered.*] Ah, Judge—what a liberation it is, this act of Eilert Løvborg's.

BRACK. Liberation, Mrs. Hedda? Well, yes, for him; you could certainly say he's been liberated—

HEDDA. I mean for me. It's liberating to know that there can still actually be a free and courageous action in this world. Something that shimmers with spontaneous beauty.

BRACK. [*Smiling.*] Hm—my dear Mrs. Hedda—

HEDDA. Oh, I already know what you're going to say. Because you're a kind of specialist too, you know, just like— Oh, well!

BRACK. [*Looking fixedly at her.*] Eilert Løvborg meant more to you than you're willing to admit, perhaps even to yourself. Or am I wrong about that?

HEDDA. I won't answer that sort of question. I simply know that Eilert Løvborg's had the courage to live life after his own mind. And now—this last great act, filled with beauty! That he had the strength and the will to break away from the banquet of life—so young.

BRACK. It grieves me, Mrs. Hedda—but I'm afraid I have to disburden you of this beautiful illusion.

HEDDA. Illusion?

BRACK. One that, in any case, you'd soon be deprived of.

HEDDA. And what's that?

BRACK. He didn't shoot himself—of his own free will.

HEDDA. He didn't—!

BRACK. No. This whole affair didn't go off quite the way I described it.

HEDDA. [*In suspense.*] You've hidden something? What is it?

BRACK. For poor Mrs. Elvsted's sake, I did a little editing here and there.

HEDDA. Where?

BRACK. First, the fact that he's already dead.

HEDDA. In the hospital?

BRACK. Yes. Without regaining consciousness.

HEDDA. What else did you hide?

BRACK. That the incident didn't occur in his room.

HEDDA. Well, that's rather unimportant.

BRACK. Not entirely. Suppose I were to tell you that Eilert Løvborg was found shot in—in Mademoiselle Diana's boudoir.

HEDDA. [*Half rises, then sinks back again.*] That's impossible, Judge! He wouldn't have gone there again today!

BRACK. He was there this afternoon. He went there, demanding something he said they'd stolen from him. Kept raving about a lost child—

HEDDA. Ah—so that was it—

BRACK. I thought perhaps that might be his manuscript. But, I hear now, he destroyed that himself. So it must have been his wallet.

HEDDA. I suppose so. Then, there— that's where they found him.

BRACK. Yes, there. With a discharged pistol in his breast pocket. The bullet had wounded him fatally.

HEDDA. In the chest—yes.

BRACK. No—in the stomach—more or less.

HEDDA. [*Stares up at him with a look of revulsion.*] That too! What is it, this— this curse—that everything I touch turns ridiculous and vile?

BRACK. There's something else, Mrs. Hedda. Another ugly aspect to the case.

HEDDA. What's that?

BRACK. The pistol he was carrying—

HEDDA. [*Breathlessly.*] Well! What about it?

BRACK. He must have stolen it.
HEDDA. [*Springs up.*] Stolen! That's not true! He didn't!
BRACK. It seems impossible otherwise. He must have stolen it—shh! [TESMAN *and* MRS. ELVSTED *have gotten up from the table in the inner room and come into the drawing room.*]
TESMAN. [*With both hands full of papers.*] Hedda dear—it's nearly impossible to see in there under that overhead lamp. You know?
HEDDA. Yes, I know.
TESMAN. Do you think it would be all right if we used your table for a while? Hm?
HEDDA. Yes, I don't mind. [*Quickly.*] Wait! No, let me clear it off first.
TESMAN. Oh, don't bother, Hedda. There's plenty of room.
HEDDA. No, no, let me just clear it off, can't you? I'll put all this in by the piano. There! [*She has pulled out an object covered with sheet music from under the bookcase, adds more music to it, and carries the whole thing into the inner room and off left.* TESMAN *puts the scraps of paper on the writing table and moves the lamp over from the corner table. He and* MRS. ELVSTED *sit down and go on with their work.* HEDDA *comes back.*]
HEDDA. [*Behind* MRS. ELVSTED's *chair, gently ruffling her hair.*] Well, my sweet little Thea—how is it going with Eilert Løvborg's monument?
MRS. ELVSTED. [*Looking despondently up at her.*] Oh, dear—it's going to be terribly hard to set these in order.
TESMAN. It's got to be done. There's just no alternative. Besides, setting other people's papers in order—it's exactly what I can do best. [HEDDA *goes over by the stove and sits on one of the taborets.* BRACK *stands over her, leaning on the armchair.*]
HEDDA. [*Whispering.*] What did you say about the pistol?
BRACK. [*Softly.*] That he must have stolen it.
HEDDA. Why, necessarily, that?
BRACK. Because every other explanation would seem impossible, Mrs. Hedda.
HEDDA. I see.
BRACK. [*Glancing at her.*] Of course, Eilert Løvborg was here this morning. Wasn't he?

HEDDA. Yes.
BRACK. Were you alone with him?
HEDDA. Yes, briefly.
BRACK. Did you leave the room while he was here?
HEDDA. No.
BRACK. Consider. You didn't leave, even for a moment.
HEDDA. Well, yes, perhaps, just for a moment—into the hall.
BRACK. And where did you have your pistol case?
HEDDA. I had it put away in—
BRACK. Yes, Mrs. Hedda?
HEDDA. It was lying over there, on the writing table.
BRACK. Have you looked since to see if both pistols are there?
HEDDA. No.
BRACK. No need to. I saw the pistol. Løvborg had it on him. I knew it immediately, from yesterday. And other days too.
HEDDA. Do you have it, maybe?
BRACK. No, the police have it.
HEDDA. What will they do with it?
BRACK. Try to trace it to the owner.
HEDDA. Do you think they'll succeed?
BRACK. [*Bending over her and whispering.*] No, Hedda Gabler—as long as I keep quiet.
HEDDA. [*Looking at him anxiously.*] And if you don't keep quiet—then what?
BRACK. [*With a shrug.*] Counsel could always claim that the pistol was stolen.
HEDDA. [*Decisively.*] I'd rather die!
BRACK. [*Smiling.*] People *say* such things. But they don't *do* them.
HEDDA. [*Without answering.*] And what, then, if the pistol wasn't stolen? And they found the owner? What would happen?
BRACK. Well, Hedda—there'd be a scandal.
HEDDA. A scandal!
BRACK. A scandal, yes—the kind you're so deathly afraid of. Naturally, you'd appear in court—you and Mademoiselle Diana. She'd have to explain how the whole thing occurred. Whether it was an accident or homicide. Was he trying to pull the pistol out of his pocket to threaten her? Is that why it went off? Or had she torn the pistol out of his hand,

HEDDA. But all that sordid business is no concern of mine.

BRACK. No. But you'll have to answer the question: why did you give Eilert Løvborg the pistol? And what conclusions will people draw from the fact that you did give it to him?

HEDDA. [*Her head sinking.*] That's true. I hadn't thought of that.

BRACK. Well, luckily there's no danger, as long as I keep quiet.

HEDDA. So I'm in your power, Judge. You have your hold over me from now on.

BRACK. [*Whispers more softly.*] My dearest Hedda—believe me—I won't abuse my position.

HEDDA. All the same, I'm in your power. Tied to your will and desire. Not free. Not free, then! [*Rises impetuously.*] No—I can't bear the thought of it. Never!

BRACK. [*Looks at her half mockingly.*] One usually manages to adjust to the inevitable.

HEDDA. [*Returning his look.*] Yes, perhaps so. [*She goes over to the writing table. Suppressing an involuntary smile, she imitates* TESMAN'*s intonation.*] Well? Getting on with it, George? Uh?

TESMAN. Goodness knows, dear. It's going to mean months and months of work, in any case.

HEDDA. [*As before.*] Imagine that! [*Runs her hand lightly through* MRS. ELVSTED'*s hair.*] Don't you find it strange, Thea? Here you are, sitting now beside Tesman—just as you used to sit with Eilert Løvborg.

MRS. ELVSTED. Oh, if I could only inspire your husband in the same way.

HEDDA. Oh, that will surely come—in time.

TESMAN. Yes, you know what, Hedda—I really think I'm beginning to feel something of the kind. But you go back and sit with Judge Brack.

HEDDA. Is there nothing the two of you need from me now?

TESMAN. No, nothing in the world. [*Turning his head.*] From now on, Judge, you'll have to be good enough to keep Hedda company.

BRACK. [*With a glance at* HEDDA.] I'll take the greatest pleasure in that.

HEDDA. Thanks. But I'm tired this evening. I want to rest a while in there on the sofa.

TESMAN. Yes, do that, dear. Uh? [HEDDA *goes into the inner room, pulling the curtains closed after her. Short pause. Suddenly she is heard playing a wild dance melody on the piano.*]

MRS. ELVSTED. [*Starting up from her chair.*] Oh—what's that?

TESMAN. [*Running to the center doorway.*] But Hedda dearest—don't go playing dance music tonight! Think of Auntie Rina! And Eilert, too!

HEDDA. [*Putting her head out between the curtains.*] And Auntie Julie. And all the rest of them. From now on I'll be quiet. [*She closes the curtains again.*]

TESMAN. [*At the writing table.*] She can't feel very happy seeing us do this melancholy work. You know what, Mrs. Elvsted—you must move in with Aunt Julie. Then I can come over evenings. And then we can sit and work *there.* Uh?

MRS. ELVSTED. Yes, perhaps that would be best—

HEDDA. I can hear everything you say, Tesman. But what will I do evenings over here?

TESMAN. [*Leafing through the notes.*] Oh, I'm sure Judge Brack will be good enough to stop by and see you.

BRACK. [*In the armchair, calling out gaily.*] I couldn't miss an evening, Mrs. Tesman! We'll have great times here together, the two of us!

HEDDA. [*In a clear, ringing voice.*] Yes, you can hope so, Judge, can't you? You, the one cock of the walk—[*A shot is heard within.* TESMAN, MRS. ELVSTED, *and* BRACK *start from their chairs.*]

TESMAN. Oh, now she's fooling with those pistols again. [*He throws the curtains back and runs in.* MRS. ELVSTED *follows.* HEDDA *lies, lifeless, stretched out on the sofa. Confusion and cries.* BERTA *comes in, bewildered, from the right.*]

TESMAN. [*Shrieking to* BRACK.] Shot herself! Shot herself in the temple! Can you imagine!

BRACK. [*In the armchair, prostrated.*] But good God! People don't *do* such things!

Cyrano de Bergerac
Edmond Rostand

Although the nineteenth century in European drama opened with the triumph of romanticism and ended with realism firmly entrenched, romanticism was not simply routed. Ibsen wrote great romantic plays after the heyday of romanticism had presumably passed, and lesser writers continued to produce romantic plays throughout the century. At the very end of the century, however, there appeared a French playwright who singlehandedly restored romanticism almost to its full glory on the stage; had Rostand lived longer, or had other playwrights followed his lead, romanticism might have enjoyed a full-scale revival in the twentieth century. As it is, Rostand appears as a man somewhat out of his time.

Edmond Rostand was born in Marseilles on April 1, 1868, the son of educated and refined parents. He studied law at the Collège Stanislas in Paris, but was already actively interested in literary pursuits and published his first book of poems in 1890. He was married that same year to Rosemonde Gerard, also a writer and poet, and settled in Paris to pursue an already promising career as poet and playwright. He formed close friendships with Sarah Bernhardt and Constant Coquelin, and relied heavily upon the advice and support of these two leading actors in the writing and production of his plays.

Rostand's first play to be produced was *The Romancers* (1894), which, in its musical adaptation *The Fantasticks*, is now widely known to American audiences. The play is lightly romantic in tone, set "wherever you please, provided the costumes are pretty," and depends entirely upon the nostalgic willingness of an audience to enter into the spirit of the love story. *The Romancers* was followed by *The Faraway Princess* in 1895 and *The Woman of Samaria* in 1897; both are notable for lovely poetry and for Bernhardt's performances in their leading roles, but neither has achieved great continuing success on the stage. His next play, *Cyrano de Bergerac*, opened a long and successful run late in 1897, and secured its author's position as one of the leading playwrights of his day. Rostand was admitted to the Académie Française on May 30, 1901, the youngest person ever to receive this honor. *The Eaglet* (1900), although it starred Sarah Bernhardt in the pathetic role of Napoleon's son, was less than a complete success, and *Chantecler* (1910) was widely hailed by the critics for its philosophical profundity but has never seemed to work really effectively in the theater—perhaps in part because its characters are animals. Rostand's last play, *The Last Night of Don Juan*, was not entirely completed at the time of his death, which occurred after several years of poor health on December 2, 1918.

Cyrano de Bergerac was written specifically for and in close consultation with Coquelin. Rostand dedicated the published play to him with the note, "Cyrano's soul has been reborn in you." When the play opened at the Théâtre de la Porte Saint-Martin in Paris on December 28, 1897, Coquelin's performance in the title role was a triumph. The play was soon translated into many languages and was widely produced and acclaimed; however, early English translations failed to capture much of the spirit and beauty of the French original. Despite this limitation the play was a notable success in America with Richard Mansfield in the role of Cyrano until, in 1902, an extraordinary action was brought in the courts of Illinois charging that Rostand had plagiarized the play from a work entitled *The Merchant Prince of Cornville* by Samuel E. Gross, an eccentric millionaire and sometime author. Rostand denied the charges, but the American producers named in the suit chose not to contest it in order to avoid court expenses, and hence the Supreme Court of Illinois found for the plaintiff. Only in 1920 was this action reversed by the U.S. District Court of the Southern District of New York, which determined that, although Rostand may have seen a script of the American play (it was never produced), he was not guilty of plagiarism; any casual comparison of the two scripts reveals how ludicrous the charge was in the first place. Soon thereafter (October 1923), Walter Hampden opened in New York in the new Brian Hooker translation of the play and scored an overwhelming success. Hampden found perhaps the best role of his career in Cyrano, and the Hooker translation at last did what so few theatrical translations can ever do—measured up to the original in effectiveness and beauty. Cyrano was also a tour de force for José Ferrer in the late 1940s, and the play has been revived countless times by amateur and professional groups around the world.

The historical Cyrano de Bergerac was born in Paris in 1619. He enjoyed some small success as an author and playwright, and was, indeed, a formidable swordsman. He became a cadet in the company of Carbon de Castel-Jaloux, was involved in several major battles, on one occasion drove the actor Montfleury from the stage, defended a poet friend from attack by a large gang of thugs, and died in 1655 in Paris after a lingering illness resulting from a blow on the head from a dropped block of wood. During his last years, he was close to the widow of a friend who died in battle, although probably this relationship had nothing to do with any love affair. He did in fact write a book in 1649 entitled *Voyage to the Moon*, in which he mentioned several possible ways of getting to the moon; reference to them is made in the latter part of act 3 of Rostand's play. Cyrano de Bergerac was the first writer to suggest rocket propulsion as a means of space travel. Obviously, Rostand made great use of these and other historical facts in the delineation of his central figure, but he did not allow himself to be bound by anything approaching historical accuracy.

Cyrano de Bergerac depends almost entirely on the brilliant creation of its title character for its success in the theater. Structurally it adheres in most important respects to the romantic standards that had been in use for more than a hundred years, and its other characters are at best pasteboard figures that, by contrast, make Cyrano himself even more captivating. In that one role, however, Rostand did indeed capture a human soul. Impossibly noble, preternaturally proud, capable of feats of swordsmanship far beyond the humanly possible, Cyrano nevertheless seems truer to the human soul than many a realistic character who is more mundanely credible. Perhaps the turn-of-the-century audiences were already tired of the unrelieved gloom that so often characterized more realistic plays, but certainly audiences both then and since have embraced Cyrano out of sheer love for what they find in him rather than because he is genuinely believable. Many people have both a romantic view of their own possibilities and a deep insecurity about their presumed defects (their "noses"), which somehow prevent them from full self-realization; this would account for their readiness to identify, to love, to weep with Cyrano.

Beyond the brilliant characterization itself, Rostand also returned the beauty of the alexandrine verse form to the stage, at least for a short time. Rigid adherence to this standard during the neoclassic years may have stunted other equally exciting developments, but the nineteenth-century switch to the prose of Scribe and Zola left the French theater bereft of one of its principal sources of beauty and inspiration, its poetry. Rostand restored this poetry in a warm flood of imagery and rhyme for which audiences were more than ready. Tears flowed and cheers rang out at performances of *Cyrano de Bergerac* unlike anything encountered in a European theater for many decades. The Brian Hooker translation, with the alexandrines rendered into iambic pentameter, captures this beauty in English better than most translations do, but the patriotic fervor and excitement that brings audiences to their feet when Cyrano declaims, "The Cadets of Gascoyne, the defenders / Of Carbon de Castel-Jaloux . . ." must be experienced in French to be fully appreciated.

Rostand does not fit into any orderly discussion of the development of European drama, for his style is a reversion to that of an earlier era. Yet his success in the theater and the evident merit of *Cyrano de Bergerac*, demand attention. However truly he may be said not to fit a preconceived pattern, his success is undeniably real, and his best play has taken a permanent place in the theatrical repertory.

Cyrano de Bergerac

Translated by Brian Hooker

It was to the soul of CYRANO that I intended to dedicate this poem. But since that soul has been reborn in you, COQUELIN, it is to you that I dedicate it.

E. R.

Characters
Cyrano de Bergerac
Christian de Neuvillette
Comte de Guiche
Ragueneau
Le Bret
Carbon de Castel-Jaloux
The Cadets
Lignière
Vicomte de Valvert
A Marquis
Second Marquis
Third Marquis
Montfleury
Bellerose
Jodelet
Cuigy
Brissaille
A Meddler
A Musketeer
Another Musketeer
A Spanish Officer
A Cavalier
The Porter
A Citizen
His Son
A Cut-Purse
A Spectator
A Sentry
Bertrandou the Fifer
A Capuchin

Two Musicians
The Poets
The Pastry cooks
The Pages
Roxane
Her Duenna[1]
Lise
The Orange Girl
Mother Marguérite de Jésus
Sister Marthe
Sister Claire
An Actress
A Soubrette
The Flower Girl

The Crowd, Citizens, Marquis, Musketeers, Thieves, Pastrycooks, Poets, Cadets of Gascoyne, Actors, Violins, Pages, Children, Spanish Soldiers, Spectators, Intellectuals, Academicians, Nuns, etc.

SCENE: *The first four acts in 1640; the fifth in 1655.*

Act 1: A Performance at the Hôtel de Bourgogne
Act 2: The Bakery of the Poets
Act 3: Roxane's Kiss
Act 4: The Cadets of Gascoyne
Act 5: Cyrano's Gazette

Act 1

A Performance at the Hôtel de Bourgogne

The Hall of the Hôtel de Bourgogne in 1640. A sort of tennis court, arranged and decorated for theatrical productions.

The hall is a long rectangle; we see it diagonally, in such a way that one side of it forms the back scene, which begins at the first entrance on the right and runs up to the last entrance on the left, where it makes a right angle with the stage which is seen obliquely.

This stage is provided on either hand with benches placed along the wings. The curtain is formed by two lengths of tapestry which can be drawn apart. Above a Harlequin cloak, the royal arms. Broad steps lead from the stage down to the floor of the hall. On either side of these steps, a place for the musicians. A row of candles serving as footlights. Two tiers of galleries along the side of the hall; the upper one divided into boxes.

There are no seats upon the floor, which is the actual stage of our theater; but toward the back of the hall, on the right, a few benches are arranged; and underneath a stairway on the extreme right, which leads up to the galleries, and of which only the lower portion is visible, there is a sort of sideboard, decorated with little tapers, vases of flowers, bottles and glasses, plates of cake, et cetera.

Farther along, toward the center of our stage is the entrance to the hall; a great double door which opens slightly to admit the audience. On one of the panels of this door, as also in other places about the hall, and in particular just over the sideboard, are playbills in red, upon which we may read the title LA CLORISE.

As the curtain rises, the hall is dimly lighted and still empty. The chandeliers are lowered to the floor, in the middle of the hall, ready for lighting.

Sound of voices outside the door. Then a CAVALIER *enters abruptly.*
THE PORTER. [*Follows him.*] Halloa there!—Fifteen sols!
THE CAVALIER. I enter free.
THE PORTER. Why?
THE CAVALIER. Soldier of the Household of the King!
THE PORTER. [*Turns to another* CAVALIER *who has just entered.*] You?
SECOND CAVALIER. I pay nothing.
THE PORTER. Why not?
SECOND CAVALIER. Musketeer!
FIRST CAVALIER. [*To the* SECOND.] The play begins at two. Plenty of time— And here's the whole floor empty. Shall we try
Our exercise? [*They fence with the foils which they have brought.*]
A LACKEY. [*Enters.*] —Pst! . . . Flanquin! . . .
ANOTHER. [*Already on stage.*] What, Champagne?
FIRST LACKEY. [*Showing games which he takes out of his doublet.*] Cards. Dice. Come on. [*Sits on the floor.*]
SECOND LACKEY. [*Same action.*] Come on, old cock!
FIRST LACKEY. [*Takes from his pocket a bit of candle, lights it, sets it on the floor.*] I have stolen
A little of my master's fire.
A GUARDSMAN: [*To a* FLOWER GIRL *who comes forward.*] How sweet
Of you, to come before they light the hall! [*Puts his arm around her.*]
FIRST CAVALIER. [*Receives a thrust of the foil.*] A hit!
SECOND LACKEY. A club!
THE GUARDSMAN: [*Pursuing the girl.*] A kiss!
THE FLOWER GIRL. [*Pushing away from him.*] They'll see us!—
THE GUARDSMAN: [*Draws her into a dark corner.*] No danger!
A MAN. [*Sits on the floor, together with several others who have brought packages of food.*] When we come early, we have time to eat.
A CITIZEN. [*Escorting* HIS SON, *a boy of sixteen.*] Sit here, my son.
FIRST LACKEY. Mark the Ace!
ANOTHER MAN. [*Draws a bottle from under his cloak and sits down with the others.*] Here's the spot
For a jolly old sot to suck his Burgundy—[*Drinks.*]
Here—in the house of the Burgundians!
THE CITIZEN. [*To* HIS SON.] Would you not think you were in some den of

vice? [*Points with his cane at the* DRUNK-ARD.]
Drunkards—[*In stepping back, one of the* CAVALIERS *trips him up.*] Bullies!—[*He falls between the lackeys.*] Gamblers!—
THE GUARDSMAN: [*Behind him as he rises, still struggling with the* FLOWER GIRL.] One kiss—
THE CITIZEN. Good God!—[*Draws* HIS SON *quickly away.*]
Here!—And to think, my son, that in this hall
They play Rotrou!²
THE BOY. Yes father—and Corneille!
THE PAGES. [*Dance in, holding hands and singing.*] Tra-la-la-la-la-la-la-la-la-lère . . .
THE PORTER. You pages there—no nonsense!
FIRST PAGE. [*With wounded dignity.*] Oh, monsieur!
Really! How could you? [*To the* SECOND, *the moment the* PORTER *turns his back.*] Pst!—a bit of string?
SECOND PAGE. [*Shows fishline with hook.*] Yes—and a hook.
FIRST PAGE. Up in the gallery,
And fish for wigs?
A CUT-PURSE. [*Gathers around him several evil-looking young fellows.*] Now then, you picaroons,
Perk up, and hear me mutter. Here's your bout—
Bustle around some cull, and bite his bung . . .
SECOND PAGE. [*Calls to other pages already in the gallery.*] Hey! Brought your pea-shooters?
THIRD PAGE. [*From above.*] And our peas, too! [*Blows, and showers them with peas.*]
THE BOY. What is the play this afternoon?
THE CITIZEN. "Clorise."
THE BOY. Who wrote that?
THE CITIZEN. Balthasar Baro. What a play! . . . [*He takes the* BOY's *arm and leads him upstage.*]
THE CUT-PURSE. [*To his pupils.*] Lace now, on those long sleeves, you cut it off—[*Gesture with thumb and finger, as if using scissors.*]
A SPECTATOR. [*To another, pointing upward toward the gallery.*] Ah, *Le Cid!*—Yes, the first night, I sat there—
THE CUT-PURSE. Watches—[*Gesture as of picking a pocket.*]
THE CITIZEN. [*Coming down with* HIS SON.] Great actors we shall see today—
THE CUT-PURSE. Handkerchiefs—[*Gesture of holding the pocket with left hand, and drawing out handkerchief with right.*]
THE CITIZEN. Montfleury—
A VOICE. [*In the gallery.*] Lights! Light the lights!
THE CITIZEN. Bellerose, l'Epy, Beaupré, Jodelet—
A PAGE. [*On the floor.*] Here comes the orange girl.
THE ORANGE GIRL. Oranges, milk, Raspberry syrup, lemonade—[*Noise at the door.*]
A FALSETTO VOICE. [*Outside.*] Make way, Brutes!
FIRST LACKEY. What, the Marquis—on the floor? [*The* MARQUIS *enter in a little group.*]
SECOND LACKEY. Not long—
Only a few moments; they'll go and sit On the stage presently.
FIRST MARQUIS. [*Seeing the hall half empty.*] How now! We enter
Like tradespeople—no crowding, no disturbance!—
No treading on the toes of citizens?
Oh fie! Oh fie! [*He encounters two gentlemen who have already arrived.*]
Cuigy! Brissaille! [*Great embracings.*]
CUIGY. The faithful! [*Looks around him.*]
We are here before the candles.
FIRST MARQUIS. Ah, be still!
You put me in a temper.
SECOND MARQUIS. Console yourself, Marquis—The lamplighter!
THE CROWD. [*Applauding the appearance of the lamplighter.*] Ah! . . . [*A group gathers around the chandelier while he lights it. A few people have already taken their place in the gallery.* LIGNIÉRE *enters the hall, arm in arm with* CHRISTIAN DE NEUVILLETTE. LIGNIÉRE *is a slightly disheveled figure, dissipated and yet distinguished looking.* CHRISTIAN, *elegantly but rather unfashionably dressed, appears preoccupied and keeps looking up at the boxes.*]
CUIGY. Lignière!—
BRISSAILLE. [*Laughing.*] Still sober—at this hour?
LIGNIÈRE. [*To* CHRISTIAN.] May I present

you? [CHRISTIAN *assents.*]
Baron Christian de Neuvillette. [*They salute.*]
THE CROWD. [*Applauding as the lighted chandelier is hoisted into place.*]
CUIGY. [*Aside to* BRISSAILLE, *looking at* CHRISTIAN]. Rather
A fine head, is it not? The profile . . .
FIRST MARQUIS. [*Who has overheard.*] Peuh!
LIGNIÈRE. [*Presenting them to* CHRISTIAN.] Messieurs de Cuigy . . . de Brissaille . . .
CHRISTIAN. [*Bows.*] Enchanted!
FIRST MARQUIS. [*To the* SECOND.] He is not ill-looking; possibly a shade
Behind the fashion.
LIGNIÈRE. [*To* CUIGY.] Monsieur is recently
From the Touraine.
CHRISTIAN. Yes, I have been in Paris
Two or three weeks only. I join the Guards
Tomorrow.
FIRST MARQUIS. [*Watching the people who come into the boxes.*] Look—Madame la Présidente
Aubry!
THE ORANGE GIRL. Oranges, milk—
CUIGY. [*To* CHRISTIAN, *calling his attention to the increasing crowd.*] We have
An audience today!
CHRISTIAN. A brilliant one.
FIRST MARQUIS. Oh yes, all our own people—the gay world! [*They name the ladies who enter the boxes elaborately dressed. Bows and smiles are exchanged.*]
SECOND MARQUIS. Madame de Guéméné . . .
CUIGY. De Bois-Dauphin . . .
FIRST MARQUIS. Whom we adore—
BRISSAILLE. Madame de Chavigny . . .
SECOND MARQUIS. Who plays with all our hearts—
LIGNIÈRE. Why, there's Corneille
Returned from Rouen!
THE BOY. [*To* HIS FATHER.] Are the Academy
All here?
THE CITIZEN. I see some of them . . . there's Boudu—
Boissat—Cureau—Porchères—Colomby—
Bourzeys—Bourdon—Arbaut—Ah, those great names,
Never to be forgotten!

FIRST MARQUIS. Look—at last!
Our Intellectuals! Barthénoide,
Urimédonte, Félixérie . . .
SECOND MARQUIS. [*Languishing.*] Sweet heaven!
How exquisite their surnames are! Marquis,
You know them all?
FIRST MARQUIS. I know them all, Marquis!
LIGNIÈRE. [*Draws* CHRISTIAN *aside.*] My dear boy, I came here to serve you— Well,
But where's the lady? I'll be going.
CHRISTIAN. Not yet—
A little longer! She is always here.
Please! I must find some way of meeting her.
I am dying of love! And you—you know
Everyone, the whole court and the whole town,
And put them all into your songs—at least
You can tell me her name!
THE FIRST VIOLIN. [*Raps on his desk with his bow.*] Pst—Gentlemen! [*Raises his bow.*]
THE ORANGE GIRL. Macaroons, lemonade—
CHRISTIAN. Then she may be
One of those aesthetes . . . Intellectuals,
You call them—How can I talk to a woman
In that style? I have no wit. This fine manner
Of speaking and of writing nowadays—
Not for me! I am a soldier—and afraid.
That's her box, on the right—the empty one.
LIGNIÈRE. [*Starts for the door.*] I am going.
CHRISTIAN. [*Restrains him.*] No—wait!
LIGNIÈRE. Not I. There's a tavern
Not far away—and I am dying of thirst.
THE ORANGE GIRL. [*Passes with her tray.*] Orange juice?
LIGNIÈRE. No!
THE ORANGE GIRL. Milk?
LIGNIÈRE. Pouah!
THE ORANGE GIRL. Muscatel?
LIGNIÈRE. Here! Stop! [*To* CHRISTIAN.] I'll stay a little. [*To the* GIRL] Let me see
Your Muscatel. [*He sits down by the sideboard.* THE GIRL *pours out wine for him.*]

VOICES. [*In the crowd about the door, upon the entrance of a spruce little man, rather fat, with a beaming smile.*] Ragueneau!
LIGNIÈRE. [*To* CHRISTIAN.] Ragueneau, Poet and pastrycook—a character!
RAGUENEAU. [*Dressed like a confectioner in his Sunday clothes, advances quickly to* LIGNIÈRE.] Sir, have you seen Monsieur de Cyrano?
LIGNIÈRE. [*Presents him to* CHRISTIAN.] Permit me . . . Ragueneau, confectioner,
The chief support of modern poetry.
RAGUENEAU. [*Bridling.*] Oh—too much honor!
LIGNIÈRE. Patron of the Arts—
Mæcenas! Yes, you are—
RAGUENEAU. Undoubtedly,
The poets gather around my hearth.
LIGNIÈRE. On credit—
Himself a poet—
RAGUENEAU. So they say—
LIGNIÈRE. Maintains
The Muses.
RAGUENEAU. It is true that for an ode—
LIGNIÈRE. You give a tart—
RAGUENEAU. A tartlet—
LIGNIÈRE. Modesty!
And for a triolet you give—
RAGUENEAU. Plain bread.
LIGNIÈRE. [*Severely.*] Bread and milk!
And you love the theater?
RAGUENEAU. I adore it!
LIGNIÈRE. Well, pastry pays for all.
Your place today now—Come, between ourselves,
What did it cost you?
RAGUENEAU. Four pies; fourteen cakes. [*Looking about.*]
But—Cyrano not here? Astonishing!
LIGNIÈRE. Why so?
RAGUENEAU. Why—Montfleury plays!
LIGNIÈRE. Yes, I hear
That hippopotamus assumes the rôle
Of Phédon. What is that to Cyrano?
RAGUENEAU. Have you not heard? Monsieur de Bergerac
So hates Montfleury, he has forbidden him
For three weeks to appear upon the stage.
LIGNIÈRE. [*Who is, by this time, at his fourth glass.*] Well?
RAGUENEAU. Montfleury plays!—
CUIGY. [*Strolls over to them.*] Yes—what then?
RAGUENEAU. Ah! That
Is what I came to see.
FIRST MARQUIS. This Cyrano—
Who is he?
CUIGY. Oh, he is the lad with the long sword.
SECOND MARQUIS. Noble?
CUIGY. Sufficiently; he is in the Guards. [*Points to a gentleman who comes and goes about the hall as though seeking for someone.*]
His friend Le Bret can tell you more. [*Calls to him.*] Le Bret! [LE BRET *comes down to them.*]
Looking for Bergerac?
LE BRET. Yes. And for trouble.
CUIGY. Is he not an extraordinary man?
LE BRET. The best friend and the bravest soul alive!
RAGUENEAU. Poet—
CUIGY. Swordsman—
LE BRET. Musician—
BRISSAILLE. Philosopher—
LIGNIÈRE. Such a remarkable appearance, too!
BRISSAILLE. Truly, I should not look to find his portrait
By the grave hand of Philippe de Champagne.
He might have been a model for Callot—
One of those wild swashbucklers in a masque—
Hat with three plumes, and doublet with six points—
His cloak behind him over his long sword
Cocked, like the tail of strutting Chanticleer—
Prouder than all the swaggering Tamburlaines
Hatched out of Gascony. And to complete
This Punchinello figure—such a nose!—
My lords, there is no such nose as that nose—
You cannot look upon it without crying: "Oh, no,
Impossible! Exaggerated!" Then
You smile, and say: "Of course—I might have known;
Presently he will take it off." But that
Monsieur de Bergerac will never do.
LIGNIÈRE. [*Grimly.*] He keeps it—and God help the man who smiles!

RAGUENEAU. His sword is one half of
the shears of Fate!
FIRST MARQUIS. [*Shrugs.*] He will not
come.
RAGUENEAU. Will he not? Sir, I'll lay you
A pullet à la Ragueneau!
FIRST MARQUIS. [*Laughing.*] Done! [*Murmurs of admiration;* ROXANE *has just appeared in her box. She sits at the front of the box, and her* DUENNA *takes a seat toward the rear.* CHRISTIAN, *busy paying the Orange Girl, does not see her at first.*]
SECOND MARQUIS. [*With little excited cries.*] Ah!
Oh! Oh! Sweet sirs, look yonder! Is she not
Frightfully ravishing?
FIRST MARQUIS. Bloom of the peach—
Blush of the strawberry—
SECOND MARQUIS. So fresh—so cool,
That our hearts, grown all warm with loving her,
May catch their death of cold!
CHRISTIAN. [*Looks up, sees* ROXANE, *and seizes* LIGNIÈRE *by the arm.*] There!
Quick—up there—
In the box! Look!—
LIGNIÈRE. [*Coolly.*] Herself?
CHRISTIAN. Quickly—Her name?
LIGNIÈRE. [*Sipping his wine, and speaking between sips.*] Madeleine Robin, called
Roxane . . . refined . . .
Intellectual . . .
CHRISTIAN. Ah!—
LIGNIÈRE. Unmarried . . .
CHRISTIAN. Oh!—
LIGNIÈRE. No title . . . rich enough . . .
an orphan . . . cousin
To Cyrano . . . of whom we spoke just now . . . [*At this point, a very distinguished looking gentleman, the Cordon Bleu around his neck, enters the box, and stands a moment talking with* ROXANE.]
CHRISTIAN. [*Starts.*] And the man? . . .
LIGNIÈRE. [*Beginning to feel his wine a little; cocks his eye at them.*] Oho! That
man . . . Comte de Guiche . . .
In love with her . . . married himself, however,
To the niece of the Cardinal—
Richelieu . . .
Wishes Roxane, therefore, to marry one
Monsieur de Valvert . . . Vicomte . . .
friend of his . . .
A somewhat melancholy gentleman . . .
But . . . well, accommodating! . . . She says No . . .
Nevertheless, de Guiche is powerful . . .
Not above persecuting . . . [*He rises, swaying a little, and very happy.*] I have written
A little song about his little game . . .
Good little song, too . . . Here, I'll sing it for you . . .
Make de Guiche furious . . . naughty little song . . .
Not so bad, either—Listen! . . . [*He stands with his glass held aloft, ready to sing.*]
CHRISTIAN. No. Adieu.
LIGNIÈRE. Whither away?
CHRISTIAN. To Monsieur de Valvert!
LIGNIÈRE. Careful! The man's a swordsman . . . [*Nods toward* ROXANE, *who is watching* CHRISTIAN.] Wait! Someone
Looking at you—
CHRISTIAN. Roxane! . . . [*He forgets everything, and stands spellbound, gazing toward* ROXANE. *The* CUT-PURSE *and his crew, observing him transfixed, his eyes raised and his mouth half open, begin edging in his direction.*]
LIGNIÈRE. Oh! Very well,
Then I'll be leaving you . . . Good
day . . . Good day! . . . [CHRISTIAN *remains motionless.*]
Everywhere else, they like to hear me sing!—
Also, I am thirsty. [*He goes out, navigating carefully.* LE BRET, *having made the circuit of the hall, returns to* RAGUENEAU, *somewhat reassured.*]
LE BRET. No sign anywhere
Of Cyrano!
RAGUENEAU. [*Incredulous.*] Wait and see!
LE BRET. Humph! I hope
He has not seen the bill.
THE CROWD. The play!—The play!—
FIRST MARQUIS. [*Observing* DE GUICHE, *as he descends from* ROXANE'*s box and crosses the floor, followed by a knot of obsequious gentlemen, the* VICOMTE DE VALVERT *among them.*] This man de Guiche—what ostentation!
SECOND MARQUIS. Bah!—
Another Gascon!
FIRST MARQUIS. Gascon, yes—but cold
And calculating—certain to succeed—
My word for it. Come, shall we make our bow?

We shall be none the worse, I promise you . . . [*They go toward* DE GUICHE.]
SECOND MARQUIS. Beautiful ribbons, Count! That color, now,
What is it—"Kiss-me-Dear" or "Startled-Fawn"?
DE GUICHE. I call that shade "The Dying Spaniard."
FIRST MARQUIS. Ha!
And no false colors either—thanks to you
And your brave troops, in Flanders before long
The Spaniard will die daily.
DE GUICHE. Shall we go
And sit upon the stage? Come, Valvert.
CHRISTIAN. [*Starts at the name.*] Valvert!—
The Vicomte—Ah, that scoundrel! Quick—my glove!
I'll throw it in his face— [*Reaching into his pocket for his glove, he catches the hand of the* CUT-PURSE.]
THE CUT-PURSE. Oh!—
CHRISTIAN. [*Holding fast to the man's wrist.*] Who are you?
I was looking for a glove—
THE CUT-PURSE. [*Cringing.*] You found a hand. [*Hurriedly.*]
Let me go— I can tell you something—
CHRISTIAN. [*Still holding him.*] Well?
THE CUT-PURSE. Lignière—that friend of yours—
CHRISTIAN. [*Same business.*] Well?
THE CUT-PURSE. Good as dead—
Understand? Ambuscaded. Wrote a song
About—no matter. There's a hundred men
Waiting for him tonight—I'm one of them.
CHRISTIAN. A hundred? Who arranged this?
THE CUT-PURSE. Secret.
CHRISTIAN. Oh!
THE CUT-PURSE. [*With dignity.*] Professional secret.
CHRISTIAN. Where are they to be?
THE CUT-PURSE. Porte de Nesle. On his way home. Tell him so.
Save his life.
CHRISTIAN. [*Releases the man.*] Yes, but where am I to find him?
THE CUT-PURSE. Go round the taverns.
There's the Golden Grape,
The Pineapple, The Bursting Belt, The Two
Torches, the Three Funnels—in every one
You leave a line of writing—understand?
To warn him.
CHRISTIAN. [*Starts for the door.*] I'll go!
God, what swine—a hundred
Against one man! . . . [*Stops and looks longingly at* ROXANE.] Leave *her* here!— [*Decidedly.*]
I must save Lignière! [*Exit.*] [DE GUICHE, VALVERT, *and all the* MARQUIS *have disappeared through the curtains, to take their seats upon the stage. The floor is entirely filled; not a vacant seat remains in the gallery or in the boxes.*]
THE CROWD. The play! The play! Begin the play!
A CITIZEN. [*As his wig is hoisted into the air on the end of a fishline, in the hands of a page in the gallery.*] My wig!!
CRIES OF JOY: He's bald! Bravo, You pages! Ha ha ha!
THE CITIZEN. [*Furious, shakes his fist at the boy.*] Here, you young villain!
CRIES OF LAUGHTER. [*Beginning very loud, then suddenly repressed.*]
HA HA! Ha Ha! ha ha . . . [*Complete silence.*]
LE BRET. [*Surprised.*] That sudden hush? . . . [*A* SPECTATOR *whispers in his ear.*]
Yes?
THE SPECTATOR. I was told on good authority . . .
MURMURS. [*Here and there.*] What? . . . Here? . . . No . . . Yes . . . Look—in the latticed box—
The Cardinal! . . . The Cardinal! . . .
A PAGE. The Devil!—
Now we shall all have to behave ourselves! [*Three raps on the stage. The audience becomes motionless. Silence.*]
THE VOICE OF A MARQUIS. [*From the stage, behind the curtains.*] Snuff that candle!
ANOTHER MARQUIS. [*Puts his head out through the curtains.*] A chair! . . . [*A chair is passed from hand to hand over the heads of the crowd. He takes it, and disappears behind the curtains, not without having blown a few kisses to the occupants of the boxes.*]
A SPECTATOR. Silence!
VOICES. Hssh! . . . Hssh! . . . [*Again the three raps on the stage. The curtains part.*

Tableau. The MARQUIS *seated on their chairs to right and left of the stage, insolently posed. Backdrop representing a pastoral scene, bluish in tone. Four little crystal chandeliers light up the stage. The violins play softly.*]

LE BRET. [*In a low tone, to* RAGUENEAU.] Montfleury enters now?

RAGUENEAU. [*Nods.*] Opens the play.

LE BRET. [*Much relieved.*] Then Cyrano is not here!

RAGUENEAU. I lose . . .

LE BRET. Humph!—

So much the better! [*The melody of a musette is heard.* MONTFLEURY *appears upon the scene, a ponderous figure in the costume of a rustic shepherd, a hat garlanded with roses tilted over one ear, playing upon a beribboned pastoral pipe.*]

THE CROWD. [*Applauds.*] Montfleury! . . . Bravo! . . .

MONTFLEURY. [*After bowing to the applause, begins the rôle of Phédon.*] "Thrice happy he who hides from pomp and power
In sylvan shade or solitary bower;
Where balmy zephyrs fan his burning cheeks—"

A VOICE. [*From the midst of the hall.*] Wretch. Have I not forbade you these three weeks? [*Sensation. Everyone turns to look. Murmurs.*]

SEVERAL VOICES. What? . . . Where? . . . Who is it? . . .

CUIGY. Cyrano!

LE BRET. [*In alarm.*] Himself!

THE VOICE. King of clowns! Leave the stage—*at once!*

THE CROWD. Oh!—

MONTFLEURY. Now, Now, now—

THE VOICE. You disobey me?

SEVERAL VOICES. [*From the floor, from the boxes.*] Hsh! Go on—

Quiet!—Go on, Montfleury!—Who's afraid?—

MONTFLEURY. [*In a voice of no great assurance.*] "Thrice happy he who hides from . . ."

THE VOICE. [*More menacingly.*] Well? Well? Well? . . .

Monarch of mountebanks! Must I come and plant
A forest on your shoulders? [*A cane at the end of a long arm shakes above the heads of the crowd.*]

MONTFLEURY. [*In a voice increasingly feeble.*] "Thrice hap—" [*The cane is violently agitated.*]

THE VOICE. *GO!!!*

THE CROWD. Ah . . .

CYRANO. [*Arises in the center of the floor, erect upon a chair, his arms folded, his hat cocked ferociously, his moustache bristling, his nose terrible.*] Presently I shall grow angry! [*Sensation at his appearance.*]

MONTFLEURY. [*To the* MARQUIS.] Messieurs,
If you protect me—

A MARQUIS. [*Nonchantly.*] Well—proceed!

CYRANO. Fat swine!
If you dare breathe one balmy zephyr more,
I'll fan your cheeks for you!

THE MARQUIS. Quiet down there!

CYRANO. Unless these gentlemen retain their seats,
My cane may bite their ribbons!

ALL THE MARQUIS. [*On their feet.*] That will do!—
Montfleury—

CYRANO. Fly, goose! Shoo! Take to your wings,
Before I pluck your plumes, and draw your gorge!

A VOICE. See here—

CYRANO. Off stage!!

ANOTHER VOICE. One moment—

CYRANO. What—still there? [*Turns back his cuffs deliberately.*]
Very good—then I enter—Left—with knife—
To carve this large Italian sausage.

MONTFLEURY. [*Desperately attempting dignity.*] Sir,
When you insult me, you insult the Muse!

CYRANO. [*With great politeness.*]
Sir, if the Muse, who never knew your name,
Had the honor to meet you—then be sure
That after one glance at that face of yours,
That figure of a mortuary urn—
She would apply her buskin—toward the rear!

THE CROWD. Montfleury! . . . Montfleury! . . . The play! The Play!

CYRANO. [*To those who are shouting and

crowding about him.] Pray you, be gentle with my scabbard here—
She'll put her tongue out at you presently!— [*The circle enlarges.*]
THE CROWD. [*Recoiling.*] Keep back—
CYRANO. [*To* MONTFLEURY.] Begone!
THE CROWD. [*Pushing in closer, and growling.*] Ahr! . . . ahr! . . .
CYRANO. [*Turns upon them.*] Did someone speak? [*They recoil again.*]
A VOICE. [*In the back of the hall, sings.*]
 Monsieur de Cyrano.
  Must be another Caesar—
 Let Brutus lay him low,
  And play us "La Clorise"!
ALL IN THE CROWD. [*Singing.*]
 "La Clorise!" "La Clorise!"
CYRANO. Let me hear one more word of that same song,
And I destroy you all!
A CITIZEN. Who might you be? Samson?—
CYRANO. Precisely. Would you kindly lend me
Your jawbone?
A LADY. [*In one of the boxes.*] What an outrage!
A NOBLE. Scandalous!
A CITIZEN. Annoying!
A PAGE. What a game!
THE CROWD. Kss! Monfleury! Cyrano!
CYRANO. Silence!
THE CROWD. [*Delirious.*] Woof! Woof! Baaa! Cockadoo!
CYRANO. I—
A PAGE. Meow!
CYRANO. I say be silent!— [*His voice dominates the uproar. Momentary hush.*]
And I offer
One universal challenge to you all!
Approach, young heroes—I will take your names.
Each in his turn—no crowding! One, two, three—
Come, get your numbers—who will head the list—
You sir? No— You? Ah, no. To the first man
Who falls I'll build a monument! . . . Not one?
Will all who wish to die, please raise their hands? . . .
I see. You are so modest, you might blush
Before a sword naked. Sweet innocence! . . .
Not one name? Not one finger? . . . Very well,
Then I go on: [*Turning back toward the stage, where* MONTFLEURY *waits in despair.*] I'd have our theater cured
Of this carbuncle. Or if not, why then— [*His hand on his sword hilt.*]
The lancet!
MONTFLEURY. I—
CYRANO. [*Descends from his chair, seats himself comfortably in the center of the circle which has formed around him, and makes himself quite at home.*] Attend to me—full moon!
I clap my hands, three times—thus. At the third
You will eclipse yourself.
THE CROWD. [*Amused.*] Ah!
CYRANO. Ready? One!
MONTFLEURY. I—
A VOICE. [*From the boxes.*] No!
THE CROWD. He'll go— He'll stay—
MONTFLEURY. I really think, Gentlemen—
CYRANO. Two!
MONTFLEURY. Perhaps I had better—
CYRANO. Three! [MONTFLEURY *disappears, as if through a trapdoor. Tempest of laughter, hoots and hisses.*]
THE CROWD. Yah!—Coward— Come back—
CYRANO. [*Beaming, drops back in his chair and crosses his legs.*] Let him—if he dare!
A CITIZEN. The Manager! Speech! Speech! [BELLEROSE *advances and bows.*]
BELLEROSE. [*With elegance.*] Most noble—most fair—
THE CROWD. No! The comedian— Jodelet!—
JODELET. [*Advances, and speaks through his nose.*] Lewd fellows of the baser sort—
THE CROWD. Ha! Ha! Not bad! Bravo!
JODELET. No Bravos here!
Our heavy tragedian with the voluptuous bust
Was taken suddenly—
THE CROWD. Yah! Coward!
JODELET. I mean
He had to be excused—
THE CROWD. Call him back— No!— Yes!—
THE BOY. [*To* CYRANO.] After all, Mon-

sieur, what reason have you
To hate this Montfleury?
CYRANO. [*Graciously, still seated.*] My dear young man,
I have two reasons, either one alone
Conclusive. *Primo:* A lamentable actor,
Who mouths his verse and moans his tragedy,
And heaves up— Ugh!—like a hod-carrier, lines
That ought to soar on their own wings. *Secundo:*—
Well—that's my secret.
THE OLD CITIZEN. [*Behind him.*] But you close the play—
"La Clorise"—by Baro! Are we to miss
Our entertainment, merely—
CYRANO. [*Respectfully, turns his chair toward the old man.*] My dear old boy,
The poetry of Baro being worth
Zero, or less, I feel that I have done
Poetic justice!
THE INTELLECTUALS. Really!—our Baro!—
My dear!—Who ever?—Ah, dieu! The idea!—
CYRANO. [*Gallantly, turns his chair toward the boxes.*] Fair ladies—shine upon us like the sun,
Blossom like the flowers around us—be our songs,
Heard in a dream— Make sweet the hour of death,
Smiling upon us as you close our eyes—
Inspire, but do not try to criticize!
BELLEROSE. Quite so!—and the mere money—possibly
You would like that returned— Yes?
CYRANO. Bellerose,
You speak the first word of intelligence!
I will not wound the mantle of the Muse—
Here, catch— [*Throws him a purse.*] And hold your tongue.
THE CROWD. [*Astonished.*] Ah! Ah!
JODELET. [*Deftly catches the purse, weighs it in his hand.*] Monsieur,
You are hereby authorized to close our play
Every night, on the same terms.
THE CROWD. Boo!
JODELET. And welcome!
Let us be booed together, you and I!
BELLEROSE. Kindly pass out quietly . . .
JODELET. [*Burlesquing* BELLEROSE.]
Quietly . . . [*They begin to go out, while*

CYRANO *looks about him with satisfaction. But the exodus ceases presently during the ensuing scene. The ladies in the boxes who have already risen and put on their wraps, stop to listen, and finally sit down again.*]
LE BRET. [*To* CYRANO.] Idiot!
A MEDDLER. [*Hurries up to* CYRANO.] But what a scandal! Montfleury—
The great Montfleury! Did you know the Duc
De Candale was his patron? Who is yours?
CYRANO. No one.
THE MEDDLER. No one—no patron?
CYRANO. I said no.
THE MEDDLER. What, no great lord, to cover with his name—
CYRANO. [*With visible annoyance.*] No, I have told you twice. Must I repeat?
No sir, no patron— [*His hand on his sword.*] But a patroness!
THE MEDDLER. And when do you leave Paris?
CYRANO. That's as may be.
THE MEDDLER. The Duc de Candale has a long arm.
CYRANO. Mine
Is longer, [*Drawing his sword.*] by three feet of steel.
THE MEDDLER. Yes, yes,
But do you dream of daring—
CYRANO. I do dream
Of daring . . .
THE MEDDLER. But—
CYRANO. You may go now.
THE MEDDLER. But—
CYRANO. You may go—
Or tell me why you are staring at my nose!
THE MEDDLER. [*In confusion.*] No—I—
CYRANO. [*Stepping up to him.*] Does it astonish you?
THE MEDDLER. [*Drawing back.*] Your grace
Misunderstands my—
CYRANO. Is it long and soft
And dangling, like a trunk?
THE MEDDLER. [*Same business.*] I never said—
CYRANO. Or crooked, like an owl's beak?
THE MEDDLER. I—
CYRANO. Perhaps
A pimple ornaments the end of it?
THE MEDDLER. No—

CYRANO. Or a fly parading up and down?
What is this portent?
THE MEDDLER. Oh!—
CYRANO. This phenomenon?
THE MEDDLER. But I have been careful not to look—
CYRANO. And why
Not, if you please?
THE MEDDLER. Why—
CYRANO. It disgusts you, then?
THE MEDDLER. My dear sir—
CYRANO. Does its color appear to you
Unwholesome?
THE MEDDLER. Oh, by no means!
CYRANO. Or its form
Obscene?
THE MEDDLER. Not in the least—
CYRANO. Then why assume
This deprecating manner? Possibly
You find it just a trifle large?
THE MEDDLER. [*Babbling.*] Oh no!—
Small, very small, infinitesimal—
CYRANO. [*Roars.*] What?
How? You accuse me of absurdity?
Small—*my nose?* Why—
THE MEDDLER. [*Breathless.*] My God!—
CYRANO. Magnificent,
My nose! . . . You pug, you knob, you button-head,
Know that I glory in this nose of mine,
For a great nose indicates a great man—
Genial, courteous, intellectual,
Virile, courageous—as I am—and such
As you—poor wretch—will never dare to be
Even in imagination. For that face—
That blank, inglorious concavity
Which my right hand finds— [*He strikes him.*]
THE MEDDLER. Ow!
CYRANO. —on top of you,
Is as devoid of pride, of poetry,
Of soul, of picturesqueness, of contour,
Of character, of NOSE in short—as that
[*Takes him by the shoulders and turns him around, suiting the action to the word.*]
Which at the end of that limp spine of yours
My left foot—
THE MEDDLER. [*Escaping.*] Help! The Guard!
CYRANO. Take notice, all
Who find this feature of my countenance

A theme for comedy! When the humorist
Is noble, then my custom is to show
Appreciation proper to his rank—
More heartfelt . . . and more pointed . . .
DE GUICHE. [*Who has come down from the stage, surrounded by the* MARQUIS.] Presently
This fellow will grow tiresome.
VALVERT. [*Shrugs.*] Oh, he blows
His trumpet!
DE GUICHE. Well—will no one interfere?
VALVERT. No one? [*Looks around.*] Observe. I myself will proceed
To put him in his place. [*He walks up to* CYRANO, *who has been watching him, and stands there, looking him over with an affected air.*] Ah . . . your nose . . . hem! . . .
Your nose is . . . rather large!
CYRANO. [*Gravely.*] Rather.
VALVERT. [*Simpering.*] Oh well—
CYRANO. [*Coolly.*] Is that all?
VALVERT. [*Turns away with a shrug.*] Well, of course—
CYRANO. Ah, no young sir!
You are too simple. Why, you might have said—
Oh, a great many things! Mon dieu, why waste
Your opportunity? For example, thus:—
AGGRESSIVE: I, sir, if that nose were mine,
I'd have it amputated—on the spot!
FRIENDLY: How do you drink with such a nose?
You ought to have a cup made specially.
DESCRIPTIVE: 'Tis a rock—a crag—a cape—
A cape? say rather, a peninsula!
INQUISITIVE: What is that receptacle—
A razor-case or a portfolio?
KINDLY: Ah, do you love the little birds
So much that when they come and sing to you,
You give them this to perch on? INSOLENT:
Sir, when you smoke, the neighbors must suppose
Your chimney is on fire. CAUTIOUS: Take care—
A weight like that might make you topheavy.
THOUGHTFUL: Somebody fetch my par-

asol—
Those delicate colors fade so in the sun!
PEDANTIC: Does not Aristophanes
Mention a mythologic monster called
Hippocampelephantocamelos?
Surely we have here the original!
FAMILIAR: Well, old torchlight! Hang your hat
Over that chandelier—it hurts my eyes.
ELOQUENT: When it blows, the typhoon howls,
And the clouds darken. DRAMATIC: When it bleeds—
The Red Sea! ENTERPRISING: What a sign
For some perfumer! LYRIC: Hark—the horn
Of Roland calls to summon Charlemagne!—
SIMPLE: When do they unveil the monument?
RESPECTFUL: Sir, I recognize in you
A man of parts, a man of prominence—
RUSTIC: Hey? What? Call that a nose? Na na—
I be no fool like what you think I be—
That there's a blue cucumber! MILITARY:
Point against cavalry! PRACTICAL: Why not
A lottery with this for the grand prize?
Or—parodying Faustus in the play—
"Was this the nose that launched a thousand ships
And burned the topless towers of Ilium?"
These, my dear sir, are things you might have said
Had you some tinge of letters, or of wit
To color your discourse. But wit,—not so,
You never had an atom—and of letters,
You need but three to write you down—an Ass.
Moreover,—if you had the invention, here
Before these folks to make a jest of me—
Be sure you would not then articulate
The twentieth part of half a syllable
Of the beginning! For I say these things
Lightly enough myself, about myself,
But I allow none else to utter them.
DE GUICHE. [*Tries to lead away the amazed* VALVERT.] Vicomte—come.
VALVERT. [*Choking.*] Oh— These arrogant grand airs!—
A clown who—look at him—not even gloves!
No ribbons—no lace—no buckles on his shoes—
CYRANO. I carry my adornments on my soul.
I do not dress up like a popinjay;
But inwardly, I keep my daintiness.
I do not bear with me, by any chance,
An insult not yet washed away—a conscience
Yellow with unpurged bile—an honor frayed
To rags, a set of scruples badly worn.
I go caparisoned in gems unseen,
Trailing white plumes of freedom, garlanded
With my good name—no figure of a man,
But a soul clothed in shining armor, hung
With deeds for decorations, twirling—thus—
A bristling wit, and swinging at my side
Courage, and on the stones of this old town
Making the sharp truth ring, like golden spurs!
VALVERT. But—
CYRANO. But I have no gloves! A pity too!
I had one—the last one of an old pair—
And lost that. Very careless of me. Some
Gentleman offered me an impertinence.
I left it—in his face.
VALVERT. Dolt, bumpkin, fool,
Insolent puppy, jobbernowl!
CYRANO. [*Removes his hat and bows.*] Ah, yes?
And I—Cyrano-Savinien-Hercule
De Bergerac!
VALVERT. [*Turns away.*] Buffoon!
CYRANO. [*Cries out as if suddenly taken with a cramp.*] Oh!
VALVERT. [*Turns back.*] Well, what now?
CYRANO. [*With grimaces of anguish.*] I must do something to relieve these cramps—
This is what comes of lack of exercise—Ah!—

VALVERT. What is all this?
CYRANO. My sword has gone to sleep?
VALVERT. [*Draws.*] So be it!
CYRANO. You shall die exquisitely.
VALVERT. [*Contemptuously.*] Poet!
CYRANO. Why yes, a poet, if you will;
So while we fence, I'll make you a Ballade
Extempore.
VALVERT. A Ballade?
CYRANO. Yes. You know
What that is?
VALVERT. I—
CYRANO. The Ballade, sir, is formed
Of three stanzas of eight lines each—
VALVERT. Oh, come!
CYRANO. And a refrain of four.
VALVERT. You—
CYRANO. I'll compose
One, while I fight with you; and at the end
Of the last line—thrust home!
VALVERT. Will you?
CYRANO. I will. [*Declaims.*]
"Ballade of the duel at the Hôtel de Bourgogne
Between de Bergerac and a Boeotian."[3]
VALVERT. [*Sneering.*] What do you mean by that?
CYRANO. Oh, that? The title.
THE CROWD. [*Excited.*] Come on—A circle—Quiet—Down in front! [*Tableau. A ring of interested spectators in the center of the floor, the* MARQUIS *and the* OFFICERS *mingling with the citizens and common folk. Pages swarming up on men's shoulders to see better; the* LADIES *in the boxes standing and leaning over. To the right,* DE GUICHE *and his following; to the left,* LE BRET, CUIGY, RAGUENEAU, *and others of* CYRANO's *friends.*]
CYRANO. [*Closes his eyes for an instant.*]
Stop . . . Let me choose my rimes. . . . Now!
Here we go— [*He suits the action to the word, throughout the following.*]
Lightly I toss my hat away,
  Languidly over my arm let fall
The cloak that covers my bright array—
  Then out swords, and to work withal!
A Launcelot, in his Lady's hall . . .
A Spartacus, at the Hippodrome! . . .
  I dally awhile with you, dear jackal,
Then, as I end the refrain, thrust home! [*The swords cross—the fight is on.*]
Where shall I skewer my peacock? . . . Nay,
  Better for you to have shunned this brawl!—
Here, in the heart, thro' your ribbons gay?
  —In the belly, under your silken shawl?
Hark, how the steel rings musical!
Mark how my point floats, light as the foam,
  Ready to drive you back to the wall,
Then, as I end the refrain, thrust home!

Ho, for a rime! . . . You are white as whey—
  You break, you cower, you cringe, you . . . crawl!
Tac!—and I parry your last essay:
  So may the turn of a hand forestall
Life with its honey, death with its gall;
So may the turn of my fancy roam
  Free, for a time, till the rimes recall,
Then, as I end the refrain, thrust home! [*He announces solemnly.*]
Refrain:
  Prince! Pray God, that is Lord of all,
Pardon your soul, for your time has come!
  Beat—pass—fling you aslant, asprawl—
Then, as I end the refrain . . . [*He lunges;* VALVERT *staggers back and falls into the arms of his friends.* CYRANO *recovers, and salutes.*] —Thrust home!
[*Shouts. Applause from the boxes. Flowers and handkerchiefs come fluttering down. The* OFFICERS *surround* CYRANO *and congratulate him.* RAGUENEAU *dances for joy.* LE BRET *is unable to conceal his enthusiasm. The friends of* VALVERT *hold him up and help him away.*]
THE CROWD. [*In one long cry.*] Ah-h!
A CAVALIER. Superb!
A WOMAN. Simply sweet!
RAGUENEAU. Magnelephant!
A MARQUIS. A novelty!
LE BRET. Bah!
THE CROWD. [*Thronging around* CYRANO.]
Compliments—regards—
Bravo!—

A WOMAN'S VOICE. Why, he's a hero!
A MUSKETEER. [*Advances quickly to* CYRANO, *with outstretched hands.*] Monsieur, will you
Permit me?—It was altogether fine!
I think I may appreciate these things—
Moreover, I have been stamping for pure joy! [*He retires quickly.*]
CYRANO. [*To* CUIGY.] What was that gentleman's name?
CUIGY. Oh . . . D'Artagnan.[4]
LE BRET. [*Takes* CYRANO'S *arm.*] Come here and tell me—
CYRANO. Let this crowd go first— [*To* BELLEROSE.]
May we stay?
BELLEROSE. [*With great respect.*] Certainly! [*Cries and cat-calls offstage.*]
JODELET. [*Comes down from the door where he has been looking out.*] Hark!— Montfleury—
They are hooting him.
BELLEROSE. [*Solemnly.*] "Sic transit gloria!" [*Changes his tone and shouts to the* PORTER *and the* LAMPLIGHTER.]
—Strike! . . . Close the house! . . . Leave the lights—We rehearse
The new farce after dinner. [JODELET *and* BELLEROSE *go out after elaborately saluting* CYRANO.]
THE PORTER. [*To* CYRANO.] You do not dine?
CYRANO. I?—No! [THE PORTER *turns away.*]
LE BRET. Why not?
CYRANO. [*Haughtily.*] Because— [*Changing his tone when he sees the* PORTER *has gone.*] Because I have
No money.
LE BRET. [*Gesture of tossing.*] But—the purse of gold?
CYRANO. Farewell,
Paternal pension!
LE BRET. So you have, until
The first of next month—?
CYRANO. Nothing.
LE BRET. What a fool!—
CYRANO. But—what a gesture!
THE ORANGE GIRL. [*Behind her little counter; coughs.*] Hem! [CYRANO *and* LE BRET *look around; she advances timidly.*] Pardon, monsieur . . .
A man ought never to go hungry . . . [*Indicating the sideboard.*] See,
I have everything here . . . [*Eagerly.*] Please!—
CYRANO. [*Uncovers.*] My dear child,
I cannot bend this Gascon pride of mine
To accept such a kindness— Yet, for fear
That I may give you pain if I refuse,
I will take . . . [*He goes to the sideboard and makes his selection.*] Oh, not very much! A grape . . . [*She gives him the bunch; he removes a single grape.*]
One only! And a glass of water . . . [*She starts to pour wine into it; he stops her.*] Clear!
And . . . half a macaroon! [*He gravely returns the other half.*]
LE BRET. Old idiot!
THE ORANGE GIRL. Please!— Nothing more?
CYRANO. Why yes— Your hand to kiss. [*He kisses the hand which she holds out, as he would the hand of a princess.*]
THE ORANGE GIRL. Thank you, sir. [*She curtsys.*] Good-night. [*She goes out.*]
CYRANO. Now, I am listening. [*Plants himself before the sideboard and arranges thereon—*]
Dinner!— [—*The macaroon.*] Drink!— [—*The glass of water.*] Dessert!— [—*The grape.*] There—now I'll sit down. [*Seats himself.*]
Lord, I was hungry! Abominably! [*Eating.*] Well?
LE BRET. These fatheads with the bellicose grand airs
Will have you ruined if you listen to them;
Talk to a man of sense and hear how all
Your swagger impresses him.
CYRANO. [*Finishes his macaroon.*] Enormously.
LE BRET. The Cardinal—
CYRANO. [*Beaming.*] Was he there?
LE BRET. He must have thought you—
CYRANO. Original.
LE BRET. Well, but—
CYRANO. He is himself
A playwright. He will not be too displeased
That I have closed another author's play.
LE BRET. But look at all the enemies you have made!
CYRANO. [*Begins on the grape.*] How many—do you think?
LE BRET. Just forty-eight
Without the women.

CYRANO. Count them.
LE BRET. Montfleury,
Baro, de Guiche, the Vicomte, the Old Man,
All the Academy—
CYRANO. Enough! You make me Happy!
LE BRET. But where is all this leading you?
What is your plan?
CYRANO. I have been wandering—
Wasting my force upon too many plans.
Now I have chosen one.
LE BRET. What one?
CYRANO. The simplest—
To make myself in all things admirable!
LE BRET. Hmph!— Well, then, the real reason why you hate
Montfleury—Come, the truth, now!
CYRANO. [*Rises.*] That Silenus,[5]
Who cannot hold his belly in his arms,
Still dreams of being sweetly dangerous
Among the women—sighs and languishes,
Making sheeps' eyes out of his great frog's face—
I hate him ever since one day he dared
Smile upon—
   Oh, my friend, I seemed to see
Over some flower a great snail crawling!
LE BRET. [*Amazed.*] How,
What? Is it possible?—
CYRANO. [*With a bitter smile.*] For me to love? . . . [*Changing his tone; seriously.*]
I love.
LE BRET. May I know? You have never said—
CYRANO. Whom I love? Think a moment. Think of me—
Me, whom the plainest woman would despise—
Me, with this nose of mine that marches on
Before me by a quarter of an hour!
Whom should I love? Why—of course—it must be
The woman in the world most beautiful.
LE BRET. Most beautiful?
CYRANO. In all this world—most sweet:
Also most wise; most witty; and most fair!
LE BRET. Who and what is this woman?
CYRANO. Dangerous
Mortally, without meaning; exquisite
Without imagining. Nature's own snare
To allure manhood. A white rose wherein
Love lies in ambush for his natural prey.
Who knows her smile has known a perfect thing.
She creates grace in her own image, brings
Heaven to earth in one movement of her hand—
Nor thou, O Venus! balancing thy shell
Over the Mediterranean blue, nor thou,
Diana! marching through broad, blossoming woods,
Art so divine as when she mounts her chair,
And goes abroad through Paris!
LE BRET. Oh, well—of course,
That makes everything clear!
CYRANO. Transparently.
LE BRET. Madeleine Robin—your cousin?
CYRANO. Yes; Roxane.
LE BRET. And why not? If you love her, tell her so!
You have covered yourself with glory in her eyes
This very day.
CYRANO. My old friend—look at me,
And tell me how much hope remains for me
With this protuberance! Oh I have no more
Illusions! Now and then—bah! I may grow
Tender, walking alone in the blue cool
Of evening, through some garden fresh with flowers
After the benediction of the rain;
My poor big devil of a nose inhales
April . . . and so I follow with my eyes
Where some boy, with a girl upon his arm,
Passes a patch of silver . . . and I feel
Somehow, I wish I had a woman too,
Walking with little steps under the moon,
And holding my arm so, and smiling. Then
I dream—and I forget. . . . And then I see
The shadow of my profile on the wall!
LE BRET. My friend! . . .
CYRANO. My friend, I have my bitter

days,
Knowing myself so ugly, so alone.
Sometimes—
LE BRET. You weep?
CYRANO. [*Quickly.*] Oh, not that ever! No,
That would be too grotesque—tears trickling down
All the long way along this nose of mine?
I will not so profane the dignity
Of sorrow. Never any tears for me!
Why, there is nothing more sublime than tears,
Nothing!—Shall I make them ridiculous
In my poor person?
LE BRET. Love's no more than chance!
CYRANO. [*Shakes his head.*] No. I love Cleopatra; do I appear
Cæsar? I adore Beatrice; have I
The look of Dante?
LE BRET. But your wit—your courage—
Why, that poor child who offered you just now
Your dinner! She—you saw with your own eyes,
Her eyes did not avoid you.
CYRANO. [*Thoughtful.*] That is true . . .
LE BRET. Well then! Roxane herself, watching your duel,
Paler than—
CYRANO. Pale?—
LE BRET. Her lips parted, her hand
Thus, at her breast—I saw it! Speak to her.
Speak, man!
CYRANO. Through my nose? She might laugh at me;
That is the one thing in this world I fear!
THE PORTER. [*Followed by the* DUENNA, *approaches* CYRANO *respectfully.*] A lady asking for Monsieur.
CYRANO. Mon dieu . . . Her Duenna!—
THE DUENNA. [*A sweeping curtsy.*]
Monsieur . . . A message for you:
From our good cousin we desire to know
When and where we may see him privately.
CYRANO. [*Amazed.*] To see me?
THE DUENNA. [*An elaborate reverence.*] To see you. We have certain things
To tell you.
CYRANO. Certain—
THE DUENNA. Things.
CYRANO. [*Trembling.*] Mon dieu! . . .
THE DUENNA. We go
Tomorrow, at the first flush of the dawn,
To hear Mass at St. Roch. Then afterward,
Where can we meet and talk a little?
CYRANO. [*Catching* LE BRET's *arm.*] Where?—
I—Ah, mon dieu! . . . mon dieu! . . .
THE DUENNA. Well?
CYRANO. I am thinking . . .
THE DUENNA. And you think?
CYRANO. I . . . The shop of Ragueneau . .
Ragueneau—pastrycook . . .
THE DUENNA. Who dwells?—
CYRANO. Mon dieu! . . .
Oh, yes . . . Ah, mon dieu! . . . Rue St.-Honoré.
THE DUENNA. We are agreed.
Remember—seven o'clock. [*Reverence.*]
Until then—
CYRANO. I'll be there. [*The* DUENNA *goes out.*]
CYRANO. [*Falls into the arms of* LE BRET.]
Me . . . to see me! . . .
LE BRET. You are not quite so gloomy.
CYRANO. After all,
She knows that I exist—no matter why!
LE BRET. So now, you are going to be happy.
CYRANO. Now! . . . [*Beside himself.*]
I—I am going to be a storm—a flame—
I need to fight whole armies all alone;
I have ten hearts; I have a hundred arms; I feel
Too strong to war with mortals— [*He shouts at the top of his voice.*] BRING ME GIANTS! [*A moment since, the shadows of the comedians have been visible moving and posturing upon the stage. The violins have taken their places.*]
A VOICE. [*From the stage.*] Hey—pst—less noise! We are rehearsing here!
CYRANO. [*Laughs.*] We are going. [*He turns upstage. Through the street door enter* CUIGY, BRISSAILLE, *and a number of officers, supporting* LIGNIÈRE, *who is now thoroughly drunk.*]
CUIGY. Cyrano!
CYRANO. What is it?
CUIGY. Here—

Here's your stray lamb!
CYRANO. [*Recognizes* LIGNIÈRE.] Lignière—What's wrong with him?
CUIGY. He wants you.
BRISSAILLE. He's afraid to go home.
CYRANO. Why?
LIGNIÈRE. [*Showing a crumpled scrap of paper and speaking with the elaborate logic of profound intoxication.*] This letter—hundred against one—that's me—
I'm the one—all because of little song—
Good song—Hundred men, waiting, understand?
Porte de Nesle—way home—Might be dangerous—
Would you permit me spend the night with you?
CYRANO. A hundred—is that all? You are going home!
LIGNIÈRE. [*Astonished.*] Why—
CYRANO. [*In a voice of thunder, indicating the lighted lantern which the* PORTER *holds up curiously as he regards the scene.*] Take that lantern! [LIGNIÈRE *precipitately seizes the lantern.*] Forward march! I say
I'll be the man tonight that sees you home. [*To the* OFFICERS.]
You others follow—I want an audience!
CUIGY. A hundred against one—
CYRANO. Those are the odds
Tonight! [THE COMEDIANS *in their costumes are descending from the stage and joining the group.*]
LE BRET. But why help this—
CYRANO. There goes Le Bret Growling!
LE BRET. —This drunkard here?
CYRANO. [*His hand on* LE BRET's *shoulder.*] Because this drunkard—
This tun of sack, this butt of Burgundy—
Once in his life has done one lovely thing:
After the Mass, according to the form,
He saw, one day, the lady of his heart
Take holy water for a blessing. So
This one, who shudders at a drop of rain,
This fellow here—runs headlong to the font
Bends down and drinks it dry!
A SOUBRETTE. I say that was
A pretty thought!
CYRANO. Ah, was it not?
THE SOUBRETTE. [*To the others.*] But why
Against one poor poet, a hundred men?
CYRANO. March! [*To the* OFFICERS.]
And you gentlemen, remember now,
No rescue—Let me fight alone.
A COMEDIENNE. [*Jumps down from the stage.*] Come on!
I'm going to watch—
CYRANO. Come along!
ANOTHER COMEDIENNE. [*Jumps down, speaks to a* COMEDIAN *costumed as an old man.*] You, Cassandre?
CYRANO. Come all of you—the Doctor, Isabelle,
Léandre—the whole company—a swarm
Of murmuring, golden bees—we'll parody
Italian farce and Tragedy-of-Blood;
Ribbons for banner, masks for blazonry,
And tambourines to be our rolling drums!
ALL THE WOMEN. [*Jumping for joy.*]
Bravo!—My hood—My cloak—Hurry!
JODELET. [*Mock heroic.*] Lead on!—
CYRANO. [*To the violins.*] You violins—play us an overture—[*The violins join the procession which is forming.*
The lighted candles are snatched from the stage and distributed; it becomes a torchlight procession.]
Bravo!—Officers—Ladies in costume—
And twenty paces in advance . . . [*He takes his station as he speaks.*] Myself,
Alone, with glory fluttering over me,
Alone as Lucifer at war with heaven!
Remember—no one lifts a hand to help—Ready there? One . . . two . . . three! Porter, the doors! . . . [*The* PORTER *flings wide the great doors. We see in the dim moonlight a corner of old Paris, purple and picturesque.*]
Look—Paris dreams—nocturnal, nebulous,
Under blue moonbeams hung from wall to wall—
Naure's own setting for the scene we play!—
Yonder, behind her veil of mist, the Seine,
Like a mysterious and magic mirror
Trembles—And you shall see what you shall see!

ALL. To the Porte de Nesle!
CYRANO. [*Erect upon the threshold.*] To the Porte de Nesle! [*He turns back for a moment to the* SOUBRETTE.]
Did you not ask, my dear, why against one
Singer they send a hundred swords? [*Quietly, drawing his own sword.*] Because
They know this one man for a friend of mine! [*He goes out. The procession follows:* LIGNIÈRE *zizagging at its head, then the* COMEDIENNES *on the arms of the* OFFICERS, *then the* COMEDIANS, *leaping and dancing as they go. It vanishes into the night to the music of the violins, illuminated by the flickering glimmer of the candles.*]

Act 2

The Bakery of the Poets

The shop of Ragueneau, baker and pastrycook: a spacious affair at the corner of the rue St.-Honoré and the rue de l'Arbre Sec. The street, seen vaguely through the glass panes in the door at the back, is gray in the first light of dawn.

In the foreground, at the left, a counter is surmounted by a canopy of wrought iron from which are hanging ducks, geese, and white peacocks. Great crockery jars hold bouquets of common flowers, yellow sunflowers in particular. On the same side farther back, a huge fireplace; in front of it, between great andirons, of which each one supports a little saucepan, roast fowls revolve and weep into their dripping pans. To the right at the first entrance, a door. Beyond it, second entrance, a staircase leads up to a little dining room under the eaves, its interior visible through open shutters. A table is set there, and a tiny Flemish candlestick is lighted; there one may retire to eat and drink in private. A wooden gallery, extending from the head of the stairway, seems to lead to other little dining rooms.

In the center of the shop, an iron ring hangs by a rope over a pulley so that it can be raised or lowered; adorned with game of various kinds hung from it by hooks, it has the appearance of a sort of gastronomic chandelier.

In the shadow under the staircase, ovens are glowing. The spits revolve; the copper pots and pans gleam ruddily. Pastries in pyramids. Hams hanging from the rafters. The morning baking is in progress: a bustle of tall cooks and timid scullions and scurrying apprentices; a blossoming of white caps adorned with cock's feathers or the wings of guinea fowl. On wicker trays or on great metal platters they bring in rows of pastries and fancy dishes of various kinds.

Tables are covered with trays of cakes and rolls; others with chairs placed about them are set for guests.

One little table in a corner disappears under a heap of papers. At the curtain rise RAGUENEAU *is seated there. He is writing poetry.*

A PASTRYCOOK. [*Brings in a dish.*] Fruits en gelée!
SECOND PASTRYCOOK. [*Brings dish.*] Custard!
THIRD PASTRYCOOK. [*Brings roast peacock ornamented with feathers.*] Peacock rôti!
FOURTH PASTRYCOOK. [*Brings tray of cakes.*] Cakes and confections!
FIFTH PASTRYCOOK. [*Brings earthen dish.*] Beef en casserole!
RAGUENEAU. [*Raises his head; returns to mere earth.*] Over the coppers of my kitchen flows
The frosted-silver dawn. Silence awhile
The god who sings within thee, Ragueneau!
Lay down the lute—the oven calls for thee! [*Rises; goes to one of the cooks.*]
Here's a hiatus in your sauce; fill up
The measure.
THE COOK. How much?
RAGUENEAU. [*Measures on his finger.*] One more dactyl.
THE COOK. Huh? . . .
FIRST PASTRYCOOK. Rolls!
SECOND PASTRYCOOK. Roulades!
RAGUENEAU. [*Before the fireplace.*] Veil, O Muse, thy virgin eyes
From the lewd gleam of these terrestrial fires! [*To* FIRST PASTRYCOOK.]
Your rolls lack balance. Here's the proper form—
An equal hemistich on either side,

And the caesura in between. [*To another, pointing out an unfinished pie.*] Your house
Of crust should have a roof upon it. [*To another, who is seated on the hearth, placing poultry on a spit.*] And you—
Along the interminable spit, arrange
The modest pullet and the lordly Turk
Alternately, my son—as great Malherbe
Alternates male and female rimes. Remember,
A couplet, or a roast, should be well turned.
AN APPRENTICE. [*Advances with a dish covered by a napkin.*] Master, I thought of you when I designed
This, hoping it might please you.
RAGUENEAU. Ah! A lyre—
THE APPRENTICE. In puff-paste—
RAGUENEAU. And the jewels—candied fruit!
THE APPRENTICE. And the strings, barley-sugar!
RAGUENEAU. [*Gives him money.*] Go and drink
My health. [LISE *enters.*] St!—My Wife—
Circulate, and hide
That money! [*Shows the lyre to* LISE, *with a languid air.*] Graceful—yes?
LISE. Ridiculous! [*She places on the counter a pile of paper bags.*]
RAGUENEAU. Paper bags? Thank you . . . [*He looks at them.*] Ciel! My manuscripts!
The sacred verses of my poets—rent
Asunder, limb from limb—butchered to make
Base packages of pastry! Ah, you are one
Of those insane Bacchantes who destroyed
Orpheus!
LISE. Your dirty poets left them here
To pay for eating half our stock-in-trade:
We ought to make some profit out of them!
RAGUENEAU. Ant! Would you blame the locust for his song?
LISE. I blame the locust for his appetite! There used to be a time—before you had
Your hungry friends—you never called me Ants—
No, nor Bacchantes!
RAGUENEAU. What a way to use
Poetry!
LISE. Well, what is the use of it?
RAGUENEAU. But, my dear girl, what would you do with prose? [TWO CHILDREN *enter.*]
Well, dears?
A CHILD. Three little patties.
RAGUENEAU. [*Serves them.*] There we are! All hot and brown.
THE CHILD. Would you mind wrapping them?
RAGUENEAU. One of my paper bags! . . . Oh, certainly. [*Reads from the bag, as he is about to wrap the patties in it.*]
"Ulysses, when he left Penelope"—
Not that one! [*Takes another bag; reads.*]
"Phoebus, golden-crowned"—Not that one.
LISE. Well? They are waiting!
RAGUENEAU. Very well, very well!—
The Sonnet to Phyllis . . . Yet—it does seem hard . . .
LISE. Made up your mind—at last! Mph!—Jack-o'-Dreams!
RAGUENEAU. [*As her back is turned, calls back the* CHILDREN, *who are already at the door*] Pst!—Children—Give me back the bag. Instead
Of three patties, you shall have six of them! [*Makes the exchange. The* CHILDREN *go out. He reads from the bag, as he smooths it out tenderly.*]
"Phyllis"—A spot of butter on her name!—
"Phyllis"—
CYRANO. [*Enters hurriedly.*] What is the time?
RAGUENEAU. Six o'clock.
CYRANO. One
Hour more . . .
RAGNUENEAU. Felicitations!
CYRANO. And for what?
RAGUENEAU. Your victory! I saw it all—
CYRANO. Which one?
RAGUENEAU. At the Hôtel de Bourgogne.
CYRANO. Oh—the duel!
RAGUENEAU. The duel in rhyme!
LISE. He talks of nothing else.
CYRANO. Nonsense!
RAGUENEAU. [*Fencing and foining with a spit, which he snatches up from the hearth.*] "Then, as I end the refrain, thrust home!"
"Then, as I end the refrain"—Gods! What a line!

"Then, as I end"—
CYRANO. What time now, Ragueneau?
RAGUENEAU. [*Petrified at the full extent of a lunge, while he looks at the clock.*] Five after six—[*Recovers.*]
"—thrust home!" A Ballade, too!
LISE. [*To* CYRANO, *who in passing has mechanically shaken hands with her.*] Your hand—what have you done?
CYRANO. Oh, my hand?—Nothing.
RAGUENEAU. What danger now—
CYRANO. No danger.
LISE. I believe
He is lying.
CYRANO. Why? Was I looking down my nose?
That must have been a devil of a lie!
[*Changing his tone; to* RAGUENEAU.]
I expect someone. Leave us here alone,
When the times comes.
RAGUENEAU. How can I? In a moment,
My poets will be here.
LISE. To break their . . . fast!
CYRANO. Take them away, then, when I give the sign.
—What time?
RAGUENEAU. Ten minutes after.
CYRANO. Have you a pen?
RAGUENEAU. [*Offers him a pen.*] An eagle's feather!
A MUSKETEER. [*Enters, and speaks to* LISE *in a stentorian voice.*] Greeting!
CYRANO. [*To* RAGUENEAU.] Who is this?
RAGUENEAU. My wife's friend. A terrific warrior,
So he says.
CYRANO. Ah—I see. [*Takes up the pen; waves* RAGUENEAU *away.*] Only to write—
To fold—To give it to her—and to go . . . [*Throws down the pen.*]
Coward! And yet—the Devil take my soul
If I dare speak one word to her . . . [*To* RAGUENEAU.] What time now?
RAGUENEAU. A quarter after six.
CYRANO. [*Striking his breast.*] —One little word
Of all the many thousand I have here!
Whereas in writing . . . [*Takes up the pen.*] Come, I'll write to her
That letter I have written on my heart,
Torn up, and written over many times—
So many times . . . that all I have to do
Is to remember, and to write it down.

[*He writes. Through the glass of the door appear vague and hesitating shadows. The* POETS *enter, clothed in rusty black and spotted with mud.*]
LISE. [*To* RAGUENEAU.] Here come your scarecrows!
FIRST POET. Comrade!
SECOND POET. [*Takes both* RAGUENEAU'S *hands.*] My dear brother!
THIRD POET. [*Sniffing.*] O Lord of Roasts, how sweet thy dwellings are!
FOURTH POET. Phoebus Apollo of the Silver Spoon!
FIFTH POET. Cupid of Cookery!
RAGUENEAU. [*Surrounded, embraced, beaten on the back.*] These geniuses,
They put one at one's ease!
FIRST POET. We were delayed
By the crowd at the Porte de Nesle.
SECOND POET. Dead men
All scarred and gory, scattered on the stones,
Villainous-looking scoundrels—eight of them.
CYRANO. [*Looks up an instant.*] Eight? I thought only seven—
RAGUENEAU. Do you know
The hero of this hecatomb?
CYRANO. I? . . . No.
LISE. [*To the* MUSKETEER.] Do you?
THE MUSKETEER. Hmm—perhaps!
FIRST POET. They say one man alone
Put to flight all this crowd.
SECOND POET. Everywhere lay
Swords, daggers, pikes, bludgeons—
CYRANO. [*Writing.*] "Your eyes . . ."
THIRD POET. As far
As the Quai des Orfevres, hats and cloaks—
FIRST POET. Why, that man must have been the devil!
CYRANO. "Your lips . . ."
FIRST POET. Some savage monster might have done this thing!
CYRANO. "Looking upon you, I grow faint with fear . . ."
SECOND POET. What have you written lately, Ragueneau?
CYRANO. "Your Friend—Who loves you . . ." So. No signature;
I'll give it to her myself.
RAGUENEAU. A Recipe
In Rime.
THIRD POET. Read us your rimes!
FOURTH POET. Here's a brioche
Cocking its hat at me. [*He bites off the top*

of it.]
FIRST POET. Look how those buns
Follow the hungry poet with their eyes—
Those almond eyes!
SECOND POET. We are listening—
THIRD POET. See this cream-puff—
Fat little baby, drooling while it smiles!
SECOND POET. [*Nibbling at the pastry lyre.*]
For the first time, the lyre is my support.
RAGUENEAU. [*Coughs, adjusts his cap, strikes an attitude.*] A Recipe in Rime—
SECOND POET. [*Gives* FIRST POET *a dig with his elbow.*] Your breakfast?
FIRST POET. Dinner!
RAGUENEAU. [*Declaims.*] A Recipe for Making Almond Tarts
Beat your eggs, the yolk and white,
Very light;
Mingle with their creamy fluff
Drops of lime-juice, cool and green;
Then pour in
Milk of Almonds, just enough.
Dainty patty-pans, embraced
In puff-paste—
Have these ready within reach;
With your thumb and finger, pinch
Half an inch
Up around the edge of each—
Into these, a score or more,
Slowly pour
All your store of custard; so
Take them, bake them golden-brown—
Now sit down! . . .
Almond tartlets, Ragueneau!
THE POETS. Delicious! Melting!
A POET. [*Chokes.*] Humph!
CYRANO. [*To* RAGUENEAU.] Do you not see
Those fellows fattening themselves?—
RAGUENEAU. I know.
I would not look—it might embarrass them—
You see, I love a friendly audience.
Besides—another vanity—I am pleased
When they enjoy my cooking.
CYRANO. [*Slaps him on the back.*] Be off with you!—[RAGUENEAU *goes upstage.*]
Good little soul! [*Calls to* LISE.]
Madame!—[*She leaves the* MUSKETEER *and comes down to him.*] This musketeer—
He is making love to you?
LISE. [*Haughtily.*] If any man
Offends my virtue—all I have to do
Is look at him—once!
CYRANO. [*Looks at her gravely; she drops her eyes.*] I do not find
Those eyes of yours unconquerable.
LISE. [*Panting.*]—Ah!
CYRANO. [*Raising his voice a little.*] Now listen—I am fond of Ragueneau;
I allow no one—do you understand?—
To . . . take his name in vain!
LISE. You think—
CYRANO. [*Ironic emphasis.*] I think
I interrupt you. [*He salutes the* MUSKETEER, *who has heard without daring to resent the warning.* LISE *goes to the* MUSKETEER *as he returns* CYRANO's *salute.*]
LISE. You—you swallow that?—
You ought to have pulled his nose!
THE MUSKETEER. His nose?—His nose!
. . . [*He goes out huriedly.* ROXANE *and the* DUENNA *appear outside the door.*]
CYRANO. [*Nods to* RAGUENEAU.] Pst!—
RAGUENEAU. [*To the* POETS.] Come inside—!
CYRANO. [*Impatient.*] Pst! . . . Pst! . . .
RAGUENEAU. We shall be more
Comfortable . . . [*He leads the* POETS *into inner room.*]
FIRST POET. The cakes!
SECOND POET. Bring them along! [*They go out.*]
CYRANO. If I can see the faintest spark of hope,
Then—[*Throws door open—bows.*] Welcome! [ROXANE *enters, followed by the* DUENNA, *whom* CYRANO *detains.*] Pardon me—one word—
THE DUENNA. Take two.
CYRANO. Have you a good digestion?
THE DUENNA. Wonderful!
CYRANO. Good. Here are two sonnets, by Benserade—
THE DUENNA. Euh?
CYRANO. Which I fill for you with éclairs.
THE DUENNA. Ooo!
CYRANO. Do you like cream-puffs?
THE DUENNA. Only with whipped cream.
CYRANO. Here are three . . . six—embosomed in a poem
By Saint-Amant. This ode of Chapelin
Looks deep enough to hold—a jelly roll.
—Do you love Nature?
THE DUENNA. Mad about it.
CYRANO. Then

Go out and eat these in the street. Do not
Return—
THE DUENNA. Oh, but—
CYRANO. Until you finish them. [*Down to* ROXANE.]
Blessed above all others be the hour
When you remembered to remember me,
And came to tell me . . . what?
ROXANE. [*Takes off her mask.*] First let me thank you
Because . . . That man . . . that creature, whom your sword
Made sport of yesterday—His patron, one—
CYRANO. De Guiche?—
ROXANE. —who thinks himself in love with me
Would have forced that man upon me for—a husband—
CYRANO. I understand—so much the better then!
I fought, not for my nose, but your bright eyes.
ROXANE. And then, to tell you—but before I can
Tell you—Are you, I wonder, still the same
Big brother—almost—that you used to be
When we were children, playing by the pond
In the old garden down there—
CYRANO. I remember—
Every summer you came to Bergerac! . . .
ROXANE. You used to make swords out of bulrushes—
CYRANO. You dandelion-dolls with golden hair—
ROXANE. And those green plums—
CYRANO. And those black mulberries—
ROXANE. In those days, you did everything I wished!
CYRANO. Roxane, in short skirts, was called Madeleine.
ROXANE. Was I pretty?
CYRANO. Oh—not too plain!
ROXANE. Sometimes
When you had hurt your hand you used to come
Running to me—and I would be your mother,
And say—Oh, in a very grown-up voice: [*She sees the hand—starts.*] Oh!—
Wait—I said, "Let me see!"
Still—at your age! How did you do that?
CYRANO. Playing
With the big boys, down by the Porte de Nesle.
ROXANE. [*Sits at a table and wets her handkerchief in a glass of water.*] Come here to me.
CYRANO. —Such a wise little mother!
ROXANE. And tell me, while I wash this blood away,
How many you—played with?
CYRANO. Oh, about a hundred.
ROXANE. Tell me.
CYRANO. No. Let me go. Tell me what you
Were going to tell me—if you dared?
ROXANE. [*Still holding his hand.*] I think I do dare—now. It seems like long ago
When I could tell you things. Yes—I dare . . . Listen:
I . . . love someone.
CYRANO. Ah! . . .
ROXANE. Someone who does not know.
CYRANO. Ah! . . .
ROXANE. At least—not yet.
CYRANO. Ah! . . .
ROXANE. But he will know
Some day.
CYRANO. Ah! . . .
ROXANE. A big boy who loves me too,
And is afraid of me, and keeps away,
And never says one word.
CYRANO. Ah! . . .
ROXANE. Let me have
Your hand a moment—why how hot it is!—
I know. I see him trying . . .
CYRANO. Ah! . . .
ROXANE. There now!
Is that better?—[*She finishes bandaging the hand with her handkerchief.*] Besides—only to think—
(This is a secret.) He is a soldier too,
In your own regiment—
CYRANO. Ah! . . .
ROXANE. Yes, in the Guards,
Your company too.
CYRANO. Ah! . . .
ROXANE. And such a man!—
He is proud—noble—young—brave—beautiful—
CYRANO. [*Turns pale; rises.*] Beautiful!—
ROXANE. What's the matter?
CYRANO. [*Smiling.*] Nothing—this—

My sore hand!
ROXANE. Well, I love him. That is all.
Oh—and I never saw him anywhere
Except the *Comédie*.
CYRANO. You have never spoken?
ROXANE. Only our eyes . . .
CYRANO. Why, then—How do you know?—
ROXANE. People talk about people; and I hear
Things . . . and I know.
CYRANO. You say he is in the Guards: His name?
ROXANE. Baron Christian de Neuvillette.
CYRANO. He is not in the Guards.
ROXANE. Yes. Since this morning.
Captain Carbon de Castel-Jaloux.
CYRANO. So soon! . . .
So soon we lose our hearts!—But, my dear child,—
THE DUENNA. [*Opens the door.*] I have eaten the cakes, Monsieur de Bergerac!
CYRANO. Good! Now go out and read the poetry! [*The* DUENNA *disappears.*]
—But, my dear child! You, who love only words,
Wit, the grand manner—Why, for all you know,
The man may be a savage, or a fool.
ROXANE. His curls are like a hero from D'Urfé.
CYRANO. His mind may be as curly as his hair.
ROXANE. Not with such eyes. I read his soul in them.
CYRANO. Yes, all our souls are written in our eyes!
But—if he be a bungler?
ROXANE. Then I shall die— There!
CYRANO. [*After a pause.*] And you brought me here to tell me this?
I do not yet quite understand, Madame,
The reason for your confidence.
ROXANE. They say
That in your company—It frightens me—
You are all Gascons . . .
CYRANO. And we pick a quarrel
With any flat-foot who intrudes himself.
Whose blood is not pure Gascon like our own?
Is this what you have heard?
ROXANE. I am so afraid
For him!
CYRANO. [*Between his teeth.*] Not without reason!—
ROXANE. And I thought
You . . . You were so brave, so invincible
Yesterday, against all of those brutes!—
If you,
Whom they all fear—
CYRANO. Oh well—I will defend
Your little Baron.
ROXANE. Will you? Just for me?
Because I have always been—your friend!
CYRANO. Of course . . .
ROXANE. Will you be *his* friend?
CYRANO. I will be his friend.
ROXANE. And never let him fight a duel?
CYRANO. No—never.
ROXANE. Oh, but you are a darling!—I must go—
You never told me about last night—
Why,
You must have been a hero! Have him write
And tell me all about it—will you?
CYRANO. Of course . . .
ROXANE. [*Kisses her hand.*] I always did love you!—A hundred men
Against one—Well. . . . Adieu. We are great friends,
Are we not?
CYRANO. Of course . . .
ROXANE. He *must* write to me—
A hundred—You shall tell me the whole story
Some day, when I have time. A hundred men—
What courage—
CYRANO. [*Salutes as she goes out.*] Oh . . . I have done better since! [*The door closes after her.* CYRANO *remains motionless, his eyes on the ground. Pause. The other door opens;* RAGUENEAU *puts in his head.*]
RAGUENEAU. May I come in?
CYRANO. [*Without moving.*] Yes . . .
[RAGUENEAU *and his friends re-enter. At the same time,* CARBON DE CASTEL-JALOUX *appears at the street door in uniform as Captain of the Guards; recognizes* CYRANO *with a sweeping gesture.*]
CARBON. Here he is!—Our hero!

CYRANO. [*Raises his head and salutes.*]
Our Captain!
CARBON. We know! All our company
Are here—
CYRANO. [*Recoils.*] No—
CARBON. Come! They are waiting for
you.
CYRANO. No!
CARBON. [*Tries to lead him out.*] Only
across the street— Come!
CYRANO. Please—
CARBON. [*Goes to the door and shouts in a
voice of thunder.*] Our champion
Refuses! He is not feeling well today!
A VOICE OUTSIDE. Ah! Sandious! [*Noise
outside of swords and trampling feet approaching.*]
CARBON. Here they come now!
THE CADETS. [*Entering the shop.*] Mille
dious!—
Mordious!—Capdedious!—Pocapdedious!
RAGUENEAU. [*In astonishment.*] Gentlemen—
You are all Gascons?
THE CADETS. All!
FIRST CADET. [*To* CYRANO.] Bravo!
CYRANO. Baron!
ANOTHER CADET. [*Takes both his hands.*]
Vivat!
CYRANO. Baron!
THIRD CADET. Come to my arms!
CYRANO. Baron!
OTHERS. To mine!— To mine!—
CYRANO. Baron . . . Baron . . . Have
mercy—
RAGUENEAU. You are all Barons too?
THE CADETS. *Are* we?
RAGUENEAU. Are they? . . .
FIRST CADET. Our coronets would star
the midnight sky!
LE BRET. [*Enters. Hurries to* CYRANO.]
The whole town's looking for you!
Raving mad—
A triumph! Those who saw the fight—
CYRANO. I hope!
You have not told them where I—
LE BRET. [*Rubbing his hands.*] Certainly
I told them!
CITIZEN. [*Enters, followed by a group.*]
Listen! Shut the door!—Here comes
All Paris! [*The street outside fills with a
shouting crowd. Chairs and carriages stop
at the door.*]
LE BRET. [*Aside to* CYRANO, *smiling.*] And
Roxane?

CYRANO. [*Quickly.*] Hush.
THE CROWD OUTSIDE. Cyrano! [*A mob
bursts into the shop. Shouts, acclamations,
general disturbance.*]
RAGUENEAU. [*Standing on a table.*] My
shop invaded— They'll break everything—
Glorious!
SEVERAL MEN. [*Crowding about* CYRANO.]
My friend! . . . My friend! . . .
CYRANO. Why, yesterday
I did not have so many friends!
LE BRET. Success
At last!
A MARQUIS. [*Runs to* CYRANO, *with outstretched hands.*] My dear—really!—
CYRANO. [*Coldly.*] So? And how long
Have I been dear to you?
ANOTHER MARQUIS. One moment—
pray!
I have two ladies in my carriage here;
Let me present you—
CYRANO. Certainly! And first,
Who will present you, sir—to me?
LE BRET. [*Astounded.*] Why, what
The devil?—
CYRANO. Hush!
A MAN OF LETTERS. [*With a portfolio.*]
May I have the details? . . .
CYRANO. You may not.
LE BRET. [*Plucking* CYRANO's *sleeve.*] Theophraste Renaudot!—Editor
Of the *Gazette*—your reputation! . . .
CYRANO. No!
A POET. [*Advances.*] Monsieur—
CYRANO. Well?
THE POET. Your full name? I will compose
A pentacrostic—
ANOTHER. Monsieur—
CYRANO. That will do! [*Movement. The
crowd arranges itself.* DE GUICHE *appears, escorted by* CUIGY, BRISSAILE, *and
the other* OFFICERS *who were with*
CYRANO *at the close of the first act.*]
CUIGY. [*Goes to* CYRANO.] Monsieur de
Guiche!— [*Murmur. Everyone moves.*]
A message from the Marshal
De Gassion—
DE GUICHE. [*Saluting* CYRANO.] Who
wishes to express
Through me his admiration. He has
heard
Of your affair—
THE CROWD. Bravo!
CYRANO. [*Bowing.*] The Marshal speaks

As an authority.
DE GUICHE. He said just now
The story would have been incredible
Were it not for the witness—
CUIGY. Of our eyes!
LE BRET. [*Aside to* CYRANO.] What is it?
CYRANO. Hush!—
LE BRET. Something is wrong with you;
Are you in pain?
CYRANO. [*Recovering himself.*] In pain?
Before this crowd? [*His moustache bristles. He throws out his chest.*]
I? In pain? You shall see!
DE GUICHE. [*To whom* CUIGY *has been whispering.*] Your name is known
Already as a soldier. You are one
Of those wild Gascons, are you not?
CYRANO. The Guards,
Yes. A Cadet.
A CADET. [*In a voice of thunder.*] One of ourselves!
DE GUICHE. Ah! So—
Then all these gentlemen with the haughty air,
These are the famous—
CARBON. Cyrano!
CYRANO. Captain?
CARBON. Our troop being all present, be so kind
As to present them to the Comte de Guiche!
CYRANO. [*With a gesture presenting the* CADETS *to* DE GUICHE, *declaims.*] The Cadets of Gascoyne—the defenders of Carbon de Castel-Jaloux:
Free fighters, free lovers, free spenders—
The Cadets of Gascoyne—the defenders
Of old homes, old names, and old splendors—
A proud and a pestilent crew!
The Cadets of Gascoyne, the defenders
Of Carbon de Castel-Jaloux.

Hawk-eyed, they stare down all contenders—
The wolf bares his fangs as they do—
Make way there, you fat moneylenders!
(Hawk-eyed, they stare down all contenders)
Old boots that have been to the menders,
Old cloaks that are worn through and through—
Hawk-eyed, they stare down all contenders—
The wolf bares his fangs as they do!

Skull-breakers they are, and sword-benders;
Red blood is their favorite brew;
Hot haters and loyal befrienders,
Skull-breakers they are, and sword-benders.
Wherever a quarrel engenders,
They're ready and waiting for you!
Skull-breakers they are, and sword-benders;
Red blood is their favorite brew!
Behold them, our Gascon defenders
Who win every woman they woo!
There's never a dame but surrenders—
Behold them, our Gascon defenders!
Young wives who are clever pretenders—
Old husbands who house the cuckoo—
Behold them—our Gascon defenders
Who win every woman they woo!
DE GUICHE. [*Languidly, sitting in a chair.*]
Poets are fashionable nowadays
To have about one. Would you care to join
My following?
CYRANO. No, sir. I do not follow.
DE GUICHE. Your duel yesterday amused my uncle
The Cardinal. I might help you there.
LE BRET. Grand Dieu!
DE GUICHE. I suppose you have written a tragedy—
They all have.
LE BRET. [*Aside to* CYRANO.] Now at last you'll have it played—
Your "Agrippine!"
DE GUICHE. Why not? Take it to him.
CYRANO. [*Tempted.*] Really—
DE GUICHE. He is himself a dramatist;
Let him rewrite a few lines here and there,
And he'll approve the rest.
CYRANO. [*His face falls again.*] Impossible.
My blood curdles to think of altering
One comma.
DE GUICHE. Ah, but when he likes a thing
He pays well.
CYRANO. Yes—but not so well as I—
When I have made a line that sings itself
So that I love the sound of it—I pay

Myself a hundred times.
DE GUICHE. You are proud, my friend.
CYRANO. You have observed that?
A CADET. [*Enters with a drawn sword, along the whole blade of which is transfixed a collection of disreputable hats, their plumes draggled, their crowns cut and torn.*] Cyrano! See here—
Look what we found this morning in the street—
The plumes dropped in their flight by those fine birds
Who showed the white feather!
CARBON. Spoils of the hunt—
Well mounted!
THE CROWD. Ha-ha-ha!
CUIGY. Whoever hired
Those rascals, he must be an angry man
Today!
BRISSAILLE. Who was it? Do you know?
DE GUICHE. Myself!—[*The laughter ceases.*]
I hired them to do the sort of work
We do not soil our hands with—punishing
A drunken poet. . . . [*Uncomfortable silence.*]
THE CADET. [*To* CYRANO.] What shall we do with them?
They ought to be preserved before they spoil—
CYRANO. [*Takes the sword, and in the gesture of saluting* DE GUICHE *with it, makes all the hats slide off at his feet.*] Sir, will you not return these to your friends?
DE GUICHE. My chair—my porters here—immediately! [*To* CYRANO *violently.*]
—As for you, sir—
A VOICE. [*In the street.*] The chair of Monseigneur
Le Comte de Guiche!—
DE GUICHE. [*Who has recovered his self-control; smiling.*] Have you read *Don Quixote*?
CYRANO. I have—and found myself the hero.
A PORTER. [*Appears at the door.*] Chair Ready!
DE GUICHE. Be so good as to read once more
The chapter of the windmills.
CYRANO. [*Gravely.*] Chapter Thirteen.
DE GUICHE. Windmills, remember, if you fight with them—

CYRANO. My enemies change, then, with every wind?
DE GUICHE. —May swing round their huge arms and cast you down
Into the mire.
CYRANO. Or up—among the stars! [DE GUICHE *goes out. We see him get into the chair. The* OFFICERS *follow murmuring among themselves.* LE BRET *goes up with them. The crowd goes out.*]
CYRANO. [*Saluting with burlesque politeness, those who go out without daring to take leave of him.*] Gentlemen. . . .
Gentlemen. . . .
LE BRET. [*As the door closes, comes down, shaking his clenched hands to heaven.*]
You have done it now—
You have made your fortune!
CYRANO. There you go again,
Growling!—
LE BRET. At least this latest pose of yours—
Ruining every chance that comes your way—
Becomes exaggerated—
CYRANO. Very well,
Then I exaggerate!
LE BRET. [*Triumphantly.*] Oh, you do!
CYRANO. Yes;
On principle. There are things in this world
A man does well to carry to extremes.
LE BRET. Stop trying to be Three Musketeers in one!
Fortune and glory—
CYRANO. What would you have me do?
Seek for the patronage of some great man,
And like a creeping vine on a tall tree
Crawl upward, where I cannot stand alone?
No thank you! Dedicate, as others do,
Poems to pawnbrokers? Be a buffoon
In the vile hope of teasing out a smile
On some cold face? No thank you! Eat a toad
For breakfast every morning? Make my knees
Callous, and cultivate a supple spine,—
Wear out my belly groveling in the dust?
No thank you! Scratch the back of any swine
That roots up gold for me? Tickle the horns
Of Mammon with my left hand, while

my right,
Too proud to know his partner's business,
Takes in the fee? No thank you! Use the fire
God gave me to burn incense all day long
Under the nose of wood and stone? No thank you!
Shall I go leaping into ladies' laps
And licking fingers?—or—to change the form—
Navigating with madrigals for oars,
My sails full of the sighs of dowagers?
No thank you! Publish verses at my own
Expense? No thank you! Be the patron saint
Of a small group of literary souls
Who dine together every Tuesday? No
I thank you! shall I labor night and day
To build a reputation on one song,
And never write another? Shall I find
True genius only among Geniuses,
Palpitate over little paragraphs,
And struggle to insinuate my name
In the columns of the *Mercury*?
No thank you! Calculate, scheme, be afraid,
Love more to make a visit than a poem,
Seek introductions, favors, influences?—
No thank you! No, I thank you! And again
I thank you!—But . . . To sing, to laugh, to dream,
To walk in my own way and be alone,
Free, with an eye to see things as they are,
A voice that means manhood—to cock my hat
Where I choose— At a word, a *Yes*, a *No*,
To fight—or write. To travel any road
Under the sun, under the stars, nor doubt
If fame or fortune lie beyond the bourn—
Never to make a line I have not heard
In my own heart; yet, with all modesty
To say: "My soul, be satisfied with flowers,
With fruit, with weeds even; but gather them
In the one garden you may call your own."

So, when I win some triumph, by some chance,
Render no share to Caesar—in a word,
I am too proud to be a parasite,
And if my nature wants the germ that grows
Towering to heaven like the mountain pine,
Or like the oak, sheltering multitudes—
I stand, not high it may be—but alone!
LE BRET. Alone, yes!—But why stand against the world?
What devil has possessed you now, to go
Everywhere making yourself enemies?
CYRANO. Watching you other people making friends
Everywhere—as a dog makes friends! I mark
The manner of these canine courtesies
And think: "My friends are of a cleaner breed;
Here comes—thank God!—another enemy!"
LE BRET. But this is madness!
CYRANO. Method, let us say.
It is my pleasure to displease. I love
Hatred. Imagine how it feels to face
The volley of a thousand angry eyes—
The bile of envy and the froth of fear
Spattering little drops about me—
You—
Good nature all around you, soft and warm—
You are like those Italians, in great cowls
Comfortable and loose—your chin sinks down
Into the folds, your shoulders droop.
But I—
The Spanish ruff I wear around my throat
Is like a ring of enemies; hard, proud,
Each point another pride, another thorn—
So that I hold myself erect perforce
Wearing the hatred of the common herd
Haughtily, the harsh collar of Old Spain,
At once a fetter and —a halo!
LE BRET. Yes . . . [*After a silence, draws* CYRANO'*s arm through his own.*]
Tell this to all the world—And then to me

Say very softly that . . . She loves you not.
CYRANO. [*Quickly.*] Hush! [*A moment since,* CHRISTIAN *has entered and mingled with the* CADETS, *who do not offer to speak to him. Finally, he sits down alone at a small table, where he is served by* LISE.]
A CADET. [*Rises frm a table upstage, his glass in his hand.*] Cyrano!—Your story!
CYRANO. Presently . . . [*He goes up, on the arm of* LE BRET, *talking to him. The* CADET *comes downstage.*]
THE CADET. The story of the combat! An example
For—[*He stops by the table where* CHRISTIAN *is sitting.*]—this young tadpole here.
CHRISTIAN. [*Looks up.*] Tadpole?
ANOTHER CADET. Yes, you!—
You narrow-gutted Northerner!
CHRISTIAN. Sir?
FIRST CADET. Hark ye,
Monsieur de Neuvillette: You are to know
There is a certain subject—I would say,
A certain object—never to be named
Among us: utterly unmentionable!
CHRISTIAN. And that is?
THIRD CADET. [*In an awful voice.*] Look at me! . . . [*He strikes his nose three times with his finger, mysteriously.*] You understand?
CHRISTIAN. Why, yes; the—
FOURTH CADET. Sh! . . . We never speak that word—[*Indicating* CYRANO *by a gesture.*]
To breathe it is to have to do with HIM!
FIFTH CADET. [*Speaks through his nose.*] He has exterminated several
Whose tone of voice suggested . . .
SIX CADET. [*In a hollow tone; rising from under the table on all fours.*] Would you die
Before your time? Just mention anything
Convex . . . or cartilaginous . . .
SEVENTH CADET. [*His hand on* CHRISTIAN's *shoulder.*] One word—
One syllable—one gesture—nay, one sneeze—
Your handkerchief becomes your windingsheet! [*Silence. In a circle around* CHRISTIAN, *arms crossed, they regard him expectantly.*]

CHRISTIAN. [*Rises and goes to* CARBON, *who is conversing with an* OFFICER, *and pretending not to see what is taking place.*] Captain!
CARBON. [*Turns, and looks him over.*] Sir?
CHRISTIAN. What is the proper thing to do
When Gascons grow too boastful?
CARBON. Prove to them
That one may be a Norman, and have courage. [*Turns his back.*]
CHRISTIAN. I thank you.
FIRST CADET. [*To* CYRANO.] Come—the story!
ALL. The story!
CYRANO. [*Comes down.*] Oh,
My story? Well . . . [*They all draw up their stools and group themselves around him, eagerly.* CHRISTIAN *places himself astride of a chair, his arms on the back of it.*] I marched on, all alone
To meet those devils. Overhead, the moon
Hung like a gold watch at the fob of heaven,
Till suddenly some Angel rubbed a cloud,
As it might be his handkerchief, across
The shining crystal, and—the night came down.
No lamps in those back streets—It was so dark—
Mordious! You could not see beyond—
CHRISTIAN. Your nose. [*Silence. Every man slowly rises to his feet. They look at* CYRANO *almost with terror. He has stopped short, utterly astonished. Pause.*]
CYRANO. Who is that man there?
A CADET. [*In a low voice.*] A recruit—arrived
This morning.
CYRANO. [*Takes a step toward* CHRISTIAN.] A recruit—
CARBON. [*In a low voice.*] His name is Christian
De Neuvil—
CYRANO. [*Suddenly motionless.*] Oh . . . [*He turns pale, flushes, makes a movement as if to throw himself upon* CHRISTIAN.] I—[*Controls himself, and goes on in a choking voice.*] I see. Very well,
As I was saying—[*With a sudden burst of rage.*] Mordious! . . . [*He goes on in a natural tone.*] It grew dark,
You could not see your hand before

your eyes.
I marched on, thinking how, all for the sake
Of one old souse [*They slowly sit down, watching him.*] who wrote a bawdy song
Whenever he took—
CHRISTIAN. A noseful—[*Everyone rises.* CHRISTIAN *balances himself on two legs of his chair.*]
CYRANO. [*Half strangled.*] —Took a notion.
Whenever he took a notion—For his sake,
I might antagonize some dangerous man,
One powerful enough to make me pay—
CHRISTIAN. Through the nose—
CYRANO. [*Wipes the sweat from his forehead.*] —Pay the Piper. After all,
I thought, why am I putting in my—
CHRISTIAN. Nose—
CYRANO. —My oar . . . Why am I putting in my oar?
The quarrel's none of mine. However—now
I am here, I may as well go through with it.
Come Gascon—do your duty!—Suddenly
A sword flashed in the dark. I caught it fair—
CHRISTIAN. On the nose—
CYRANO. On my blade. Before I knew it,
There I was—
CHRISTIAN. Rubbing noses—
CYRANO. [*Pale and smiling.*] Crossing swords
With half a score at once. I handed one—
CHRISTIAN. A nosegay—
CYRANO. [*Leaping at him.*] Ventre-Saint Gris! . . . [*The Gascons tumble over each other to get a good view. Arrived in front of* CHRISTIAN, *who has not moved an inch,* CYRANO *masters himself again, and continues.*] He went down;
The rest gave way; I charged—
CHRISTIAN. Nose in the air—
CYRANO: I skewered two of them—disarmed a third—
Another lunged— Paf! And I countered—
CHRISTIAN. Pif!

CYRANO. [*Bellowing.*] TONNERRE! Out of here!—All of you! [*All the* CADETS *rush for the door.*]
FIRST CADET. At last—
The old lion wakes!
CYRANO. All of you! Leave me here
Alone with that man! [*The lines following are heard brokenly in the confusion of getting through the door.*]
SECOND CADET. Bigre! He'll have the fellow
Chopped into sausage—
RAGUENEAU. Sausage?—
THIRD CADET. Mince-meat, then—
One of your pies!—
RAGUENEAU. Am I pale? You look white
As a fresh napkin—
CARBON. [*At the door.*] Come!
FOURTH CADET. He'll never leave
Enough of him to—
FIFTH CADET. Why, it frightens ME
To think of what will—
SIXTH CADET. [*Closing the door.*] Something horrible
Beyond imagination . . . [*They are all gone; some through the street door, some by the inner doors to right and left. A few disappear up the staircase.* CYRANO *and* CHRISTIAN *stand face to face a moment, and look at each other.*]
CYRANO. To my arms!
CHRISTIAN. Sir?
CYRANO. You have courage!
CHRISTIAN. Oh, that! . . .
CYRANO. You are brave—
That pleases me.
CHRISTIAN. You mean? . . .
CYRANO. I am her brother? Come!
CHRISTIAN. Whose?
CYRANO. Hers—Roxane!
CHRISTIAN. Her . . . brother? You? [*Hurries to him.*]
CYRANO. Her cousin. Much the same.
CHRISTIAN. And has she told you? . . .
CYRANO. Everything.
CHRISTIAN. She loves me?
CYRANO. Perhaps.
CHRISTIAN. [*Takes both his hands.*] My dear sir—more than I can say,
I am honored—
CYRANO. This is rather sudden.
CHRISTIAN. Please
Forgive me—
CYRANO. [*Holds him at arm's length, looking at him.*] Why, he is a handsome devil.

This fellow!
CHRISTIAN. On my honor—if you knew
How much I have admired—
CYRANO. Yes, yes—and all
Those Noses which—
CHRISTIAN. Please! I apologize.
CYRANO. [*Change of tone.*] Roxane expects a letter—
CHRISTIAN. Not from me?—
CYRANO. Yes. Why not?
CHRISTIAN. Once I write, that ruins all!
CYRANO. And why?
CHRISTIAN. Because . . . because I am a fool!
Stupid enough to hang myself!
CYRANO. But no—
You are no fool; you call yourself a fool,
There's proof enough in that. Besides, you did not
Attack me like a fool.
CHRISTIAN. Bah! Anyone
Can pick a quarrel. Yes, I have a sort
Of rough and ready soldier's tongue. I know
That. But with any woman—paralyzed,
Speechless, dumb. I can only look at them.
Yet sometimes, when I go away, their eyes . . .
CYRANO. Why not their hearts, if you should wait and see?
CHRISTIAN. No. I am one of those—I know—those men
Who never can make love.
CYRANO. Strange. . . . Now it seems
I, if I gave my mind to it, I might
Perhaps make love well.
CHRISTIAN. Oh, if I had words
To say what I have here!
CYRANO. If I could be
A handsome little Musketeer with eyes!—
CHRISTIAN. Besides—you know Roxane—how sensitive—
One rough word, and the sweet illusion—gone!
CYRANO. I wish you might be my interpreter.
CHRISTIAN. I wish I had your wit—
CYRANO. Borrow it, then!—
Your beautiful young manhood—lend me that,
And we two make one hero of romance!
CHRISTIAN. What?

CYRANO. Would you dare repeat to her the words
I gave you, day by day?
CHRISTIAN. You mean?
CYRANO. I mean
Roxane shall have no disillusionment!
Come, shall we win her both together? Take
The soul within this leathern jack of mine,
And breathe it into you? [*Touches him on the breast.*] So—there's my heart
Under your velvet, now!
CHRISTIAN. But— Cyrano!—
CYRANO. But—Christian, why not?
CHRISTIAN. I am afraid—
CYRANO. I know—
Afraid that when you have her all alone,
You lose all. Have no fear. It is yourself
She loves—give her yourself put into words—
My words, upon your lips!
CHRISTIAN. But . . . but your eyes! . . .
They burn like—
CYRANO. Will you? . . . Will you?
CHRISTIAN. Does it mean
So much to you?
CYRANO. [*Beside himself.*] It means—[*Recovers, changes tone.*] A Comedy,
A situation for a poet! Come.
Shall we collaborate? I'll be your cloak
Of darkness, your enchanged sword, your ring
To charm the fairy Princess!
CHRISTIAN. But the letter—
I cannot write—
CYRANO. Oh yes, the letter. [*He takes from his pocket the letter which he has written.*] Here.
CHRISTIAN. What is this?
CYRANO. All there; all but the address.
CHRISTIAN. I—
CYRANO. Oh, you may send it. It will serve.
CHRISTIAN. But why
Have you done this?
CYRANO. I have amused myself
As we all do, we poets—writing vows
To Chloris, Phyllis—any pretty name—
You might have had a pocketful of them!
Take it, and turn to facts my fantasies—
I loosed these loves like doves into the air;
Give them a habitation and a home.

Here, take it—You will find me all the more
Eloquent, being insincere! Come!
CHRISTIAN. First,
There must be a few changes here and there—
Written at random, can it fit Roxane?
CYRANO. Like her own glove.
CHRISTIAN. No, but—
CYRANO. My son, have faith—
Faith in the love of women for themselves—
Roxane will know this letter for her own!
CHRISTIAN. [*Throws himself into the arms of* CYRANO. *They stand embraced.*] My friend! [*The door upstage opens a little. A* CADET *steals in.*]
THE CADET. Nothing. A silence like the tomb . . .
I hardly dare look—[*He sees the two.*] Wha-at? [*The other* CADETS *crowd in behind him and see.*]
THE CADETS. No!—No!
SECOND CADET. Mon dieu!
THE MUSKETEER. [*Slaps his knee.*] Well, well, well!
CARBON. Here's our devil . . . Christianized!
Offend one nostril, and he turns the other.
THE MUSKETEER. Now we are allowed to talk about his nose! [*Calls.*] Hey, Lise! Come here— [*Affectedly.*] Snf! What a horrid smell!
What is it? . . . [*Plants himself in front of* CYRANO, *and looks at his nose in an impolite manner.*] You ought to know about such things;
What seems to have died around here?
CYRANO. [*Knocks him backward over a bench.*] Cabbage-heads! [*Joy. The* CADETS *have found their old* CYRANO *again. General disturbance.*]

Act 3

Roxane's Kiss

A little square in the old Marais: old houses, and a glimpse of narrow streets. On the right, the house of Roxane and her garden wall, overhung with tall shubbery. Over the door of the house a balcony and a tall window; to one side of the door, a bench.

Ivy clings to the wall; jasmine embraces the balcony, trembles, and falls away.
By the bench and the jutting stonework of the wall one might easily climb up to the balcony.
Opposite, an ancient house of the like character, brick and stone, whose front door forms an entrance. The knocker on this door is tied up in linen like an injured thumb.
At the curtain rise the DUENNA *is seated on the bench beside the door. The window is wide open on* ROXANE'S *balcony; a light within suggests that it is early evening. By the* DUENNA *stands* RAGUENEAU *dressed in what might be the livery of one attached to the household. He is by way of telling her something, and wiping his eyes meanwhile.*

RAGUENEAU. And so she ran off with a Musketeer!
I was ruined—I was alone—Remained
Nothing for me to do but hang myself,
So I did that. Presently along comes
Monsieur de Bergerac, and cuts me down,
And makes me steward to his cousin.
THE DUENNA. Ruined?—
I thought your pastry was a great success!
RAGUENEAU. [*Shakes his head.*] Lise loved the soldiers, and I loved the poets—
Mars ate up all the cakes Apollo left;
It did not take long. . . .
THE DUENNA. [*Calls up to window.*] Roxane! Are you ready?
We are late!
VOICE OF ROXANE. [*Within.*] Putting on my cape—
THE DUENNA. [*To* RAGUENEAU, *indicating the house opposite.*] Clomire
Across the way receives on Thursday nights—
We are to have a psycho-colloquy
Upon the Tender Passion.
RAGUENEAU. Ah—the Tender . . .
THE DUENNA. [*Sighs.*] —Passion! . . .
[*Calls up to window.*] Roxane!—Hurry, dear—we shall miss
The Tender Passion!
ROXANE. Coming!—[*Music of stringed instruments offstage approaching.*]
THE VOICE OF CYRANO. [*Singing.*] La, la, la!—
THE DUENNA. A serenade?—How pleasant—
CYRANO. No, no, no!—

F natural, you natural born fool! [*Enters, followed by two* PAGES, *carrying theorbos.*]
FIRST PAGE. [*Ironically.*] No doubt your honor knows F natural
When he hears—
CYRANO. I am a musician, infant!—
A pupil of Gassendil.
THE PAGE. [*Plays and sings.*] La, la,—
CYRANO. Here—
Give me that—[*He snatches the instrument from the* PAGE *and continues the tune.*]
La, la, la, la—
ROXANE. [*Appears on the balcony.*] Is that you,
Cyrano?
CYRANO. [*Singing.*] I, who praise your lilies fair,
But long to love your ro . . . ses!
ROXANE. I'll be down—
Wait— [*Goes in through window.*]
THE DUENNA. Did you train these virtuosi?
CYRANO. No—
I won them on a bet from D'Assoucy.
We were debating a fine point of grammar
When, pointing out these two young nightingales
Dressed up like peacocks, with their instruments,
He cries: "No, but I KNOW! I'll wager you
A day of music." Well, of course he lost;
And so until tomorrow they are mine,
My private orchestra. Pleasant at first,
But they become a trifle— [*To the* PAGES.] Here! Go play
A minuet to Montfluery—and tell him I sent you! [*The* PAGES *go up to the exit.* CYRANO *turns to the* DUENNA.] I came here as usual
To inquire after our friend—[*To* PAGES.] Play out of tune.
And keep on playing! [*The* PAGES *go out. He turns to the* DUENNA.] Our friend with the great soul.
ROXANE. [*Enters in time to hear the last words.*] He is beautiful and brilliant— and I love him!
CYRANO. Do you find Christian . . . intellectual?
ROXANE. More so than you, even.
CYRANO. I am glad.
ROXANE. No man
Ever so beautifully said those things—
Those pretty nothings that are everything.
Sometimes he falls into a reverie;
His inspiration fails—then all at once,
He will say something absolutely . . . Oh! . . .
CYRANO. Really!
ROXANE. How like a man! You think a man
Who has a handsome face must be a fool.
CYRANO. He talks well about . . . matters of the heart?
ROXANE. He does not *talk;* he rhapsodizes . . . dreams . . .
CYRANO. [*Twisting his mustache.*] He . . . writes well?
ROXANE. Wonderfully. Listen now: [*Reciting as from memory.*]
"Take my heart; I shall have it all the more;
Plucking the flowers, we keep the plant in bloom—"
Well?
CYRANO. Pooh!
ROXANE. And this: "Knowing you have in store
More heart to give than I to find heart-room—"
CYRANO. First he has too much, then too little; just
How much heart does he need?
ROXANE. [*Tapping her foot.*] You are teasing me!
You are jealous!
CYRANO. [*Startled.*] Jealous?
ROXANE. Of his poetry—
You poets are like that . . . And these last lines
Are they not the last word in tenderness?—
"There is no more to say: only believe
That unto you my whole heart gives one cry,
And writing, writes down more than you receive;
Sending you kisses through my fingertips—
Lady, O read my letter with your lips!"
CYRANO. H'm, yes—those last lines . . . but he overwrites!
ROXANE. Listen to this—
CYRANO. You know them all by heart?
ROXANE. Every one!
CYRANO. [*Twisting his mustache.*] I may call that flattering . . .

ROXANE. He is a master!
CYRANO. Oh—come!
ROXANE. Yes—a master!
CYRANO. [*Bowing.*] A master—if you will!
THE DUENNA. [*Comes downstage quickly.*] Monsieur de Guiche!—[*To* CYRANO, *pushing him toward the house.*]
Go inside—If he does not find you here,
It may be just as well. He may suspect—
ROXANE. —My secret! Yes; he is in love with me
And he is powerful. Let him not know—
One look would frost my roses before bloom.
CYRANO. [*Going into house.*] Very well, very well!
ROXANE. [*To* DE GUICHE, *as he enters.*] We were just going—
DE GUICHE. I came only to say farewell.
ROXANE. You leave Paris?
DE GUICHE. Yes—for the front.
ROXANE. Ah!
DE GUICHE. And tonight!
ROXANE. Ah!
DE GUICHE. We have orders to besiege Arras.
ROXANE. Arras?
DE GUICHE. Yes. My departure leaves you . . . cold?
ROXANE. [*Politely.*] Oh! Not that.
DE GUICHE. It has left me desolate—
When shall I see you? Ever? Did you know
I was made Colonel?
ROXANE. [*Indifferent.*] Bravo.
DE GUICHE. Regiment
Of the Guards.
ROXANE. [*Catching her breath.*] Of the Guards?—
DE GUICHE. His regiment
Your cousin, the mighty man of words!—[*Grimly.*] Down there
We may have an accounting!
ROXANE. [*Suffocating.*] Are you sure
The Guards are ordered?
DE GUICHE. Under my command!
ROXANE. [*Sinks down, breathless, on the bench; aside.*] Christian!—
DE GUICHE. What is it?
ROXANE. [*Losing control of herself.*] To the war—perhaps
Never again to—When a woman cares,
Is that nothing?
DE GUICHE. [*Surprised and delighted.*] You say this now—to me—
Now, at the very moment?—!
ROXANE. [*Recovers—changes her tone.*] Tell me something:
My cousin—You say you mean to be revenged
On him. Do you mean that?
DE GUICHE. [*Smiles.*] Why? Would you care?
ROXANE. Not for him.
DE GUICHE. Do you see him?
ROXANE. Now and then.
DE GUICHE. He goes about everywhere nowadays
With one of the Cadets—de Neuve—Neuville—
Neuvillers—
ROXANE. [*Coolly.*] A tall man?—
DE GUICHE. Blond—
ROXANE. Rosy cheeks?—
DE GUICHE. Handsome!—
ROXANE. Pooh!—
DE GUICHE. And a fool.
ROXANE. [*Languidly.*] So he appears . . . [*Animated.*]
But Cyrano? What will you do to him?
Order him into danger? He loves that!
I know what *I* should do.
DE GUICHE. What?
ROXANE. Leave him here
With his Cadets, while all the regiment
Goes on to glory! That would torture him—
To sit all through the war with folded arms—
I know his nature. If you hate that man,
Strike at his self-esteem.
DE GUICHE. Oh woman—woman!
Who but a woman would have thought of this?
ROXANE. He'll eat his heart out, while his Gascon friends
Bite their nails all day long in Paris here.
And you will be avenged!
DE GUICHE. You love me then,
A little? . . . [*She smiles.*] Making my enemies your own,
Hating them—I should like to see in that
A sign of love, Roxane.
ROXANE. Perhaps it is one . . .

DE GUICHE. [*Shows a number of folded dispatches.*] Here are the orders—for each company—
Ready to send . . . [*Selects one.*] So—
This is for the Guards—
I'll keep that. Aha, Cyrano! [*To* ROXANE.] You too,
You play your little games, do you?
ROXANE. [*Watching him.*] Sometimes . . .
DE GUICHE. [*Close to her, speaking hurriedly.*] And you!—Oh, I am mad over you!—Listen—
I leave tonight—but—let you through my hands
Now, when I feel you trembling?—Listen—Close by,
In the Rue d'Orléans, the Capuchins
Have their new convent. By their law, no layman
May pass inside those walls. I'll see to that—
Their sleeves are wide enough to cover me—
The servants of my Uncle-Cardinal
Will fear his nephew. So—I'll come to you
Masked, after everyone knows I have gone—Oh, let me wait one day!—
ROXANE. If this be known,
Your honor—
DE GUICHE. Bah!
ROXANE. The war—your duty—
DE GUICHE. [*Blows away an imaginary feather.*] Phoo!—
Only say yes!
ROXANE. No!
DE GUICHE. Whisper . . .
ROXANE. [*Tenderly.*] I ought not
To let you . . .
DE GUICHE. Ah! . . .
ROXANE. [*Pretends to break down.*] Ah, go!
[*Aside.*]—Christian remains—[*Aloud—heroically.*]
I must have you a hero—Antoine . . .
DE GUICHE. Heaven! . . .
So you can love—
ROXANE. One for whose sake I fear.
DE GUICHE. [*Triumphant.*] I go!
Will that content you?
[*Kisses her hand.*]
ROXANE. Yes—my friend! [*He goes out.*]
THE DUENNA. [*As* DE GUICHE *disappears, making a deep curtsy behind his back, and imitating* ROXANE's *intense tone.*] Yes—my friend!
ROXANE. [*Quickly, close to her.*] Not a word to Cyrano—
He would never forgive me if he knew
I stole his war! [*She calls toward the house.*] Cousin! [CYRANO *comes out of the house; she turns to him indicating the house opposite.*] We are going over—
Alcandre speaks tonight—and Lysimon.
THE DUENNA. [*Puts finger in her ear.*] My little finger says we shall not hear Everything.
CYRANO. Never mind me—
THE DUENNA. [*Across the street.*] Look—Oh, look!
The knocker tied up in a napkin—Yes,
They muzzled you because you bark too loud
And interrupt the lecture—little beast!
ROXANE. [*As the door opens.*] Enter . . .
[*To* CYRANO.] If Christian comes, tell him to wait.
CYRANO. Oh—[ROXANE *returns.*] When he comes, what will you talk about?
You always know beforehand.
ROXANE. About . . .
CYRANO. Well?
ROXANE. You will not tell him, will you?
CYRANO. I am dumb.
ROXANE. About nothing! Or about everything—
I shall say: "Speak of love in your own words—
Improvise! Rhapsodize! Be eloquent!"
CYRANO. [*Smiling.*] Good!
ROXANE. Sh!—
CYRANO. Sh!—
ROXANE. Not a word! [*She goes in; the door closes.*]
CYRANO. [*Bowing.*] Thank you so much—
ROXANE. [*Opens door and puts out her head.*] He must be unprepared—
CYRANO. Of course!
ROXANE. Sh!— [*Goes in again.*]
CYRANO. [*Calls.*] Christian! [CHRISTIAN *enters.*]
I have your theme—bring on your memory!—
Here is your chance now to surpass yourself,
No time to lose—come! Look intelligent—
Come home and learn your lines.
CHRISTIAN. No.
CYRANO. What?
CHRISTIAN. I'll wait

Here for Roxane.
CYRANO. What lunacy is this?
Come quickly!
CHRISTIAN. No, I say! I have had enough—
Taking my words, my letters, all from you—
Making our love a little comedy!
It was a game at first; but now—she cares . . .
Thanks to you. I am not afraid. I'll speak
For myself now.
CYRANO. Undoubtedly!
CHRISTIAN. I will!
Why not? I am no such fool—you shall see!
Besides—my dear friend—you have taught me much.
I ought to know something . . . By God, I know
Enough to take a woman in my arms!
[ROXANE *appears in the doorway, opposite.*]
There she is now . . . Cyrano, wait! Stay here!
CYRANO. [*Bows.*] Speak for yourself, my friend! [*He goes out.*]
ROXANE. [*Taking leave of the company.*]—
Barthénoide!
Alcandre! . . . Grémione! . . .
THE DUENNA. I told you so—
We missed the Tender Passion! [*She goes into* ROXANE'S *house.*]
ROXANE. Urimédonte!—
Adieu! [*As the guests disappear down the street, she turns to* CHRISTIAN.] Is that you, Christian? Let us stay
Here, in the twilight. They are gone. The air
Is fragrant. We shall be alone. Sit down
There—so . . . [*They sit on the bench.*]
Now tell me things.
CHRISTIAN. [*After a silence.*] I love you.
ROXANE. [*Closes her eyes.*] Yes,
Speak to me about love . . .
CHRISTIAN. I love you.
ROXANE. Now
Be eloquent! . . .
CHRISTIAN. I love—
ROXANE. [*Opens her eyes.*] You have your theme—
Improvise! Rhapsodize!
CHRISTIAN. I love you so!
ROXANE. Of course. And then? . . .
CHRISTIAN. And then . . . Oh, I should be
So happy if you loved me too! Roxane,
Say that you love me too!
ROXANE. [*Making a face.*] I ask for cream—
You give me milk and water. Tell me first
A little, how you love me.
CHRISTIAN. Very much.
ROXANE. Oh—tell me how you *feel!*
CHRISTIAN. [*Coming nearer, and devouring her with his eyes.*] Your throat . . . If only
I might . . . kiss it—
ROXANE. Christian!
CHRISTIAN. I love you so!
ROXANE. [*Makes as if to rise.*] Again?
CHRISTIAN. [*Desperately, restraining her.*]
No, not again—I do not love you—
ROXANE. [*Settles back.*] That is better . . .
CHRISTIAN. I adore you!
ROXANE. Oh!— [*Rises and moves away.*]
CHRISTIAN. I know;
I grow absurd.
ROXANE. [*Coldly.*] And that displeases me
As much as if you had grown ugly.
CHRISTIAN. I—
ROXANE. Gather your dreams together into words!
CHRISTIAN. I love—
ROXANE. I know; you love me. Adieu.
[*She goes to the house.*]
CHRISTIAN. No,
But wait—please—let me—I was going to say—
ROXANE. [*Pushes the door open.*] That you adore me. Yes; I know that too.
No! . . . Go away! . . . [*She goes in and shuts the door in his face.*]
CHRISTIAN. I . . . I . . .
CYRANO. [*Enters.*] A great success!
CHRISTIAN. Help me!
CYRANO. Not I.
CHRISTIAN. I cannot live unless
She loves me—now, this moment!
CYRANO. How the devil
Am I to teach you now—this moment?
CHRISTIAN. [*Catches him by the arm.*]—
Wait!—
Look! Up there!—Quick—[*The light shows in* ROXANE'S *window.*]
CYRANO. Her window—
CHRISTIAN. [*Wailing.*] I shall die!—
CYRANO. Less noise!
CHRISTIAN. Oh, I—

CYRANO. It does seem fairly dark—
CYRANO. [*Excitedly.*] Well?—Well?—Well?—
CYRANO. Let us try what can be done; It is more than you deserve—stand over there,
Idiot—there!—before the balcony—
Let me stand underneath. I'll whisper you
What to say.
CHRISTIAN. She may hear—she may—
CYRANO. Less noise! [*The* PAGES *appear upstage.*]
FIRST PAGE. Hep!—
CYRANO. [*Finger to lips.*] Sh!—
FIRST PAGE. [*Low voice.*] We serenaded Montfleury!—
What next?
CYRANO. Down to the corner of the street—
One this way—and the other over there—If anybody passes, play a tune!
PAGE. What tune, O musical Philosopher?
CYRANO. Sad for a man, or merry for a woman—
Now go! [*The* PAGES *disappear, one toward each corner of the street.*]
CYRANO. [*To* CHRISTIAN.] Call her!
CHRISTIAN. Roxane!
CYRANO. Wait . . . [*Gathers up a handful of pebbles.*] Gravel . . . [*Throws it at the window.*] There!—
ROXANE. [*Opens the window.*] Who is calling?
CHRISTIAN. I—
ROXANE. Who?
CHRISTIAN. Christian.
ROXANE. You again?
CHRISTIAN. I had to tell you—
CYRANO. [*Under the balcony.*] Good— Keep your voice down.
ROXANE. No. Go away. You tell me nothing.
CHRISTIAN. Please!—
ROXANE. You do not love me any more—
CHRISTIAN. [*To whom* CYRANO *whispers his words.*] No—no—
Not any more—I love you . . . evermore . . .
And ever . . . more and more!
ROXANE. [*About to close the window—pauses.*] A little better . . .
CHRISTIAN. [*Same business.*] Love grows
and struggles like . . . an angry child . . .
Breaking my heart . . . his cradle . . .
ROXANE. [*Coming out on the balcony.*] Better still—
But . . . such a babe is dangerous; why not
Have smothered it newborn?
CHRISTIAN. [*Same business.*] And so I do . . .
And yet he lives . . . I found . . . as you shall find . . .
This newborn babe . . . an infant . . . Hercules!
ROXANE. [*Further forward.*] Good!—
CHRISTIAN. [*Same business.*] Strong enough . . . at birth . . . to strangle those
Two serpents—Doubt and . . . Pride.
ROXANE. [*Leans over balcony.*] Why, very well!
Tell me now why you speak so haltingly—
Has your imagination gone lame?
CYRANO. [*Thrusts* CHRISTIAN *under the balcony, and stands in his place.*] Here— This grows too difficult!
ROXANE. Your words tonight
Hesitate. Why?
CYRANO. [*In a low tone, imitating* CHRISTIAN.] Through the warm summer gloom
They grope in darkness toward the light of you.
ROXANE. My words, well aimed, find you more readily.
CYRANO. My heart is open wide and waits for them—
Too large a mark to miss! My words fly home,
Heavy with honey like returning bees,
To your small secret ear. Moreover— yours
Fall to me swiftly. Mine more slowly rise.
ROXANE. Yet not so slowly as they did at first.
CYRANO. They have learned the way, and you have welcomed them.
ROXANE. [*Softly.*] Am I so far above you now?
CYRANO. So far—
If you let fall upon me one hard word,
Out of that height—you crush me!
ROXANE. [*Turns.*] I'll come down—
CYRANO. [*Quickly.*] No!

ROXANE. [*Points out the bench under the balcony.*] Stand you on the bench. Come nearer!
CYRANO. [*Recoils into the shadow.*] No!—
ROXANE. And why—so great a *No?*
CYRANO. [*More and more overcome by emotion.*] Let me enjoy
The one moment I ever—my one chance
To speak to you . . . unseen!
ROXANE. Unseen?—
CYRANO. Yes!—Yes . . .
Night, making all things dimly beautiful,
One veil over us both— You only see
The darkness of a long cloak in the gloom,
And I the whiteness of a summer gown—
You are all light— I am all shadow! . . . How
Can you know what this moment means to me?
If I was ever eloquent—
ROXANE. You were
Eloquent—
CYRANO. —You have never heard till now
My own heart speaking!
ROXANE. Why not?
CYRANO. Until now,
I spoke through . . .
ROXANE. Yes?—
CYRANO. —through that sweet drunkenness
You pour into the world out of your eyes!
But tonight . . . But tonight, I indeed speak
For the first time!
ROXANE. For the first time— Your voice, Even, is not the same.
CYRANO. [*Passionately; moves nearer.*] How should it be?
I have another voice—my own,
Myself, daring— [*He stops, confused; then tries to recover himself.*] Where was I?
. . . I forget! . . .
Forgive me. This is all sweet like a dream . . .
Strange—like a dream . . .
ROXANE. How, strange?
CYRANO. Is it not so
To be myself to you, and have no fear
Of moving you to laughter?
ROXANE. Laughter—why?
CYRANO. [*Struggling for an explanation.*] Because . . . What am I . . . What is any man,
That he dare ask for you? Therefore my heart
Hides behind phrases. There's a modesty
In these things too— I come here to pluck down
Out of the sky the evening star—then smile,
And stoop to gather little flowers.
ROXANE. Are they
Not sweet, those little flowers?
CYRANO. Not enough sweet
For you and me, tonight!
ROXANE. [*Breathless.*] You never spoke
To me like this . . .
CYRANO. Little things, pretty things—
Arrows and hearts and torches—roses red,
And violets blue—are these all? Come away,
And breathe fresh air! Must we keep on and on
Sipping stale honey out of tiny cups
Decorated with golden tracery,
Drop by drop, all day long? We are alive;
We thirst— Come away, plunge, and drink, and drown
In the great river flowing to the sea!
ROXANE. But . . . Poetry?
CYRANO. I have made rimes for you—
Not now— Shall we insult Nature, this night,
These flowers, this moment—shall we set all these
To phrases from a letter by Voiture?
Look once at the high stars that shine in heaven,
And put off artificiality!
Have you not seen great gaudy hothouse flowers,
Barren, without fragrance?—Souls are like that:
Forced to show all, they soon become all show—
The means to Nature's end ends meaningless!
ROXANE. But . . . Poetry?
CYRANO. Love hates that game of words!
It is a crime to fence with life— I tell you,
There comes one moment, once—and

God help those
Who pass that moment by!—when
  Beauty stands
Looking into the soul with grave, sweet
  eyes
That sicken at pretty words!
ROXANE. If that be true—
And when that moment comes to you
  and me—
What words will you? . . .
CYRANO. All those, all those, all those
That blossom in my heart, I'll fling to
  you—
Armfuls of loose bloom! Love, I love
  beyond
Breath, beyond reason, beyond love's
  own power
Of loving! Your name is like a golden
  bell
Hung in my heart; and when I think of
  you,
I tremble, and the bell swings and
  rings—"Roxane!" . . .
"Roxane!" . . . along my veins, "Rox-
  ane!" . . . I know
All small forgotten things that once
  meant You—
I remember last year, the First of May,
A little before noon, you had your hair
Drawn low, that one time only. Is that
  strange?
You know how, after looking at the sun,
One sees red spots everywhere—so, for
  hours
After the flood of sunshine that you
  are,
My eyes are blinded by your burning
  hair!
ROXANE. [*Very low.*] Yes . . . that is . . .
  Love—
CYRANO. Yes, that is Love—that wind
Of terrible and jealous beauty, blowing
Over me—that dark fire, that music . . .
  Yet
Love seeketh not his own! Dear, you
  may take
My happiness to make you happier,
Even though you never know I gave it
  you—
Only let me hear sometimes, all alone,
The distant laughter of your joy! . . . I
  never
Look at you, but there's some new vir-
  tue born
In me, some new courage. Do you
  begin
To understand, a little? Can you feel
My soul, there in the darkness, breathe
  on you?
—Oh, but tonight, now, I dare say
  these things—
I . . . to you . . . and you hear them!
  . . . It is too much!
In my most sweet unreasonable
  dreams,
I have not hoped for this! Now let me
  die,
Having lived. It is my voice, mine, my
  own,
That makes you tremble there in the
  green gloom
Above me—for you do tremble, as a
  blossom
Among the leaves— You tremble, and I
  can feel,
All the way down along these jasmine
  branches,
Whether you will or no, the passion of
  you
Trembling . . . [*He kisses wildly the end of
  a drooping spray of jasmine.*]
ROXANE. Yes, I do tremble . . . and I
  weep . . .
And I love you . . . and I am yours . . .
  and you
Have made me thus!
CYRANO. [*After a pause; quietly.*] What is
  death like, I wonder?
I know everything else now . . . I have
  done
This to you—I, myself . . . Only let me
Ask one thing more—
CHRISTIAN. [*Under the balcony.*] One kiss!
ROXANE. [*Startled.*] One?—
CYRANO. [*To* CHRISTIAN.] You! . . .
ROXANE. You ask me
For—
CYRANO. I . . . Yes, but—I mean— [*To*
  CHRISTIAN.] You go too far!
CHRISTIAN. She is willing!— Why not
  make the most of it?
CYRANO. [*To* ROXANE.] I did ask . . . but
  I know I ask too much . . .
ROXANE. Only one— Is that all?
CYRANO. All!—How much more
Than all!—I know—I frighten you—I
  ask . . .
I ask you to refuse—
CHRISTIAN. [*To* CYRANO.] But why?
  Why? Why?
CYRANO. Christian, be quiet!
ROXANE. [*Leaning over.*] What is that you

say
To yourself?
CYRANO. I am angry with myself
Because I go too far, and so I say
To myself: "Christian, be quiet!"— [*The theorbos begin to play.*] Hark—someone
Is coming— [ROXANE *closes her window.* CYRANO *listens to the theorbos, one of which plays a gay melody, the other a mournful one.*] A sad tune, a merry tune—
Man, woman—what do they mean?— [*A* CAPUCHIN *enters; he carries a lantern, and goes from house to house, looking at the doors.*] Aha!—a priest! [*To the* CAPUCHIN.]
What is this new game of Diogenes?
THE CAPUCHIN. I am looking for the house of Madame—
CHRISTIAN. [*Impatient.*] Bah!—
THE CAPUCHIN. Madeleine Robin—
CHRISTIAN. What does he want?
CYRANO. [*To the* CAPUCHIN; *points out a street.*] This way—
To the right—keep to the right—
THE CAPUCHIN. I thank you, sir!—
I'll say my beads for you to the last grain.
CYRANO. Good fortune, father, and my service to you! [*The* CAPUCHIN *goes out.*]
CHRISTIAN. Win me that kiss!
CYRANO. No.
CHRISTIAN. Sooner or later—
CYRANO. True . . .
That is true . . . Soon or late, it will be so
Because you are young and she is beautiful— [*To himself.*]
Since it must be, I had rather be myself [*The window re-opens.* CHRISTIAN *hides under the balcony.*]
The cause of . . . what must be.
ROXANE. [*Out on the balcony.*] Are you still there?
We were speaking of—
CYRANO. A kiss. The word is sweet—
What will the deed be? Are your lips afraid
Even of its burning name? Not much afraid—
Not too much! Have you not unwittingly
Laid aside laughter, slipping beyond speech
Insensibly, already, without fear,
From words to smiles . . . from smiles to sighs . . . from sighing,
Even to tears? One step more—only one—
From a tear to a kiss—one step, one thrill!
ROXANE. Hush—
CYRANO. And what is a kiss, when all is done?
A promise given under seal—a vow
Taken before the shrine of memory—
A signature acknowledged—a rosy dot
Over the i of Loving—a secret whispered
To listening lips apart—a moment made
Immortal, with a rush of wings unseen—
A sacrament of blossoms, a new song
Sung by two hearts to an old simple tune—
The ring of one horizon around two souls
Together, all alone!
ROXANE. Hush! . . .
CYRANO. Why, what shame?—
There was a Queen of France, not long ago,
And a great lord of England—a queen's gift.
A crown jewel!
ROXANE. Indeed!
CYRANO. Indeed, like him,
I have my sorrows and my silences;
Like her, you are the queen I dare adore;
Like him I am faithful and forlorn—
ROXANE. Like him,
Beautiful—
CYRANO. [*Aside.*] So I am—I forgot that!
ROXANE. Then— Come; . . . Gather your sacred blossom . . .
CYRANO. [*To* CHRISTIAN.] Go!—
ROXANE. Your crown jewel . . .
CYRANO. Go on!
ROXANE. Your old new song . . .
CYRANO. Climb!
CHRISTIAN. [*Hesitates.*] No— Would you?—not yet—
ROXANE. Your moment made Immortal . . .
CYRANO. [*Pushing him.*] Climb up, animal! [CHRISTIAN *springs on the bench, and climbs by the pillars, the branches, the vines, until he bestrides the balcony railing.*]

CHRISTIAN. Roxane! . . . [*He takes her in his arms and bends over her.*]
CYRANO. [*Very low.*] Ah! . . . Roxanne!
. . . I have won what I have won—
The feast of love—and I am Lazarus!
Yet . . . I have something here that is mine now
And was not mine before I spoke the words
That won her—not for me! . . . Kissing my words
My words, upon your lips! [*The theorbos begin to play.*] A merry tune—
A sad tune— So! The Capuchin! [*He pretends to be running, as if he had arrived from a distance; then calls up to the balcony.*] Hola!
ROXANE. Who is it?
CYRANO. I. Is Christian there with you?
CHRISTIAN. [*Astonished.*] Cyrano!
ROXANE. Good morrow, Cousin!
CYRANO. Cousin, . . . good morrow!
ROXANE. I am coming down. [*She disappears into the house. The* CAPUCHIN *enters upstage.*]
CHRISTIAN. [*Sees him.*] Oh—again!
THE CAPUCHIN. [*To* CYRANO.] She lives here,
Madeleine Robin!
CYRANO. You said RO-LIN.
THE CAPUCHIN. No—
R-O-B-I-N
ROXANE. [*Appears on the threshold of the house, followed by* RAGUENEAU *with a lantern, and by* CHRISTIAN.] What is it?
THE CAPUCHIN. A letter.
CHRISTIAN. Oh! . . .
THE CAPUCHIN. [*To* ROXANE.] Some matter profitable to the soul—
A very noble lord gave it to me!
ROXANE. [*To* CHRISTIAN.] De Guiche!
CHRISTIAN. He dares?—
ROXANE. It will not be for long;
When he learns that I love you . . . [*By the light of the latern which* RAGUENEAU *holds, she reads the letter in a low tone, as if to herself.*] "Mademoiselle
The drums are beating, and the regiment
Arms for the march. Secretly I remain
Here, in the Convent. I have disobeyed;
I shall be with you soon. I send this first
By an old monk, as simple as a sheep,
Who understands nothing of this. Your smile
Is more than I can bear, and seek no more.
Be along tonight, waiting for one who dares
To hope you will forgive . . . —" etcetera— [*To the* CAPUCHIN.]
Father, this letter concerns you . . . [*To* CHRISTIAN.] —and you.
Listen: [*The others gather around her. She pretends to read from the letter, aloud.*]
"Mademoiselle: The Cardinal
Will have his way, although against your will;
That is why I am sending this to you
By a most holy man, intelligent,
Discreet. You will communicate to him
Our order to perform, here and at once
The rite of . . . [*Turns the page.*] —Holy Matrimony. You
And Christian will be married privately
In your house. I have sent him to you. I know
You hesitate. Be resigned, nevertheless,
To the Cardinal's command, who sends herewith
His blessing. Be assured also of my own
Respect and high consideration—*signed,*
Your very humble and—etcetera—"
THE CAPUCHIN. A noble lord! I said so—never fear—
A worthy lord!—a very worthy lord!—
ROXANE. [*To* CHRISTIAN.] Am I a good reader of letters?
CHRISTIAN. [*Motions toward the* CAPUCHIN.] Careful!—
ROXANE. [*In a tragic tone.*] Oh, this is terrible!
THE CAPUCHIN. [*Turns the light on his lantern on* CYRANO.] You are to be—
CHRISTIAN. I am the bridegroom!
THE CAPUCHIN. [*Turns his lantern upon* CHRISTIAN; *then, as if some suspicion crossed his mind, upon seeing the young man so handsome.*] Oh—why, you . . .
ROXANE. [*Quickly.*] Look here—
"Postscript: Give to the Convent in my name
One hundred and twenty pistoles"—
THE CAPUCHIN. Think of it!
A worthy lord—a worthy lord! . . . [*To* ROXANE, *solemnly.*]
Daughter, resign yourself!
ROXANE. [*With an air of martyrdom.*] I am resigned . . . [*While* RAGUENEAU *opens*

the door for the CAPUCHIN *and* CHRISTIAN *invites him to enter, she turns to* CYRANO.]
De Guiche may come. Keep him out here with you
Do not let him—
CYRANO. I understand! [*To the* CAPUCHIN.] How long
Will you be?—
THE CAPUCHIN. Oh, a quarter of an hour.
CYRANO. [*Hurrying them into the house.*] Hurry—I'll wait here—
ROXANE. [*To* CHRISTIAN.] Come! [*They go into the house.*]
CYRANO. Now then, to make
His Grace delay that quarter of an hour . . .
I have it!—up here— [*He steps on the bench, and climbs up the wall toward the balcony. The theorbos begin to play a mournful melody.*] Sad music— Ah, a man! . . . [*The music pauses on a sinister tremolo.*]
Oh—very much a man! [*He sits astride of the railing and, drawing toward him a long branch of one of the trees which border the garden wall, he grasps it with both hands, ready to swing himself down.*] So—not too high— [*He peers down at the ground.*]
I must float gently through the atmosphere—
DE GUICHE. [*Enters, masked, groping in the dark toward the house.*] Where is that cursed, bleating Capuchin?
CYRANO. What if he knows my voice?— the devil!—Tic-tac,
Bergerac—we unlock our Gascon tongue;
A good strong accent—
DE GUICHE. Here is the house—all dark—Damn this mask!— [*As he is about to enter the house,* CYRANO *leaps from the balcony, still holding fast to the branch, which bends and swings him between* DE GUICHE *and the door; then he releases the branch and pretends to fall heavily as though from a height. He lands flatly on the ground, where he lies motionless, as if stunned.* DE GUICHE *leaps back.*] What is that? [*When he lifts his eyes, the branch has sprung back into place. He can see nothing but the sky; he does not understand.*] Why . . . where did this man
Fall from?
CYRANO. [*Sits up, and speaks with a strong accent.*] —The moon!
DE GUICHE. You—
CYRANO. From the moon, the moon! I fell out of the moon!
DE GUICHE. The fellow is mad—
CYRANO. [*Dreamily.*] Where am I?
DE GUICHE. Why—
CYRANO. What time is it? What place
Is this? What day? What season?
DE GUICHE. You—
CYRANO. I am stunned!
DE GUICHE. My dear sir—
CYRANO. Like a bomb—a bomb—I fell
From the moon!
DE GUICHE. Now, see here—
CYRANO. [*Rising to his feet, and speaking in a terrible voice.*] I say, the moon!
DE GUICHE. [*recoils.*] Very well—if you say so— [*Aside.*] Raving mad!—
CYRANO. [*Advancing upon him.*] I am not speaking metaphorically!
DE GUICHE. Pardon.
CYRANO. A hundred years—an hour ago—
I really cannot say how long I fell—
I was in yonder shining sphere—
DE GUICHE. [*Shrugs.*] Quite so.
Please let me pass.
CYRANO. [*Interposes himself.*] Where am I? Tell the truth—
I can bear it. In what quarter of the globe
Have I descended like a meteorite?
DE GUICHE. Morbleu!
CYRANO. I could not choose my place to fall—
The earth spun round so fast— Was it the Earth,
I wonder?—Or is this another world?
Another moon? Whither have I been drawn
By the dead weight of my posterior?
DE GUICHE. Sir, I repeat—
CYRANO. [*With a sudden cry, which causes* DE GUICHE *to recoil again.*] His face! My God—black!
DE GUICHE. [*Carries his hand to his mask.*] Oh!—
CYRANO. [*Terrified.*] Are you a native? Is this Africa?
DE GUICHE. —This mask!
CYRANO. [*Somewhat reassured.*] Are we in Venice? Genoa?
DE GUICHE. [*Tries to pass him.*] A lady is

CYRANO. [*Quite happy again.*] So this is Paris!
DE GUICHE. [*Smiling in spite of himself.*] This fool becomes amusing.
CYRANO. Ah! You smile?
DE GUICHE. I do. Kindly permit me—
CYRANO. [*Delighted.*] Dear old Paris— Well, well!— [*Wholly at his ease, smiles, bows, arranges his dress.*] Excuse my appearance. I arrive
By the last thunderbolt—a trifle singed
As I came through the ether. These long journeys—
You know! There are so few conveniences!
My eyes are full of star-dust. On my spurs,
Some sort of fur . . . Planet's apparently . . . [*Plucks something from his sleeve.*]
Look—on my doublet—That's a Comet's hair! [*He blows something from the back of his hand.*]
Phoo!
DE GUICHE. [*Grows angry.*] Monsieur—
CYRANO. [*As DE GUICHE is about to push past, thrusts his leg in the way.*] Here's a tooth, stuck in my boot,
From the Great Bear. Trying to get away,
I tripped over the Scorpion and came down
Slap, into one scale of the Balances—
The pointer marks my weight this moment . . . [*Pointing upward.*] See? [DE GUICHE *makes a sudden movement.* CYRANO *catches his arm.*]
Be careful, If you struck me on the nose,
It would drip milk!
DE GUICHE. Milk?
CYRANO. From the Milky Way!
DE GUICHE. Hell!
CYRANO. No, no—Heaven. [*Crossing his arms.*] Curious place up there—
Did you know Sirius wore a nightcap? True! [*Confidentially.*]
The Little Bear is still too young to bite. [*Laughing.*]
My foot caught in the Lyre, and broke a string. [*Proudly.*]
Well—when I write my book, and tell the tale
Of my adventures—all these little stars
That shake out of my cloak—I must save those
To use for asterisks!
DE GUICHE. That will do now— I wish—
CYRANO. Yes, yes—I know—
DE GUICHE. Sir—
CYRANO. You desire
To learn from my own lips the character
Of the moon's surface—its inhabitants If any—
DE GUICHE. [*Loses patience and shouts.*] I desire no such thing! I—
CYRANO. [*Rapidly.*] You wish to know by what mysterious means
I reached the moon?—well—confidentially—
It was a new invention of my own.
DE GUICHE. [*Discouraged.*] Drunk too— as well as mad!
CYRANO. I scorned the eagle
Of Regiomontanus, and the dove
Of Archytas!
DE GUICHE. A learned lunatic!
CYRANO. I imitated no one. I myself
Discovered not one scheme merely, but six—
Six ways to violate the virgin sky! [DE GUICHE *has succeeded in passing him, and moves toward the door of* ROXANE'S *house.* CYRANO *follows, ready to use violence if necessary.*]
DE GUICHE. [*Looks around.*] Six?
CYRANO. [*With increasing volubility.*] As for instance—Having stripped myself
Bare as a wax candle, adorn my form
With crystal vials filled with morning dew,
And so be drawn aloft, as the sun rises
Drinking the mist of dawn!
DE GUICHE. [*Takes a step toward* CYRANO.] Yes—that makes one.
CYRANO. [*Draws back to lead him away from the door; speaks faster and faster.*]
Or, sealing up the air in the cedar chest,
Rarefy it by means of mirrors, placed
In an icosahedron.
DE GUICHE. [*Takes another step.*] Two.
CYRANO. [*Still retreating.*] Again,
I might construct a rocket, in the form
Of a huge locust, driven by impulses
Of villainous saltpeter from the rear,
Upward, by leaps and bounds.
DE GUICHE. [*Interested in spite of himself, and counting on his fingers.*] Three.

CYRANO. [*Same business.*] Or again,
Smoke having a natural tendency to rise,
Blow in a globe enough to raise me.
DE GUICHE. [*Same business, more and more astonished.*] Four!
CYRANO. Or since Diana, as old fables tell,
Draws forth to fill her crescent horn, the marrow
Of bulls and goats—to anoint myself therewith.
DE GUICHE. [*Hypnotized.*] Five!—
CYRANO. [*Has by this time led him all the way across the street, close to a bench.*]
Finally—seated on an iron plate,
To hurl a magnet in the air—the iron
Follows—I catch the magnet—throw again—
And so proceed indefinitely.
DE GUICHE. Six!—
All excellent,—and which did you adopt?
CYRANO. [*Coolly.*] Why, none of them . . . A seventh.
DE GUICHE. Which was?—
CYRANO. Guess!—
DE GUICHE. An interesting idiot, this!
CYRANO. [*Imitates the sound of waves with his voice, and their movement by large, vague gestures.*] Hoo! . . . Hoo! . . .
DE GUICHE. Well?
CYRANO. Have you guessed it yet?
DE GUICHE. Why, no.
CYRANO. [*Grandiloquent.*] The ocean! . . .
What hour its rising tide seeks the full moon,
I laid me on the strand, fresh from the spray,
My head fronting the moonbeams, since the hair
Retains moisture—and so I slowly rose
As upon angels' wings, effortlessly,
Upward—then suddenly I felt a shock!—And then . . .
DE GUICHE. [*Overcome by curiosity, sits down on the bench.*] And then?
CYRANO. And then— [*Changes abruptly to his natural voice.*] The time is up!—
Fifteen minutes, your Grace!—You are now free;
And—they are bound—in wedlock.
DE GUICHE. [*Leaping up.*] Am *I* drunk?
That voice . . . [*The door of* ROXANE'S *house opens; lackeys appear, bearing lighted candles. Lights up.* CYRANO *removes his hat.*] And that nose!—
Cyrano!
CYRANO. [*Saluting.*] Cyrano! . . .
This very moment, they have exchanged rings.
DE GUICHE. Who? [*He turns upstage. Tableau. Between the lackeys,* ROXANE *and* CHRISTIAN *appear, hand in hand. The* CAPUCHIN *follows them, smiling.* RAGUENEAU *holds aloft a torch. The* DUENNA *brings up the rear, in a negligée, and a pleasant flutter of emotion.*]
Zounds! [*To* ROXANE.] You?—
[*Recognizes* CHRISTIAN.] He?—
[*Saluting* ROXANE.] My sincere compliments! [*To* CYRANO.]
You also, my inventor of machines!
Your rigmarole would have detained a saint
Entering Paradise—decidedly
You must not fail to write that book some day!
CYRANO. [*Bowing.*] Sir, I engage myself to do so. [*Leads the bridal pair down to* DE GUICHE *and strokes, with great satisfaction his long white beard.*] My lord,
The handsome couple you—and God—have joined
Together!
DE GUICHE. [*Regarding him with a frosty eye.*] Quite so. [*Turns to* ROXANE.]
Madame, kindly bid
Your . . . husband farewell.
ROXANE. Oh!—
DE GUICHE. [*To* CHRISTIAN.] Your regiment
Leaves tonight, sir. Report at once!
ROXANE. You mean
For the front? The war?
DE GUICHE. Certainly!
ROXANE. I thought
The Cadets were not going—
DE GUICHE. Oh yes, they are!— [*Taking out the dispatch from his pocket.*]
Here is the order— [*To* CHRISTIAN.]
Baron! Deliver this.
ROXANE. [*Throws herself into* CHRISTIAN'S *arms.*] Christian!
DE GUICHE. [*To* CYRANO, *sneering.*] The bridal night is not so near!
CYRANO. [*Aside*] Somehow that news fails to disquiet me.
CHRISTIAN. [*To* ROXANE.] Your lips again . . .
CYRANO. There . . . That will do now—

Come!
CHRISTIAN. [*Still holding* ROXANE.] You do not know how hard it is—
CYRANO. [*Tries to drag him away.*] I know! [*The beating of drums is heard in the distance.*]
DE GUICHE. [*Upstage.*] The regiment—on the march!
ROXANE. [*As* CYRANO *tries to lead* CHRISTIAN *away, follows, and detains them.*] Take care of him
For me— [*Appealingly.*] Promise me never to let him do
Anything dangerous!
CYRANO. I'll do my best—
I cannot promise—
ROXANE. [*Same business.*] Make him be careful!
CYRANO. Yes—
I'll try—
ROXANE. [*Same business.*] Be sure to keep him dry and warm!
CYRANO. Yes, yes—if possible—
ROXANE. [*Same business; confidentially, in his ear.*] See that he remains
Faithful!—
CYRANO. Of course! If—
ROXANE. [*Same business.*] And have him write to me
Every single day!
CYRANO. [*Stops.*] That, I promise you!

Act 4

The Cadets of Gascoyne

The post occupied by the Company of CARBON DE CASTEL-JALOUX *at the siege of Arras.*

In the background, a rampart traversing the entire scene; beyond this, and apparently below, a plain stretches away to the horizon. The country is cut up with earthworks and other suggestions of the siege. In the distance, against the skyline, the houses and the walls of Arras.

Tents; scattered weapons; drums, et cetera. It is near daybreak, and the east is yellow with approaching dawn. SENTRIES *at intervals. Camp-fires.*

Curtain rise discovers the cadets asleep, rolled in their cloaks. CARBON DE CASTEL-JALOUX *and* LE BRET *keep watch. They are both very thin and pale.* CHRISTIAN *is asleep among the others, wrapped in his cloak, in the foreground, his face lighted by the flickering fire. Silence.*

LE BRET. Horrible!
CARBON. Why, yes. All of that.
LE BRET. Mordious!
CARBON. [*Gesture toward the sleeping* CADETS.] Swear gently—You might wake them. [*To* CADETS.] Go to sleep—
Hush! [*To* LE BRET.] Who sleeps dines.
LE BRET. I have insomnia.
God! What a famine. [*Firing offstage.*]
CARBON. Curse that musketry!
They'll wake my babies. [*To the men.*] Go to sleep!—
A CADET. [*Rouses.*] Diantre!
Again?
CARBON. No—only Cyrano coming home. [*The heads which have been raised sink back again.*]
A SENTRY. [*Offstage.*] Halt! Who goes there?
VOICE OF CYRANO. Bergerac!
THE SENTRY ON THE PARAPET. Halt! Who goes!—
CYRANO. [*Appears on the parapet.*] Bergerac, idiot!
LE BRET. [*Goes to meet him.*] Thank God again!
CYRANO. [*Signs to him not to wake anyone.*] Hush!
LE BRET. Wounded?—
CYRANO. No—They always miss me—quite
A habit by this time!
LE BRET. Yes—Go right on—
Risk your life every morning before breakfast
To send a letter!
CYRANO. [*Stops near* CHRISTIAN.] I promised he should write
Every single day . . . [*Looks down at him.*] Hm— The boy looks pale
When he is asleep—thin too—starving to death—
If that poor child knew! Handsome, none the less . . .
LE BRET. Go and get some sleep!
CYRANO. [*Affectionately.*] Now, now—you old bear,
No growling!—I am careful—you know I am—

Every night, when I cross the Spanish
  lines
I wait till they are all drunk.
LE BRET. You might bring
Something with you.
CYRANO. I have to travel light
To pass through—By the way, there will
  be news
For you today: the French will eat or
  die,
If what I saw means anything.
LE BRET. Tell us!
CYRANO. No—
I am not sure—we shall see!
CARBON. What a war,
When the besieger starves to death!
LE BRET. Fine war—
Fine situation! We besiege Arras—
The Cardinal Prince of Spain besieges
  us—
And—here we are!
CYRANO. Someone might besiege *him*.
CARBON. A hungry joke!
CYRANO. Ho, ho!
LE BRET. Yes, you can laugh—
Risking a life like yours to carry let-
  ters—
Where are you going now?
CYRANO. [*At the tent door.*] To write an-
  other. [*Goes into tent. A little more
  daylight. The clouds redden. The town of
  Arras shows on the horizon. A cannon
  shot is heard, followed immediately by a
  roll of drums, far away to the left. Other
  drums beat a little nearer. The drums go
  on answering each other here and there,
  approach, beat loudly almost on the stage,
  and die away toward the right, across the
  camp. The camp awakes. Voices of officers
  in the distance.*]
CARBON. [*Sighs.*] Those drums! another
  good nourishing sleep
Gone to the devil. [*The* CADETS *rouse
  themselves.*] Now then!—
FIRST CADET. [*Sits up, yawns.*] God! I'm
  hungry!
SECOND CADET. Starving!
ALL. [*Groan.*] Aoh!
CARBON. Up with you!
THIRD CADET. Not another step!
FOURTH CADET. Not another move-
  ment!
FIRST CADET. Look at my tongue—
I said this air was indigestible!
FIFTH CADET. My coronet for a half a
  pound of cheese!
SIXTH CADET. I have no stomach for this
  war—I'll stay
In my tent—like Achilles.
ANOTHER. Yes—no bread,
No fighting—
CARBON. Cyrano!
OTHERS. May as well die—
CARBON. Come out here!—You know
  how to talk to them.
Get them laughing—
SECOND CADET. [*Rushes up to* FIRST CA-
  DET *who is eating something.*] What are
  you gnawing there!
FIRST CADET. Gun wads and axle-
  grease. Fat country this
Around Arras.
ANOTHER. [*Enters.*] I have been out
  hunting!
ANOTHER. [*Enters.*] Went fishing, in the
  Scarpe!
ALL. [*Leaping up and surrounding the new-
  comers.*] Find anything?
Any fish? Any game? Perch? Par-
  tridges?
Let me look!
THE FISHERMAN. Yes—one gudgeon.
  [*Shows it.*]
THE HUNTER. One fat . . . sparrow.
  [*Shows it.*]
ALL. Ah!—See here, this—mutiny!—
CARBON. Cyrano!
Come and help!
CYRANO. [*Enters from tent.*] Well? [*Silence.
  To the* FIRST CADET *who is walking
  away, with his chin on his chest.*] You
  there, with the long face?
FIRST CADET. I have something on my
  mind that troubles me.
CYRANO. What is that?
FIRST CADET. My stomach.
CYRANO. So have I.
FIRST CADET. No doubt
You enjoy this!
CYRANO. [*Tightens his belt.*] It keeps me
  looking young.
SECOND CADET. My teeth are growing
  rusty.
CYRANO. Sharpen them!
THIRD CADET. My belly sounds as hol-
  low as a drum.
CYRANO. Beat the long roll on it!
FOURTH CADET. My ears are ringing.
CYRANO. Liar! A hungry belly has no
  ears.
FIFTH CADET. Oh for a barrel of good
  wine!

CYRANO. [*Offers him his own helmet.*] Your casque.
SIXTH CADET. I'll swallow anything!
CYRANO. [*Throws him the book which he has in his hand.*] Try the "Iliad."
SEVENTH CADET. The Cardinal, he has four meals a day—
What does he care!
CYRANO. Ask him; he really ought
To send you . . . a spring lamb out of his flock,
Roasted whole—
THE CADET. Yes, and a bottle—
CYRANO. [*Exaggerates the manner of one speaking to a servant.*] If you please, Richelieu—a little more of the Red Seal . . .
Ah, thank you!
THE CADET. And the salad—
CYRANO. Of course—Romaine!
ANOTHER CADET. [*Shivering.*] I am as hungry as a wolf.
CYRANO. [*Tosses him a cloak.*] Put on Your sheep's clothing.
FIRST CADET. [*With a shrug.*] Always the clever answer!
CYRANO. Always the answer—yes! Let me die so—
Under some rosy-golden sunset, saying
A good thing, for a good cause! By the sword,
The point of honor—by the hand of one
Worthy to be my foeman, let me fall—
Steel in my heart, and laughter on my lips!
VOICES HERE AND THERE. All very well—
We are hungry!
CYRANO. Bah! You think
Of nothing but yourselves. [*His eye singles out the old* FIFER *in the background.*]
Here, Bertrandou,
You were a shepherd once—Your pipe now! Come,
Breathe, blow,—Play to these belly-worshippers
The old airs of the South—"Airs with a smile in them,
Airs with a sigh in them, airs with the breeze
And the blue of the sky in them—"
Small, demure tunes
Whose every note is like a little sister—
Songs heard only in some long silent voice
Not quite forgotten—Mountain melodies
Like thin smoke rising from brown cottages
In the still noon, slowly—Quaint lullabies,
Whose very music has a Southern tongue—[*The* OLD MAN *sits down and prepares his fife.*]
Now let the fife, that dry old warrior,
Dream, while over the stops your fingers dance
A minuet of little birds—let him
Dream beyond ebony and ivory;
Let him remember he was once a reed
Out of the river, and recall the spirit
Of innocent, untroubled country days
. . . [*The* FIFER *begins to play a Provençal melody.*]
Listen, you Gascons! Now it is no more
The shrill fife—It is the flute, through woodlands far
Away, calling—no longer the hot battle-cry,
But the cool, quiet pipe our goatherds play!
Listen—the forest glens . . . the hills . . . the downs . . .
The green sweetness of night on the Dordogne . . .
Listen, you Gascons! It is all Gascoyne! . . . [*Every head is bowed; every eye cast down. Here and there a tear is furtively brushed away with the back of a hand, the corner of a cloak.*]
CARBON. [*Softly to* CYRANO.] You make them weep—
CYRANO. For homesickness—a hunger
More noble than that hunger of the flesh;
It is their hearts now that are starving.
CARBON. Yes,
But you melt down their manhood.
CYRANO. [*Motions the* DRUMMER *to approach.*] You think so?
Let them be. There is iron in their blood
Not easily dissolved in tears. You need
Only—[*He makes a gesture; the drum beats.*]
ALL. [*Spring up and rush toward their weapons.*] What's that? Where is it?—What?—
CYRANO. [*Smiles.*] You see—
Let Mars snore in his sleep once—and farewell
Venus—sweet dreams—regrets—dear

thoughts of home—
All the fife lulls to rest wakes at the drums!
A CADET. [*Looks upstage.*] Aha—Monsieur de Guiche!
THE CADETS. [*Mutter among themselves.*] Ugh! . . .
CYRANO. [*Smiles.*] Flattering Murmur!
A CADET. He makes me weary!
ANOTHER. With his collar
Of lace over his corselet—
ANOTHER. Like a ribbon
Tied round a sword!
ANOTHER. Bandages for a boil
On the back of his neck—
SECOND CADET. A courtier always!
ANOTHER. The Cardinal's nephew!
CARBON. None the less—a Gascon.
FIRST CADET. A counterfeit! Never you trust that man—
Because we Gascons, look you, are all mad—
This fellow is reasonable—nothing more
Dangerous than a reasonable Gascon!
LE BRET. He looks pale.
ANOTHER. Oh, he can be hungry too,
Like any other poor devil—but he wears
So many jewels on that belt of his
That his cramps glitter in the sun!
CYRANO. [*Quickly.*] Is he
To see us looking miserable? Quick—
Pipes!—Cards!—Dice!— [*They all hurriedly begin to play, on their stools, on the drums, or on their cloaks spread on the ground, lighting their long pipes meanwhile.*] As for me, I read Descartes.
[*He walks up and down, reading a small book which he takes from his pocket.* TABLEAU: DE GUICHE *enters, looking pale and haggard. All are absorbed in their games. General air of contentment.* DE GUICHE *goes to* CARBON. *They look at each other askance, each observing with satisfaction the condition of the other.*]
DE GUICHE. Good morning! [*Aside.*] He looks yellow.
CARBON. [*Same business.*] He is all eyes.
DE GUICHE. [*Looks at the* CADETS.] What have we here? Black looks? Yes, gentlemen—
I am informed I am not popular;
The hill-nobility, barons of Béarn,
The pomp and pride of Périgord—I learn
They disapprove their colonel; call him courtier,
Politician—they take it ill that I
Cover my steel with lace of Genoa.
It is a great offense to be a Gascon
And not to be a beggar! [*Silence. They smoke. They play.*] Well—Shall I have
Your captain punish you? . . . No.
CARBON. As to that,
It would be impossible.
DE GUICHE. Oh?
CARBON. I am free;
I pay my company; it is my own;
I obey military orders.
DE GUICHE. Oh!
That will be quite enough. [*To the* CADETS.] I can afford
Your little hates. My conduct under fire
Is well known. It was only yesterday
I drove the Count de Bucquoi from Bapaume,
Pouring my men down like an avalanche,
I myself led the charge—
CYRANO. [*Without looking up from his book.*] And your white scarf?
DE GUICHE. [*Surprised and gratified.*] You heard that episode? Yes—rallying
My men for the third time, I found myself
Carried among a crowd of fugitives
Into the enemy's lines. I was in danger
Of being shot or captured: but I thought
Quickly—took off and flung away the scarf
That marked my military rank—and so
Being inconspicuous, escaped among
My own force, rallied them, returned again
And won the day! . . . [*The* CADETS *do not appear to be listening, but here and there the cards and the dice boxes remain motionless, the smoke is retained in their cheeks.*] What do you say to that?
Presence of mind—yes?
CYRANO. Henry of Navarre
Being outnumbered, never flung away
His white plume. [*Silent enjoyment. The cards flutter, the dice roll, the smoke puffs out.*]
DE GUICHE. My device was a success,
However! [*Same attentive pause, interrupting the games and the smoking.*]
CYRANO. Possibly . . . An officer

Does not lightly resign the privilege
Of being a target. [*Cards, dice, and smoke
fall, roll, and float away with increasing
satisfaction.*] Now, if I had been
there—
Your courage and my own differ in
this—
When your scarf fell, I should have put
it on.
DE GUICHE. Boasting again!
CYRANO. Boasting? Lend it to me
Tonight; I'll lead the first charge, with
your scarf
Over my shoulder!
DE GUICHE. Gasconnade once more!
You are safe making that offer, and you
know it—
My scarf lies on the river bank between
The lines, a spot swept by artillery
Impossible to reach alive!
CYRANO. [*Produces the scarf from his
pocket.*] Yes. Here . . . [*Silence. The
CADETS stifle their laughter behind their
cards and their dice boxes.* DE GUICHE
*turns to look at them. Immediately they
resume their gravity and their game. One
of them whistles carelessly the mountain
air which the* FIFER *was playing.*]
DE GUICHE. [*Takes the scarf.*] Thank you!
That bit of white is what I need
To make a signal. I was hesitating—
You have decided me. [*He goes up to the
parapet, climbs upon it, and waves the
scarf at arm's length several times.*]
ALL. What is he doing?—
What?—
THE SENTRY ON THE PARAPET. There's a
man down there running away!
DE GUICHE. [*Descending.*] A Spaniard.
Very useful as a spy
To both sides. He informs the enemy
As I instruct him. By his influence
I can arrange their dispositions.
CYRANO. Traitor!
DE GUICHE. [*Folding the scarf.*] A traitor,
yes; but useful . . . We were saying?
Oh, yes—Here is a bit of news for you:
Last night we had hopes of reprovisioning
The army. Under cover of the dark,
The Marshall moved to Dourlens. Our
supplies
Are there. He may reach them. But to
return
Safely, he needs a large force—at least
half

Our entire strength. At present, we
have here
Merely a skeleton.
CARBON. Fortunately,
The Spaniards do not know that.
DE GUICHE. Oh, yes; they know.
They will attack.
CARBON. Ah!
DE GUICHE. From that spy of mine
I learned of their intention. His report
Will determine the point of their advance.
The fellow asked me what to say! I told
him:
"Go out between the lines; watch for
my signal;
Where you see that, let them attack
there."
CARBON. [*To the* CADETS.] Well.
Gentlemen! [*All rise. Noise of sword belts
and breastplates being buckled on.*]
DE GUICHE. You may have perhaps an
hour.
FRIST CADET. Oh—An hour! [*They all sit
down and resume their games once more.*]
DE GUICHE. [*To* CARBON.] The great
thing is to gain time.
Any moment the Marshall may return.
CARBON. And to gain time?
DE GUICHE. You will all be so kind
As to lay down your lives!
CYRANO. Ah! Your revenge?
DE GUICHE. I make no great pretence of
loving you!
But—since you gentlemen esteem
yourselves
Invincible, the bravest of the brave,
And at that—why need we be personal?
I serve the king in choosing . . . as I
choose!
CYRANO. [*Salutes.*] Sir, permit me to offer—all our thanks.
DE GUICHE. [*Returns the salute.*] You love
to fight a hundred against one;
Here is your opportunity! [*He goes upstage with* CARBON.]
CYRANO. [*To the* CADETS.] My friends,
We shall add now to our old Gascon
arms
With their six chevrons, blue and gold,
a seventh—
Blood-red! [DE GUICHE *talks in a low tone
to* CARBON *upstage. Orders are given.
The defense is arranged.* CYRANO *goes to*
CHRISTIAN *who has remained motionless
with folded arms.*] Christian?

[*Lays a hand on his shoulder.*]
CHRISTIAN. [*Shakes his head.*] Roxane . . .
CYRANO. Yes.
CHRISTIAN. I should like
To say farewell to her, with my whole heart
Written for her to keep.
CYRANO. I thought of that—[*Takes a letter from his doublet.*]
I have written your farewell.
CHRISTIAN. Show me!
CYRANO. You wish
To read it?
CHRISTIAN. Of course! [*He takes the letter; begins to read, looks up suddenly.*] What?—
CYRANO. What is it?
CHRISTIAN. Look—
This little circle—
CYRANO. [*Takes back the letter quickly, and looks innocent.*] Circle?—
CHRISTIAN. Yes—a tear!
CYRANO. So it is! . . . Well—a poet while he writes
Is like a lover in his lady's arms,
Believing his imagination—all
Seems true—you understand? There's half the charm
Of writing—Now, this letter as you see
I have made so pathetic that I wept
While I was writing it!
CHRISTIAN. You—wept?
CYRANO. Why, yes—
Because . . . it is a little thing to die,
But—not to see her . . . that is terrible!
And I shall never—[CHRISTIAN *looks at him.*] We shall never—[*Quickly.*] You Will never—
CHRISTIAN. [*Snatches the letter.*] Give me that! [*Noise in the distance on the outskirts of the camp.*]
VOICE OF A SENTRY. Halt—who goes there?
[*Shots, shouting, jingle of harness.*]
CARBON. What is it?
THE SENTRY ON THE PARAPET. Why, a coach. [*The rush to look.*]
CONFUSED VOICES. What? In the Camp?
A coach? Coming this way—It must have driven
Through the Spanish lines—what the devil—Fire!—
No—Hark! The driver shouting—what does he say?
Wait—He said: "On the service of the King!" [*They are all on the parapet looking over. The jingling comes nearer.*]
DE GUICHE. Of the King? [*They come down and fall into line.*]
CARBON. Hats off, all!
DE GUICHE. [*Speaks offstage.*] The King! Fall in,
Rascals!—[*The coach enters at full trot. It is covered with mud and dust. The curtains are drawn. Two footmen are seated behind. It stops suddenly.*]
CARBON. [*Shouts.*] Beat the assembly—
[*Roll of drums. All the* CADETS *uncover.*]
DE GUICHE. Two of you,
Lower the steps—open the door—[*Two men rush to the coach. The door opens.*]
ROXANE. [*Comes out of the coach.*] Good Morning! [*At the sound of a woman's voice, every head is raised. Sensation.*]
DE GUICHE. On the King's service—You?
ROXANE. Yes—my own king—
Love!
CYRANO. [*Aside.*] God is merciful . . .
CHRISTIAN. [*Hastens to her.*] You! Why have you—
ROXANE. Your war lasted so long!
CHRISTIAN. But why?!
ROXANE. Not now—
CYRANO. [*Aside.*] I wonder if I dare to look at her . . .
DE GUICHE. You cannot remain here!
ROXANE. Why, certainly!
Roll that drum here, somebody . . . [*She sits on the drum, which is brought to her.*]
Thank you—There! [*She laughs.*]
Would you belive—they fired upon us?—My coach
Looks like the pumpkin in the fairy tale,
Does it not? And my footmen—[*She throws a kiss to* CHRISTIAN.] How do you do? [*She looks about.*]
How serious you all are! Do you know,
It is a long drive here—from Arras?
[*See* CYRANO.] Cousin,
I am glad to see you!
CYRANO. [*Advances.*] Oh—How did you come?
ROXANE. How did I find you? Very easily—
I followed where the country was laid waste
—Oh, but I saw such things! I had to see
To believe. Gentlemen, is that the service
Of your King? I prefer my own!

CYRANO. But how
Did you come through?
ROXANE. Why, through the Spanish lines
Of course!
FIRST CADET. They let you pass?—
DE GUICHE. What did you say?
How did you manage?
LE BRET. Yes, that must have been
Difficult!
ROXANE. No—I simply drove along.
Now and then some hidalgo scowled at me
And I smiled back—my best smile; whereupon,
The Spaniards being (without prejudice
To the French) the most polished gentlemen
In the world—I passed!
CARBON. Certainly that smile
Should be a passport! Did they never ask
You errand or your destination?
ROXANE. Oh,
Frequently! Then I dropped my eyes and said:
"I have a lover . . ." Whereupon, the Spaniard
With an air of ferocious dignity
Would close the carriage door—with such a gesture
As any king might envy, wave aside
The muskets that were levelled at my breast,
Fall back three paces, equally superb
In grace and gloom, draw himself up, thrust forth
A spur under his cloak, sweeping the air
With his long plumes, bow very low, and say:
"Pass, Señorita!"
CHRISTIAN. But Roxane—
ROXANE. I know—
I said "a lover"—but you understand—
Forgive me!—If I said "I am going to meet
My husband," no one would believe me!
CHRISTIAN. Yes,
But—
ROXANE. What then?
DE GUICHE. You must leave this place.
CYRANO. At once.
ROXANE. I?

LE BRET. Yes—immediately.
ROXANE. And why?
CHRISTIAN. [*Embarrassed.*] Because . . .
CYRANO. [*Same.*] In half an hour . . .
DE GUICHE. [*Same.*] Or three-quarters . . .
CARBON. [*Same.*] Perhaps
It might be better . . .
LE BRET. If you . . .
ROXANE. Oh—I see!
You are going to fight. I remain here.
ALL. No—no!
ROXANE. He is my husband—[*Throws herself in* CHRISTIAN's *arms.*] I will die with you!
CHRISTIAN. Your eyes! . . . Why do you?—
ROXANE. You know why . . .
DE GUICHE. [*Desperate.*] This post
Is dangerous—
ROXANE. [*Turns.*] How—dangerous?
CYRANO. The proof
Is, we are ordered—
ROXANE. [*To* DE GUICHE.] Oh—you wish to make
A widow of me?
DE GUICHE. On my word of honor—
ROXANE. No matter. I am just a little mad—
I will stay. It may be amusing.
CYRANO. What,
A heroine—our intellectual?
ROXANE. Monsieur de Bergerac, I am your cousin!
A CADET. We'll fight now! Hurrah!
ROXANE. [*More and more excited.*] I am safe with you—my friends!
ANOTHER. [*Carried away.*] The whole camp breathes of lilies!—
ROXANE. And I think,
This hat would look well on the battlefield! . . .
But perhaps—[*Looks at* DE GUICHE.]
The Count ought to leave us. Any moment
Now, there may be danger.
DE GUICHE. This is too much!
I must inspect my guns. I shall return—
You may change your mind—There will yet be time—
ROXANE. Never!— [DE GUICHE *goes out.*]
CHRISTIAN. [*Imploring.*] Roxane! . . .
ROXANE. No!
FIRST CADET. [*To the rest.*] She stays here!

ALL. [*Rushing about, elbowing each other, brushing off their clothes.*] A comb!—Soap!—Here's a hole in my—A needle!—Who
Has a ribbon?—Your mirror, quick!—My cuffs—
A razor—
ROXANE. [*To* CYRANO, *who is still urging her.*] No! I shall not stir one step!
CARBON. [*Having, like the others, tightened his belt, dusted himself, brushed off his hat, smoothed out his plume and put on his lace cuffs, advances to* ROXANE *ceremoniously.*] In that case, may I not present to you
Some of these gentlemen who are to have
The honor of dying in your presence?
ROXANE. [*Bows.*] Please!—[*She waits, standing, on the arm of* CHRISTIAN.]
CARBON. [*Presents.*] Baron de Peyrescous de Colignac!
THE CADET. [*Salutes.*] Madame . . .
ROXANE. Monsieur . . .
CARBON. [*Continues.*] Baron de Casterac De Cahuzac—Vidame de Malgouyre Estressac Lésbas d'Escarabiot—
THE VIDAME. Madame . . .
CARBON. Chevalier d'Antignac-Juzet—Baron Hillot de Blagnac-Saléchan De Castel-Crabioules—
THE BARON. Madame . . .
ROXANE. How many
Names you all have!
THE BARON. Hundreds!
CARBON. [*To* ROXANE.] Open the hand That holds your handerchief.
ROXANE. [*Open her hand; the handkerchief falls.*] Why? [*The whole company makes a movement toward it.*]
CARBON. [*Picks it up quickly.*] My company
Was in want of a banner. We have now The fairest in the army!
ROXANE. [*Smiling.*] Rather small—
CARBON. [*Fastens the handerchief to his lance.*]
Lace—and embroidered!
A CADET. [*To the others.*] With her smiling on me,
I could die happy, if I only had Something in my—
CARBON. [*Turns upon him.*] Shame on you! Feast your eyes
And forget your—
ROXANE. [*Quickly.*] It must be this fresh air—
I am starving! Let me see . . . Cold partridges,
Pastry, a little white wine—that would do.
Will some one bring that to me?
A CADET. [*Aside.*] Will some one!—
ANOTHER. Where the devil are we to find—
ROXANE. [*Overhears; sweetly.*] Why, there—
In my carriage.
ALL. Wha-at?
ROXANE. All you have to do
Is to unpack, and carve, and serve things. Oh,
Notice my coachman; you may recognize
An old friend.
THE CADETS. [*Rush to the coach.*] Ragueneau!
ROXANE. [*Follows them with her eyes.*] Poor fellows . . .
THE CADETS. [*Acclamations.*] Ah! Ah!
CYRANO. [*Kisses her hand.*] Our good fairy!
RAGUENEAU. [*Standing on his box, like a mountebank before a crowd.*] Gentlemen!— [*Enthusiasm.*]
THE CADETS. Bravo! Bravo!
RAGUENEAU. The Spaniards, basking in our smiles,
Smiled on our baskets! [*Applause.*]
CYRANO. [*Aside, to* CHRISTIAN.] Christian!—
RAGUENEAU. They adored
The Fair, and missed— [*He takes from under the seat a dish, which he holds aloft.*] the Fowl! [*Applause. The dish is passed from hand to hand.*]
CYRANO. [*As before to* CHRISTIAN.] One moment—
RAGUENEAU. Venus
Charmed their eyes, while Adonis quietly [*Brandishing a ham.*]
Brought home the Boar! [*Applause; the ham is seized by a score of hands outstretched.*]
CYRANO. [*As before.*] Pst—Let me speak to you—
ROXANE. [*As the* CADETS *return, their arms full of provisions.*] Spread them out on the ground. [*Calls.*] Christian! Come here;

Make yourself useful. [CHRISTIAN *turns to her, at the moment when* CYRANO *was leading him aside. She arranges the food, with his aid and that of the two imperturbable footmen.*]
RAGUENEAU. Peacock, aux truffes!
FIRST CADET. [*Comes down, cutting a huge slice of the ham.*] Tonnere!
We are not going to die without a gorge—[*Sees* ROXANE; *corrects himself hastily.*]
Pardon—a banquet!
RAGUENEAU. [*Tossing out the cushions of the carriage.*] Open these—they are full
Of ortolans! [*Tumult; laughter; the cushions are eviscerated.*]
THIRD CADET. Lucullus!
RAGUENEAU. [*Throws out bottles of red wine.*] Flasks of ruby—[*And of white.*]
Flasks of topaz—
ROXANE. [*Throws a tablecloth at the head of* CYRANO.] Come back out of your dreams!
Unfold this cloth—
RAGUENEAU. [*Takes off one of the lanterns of the carriage, and flourishes it.*] Our lamps are bonbonnières!
CYRANO. [*To* CHRISTIAN.] I must see you before you speak with her—
RAGUENEAU. [*More and more lyrical.*] My whip-handle is one long sausage!
ROXANE. [*Pouring wine; passing the food.*] We
Being about to die, first let us dine!
Never mind the others—all for Gascoyne!
And if De Guiche comes, he is not invited! [*Going from one to another.*]
Plenty of time—you need not eat so fast—
Hold your cup—[*To another.*] What's the matter?
THE CADET. [*Sobbing.*] You are so good
To us . . .
ROXANE. There, there! Red or white wine?—Some bread
For Monsieur de Carbon!—Napkins—
A knife—
Pass your plate—Some of the crust? A little more—
Light or dark?—Burgundy?—
CYRANO. [*Follows her with an armful of dishes, helping to serve.*] Adorable!
ROXANE. [*Goes to* CHRISTIAN.] What would you like?
CHRISTIAN. Nothing.
ROXANE. Oh, but you must!—
A little wine? A biscuit?
CHRISTIAN. Tell me first
Why you came—
ROXANE. By and by. I must take care
Of these poor boys—
LE BRET. [*Who has gone upstage to pass up food to the sentry on the parapet, on the end of a lance.*] De Guiche!—
CYRANO. Hide everything
Quick!—Dishes, bottles, tablecloth—
Now look
Hungry again—[*To* RAGUENEAU.] You there! Up on your box—
—Everything out of sight? [*In a twinkling, everything has been pushed inside the tents, hidden in their hats or under their cloaks.* DE GUICHE *enters quickly, then stops, sniffing the air. Silence.*]
DE GUICHE. It smells good here.
A CADET. [*Humming with an air of great unconcern.*] Sing ha-ha-ha and ho-ho-ho—
DE GUICHE. [*Stares at him; he grows embarrassed.*] You there—
What are you blushing for?
THE CADET. Nothing—my blood
Stirs at the thought of battle.
ANOTHER. Pom . . . pom . . . pom! . . .
DE GUICHE. [*Turns upon him.*] What is that?
THE CADET. [*Slightly stimulated.*] Only song—only little song—
DE GUICHE. You appear happy!
THE CADET. Oh yes—always happy
Before a fight—
DE GUICHE. [*Calls to* CARBON, *for the purpose of giving him an order.*] Captain! I—[*Stops and looks at him.*] What the devil—You are looking happy too!—
CARBON. [*Pulls a long face and hides a bottle behind his back.*] No!
DE GUICHE. Here—I had
One gun remaining. I have had it placed [*He points offstage.*]
There—in that corner—for your men.
A CADET. [*Simpering.*] So kind!—
Charming attention!
ANOTHER. [*Same business; burlesque.*]
Sweet solicitude!—
DE GUICHE. [*Contemptuous.*] I believe you are both drunk— [*Coldly.*] Being unaccustomed
To guns—take care of the recoil!

FIRST CADET. [*Gesture.*] Ah-h . . . Pfft!
DE GUICHE. [*Goes up to him, furious.*] How dare you?
FIRST CADET. A Gascon's gun never recoils!
DE GUICHE. [*Shakes him by the arm.*] You are drunk—
FIRST CADET. [*Superbly.*] With the smell of powder!
DE GUICHE. [*Turns away with a shrug.*] Bah! [*To* ROXANE.] Madame, have you decided?
ROXANE. I stay here.
DE GUICHE. You have time to escape—
ROXANE. No!
DE GUICHE. Very well—
Someone give me a musket!
CARBON. What?
DE GUICHE. *I* stay
Here also.
CYRANO. [*Formally.*] Sir, you show courage!
FIRST CADET. A Gascon
In spite of all that lace!
ROXANE. Why—
DE GUICHE. Must I run
Away, and leave a woman?
SECOND CADET. [*To* FIRST CADET.] We might give him
Something to eat—what do you say?
[*All the food re-appears, as if by magic.*]
DE GUICHE. [*His face lights up.*] A feast!
THIRD CADET. Here a little, there a little—
DE GUICHE. [*Recovers his self-control; haughtily.*] Do you think I want your leavings?
CYRANO. [*Saluting.*] Colonel—you improve!
DE GUICHE. I can fight as I am!
FIRST CADET. [*Delighted.*] Listen to him—
He has an accent!
DE GUICHE. [*Laughs.*] Have I so?
FIRST CADET. A Gascon!—
A Gascon after all! [*They all begin to dance.*]
CARBON. [*Who has disappeared for a moment behind the parapet, reappears on top of it.*] I have placed my pikemen Here. [*Indicates a row of pikes showing above the parapet.*]
DE GUICHE. [*Bows to* ROXANE.] We'll review them; will you take my arm? [*She takes his arm; they go up on the parapet. The rest uncover, and follow them upstage.*]
CHRISTIAN. [*Goes hurriedly to* CYRANO.] Speak quickly! [*At the moment when* ROXANE *appears on the parapet the pikes are lowered in salute, and a cheer is heard. She bows.*]
THE PIKEMEN. [*Offstage.*] Hurrah!
CHRISTIAN. What is it?
CYRANO. If Roxane . . .
CHRISTIAN. Well?
CYRANO. Speaks about your letters . . .
CHRISTIAN. Yes—I know!
CYRANO. Do not make the mistake of showing . . .
CHRISTIAN. What?
CYRANO. Showing surprise.
CHRISTIAN. Surprise—why?
CYRANO. I must tell you! . . .
It is quite simple—I had forgotten it
Until just now. You have . . .
CHRISTIAN. Speak quickly!—
CYRANO. You
Have written oftener than you think.
CHRISTIAN. Oh—Have I!
CYRANO. I took upon me to interpret you;
And wrote—sometimes . . . without . . .
CHRISTIAN. My knowing. Well?
CYRANO. Perfectly simple!
CHRISTIAN. Oh yes, perfectly!—
For a month, we have been blockaded here!—
How did you send all these letters?
CYRANO. Before
Daylight, I managed—
CHRISTIAN. I see. That was also
Perfectly simple!—So I wrote to her,
How many times a week? Twice? Three times? Four?
CYRANO. Oftener.
CHRISTIAN. Every day?
CYRANO. Yes—every day . . .
Every single day . . .
CHRISTIAN. [*Violently.*] And that wrought you up
Into such a flame that you faced death—
CYRANO. [*Sees* ROXANE *returning.*] Hush—
Not before her! [*He goes quickly into the tent.* ROXANE *comes up to* CHRISTIAN.]
ROXANE. Now—Christian!
CHRISTIAN. [*Takes her hands.*] Tell me now
Why you came here—over these ruined roads—
Why you made your way among moss-

troopers
And ruffians—you—to join me here?
ROXANE. Because—
Your letters . . .
CHRISTIAN. Meaning?
ROXANE. It was your own fault
If I ran into danger! I went mad—
Mad with you! Think what you have written me,
How many times, each one more wonderful
Than the last!
CHRISTIAN. All this for a few absurd
Love-letters—
ROXANE. Hush—absurd! How can you know?
I thought I loved you, ever since one night
When a voice that I never would have known
Under my window breathed your soul to me . . .
But—all this time, your letters—every one
Was like hearing your voice there in the dark,
All around me, like your arms around me . . . [*More lightly.*] At last,
I came. Anyone would! Do you suppose
The prim Penelope had stayed at home
Embroidering,—if Ulysses wrote like you?
She would have fallen like another Helen—
Tucked up those linen petticoats of hers
And followed him to Troy!
CHRISTIAN. But you—
ROXANE. I read them
Over and over. I grew faint reading them.
I belonged to you. Every page of them
Was like a petal fallen from your soul—
Like the light and the fire of a great love,
Sweet and strong and true—
CHRISTIAN. Sweet . . . and strong . . . and true . . .
You felt that, Roxane?
ROXANE. You know how I feel! . . .
CHRISTIAN. So—you came . . .
ROXANE. Oh, my Christian, oh my king,—
Lift me up if I fall upon my knees—
It is the heart of me that kneels to you,
And will remain forever at your feet—
You cannot lift that!—
I came here to say
"Forgive me"—(It is time to be forgiven
Now, when we may die presently)—
forgive me
For being light and vain and loving you
Only because you were beautiful.
CHRISTIAN. [*Astonished.*] Roxane! . . .
ROXANE. Afterward I knew better. Afterward
(I had to learn to use my wings) I loved you
For yourself too—knowing you more, and loving
More of you. And now—
CHRISTIAN. Now? . . .
ROXANE. It is yourself
I love now: you own self.
CHRISTIAN. [*Taken aback.*] Roxane!
ROXANE. [*Gravely.*] Be happy!—
You must have suffered; for you must have seen
How frivolous I was; and to be loved
For the mere costume, the poor casual body
You went about in—to a soul like yours,
That must have been torture! Therefore with words
You revealed your heart. Now that image of you
Which filled my eyes first—I see better now,
And I see it no more!
CHRISTIAN. Oh!—
ROXANE. You still doubt
Your victory?
CHRISTIAN. [*Miserably.*] Roxane!—
ROXANE. I understand:
You cannot perfectly believe in me—
A love like this—
CHRISTIAN. I want no love like this! I want love only for—
ROXANE. Only for what
Every woman sees in you? I can do
Better than that!
CHRISTIAN. No—it was best before!
ROXANE. You do not altogether know me . . . Dear,
There is more of me than there was—with this,
I can love more of you—more of what makes
You your own self—Truly! . . . If you were less
Lovable—

CHRISTIAN. No!
ROXANE. —Less charming—ugly even—
I should love you still.
CHRISTIAN. You mean that?
ROXANE. I do
Mean that!
CHRISTIAN. Ugly? . . .
ROXANE. Yes. Even then!
CHRISTIAN. [*Agonized.*] Oh . . . God! . . .
ROXANE. Now are you happy?
CHRISTIAN. [*Choking.*] Yes . . .
ROXANE. What is it?
CHRISTIAN. [*Pushes her away gently.*]
Only . . .
Nothing . . . one moment . . .
ROXANE. But—
CHRISTIAN. [*Gesture toward the* CADETS.] I am keeping you
From those poor fellows—Go and smile at them;
They are going to die!
ROXANE. [*Softly.*] Dear Christian!
CHRISTIAN. Go—[*She goes up among the Gascons who gather round her respectfully.*]
Cyrano!
CYRANO. [*Comes out of the tent, armed for the battle.*] What is wrong? You look—
CHRISTIAN. She does not
Love me any more.
CYRANO. [*Smiles.*] You think not?
CHRISTIAN. She loves
You.
CYRANO. No!—
CHRISTIAN. [*Bitterly.*] She loves only my soul.
CYRANO. No!
CHRISTIAN. Yes—
That means you. And you love her.
CYRANO. I?
CHRISTIAN. I see—
I know!
CYRANO. That is true . . .
CHRISTIAN. More than—
CYRANO. [*Quietly.*] More than that.
CHRISTIAN. Tell her so!
CYRANO. No.
CHRISTIAN. Why not?
CYRANO. Why—look at me!
CHRISTIAN. She would love me if I were ugly.
CYRANO. [*Startled.*] She—
Said that?
CHRISTIAN. Yes. Now then!
CYRANO. [*Half to himself.*] It was good of her
To tell you that . . . [*Change of tone.*]
Nonsense! Do not believe
Any such madness—It was good of her
To tell you. . . . Do not take her at her word!
Go on—you never will be ugly—Go!
She would never forgive me.
CHRISTIAN. That is what
We shall see.
CYRANO. No, no—
CHRISTIAN. Let her choose between us!—
Tell her everything!
CYRANO. No—you torture me—
CHRISTIAN. Shall I ruin your happiness, because
I have a cursed pretty face? That seems
Too unfair!
CYRANO. And am I to ruin yours
Because I happen to be born with power
To say what you—perhaps—feel?
CHRISTIAN. Tell her!
CYRANO. Man—
Do not try me too far!
CHRISTIAN. I am tired of being
My own rival!
CYRANO. Christian!—
CHRISTIAN. Our secret marriage—
No witnesses—fraudulent—that can be
Annulled—
CYRANO. Do not try me—
CHRISTIAN. I want her love
For the poor fool I am—or not at all!
Oh, I am going through with this! I'll know,
One way or the other. Now I shall walk down
To the end of the post. Go tell her. Let her choose
One of us.
CYRANO. It will be you.
CHRISTIAN. God—I hope so! [*He turns and calls.*]
Roxane!
CYRANO. No—no—
ROXANE. [*Hurries down to him.*] Yes, Christian?
CHRISTIAN. Cyrano
Has news for you—important. [*She turns to* CYRANO, CHRISTIAN *goes out.*]
ROXANE. [*Lightly.*] Oh—important?
CYRANO. He is gone . . . [*To* ROXANE.]
Nothing—only Christian thinks
You ought to know—
ROXANE. I do know. He still doubts

What I told him just now. I saw that.
CYRANO. [*Takes her hand.*] Was it
True—what you told him just now?
ROXANE. It was true!
I said that I should love him even . . .
CYRANO. [*Smiling sadly.*] The word
Comes hard—before me?
ROXANE. Even if he were . . .
CYRANO. Say it—
I shall not be hurt!—Ugly?
ROXANE. Even then
I should love him. [*A few shots, offstage in the direction in which* CHRISTIAN *disappeared.*] Hark! The guns—
CYRANO. Hideous?
ROXANE. Hideous.
CYRANO. Disfigured?
ROXANE. Or disfigured.
CYRANO. Even
Grotesque?
ROXANE. How could he ever be grotesque—
Ever—to me!
CYRANO. But you could love him so,
As much as?—
ROXANE. Yes—and more!
CYRANO. [*Aside, excitedly.*] It is true!—true!—
Perhaps—God! This is too much happiness . . . [*To* ROXANE.]
I—Roxane—listen—
LE BRET. [*Enters quickly; calls to* CYRANO *in a low tone.*] Cyrano—
CYRANO. [*Turns.*] Yes?
LE BRET. Hush! . . . [*Whispers a few words to him.*]
CYRANO. [*Lets fall* ROXANE'S *hand.*] Ah!
ROXANE. What is it?
CYRANO. [*Half stunned, and aside.*] All gone . . .
ROXANE. [*More shots.*] What is it? Oh,
They are fighting!—[*She goes up to look offstage.*]
CYRANO. All gone. I cannot ever
Tell her, now . . . ever . . .
ROXANE. [*Starts to rush away.*] What has happened?
CYRANO. [*Restrains her.*] Nothing. [*Several* CADETS *enter. They conceal something which they are carrying, and form a group so as to prevent* ROXANE *from seeing their burden.*]
ROXANE. These men—
CYRANO. Come away . . . [*He leads her away from the group.*]
ROXANE. You were telling me
Something—
CYRANO. Oh, that? Nothing. . . .
[*Gravely.*] I swear to you
That the spirit of Christian—that his soul
Was—[*Corrects himself quickly.*] That his soul is no less great—
ROXANE. [*Catches at the word.*] Was? [*Crying out. She rushes among the men, and scatters them.*]
CYRANO. All gone . . .
ROXANE. [*Sees* CHRISTIAN *lying upon his cloak.*] Christian!
LE BRET. [*To* CYRANO.] At the first volley.
[ROXANE *throws herself upon the body of* CHRISTIAN. *Shots; at first scattered, then increasing. Drums. Voices shouting.*]
CARBON. [*Sword in hand.*] Here
They come!—Ready!—[*Followed by the* CADETS, *he climbs over the parapet and disappears.*]
ROXANE. Christian!
CARBON. [*Off stage.*] Come on, here,
You!
ROXANE. Christian!
CARBON. Fall in!
ROXANE. Christian!
CARBON. Measure your fuse!
[RAGUENEAU *hurries up, carrying a helmet full of water.*]
CHRISTIAN. [*Faintly.*] Roxane! . . .
CYRANO. [*Low and quick, in* CHRISTIAN'S *ear, while* ROXANE *is dipping into the water a strip of linen torn from her dress.*]
I have told her; she loves you.
[CHRISTIAN *closes his eyes.*]
ROXANE. [*Turns to* CHRISTIAN.] Yes,
My darling?
CARBON. Draw your ramrods!
ROXANE. [*To* CYRANO.] He is not dead? . . .
CHRISTIAN. Open your charges!
ROXANE. I can feel his cheek
Growing cold against mine—
CARBON. Take aim!
ROXANE. A letter—
Over his heart—[*She opens it.*] For me.
CYRANO. [*Aside.*] My letter . . .
CARBON. Fire! [*Musketry, cries and groans. Din of battle.*]
CYRANO. [*Trying to withdraw his hand, which* ROXANE, *still upon her knees, is holding.*] But Roxane—they are fighting—
ROXANE. Wait a little . . .
He is dead. No one else knew him but

you . . . [*She weeps quietly.*]
Was he not a great lover, a great man,
A hero?
CYRANO. [*Standing, bareheaded.*] Yes,
Roxane.
ROXANE. A poet, unknown,
Adorable?
CYRANO. Yes, Roxane,
ROXANE. A fine mind?
CYRANO. Yes, Roxane.
ROXANE. A heart deeper than we
knew—
A soul magnificently tender?
CYRANO. [*Firmly.*] Yes,
Roxane!
ROXANE. [*Sinks down upon the breast of*
CHRISTIAN.] He is dead now . . .
CYRANO. [*Aside; draws his sword.*] Why, so
am I—
For I am dead, and my love mourns for
me
And does not know . . . [*Trumpets in
distance.*]
DE GUICHE. [*Appears on the parapet, disheveled, wounded on the forehead, shouting.*] The signal—hark—the
trumpets!
The army has returned—Hold them
now!—Hold them!
The army!—
ROXANE. On his letter—blood . . . and
tears.
A VOICE. [*Off stage.*] Surrender!
THE CADETS. No!
RAGUENEAU. This place is dangerous!—
CYRANO. [*To* DE GUICHE.] Take her
away—I am going—
ROXANE. [*Kisses the letter; faintly.*] His
blood . . . his tears . . .
RAGUENEAU. [*Leaps down from the coach
and runs to her.*] She has fainted—
DE GUICHE. [*On the parapet; savagely, to
the* CADETS.] Hold them!
VOICE OFFSTAGE. Lay down your arms!
VOICES. No! No!
CYRANO. [*To* DE GUICHE.] Sir, you have
proved yourself—Take care of her.
DE GUICHE. [*Hurries to* ROXANE *and takes
her up in his arms.*] As you will—we
can win, if you hold on
A little longer—
CYRANO. Good!
[*Calls out to* ROXANE, *as she is carried
away, fainting, by* DE GUICHE *and*
RAGUENEAU.] Adieu, Roxane! [*Tumult,
outcries. Several* CADETS *come back
wounded and fall on the stage.* CYRANO,
*rushing to the fight, is stopped on the crest
of the parapet by* CARBON, *covered with
blood.*]
CARBON. We are breaking—I am twice
wounded—
CYRANO. [*Shouts to the Gascons.*] Hardi!
Reculez pas, Drollos! [*To* CARBON, *holding him up.*] So—never fear!
I have two deaths to avenge now—
Christian's
And my own! [*They come down.* CYRANO
takes from him the lance with ROXANE's
handkerchief still fastened to it.] Float,
little banner, with her name! [*He
plants it on the parapet; then shouts to the
*CADETS.]
Toumbé dessus! Escrasas lous! [*To the*
FIFER.] Your fife!
Music! [*Fife plays. The wounded drag
themselves to their feet. Other* CADETS
*scramble over the parapet and group
themselves around* CYRANO *and his tiny
flag. The coach is filled and covered with
men, bristling with muskets, transformed
into a redoubt.*]
A CADET. [*Reels backward over the wall,
still fighting. Shouts.*] The are climbing
over!— [*And falls dead.*]
CYRANO. Very good—
Let them come!—A salute now—[*The
parapet is crowned for an instant with a
rank of enemies. The imperial banner of
Spain is raised aloft.*] Fire! [*General
volley.*]
VOICE. [*Among the ranks of the enemy.*]
Fire! [*Murderous counter-fire; the* CADETS *fall on every side.*]
A SPANISH OFFICER. [*Uncovers.*] Who are
these men who are so fond of death?
CYRANO. [*Erect amid the hail of bullets,
declaims.*] The Cadets of Gascoyne,
the defenders
Of Carbon de Castel-Jaloux—
Free fighters, free lovers, free spenders— [*He rushes forward, followed by a
few survivors.*]
The Cadets of Gascoyne . . . [*The rest is
lost in the din of battle.*]

Act 5

Cyrano's Gazette

Fifteen years later, in 1655: the park of the convent occupied by the Ladies of the Cross, at Paris.

Magnificent foliage. To the left, the house upon a broad terrace at the head of a flight of steps, with several doors opening upon the terrace. In the center of the scene an enormous tree alone in the center of a little open space. Toward the right, in the foreground, among boxwood bushes, a semicircular bench of stone.

All the way across the background of the scene, an avenue overarched by the chestnut trees, leading to the door of a chapel on the right, just visible among the branches of the trees. Beyond the double curtain of the trees, we catch a glimpse of bright lawns and shaded walks, masses of shrubbery; the perspective of the park; the sky.

A little side door of the chapel opens upon a colonnade, garlanded with autumnal vines, and disappearing on the right behind the boxtrees.

It is late October. Above the still living green of the turf all the foliage is red and yellow and brown. The evergreen masses of box and yew stand out darkly against this autumnal coloring. A heap of dead leaves under every tree. The leaves are falling everywhere. They rustle underfoot along the walks; the terrace and the bench are half covered with them.

Before the bench on the right, on the side toward the tree, is placed a tall embroidery frame and beside it a little chair. Baskets filled with skeins of many-colored silks and balls of wool. Tapestry unfinished on the frame.

At the curtain rise the NUNS *are coming and going across the park; several of them are seated on the bench around* MOTHER MARGUÉRITE DE JÉSUS. *The leaves are falling.*

SISTER MARTHE. [*To* MOTHER MARGUÉRITE.] Sister Claire has been looking in the glass
At her new cap; twice!
MOTHER MARGUÉRITE. [*To* SISTER CLAIRE.] It is very plain;
Very.
SISTER CLAIRE. And Sister Marthe stole a plum
Out of the tart this morning!
MOTHER MARGUÉRITE. [*To* SISTER MARTHE.] That was wrong;
Very wrong.
SISTER CLAIRE. Oh, but such a little look!
SISTER MARTHE. Such a little plum!
MOTHER MARGUÉRITE. [*Severely.*] I shall tell Monsieur
De Cyrano, this evening.
SISTER CLAIRE. No! Oh, no!—
He will make fun of us.
SISTER MARTHE. He will say nuns
Are so gay!
SISTER CLAIRE. And so greedy!
MOTHER MARGUÉRITE. [*Smiling.*] And so good . . .
SISTER CLAIRE. It must be ten years, Mother Marguérite,
That he has come here every Saturday, Is it not?
MOTHER MARGUÉRITE. More than ten years; ever since
His cousin came to live among us here—
Her worldly weeds among our linen veils,
Her widowhood and our virginity—
Like a black dove among white doves.
SISTER MARTHE. No one
Else ever turns that happy sorrow of hers
Into a smile.
ALL THE NUNS. He is such fun!—He makes us
Almost laugh!—And he teases everyone—
And pleases everyone—And we all love him—
And he likes our cake, too—
SISTER MARTHE. I am afraid
He is not a good Catholic.
SISTER CLAIRE. Some day
We shall convert him.
THE NUNS. Yes—yes!
MOTHER MARGUÉRITE. Let him be;
I forbid you to worry him. Perhaps
He might stop coming here.
SISTER MARTHE. But . . . God?
MOTHER MARGUÉRITE. You need not
Be afraid. God knows all about him.
SISTER MARTHE. Yes . . .
But every Saturday he says to me,

Just as if he were proud of it: "Well, Sister,
I ate meat yesterday!"
MOTHER MARGUÉRITE. He tells you so?
The last time he said that, he had not eaten
Anything, for two days.
SISTER MARTHE. Mother!—
MOTHER MARGUÉRITE. He is poor;
Very poor.
SISTER MARTHE. Who said so?
MOTHER MARGUÉRITE. Monsieur Le Bret.
SISTER MARTHE. Why does not someone help him?
MOTHER MARGUÉRITE. He would be
Angry; very angry . . . [*Between the trees upstage,* ROXANE *appears, all in black, with a widow's cap and long veils.* DE GUICHE, *magnificently grown old, walks beside her. They move slowly.* MOTHER MARGUÉRITE *rises.*] Let us go in—
Madame Madeleine has a visitor.
SISTER MARTHE. [*To* SISTER CLAIRE.] The Duc de Grammont, is it not? The Marshal?
SISTER CLAIRE. [*Looks toward* DE GUICHE.] I think so—yes.
SISTER MARTHE. He has not been to see her
For months—
THE NUNS. He is busy—the Court!—the Camp!—
SISTER CLAIRE. The world! . . . [*They go out.* DE GUICHE *and* ROXANE *come down in silence, and stop near the embroidery frame. Pause.*]
DE GUICHE. And you remain here, wasting all that gold—
For ever in mourning?
ROXANE. For ever.
DE GUICHE. And still faithful?
ROXANE. And still faithful . . .
DE GUICHE. [*After a pause.*] Have you forgiven me?
ROXANE. [*Simply, looking up at the cross of the Convent.*] I am here. [*Another pause.*]
DE GUICHE. Was Christian . . . all that?
ROXANE. If you knew him.
DE GUICHE. Ah? We were not precisely . . . intimate . . .
And his last letter—always at your heart?
ROXANE. It hangs here, like a holy reliquary.
DE GUICHE. Dead—and you love him still!
ROXANE. Sometimes I think
He has not altogether died; our hearts
Meet, and his love flows all around me, living.
DE GUICHE. [*After another pause.*] You see Cyrano often?
ROXANE. Every week.
My old friend takes the place of my Gazette,
Brings me all the news. Every Saturday,
Under that tree where you are now, his chair
Stands, if the day be fine. I wait for him,
Embroidering; the hour strikes; then I hear,
(I need not turn to look!) at the last stroke,
His cane tapping the steps. He laughs at me
For my eternal needlework. He tells
The story of the past week— [LE BRET *appears on the steps.*] There's Le Bret!— [LE BRET *approaches.*]
How is it with our friend?
LE BRET. Badly.
DE GUICHE. Indeed?
ROXANE. [*To* DE GUICHE.] Oh, he exaggerates!
LE BRET. Just as I said—
Loneliness, misery—I told him so!—
His satires make a host of enemies—
He attacks the false nobles, the false saints,
The false heroes, the false artists—in short,
Everyone!
ROXANE. But they fear that sword of his
No one dare touch him!
DE GUICHE. [*With a shrug.*] H'm—that may be so.
LE BRET. It is not violence I fear for him,
But solitude—poverty—old gray December,
Stealing on wolf's feet, with a wolf's green eyes,
Into his darkening room. Those bravoes yet
May strike our Swordsman down! Every day now,
He draws his belt up one hole; his poor nose
Looks like old ivory; he has one coat

Left—his old black serge.
DE GUICHE. That is nothing strange
In this world! No, you need not pity him
Overmuch.
LE BRET. [*With a bitter smile.*] My lord Marshal! . . .
DE GUICHE. I say, do not
Pity him overmuch. He lives his life,
His own life, his own way—thought, word, and deed
Free!
LE BRET. [*As before.*] My lord Duke! . . .
DE GUICHE. [*Haughtily.*] Yes, I know—I have all;
He has nothing. Nevertheless, today
I should be proud to shake his hand . . . [*Saluting* ROXANE.] Adieu.
ROXANE. I will go with you. [DE GUICHE *salutes* LE BRET, *and turns with* ROXANE *toward the steps.*]
DE GUICHE. [*Pauses on the steps, as she climbs.*] Yes—I envy him
Now and then . . . Do you know, when a man wins
Everything in this world, when he succeeds
Too much—he feels, having done nothing wrong
Especially, Heaven knows!—he feels somehow
A thousand small displeasures with himself,
Whose whole sum is not quite Remorse, but rather
A sort of vague disgust . . . The ducal robes
Mounting up, step by step, to pride and power,
Somewhere among their folds draw after them
A rustle of dry illusions, vain regrets,
As your veil, up the stairs here, draws along
The whisper of dead leaves.
ROXANE. [*Ironical.*] The sentiment
Does you honor.
DE GUICHE. Oh, yes . . . [*Pausing suddenly.*] Monsieur Le Bret!— [*To* ROXANE.]
You pardon us?— [*He goes to* LE BRET, *and speaks in a low tone.*] One moment— It is true
That no one dares attack your friend. Some people
Dislike him, none the less. The other day
At Court, such a one said to me: "This man
Cyrano may die—accidentally."
LE BRET. [*Coldly.*] Thank you.
DE GUICHE. You may thank me. Keep him at home
All you can. Tell him to be careful.
LE BRET. [*Shaking his hands to heaven.*] Careful!—
He is coming here. I'll warn him—yes, but! . . .
ROXANE. [*Still on the steps, to a* NUN *who approaches her.*] Here
I am—what is it?
THE NUN. Madame, Ragueneau
Wishes to see you.
ROXANE. Bring him here. [*To* LE BRET *and* DE GUICHE.] He comes
For sympathy—having been first of all
A Poet, he became since then, in turn,
A Singer—
LE BRET. Bath-house keeper—
ROXANE. Sacristan—
LE BRET. Actor—
ROXANE. Hairdresser—
LE BRET. Music-master—
ROXANE. Now,
Today—
RAGUENEAU. [*Enters hurriedly.*]
Madame!— [*He sees* LE BRET.] Monsieur!—
ROXANE. [*Smiling.*] First tell your troubles
To Le Bret for a moment.
RAGUENEAU. But Madame— [*She goes out, with* DE GUICHE, *not hearing him.* RAGUENEAU *comes to* LE BRET.]
After all, I had rather— You are here—
She need not know so soon— I went to see him
Just now— Our friend— As I came near his door,
I saw him coming out. I hurried on
To join him. At the corner of the street,
As he passed— Could it be an accident?—
I wonder!—At the window overhead,
A lackey with a heavy log of wood
Let it fall—
LE BRET. Cyrano!
RAGUENEAU. I ran to him—
LE BRET. God! The cowards!
RAGUENEAU. I found him lying there—
A great hole in his head—
LE BRET. Is he alive?

RAGUENEAU. Alive—yes. But . . . I had to carry him
Up to his room—Dieu! Have you seen his room?—
LE BRET. Is he suffering?
RAGUENEAU. No; unconscious.
LE BRET. Did you
Call a doctor?
RAGUENEAU. One came—for charity.
LE BRET. Poor Cyrano!—We must not tell Roxane
All at once . . . Did the doctor say?—
RAGUENEAU. He said
Fever, and lesions of the— I forget
Those long names— Ah, if you had seen him there,
His head all white bandages!—Let us go
Quickly—there is no one to care for him—
All alone— If he tries to raise his head,
He may die!
LE BRET. [*Draws him away to the right.*] This way— It is shorter—through The Chapel—
ROXANE. [*Appears on the stairway, and calls to* LE BRET *as he is going out by the colonnade which leads to the small door of the Chapel.*] Monsieur Le Bret!— [LE BRET *and* RAGUENEAU *rush off without hearing.*] Running away
When I call to him? Poor dear Ragueneau
Must have been very tragic! [*She comes slowly down the stair, toward the tree.*]
What a day! . . .
Something in these bright autumn afternoons
Happy and yet regretful—an old sorrow
Smiling . . . as though poor little April dried
Her tears long ago—and remembered . . . [*She sits down at her work. Two* NUNS *come out of the house carrying a great chair and set it under the tree.*]
Ah—
The old chair, for my old friend!—
SISTER MARTHE. The best one
In our best parlor!—
ROXANE. Thank you, Sister— [*The* NUNS *withdraw.*] There— [*She begins embroidering. The clock strikes.*]
The hour!—He will be coming now— my silks—
All done striking? He never was so late

Before! The sister at the door—my thimble . . .
Here it is—she must be exhorting him
To repent all his sins . . . [*A pause.*] He ought to be
Converted, by this time— Another leaf— [*A dead leaf falls on her work; she brushes it away.*]
Certainly nothing could—my scissors— ever
Keep him away—
A NUN. [*Appears on the steps.*] Monsieur de Bergerac.
ROXANE. [*Without turning.*] What was I saying? . . . Hard, sometimes, to match
These faded colors! . . . [*While she goes on working,* CYRANO *appears at the top of the steps, very pale, his hat drawn over his eyes. The* NUN *who has brought him in goes away. He begins to descend the steps leaning on his cane, and holding himself on his feet only by an evident effort.* ROXANE *turns to him, with a tone of friendly banter.*] After fourteen years,
Late—for the first time!
CYRANO. [*Reaches the chair, and sinks into it; his gay tone contrasting with his tortured face.*] Yes, yes—maddening!
I was detained by—
ROXANE. Well?
CYRANO. A visitor,
Most unexpected.
ROXANE. [*Carelessly, still sewing.*] Was your visitor
Tiresome?
CYRANO. Why, hardly that—inopportune,
Let us say—an old friend of mine—at least
A very old acquaintance.
ROXANE. Did you tell him
To go away?
CYRANO. For the time being, yes.
I said: "Excuse me—this is Saturday—
I have a previous engagement, one
I cannot miss, even for you— Come back
An hour from now."
ROXANE. Your friend will have to wait;
I shall not let you go till dark.
CYRANO. [*Very gently.*] Perhaps
A little before dark, I must go . . . [*He leans back in the chair, and closes his eyes.* SISTER MARTHE *crosses above the stairway.* ROXANE *sees her, motions her to*

wait, then turns to CYRANO.]
ROXANE. Look—
Somebody waiting to be teased.
CYRANO. [*Quickly, opens his eyes.*] Of
course! [*In a big, comic voice.*]
Sister, approach! [SISTER MARTHE *glides toward him.*] Beautiful downcast eyes!—
So shy—
SISTER MARTHE. [*Looks up, smiling.*]
You—[*She sees his face.*] Oh!—
CYRANO. [*Indicates* ROXANE.] Sh!—Careful! [*Resumes his burlesque tone.*]
Yesterday,
I ate meat again!
SISTER MARTHE. Yes, I know. [*Aside.*]
That is why
He looks so pale . . . [*To him: low and quickly.*] In the refectory,
Before you go— come to me there—I'll make you
A great bowl of hot soup—will you come?
CYRANO. [*Boisterously.*] Ah—
Will I come!
SISTER MARTHE. You are quite reasonable
Today!
ROXANE. Has she converted you?
SISTER MARTHE. Oh, no—
Not for the world!—
CYRANO. Why, now I think of it,
That is so— You, bursting with holiness,
And yet you never preach! Astonishing
I call it . . . [*With burlesque ferocity.*]
Ah—now I'll astonish you—
I am going to— [*With the air of seeking for a good joke and finding it.*] —let you pray for me
Tonight, at vespers!
ROXANE. Aha!
CYRANO. Look at her—
Absolutely struck dumb!
SISTER MARTHE. [*Gently.*] I did not wait
For you to say I might. [*She goes out.*]
CYRANO. [*Returns to* ROXANE, *who is bending over her work.*] Now, may the devil
Admire me, if I ever hope to see
The end of that embroidery!
ROXANE. [*Smiling.*] I thought
It was time you said that. [*A breath of wind causes a few leaves to fall.*]
CYRANO. The leaves—
ROXANE. [*Raises her head and looks away through the trees.*] What color—
Perfect Venetian red! Look at them fall.
CYRANO. Yes—they know how to die. A little way
From the branch to the earth, a little fear
Of mingling with the common dust—and yet
They go down gracefully—a fall that seems
Like flying!
ROXANE. Melancholy—you?
CYRANO. Why, no,
Roxane!
ROXANE. Then let the leaves fall. Tell me now
The Court news—my Gazette!
CYRANO. Let me see—
ROXANE. Ah!
CYRANO. [*More and more pale, struggling against pain.*] Saturday, the nineteenth; the King fell ill,
After eight helpings of grape marmalade.
His malady was brought before the court,
Found guilty of high treason; whereupon
His Majesty revived. The royal pulse
Is now normal. Sunday, the twentieth:
The Queen gave a grand ball, at which they burned
Seven hundred and sixty-three wax candles.
Note: They say our troops have been victorious
In Austria. Later: Three sorcerers
Have been hung. Special post: The little dog
Of Madame D'Athis was obliged to take
Four pills before—
ROXANE. Monsieur de Bergerac,
Will you kindly be quiet!
CYRANO. Monday . . . nothing
Lygdamire has a new lover.
ROXANE. Oh!
CYRANO. [*His face more and more altered.*]
Tuesday,
The twenty-second: All the court has gone
To Fontainebleau. Wednesday: The Comte de Fiesque
Spoke to Madame de Montglat: she said No.
Thursday: Mancini was the Queen of France
Or—very nearly! Friday: La Montglat

Said Yes. Saturday, twenty-sixth . . .
[*His eyes close; his head sinks back; silence.*]
ROXANE. [*Surprised at not hearing any more, turns, looks at him, and rises, frightened.*] He has fainted— [*She runs to him crying out.*]
Cyrano!
CYRANO. [*Opens his eyes.*] What . . . What is it? . . . [*He sees* ROXANE *leaning over him, and quickly pulls his hat down over his head and leans back away from her in the chair.*] No—oh no—
It is nothing—truly!
ROXANE. But—
CYRANO. My old wound—
At Arras—sometimes—you know. . . .
ROXANE. My poor friend!
CYRANO. Oh it is nothing; it will soon be gone. . . . [*Forcing a smile.*]
There! It is gone!
ROXANE. [*Standing close to him.*] We all have our old wounds
I have mine—here . . . [*Her hand at her breast.*] under this faded scrap
Of writing. . . . It is hard to read now—all
But the blood—and the tears. . . . [*Twilight begins to fall.*]
CYRANO. His letter! . . . Did you
Not promise me that some day . . . that some day. . . .
You would let me read it?
ROXANE. His letter?—You . . .
You wish—
CYRANO. I do wish it-today.
ROXANE. [*Gives him the little silken bag from around her neck.*] Here. . . .
CYRANO. May I . . . open it?
ROXANE. Open it, and read. [*She goes back to her work, folds it again, rearranges her silks.*]
CYRANO. [*Unfolds the letter; reads.*]
"Farewell Roxane, because today I die—"
ROXANE. [*Looks up, surprised.*] Aloud?
CYRANO. [*Reads.*] "I know that it will be today,
My own dearly beloved—and my heart
Still so heavy with love I have not told,
And I die without telling you! No more
Shall my eyes drink the sight of you like wine,
Never more, with a look that is a kiss,
Follow the sweet grace of you—"
ROXANE. How you read it—
His letter!
CYRANO. [*Continues.*] "I remember now the way
You have, of pushing back a lock of hair
With one hand, from your forehead—and my heart
Cries out—"
ROXANE. His letter . . . and you read it so . . . [*The darkness increases imperceptibly.*]
CYRANO. "Cries out and keeps crying: 'Farewell, my dear,
My dearest—'"
ROXANE. In a voice. . . .
CYRANO. "—My own heart's own,
My own treasure—"
ROXANE. [*Dreamily.*] In such a voice. . . .
CYRANO. —"My Love—"
ROXANE. —As I remember hearing . . . [*She trembles.*] —long ago. . . . [*She comes near him, softly, without his seeing her; passes the chair, leans over silently, looking at the letter. The darkness increases.*]
CYRANO. "—I am never away from you. Even now,
I shall not leave you. In another world,
I shall be still that one who loves you, loves you
Beyond measure, beyond—"
ROXANE. [*Lays her hand on his shoulder.*] How can you read
Now? It is dark . . . [*He starts, turns, and sees her there close to him. A little movement of surprise, almost of fear; then he bows his head. A long pause; then in the twilight now completely fallen, she says very softly, clasping her hands.*] And all these fourteen years,
He has been the old friend, who came to me
To be amusing.
CYRANO. Roxane!—
ROXANE. It was you.
CYRANO. No, no, Roxane, no!
ROXANE. And I might have known,
Every time that I heard you speak my name! . . .
CYRANO. No—It was not I—
ROXANE. It was . . . you!
CYRANO. I swear—
ROXANE. I understand everything now: The letters—
That was you . . .
CYRANO. No!

ROXANE. And the dear, foolish words—
That was you. . . .
CYRANO. No!
ROXANE. And the voice . . . in the dark. . . .
That was . . . you!
CYRANO. On my honor—
ROXANE. And . . . the Soul!—
That was all you.
CYRANO. I never loved you—
ROXANE. Yes,
You loved me.
CYRANO. [*Desperately.*] No— He loved you—
ROXANE. Even now,
You love me!
CYRANO. [*His voice weakens.*] No!
ROXANE. [*Smiling.*] And why . . . so great a "No"?
CYRANO. No, no, my own dear love, I love you not! . . . [*Pause.*]
ROXANE. How many things have died . . . and are newborn! . . .
Why were you silent for so many years,
All the while, every night and every day,
He gave me nothing—you knew that—
You knew
Here, in this letter lying on my breast,
Your tears—You knew they were your tears—
CYRANO. [*Holds the letter out to her.*] The blood
Was his.
ROXANE. Why do you break that silence now,
Today?
CYRANO. Why? Oh, because— [LE BRET *and* RAGUENEAU *enter, running.*]
LE BRET. What recklessness—I knew it! He is here!
CYRANO. [*Smiling, and trying to rise.*] Well? Here I am!
RAGUENEAU. He has killed himself, Madame, coming here!
ROXANE. He—Oh, God. . . . And that faintness . . . was that?—
CYRANO. No,
Nothing! I did not finish my Gazette—
Saturday, twenty-sixth: An hour or so
Before dinner, Monsieur de Bergerac
Died, foully murdered. [*He uncovers his head, and shows it swathed in bandages.*]
ROXANE. Oh, what does he mean?—
Cyrano!— What have they done to you?—
CYRANO. "Struck down
By the sword of a hero, let me fall—
Steel in my heart, and laughter on my lips!"
Yes, I said that once. How Fate loves a jest!—
Behold me ambushed—taken in the rear—
My battlefield a gutter—my noble foe
A lackey, with a log of wood! . . . It seems
Too logical—I have missed everything,
Even my death!
RAGUENEAU. [*Breaks down.*] Ah, monsieur!—
CYRANO. Ragueneau,
Stop blubbering! [*Takes his hand.*] What are you writing nowadays,
Old poet?
RAGUENEAU. [*Through his tears.*] I am not a poet now;
I snuff the—light the candles—for Molière!
CYRANO. Oh—Molière!
RAGUENEAU. Yes, but I am leaving him
Tomorrow. Yesterday they played "Scapin"—
He has stolen your scene—
LE BRET. The whole scene—word for word!
RAGUENEAU. Yes: "What the devil was he doing there"[6]—
That one!
LE BRET. [*Furious.*] And Molière stole it all from you—Bodily!—
CYRANO. Bah—He showed good taste. . . . [*To* RAGUENEAU.] The scene
Went well? . . .
RAGUENEAU. Ah, monsieur, they laughed—and laughed—
How they did laugh!
CYRANO. Yes—that has been my life. . . .
Do you remember that night Christian spoke
Under your window? It was always so!
While I stood in the darkness underneath,
Others climbed up to win the applause—the kiss!—
Well—that seems only justice—I still say,
Even now, on the threshold of my tomb—
"Molière has genius—Christian had good looks—" [*The chapel bell is ringing. Along the avenue of trees above the*

stairway, the NUNS *pass in procession to their prayers.*]
They are going to pray now; there is the bell.
ROXANE. [*Raises herself and calls to them.*] Sister!—Sister!—
CYRANO. [*Holding on to her hand.*] No,—do not go away—
I may not still be here when you return. . . . [*The* NUNS *have gone into the chapel. The organ begins to play.*]
A little harmony is all I need—
Listen. . . .
ROXANE. You shall not die! I love you!—
CYRANO. No—
That is not in the story! You remember
When Beauty said "I love you" to the Beast
That was a fairy prince, his ugliness
Changed and dissolved, like magic. . . . But you see
I am still the same.
ROXANE. And I—I have done
This to you! All my fault—mine!
CYRANO. You? Why no,
On the contrary! I had never known
Womanhood and its sweetness but for you.
My mother did not love to look at me—
I never had a sister—Later on,
I feared the mistress with a mockery
Behind her smile. But you—because of you I have had one friend not quite all a friend—
Across my life, one whispering silken gown! . . .
LE BRET. [*Points to the rising moon which begins to shine down between the trees.*]
Your other friend is looking at you.
CYRANO. [*Smiling at the moon.*] I see. . . .
ROXANE. I never loved but one man in my life,
And I have lost him—twice. . . .
CYRANO. Le Bret—I shall be up there presently
In the moon—without having to invent
Any flying machines!
ROXANE. What are you saying? . . .
CYRANO. The moon—yes, that would be the place for me—
My kind of paradise! I shall find there
Those other souls who should be friends of mine—
Socrates—Galileo—
LE BRET. [*Revolting.*] No! No! No!
It is too idiotic—too unfair—
Such a friend—such a poet—such a man
To die so—to die so!—
CYRANO. [*Affectionately.*] There goes Le Bret,
Growling!
LET BRET. [*Breaks down.*] My friend!
CYRANO. [*Half raises himself, his eye wanders.*] The Cadets of Gascoyne,
The Defenders. . . . The elementary mass—
Ah—there's the point! Now, then . . .
LE BRET. Delirious—
And all that learning—
CYRANO. On the other hand,
We have Copernicus—
ROXANE. Oh!
CYRANO. [*More and more delirious.*] "Very well,
But what the devil was he doing there?—
What the devil was he doing there, up there?" . . . [*He declaims.*]
Philosopher and scientist,
Poet, musician, duellist—
He flew high, and fell back again!
A pretty wit—whose like we lack—
A lover . . . not like other men. . . .
Here lies Hercule-Savinien
De Cyrano de Bergerac—
Who was all things—and all in vain!
Well, I must go—pardon—I cannot stay!
My moonbeam comes to carry me away. . . . [*He falls back into the chair, half fainting. The sobbing of* ROXANE *recalls him to reality. Gradually his mind comes back to him. He looks at her, stroking the veil that hides her hair.*]
I would not have you mourn any the less
That good, brave, noble Christian; but perhaps—
I ask you only this—when the great cold
Gathers around my bones, that you may give
A double meaning to your widow's weeds
And the tears you let fall for him may be
For a little—my tears. . . .
ROXANE. [*Sobbing.*] Oh, my love! . . .
CYRANO. [*Suddenly shaken as with a fever fit, he raises himself erect and pushes her*

away.] —Not here!—
Not lying down! . . . [*They spring forward to help him; he motions them back.*] Let no one help me—no one!—
Only the tree . . . [*He sets his back against the trunk. Pause.*] It is coming . . . I feel
Already shod with marble . . . gloved with lead . . . [*Joyously.*]
Let the old fellow come now! He shall find me
On my feet—sword in hand—[*Draws his sword.*]
LE BRET. Cyrano!—
ROXANE. [*Half fainting.*] Oh, Cyrano!
CYRANO. I can see him there—he grins—
He is looking at my nose—that skeleton
—What's that you say? Hopeless?— Why, very well!—
But a man does not fight merely to win!
No—no——better to know one fights in vain! . . .
You there—Who are you? A hundred against one—
I know them now, my ancient enemies—[*He lunges at the empty air.*]
Falsehood! . . . There! There! Prejudice—Compromise—
Cowardice—[*Thrusting.*] What's that? No! Surrender? No!
Never-never! . . . Ah, you too, Vanity!
I knew you would overthrow me in the end—
No! I fight on! I fight on! I fight on!
[*He swings the blade in great circles, then pauses, gasping. When he speaks again, it is in another tone.*]
Yes, all my laurels you have riven away
And all my roses; yet in spite of you,
There is one crown I bear away with me,
And tonight, when I enter before God,
My salute shall sweep all the stars away
From the blue threshold! One thing without stain,
Unspotted from the world, in spite of doom
Mine own!—[*He springs forward, his sword aloft.*] And that is . . . [*The sword escapes from his hand; he totters, and falls into the arms of* LE BRET *and* RAGUENEAU.]
ROXANE. [*Bends over him and kisses him on the forehead.*] —That is . . .
CYRANO. [*Opens his eyes and smiles up at her.*] My white plume . . .

1. Governess.
2. French dramatist (1609–50) considered in his day second only to Corneille.
3. The natives of Boeotia, an ancient Greek state, were reputedly dull and stupid.
4. The hero of Alexander Dumas's popular novel, *The Three Musketeers*.
5. In Greek mythology, the leader of the satyrs.
6. See *Our Dramatic Heritage*, 2:579–80.

The Lower Depths

Maxim Gorky

During the last quarter of the nineteenth century and well into the twentieth, there were a great many excellent naturalistic plays written in Europe. As social consciousness was awakened to the sad lot of the lowest classes, naturalism proved an especially effective style for rendering on stage what people had long neglected in real life. An excellent example with which to illustrate this widely practiced dramatic genre and at the same time to turn attention to a burgeoning new theatrical life in Russia, is Maxim Gorky's *The Lower Depths*.

Maxim Gorky was the pen name of Alexei Maximovich Peshkov, who was born on March 28, 1868, in Nizhny Novgorod in central Russia. (In 1932, the town was renamed Gorky in his honor.) At the age of three, he suffered an attack of cholera; his father caught the disease from him and died, and his mother, resentful of his having "caused" his father's death, placed the boy with his maternal grandparents and showed little further interest in him. She later remarried, but died in 1879, and the boy was shuttled from one family to another and forced to work for a living from the age of eleven. Although of bourgeois parentage, he was reduced to abject poverty and lived among the lowest elements of society, rarely knowing where his next meal might come from and changing jobs almost more frequently than he changed clothes. At the age of nineteen he attempted suicide, and at twenty he was arrested for the first of many times for revolutionary activity. He journeyed through Russia on foot, learning the ways of the Russian people and somehow educating himself at the same time. He became an avid reader and then turned to writing, publishing his first short stories in 1892. Small wonder that, when he needed a pen name, he chose one that may be translated as Maxim the Bitter.

Gorky worked on a newspaper for a time, but soon achieved enough success with his writing that he was able to live on the income from it. His stories were immensely popular from the beginning, for they pictured the Russian people whom he had come to know so well—miserable and downtrodden, but with an almost romantic determination to build a better future. Revolution was already in the air in Russia, and Gorky's writing both fed the flames and reaped the profit. Gorky's income was one of the major sources of financing for the Marxist cause in those years. Gorky married in 1896 and fathered two children, but neither of them outlived him. He was at the height of his success as a popular writer when, in 1900, he began to consider writing for the theater.

The Moscow Art Theater had already established its reputation with the success of Chekhov's *The Sea Gull* and with Stanislavski's important new approaches to naturalistic acting when Chekhov introduced Gorky to Stanislavski. The latter urged Gorky to write a play for them, and he responded by writing *The Smug Citizens*, which was produced in 1902. *The Lower Depths* followed later that same year, and is almost the sole basis for Gorky's playwriting reputation outside the Soviet Union. Gorky went on to write some fifteen plays in all, but they are little known outside Russia. Many are produced regularly in Russia, but the Russian government has officially heralded Gorky as the father of socialist realism and has virtually canonized his work, so it is a little difficult to assess how popular his plays might be even in Russia under less controlled circumstances. Certainly his worldwide literary reputation depends primarily on factors other than theatrical. Gorky remained an ardent, though certainly not docile, exponent of the Marxist cause throughout the revolutionary period and was an honored citizen of the Soviet Union and first chairman of the Congress of Soviet Writers. Critics outside Russia generally agree, however, that the quality of his writing declined as he tried to adhere to the party line during the Stalin years. There is some suspicion that his death on June 18, 1936, was not a natural one and was politically motivated, but that has never been proved.

The first performance of *The Lower Depths* took place in the Moscow Art Theater on December 18, 1902, less than three years before the revolution of 1905. Since Gorky was a known political dissident, the police and the censors were alert for possible trouble; according to Nemirovich-Danchenko, codirector with Stanislavski of the Moscow Art Theater, "I was left with the impression that *The Lower Depths* was authorized only because the authorities were counting on the play's complete failure." If so, the authorities had seriously miscalculated, for *The Lower Depths* was not only an overwhelming success that night, but has remained so in Russia and abroad ever since. Audiences were stunned by its stark realism on which Stanislavski and his acting company had lavished endless attention to detail. They had visited the worst flophouses to learn about their denizens at first hand, and Gorky had filled in any missing details from his personal experience. Even the actors' rags were authentic, and it is reported that audience members in the first few rows were afraid of getting lice. Not only was the play a landmark in realism, but also, despite heavy censorship, it was perceived as a stirring revolutionary message. The down-and-out members of society, seething with unrest and still clinging to dreams of a brighter future, were a powder keg waiting to explode, and the intelligentsia in 1902 Moscow had no difficulty in recognizing the writer's viewpoint. Obviously, the intensity of this fervor can no longer attend a modern production of the play, but its realistic look into the human condition, as well as its historical insights, continue to make it timely.

The Lower Depths has been accused of being structurally loose and disorganized, but this is true more in appearance than in reality. The slice-of-life technique demanded that a naturalistic play appear to be nothing more than several hours in the lives of its characters, viewed objectively and with a minimum of artistic selection; *The Lower Depths* certainly makes this impression. In fact, however, within this apparent formlessness, Gorky has planned a neat dichotomy between Luka and Satin that may have only been apparent with actors like Moskvin and Stanislavski in these pivotal roles. The central action of the play is a philosophical struggle between these two for the hearts and souls of the other residents of the cave-like cellar. Luka's arrival and his magnetic personality for a while seduce the others into false optimism and impossible dreams about their futures; when Luka disappears, Satin's cynical but practical views prevail, with severe damage to those who had been most prevailed upon by Luka's illusions. Thus, the last act is not an anticlimax, as it has occasionally been described by some critics, but rather the completion of the action, as the results of Luka's meddling become apparent.

Luka is an attractive rascal, in line with a long stage tradition of such rascals and with Gorky's own habits in his short stories. In his way, Luka evidently means well, and much that he offers in the way of comfort and hope represents the standard bourgeois position on such matters. Luka has been subject to an unusually wide variety of interpretations by later actors; he has been portrayed as a near saint by those who believe Luka's views represent what the author is trying to say and as a crafty villain by those who believe he has no redeeming qualities. Soviet revisionism has forced something akin to the latter view in Russian productions, and Gorky himself in a 1933 essay tried to picture Luka in a completely negative light; but neither Moskvin's reputation as an outstanding clown nor a close reading of the uncensored text will bear this interpretation. The play is much the richer for not yielding to such simplistic explications. Satin, on the other hand, is tough-minded and realistic, recognizing that, although illusions may offer one a temporary kind of comfort, only an honest facing of the truth leads to genuine improvement in the human condition. Satin's eloquent defense in the last act of man as the ultimate end and meaning in life was widely quoted in Russia and recognized as a call to revolt, as an unwillingness to accept forever the repressions and inequities of the czarist regime.

In the best Marxist sense, Luka's platitudinous optimism is indeed an opiate of the people, a pleasant masking of reality calculated to keep the downtrodden contented with their lot and to encourage them not to take up arms against their troubles. Satin's views, on the other hand, though they may be cynical (as well they might be, coming from "Maxim the Bitter"), represent a call to action, at least in the sense of keeping one's self prepared for that day when the downtrodden shall finally unite. Interestingly, Satin finds real good in much that Luka has said, especially endorsing the latter's insistence on kindness to one's fellow creatures; it is by concerted action by the people, united as comrades, that social ills can finally be corrected. It is only when Luka's good intentions turn into lies and illusions that control one's life that they wreak havoc; the Actor's shocking suicide is the result chiefly of withdrawal pains, when he finds that he cannot live with the drug that Luka's well-meaning lie had become for him. Eugene O'Neill deals with the same theme in *The Iceman Cometh,* concluding that such "pipedreams" are essential for human life; the philosophical, as well as the political, issue is not completely resolved by either writer.

Ultimately, the success of *The Lower Depths* depends on its realistic evocation of human character among the very dregs of humanity. Gorky's world is an unpleasant one, but it rings true, and Gorky suggests a large measure of human compassion in his portrayal of these outcasts. The thief and the prostitute, the fallen aristocrat and the foreign migrant laborer, all are portrayed with tough but loving insight and all are extraordinarily well-drawn theatrical portraits. Theatrical companies around the world have responded with enthusiasm to the ensemble acting challenge that *The Lower Depths* offers, and the play has been one of the most frequently translated and produced works in the Soviet theater.

N.B. The notes to *The Lower Depths* were prepared by the translators.

The Lower Depths

Translated by Alexander Bakshy in collaboration with Paul S. Nathan

GORKY's original title for this play was *At the Bottom of Life*. On the advice of a friend he soon shortened it to *At the Bottom*, under which name the play was given its first production on the stage of the Moscow Art Theater. The play has been translated into English under a variety of titles, but *The Lower Depths* is the one best known in English-speaking countries.

The action of the play is laid in a Volga town at the turn of the century. The characters inhabiting Kostylyov's lodging house are representatives of the type known in Russia as *bosyák*, the name, literally meaning "a barefoot," having come to be applied to the whole class of people who did occasional odd jobs but lived mostly by their wits. They formed a motley, shiftless, and often criminal fringe of the population of most Russian towns and used to be particularly numerous in port towns.

Three of the characters in *The Lower Depths* (the Baron, Satin, and Peppel), are former jailbirds, and Luka (judging by Gorky's film scenario based on the play) is one of them, too, though obviously reformed. Three other characters, the locksmith Klestch and the two longshoremen, the Tartar and the Goiter, typify the conscientious, upright working man. Even the cynical capmaker, Bubnov, is honest in his own way. The contrast is significant. But it is Satin, Luka, and Peppel through whom the moral message of the play is mostly conveyed. The translator must own to inconsistency in retaining the Russian nickname *Kvashnya* (which means "a tub for leavening dough") for one of the characters, while translating the nickname of another character, "Goiter" (which is *Krivoy Zob* in Russian, meaning "a lopsided Adam's apple.") His main excuse, aside from reasons of convenience, is that in the play *Kvashnya* takes on almost the quality of a proper name.

A.B.

Characters

The Baron, age thirty-three
Kvashnya, peddles dumplings in the market, age close to forty
Bubnov, a capmaker, age forty-five
Andrey Dmitrich Klestch, a locksmith, age forty
Nastya, a girl of the streets, age twenty-four
Anna, Klestch's wife, age thirty
Satin, age close to forty
The Actor, age close to forty
Mikhail Ivanovich Kostylyov, keeper of the lodgings, age fifty-four
Vassily (Vassya) Peppel, age twenty-eight
Natasha, sister of Vassilissa Kostylyova, age twenty
Luka, a pilgrim, age sixty
Alyoshka, a cobbler, age twenty
Vassilissa Karpovna Kostylyova, wife of Mikhail Kostylyov, age twenty-six
Abram Ivanych Medvedev, a policeman, Vassilissa's and Natasha's uncle, age fifty
The Tartar } *longshoremen*
The Goiter

Act 1

A cavelike basement. A heavy vaulted ceiling, blackened with smoke, with patches where the plaster has fallen off. The light comes from the direction of the audience and from a square window high up the wall, right. The right corner is cut off by a thin partition behind which is PEPPEL's *room. Near the door leading into it is* BUBNOV's *plank bed.*[1] *In the left corner is a big Russian stove. In the stone wall, left, is a door to the kitchen, where* KVASHNYA, *the* BARON, *and* NASTYA *live. By the wall between the stove and the door stands a wide bed screened off by a dirty cotton-print curtain. Everywhere along the walls are plank beds. Near the left wall, downstage, stands a block of wood with a vise and a small anvil mounted upon it. Sitting before it, on a smaller block of wood, is* KLETSCH, *who is busy trying keys in old locks. On the floor lie two bunches of keys strung on wire rings, a battered tin samovar, a hammer, and some files. In the center of the basement stand a big table with a samovar, two benches, and a square stool—all unpainted and dirty. At the table* KVASHNYA *is serving tea, the* BARON *is munching black bread, and* NASTYA, *seated on the stool and leaning on the table, is reading a battered book.* ANNA, *lying on the bed behind the curtain, is heard coughing. On his plank bed the capmaker* BUBNOV, *holding a hat block between his legs, is fitting a ripped pair of pants over it, figuring out the best way to cut the cloth. Scattered about him are a torn hatbox containing cap visors, scraps of oilcloth, and cast-off clothing.* SATIN, *just awake, lies on a plank bed emitting loud guttural sounds. On top of the stove, unseen by the audience, the* ACTOR *is puttering around and coughing. It is morning in early spring.*

BARON. Go on.

KVASHNYA. Oh, no, my friend, says I, keep away from me with that. I went through all that before, says I, and now you won't make me go to the altar even if you give me a hundred boiled crawfish.

BUBNOV. [*To* SATIN.] What are you snorting about? [SATIN *continues to grunt.*]

KVASHNYA. That I, a free woman and my own mistress, says I—that I should enter myself in somebody else's passport and make myself a man's slave—never! I wouldn't marry him even if he were an American prince.

KLETSCH. Liar.

KVASHNYA. What's that?

KLETSCH. You're lying. You'll marry Abram all right.

BARON. [*Snatches* NASTYA's *book and reads the title.*] Fatal Love. [*He laughs.*]

NASTYA. [*Stretching out her hand.*] Oh, give it back. Don't be childish. [*The* BARON *gazes at her, waving the book in the air.*]

KVASHNYA. [*To* KLETSCH.] You red-haired goat! I'm lying, am I? How dare you speak to me like that?

BARON. [*Hitting* NASTYA *on the head with the book.*] You *are* a fool, Nastya—

NASTYA. [*Wresting the book from him.*] Let me have it.

KLETSCH. Ha! A great lady. And you *will* marry Abram all the same—that's all you've been waiting for.

KVASHNYA. Oh, of course! I haven't got anything better to do. You've driven your wife till she's nearly dead—

KLETSCH. Shut up, you old sow! It's none of your business!

KVASHNYA. Oh, you don't like to hear the truth!

BARON. There it goes! What's doing, Nastya?

NASTYA. [*Without lifting her head.*] Go away!

ANNA. [*Thrusting her head out from behind the curtain.*] Another day starting! For heaven's sake, stop shouting and quarreling!

KLETSCH. Now she's whining again.

ANNA. Every day it's the same thing. Won't you let me die in peace?

BUBNOV. Noise never stopped anybody from dying.

KVASHNYA. [*Walking up to* ANNA.] How could you live with such a brute?

ANNA. Leave me alone—

KVASHNYA. Well, you *are* a patient sufferer, poor soul. How does your chest feel? Any easier?

BARON. Kvashnya! It's time to go to market!

KVASHNYA. I'm coming. [*To* ANNA.]

Would you like some hot meat dumplings?

ANNA. No, thank you. Why should I bother to eat?

KVASHNYA. Never you mind. Heat softens your innards. I'll put some in a cup and leave it for you—eat them when you feel like it. Come on, nobleman— [*To* KLESTCH.] You devil, you! [*Goes off to the kitchen.*]

ANNA. [*Coughing.*] Oh, Lord—

BARON. [*Giving* NASTYA *a nudge on the back of the neck.*] Drop it, silly!

NASTYA. [*In a loud voice.*] Go away—I'm not keeping you. [*The* BARON *follows* KVASHNYA *off, whistling.*]

SATIN. [*Half rising from his plank bed.*] Who beat me up last night?

BUBNOV. Does it make any difference?

SATIN. You're right, I suppose. But why did they beat me?

BUBNOV. Did you have a card game?

SATIN. I did.

BUBNOV. That's why they beat you up.

SATIN. The dirty swine!

ACTOR. [*Poking his head down from the stove.*] They'll beat you to death one time—

SATIN. You're a blockhead.

ACTOR. Why?

SATIN. Because you can't kill a man two times.

ACTOR. [*After a pause.*] I don't understand—why not?

KLESTCH. You'd better come down off the stove and clean the place up— You've been loafing up there long enough.

ACTOR. That's none of your business.

KLESTCH. Wait till Vassilissa comes in— she'll show you whose business it is.

ACTOR. To hell with Vassilissa! Today it's the Baron's turn to clean. Baron!

BARON. [*Coming in from the kitchen.*] I've no time for cleaning—I'm going to market with Kvashnya.

ACTOR. That has nothing to do with me—you can go to jail for all I care, but it's your turn to sweep the floor— I'm not going to do other people's work.

BARON. Oh, the devil with it! Nastya will sweep up. Hey, you, fatal love! Wake up! [*Snatches* NASTYA's *book from her.*]

NASTYA. [*Rising.*] What do you want? Give it back, you boor. Call yourself a nobleman.

BARON. [*Returning the book.*] Nastya, sweep the floor for me, will you?

NASTYA. [*Going off to the kitchen.*] No, thank you! [KVASHNYA *appears at the door.*]

KVASHNYA. [*To the* BARON.] Come along with me. They can clean up without you. You've been asked, Actor, and you should do it. It won't break your back.

ACTOR. It's always me—I don't get it.

BARON. [*Coming in with a yoke over his shoulders, two baskets containing large cloth-covered pots hanging from the ends.*] It's rather heavy today.

SATIN. Hardly worth your while to have been born a baron.

KVASHNYA. [*To the* ACTOR.] No, mind you sweep the floor. [*Preceded by the* BARON, KVASHNYA *goes off.*]

ACTOR. [*Coming down from the stove.*] It's hard for me to breathe dust. [*Speaking with pride.*] My organism is poisoned with alcohol. [*He sits on a plank bed, sunk in thought.*]

SATIN. Organism—organon—

ANNA. Andrey Dmitrich—

KLESTCH. What is it now?

ANNA. Kvashyna has left me some dumplings in there—you eat them.

KLESTCH. [*Walking up to her.*] Aren't you going to?

ANNA. No, I don't want any. Why should I eat? You work—you need it.

KLESTCH. Are you afraid? Don't be. You may pull through—

ANNA. Go eat the dumplings. I feel all in. Seems as though it's coming soon—

KLESTCH. [*Moving away.*] Never mind— you may get up yet—that happens sometimes. [*Goes off into the kitchen.*]

ACTOR. [*In a loud voice, as if waking up suddenly.*] Yesterday, in the hospital, the doctor said to me: Your organism, he said, is completely poisoned with alcohol—

SATIN. [*Smiling.*] Organon—

ACTOR. [*Insistently.*] Not organon, but or-gan-ism—

SATIN. Sycamore—

ACTOR. [*Waving his hand at him.*] You and your nonsense. I'm speaking seriously—I am. If my organism is poisoned, then it's bad for me to

sweep the floor—to breathe dust—
SATIN. Macrobiotics— Ha!
BUBNOV. What are you mumbling about?
SATIN. Words— Here's another—tran-sit-dental—
BUBNOV. What does that mean?
SATIN. Don't know—I can't remember.
BUBNOV. Why do you say them then?
SATIN. Because. I'm tired, my friend, of all human words, our words. I'm fed up with them. I've heard every one of them a thousand times, if I've heard them once.
ACTOR. There's a line in the play *Hamlet:* "Words—words—words!" A fine piece of work. I played the gravedigger.
KLESTCH. [*Coming in from the kitchen.*] How soon are you going to play with the broom?
ACTOR. None of your business. [*Striking himself on the chest.*] The fair Ophelia! Nymph, in thy orisons be all my sins remembered! [*From offstage, somewhere in the distance, can be heard a muffled noise—followed by shouts and a policeman's whistle.* KLESTCH *resumes his work, rasping with a file.*]
SATIN. I love rare words I can't understand. When I was a boy I had a job in a telegraph office—used to read lots of books—
BUBNOV. So you were a telegrapher too?
SATIN. I was. There are some fine books—with lots of odd words. I was an educated man, you know.
BUBNOV. I've heard that a hundred times. So you were. So what? I was a fur-dresser at one time—had my own shop. My hands and arms got so yellow from dyeing furs—oh, so yellow—up to the elbow, I tell you. I thought I'd never wash it off—even go to my grave with yellow arms. Well, look at them now—they're just dirty. Yes.
SATIN. And so?
BUBNOV. Nothing. That's all.
SATIN. Well, what are you driving at?
BUBNOV. Oh, just something to think over. It comes to this—no matter how you paint yourself up, it'll all rub off—yes, it'll all rub off.
SATIN. Oh—my bones are sore.

ACTOR. [*Sitting with his arms around his knees.*] Education is rubbish. The main thing is talent. I knew an actor—he could scarcely read—but when he played his part the theater shook and rattled with the audience's raptures.
SATIN. Bubnov, give me five kopecks.
BUBNOV. All I've got is two kopecks.
ACTOR. Talent, I say, is what an actor needs. And talent is faith in oneself, in one's own powers.
SATIN. Give me five kopecks and I'll believe you're a talent, a hero, a crocodile, a bailiff— Klestch, give me five kopecks.
KLESTCH. Go to hell! There are too many of your kind around here.
SATIN. What are you cursing for? I know you haven't a kopeck.
ANNA. Andrey Dmitrich—I'm suffocating, I feel awful—
KLESTCH. What can I do?
BUBNOV. Open the door to the front hall.
KLESTCH. Thank you. You sit there on a plank bed, and I'm on the floor. Let me have your place, and you can open the door all you want. I have a cold as it is.
BUBNOV. [*Calmly.*] There's no reason for me to open the door. It's your own wife asking.
KLESTCH. [*Sullenly.*] People will ask for anything.
SATIN. Wow, my head's ringing! Why, I'd like to know, do people punch each other in the head?
BUBNOV. Not only heads—they do it to the rest of the body too. [*Rising.*] Got to go buy myself some thread. Funny, our landlord and his lady haven't shown up today—maybe they've dropped in their tracks. [*Goes off.*] [ANNA *coughs.* SATIN *lies motionless, his arms under his head.*]
ACTOR. [*Looks around with sad eyes and walks up to* ANNA.] Feeling bad?
ANNA. It's too stuffy in here.
ACTOR. If you like, I'll take you out into the hallway. Here, get up. [*He helps* ANNA *to rise, throws some old garment over her shoulders, and, holding her under the arm, leads her out to the hallway.*] Come, come—step out. I'm sick myself—poisoned with alcohol.

[KOSTYLYOV *appears in the doorway.*]

KOSTYLYOV. Going out for a walk? A fine couple—a ram and a lamb.

ACTOR. Make way—you see invalids are going out, don't you?

KOSTYLYOV. Pass on, if you please. [*Humming some hymn, he looks the place over suspiciously and inclines his head to the left as if trying to hear something in* PEPPEL's *room.* KLESTCH *tinkles his keys and rasps his file with great firmness, meanwhile watching his landlord from under his brows.*] Grating away, are you?

KLESTCH. What?

KOSTYLYOV. You're grating, I say. [*After a pause.*] Oh—yes—what is it I wanted to ask you? [*Quickly, in a low voice.*] Has my wife been here?

KLESTCH. I haven't seen her.

KOSTYLYOV. [*Moving cautiously toward* PEPPEL's *room.*] What a lot of space you get from me for two rubles a month! A bed—a place to sit—h'm—it's worth all of five rubles, I swear! I think I'll raise you half a ruble.

KLESTCH. Raise me by the neck and strangle me while you're at it. You'll be dead soon, but all you think about is half rubles.

KOSTYLYOV. Why should I strangle you? What good will it do anybody? God be with you, my good man, live to your heart's content. But I *will* raise your rent a half ruble. That'll buy me more oil for my icon lamp—and my sacrifice will burn before the holy icon. That sacrifice will be reckoned for me as amends for my sins, and for yours too. You never think of your sins, do you? So there it is. Oh, Andrey! You're such a spiteful man. Your wife has withered away because of your spitefulness. Nobody likes or respects you—and your work grates on people's ears, disturbs everybody—

KLESTCH. [*Shouting.*] Have you come to plague me? [SATIN *emits a loud roar.*]

KOSTYLYOV. [*Startled.*] My goodness! [*Enter the* ACTOR.]

ACTOR. I've seated the lady in the hallway, wrapped her up—

KOSTYLYOV. You have a kind heart, my friend. That's fine—that'll be credited to you.

ACTOR. When?

KOSTYLYOV. In the next world, my friend. Every deed, everything, is entered in a man's account there.

ACTOR. That's there. You ought to reward me for my kindness here.

KOSTYLYOV. Now, how could I do that?

ACTOR. Slash my debt in half.

KOSTYLYOV. Hee-hee! You will have your little joke, my dear fellow, you will keep play acting. Why, is kindness of heart comparable to money? Kindness stands above all benefits. And your debt to me is just what it is—a debt. Therefore you have to pay it back. To me who am an old man you must show kindness without looking for rewards—

ACTOR. Old man, you're a rogue. [*The* ACTOR *goes off to the kitchen.* KLESTCH *rises and exits to the hallway.*]

KOSTYLYOV. [*To* SATIN.] He's run away, that grater—hee-hee! He doesn't like me.

SATIN. Who does like you, outside the devil?

KOSTYLYOV. [*Laughingly.*] You *are* sharp. For myself, I like all of you—I understand you, my wretched, worthless, ruined brethren. [*Suddenly, quickly.*] Is Vassily in?

SATIN. Go look.

KOSTYLYOV. [*Walks up to* PEPPEL's *door and knocks.*] Vassya! [*The* ACTOR *appears at the kitchen door, munching.*]

PEPPEL. [*Offstage.*] Who's there?

KOSTYLYOV. It's me, Vassya.

PEPPEL. [*From his room.*] What do you want?

KOSTYLYOV. [*Moving back from the door.*] Open the door—

SATIN. [*Without looking at* KOSTYLYOV.] He'll open, and she's there. [*The* ACTOR *laughs.*]

KOSTYLYOV. [*Alarmed, in a low voice.*] What's that? Who's there? What do you mean?

SATIN. Are you speaking to me?

KOSTYLYOV. What was it you just said?

SATIN. I was talking to myself.

KOSTYLYOV. Look out, my friend. Know when to stop with your jokes—yes! [*Knocks loudly on* PEPPEL's *door.*] Vassily! [PEPPEL *opens his door.*]

PEPPEL. Well? What's the idea of disturbing me?

KOSTYLYOV. [*Peeking into the room.*] You see, I have—
PEPPEL. Have you brought the money?
KOSTYLYOV. I have some business to talk over with you.
PEPPEL. Have you brought the money?
KOSTYLYOV. What money? Wait—
PEPPEL. I say the money, the seven rubles for the watch. Come on.
KOSTYLYOV. What watch? Oh, Vassya—
PEPPEL. Now look! Yesterday, before witnesses, I sold you a watch for ten rubles. I received three rubles, now hand over the other seven. Why are you blinking at me like that? You wander around here, disturb other people's sleep, but don't know your business.
KOSTYLYOV. Sh-sh! Don't lose your temper, Vassya. The watch—that's—
SATIN. Stolen goods—
KOSTYLYOV. [*Sternly.*] I don't take stolen goods—how can you say—
PEPPEL. [*Seizing* KOSTYLYOV *by the shoulder.*] Why did you wake me up? What do you want?
KOSTYLYOV. I don't want anything—I'll go—if you feel that way.
PEPPEL. Go bring the money.
KOSTYLYOV. Such rude people! I must say! [*Goes off.*]
ACTOR. A regular comedy!
SATIN. Wonderful! I love it!
PEPPEL. What brought him here?
SATIN. Don't you understand? He's looking for his wife. Why don't you finish him off, Vassily?
PEPPEL. It's not worth spoiling my life over trash like him.
SATIN. You ought to make a neat job of it. Then you can marry Vassilissa—become our landlord—
PEPPEL. I can hardly wait! With your kind hearts you'll drink up all my property in a barroom, and me too. [*He sits down on a plank bed.*] The old pest—woke me up! And I had such a fine dream. I was fishing some place and caught a huge perch. It was such a size, it could only happen in a dream. Well, I pull it along on the hook and all the time I'm afraid the line will snap. I keep the bag ready hoping to get the perch in any minute—
SATIN. It wasn't a perch—it was Vassilissa.
ACTOR. He caught Vassilissa a long time ago.
PEPPEL. Go to hell, all of you—you *and* Vassilissa! [KLESTCH *enters from the front hall.*]
KLESTCH. Damn cold out!
ACTOR. Why didn't you bring Anna in? She'll freeze to death.
KLESTCH. Natasha took her into her kitchen.
ACTOR. The old man will throw her out.
KLESTCH. [*Sitting down to resume his work.*] Well, then Natasha will bring her here.
SATIN. Let me have five kopecks, Vassily.
ACTOR. [*To* SATIN.] Five kopecks! Look, Vassya! Give us a quarter of a ruble.
PEPPEL. I'd better give it to you quick—before you ask for a ruble. Here!
SATIN. Gibraltar! There are no better people in the world than thieves.
KLESTCH. Money comes easy to them—they don't have to work.
SATIN. Money comes easy to many people, but it doesn't come so easy to let it go. As for work, just you make it pleasant for me and I'll probably work— Yes. I probably will. When work is a pleasure, life is a joy! When work is a duty, life is slavery. [*To* ACTOR.] Let's go, Sardanapalus.
ACTOR. Let's go, Nebuchadnezzar. I'm going to get boiled—like forty thousand sots. [SATIN *and the* ACTOR *go off.*]
PEPPEL. [*Yawning.*] Well, how's your wife?
KLESTCH. [*After a pause.*] Looks like it'll be pretty soon now.
PEPPEL. You know, looking at you—I can't see any sense to your grating.
KLESTCH. What else can I do?
PEPPEL. Do nothing.
KLESTCH. How am I supposed to eat?
PEPPEL. Other people manage to live.
KLESTCH. You mean the ones here? They're not people. Scum, hoodlums—that's all they are. I'm a worker—I feel ashamed to set eyes on them—I've been working since I was a kid. You think I won't get out of here? I'll wriggle out of this hole even if it tears my skin off. Just wait till my wife dies— I've lived six months here, but it feels more like six years—

PEPPEL. Nobody here is any worse than you are—you're wrong about that.
KLESTCH. They're not! These men with no honor or conscience—
PEPPEL. [*Indifferently.*] What good are honor and conscience? You can't put them on your feet instead of boots. Honor and conscience are only important to those who have power—force— [*Enter* BUBNOV.]
BUBNOV. Whew, I'm shivering!
PEPPEL. Bubnov, have you got a conscience?
BUBNOV. What? Conscience?
PEPPEL. That's what I said.
BUBNOV. What do I want a conscience for? I'm no moneybags.
PEPPEL. That's just what I say. Only rich people need honor and conscience. And Klestch here criticizes us, says we have no conscience.
BUBNOV. Why, does he want to borrow some?
PEPPEL. He has plenty of his own.
BUBNOV. [*To* KLESTCH.] Then you're selling it? Well, you'll have a tough time finding customers here. There's one thing I would buy—marked cards—but even those would have to be on credit.
PEPPEL. [*Lecturing him.*] You're a fool, Andrey. You ought to listen to Satin—or the Baron about conscience.
KLESTCH. I have nothing to talk to them about.
PEPPEL. They've got more brains than you have—even if they are drunks.
BUBNOV. Be both drunk and smart—you've got a good start.
PEPPEL. Satin says—everybody wants his neighbor to have a conscience, but it turns out nobody can afford one. And it's the truth. [*Enter* NATASHA. *She is followed by* LUKA *who has a stick in his hand, a peasant knapsack on his back, and a kettle and teapot hanging from his waist.*]
LUKA. Good health to you, honest people.
PEPPEL. [*Smoothing down his mustache.*] Ah, Natasha!
BUBNOV. [*To* LUKA.] We were honest, you bet—so far back we forget.
NATASHA. This is a new lodger.
LUKA. It's all the same to me. I have just as much respect for crooks. To my way of thinking, every flea is a good flea—they're all dark and all good jumpers. Where do I accommodate myself here, my dear?
NATASHA. [*Pointing to the kitchen door.*] Step in there, grandpa.
LUKA. Thank you, girlie. Anywhere you say. To an old man any place that's warm is homeland. [LUKA *goes off.*]
PEPPEL. What an interesting old man you've brought, Natasha.
NATASHA. More interesting than you are. Your wife's in our kitchen. Andrey. Come get her in a little while.
KLESTCH. All right, I will.
NATASHA. You ought to treat her more kindly, Andrey. It won't be long now—
KLESTCH. I know.
NATASHA. You know. It's not enough to know—you have to understand. It's a frightening thing to die.
PEPPEL. I'm not afraid of death.
NATASHA. You *are* a brave man.
BUBNOV. [*Whistles.*] This thread is rotten.
PEPPEL. Really, I'm not afraid. I'll accept my death any time—right now. Take a knife and stab me to the heart, I'll die without a sigh of regret. Even with joy, because it comes from a pure hand.
NATASHA. [*As she turns to go off.*] Well—you better pull the wool over somebody else's eyes.
BUBNOV. [*Drawling.*] The thread is rotten, it's a fact.
NATASHA. [*At the door.*] Don't forget about your wife, Andrey.
KLESTCH. All right. [NATASHA *goes off.*]
PEPPEL. A fine girl.
BUBNOV. Not bad.
PEPPEL. Why is she so uppity with me—turning me down? She'll get ruined here anyway.
BUBNOV. She will—through you.
PEPPEL. Why through me? I feel sorry for her.
BUBNOV. Like a wolf for a sheep.
PEPPEL. That's a lie. I feel very sorry for her. She has a hard time of it here—I see it.
KLETSCH. Wait till Vassilissa catches you talking to her.
BUBNOV. Vassilissa? Y-yes, that one

doesn't make anybody a present of what's hers.

PEPPEL. [*Lying down on a plank bed.*] Go to hell, both of you—Prophets, too!

KLESTCH. You'll see—just wait.

LUKA. [*In the kitchen, singing.*] In the darkness of the night you can't see the road aright—

KLESTCH. Listen to that howling. New lodger! Hmph! [*Goes off into the hall.*]

PEPPEL. God, I'm bored. What is it makes me feel bored? You go on living, everything is fine. Suddenly, as if you'd caught a chill—you feel bored.

BUBNOV. Bored? H'm!

PEPPEL. Up to here.

LUKA. [*Singing in the kitchen.*] No, sir, you can't see your road aright—

PEPPEL. Hey, there, old man!

LUKA. [*Peeping out of the kitchen.*] You mean me?

PEPPEL. Yes, you. Stop singing.

LUKA. [*Coming in.*] Don't you like it?

PEPPEL. I do when the singing's good.

LUKA. Then mine is bad?

PEPPEL. It seems so.

LUKA. Imagine! And I thought I sang well. It's always like that. A man thinks to himself: I'm doing a good job. Then bang—everybody is displeased.

PEPPEL. [*Laughing.*] That's true!

BUBNOV. You say you're bored, and there you're laughing.

PEPPEL. What's that to you? The croaking raven.

LUKA. Who's bored around here?

PEPPEL. I am. [*Enter the* BARON.]

LUKA. Imagine that! In the kitchen there a girl is sitting. She's reading a book and crying—yes, crying! Tears roll down from her eyes. I say to her, What's the matter, my dear? And she answers, I feel so sorry for him. For who? I ask her. And she says—the man here, in this book. Some people find strange things to bother them, don't they? Must be from boredom too.

BARON. That one is a fool.

PEPPEL. Baron, have you had tea?

BARON. Yes. Go on.

PEPPEL. Would you like me to treat you to half a bottle?

BARON. Of course I would. Go on.

PEPPEL. Get down on all fours and bark like a dog.

BARON. Idiot! Who are you—a wealthy merchant? Or are you drunk?

PEPPEL. Oh, come on—do some barking. It'll amuse me. You're one of the high and mighty. Time was when you looked upon the common folk like me as if we weren't human beings and all that sort of thing—

BARON. Go on.

PEPPEL. Well, today I'll make you bark like a dog, and you will bark. You know you will.

BARON. So I will. Fathead! What sort of pleasure can you derive from that, when I know myself I've grown perhaps even worse than you. You should have tried to make me walk on all fours when you weren't my equal.

BUBNOV. That's true.

LUKA. Very good, if you ask me.

BUBNOV. What's gone is gone, and what's left isn't worth talking about. We have no high and mighty gentlemen here—everything has washed off—only the naked man remains.

LUKA. Therefore all are equal. Were you a baron, dear fellow?

BARON. What is this? Who are you, you old goblin?

LUKA. I've met a count, and a prince too—but this is the first time I've ever seen a baron, and a damaged one at that.

PEPPEL. [*Laughs*] You know, Baron, you've made me feel a bit ashamed of myself.

BARON. It's time you showed more intelligence, Vassily.

LUKA. Oh-ho-ho! Just to look at you, my good friends, one can see what kind of a life—

BUBNOV. Every morning's so foul we wake up with a howl.

BARON. We knew better times too. I used to wake up in the morning and drink coffee in bed—yes, coffee with cream!

LUKA. Yet all of you are just human beings. Yes, put on as much as you like, wriggle as much as you can, but just as you were born a man, so you'll die a man. And as I look on I see everybody getting cleverer and more interesting. They all live worse, it's true, but they all want something better—a stubborn lot.

BARON. Who are you, old man? Where do you come from?

LUKA. Who, me?

BARON. Are you a pilgrim?

LUKA. All of us are pilgrims on this earth. I've even heard people say that the earth itself is a pilgrim in the heavens.

BARON. [*Sternly.*] That may be, but how about a passport? Have you got one?

LUKA. And who are you, a detective?

PEPPEL. [*Delightedly.*] That's the ticket, old man. Got it in the neck, eh, Baron?

BUBNOV. Y-yes, our gentleman got it good and proper.

BARON. [*Embarrassed.*] What's the matter? I'm only joking, old man. Why, my friend, I have no papers myself.

BUBNOV. Liar.

BARON. That is, I have papers, but they're no good for anything.

LUKA. All papers are like that—no good for anything.

PEPPEL. Baron, let's go have a drink.

BARON. I'm ready. Good-by, old man. You are a rogue, though.

LUKA. All's possible, my friend.

PEPPEL. [*At the hallway door.*] Well, come on. [PEPPEL *goes off, the* BARON *hurrying after him.*]

LUKA. The fellow actually was a baron?

BUBNOV. God knows! But he's an aristocrat all right. Even now it breaks out all of a sudden. Seems it never got completely rubbed off.

LUKA. Maybe aristocracy is just like smallpox. A man gets well, but the pock marks remain.

BUBNOV. He's not bad, though. Only sometimes he's got to kick up a fuss—like about your passport today. [*Enter* ALYOSHKA. *He is tipsy, carries an accordion, and is whistling as he comes in.*]

ALYOSHKA. Hey, inhabitants!

BUBNOV. What are you yelling for?

ALYOSHKA. Excuse me. Pardon me. I'm a polite man—

BUBNOV. Off on a binge again?

ALYOSHKA. All I can hold! Just a minute ago subinspector Medyakin threw me out of the police station. Don't let me even get the smell of you in the streets, says he, ever! And I'm a man of character. My boss spits at me like a cat. And what's a boss? Pooh! He's a drunkard, my boss is. And I'm a man—who wants nothing. Nothing—and that's that! You can have me for a ruble twenty! But I want nothing! Give me a million—I don't want it. And to let my fellow worker who's a drunkard order me around—I won't have it. I won't, no, I won't! [NASTYA *appears in the kitchen doorway and shakes her head as she watches* ALYOSHKA.]

LUKA. [*Good-humoredly.*] You *have* got yourself in a tangle, young man—

BUBNOV. Just human foolishness.

ALYOSHKA. [*Stretching himself out on the floor.*] There, you can eat me up for all I care. But I want nothing. I'm a reckless man. Explain to me—why am I worse than other people, and who are they? Medyakin says: Keep off the street or I'll knock your block off. But I will go out. I'll lie in the middle of the street—let them run over me! I want nothing!

NASTYA. Poor thing! So young, and already—makes a fool of himself.

ALYOSHKA. [*Noticing* NASTYA, *raises himself to his knees.*] Mamsel! Parlez français? Prix-fixe? I'm painting the town red—

NASTYA. [*In a loud whisper.*] Vassilissa! [*Flinging open the hallway door,* VASSILISSA *enters.*]

VASSILISSA. [*To* ALYOSHKA.] You here again.

ALYOSHKA. Good morning—please step right in—

VASSILISSA. I told you, dog, not to show your face around here, didn't I? And you're here again?

ALYOSHKA. Vassilissa Karpovna—I'll play you a funeral march, shall I?

VASSILISSA. [*Pushing him by the shoulder.*] Get out!

ALYOSHKA. [*Moving toward the door.*] Now wait—you can't do that. A funeral march—I've just learned it—fresh music. No, wait—you can't do that.

VASSILISSA. I'll show you what I can't do. I'll set the whole street on you, you dirty prattler. You're too young to go around yapping about me.

ALYOSHKA. All right. I'm going. [*Runs out.*]
VASSILISSA. Don't let him set foot in here ever again. You hear me?
BUBNOV. I'm not your watchman.
VASSILISSA. I don't care who you are. You're living here on charity, remember that. How much do you owe me?
BUBNOV. [*Calmly.*] I haven't counted it.
VASSILISSA. Look out, or I will! [ALYOSHKA *opens the door.*]
ALYOSHKA. [*Shouting.*] Vassilissa Karpovna! I'm not afraid of you—not that much! [*He sneaks into the kitchen.* LUKA *laughs.*]
VASSILISSA. Who are you?
LUKA. A wayfarer—a pilgrim.
VASSILISSA. For a night or to stay?
LUKA. That depends.
VASSILISSA. Your passport.
LUKA. You shall have it.
VASSILISSA. Let me see.
LUKA. I'll bring it to you—drag it up to your very own door.
VASSILISSA. Wayfarer indeed! You should have called yourself a tramp—that would have been nearer the truth.
LUKA. [*With a sigh.*] Not much kindliness in you, woman. [VASSILISSA *moves toward* PEPPEL'S *room.* ALYOSHKA *peeps out of the kitchen.*]
ALYOSHKA. [*In a whisper.*] Has she gone?
VASSILISSA. [*Turning toward him.*] You still here? [ALYOSHKA *disappears, whistling.* NASTYA *and* LUKA *laugh.*]
BUBNOV. [*To* VASSILISSA.] He's out.
VASSILISSA. Who is?
BUBNOV. Vassily.
VASSILISSA. Have I asked you about him?
BUBNOV. I see you're looking in everywhere.
VASSILISSA. I'm looking to see that things are in order—understand? And why hasn't the floor been swept at this hour? How many times have I ordered you to keep the place clean?
BUBNOV. It's the Actor's turn—
VASSILISSA. I don't care whose it is. But if the sanitation inspectors come and I'm fined, I'll throw the whole damn lot of you out!
BUBNOV. [*Calmly.*] What will you live on then?

VASSILISSA. Don't let me see a speck of dust here! [*Walks toward the kitchen and stops before* NASTYA.] What are you sticking around for? And your face all swollen up too. Don't stand there like a stump. Sweep the floor. Have you seen—Natasha! Has she been here?
NASTYA. I don't know—I haven't seen her.
VASSILISSA. Bubnov! Has my sister been here?
BUBNOV. [*Pointing at* LUKA.] She brought him in.
VASSILISSA. And that one—was he in?
BUBNOV. Vassily? Yes, he was. She talked to Klestch here, your Natasha.
VASSILISSA. I'm not asking you who she talked to. Dirt—filth everywhere! Oh, pigs! See that this place is clean, hear me? [*She goes off quickly.*]
BUBNOV. God, what a brute that woman is!
LUKA. A peppery madam.
NASTYA. Anybody would be a brute leading such a life. Tie any live human being to a husband like here—
BUBNOV. Well, she's not tied too fast—
LUKA. Does she always act up like this?
BUBNOV. Always. You see, she came to see her lover, and he's out.
LUKA. So she felt hurt— I see. Oh-ho! So many different people order others around on this earth—and try to throw all sorts of scares into each other, but still there's no order in life—nor cleanliness.
BUBNOV. Everybody wants order, but their brains are in disorder. Anyway—somebody's got to sweep the floor. Nastya, you take care of it.
NASTYA. Oh, of course! I'm not your maid here. [*After a pause.*] I'm going to get drunk today—gloriously drunk!
BUBNOV. That's an idea.
LUKA. Why do you want to get drunk, girlie? Just a while ago you were crying—now you say you want to get drunk.
NASTYA. [*Challengingly.*] And when I'm drunk I'll cry again—that's all.
BUBNOV. All—that isn't much.
LUKA. But what's the reason, tell me? Even a pimple doesn't just spring up,

without a reason. [NASTYA *makes no answer, only shakes her head.*] I see— Oh-ho-ho! You human beings! What's going to happen to you? Well, let me sweep up here then. Where's your broom?

BUBNOV. Behind the door, in the hallway. [LUKA *goes into the hallway.*] Nastya!

NASTYA. Yes?

BUBNOV. Why did Vassilissa jump on Alyoshka?

NASTYA. He's been telling everybody Vassily's sick of her and wants to drop her for Natasha. I'm going to get out of here and move to other lodgings.

BUBNOV. What for? And where?

NASTYA. I'm fed up—I'm not needed here.

BUBNOV. [*Calmly.*] You're not needed anywhere. For that matter all humans on this earth are not needed. [NASTYA *shakes her head, rises, and goes out into the hallway. Enter* MEDVEDEV, *a policeman, followed by* LUKA *carrying a broom.*]

MEDVEDEV. I don't think I know you.

LUKA. Do you know everybody else?

MEDVEDEV. On my beat I have to know everybody. But I don't know you.

LUKA. That's because the earth couldn't squeeze all of itself into your beat, uncle—a bit of it has remained outside. [*He goes off to the kitchen.*]

MEDVEDEV. [*Walking up to* BUBNOV.] He's right, mine is a small beat—though it's worse than any big one. Just a while ago, before going off duty, I took the cobbler Alyoshka to the station. He stretched himself out in the middle of the street, began playing his accordion, and yelled—I don't want anything—I don't want anything. There were horses in the street and all sorts of traffic—he could have been crushed to death and all that. A wild fellow. Well, I took him in—he's too fond of disorder.

BUBNOV. Coming for a game of checkers tonight?

MEDVEDEV. I am. Y-yes. And how is—Vassily?

BUBNOV. He's all right. The same as always.

MEDVEDEV. Then he's still carrying on?

BUBNOV. Why shouldn't he? He can carry on—

MEDVEDEV. [*Doubtfully.*] Can he? [LUKA, *carrying a bucket, crosses the room to the hallway.*] Y-yes— There's been some talk about Vassily around here—have you heard it?

BUBNOV. I hear all sorts of talk—

MEDVEDEV. About him and Vassilissa— Have you noticed anything?

BUBNOV. Noticed what?

MEDVEDEV. Just in general— Or maybe you know and are lying to me? Everybody knows it—[*Severely.*] One mustn't lie, my friend.

BUBNOV. Why should I lie?

MEDVEDEV. Glad you see it my way. Oh, the swine! They say Peppel and Vassilissa—are like that—What's that got to do with me? I'm not her father—only her uncle. Why should they make fun of me? [*Enter* KVASHNYA.] God knows what people are coming to—they laugh at everything. Ah! It's you!

KVASHNYA. It's me, my precious uniform! Bubnov, he pestered me again at the market to marry him—

BUBNOV. Why not? Go to it! He's got money, and still makes a presentable swain.

MEDVEDEV. Me? Ho! Ho!

KVASHNYA. Ah, so? Don't touch my sore spot, policeman, I went through it once before, dear man. When a woman gets married it's like jumping into a hole in the ice in the middle of winter: you do it once, and you remember it the rest of your days.

MEDVEDEV. Wait a minute. Husbands aren't all alike.

KVASHNYA. But I'm always the same. When my darling husband—God blast his soul—gave up the ghost, I was so happy I stayed in alone the whole day—I sat and couldn't believe my good luck.

MEDVEDEV. If your husband beat you—for no good reason, you should have complained to the police.

KVASHNYA. I kept complaining to God for eight years—he never helped.

MEDVEDEV. Today wife-beating is forbidden. Today there's law and order in everything. You can't beat anybody for nothing. If you do beat anyone, it's got to be for the sake of order. [*Enter* LUKA, *leading* ANNA.]

LUKA. Here, we've made it. Don't you know you mustn't walk around alone with your weak constitution? Where's your place?

ANNA. [*Pointing to her bed.*] Thank you, grandpa!

KVASHNYA. There's a married one. Look at her.

LUKA. The little woman has a very weak constitution. She was walking along the hallway, clinging to the walls, and moaning. Why do you let her walk by herself.?

KVASHNYA. It was careless of us, sir, please forgive us. And her chambermaid must have gone out for a stroll.

LUKA. You're making a joke of it—but how can anybody cast off a human being? Whatever condition he's in, a human being is always worth something.

MEDVEDEV. You have to keep your eye on a person. What if she dies? There'll be a lot of complications. Yes, you have to keep an eye open.

LUKA. Very true, master sergeant.

MEDVEDEV. Y-yes—though I'm not quite a master sergeant yet—

LUKA. Ain't you? You look like a hero. [*There is noise and a stamping of feet in the hallway. Muffled sounds of shouting are heard.*]

MEDVEDEV. Must be a brawl?

BUBNOV. Sounds like it.

KVASHNYA. I'm going to take a look.

MEDVEDEV. I'll have to be going too. Duty is duty! I wish when people started a fight other people would leave them alone. They'd stop fighting themselves—when they got tired. They should be allowed to knock each other around without interference, for all they're worth. They wouldn't be so keen to get into scrapes again—they'd remember their bruises—

BUBNOV. [*Getting up from his plank bed.*] You ought to tell that to the Chief of Police— [*The door bursts wide open, revealing* KOSTYLYOV *on the threshold.*]

KOSTYLYOV. [*Shouting.*] Abram! Come quick! Vassilissa's—killing—Natasha! Quick! [KVASHNYA, MEDVEDEV, *and* BUBNOV *rush out into the hallway.* LUKA *gazes after them, shaking his head.*]

ANNA. Oh, God! Poor little Natasha!

LUKA. Who's fighting out there?

ANNA. Our landladies—sisters—

LUKA. [*Walking up to* ANNA.] What are they dividing up?

ANNA. They've nothing better to do—they're well fed and strong—

LUKA. What's your name?

ANNA. Anna. You know, as I look at you, you remind me of my father—just as kind—and soft.

LUKA. I've been through the wringer—that's why I'm soft. [*He laughs with a cracked senile laugh.*]

Act 2

The same basement. On the plank bed near the stove SATIN, *the* BARON, *the* GOITER, *and the* TARTAR *are playing cards.* KLESTCH *and the* ACTOR *are watching the game. On his plank bed* BUBNOV *is playing checkers with* MEDVEDEV. LUKA *is sitting on a square stool by* ANNA's *bed. It is evening. The place is lighted by two lamps: one hanging from the wall near the cardplayers, the other on* BUBNOV's *plank bed.*

TARTAR. I play one more game—then I play no more—

BUBNOV. Goiter, sing! [*Striking up.*] The sun comes up, the sun goes down again—

GOITER. [*Continuing.*] But in my cell it's never light—

TARTAR. [*To* SATIN.] Mix cards—mix 'em good! I know good what you are.

BUBNOV AND GOITER. [*Singing together.*] The guards are watching my barred window—e-eh! Watching closely day and night—

ANNA. Beatings—harsh words, that's all I've ever known in my life. Nothing but that—

LUKA. Forget it, my good woman. Don't upset yourself.

MEDVEDEV. Where are you moving your man? Are you blind?

BUBNOV. A-ah! I see—I see—
TARTAR. [*Threatening* SATIN *with his fist.*] Why you try hide a card? I see it—Oh!
GOITER. Don't bother, Assan! They'll clean up on us anyway! Bubnov, sing.
ANNA. I don't remember a time I didn't feel hungry. I counted every piece of bread. All my life I've trembled and worried that I might eat more than my share. All my life I've been wearing rags—all my miserable life. What have I done to deserve this?
LUKA. Poor child! You are worn out. Never mind.
ACTOR. [*To the* GOITER.] Play the jack—the jack, you fool!
BARON. And we have a king.
KLESTCH. They'll always beat your card.
SATIN. Such is our habit.
MEDVEDEV. King!
BUBNOV. Mine too. Well—
ANNA. I'm dying now—
KLESTCH. Oh, oh! Stop playing, Assan, take a tip from me and get out of the game.
ACTOR. He can't do without your advice, can he?
BARON. Watch out, Andrey, or I'll send you packing to hell!
TARTAR. Deal again. The jug went for water—broke himself—and me too! [*Shaking his head,* KLESTCH *moves over to* BUBNOV.]
ANNA. I keep thinking: O God! Am I to be punished with suffering in the next world too? Even there, O God?
LUKA. You won't be. Don't worry. Nothing will happen to you. You'll have a good rest there. Just bear up a little more. Everybody bears his life, my dear, each in his own way. [*He rises and walks quickly to the kitchen.*]
BUBNOV. [*Singing.*] You guards can watch my window closely—
GOITER. [*Singing.*] I will not try my leave to take—
BUBNOV AND GOITER. [*Together.*] I'd surely like to get my freedom—e-eh! But no—my chains I cannot break.
TARTAR. [*Shouting.*] Ah! You push a card up your sleeve.
BARON. [*Embarrassed.*] Well—where do you want me to push it—up your nose?
ACTOR. You're wrong, Assan—nobody would do that—never.
TARTAR. I saw it. Crook. I no play.
SATIN. [*Gathering the cards.*] Leave off, Assan. You knew we were crooks. If so, why did you play with us?
BARON. You've lost two quarter rubles, but make three rubles' worth of noise. Ah!
TARTAR. [*Heatedly.*] You must play honest.
SATIN. What for?
TARTAR. What you mean, what for?
SATIN. Just that—what for?
TARTAR. You not know?
SATIN. I don't. Do you? [*The* TARTAR *spits in bitter disgust. The others laugh at him.*]
GOITER. [*Good-humoredly.*] You're a funny man, Assan. Can't you understand? If they're going to start living honestly, they'll die of hunger in three days.
TARTAR. That no my business. People must live honest.
GOITER. There he goes—like a parrot. We'll do better to go have tea. Bubnov! [*Singing.*] O chains, you heavy chains that bind me—
BUBNOV. You are my iron guards in truth—
GOITER. Come on, Assan. [*Goes off, singing.*] I know I cannot break you ever—e-eh! [*The* TARTAR *shakes his fist at the* BARON *and follows his friend.*]
SATIN. [*To the* BARON.] Your Excellency, you made a magnificent fool of yourself once again. You're an educated man, and still you can't do a proper job of cheating at cards—
BARON. [*Spreading his hands.*] Devil knows how I muffed it.
ACTOR. You lack talent—faith in yourself—and without that a man can do nothing—ever.
MEDVEDEV. I have one king, and you have two. H'mm!
BUBNOV. Even one is all right if he's clever and bright. Your move.
KLESTCH. Your game is lost, Abram Ivanych.
MEDVEDEV. Mind your own business, understand? Hold your tongue.
SATIN. Winnings—fifty-three kopecks.
ACTOR. Three kopecks go to me. Though what do I want three kopecks for? [*Enter* LUKA *from the*

kitchen.]

LUKA. Well, you've cleaned up the Tartar. Now you'll go drink some vodka, I take it?

BARON. Come with us.

SATIN. I'd like to see what sort of a man you are when drunk.

LUKA. No better than when I'm sober.

ACTOR. Come along, grandpa—I'll recite some verses to you.

LUKA. What are those?

ACTOR. You know—poems.

LUKA. Oh, poems! And what do I want poems for?

ACTOR. They make one laugh—or sometimes sad.

SATIN. Are you coming, reciter? [SATIN *and the* BARON *go off.*]

ACTOR. In a minute. I'll catch up with you. Here, grandpa, is something from a poem—I forget how it begins— H'm, I forget— [*He rubs his forehead.*]

BUBNOV. There! It's good-by to your king. Your move.

MEDVEDEV. Damn it—I made the wrong move.

ACTOR. In the old days, old man, when my organism wasn't yet poisoned with alcohol, I had a good memory. Now it's all over with me—it's all over. I always read that poem with great success—it brought the house down. You don't know what applause is— It's like vodka, my friend. I would come on the stage, stand like this— [*Assumes a pose.*] Yes, stand like this and— [*A long pause.*] I can't remember a thing—not a single word! And it's the poem I loved best of all— That's bad, old man, isn't it?

LUKA. It can't be good if you've forgotten something you loved best. All our soul is in what we love.

ACTOR. I've drunk up my soul, old man. I'm lost. And why am I lost? Because I had no faith in myself. I'm finished.

LUKA. Why finished? You get yourself treated. They treat for drunkenness today, so I hear. Free of charge, too. There's a special hospital for drunkards—so they can be treated for nothing. They've decided, you see, that a drunkard is a human being like everybody else, and they're even glad when he wants to be treated. There's a chance for you—go there right away.

ACTOR. [*Reflectively.*] Go where? Where is it?

LUKA. It's—in a town—what's its name? It's called— Never mind. I'll give you the name! Only you know what—you prepare yourself in the meantime. Keep away from vodka. Pull yourself together and bear up! Then later you'll be cured—and you'll start your life all over again. Yes, all over again—wouldn't it be fine, my friend? Well, make up your mind—and be quick about it!

ACTOR. [*Smiling.*] All over again—from the start— That'll be fine— Yes, yes. Again. [*He laughs.*] Of course. I can do that. Surely I can, don't you think?

LUKA. Why certainly. A man can do anything, if he only wants to.

ACTOR. [*As if suddenly awakened.*] You're a queer fellow. So long! [*Whistles.*] So long, old man. [*Goes off.*]

ANNA. Grandpa!

LUKA. What is it, my dear?

ANNA. Talk to me.

LUKA. [*Coming up to her.*] All right, let's talk. [KLESTCH *looks about, walks up to his wife, gazes at her, and gesticulates as if wishing to say something.*] What is it, my friend?

KLESTCH. [*In a low voice.*] Nothing. [*He walks slowly toward the hallway, stops for a few seconds at the threshold, and goes off.*]

LUKA. [*After following* KLESTCH *with his eyes.*] Your husband finds it hard to bear.

ANNA. I have other things than him to think of now.

LUKA. Did he beat you?

ANNA. Didn't he though! It's through him, I think, that I took sick—

BUBNOV. My wife—had a lover. The rascal was awfully good at checkers—

MEDVEDEV. H'm—

ANNA. Talk to me, grandpa dear. I feel sick—

LUKA. It's all right. It's before death, dear. It's all right. You keep hoping. You'll die, you see, and then you'll have peace. You'll have nothing to fear—nothing at all. There'll be peace and quiet—and you'll have nothing to do but lie. Death quiets everything. It's kind to us humans. When you die you'll have rest, folks say. It's true, my dear. For where can a human being find rest in this world? [*Enter* PEPPEL. *He is slightly tipsy, and looks disheveled and sullen. He sits down on a plank bed near the door and remains silent and motionless.*]

ANNA. But has one to suffer there too?

LUKA. There'll be nothing there, nothing. Believe me. Peace and nothing more. They'll call you before the Lord and say: Look, O Lord, here's your servant Anna—

MEDVEDEV. [*Sharply.*] How do you know what they'll say there? [*At the sound of* MEDVEDEV's *voice* PEPPEL *raises his head and listens.*]

LUKA. It must be I do, master sergeant—

MEDVEDEV. [*In a conciliatory tone.*] I—see. Well, it's your business. Though I'm not quite a master sergeant yet—

BUBNOV. I take two.

MEDVEDEV. Drat it.

LUKA. And the Lord will look at you gently and caressingly and will say: I know this Anna. Well, he'll say, conduct Anna to heaven. Let her rest—I know she's had a very hard life and is very tired. Give Anna rest—

ANNA. [*Gasping.*] Oh, grandpa dear—if it were only like that! If I could only have rest—feel nothing—

LUKA. You won't, I tell you. You have to believe. You have to die with joy, without fear. To us, I tell you, death is like a mother to little children.

ANNA. But maybe—I'll get better?

LUKA. [*Ironically.*] What for? For more suffering?

ANNA. Well—just to live a little longer—just a little. If there isn't going to be any suffering there, I can bear it here—yes, I can.

LUKA. There'll be nothing there. Just—

PEPPEL. [*Rising.*] That's true— Or maybe it isn't.

ANNA. [*In a frightened voice.*] O God—

LUKA. Hello, handsome—

MEDVEDEV. Who's hollering?

PEPPEL. [*Walking up to him.*] I am. Why?

MEDVEDEV. There's no call for your hollering—that's why. Every man must behave himself quietly.

PEPPEL. Blockhead! Call yourself an uncle— Ho! Ho!

LUKA. [*To* PEPPEL, *in a low voice.*] You there—don't shout. There's a woman dying here—her lips are already brushed with earth—don't interfere.

PEPPEL. For you, grandfather, I'll be glad to do it. You're a smart fellow. You tell lies and pleasant tales mighty well. That's all right with me. Go on lying. There's damn little in this world that's pleasant.

BUBNOV. Is the woman really dying?

LUKA. She doesn't look like she's joking—

BUBNOV. Well, then she'll stop coughing. Her coughing's been disturbing everybody. I take two.

MEDVEDEV. Ah, blast your hide!

PEPPEL. Abram.

MEDVEDEV. I'm no Abram to you.

PEPPEL. Abrashka, is Natasha ill?

MEDVEDEV. What business is that of yours?

PEPPEL. Come on, tell me: did Vassilissa beat her up badly?

MEDVEDEV. That has nothing to do with you either. It's a family affair. And who are you, anyway?

PEPPEL. Never mind who I am. But if I decide so, you'll never see Natasha again.

MEDVEDEV. [*Interrupting his game.*] What's that? Do you know who you're talking about? That my niece should ever become— You thief!

PEPPEL. I may be a thief, but you never caught me—

MEDVEDEV. You wait. I'll catch you yet—it won't be long!

PEPPEL. If you catch me, it will be so much the worse for your whole brood. Do you think I'm going to keep mum before the court examiner? Expect good deeds from a wolf! Who kept after me to start thieving and who showed me the places? Mishka Kostylyov and his wife. Who took in what I stole? Mishka Kostylyov and his wife.

MEDVEDEV. Liar. They won't believe you.

PEPPEL. They will—because it's the truth. I'll drag you into it too—ha! I'll ruin all of you, you scoundrel,

you'll see.
MEDVEDEV. [*Taken aback.*] You're lying. Just lying. And when have I done you any harm? A mad dog, that's what you are.
PEPPEL. And when have you done me any good?
LUKA. Aha—
MEDVEDEV. [*To* LUKA.] What are you croaking about? You have no business here. This is a family affair.
BUBNOV. [*To* LUKA.] Leave off. They're not tying nooses for you and me.
LUKA. [*Meekly.*] I know. I only say if a man hasn't done somebody good, he's done him ill.
MEDVEDEV. [*Missing* LUKA's *point.*] That's better. Around here we all know one another. And who are you? [*Spitting like an angry cat, he goes off quickly.*]
LUKA. The gentleman lost his temper. Oh-ho-ho! You *have* got yourselves into all sorts of mix-ups, my friends—
PEPPEL. He's run to complain to Vassilissa.
BUBNOV. You're playing the fool, Vassily. What's all this showing off how brave you are? Bravery is all right when you go picking mushrooms in the woods. It's not much use in these parts. They'll wring your neck in no time here.
PEPPEL. Oh, no. We folks from Yaroslavl don't knuckle down without a fight. And if it's going to be a fight, I'm ready for it.
LUKA. Really, young man, why don't you go away from here?
PEPPEL. Where to? Can you tell me?
LUKA. Go to—Siberia.
PEPPEL. Oh, yes? No, I'll wait until I'm sent there at government expense.
LUKA. You listen to me—go to Siberia. New paths will open for you there. Men like you are needed there.
PEPPEL. My life is cut out for me. My father spent all his life in prisons and taught me to do the same. I was only a tyke when everybody already called me a thief, a thief's son—
LUKA. Well, Siberia's a fine place—a golden land. For a man who's strong and has a good head on his shoulders it's like a hothouse for a cucumber.
PEPPEL. Why do you tell lies, old man?
LUKA. What?
PEPPEL. Gone deaf suddenly. Why do you lie, I say?
LUKA. Where do you see me lying?
PEPPEL. Everywhere. You keep saying it's fine here and it's fine there, but you know you're lying. What for?
LUKA. Well, take my word for it and go look it over for yourself. You'll thank me for it. What's the good of sticking around here? Anyway, what do you want the truth for? The truth might come down on you like an ax.
PEPPEL. I don't care. An ax is all right with me.
LUKA. You're a queer fellow. Why be your own killer?
BUBNOV. I don't understand what all this silly talk is about. What truth do you want, Vassily? And what for? You know the truth about yourself—everybody knows it.
PEPPEL. Shut up, Bubnov, don't croak. I want him to tell me— Listen, old man: Does God exist? [LUKA *smiles, making no answer.*]
BUBNOV. People live like chips floating down the river. The house is built, but the chips are thrown away to take care of themselves.
PEPPEL. Well? Does he? Answer me.
LUKA. [*In a low voice.*] If you believe in him, he exists. If you don't, he doesn't. Whatever you believe in exists. [PEPPEL, *puzzled, stares at* LUKA *in silence.*]
BUBNOV. I'm going to have some tea. Come along, you two!
LUKA. Why are you looking at me?
PEPPEL. Well—wait. So you say—
BUBNOV. I'll go alone then— [*He walks toward the door as* VASSILISSA *enters.*]
PEPPEL. So you mean to say—
VASSILISSA. [*To* BUBNOV.] Is Nastya in?
BUBNOV. No. [*He goes off.*]
PEPPEL. Oh, it's you.
VASSILISSA. [*Going up to* ANNA.] Still alive?
LUKA. Don't disturb her.
VASSILISSA. Why are you hanging around here?
LUKA. I can leave, if necessary.
VASSILISSA. [*Walking toward* PEPPEL's *room.*] I want to talk over some business with you, Vassily. [*She enters*

PEPPEL's *room, while* LUKA *moves to the hallway door, opens it, slams it loudly, and cautiously climbs over a plank bed onto the stove.*] Come here, Vassya.

PEPPEL. I don't want to.

VASSILISSA. [*Coming out.*] Why not? What makes you cross with me?

PEPPEL. I'm bored—fed up with all this business.

VASSILISSA. Fed up with me too?

PEPPEL. Yes, with you too. [VASSILISSA *pulls her shoulder kerchief tight, pressing her hands to her breast, then walks to* ANNA's *bed, peeps silently behind the curtain, and returns to* PEPPEL.] Well, if you have anything to say—

VASSILISSA. What is there to say? You can't force one to like you—and it's not in my character to beg for alms. Thank you for speaking the truth.

PEPPEL. What truth?

VASSILISSA. That you're fed up with me. Or isn't it true? [PEPPEL *gazes at her in silence. She moves up to him.*] Why are you staring at me? Don't you recognize me?

PEPPEL. [*With a sigh.*] You *are* beautiful to look at, Vassilissa—VASSILISSA *puts an arm around his neck, but he shakes it off with a shrug of his shoulders.*] But you never touched my heart. I lived with you and all that sort of thing—but I never really cared for you—

VASSILISSA. [*In a low voice.*] I see—Well?

PEPPEL. Well—there's nothing we can talk about—nothing at all! Just leave me.

VASSILISSA. You've taken a fancy to somebody else?

PEPPEL. That's none of your business. If I have, I won't ask you to be my matchmaker.

VASSILISSA. [*Significantly.*] That's a pity. I could probably get you the right party.

PEPPEL. [*Suspiciously.*] Who do you mean?

VASSILISSA. You know who—why pretend? Vassily, I'm a straightforward person—[*Lowering her voice.*] I won't hide it—you've hurt me. For no reason whatever you struck me as if with a whip. You were telling me you loved me and then all of a sudden—

PEPPEL. It wasn't sudden at all. I've felt like that for a long time. There's no soul in you, Vassilissa. A woman must have a soul. We men are brutes. We should be—we have to be tamed and trained. And what kind of training have you been giving me?

VASSILISSA. What's gone is gone. I know we're not masters of our feelings. If you don't love me any more—all right—so be it.

PEPPEL. Well, then, that's that. We'll each go our own way, quietly, without any fuss, and that's fine.

VASSILISSA. No, wait. That's not all. When I lived with you I was always counting on you to help me get out of this mess—free me from my husband, my uncle—this whole life. Maybe it wasn't you I loved, Vassya, but this hope, this constant thought on my mind, that I loved in you. You understand? I was waiting for you to pull me out of here—

PEPPEL. You're no nail, and I'm no pair of pliers. I thought myself that with your brains—you *are* clever—and smart too—aren't you?

VASSILISSA. [*Bending closer to him.*] Vassya, let's—help each other.

PEPPEL. How?

VASSILISSA. [*Quietly, but strongly.*] I know you like—my sister.

PEPPEL. That's why you're so brutal—always beating her. Look out, Vassilissa. Keep your hands off her.

VASSILISSA. Wait. Don't excite yourself. It can all be done quietly—arranged in a friendly way. You want to marry Natasha? All right—marry her. I'll even give you some money—say three hundred rubles. When I've saved more, I'll give you more.

PEPPEL. [*Moving away from* VASSILISSA.] Now just a minute—What's that for? What's the idea?

VASSILISSA. Free me from my husband—Take that noose off my neck.

PEPPEL. [*Whistles quietly.*] So that's it? I see. Very neat on your part—the husband packed off into the grave, the lover to Siberia, and you youself—

VASSILISSA. No, Vassya—why Siberia? You don't have to do it yourself—you can get others. And even if you do it, who'll know? Think of Natasha. And you'll have money—you'll go away somewhere—you'll free me for life—

and as far as my sister's concerned, it'll be better for her, too, to be away from me. It's hard for me to see her—I get bitter because of you—and I can't restrain myself. I torment her, beat her—beat her so hard I cry myself for pity of her. But I keep beating her and will go right on doing it.
PEPPEL. A demon—that's what you are. And you're boasting about it.
VASSILISSA. I'm not boasting—I'm speaking the truth. Think, Vassya. Twice you did time on account of my husband—because of his greed. He's sucking my blood like a bedbug—been doing it for four years. What sort of a husband is that? And he's harsh with Natasha, taunts her, calls her a beggar. He's poison to everybody.
PEPPEL. There's something too clever in all this.
VASSILISSA. My meaning is clear—only a fool can fail to understand what I want. [KOSTYLYOV *enters cautiously and moves stealthily forward.*]
PEPPEL. [*To* VASSILISSA.] Well, you'd better go now.
VASSILISSA. Think it over. [*Noticing her husband.*] What brings you here? Looking for me? [PEPPEL *jumps to his feet and stares wildly at* KOSTYLYOV.]
KOSTYLYOV. It's me—it's me. And you're alone here? Ah—you have been having a chat? [*Suddenly stamps his feet and squeals at* VASSILISSA.] You slut! You dirty trash! [*He is frightened by his own voice, as the other two look at him silently without moving.*] God forgive me—you've led me into sin again, Vassilissa. I've been looking for you everywhere. [*Squealing again.*] Time to go to bed! You've forgotten to put oil in the icon lamps! You—miserable swine. [*He shakes his trembling hands at* VASSILISSA. *She walks slowly to the hallway, looking back at* PEPPEL.]
PEPPEL. [*To* KOSTYLYOV.] Get out of here!
KOSTYLYOV. [*Shouting.*] It's my house! You get out of here! Thief!
PEPPEL. [*In a low voice.*] Get out. Mishka!
KOSTYLYOV. Don't you dare! I'll—I'll—[PEPPEL *grabs him by the collar and shakes him. A loud shuffling and a long animal-like yawn are heard from the top of the stove.* PEPPEL *releases* KOSTYLYOV, *who runs into the hallway screaming.*]
PEPPEL. [*Jumping onto the plank bed.*] Who's up there—on the stove?
LUKA. [*Popping out.*] What?
PEPPEL. You?
LUKA. [*Calmly.*] Yes—it's me—none other—O Lord Jesus Christ!
PEPPEL. [*Closes the hallway door and looks for the bolt, but cannot find it.*] Ah, those devils! Come down, old man!
LUKA. I'm coming—right away. [*He comes down.*]
PEPPEL. [*Roughly.*] Why did you get up on top of the stove?
LUKA. Was there somewhere else I should have gone?
PEPPEL. But you went into the hall?
LUKA. It's too cold out there for an old man like me.
PEPPEL. Did you—hear?
LUKA. I heard. How could I help hearing? I ain't deaf. Ah, what luck has come to you, my boy—what luck!
PEPPEL. [*Suspiciously.*] What sort of luck?
LUKA. That I got up on the stove.
PEPPEL. And why did you start shuffling around up there?
LUKA. Because I felt hot—fortunately for you, my boy. Besides, I figured the fellow can make a mistake and squeeze the old man to death.
PEPPEL. Yes—I could've done that—I hate him—
LUKA. Nothing easier. Anybody could do it. People often make that mistake.
PEPPEL. [*Smiling.*] Say, maybe you made it yourself once?
LUKA. Listen to what I'm going to tell you, my boy. You've got to cut yourself off from that woman. Don't let her come near you—ever. She'll drive her husband into the grave herself, and she'll do a neater job of it than you can—believe me! Don't listen to that witch. Look at my head. Bald, isn't it? And why? Because of these same women. I've known more of them maybe than I had hair on my head. And this Vassilissa woman is worse than a savage.
PEPPEL. I don't understand. Am I supposed to say thank you, or are you

just another—

LUKA. Don't say anything. You can't improve on what I said. Better listen to me—whoever she is, the girl you like around here, take her by the arm and be off with you! Get away from here—as fast as you can!

PEPPEL. [*Somberly.*] I can't make people out—which are kind and which are out to get you—I can't understand anything.

LUKA. What is there to understand? A man can live any which way—however his heart tells him—kind today, mean tomorrow. If that girl here has touched your heart real strong, go away with her and that's all there is to that. Or you can go away alone. You're still young—you have plenty of time to settle down with a woman.

PEPPEL. [*Taking* LUKA *by the shoulder.*] No, tell me what are you getting out of all this?

LUKA. Now wait—let go. I want to have a look at Anna—there's been too much rattle in her breathing. [*Walks up to* ANNA's *bed, draws the curtain, looks, touches her with his hand.* PEPPEL *watches him attentively, with a puzzled air.*] Jesus Christ, the all-merciful. Receive the soul of thy newly departed servant, Anna, with peace.

PEPPEL. [*Quietly.*] Is she dead? [*Staying where he is, he straightens up and gazes at the bed.*]

LUKA. [*Quietly.*] Her suffering has ended. Where's her man?

PEPPEL. Over at the inn, most likely.

LUKA. I must go tell him.

PEPPEL. [*With a shudder.*] I don't like dead people.

LUKA. [*Walking toward the hall door.*] What's there to like them for? It's the living people we should like—yes, the living ones.

PEPPEL. I'll go along with you.

LUKA. Are you afraid?

PEPPEL. I don't like—[*They hurry out. The place is deserted and quiet. After a time a noise is heard beyond the hallway door—it is indistinct, uneven, and unintelligible. Then the* ACTOR *enters.*]

ACTOR. [*Stops just across the threshold without closing the door, and, holding onto the jamb with both hands, shouts.*] Hey, old man! Where are you? It's come back to me—listen. [*Staggering, takes two steps forward and, assuming a stage pose, recites.*]

If the world, my friends, is unable to find
The road to justice and truth,
Honor be to the madman who weaves golden dreams
Giving mankind surcease.

[NATASHA *appears at the door behind the* ACTOR.]

Old man, listen.

If tomorrow the sun should forget to light up
Our planet's eternal path,
A thought of some madman will instantly flash
To illumine the darkened earth.

NATASHA. [*Laughing.*] You loon! Been out getting crocked?

ACTOR. [*Turning to* NATASHA.] Ah! It's you? And where's the old man, the darling little old man? There's nobody here, it seems. Well, farewell Natasha—yes, farewell!

NATASHA. [Stepping forward.] You never said good evening, and now you're saying farewell.

ACTOR. [*Barring her way.*] I'm leaving, going away. Spring will come, but I'll be here no more.

NATASHA. Let me pass. Where are you off to?

ACTOR. I'm going to look for a town—to get treatment. You should go too. Ophelia—get thee to a nunnery. You see, there's a hospital for organisms—for drunkards. A splendid hospital—marble everywhere—marble floors—bright, clean rooms—food—everything free! And yes, marble floors! I'll find this hospital, get cured, and once again I'll—act. I'm on the road to rebirth, as King—Lear said. My stage name is Sverchkov-Zavolzhsky—nobody knows that—nobody. I have no name here. Do you realize how it hurts to lose one's name? Even dogs have names. [NATASHA *quietly moves around the* ACTOR, *stops at* ANNA's *bed, and looks.*] Without a name there's no man.

NATASHA. Look—but she's dead!

ACTOR. [*Shaking his head.*] That can't be.
NATASHA. [*Stepping back.*] Really—look. [BUBNOV *appears at the door.*]
BUBNOV. Look at what?
NATASHA. Anna's—dead.
BUBNOV. That means the end of her coughing. [*Walks up to* ANNA's *bed, looks at her, and proceeds to his own place.*] Somebody should tell Klestch about it—it's his business.
ACTOR. I'm going—I'll tell him—She's lost her name! [*He goes off.*]
NATASHA. [*Standing in the center of the room.*] Some day I will end like that—in a basement—forgotten by everybody—
BUBNOV. [*Spreading some tattered clothes on his plank bed.*] What? What are you mumbling there?
NATASHA. Nothing—I was talking to myself.
BUBNOV. Waiting for Vassily? Look out! He'll break your neck for you.
NATASHA. What's the difference who breaks it? I'd rather it's him.
BUBNOV. [*Lying down.*] Well, it's up to you.
NATASHA. It's a good thing she died—but I can't help feeling sorry for her. God! What did she live for?
BUBNOV. It's like that with everybody—a man is born, lives a while, and dies. I'll die too—and so will you. Nothing to be sorry about. [*Enter* LUKA, *the* TARTAR, *the* GOITER, *and* KLESTCH, KLESTCH *walks slowly behind the others, stooped over.*]
NATASHA. Sh-sh! Anna—
GOITER. We know—God rest her soul, if she's dead.
TARTAR. [*To* KLESTCH.] You must pull her out! Pull her out hallway! Here no dead people. Here live people will sleep.
KLESTCH. [*In a low voice.*] I'll pull her out. [*They all walk up to the bed.* KLESTCH *gazes at his wife over the shoulders of the others.*]
GOITER. [*To the* TARTAR.] You think there'll be a bad smell from her? No! She dried up while she was still alive.
NATASHA. God! Not one to feel sorry for her—not a single kind word from anybody—Shame on you!
LUKA. Don't take it that way, girlie—It's all right. How can we feel sorry for the dead? Why, girlie, we don't feel sorry for the living—even for ourselves. So what can you expect?
BUBNOV. [*Yawning.*] And another thing—death isn't afraid of words—Sickness is, but not death.
TARTAR. [*Moving away.*] Must call police.
GOITER. The police? Positively. Did you report to the police, Klestch?
KLESTCH. No. I have to bury her—and all I have is forty kopecks.
GOITER. Well, in a case like that borrow somewhere. Or we can take up a collection—five kopecks from this one, as much as he can spare from that. But you have to report to the police—and do it quick—or they'll think you've killed the woman—or something—[*Walks to his plank bed and prepares to lie down alongside the* TARTAR.]
NATASHA. [*Moving away toward* BUBNOV's *plank bed.*] Now I'll be seeing her in my dreams. I always see dead people in my dreams—I'm afraid to go back alone—it's dark in the hall.
LUKA. [*Following her.*] The people to fear are the living ones—take it from me—
NATASHA. Come with me to the door, grandpa.
LUKA. All right—let's go. [*The two exit. There is a pause.*]
GOITER. Oh-ho-ho! Assan! Spring is coming, friend—life will be warm again! In the villages the peasants are already mending their plows, harrows—getting ready to turn the earth—y-yes! And we? Assan! The cursed Mohammed, he's dead to the world.
BUBNOV. Tartars love to sleep.
KLESTCH. [*Standing in the center of the room and gazing dully into space.*] What am I to do now?
GOITER. Lie down and sleep—that's all.
KLESTCH. [*In a low voice.*] And how—about her? [*Nobody answers him. Enter* SATIN *and the* ACTOR.]
ACTOR. [*Shouts.*] Old man! Come here, my faithful Kent!
SATIN. Behold the great explorer! Ho-ho!
ACTOR. It's all settled and done with! Where's the town, old man? Where are you?

SATIN. Fata-morgana! The old man lied to you. There's nothing! No town, no people—nothing!
ACTOR. You're lying!
TARTAR. [*Jumping up from his bed.*] Where's landlord? I go see landlord. I not sleep, I not pay money. Dead people—drunken people—[*He rushes out.* SATIN *whistles after him.*]
BUBNOV. [*In a sleepy voice.*] Come to bed, fellows, stop making so much noise. People are supposed to sleep at night.
ACTOR. Oh, yes—there's a dead body here. "Daddy, Daddy, have you heard? Our nets have caught a corpse"—a poem by—Shakespeare.
SATIN. [*Shouts.*] Corpses don't hear! Corpses don't feel! Shout—yell—corpses don't hear! [LUKA *appears at the door.*]

Act 3

A vacant plot of ground littered with junk and overgrown with weeds. At the rear a high red-brick wall cuts off the sky. Near the wall is a cluster of elder. To the right of it runs a dark log wall which is part of some kind of shed or stables. To the left is a gray wall with patches of plaster. This belongs to the KOSTYLYOV *lodging house and stands at an angle, its far corner jutting out almost to the center of the plot, and a narrow passage showing between it and the red-brick wall. In the gray wall are two windows, one at ground level, the other up about five feet and nearer the corner. Alongside this wall lie a country sledge, turned upside down, and a log about ten feet long. Piled against the wall on the right are some beams and old wooden planks.*

It is early spring, and the snow has already melted away. The black twigs of the elder bush have not yet budded. The setting sun casts a red glow on the brick wall, rear. Sitting on the log, side by side, are NATASHA *and* NASTYA. LUKA *and the* BARON *are seated on the sledge.* KLESTCH *is lying on the heap of wood across from them.* BUBNOV's *head is visible in the lower window.*

NASTYA. [*Speaking in a singsong voice, her eyes closed and her head beating time to her words.*] So one night he comes to the garden, to the arbor, as we arranged—and I'm already there waiting for him a long time, trembling with fear and grief. He too is trembling all over, his face white as chalk, and a revolver in his hand—
NATASHA. [*Cracking sunflower seeds.*] Imagine that! It seems to be true what people say about students being desperate—
NASTYA. And he says to me in a ghastly voice: My dearest, my previous love—
BUBNOV. Ho-Ho! Precious?
BARON. Just a minute. Don't like it, don't listen—but don't spoil a good lie. Go on.
NASTYA. My adorable one, says he. My parents refuse to give their consent, says he, to my taking you for my spouse and threaten to put an eternal curse on me for my love of you. On account of this, says he, I'm obliged to take my life. And the revolver in his hand is ever so big and has ten bullets in it. Farewell, dear heart, says he, nothing can make me change my mind, for I could never live without you—never! And I answered him: My never-to-be-forgotten friend—Marcel—
BUBNOV. [*With surprise.*] Morsel? What's that? Something to eat?
BARON. [*Laughing.*] But listen, Nastya—last time it was Gaston!
NASTYA. [*Jumping to her feet.*] Keep quiet, you miserable things! You're nothing but stray dogs! How can you understand what love—real love is? And I did have real love! [*To the* BARON.] You pitiful wretch! You're an educated man. You drank coffee in bed, you say—
LUKA. Now wait, folks! You mustn't interrupt her. Oblige the girl, let her have her way. It doesn't matter what's said, but why it's said. Never mind them, girlie, go on with your story.
BUBNOV. Paint your feathers, crow. Fire away!

BARON. Well, go on.
NATASHA. Take no notice of them. Who are they? They're just envious—they have nothing to say about themselves.
NASTYA. [*Resuming her seat.*] I don't want to talk any more. No, I won't. If they don't belive me—if they laugh at me—[*She stops abruptly, pauses for a few seconds, then, closing her eyes again, continues in a fervent, loud voice, waving her hand to the beat of her speech as if listening to distant music.*] And so I reply to him: Joy of my life! My bright star! For me too it's positively impossible to live in this world—because I love you madly and will go on loving you as long as my heart beats in my breast. But, says I, you mustn't destroy your young life—as it's needed by your dear parents for whom you are their only joy—Forget me! Better that I suffer—the heartache of mssing you—for I have nobody—my kind never has! Better let me be destroyed—it won't matter now! I'm not fit for anything and I've nothing—nothing—[*She covers her face with her hands and weeps silently.*]
NATASHA. [*Turning away from* NASTYA, *in a low voice.*] Don't cry—don't! [*A smile on his face,* LUKA *strokes* NASTYA'*s head.*]
BUBNOV. [*Roars with laughter.*] Damn fool!
BARON. [*Laughing.*] Do you think this true, grandpa? She took it all from the book *Fatal Love*—It's all bunk! Don't bother with her!
NATASHA. What's that to you? Better hold your tongue—if you have no heart left in you.
NASTYA. [*Fiercely.*] You godforsaken, empty man! Where's your soul?
LUKA. [*Taking* NASTYA *by the arm.*] Come along, dear. Don't mind them—calm yourself. I know—I believe you. Yours is the truth, not theirs. If you believe you had a real love, then you did have it—you certainly did. And don't be angry with your Baron. Maybe he does laugh from plain envy—maybe he never knew anything true and real in his life. Come along.
NASTYA. [*Pressing her hands to her breast.*] Honest, grandpa, it's true, it did happen. He was a student, a Frenchman—Gaston was his name—He had a small black beard—and wore patent leather boots—may lightning strike me dead! And he loved me so dearly—so dearly!
LUKA. I know. I believe you. You say he wore patent leather boots? My goodness! And you loved him too? [*The two go off around the corner.*]
BARON. That girl is so stupid—kind, but so unbearably stupid.
BUBNOV. What is it that makes human beings so fond of lying? As if they were always facing a court examiner—
NATASHA. Lies must be more pleasant than the truth, it seems. I too—
BARON. Well—go on.
NATASHA. I too like to imagine things. I imagine them and—wait.
BARON. For what?
NATASHA. [*Smiling embarrassedly.*] Oh, I don't know. Maybe tomorrow, I think, somebody will come—somebody—quite different—Or maybe something will happen—something that's never happened before. I wait and wait—I'm always waiting. But really, come to think of it, what have I to wait for? [*A pause.*]
BARON. [*Ironically.*] There's nothing to wait for. I don't expect anything. Everything has already happened. It's over—and done with! Go on.
NATASHA. Or sometimes I imagine that tomorrow—I'll suddenly die. It gives you such a creepy feeling. Summer is a fine time for imagining death—All those thunderstorms in summer—it's easy to get killed by lightning.
BARON. You have a hard life. That sister of yours has a devilish character.
NATASHA. And who has a good life? Nobody. I see it all around me.
KLESTCH. [*Until this moment motionless and indifferent, suddenly springing to his feet.*] Nobody? That's a lie! Some people have it! If everybody suffered, it'd be all right. You wouldn't feel then that life's been unfair to you.
BUBNOV. What's got into you? The devil? Howling like that! Huh!
KLESTCH. [*Lies down on the heap, as before, mumbling to himself.*]
BARON. I suppose I have to go and

make up with Nastya—or she won't give me anything for a drink.

BUBNOV. H'mm—People do love telling lies. With Nastya, I can understand it. She's used to painting her face—so she wants to paint her soul too—put rouge on it. But why do others do it? Take Luka for instance—he lies an awful lot—gets nothing out of it. And he's already an old man. What does he do it for?

BARON. [*Moving away, with a smile.*] All human beings have gray little souls—and they all want to rouge them up.

LUKA. [*Returning from around the corner.*] Look, my dear man, why do you upset the girl? You should leave her alone. Let her amuse herself by crying. You know she cries for her own pleasure—what harm does it do you?

BARON. The whole thing is stupid, old man. I'm tired of it. Today it's Marcel, tomorrow Gaston—and every day it's the same story! However, I'm off to make up with her. [*He goes.*]

LUKA. Go and be gentle with her. It never does any harm to be gentle to a human being.

NATASHA. You're a kind man, grandpa. What makes you that way?

LUKA. Kind, you say? That's all right, if it's true. [*Soft sounds of an accordion and a song drift on from behind the red wall.*] Somebody has to be kind, my girl—we have to feel sorry for people. Christ felt sorry for everybody and bid us do the same. Believe me—feeling sorry for a man at the right moment can do a lot of good. One time, for instance, I was a watchman in a country house in Siberia, near Tomsk, working for an engineer, you know. Well, the house stood in the woods, all by itself—no other homes around. It was winter and I was all alone in the house. I felt fine. One day I hear noises at a window!

NATASHA. Burglars?

LUKA. That's right. Trying to break in. Well, I picked up my rifle and went out. I look around and there I see—two men trying to open the window—and working so hard at it they didn't even notice me. I shout at them: Hey, you! Get out of here! And what do they do?— They turn around and rush at me with an ax. I warn them, Keep away, I say, or I'll shoot, and at the same time I cover them with my rifle, now one, now the other. Down on their knees they went as if begging me to let them go. But by now I felt very cross with them—for the ax, you know. You devils wouldn't go away when I told you, says I, now, says I, break off some twigs from a tree, one of you. That was done. And now, I order, one of you lie down and let the other lash him with the twigs. So by my order they gave each other a fine lashing. And after they did it they say to me, Grandpa, they say, for mercy's sake give us some bread. We've been tramping around on an empty belly. So there are your burglars, my dear— [*Laughing.*] And with an ax too! Yes, fine fellows they were, both of them. I say to them: You devils should have asked for bread right away. And they answer me— We're tired of asking. You keep asking people—and nobody gives you anything—it makes you feel pretty sore. And so they stayed with me right through the winter. One of them, Stepan, would take a rifle sometimes and go into the woods for days. The other, Yakov, was poorly, coughed all the time. And so the three of us kept watch over that country house. When spring came they said, good-by, grandpa! and left—to tramp their way to Russia.

NATASHA. Were they runaway convicts?

LUKA. They were—they ran away from a convict camp. Fine fellows! If I hadn't felt sorry for them, they might have killed me—or something. And then they would have been tried, sent to jail, to Siberia—what sense in that? Jail doesn't teach anyone to do good, nor Siberia, but a man—yes! A man can teach another man to do good—believe me! [*A pause.*]

BUBNOV. Y-yes! Now *I* don't know how to tell lies. What good are they? What I say is—give 'em the whole truth just as it is. Why feel shy about it?

KLESTCH. [*Again jumping suddenly to his feet, as if burned, and shouting.*] What truth? Where's the truth? [*Running his hands through his tatters.*] Here's the truth! No work, no strength, not even a place to live. The only thing left is to die like a dog! This is the truth! Good God! What do I want the truth for? I want to breathe more freely—that's all I ask. What have I done wrong? Why should I have been given the truth? No chance to live—Christ Almighty—not a chance—that's the truth!

BUBNOV. Whew! It certainly got him!

LUKA. Lord Jesus— Look, my friend, you should—

KLESTCH. [*Shaking with emotion.*] You keep saying, The truth—the truth! And you, old man, keep comforting everybody. So I tell you—I hate you all—and this truth too—to hell with it. Understand? To hell with it! [*Rushes off around the corner, glancing back as he goes.*]

LUKA. My, my! How upset he got! And where is he off to?

NATASHA. He acted as if he suddenly went off his nut.

BUBNOV. A fine show, I call it. Just like on the stage— That kind of thing happens, though, every once in a while. The man hasn't got used to life yet— [PEPPEL *enters slowly from around the corner.*]

PEPPEL. Peace to you honest people! Well, Luka, you sly old man—still telling stories?

LUKA. You should have been here—a man was screaming his lungs out.

PEPPEL. Was it Klestch? What got into him? I saw him running as if he was on fire.

LUKA. Who won't run when it gets you right in the heart?

PEPPEL. I don't like him—he's too bitter and proud. [*Imitating* KLESTCH.] "I'm a working man"—and everybody's below him, he'll have you think. Well, work if you like it—what's there to be proud of? If we're supposed to judge people by their work, the horse is better than any man—you drive it—and it doesn't speak. Are your folks at home, Natasha?

NATASHA. They've gone to the cemetery—said they'd go to the evening mass afterward.

PEPPEL. And I've been wondering why you're free. It's a rare sight.

LUKA. [*To* BUBNOV, *reflectively.*] You've been saying we need the truth. But it isn't always that truth is good for what ails a man—you can't always cure the soul with truth. I remember this case, for instance, I knew a man who believed in the true and just land—

BUBNOV. Believed in what?

LUKA. In the true and just land. There must be such a land in the world, he'd say. The people in that land, says he, are of a special kind—a fine people. They respect one another, help one another, and everything they do is decent and fine. And so every day this man was thinking of going to look for that true and just land. He was a poor man, and had a hard life. But whenever things were so bad he was ready to lie down and die, he didn't let himself lose heart; he just smiled and said: It's all right—I can bear it. I'll wait a while, and then I'll give up this life and go to the true and just land. He had only one joy in life—that land—

PEPPEL. Did he go?

BUBNOV. Where? Ho! Ho!

LUKA. Then there came to that place—all this happened in Siberia—a man exiled by the government, a learned man, with books, maps, and all sorts of things like that. So our man says to the scientist: Do me a favor, please, show me where the true and just land lies and how to get there. The scientist at once opens his books, spreads his maps—looks here, looks there—there's no true and just land anywhere. Everything is right, all the lands are shown—but the true and just land is just not there.

PEPPEL. [*In a low voice.*] Not there? Really? [BUBNOV *laughs.*]

NATASHA. Don't interrupt. Go on, grandpa.

LUKA. My man doesn't believe him. It must be there, says he, look harder for it. Otherwise your books and maps, says he—they're all worthless if they fail to show the true and just land. The scientist is sore at that. My maps, says he, are the truest of all, and the true and just land doesn't exist anywhere. Hearing that, my man too gets angry. What? says he. I've lived and suffered all these years believing it exists, and your maps make out it doesn't? It's robbery! And he says to the scientist: You dirty swine. You're a crook, not a scientist. And bang! he punches him in the nose, and bang! again! [*He pauses.*] After that he went home—and hung himself. [*All are silent.* LUKA *looks at* PEPPEL *and* NATASHA *with a smile.*]

PEPPEL. [*In a low voice.*] What the devil! That's not what I'd call a gay story—

NATASHA. He couldn't bear having been deceived.

BUBNOV. [*Somberly.*] It's all tales.

PEPPEL. Y-yes. There is the true and just land for you. None such, it turns out.

NATASHA. I feel sorry for the man.

BUBNOV. It's all make-believe. Ho! Ho! The true and just land! How do you like that? Ho! Ho! Ho! [*He vanishes from his window.*]

LUKA. [*Nodding in the direction of* BUBNOV's *window.*] He's laughing. Hee-hee! [*He pauses.*] Well, friends, may you come to good ends. I'm leaving you soon.

PEPPEL. Where are you off to now?

LUKA. To the Ukrainians. I've heard they've discovered a new faith down there—I must have a look at it. Yes, people keep looking—keep wishing for something better. God give them patience!

PEPPEL. What's your opinion? Will they find it?

LUKA. Who, people? They'll find it. Look for something—want something with all your heart—you'll find it.

NATASHA. If they would only find something—think up something good—

LUKA. They'll think it up. Only we have to help them, girlie—make it easier for them.

NATASHA. How can I help? I get no help myself.

PEPPEL. [*Resolutely.*] I'm going to—I will talk to you again, Natasha— Let him hear it too—he knows all about it. Come—with me!

NATASHA. Where? From one jail to another?

PEPPEL. I said I'd give up thieving. I swear I will. And I mean it. I'm not an illiterate—I'll work. Luka here says one ought to go to Siberia of his own free will. Let's go there. Don't you think I'm sick of my life? I know, Natasha, I see it all. I try to make myself feel better thinking others steal much more than I do and have honors heaped on them—but that doesn't help me—it's no answer. I'm not letting conscience prick me into saying this—I don't believe in conscience. But one thing I do know—this is not the way to live. I must live a better life. I must live—in such a way that I can respect myself—

LUKA. You're right, my boy. May the Lord Jesus Christ help you. You're right—a man must respect himself.

PEPPEL. I've been a thief from the time I was a kid. Everybody called me Vassya the thief! Vassya the thief's son! Ah, so? Then have it your way. Here I am—a thief! You must understand—I'm a thief maybe only out of spite—only because nobody ever thought of calling me by any other name. You'll call me something else, Natasha, won't you?

NATASHA. [*In a melancholy tone.*] I can't believe any words—somehow. And I feel uneasy today—my heart aches—as if I were expecting something to happen. I'm sorry you've started this conversation, Vassily—

PEPPEL. How long should I have waited? This isn't the first time I've brought it up.

NATASHA. Well, I don't know how I could go with you. Frankly, I can't say I love you very much. Sometimes I seem to like you. Other times it makes me sick to look at you. It must be I don't really love you. When you love somebody you don't see anything wrong with them. I do.

PEPPEL. You'll love me all right—don't worry. I'll see you get to like me—if you'll only say yes. I've been watching you for over a year—I can see you're a good girl—strict with yourself—dependable—and I've fallen in love with you—deeply. [VASSILISSA, *in her best finery, appears at the higher window*

and listens, standing by the jamb.]
NATASHA. I see. You say you love me—and what about my sister?
PEPPEL. [*Embarrassed.*] Oh, she's nothing to me. There are lots of her kind—
LUKA. Don't mind that, girlie. When there's no bread, you eat grass—
PEPPEL. [*Somberly.*] I ask you to bear with me. Mine is a bitter life—a hungry wolf's life—there's no joy in it. I feel as if I'm sinking in a bog—whatever I lay hold of is rotten, nothing can keep me from going down. Your sister—I thought she was different. If she weren't so greedy for money—I'd have done anything for her. Only she had to be all mine. But she's after something else—she wants money—and freedom too—freedom to play around with men. She can't help me. But you—you're like a young fir tree—prickly to touch, but strong to hold on to—
LUKA. My advice too, girlie—marry him. He's all right—he's a good fellow. Only you have to remind him as often as you can that he's a good fellow—so he doesn't forget it. He'll believe you. Just keep telling him—you're a good man, Vassya, remember that! And besides, my dear, where else can you go? Your sister is a wicked wild beast, and as for her husband—well, nothing you can say about him can be as bad as he is. Then, all this life around here—it can take you nowhere. And Vassily—he's substantial, there's something to him.
NATASHA. I know I have nowhere else to go—I've thought of that myself. Only—I have no faith in anybody. But you're right, I've nowhere to go—
PEPPEL. There's one road for you here—but I won't let you go that way—I'd rather kill you.
NATASHA. There! I'm not your wife yet, and you already want to kill me.
PEPPEL. [*Putting his arms around her.*] Stop it, Natasha. Let's not say any more!
NATASHA. [*Pressing close to him.*] I'll say one thing, Vassily—and let God be my witness—the very first time you strike me—or wrong me in some other way—I won't spare my life—I'll either hang myself or—
PEPPEL. May my hand wither away, if I ever touch you!
LUKA. Have no doubts, dear. He needs you more than you need him.
VASSILISSA. [*From the window.*] Congratulations on the happy ending!
NATASHA. They're back! God, they've seen us. Oh, Vassily!
PEPPEL. What are you scared of? Nobody will dare touch you now.
VASSILISSA. Don't be afraid, Natasha. He won't beat you. He can neither beat nor love—I know.
LUKA. [*In a low voice.*] Oh, what a woman—a regular viper—
VASSILISSA. He's brave mostly with words—[*Enter* KOSTYLYOV.]
KOSTYLYOV. Natashka! What are you doing here, loafer? Scandalmongering? Complaining about your family? And all this time the samovar hasn't been prepared, the table hasn't been cleared—ah?
NATASHA. But you said you wanted to go to church.
KOSTYLYOV. What we wanted to do is none of your business! You have to see to your own work—do what you're told!
PEPPEL. You shut up! She's not your servant any more. Don't go, Natasha—don't do anything!
NATASHA. Don't you give orders—it's too early for you. [*She goes off.*]
PEPPEL. [*To* KOSTYLOV.] Enough! You've bullied the girl all you're going to. Now she's mine.
KOSTYLYOV. Yours? When did you buy her? How much did you pay? [VASSILISSA *laughs loudly.*]
LUKA. Go away, Vassya.
PEPPEL. Watch out you—laughers! See you don't have to cry!
VASSILISSA. Oh, how frightening! Oh, I'm so scared!
LUKA. Go away, Vassily. Don't you see she's egging you on, trying to get you worked up?
PEPPEL. Oh, so? Not me! I'll be damned if you have your own way!
VASSILISSA. And I'll be damned if I don't, Vassya!
PEPPEL. [*Shaking his fist at her.*] We'll see about that! [*He goes off.*]

VASSILISSA. [*Disappearing from the window.*] I'll fix you a nice wedding!
KOSTYLYOV. [*Walking up to* LUKA.] What's doing, old man?
LUKA. Nothing doing, old man.
KOSTYLYOV. Really. I hear you're leaving?
LUKA. It's time to go.
KOSTYLYOV. Where to?
LUKA. Where my nose leads me.
KOSTYLYOV. I see, tramping about. Seems you find it uncomfortable to stay in one place?
LUKA. That's for stones. And they say even water won't flow under a stone.
KOSTYLYOV. We're not talking about stones. A man must live in one place. You can't let people live like cockroaches—crawling every which way. A man ought to stick to his place—not wander about the earth for nothing.
LUKA. What if a man's place is everywhere?
KOSTYLYOV. Then he's a tramp, a useless man. A man must be useful, he must work—
LUKA. You don't say.
KOSTYLYOV. Yes—certainly. What's a pilgrim? A pilgrim, I've heard tell, means a foreigner, a stranger. He's a strange man, not like other people. If he's really strange—if he knows something—has learned something that's of no use to anybody—it may even be some truth—but not every truth is useful—not by a long shot—Well, let him keep what he knows to himself—and hold his tongue. If he's a real pilgrim he doesn't talk—or talks so nobody understands him. He doesn't want anything, minds his own business, and doesn't stir up trouble for nothing. It's none of his business how people live. Let him follow a righteous life—live in the woods—in the thickets—out of everybody's sight. It's not for him to interfere or criticize, but to pray for everybody—for all worldly sins—mine and yours—for everything. That's why he puts worldly vanity behind him—just so he can pray. Exactly! [*He pauses.*] And what sort of pilgrim are you? You have no passport. A good man must have a passport. All good people have passports—yes.
LUKA. There are people, and there are also just plain men.
KOSTYLYOV. Don't try to be funny. And don't talk to me in riddles. I'm no more stupid than you are. What do you mean by people and men?
LUKA. This is no riddle. I say there's soil unfit for sowing, and there's fertile soil—whatever you sow on it grows—That's all the difference.
KOSTYLYOV. Well? What do you mean by that?
LUKA. Take yourself, for instance. If the Lord God himself says to you: Mikhail, be a man!—he'll be wasting his breath—as you are, so you'll stay—
KOSTYLYOV. And do you know my wife has an uncle who's a policeman? And if I—[*Enter* VASSILISSA.]
VASSILISSA. Come have tea, Mikhail Ivanovich.
KOSTYLYOV. [*To* LUKA.] Listen, you—get out of here! Clear out of the house!
VASSILISSA. Yes, old man, be off with you. Your tongue is much too sharp. And who knows—maybe you're a fugitive—
KOSTYLYOV. If I see hide or hair of you after today—I'll take steps!
LUKA. Call your uncle? Call him. Tell him you've caught a fugitive. He may get a reward—about three kopecks—[BUBNOV *reappears in the lower window.*]
BUBNOV. What's up? What's being sold for three kopecks?
LUKA. He's threatening to sell me.
VASSILISSA. [*To* KOSTYLYOV.] Come on.
BUBNOV. For three kopecks? Watch out, old man, they'll sell you for one kopeck.
KOSTYLYOV. [*To* BUBNOV.] You would pop your head out like a devil in an oven!
VASSILISSA. [*As she goes.*] The world seems to be full of suspicious characters—and all sorts of crooks.
LUKA. Hope you'll enjoy your tea.
VASSILISSA. [*Glancing back.*] Hold your tongue—you dirty toadstool!
[*She and* KOSTYLYOV *disappear around the corner.*]
LUKA. Tonight I'll be out of here.
BUBNOV. The best thing you can do. It's

always better to go away while there's still time.

LUKA. You're right.

BUBNOV. I know what I'm talking about. I probably saved myself from Siberia by going away in time.

LUKA. Did you?

BUBNOV. That's the truth. It was this way. My wife got mixed up with a furrier. He was a fine worker—I must say—very clever in dyeing dog skins to look like raccoon—also turning cat skins into kangaroo fur—muskrat—and all sorts of other furs. He *was* clever. Well, my wife got mixed up with him, and the two of them were so close I began to be afraid they'd poison me any minute or think up some other way to get rid of me. I started beating my wife, and the furrier beat me. He was a fierce fighter. Once he pulled half my beard out and broke a rib. I got angry too—one day I whacked my wife on the head with a poker—and all in all it was quite a war going on. Well, I realized I couldn't get any place that way—they were getting the best of me. So I made up my mind to kill my wife—I was in dead earnest about it. But I woke up in time and went away instead.

LUKA. That was a better idea. Let them make dogs into raccoons.

BUBNOV. Only, my workshop was in my wife's name—and I was left—as you see me now. Though, to tell the truth, I'd have drunk up my shop anyway. You see, I have spells of heavy drinking—

LUKA. Have you? A-ah!

BUBNOV. Terrific spells. When it comes over me I drink up every little thing I have—about all I end up with is my skin. And another thing—I'm lazy. You can't imagine how I hate work. [SATIN *and the* ACTOR *enter, arguing.*]

SATIN. Bunk! You'll go nowhere. It's nothing but a damn pipe dream. Look here, old man. What sort of ideas have you been giving this broken-down old windbag?

ACTOR. You lie. Grandpa, tell him he's lying. I'm going. I had work today, I swept the street—but I haven't touched vodka. How's that? Here are the thirty kopecks, but I'm sober.

SATIN. It's crazy, that's all. Give them to me—I'll drink them up for you—or gamble them away—

ACTOR. Go away! It's for the trip.

LUKA. [*To* SATIN.] Now why do you discourage the poor fellow?

SATIN. Tell me, O wizard, belov'd by the gods, what fate do my stars hold in store? I lost every kopeck I had, brother. The world hasn't entirely gone to the dogs, grandpa—there are still cardsharpers cleverer than I am.

LUKA. You're a jolly fellow, Konstantin, and a real pleasant one.

BUBNOV. Come here, Actor. [*The* ACTOR *walks over to the window and squats before* BUBNOV. *They talk in low voices.*]

SATIN. In my young days I was quite amusing, old man. It's pleasant to think back to those days. I was a happy-go-lucky sort of fellow—danced beautifully, performed on the stage, liked to make people laugh—it was a fine time.

LUKA. What made you stray from the path then?

SATIN. You're very curious, old man. You want to know everyting—What for?

LUKA. To understand the affairs of human beings, my man. Now I look at you and can't make you out. You're so manly, Konstantin, and you've got brains too. Why, then, suddenly—

SATIN. It's jail, old man. I was four years and seven months in jail—and after jail a man can go nowhere.

LUKA. So. And what did you do time for?

SATIN. For a dirty swine—I killed him in a fit of temper. It was in jail that I learned to play cards too.

LUKA. Did you kill because of a woman?

SATIN. Because of my sister. But don't bother me. I don't like being questioned. Besides, it was all long ago—my sister's dead—nine years since. A fine little person my sister was.

LUKA. I must say you take life lightly. Now the locksmith here let out such a scream a while ago, it was something frightful.

SATIN. Who, Klestch?

LUKA. That's the one. No work, he shouts, no nothing!

SATIN. He'll get used to it. What shall I do with myself now, I wonder?

LUKA. [*Quietly.*] Look, here he comes. [*His head bent low,* KLESTCH *enters slowly.*]

SATIN. Hey, widower! Why so down in the dumps? What's on your mind?

KLESTCH. I'm trying to think what to do. I've no tools. The funeral swallowed up everything.

SATIN. I'll give you a word of advice—don't do anything. Just let yourself be a burden on the world at large!

KLESTCH. You with your talk. I have some shame before other people.

SATIN. Forget it. People aren't ashamed at your living worse than a dog. Think this over—you stop working—I stop—hundreds and thousands of others—everybody—understand?—everybody stops working. Nobody wants to do any work—what'll happen then?

KLESTCH. Everybody will drop dead from hunger.

LUKA. [*To* SATIN.] You ought to join the Wanderers with your ideas. There are such people, called Wanderers.[2]

SATIN. I know—they're no fools, grandpa. [*From the* KOSTYLYOVS' *window come* NATASHA's *cries:* "What have I done wrong? Please, what have I done?"]

LUKA. [*With alarm.*] Sounds like Natasha. Oh, God! [*Noise, uproar, the sound of dishes being smashed in the* KOSTYLYOVS' *apartment.*]

KOSTYLYOV. [*Off stage.*] You heathen—you slut—

VASSILISSA. [*Off.*] Wait, I'll fix her—

NATASHA. [*Off.*] They're beating me! They're killing me!

SATIN. [*Shouting through the window.*] Hey, you there!

LUKA. [*Fidgeting.*] We ought to call Vassily— Oh, God! Boys, friends'—

ACTOR. [*Running off.*] I'll get him—

BUBNOV. They do beat her an awful lot now.

SATIN. Come on, old man—we'll be witnesses.

LUKA. [*Following* SATIN.] I'm no good as a witness—no! If only Vassily would come quick— [*The two go off.*]

NATASHA. [*Off stage.*] Vassilissa! Sister! Vassi—

BUBNOV. They've gagged her—I'll go look— [*The disturbance in the* KOSTYLYOV *apartment dies down, apparently moving out of the room into the hall.* LUKA's *shout, "Stop!" is heard. A door is slammed loudly, chopping off the noise as with a hatchet. All is quiet on the stage. Twilight.*]

KLESTCH. [*He is sitting indifferently on the upturned sleigh, rubbing his hands hard. Then he begins muttering something—at first indistinctly.*] How now? I have to live—[*Raising his voice.*] I have to have a place to live in—don't I? I haven't one. I have nothing. Only myself. Just one solitary being. No help from anybody. [*Hunching over, he goes off slowly. There are a few seconds of sinister silence. Then a low, confused din rises somewhere in the passage. It swells and draws nearer. Individual voices can be distinguished offstage.*]

VASSILISSA. I'm her sister! Let go!

KOSTYLYOV. What right have you?

VASSILISSA. Jailbird!

SATIN. Call Vassya, quick! Lay into him, Goiter! [*A police whistle is heard. The* TARTAR, *his right arm in a sling, rushes on.*]

TARTAR. What such law is there—kill in daytime? [*The* GOITER *enters, followed by* MEDVEDEV.]

GOITER. Ah, what a wallop I gave him!

MEDVEDEV. How dare you strike people?

TARTAR. And you? What's your duty?

MEDVEDEV. [*Running after the* GOITER.] Stop. Give me my whistle. [KOSTYLYOV *runs on.*]

KOSTYLYOV. Abram! Catch him—arrest him! [KVASHNYA *and* NASTYA *come on from around the corner, supporting a disheveled* NATASHA *under the arms. They are followed by* SATIN, *stepping backward as he fends off* VASSILISSA, *who, arms waving, tries to reach out and hit* NATASHA. ALYOSHKA *skips madly around* VASSILISSA, *blowing a whistle into her ears, shouting, and yelling. A few tattered figures, men and women, drift on to join the others.*]

SATIN. [*To* VASSILISSA.] Where are you pushing? You damned hoot owl—

VASSILISSA. Keep away, jailbird! I'll tear

her to pieces if it kills me too!
KVASHNYA. [*Moving* NATASHA *away.*] Come, Vassilissa. You ought to be ashamed. Stop acting like a wild animal.
MEDVEDEV. [*Catching hold of* SATIN.] Now I've got you!
SATIN. Goiter! give it to them! Vassya! Vassya! [NATASHA *is led to the pile of wood, right, where she can sit down. The rest are bunched together near the passage, against the red wall.* PEPPEL, *rushing out of the passage, elbows his way through the crowd silently and vigorously.*]
PEPPEL. Where's Natasha? Ah, it's you— [KOSTYLYOV *slips around the corner.*]
KOSTYLYOV. [*Offstage.*] Abram! Get hold of Vassya! Boys, help him catch Vassya! He's a robber, a thief!
PEPPEL. Ah, you old goat! [*Swinging his fist, he belabors* KOSTYLYOV. *The latter falls to the ground, only the upper part of his body showing around the corner.* PEPPEL *dashes over to* NATASHA.]
VASSILISSA. Do something to Vassya! All you good people, beat him up—the dirty thief!
MEDVEDEV. [*Shouting to* SATIN.] Keep out of this! This is a family affair! They're relations—and who are you?
PEPPEL. What did she do to you? Stab you?
KVASHNYA. Just look what the brutes did—scalded the girl's feet with boiling water.
NASTYA. Toppled the samovar on her.
TARTAR. Maybe accident— You must know certain—you mustn't talk if you not know—
NATASHA. [*Almost fainting.*] Take me away, Vassily—hide me—
VASSILISSA. My God! Look! He's dead. They've killed him— [*Everybody crowds around* KOSTYLYOV *in the passage.* BUBNOV *comes out of the crowd and walks up to* PEPPEL.]
BUBNOV. [*In a low voice.*] Look, Vassya. The old man is—you know what—finished.
PEPPEL. [*Looking at* BUBNOV *without understanding a word.*] Go call somebody—to take her to a hospital—Well, I'll get even with them!
BUBNOV. I was saying—somebody has flattened the old man—[*The noise on the stage dies down like a campfire doused with water. Random exclamations uttered in undertones can be heard:* "Is it really?" "What do you know!" "Well?" "Let's get away from here." "Oh, hell!" "Now look out!" *The crowd dwindles.* BUBNOV, *the* TARTAR, NASTYA, *and* KVASHNYA *rush over to* KOSTYLYOV's *body.*]
VASSILISSA. [*Rises from the ground and shouts.*] They've killed him! They've killed my husband! [*In a triumphant voice.*] Here's the murderer. Vassya did it. I saw it. Good people, I saw it with my own eyes. Well, Vassya? What'll you say to the police now?
PEPPEL. [*Leaving* NATASHA.] Get out of the way! [*Gazes at the dead man. To* VASSILISSA.] Well? You're glad? [*Touches the body with his foot.*] The old pig has popped off! You've had your way. Well, I'd better finish you off too! [*He makes a dash for her, but* SATIN *and the* GOITER *stop him quickly.* VASSILISSA *flees into the passage.*]
SATIN. Come to your senses!
GOITER. Whoa! Where are you galloping? [VASSILISSA *returns.*]
VASSILISSA. Now what, my dear friend Vassya? One can't escape his fate. Call the police inspector, Abram! Blow your whistle!
MEDVEDEV. They've swiped my whistle, those bastards!
ALYOSHKA. Here it is— [*He blows the whistle.* MEDVEDEV *runs after him.*]
SATIN. [*Leading* PEPPEL *to* NATASHA.] Don't be afraid, Vassya! Killing a man in a fight is nothing serious. It doesn't cost much—
VASSILISSA. Hold Vassya! He killed him— I saw him do it!
SATIN. I punched the old man a few times myself. He didn't need much to keel over. Call me as a witness, Vassya.
PEPPEL. I need no alibis. What I need is to get Vassilissa into it, and that I will do. It was she who wanted all this—egged me on to kill her husband!
NATASHA. [*Suddenly, in a loud voice.*] Oh, now I understand! So that's it, Vassily? Kind people! They're in this together! My sister and him—they're together! They've plotted all this. Isn't that so, Vassily? You talked to

me today the way you did—so she'd hear everything? Kind people! She's his mistress—you know that—everybody knows it—they're both guilty! It was she who got him to kill her husband—He was in their way—and I was too. So they've maimed me—
PEPPEL. Natasha—what are you saying?
SATIN. What the hell.
VASSILISSA. Liar! She lies—I—it was he, Vassya—he killed him!
NATASHA. They're in it together! I curse you! I curse you both!
SATIN. Such goings on! Watch out, Vassily! They'll be the death of you.
GOITER. This is more than I can understand. Good God, what a business!
PEPPEL. Do you really mean it, Natasha? Do you really believe that I and she—
SATIN. Honest, Natasha, think—
VASSILISSA. [*In the passage.*] My husband has been killed, sir. Vassya Peppel, the thief—he killed him, Inspector. I saw it—everybody saw it—
NATASHA. [*Tossing about, almost unconscious.*] Kind people! My sister and Vassya killed him. Listen to me, police! That one, my sister, taught—got him—her lover—there he is, damn him—they killed the man! Arrest them—try them. Take me too—to jail! For Christ's sake, take me to jail!

Act 4

The same setting as the first act. The partitions forming PEPPEL's *room have been removed, and the room no longer exists. Lying in that corner now is the* TARTAR; *he is restless and groans occasionally. The wood block with anvil, at which* KLESTCH *used to work, is also gone.* KLESTCH *himself is sitting at the table tinkering with an accordion and trying the scales. At the other end of the table are* SATIN, *the* BARON, *and* NASTYA. *In front of them they have a bottle of vodka, three bottles of beer, and a big chunk of black bread. The* ACTOR *is on the stove, and can be heard moving about and coughing. It is night.*

The place is lit by a lamp standing in the center of the table. Outside a wind is blowing.

KLESTCH. Y-yes—it was during all that mix-up that he disappeared.
BARON. Vanished from the police—like unto smoke fleeing from the face of fire.
SATIN. Thus do sinners vanish from the sight of the righteous.
NASTYA. He was a good old man. And you—you're not men, you're just rust.
BARON. [*Drinking.*] Here's to you, your ladyship!
SATIN. Yes, he was an interesting old gaffer. Nastya fell plumb in love with him.
NASTYA. I did fall in love with him. I won't deny it. He saw—he understood everything—
ACTOR. [*Laughing.*] And, all in all, to quite a few people he was like soft bread to the toothless.
BARON. [*Laughing.*] Like plaster to an abscess.
KLESTCH. He had pity for other people. You haven't.
SATIN. What good will it do you if I pity you?
KLESTCH. You know—well, if not how to pity a man—you know how not to hurt him.
TARTAR. [*Sitting up on his plank bed and rocking his wounded arm, as if it were a baby.*] Old man was good. He had the law in his soul. Who has the law in his soul—he is good. Who lost the law, he is lost.
BARON. What kind of law, Assan?
TARTAR. Different kind. You know what kind.
BARON. Go on.
TARTAR. Not hurt a man—this is the law!
SATIN. It's called "The code of criminal and reformatory penalties."
BARON. Also "The code of penalties imposed by Justices of the Peace."
TARTAR. Is called Koran. Your Koran called the law. In every soul must be Koran—yes.
KLESTCH. [*Trying the accordion.*] Damn it, listen to it hiss. Assan is right. We must live according to the law—according to the Gospels—

SATIN. Do that.
BARON. Yes, try it.
TARTAR. Mohammed gave Koran, said: Here is law! Do as written here. Then time come—Koran is not enough—time will give new law. Every new time will give its law.
SATIN. That's right. Time came, and it gave us the Penal Code. A strong law—not to be worn out in a hurry.
NASTYA. [*Banging on the table with her glass.*] Why do I go on living with you—here? I'm going away—anywhere—to the world's end!
BARON. Without shoes, your ladyship?
NASTYA. Stark naked! Even if I have to crawl on all fours!
BARON. It'll make a delightful picture, your ladyship—particularly on all fours.
NASTYA. Yes, I'm willing to crawl—just so long as I don't have to see your pan any more. Oh, I'm so disgusted with everything—with all life—all people!
SATIN. When you leave, take the Actor with you. He's about ready to go there too. It's come to his knowledge that half a mile from the world's end there is a hospital for organons—
ACTOR. [*Peeping out from the top of the stove.*] For organisms, you fool!
SATIN. For organons poisoned by alcohol—
ACTOR. And he will go! Yes, he will. Just wait!
BARON. Who's he, sir?
ACTOR. I!
BARON. Thank you, servant of the goddess—what's her name?—the goddess of drama, of tragedy—what was she called?
ACTOR. A muse, fathead! A muse, not a goddess.
SATIN. Lachesis—Hera—Aphrodite—Atropos—devil knows which. Do you see what the old man did, Baron? It was he who worked the Actor up to this state.
BARON. The old man is a fool—
ACTOR. Savages! Ignoramuses! Mel-po-me-ne! Clods! He'll go, you'll see. "Guzzle ye, O somber minds"—a poem by Béranger—yes! He'll find himself a place where there's no—no—
BARON. Where there's nothing, sir?
ACTOR. Yes, nothing! "This hole—my grave will be—I die of sickness and infirmity!" Why do you live? Why?
BARON. You, Edmund Kean or Genius and Dissipation! Stop yelling!
ACTOR. Not on your life! I will yell!
NASTYA. [*Lifts her head from the table and flings her arms out.*] Yell! Let 'em hear you!
BARON. What's the sense, your ladyship?
SATIN. Leave them alone, Baron! To hell with them! Let them holler! Let them split their heads wide open! There's sense enough in that! Keep out of people's way, as the old man used to say. Yes, he was like yeast, leavening our crowd here—
KLESTCH. He beckoned them to go somewhere, but he didn't show them the road.
BARON. The old man is a faker.
NASTYA. Liar! You're a faker yourself.
BARON. Shush, your ladyship.
KLESTCH. The old man didn't like the truth—dead set against it, he was—And he was right. I say too—what can we do with the truth when even without it we can't breathe? There's Assan—had his arm crushed on the job—it'll have to be cut off, I suppose—that's truth for you.
SATIN. [*Banging on the table with his fist.*] Shut up, you brutes, numskulls! That's enough about the old man! [*In a calmer tone.*] You're the worst of all, Baron. You understand nothing—and lie. The old man is not a faker. What's truth? Man—that's the truth! He understood this—you don't. You're dull, like a brick. I understand the old man—I do. Certainly he lied—but it was out of pity for you, the devil take you! There are lots of people who lie out of pity for others—I know it—I've read about it. They lie beautifully, excitingly, with a kind of inspiration. There are lies that soothe, that reconcile one to his lot. There are lies that justify the load that crushed a worker's arm—and hold a man to blame for dying of starvation—I know lies! People weak in spirit—and those who live on the sweat of others—these need lies—the weak find support in them,

the exploiters use them as a screen. But a man who is his own master, who is independent and doesn't batten on others—he can get along without lies. Lies are the religion of slaves and bosses. Truth is the god of the free man.

BARON. Bravo! Splendid! I agree with you. You speak—like a decent man.

SATIN. Why shouldn't a cheat speak well sometimes, when the decent people—speak like cheats? Yes, I've forgotten a lot, but I still know some things. The old man had a head on his shoulders. He had the same effect on me as acid on an old, dirty coin. Let's drink to his health! Fill the glasses— [NASTYA *pours a glass of beer and hands it to* SATIN, *who continues with a smile.*] The old man lives from within—he looks at everything through his own eyes. I asked him once: Grandpa, what do people live for? [*Trying to imitate* LUKA's *voice and manner.*] "They live for something better to come, my friend. Let's say, there are cabinetmakers. They live on, and all of them are just trash. But one day a cabinetmaker is born—such a cabinetmaker as has never been seen on this earth—there's no equal to him—he outshines everybody. The whole cabinetmaking trade is changed by him—and in one jump it moves twenty years ahead. Likewise, all the rest—locksmiths, say—cobblers and other working people—and peasants, too—and even the masters—they all live for something better to come. They live a hundred—and maybe more years for a better man." [NASTYA *regards* SATIN *fixedly.* KLESTCH *stops work on the accordion and listens. The* BARON, *his head bowed low, drums quietly with his fingers on the table. The* ACTOR, *leaning over from the stove, cautiously tries to lower himself onto the plank bed.*] "Everybody, my friend, everybody lives for something better to come. That's why we have to be considerate of every man— Who knows what's in him, why he was born and what he can do? Maybe he was born for our good fortune—for our greater benefit. And most especially we have to be considerate of youngsters. Kids need plenty of elbowroom. Don't interfere with their life. Be kind to them."

BARON. [*Reflectively.*] H'm—for something better to come? That reminds me of our family. An old family—goes back to the time of Catherine the Great—noblemen—warriors! The founders came from France. They served the government, kept rising higher and higher. In the reign of Nicholas I my grandfather, Gustave Debil, held a high post— There was wealth—hundreds of serfs—horses—cooks—

NASTYA. Liar! There was not!

BARON. [*Jumping to his feet.*] What? Well, go on.

NASTYA. There wasn't.

BARON. [*Shouting.*] A house in Moscow! A house in St. Petersburg! Carriages—with the coat of arms! [KLESTCH *picks up the accordion and, moving to one side, watches the scene.*]

NASTYA. There wasn't!

BARON. Shut up! I say dozens of flunkies!

NASTYA. [*With relish.*] There wasn't.

BARON. I'll kill you.

NASTYA. [*Ready to run off.*] There weren't any carriages!

SATIN. Chuck it, Nastya! Don't tease him.

BARON. Just wait—you scum! My grandfather—

NASTYA. There was no grandfather! There was nothing! [SATIN *laughs.*]

BARON. [*Exhausted by his outburst, sits down on the bench.*] Satin, tell this slut— You're laughing too? You don't believe me either? [*Shouts in despair, banging the table.*] There was, the devil take you!

NASTYA. [*Triumphantly.*] A-ah, you scream? You understand now how it feels when somebody doesn't believe you?

KLESTCH. [*Returning to the table.*] I thought there was going to be a fight—

TARTAR. A-ah, people are stupid. Very bad.

BARON. I can't permit anybody to insult me! I have proofs—documents, damn it!

SATIN. Chuck them! And forget about your grandfather's carriages. In the carriages of the past you can't go anywhere.

BARON. But how dare she?

NASTYA. Imagine! How dare I!

SATIN. You see, she dares. Is she any worse than you? Although, in her past—she certainly didn't have not only carriages and a grandfather, but even a father and mother—

BARON. [*Calming down.*] Damn you—you can reason calmly. I don't seem to have any character—

SATIN. Get yourself one. They're useful. [*A pause.*] Have you been visiting the hospital, Nastya?

NASTYA. What for?

SATIN. To see Natasha.

NASTYA. A little late, aren't you? She left the hospital a long time ago. She came out—and vanished. Nobody's seen her anywhere.

SATIN. She must have evaporated—fizzed out.

KLESTCH. It'll be interesting to see which one does the most to ruin the other one—whether Vassya drags Vassilissa down, or the other way around.

NASTYA. Vassilissa will wriggle out of it—she's clever. And Vassya will go to Siberia.

SATIN. The penalty for killing in a fight is only jail.

NASTYA. That's a pity. Siberia's more his style. I wish you'd all be packed off to Siberia—or swept off like dirt—into some pit.

SATIN. [*Startled.*] Have you gone raving mad?

BARON. I'll bloody her nose—for her impertinence.

NASTYA. You try—just touch me.

BARON. I certainly will.

SATIN. Drop it. Don't touch her. Don't hurt another human being! I can't get that old man out of my head. [*Laughs.*] Don't hurt another human being! But I was hurt once—hurt for the rest of my life with a single blow. What am I supposed to do? Forgive it? Not on your life! Never!

BARON. [*To* NASTYA.] You have to understand once and for all, you're not my equal. You're—dirt under my feet!

NASTYA. You good-for-nothing! Why, you're living off me like a worm off an apple. [*The men all burst into laughter.*]

KLESTCH. A sweet little apple! Ah, what a crackbrain!

BARON. You can't be cross with this idiot!

NASTYA. You're laughing? You faker! You don't think it's funny.

ACTOR. [*Somberly.*] Give it to them good!

NASTYA. If I had the power—I'd smash you all like this! [*She picks up a cup from the table and smashes it on the floor.*]

TARTAR. Why break cup? Such—pighead!

BARON. [*Rising.*] I'll teach her good manners!

NASTYA. [*Running toward the hall door.*] You go to hell!

SATIN. [*After her.*] Hey! Stop it! Who are you scaring? And what's it all about, anyway?

NASTYA. Beasts! I hope you'll be struck dead! Beasts! [*She disappears into the hallway.*]

ACTOR. [*Somberly.*] Amen.

TARTAR. Oh! Russian woman, spiteful woman! Too free! Tartar woman—no! She know the law! Nothing stop her!

KLESTCH. She needs a good beating.

BARON. What a bitch!

KLESTCH. [*Trying the accordion.*] It's finished. But no sign of the owner. The boy is on a binge again.

SATIN. Have a drink.

KLESTCH. Thanks! It's time to turn in too.

SATIN. Getting used to us?

KLESTCH. [*Downs his drink and moves to his plank bed in the corner.*] It's all right. It's the same human beings everywhere. At first, you don't see it. Then, you get a good look at them, and it turns out they're all human beings—they're all right. [*The* TARTAR *spreads out some garment on his plank bed, kneels down, and begins to pray.*]

BARON. [*To* SATIN, *pointing at the* TARTAR.] Look.

SATIN. Leave him alone. He's a good fellow. [*Laughs.*] I'm in a kind mood today—the devil knows why.

BARON. You're always kind when you're

oiled—kind and brainy.

SATIN. When I'm drunk I like everything. Yes, sir. He's praying? Fine. A man can believe or not believe—it's his own affair. A man is free—he pays for everything himself—for belief and disbelief, for love, for intelligence, and that makes him free. Man—that's the truth. What is man? It's not you, nor I, nor they— No, it's you, I, they, the old man, Napoleon, Mohammed—all in one. [*Outlines the figure of a man in the air.*] You understand? It's tremendous! In this are all the beginnings and all the ends. Everything in man, everything for man. Only man exists, the rest is the work of his hands and his brain. Man! It's magnificent! It has a proud ring! Man! We have to respect man, not pity him, not demean him— Respect him, that's what we have to do. Let's drink to man, Baron! [*Rises.*] It's good to feel oneself a man! I'm a jailbird, a murderer, a cheat—granted! When I walk down the street, people look at me as at a crook—they side-step and glance back at me—and often say to me: Scoundrel! Charlatan! Work! Work? For what? So that I have what my body needs and feel satisfied? [*Laughs.*] I've always despised people whose main thought in life is to feel satisfied. That's not important, Baron—no! Man is above that! Man is above satisfaction!

BARON. [*Shaking his head.*] You can reason. It's a fine thing—it must warm your heart. I haven't got that—I can't reason. [*Looks around and speaks in a low voice, cautiously.*] I feel scared sometimes, old fellow. You know? I get panicky. Because, what's to become of me?

SATIN. [*Walking up and down.*] Nonsense! What can a man fear?

BARON. You know, ever since I can remember myself I've always felt a sort of fog in my head. I could never understand anything. I have an awkward feeling as if all my life I've done nothing but change clothes—but to what end? I can't figure it out. I was given education, wore the uniform of a college for the nobility— but what did I study? I don't remember. I got married—to a woman who was no good, wore tails, then a dressing gown—why? I don't know. I went through my fortune—came to wear an old gray jacket and faded pants— But how did I go broke? I didn't notice. I got a job on a government board—wore a uniform, a cap with a badge—then embezzled government money, had prison clothes put on me, and later changed into this. And all that as if in a dream. It's funny.

SATIN. Not very. Stupid, rather.

BARON. Yes—I too think it's stupid. Yet there must have been some purpose that I was born for—don't you think?

SATIN. [*Laughing.*] Probably. A man is born for something better to come. [*Nods his head.*]

BARON. That Nastya! Where did she run off to? I'd better go look. After all, she's— [*He goes out. There is a pause.*]

ACTOR. Tartar! [*A pause.*] Assan! [*The* TARTAR *turns his head.*] Pray—for me.

TARTAR. What?

ACTOR. [*In a lower voice.*] Pray—for me.

TARTAR. [*After a pause.*] Pray yourself.

ACTOR. [*Coming down hurriedly from the stove, walks up to the table, pours himself some vodka with a trembling hand, downs it, and almost runs into the hallway.*] I'm gone.

SATIN. Hey you, sycamore! Where are you going? [*He whistles.*] [*Enter* MEDVEDEV, *wearing a woman's quilted jacket, and* BUBNOV. *They are both slightly drunk.* BUBNOV *carries a string of pretzels in one hand and a few small smoked fishes in the other, with a bottle of vodka under his arm and another sticking out of his pocket.*]

MEDVEDEV. The camel is a kind of—donkey, only without ears.

BUBNOV. Forget it. You're kind of a donkey yourself.

MEDVEDEV. The camel has no ears at all—he hears with his nostrils.

BUBNOV. [*To* SATIN.] Friend! I've been looking for you in all the barrooms. Take a bottle, my hands are full.

SATIN. Put the pretzels on the table and that'll free your hand.

BUBNOV. You're right, by God! Look,

policeman—here's a clever fellow, isn't he?

MEDVEDEV. Crooks are all clever—I know. They can't do without brains. A good man can be stupid and still be good. But a bad man must have brains—absolutely. As for the camel, you're wrong. He's a beast of burden, and has no horns—nor teeth—

BUBNOV. Where is everybody? Why isn't there anybody here? Hey you! Come out! I'm treating everybody! Who's over in the corner?

SATIN. How soon are you going to drink up your money? Scarecrow!

BUBNOV. It'll be soon. This time I've saved up only a little capital. Goiter! Where's Goiter?

KLESTCH. [*Walking up to the table.*] He's out.

BUBNOV. B-rr! Fido! Brlyn—brlyn—brlyn! Turkey! Don't bark, don't cackle! Drink! Enjoy yourselves! Get out of the dumps! I'm treating everybody. I love treating people. If I was rich—I'd have a free barroom—you bet I would. With music—and a choir singing too. Everybody could come, drink, eat, listen to songs—ease their hearts! You're a poor man? Step right in—into my free barroom! Satin! I'd make you—I'd give you half of all my capital! There!

SATIN. Give me all you have now.

BUBNOV. My whole capital? Now? Take it. Here's a ruble—here's a quarter—here are the coppers—everything!

SATIN. That's fine. They'll be safer in my hands—I'll have a game with them—

MEDVEDEV. I'm witness—the money's been given for safekeeping—to what amount?

BUBNOV. You? You're a camel. We don't need witnesses. [*Enter* ALYOSHKA, *barefoot.*]

ALYOSHKA. Folks! I got my feet wet.

BUBNOV. Come! Wet your whistle! That'll set you right. My dear fellow—you sing and play—that's fine. But you shouldn't drink. Drinking's bad for a person, my friend. It certainly is.

ALYOSHKA. I can tell that by looking at you. The only time you look like a man is when you're drunk. Klestch, have you fixed my accordion? [*Sings, dancing.*]

> If this here phiz
> Weren't so fair to see,
> My girl wouldn't be
> So sweet on me.

I'm shivering, boys. It's cold.

MEDVEDEV. H'mm!—And may I ask who the girl friend is?

BUBNOV. Leave him alone. You're off the police force now, my friend. It's all over, finished. You're neither a policeman nor an uncle any more.

ALYOSHKA. Just Aunt Kvashnya's husband.

BUBNOV. One of your nieces is in jail, the other is dying.

MEDVEDEV. [*Haughtily.*] Liar! She's not dying—she's missing! [SATIN *laughs.*]

BUBNOV. It's all the same, brother. A man without nieces is no uncle.

ALYOSHKA. Your Excellency! [*Sings.*]

> My girl friend has money,
> I haven't a sou!
> But I'm a gay lad,
> And the girls think so too!

Damn, it's cold. [*Enter the* GOITER. *From time to time, up till the end of the act, other figures, men and women, come in. They undress for sleep and take their places on the plank beds, muttering to themselves.*]

GOITER. Bubnov! Why did you run away?

BUBNOV. Come here! Sit down. Now let's sing—you know, my favorite—eh?

TARTAR. Night all must sleep. Sing song daytime.

SATIN. It's all right, Assan! Come over here!

TARTAR. How is all right? Will be noise. When you sing song, is noise.

BUBNOV. [*Walking up to the* TARTAR.] How's your hand, Assan? Have they cut it off?

TARTAR. Why cut off? I wait. Maybe they no have cut it off. Hand is not iron, you cut it off quick.

GOITER. You're in a rotten way, Assan. Without a hand you're no good for anything. The likes of us are valued for their hands and their backs. No hand, no man. Yes, yours is a bad case. Come have some vodka—and to hell with it all! [*Enter* KVASHNYA.]

KVASHNYA. Ah, my dear lodgers! And isn't it terrible outdoors? Cold—wet! Is my policeman here? Policeman!

MEDVEDEV. Here I am.

KVASHNYA. Wearing my blouse again? And from the looks of it—a bit under the influence, ain't you? How does that happen?

MEDVEDEV. It's on account of his birthday—Bubnov's— And it's cold and wet.

KVASHNYA. Wet! Look out! Don't give me any of that! Go to bed.

MEDVEDEV. [*Going off to the kitchen.*] To bed—that I can—I want to go to bed—it's time.

SATIN. You *are* strict with him. Why?

KVASHNYA. You can't be otherwise, my friend. A man like him has to be kept in line. I took him on for a companion thinking I'd benefit by it—after all, he's a military man, and you're wild people, while I'm only a woman— And right off the bat he takes to drink! That's of no use to me.

SATIN. You didn't choose your assistant very well.

KVASHNYA. No, you're wrong. You wouldn't want to live with me—you wouldn't have me. And if you did, within a week you'd gamble me away at cards—me and my tripe!

SATIN. [*Laughing.*] You're right there, landlady. I certainly would.

KVASHNYA. There you are, Alyoshka!

ALYOSHKA. Here he is—that's me.

KVASHNYA. What sort of tales are you telling about me?

ALYOSHKA. Me? I tell everything—just as it is, honestly. There's a woman, says I. A remarkable woman. In flesh, fat, and bones she's a heavyweight twice over. But she hasn't an ounce of brains!

KVASHNYA. Now, that's a lie. I have plenty of brains. But why do you say I beat my policeman?

ALYOSHKA. I thought you were beating him when you pulled his hair.

KVASHNYA. [*Laughing.*] You're a fool! As if you didn't see. Why carry dirt out of the house? Besides, it hurt his pride. He took to drink because of your tales.

ALYOSHKA. Then it's true what they say—hens drink too. [SATIN *and* KLESTCH *laugh.*]

KVASHNYA. You do have a wicked tongue! I can't make out what sort of man you are, Alyoshka.

ALYOSHKA. The very finest sort of man! Can do anything. Something catches my eye, and off I fly.

BUBNOV. [*Near the* TARTAR's *plank bed.*] Come along. We'll keep you awake anyway. We'll be singing—all night, Goiter!

GOITER. Want a song? All right.

ALYOSHKA. I'll play the accompaniment.

SATIN. I'm all ears.

TARTAR. [*Smiling.*] Well, devil Bubnov—now we have some your vodka. Drink we will, play we will, death will come, die we will!

BUBNOV. Fill his glass, Satin. Sit down, Goiter. Ah, friends! A man doesn't need much, does he? Here am I—I've had some drink—and I'm happy. Goiter, start my favorite one. I'll sing and weep!

GOITER. [*Sings.*] The sun comes up, the sun goes down again—

BUBNOV. [*Picking it up.*] But in my cell it's never light— [*The hallway door is flung open. The* BARON, *standing on the threshold, shouts.*]

BARON. Hey, you! Come—come here! Out there—in the vacant lot the Actor—has hanged himself! [*There is a general silence. Everybody gazes at the* BARON. NASTYA *appears from behind the* BARON's *back and slowly, her eyes wide open, walks up to the table.*]

SATIN. [*In a low voice.*] Ah, spoiled the song—the fool!

---

1. A plank bed is a low wooden platform, which was used in Russian prisons and cheap lodging houses to provide sleeping accommodations, generally for several persons lying alongside one another. In the play Bubnov has a small plank bed to himself.

2. A Russian religious sect dating from the time of Peter the Great and called Wanderers (or sometimes Runners) because they preached running away from places where the government-instituted religious reforms were being enforced.

The Cherry Orchard

Anton Chekhov

Unquestionably the finest playwright Russia has yet produced, Anton Pavlovich Chekhov was born in Taganrog on January 29, 1860, the son and grandson of serfs. The industrious grandfather had saved enough money to buy the family's freedom, but the father, who owned a small grocery shop, was more interested in music and local politics, and in 1876 had to flee Taganrog with his family to avoid imprisonment for debt. Anton, who had been educated at a local Greek preparatory school, needed three more years to finish secondary school in Taganrog, so he remained behind while the rest of the family lived in a Moscow slum. In 1879, Chekhov went to Moscow on a scholarship to study medicine, and, moving in with his family, assumed financial responsibility for supporting them. Going to school in the daytime and writing at night, Chekhov began to crank out countless potboiling short stories and articles as a means of earning a livelihood. In 1886, when Chekhov became a doctor, he was astonished to learn that he had also become a literary figure of considerable prominence and promise, as well as the means of raising the family fortunes to a tolerable living level. It was during this period also that he contracted tuberculosis; although he concealed his illness from his family for years, it eventually killed him.

Chekhov practiced medicine intermittently for several years, dividing his time between that and his more lucrative writing career and frequently giving medical care free to those in need. By the mid-1890s his wealth was sufficient to allow retirement, and his tuberculosis was so severe as to forbid further medical practice, but he continued to write to the end of his life. Feeling a deep sense of social responsibility, he fought a cholera plague while he was able, endowed three schools, and traveled across Siberia in 1890 to devote several months to studying health conditions on the prison island of Sakhalin; his report shocked the government into at least some corrective action.

From his youth, Chekhov had been fascinated by the theater, but his first several attempts to write plays were unsuccessful. His first major play, *Ivanov*, was a failure in its first production in Moscow in 1887, but he rewrote it and scored a significant theatrical success with it in St. Petersburg in 1889. During these years, he also wrote a number of one-act farces, the best known of which are *The Bear* (1888) and *The Marriage Proposal* (1889), that are delightfully entertaining and that are frequently produced today. In 1896, *The Sea Gull* was also a failure in a production in St. Petersburg, owing chiefly to insensitive directing, and Chekhov vowed never to write for the theater again. Reluctantly, however, he allowed himself to be persuaded to authorize a second production of *The Sea Gull* by a struggling young Moscow theater group headed by Konstantin Stanislavski and Vladimir Nemirovich Danchenko. The opening night performance on December 29, 1898, made theatrical history, for it was so successful that it established the Moscow Art Theater as one of the major realistic theater ensembles in Europe (the group adopted the sea gull as its emblem) and rededicated Chekhov to writing what were to become the masterworks of his career. The Moscow Art Theater premiered *Uncle Vanya* on November 7, 1899; *The Three Sisters* on February 13, 1901; and *The Cherry Orchard* on January 30, 1904 (all dates according to the Gregorian calendar, not officially adopted in Russia until a few years later).

Despite the importance of Chekhov and the Moscow Art Theater to each other, their relationship was frequently a stormy one. Chekhov's tuberculosis was by this time so advanced that he needed to remain most of the time in the south, communicating with his producers by mail—never a very satisfactory arrangement. When he did see performances or rehearsals, he often felt that his work was being badly misinterpreted, charging, for example, that Stanislavski had "ruined" *The Cherry Orchard*. The trouble lay in part in the fact that Chekhov was attempting a new kind of drama, realistic in its exterior details in the best slice-of-life fashion, but rooted in the psychological lives of his characters rather than in their external actions. Subtext took on a vastly greater significance, as did careful nuances of pace and rhythm. Chekhov followed in a general way the well-made play structure as adapted by Ibsen, but without the twists and surprises of plot that had been the most overt features of the Scribean form. Plot in Chekhov's plays took a distant second place to intricate and subtle development of the inner lives of the characters, and this again was new to theater practitioners originally schooled in romanticism. Finally, Chekhov found rich comedy in the lives of his subtly viewed characters, whereas Stanislavski (followed by many later directors making their first acquaintance with Chekhov's work) could at first see only the serious, moody side of what he had written. Years later, Stanislavski acknowledged that he was still finding new facets in Chekhov's scripts and that Chekhov had been more nearly right than he in their quarrels, but by then Chekhov was long dead. Still, no matter how far the Moscow Art Theater productions of Chekhov's four great plays may have been from their author's ideal concept, they were unquestionably far closer to it than the more traditional companies had been able to get. Moreover, they were marked theatrical successes, enthralling audiences and establishing the international reputations of both the company and the playwright, and even Chekhov in his warmer moments acknowledged his debt to and respect for Stanislavski and his love for the Moscow Art Theater. He married Olga Knipper, one of their leading actresses, in June 1901, and died in Badenweiler, Germany (where he had traveled for treatment) on July 15, 1904.

The Cherry Orchard is widely accepted as Chekhov's finest play; J. L. Styan goes farther than that in calling it "the supreme achievement of the naturalistic movement in the modern theatre." Chekhov had used naturalism in a far different manner from anything envisioned by Zola, however; he incorporated infinite realistic detail not as an end in itself but rather as part of a poetic assimilation of theatrical elements that lays bare human psyches and brings together past, present, and future in a succession of theatrically vivid moments. As had Ibsen in his own way, Chekhov created poetry of the theater in a realistic context, but in *The Cherry Orchard* the poetic nuances are the focal point; the plot line and the environment are of secondary (but not inconsiderable) importance. Furthermore, the play is tremendously funny. Any production which emphasizes its dreamlike, lachrymose qualities to the exclusion of its genuine humor has significantly missed Chekhov's intentions. All of the characters have comic moments, but Yepikhodov, Dunyasha, Pishchik, and Gaev are brilliant comic roles that should enliven the production with a great many hearty laughs. Above all, the play is an ensemble effort. No single role is obviously a starring one, and every character must contribute meaningfully to the exquisitely delicate shifts in pace and timing that make the play work on the stage. In its rhythms, ultimately, lies the play's success or failure.

Structurally, *The Cherry Orchard* is built around a single central action in the traditional well-made play sense. That action is "to save the estate." Since it is clear at the outset that the principal characters are quite ineffectual and will not succeed in saving the estate, the bulk of the play might more effectively be described as a symphony in four movements, in which variations on the central theme are explored but in which the outcome is predetermined. The first "movement" (act) is full and vigorous with the return of the family to the home they have loved; the second is slow, nearly to the point of complete inaction; the third lively, almost frantic, as family and friends dance while the estate is sold out from under them; the fourth is somber, but carries plaintive echoes of all that has gone before, for the estate has been lost and it is painful to leave that part of life behind. Through continuous, but appropriate, suggestion, Chekhov has arranged to focus remembrances of the past almost continuously on the present, and at the same time to point to the future as the old order changes and the new inexorably takes its place. The sense that this is inherent is all human life touches every spectator, but more specifically it points to the changing social order in Russia in 1904. The serfs had been freed more than forty years earlier, but the rich landowners had been unable to adjust satisfactorily to changing conditions, the government was corrupt, and revolution was only a year away. Without ever specifically mentioning these matters, Chekhov manages brilliantly to evoke them, giving a modern audience both a historical perspective (to replace the immediacy that struck the 1904 audience) and a telling insight into human frailty.

In character creation Chekhov also broke new ground. With hint, innuendo, and subtext, he developed fully rounded, endlessly interesting human beings that were perfect roles for the inner-centered acting technique developed by Stanislavski. Frequently the lines do not at all mean what they say and a character's deeds belie his words, so that every actor must develop a rich texture of inner life for his character and must often play that inner truth contrapuntally with what is going on about him. The director must orchestrate these separate instruments so that their total impression upon an audience is symphonic in the sense implied in the play's structure. None of the characters is a particularly admirable person, but all have a combination of lovable and unattractive qualities that makes them extraordinarily believable and lifelike. Each is also something of an eccentric, which makes for marvelous comic possibilities while adding to the overall richness of character insight.

Equally as rich as the character development, and closely allied with it, is Chekhov's development of theme, but here again it is better simply to accept what the play is than to try to explicate what it says. Clearly it is a portrayal of the old order changing, of the inability of the older generation to cope with the life-style of the new. It is a depiction of people who, in a singularly twentieth-century sense, are unable to communicate with each other, although they love each other very much. It is a nostalgic evocation of life as remembered from the best days of youth, but it is also a clear-eyed look toward a better future that will erase the miseries of the past along with the evanescence of the present. It is both tears and laughter, combined in a way never before attempted in drama but that has become the sine qua non for twentieth-century theater. Chekhov promotes no political cause, preaches no moral message, and espouses no ideological viewpoint, but he captures the spirit of his own changing times and of the human soul in a manner that both ranks him among the handful of immortal dramatists and establishes new modes and directions for twentieth-century drama. Much that now seems uniquely characteristic of the modern theater can be traced to the innovative work of Anton Chekhov.

The Cherry Orchard

Translated by Michael Henry Heim

Characters
Lyubov Andreevna Ranevskaya, a landowner
Anya, her daughter, seventeen
Varya, her adopted daughter, twenty-four
Leonid Andreevich Gaev, her brother
Yermolai Alexeevich Lopakhin, a merchant
Pyotr Sergeevich Trofimov, a student
Boris Borisovich Simeonov-Pishchik, a landowner
Charlotta Ivanovna, a governess
Semyon Panteleevich Yepikhodov, a clerk
Dunyasha, a maid
Firs, a servant, eighty-seven
Yasha, a young servant
Passerby
Stationmaster
Postmaster
Guests and servants

SCENE: *The action takes place on Madame Ranevskaya's estate.*

Act 1

A room still called the nursery. One of the doors leads to ANYA's *room. Day is breaking, the sun is about to rise. It is May and the cherry trees are in bloom, but in the early morning, it is still cold. All the windows in the room are shut. Enter* DUNYASHA, *carrying a candle, and* LOPAKHIN, *with a book in his hand.*

LOPAKHIN. Thank God the train's in. What time is it?
DUNYASHA. Almost two. [*She blows out the candle.*] It's light out.
LOPAKHIN. How late does that make the train? Two hours at least. [*He yawns and stretches.*] And you know what it makes me—a first-class idiot—that's what. I come all this way just to meet them at the station, and sleep through it . . . Fell asleep in a chair. Isn't that awful? . . . Why didn't you wake me?
DUNYASHA. I thought you'd gone. [*She listens.*] That must be them now.
LOPAKHIN. [*Listening.*] No . . . They still have to get their bags and all that . . . [*Pause.*] After the five years Lyubov Andreevna's been abroad I don't know what to expect . . . But she was awfully nice then. Easy to get along with, simple. I remember once when I was fifteen or so, my father—he ran the village shop—gave me a punch in the face that made my nose bleed . . . We were here at the house for some reason, and he'd been drinking. Well, Lyubov Andreevna—I can see her now, so young and slender—she took me over to this washstand, right here in the nursery. "Don't cry, little peasant," she said. "You'll be fine again in no time . . ." [*Pause.*] Little peasant . . . My father really was a peasant, and look at me: white vest, tan shoes. A bull in a china shop . . . Oh, I'm rich, all right, I've got plenty of money. But it doesn't take much to see that down deep I'm still just a peasant. [*He leafs through the pages of the book.*] Here I spent all that time with a book and didn't understand a thing. Fell asleep over it. [*Pause.*]
DUNYASHA. The dogs have been up all night. They can tell their masters are coming.
LOPAKHIN. What's the matter, Dunyasha?

DUNYASHA. My hands are shaking. I think I'm going to faint.
LOPAKHIN. Awfully sensitive lately, aren't you, Dunyasha? Dressing like a lady, and that hair-do! It's not right. Remember who you are. [*Enter* YEPIKHODOV *carrying a bunch of flowers. He is wearing a jacket and brightly polished boots that squeak loudly. On his way into the room, he drops the flowers.*]
YEPIKHODOV. [*Picking up the flowers.*] They're from the gardener. He said to put them in the dining room. [*He hands* DUNYASHA *the flowers.*]
LOPAKHIN. And bring me some kvass.
DUNYASHA. Yes, sir. [*She exits.*]
YEPIKHODOV. It's several degrees below freezing out, and the cherry trees are all in bloom. I don't approve of our climate. [*He sighs.*] Not at all. It's not what you might call stimulative. And if I may appendix another observation, Yermolai Alexeevich, I bought these boots the day before yesterday, and—let me venture to assure you—they squeak so badly that there's no possibility whatsoever. What can I grease them with?
LOPAKHIN. Leave me alone. You bother me.
YEPIKHODOV. Every day a new disaster. But you don't hear me complain. I'm used to it. I even smile. [*Enter* DUNYASHA. *She hands* LOPAKHIN *his kvass.*] Well, I'll be off. [*He bumps into a chair and knocks it over.*] There . . . [*Almost triumphantly.*] You see? The very circumstances—if you'll pardon the expression, I mean . . . Simply remarkable, even! [*He exits.*]
DUNYASHA. You know what, Yermolai Alexeevich? Yepikhodov has proposed to me.
LOPAKHIN. Oh.
DUNYASHA. I don't know what to say . . . He's nice enough, but there are times you can't make head or tail of anything he says. It sounds all sweet and romantic, it just doesn't mean anything. I like him, kind of, and he's crazy about me. But he's so unlucky. Every day it's something else. You know what they call him for fun? Twenty-two disasters . . .
LOPAKHIN. [*Listening.*] I think they're coming.

DUNYASHA. They're coming! What's the matter with me . . . I'm all shivery.
LOPAKHIN. They're really coming. Let's go and meet them. I wonder if she'll recognize me. It's been five years now.
DUNYASHA. [*Excited.*] I'm going to faint . . . Oh dear, I'm going to faint! [*Two carriages are heard driving up to the house.* LOPAKHIN *and* DUNYASHA *exit quickly. The stage is empty. Noises start coming form the adjoining rooms.* FIRS, *who has been to the station to meet* LYUBOV ANDREEVNA, *hurries across the stage, leaning on his cane. He is wearing an old-fashioned livery and top hat and is mumbling something to himself, though it is not clear what. The backstage noise grows louder and louder. A voice says,* "Through here?" *Enter* LYUBOV ANDREEVNA, ANYA *and* CHARLOTTA IVANOVNA. CHARLOTTA *has a little dog on a leash. They are all wearing traveling clothes. They are followed by* VARYA, *wearing a coat and a kerchief,* GAEV, SIMEONOV-PISHCHIK, LOPAKHIN, DUNYASHA, *carrying a bundle and an umbrella, and other* SERVANTS *with luggage. They all walk across the room.*]
ANYA. Let's go through here. Remember what room this is, Mama?
LYUBOV ANDREEVNA. [*Joyfully, almost crying.*] The nursery!
VARYA. It's so cold. My hands are numb. [*To* LYUBOV ANDREEVNA.] Your rooms are just the way you left them, Mama. The white one and the lavender one.
LYUBOV ANDREEVNA. The nursery! My darling, precious nursery . . . This is where I slept as a child . . . [*She cries.*] It's like being a child all over again . . . [*She kisses her brother, then* VARYA, *then her brother again.*] Varya hasn't changed a bit either, still looks like a nun. I even recognized Dunyasha . . . [*She kisses* DUNYASHA.]
GAEV. The train was two hours late. It's outrageous how they run things.
CHARLOTTA. [*To* PISHCHIK.] My dog eats nuts, too.
PISHCHIK. [*Amazed.*] Unbelievable! [*They all exit but* ANYA *and* DUNYASHA.]
DUNYASHA. It's been so long . . . [*She takes off* ANYA's *coat and hat.*]
ANYA. Four nights on the train—I didn't

get any sleep . . . Now I'm frozen through.
DUNYASHA. It was snowing and cold when you left during Lent, and now look. Anya, sweet Anya! [*She laughs and kisses her.*] I've waited so long, Anya, precious . . . I have to tell you right away, I can't wait another minute . . .
ANYA. [*Without enthusiasm.*] What is it this time?
DUNYASHA. Yepikhodov, the clerk, he proposed to me just after Easter.
ANYA. That's all you ever talk about . . . [*Tidying her hair.*] I've lost all my hairpins. [*She is so exhausted she can hardly stand.*]
DUNYASHA. I really don't know what to think. He loves me so much, so much.
ANYA. [*Looking through the door into her own room, tenderly.*] My room, my windows, as if I'd never been away. Home again! Tomorrow morning I'll get up and run out into the orchard . . . Oh, I hope I can fall asleep. I didn't sleep a wink the whole way, I was so worried.
DUNYASHA. Pyotr Sergeevich has been here since the day before yesterday.
ANYA. [*Joyfully.*] Petya!
DUNYASHA. He's in the bathhouse, sleeping. That's where he's staying. Says he doesn't want to put anybody out. [*Glancing at her pocketwatch.*] Someone should go wake him, but Varvara Mikhailovna said no. "No, don't wake him," she said. [*Enter* VARYA. *She has a bunch of keys hanging from her belt.*]
VARYA. Quickly, Dunyasha, go and get some coffee . . . Mama wants some coffee.
DUNYASHA. Right away. [*She exits.*]
VARYA. Well, thank God you're home. Home again. [*Tenderly.*] My angel's back, my beauty's back!
ANYA. It was pure torture.
VARYA. I can imagine.
ANYA. It was Easter week when I left, and cold. Charlotta talked the whole way and did her magic tricks. Why did you have to saddle me with Charlotta, anyway?
VARYA. You couldn't have made the trip alone, angel. Not at seventeen.

ANYA. So we get to Paris, it's cold and snowing. My French is awful. Mama's living on the fifth floor. I walk in. She's got some French people there—ladies and an old Jesuit priest with a prayer book. Smoke everywhere, no place to sit. Suddenly I felt sorry for Mama, so sorry I took her head in my arms, held it there, and couldn't let go. Then she hugged and kissed me.
VARYA. [*Almost crying.*] That's enough, that's enough . . .
ANYA. She'd sold the villa near Menton by then so there was nothing left, nothing. I had nothing either. We barely made it home. And Mama just can't understand! Whenever we ate at a station restaurant, she'd order the most expensive thing on the menu and give the waiter a ruble tip. Charlotta too. Then Yasha would insist on some fancy dish. It was awful. You remember Mama's servant Yasha. We've brought him back with us.
VARYA. Yes, I've seen him, the good for nothing.
ANYA. Well, how is everything? Have you kept up the mortgage payments?
VARYA. Don't be silly.
ANYA. O God, O God . . .
VARYA. The estate is going up for sale in August . . .
ANYA. O God . . .
LOPAKHIN. [*Sticking his head through the door and mooing.*] Moo-oo-oo . . . [*He exits.*]
VARYA. [*Almost crying.*] I wish I could give him a taste of this . . . [*She shakes her fist at him.*]
ANYA. [*Putting her arms around* VARYA, *softly.*] Has he proposed, Varya? [VARYA *shakes her head.*] But he does love you . . . Why not talk it over between you? Why wait?
VARYA. I don't think anything will ever come of it. He's too busy, he hasn't got time for me . . . Doesn't know I'm alive. I'm through with him for good. It's too hard for me to see him. Everybody talks about our wedding, congratulates me, and there's nothing to it, it's all a dream . . . [*In a different tone of voice.*] Your brooch—it's a bee, isn't it?

ANYA. [*Sadly.*] Mama bought it. [*Walking in the direction of her room, talking cheerfully, like a child.*] Know what? In Paris I went up in a balloon.
VARYA. My angel's back, my beautiful angel! [DUNYASHA *has returned with a coffee urn and is making coffee. Standing by the door.*] All day long as I go about my work, I dream and dream. If only we could find you a rich servant, angel, my mind would be at rest. I'd go to a convent, then on to Kiev . . . to Moscow, go from one holy place to another . . . on and on. Paradise! . . .
ANYA. The birds are singing in the orchard. What time is it?
VARYA. Well past two. Time for you to go to bed, angel. [*Going into* ANYA's *room.*] Paradise! [*Enter* YASHA *with a lap robe and traveling bag.*]
YASHA. [*Crossing the stage, genteely.*] May I pass through here?
DUNYASHA. I almost didn't recognize you, Yasha, you look so French.
YASHA. Hm . . . And who might you be?
DUNYASHA. I was only so big when you left . . . [*She indicates her height with her hand.*] I'm Dunyasha, Fyodor Kozoedvov's daughter. You wouldn't remember.
YASHA. Hm . . . A juicy little morsel. [*He looks around and puts his arms around her. She cries out and drops a saucer.* YASHA *exits quickly.*]
VARYA. [*In the doorway, crossly.*] What's going on in there?
DUNYASHA. [*Almost crying.*] I've broken a saucer . . .
VARYA. A good omen.
ANYA. [*Coming out of her room.*] We'd better warn Mama that Petya's here.
VARYA. I gave orders not to wake him.
ANYA. [*Dreamily.*] It's been six years now. First Father dying, then a month later little Grisha drowning in the river. Only seven years old, my beautiful baby brother. It was too much for Mama. She picked up and left and never looked back . . . [*She shudders.*] I understand her perfectly. If only she knew. [*Pause.*] And Petya, Grisha's tutor—he might bring back memories . . . [*Enter* FIRS. *He is wearing a jacket and white vest.*]
FIRS. [*Going over to the coffee urn, anxiously.*] Madame will have her coffee here . . . [*He puts on white gloves.*] Is it ready? [*To* DUNYASHA, *sternly.*] You there! What about the cream?
DUNYASHA. Oh goodness . . . [*She rushes off.*].
FIRS. [*Fussing around the urn.*] Silly goose! [*He mumbles to himself.*] Back from Paris . . . The master used to go to Paris too . . . His own horses . . . [*He laughs.*]
VARYA. What are you laughing at, Firs?
FIRS. Pardon, Miss? [*Joyfully.*] My mistress is back! Never thought I'd live to see the day. Now I can die . . . [*He cries for joy. Enter* LYUBOV ANDREEVNA, GAEV *and* SIMEONOV-PISHCHIK. SIMEONOV-PISHCHIK *is wearing a longwaisted coat made of fine cloth and full Russian trousers tucked into his boots.* GAEV *pantomiming a billiard player with his arms and body.*]
LYUBOV ANDREEVNA. How does it go again? Wait, I remember . . . Yellow into the corner pocket! Combination into the side!
GAEV. Cut into the corner. You and I used to sleep here in this room, Lyuba, and suddenly I'm fifty-one. Strange, isn't it?
LOPAKHIN. Yes, time flies.
GAEV. What was that?
LOPAKHIN. Time, I said. It flies.
GAEV. This place reeks of cheap cologne.
ANYA. I'm going to bed. Good-night, Mama. [*She kisses her mother.*]
LYUBOV ANDREEVNA. My beautiful baby. [*She kisses her hands.*] Glad to be home? I still can't believe it.
ANYA. Good night, Uncle Leonid.
GAEV. [*Kissing her face and hands.*] God bless you. You're just like your mother! [*To* LYUBOV ANDREEVNA.] You looked just like her when you were her age, Lyuba. [ANYA *shakes hands with* LOPAKHIN *and* PISHCHIK *and exits, closing the door behind her.*]
LYUBOV ANDREEVNA. She's exhausted.
PISHCHIK. It's been a long trip, after all.
VARYA. [*To* LOPAKHIN *and* PISHCHIK.] What do you say, gentlemen? It's almost three. Time to be on your way.
LYUBOV ANDREEVNA. [*Laughing.*] Same old Varya. [*She pulls* VARYA *up to her and kisses her.*] Let me finish my coffee. Then we'll all go. [FIRS *puts a*

cushion under her feet.] Thank you, my dear. I drink coffee all the time now, day and night. Thank you, you dear old thing. [*She kisses* FIRS.]

VARYA. I'll go and make sure they've brought everything in . . . [*She exits.*]

LYUBOV ANDREEVNA. Is this really me sitting here? [*She laughs.*] I feel like jumping up and down and waving my arms. [*She covers her face with her hands.*] But what if I'm only dreaming? Dear God, how I love my country, how I cherish it! I couldn't see a thing from the train, I was crying so hard. [*Almost crying.*] But now I'd better drink my coffee. Thank you, Firs dear. Thank you, dear old Firs. I'm so glad you're still alive.

FIRS. The day before yesterday.

GAEV. He doesn't hear too well.

LOPAKHIN. Well, I'd better be going. I'm leaving for Kharkov at about four. What a shame. Here I was, hoping to have a good look at you, a chance to talk . . . You're as lovely as ever.

PISHCHIK. [*Breathing heavily.*] Even prettier . . . That Parisian outfit . . . She's in a class by herself . . .

LOPAKHIN. Your brother here—Leonid Andreevich—calls me an upstart and a boor, but I don't care. Let him talk. All I care about is that you trust me the way you used to and look at me with those wonderful gentle eyes. Dear God, my father was your father's serf and your grandfather's serf, but you—you've done so much for me that I've forgotten the past. I love you like a member of my own family . . . more.

LYUBOV ANDREEVNA. I can't sit still. I find it physically impossible . . . [*She jumps up and walks back and forth in great agitation.*] The joy is too much for me . . . Go ahead and laugh, I know I'm silly . . . Dear little bookcase . . . [*She kisses the bookcase.*] Sweet little table . . .

GAEV. Nanny died while you were away.

LYUBOV ANDREEVNA. [*She sits down and drinks some coffee.*] Yes, God rest her soul. They wrote and told me.

GAEV. Anastasy too. And cross-eyed Petrushka quit and moved to town. He's with the police now. [*He takes a box of fruit drops out of his pocket and pops one into his mouth.*]

PISHCHIK. My daughter Dashenka . . . She sends her regards.

LOPAKHIN. I have something to tell you, something good. [*He glances at his watch.*] No, I've got to go, there's no time . . . Well, I'll make it short. As you know, the cherry orchard is being sold to pay your debts; it goes up for auction on the twenty-second of August. But don't worry, dear lady. You can sleep in peace. There's a way out . . . Here's my plan. Listen carefully now. Your estate is only fifteen miles from town, the railway line is nearby, and if you divide the cherry orchard and the land along the river into individual plots and lease them for summer cottages, you'll have a yearly income of twenty-five thousand rubles at the very least.

GAEV. I'm sorry, but that's absurd.

LYUBOV ANDREEVNA. I don't think I quite follow you, Yermolai Alexeevich.

LOPAKHIN. Each acre will bring in at least ten rubles a year, and if you advertise immediately, you won't have a scrap of land left by autumn, I guarantee it. They'll grab it all up. In other words, congratulations! You're saved. The setting's magnificent, the river's deep. Of course, it needs a little work, a little fixing up . . . You'll have to tear down all the old buildings, for instance, this house too—it's of no use to anybody anyway—then chop down the cherry orchard . . .

LYUBOV ANDREEVNA. Chop down the cherry orchard? My dear man, I'm sorry, but you haven't the slightest idea what you're talking about. If there is anything interesting, anything remarkable about this province, it is our cherry orchard.

LOPAKHIN. The only thing remarkable about the orchard is its size. It only produces cherries every other year, and even then you can't do anything with them; nobody buys them.

GAEV. But it's mentioned in the encyclopedia.

LOPAKHIN. [*Glancing at his watch.*] If we don't come up with something, some kind of plan, the cherry orchard and the whole estate will be auctioned off on August twenty-second. Make up your minds! There's no other way, believe me. No other way.

FIRS. Back in the old days, forty or fifty years ago, those cherries were dried and preserved and made into jam. There was a time . . .

GAEV. Quiet, Firs.

FIRS. There was a time they sent them by the cartload to Moscow and Kharkov. The money they brought in! They were so soft and sweet and juicy, those dried cherries, they smelled so good . . . People knew the secret . . .

LYUBOV ANDREEVNA. And where's the secret now?

FIRS. Gone and forgotten. Nobody remembers anymore.

PISHCHIK. [*To* LYUBOV ANDREEVNA.] How was Paris? Eat any frogs?

LYUBOV ANDREEVNA. I ate crocodiles.

PISHCHIK. You don't say!

LOPAKHIN. Not so long ago, if you lived in the country, you were either master or peasant. Now the summer people are moving in. Every town, even the smallest, is surrounded by summer cottages, and within twenty years or so the number of summer people is bound to increase enormously. Now all they do is drink tea out on the porch, but one day they may start growing things on their plots, and then your cherry orchard will be a happy, productive, prosperous place . . .

GAEV. [*Indignant.*] Utter nonsense. [*Enter* VARYA *and* YASHA.]

VARYA. There are two telegrams waiting for you, Mama. [*After picking out the right key, she unlocks the old bookcase. The keys jangle.*] Here they are.

LYUBOV ANDREEVNA. From Paris. [*She tears up the telegrams without reading them.*] Paris is over and done with . . .

GAEV. You know how old that bookcase is, Lyuba? A week ago I pulled out the bottom drawer, and what did I see but some numbers burned into the wood. That bookcase was made exactly one hundred years ago. What do you think of that? We could even celebrate its centennial. An inanimate object, true, but a bookcase nonetheless.

PISHCHIK. A hundred years old . . . [*Amazed.*] You don't say! . . .

GAEV. Yes . . . A treasure . . . [*Running his hand over it.*] Most honorable bookcase! Allow me to salute you for more than a hundred years of service to the glorious ideals of virtue and justice. Not once in an entire century has your silent summons to productive labor faltered. [*Almost crying.*] From generation to generation you have given our family courage and faith in a better future; you have nurtured in us the ideals of goodness and social consciousness. [*Pause.*]

LOPAKHIN. Hm . . .

LYUBOV ANDREEVNA. Same old Lyonya.

GAEV. [*A little embarrassed.*] Off the right into the corner! Cut into the side!

YASHA. [*He hands* LYUBOV ANDREEVNA *her medicine.*] Care to take your pills now? . . .

PISHCHIK. Never take medicine, my dear . . . Doesn't do any good, or harm either . . . Come, let me have them. [*He takes the pills. Pours them all out into his palm, blows on them, puts them in his mouth, and washes them down with kvass.*] There!

LYUBOV ANDREEVNA. [*Alarmed.*] You're out of your mind!

PISHCHIK. So much for the pills.

LOPAKHIN. Some gullet you've got there! [*They all laugh.*]

FIRS. When the gentleman was here at Easter, he ate half a bucket of pickles . . . [*He goes on muttering.*]

LYUBOV ANDREEVNA. What's he saying?

VARYA. He's been muttering that way for three years now. We're used to it.

YASHA. It's his advancing years.

[CHARLOTTA IVANOVNA, *very thin and tightly laced, crosses the stage in a white dress with a lorgnette at her belt.*]

LOPAKHIN. Excuse me, Charlotta Ivanovna. I haven't had a chance to say hello to you yet. [*He tries to kiss her hand.*]

CHARLOTTA. [*Pulling her hand away.*] If I let you kiss my hand, you'll be wanting to kiss my elbow, then my shoulder . . .

LOPAKHIN. This is my unlucky day. [*Everyone laughs.*] Show us a trick, Charlotta Ivanovna.

LYUBOV ANDREEVNA. Yes, Charlotta. Show us a trick!
CHARLOTTA. Not now. I'm going to bed. [*She exits.*]
LOPAKHIN. See you all in three weeks. [*He kisses* LYUBOV ANDREEVNA's *hand.*] Goodbye now. Time to go. [*To* GAEV.] Goodbye. [*He shakes hands with* VARYA *and then with* FIRS *and* YASHA.] I don't really feel like going. [*To* LYUBOV ANDREEVNA.] Think it over, and when you decide about the summer houses, let me know. I can find you a loan of fifty thousand or so. Think it over seriously.
VARYA. [*Angrily.*] Well, go if you're going.
LOPAKHIN. I'm going, I'm going . . . [*He exits.*]
GAEV. The boor. Oh, I'm sorry . . . Varya's going to marry him, he's Varya's fiancé.
VARYA. Oh, Uncle Leonid, how could you!
LYUBOV ANDREEVNA. What do you mean, Varya? It would make me very happy. He's a fine man.
PISHCHIK. He certainly is . . . No doubt about it . . . My Dashenka says . . . she says . . . she says all kinds of things . . . [*He starts snoring, but wakes up almost immediately.*] By the way, my dear, could you . . . lend me two hundred forty rubles? . . . The interest on my mortgage is due tomorrow.
VARYA. [*Alarmed.*] No, no! We haven't got it!
LYUBOV ANDREEVNA. I really haven't got it.
PISHCHIK. Oh well, it'll turn up. [*He laughs.*] I never say die. Last time I thought I was done for, ruined, when suddenly they put a railway line across my property, and . . . I was in the money again. Something's bound to turn up sooner or later . . . Maybe Dashenka will win two hundred thousand . . . She's got a lottery ticket.
LYUBOV ANDREEVNA. That's the end of the coffee. Time for bed.
FIRS. [*Scolding* GAEV *while brushing his clothes.*] The wrong trousers again! What am I going to do with you?
VARYA. [*Quietly.*] Anya's asleep. [*She opens the window quietly.*] The sun is up. It's getting warm. Look how beautiful the trees are, Mama. And oh, that air! The starlings are singing!
GAEV. [*Opening another window.*] The orchard is all white. You haven't forgotten, have you, Lyuba? The long tree-lined road running on and on, straight as an arrow, shining on the moonlit nights. You remember, don't you? You haven't forgotten?
LYUBOV ANDREEVNA. [*Looking out the window at the orchard.*] Oh, my childhood, my pure, innocent childhood! Sleeping here in the nursery, looking out at the orchard, waking up happy every morning. It's just the same, nothing has changed. [*She laughs with joy.*] White, all white! Oh, my orchard! After a dark and stormy autumn, a freezing winter, here you are, young again, full of joy, the heavenly hosts have not forsaken you . . . If only I could lift the millstone from my breast, if only I could forget my past.
GAEV. Yes, and now the orchard is going to be sold to pay our debts. Strange . . .
LYUBOV ANDREEVNA. Look! It's Mama walking through the orchard . . . in a white dress! [*She laughs with joy.*] Look, there she goes!
GAEV. Where?
VARYA. Really, Mama!
LYUBOV ANDREEVNA. There's no one there. I just imagined it. See that little white tree leaning over the path where it turns off to the gazebo, there on the right? It looks like a woman . . . [*Enter* TROFIMOV *wearing a moth-eaten student's uniform and glasses.*] An amazing orchard! Banks of white blossoms against the blue sky . . . Amazing!
TROFIMOV. Lyubov Andreevna! [*She turns around and looks at him.*] I just want to welcome you back, then I'll go. [*He kisses her hand with great emotion.*] They told me not to come till morning, but I couldn't wait . . .
[LYUBOV ANDREEVNA *stares at him in bewilderment.*]
VARYA. [*Almost crying.*] It's Petya Trofimov . . .
TROFIMOV. Petya Trofimov, Grisha's tutor . . . Have I changed that much?

[LYUBOV ANDREEVNA *puts her arms around him and weeps softly.*]

GAEV. [*Embarrassed.*] Now, now, Lyuba . . .

VARYA. [*Crying.*] I told you to wait till tomorrow, Petya.

LYUBOV ANDREEVNA. Grisha . . . My baby . . . Grisha . . . My son . . .

VARYA. There's nothing we can do about it, Mama. It was God's will.

TROFIMOV. [*Gently, almost crying.*] There now, there now . . .

LYUBOV ANDREEVNA. [*Crying softly.*] My little boy—lost, drowned . . . Oh why, Petya, why? [*Lowering her voice.*] Here I am, talking away, making noise, and Anya's asleep in there . . . But what's happened to you, Petya? You used to be so handsome. You used to be so young.

TROFIMOV. A peasant woman on the train called me, "the moth-eaten gentleman."

LYUBOV ANDREEVNA. You were just a boy then, a nice, young student. And now you're losing your hair, you wear glasses. Don't tell me you're still a student. [*She moves toward the door.*]

TROFIMOV. I'm just an eternal student, I suppose.

LYUBOV ANDREEVNA. [*Kissing her brother and then* VARYA.] Well, time for bed, everybody . . . You look old too, Leonid.

PISHCHIK. [*Following her.*] Time to go to bed . . . Oh, my gout. Think I'll stay the night . . . What do you say, Lyubov Andreevna, dearest? Tomorrow morning . . . Two hundred forty rubles . . .

GAEV. Persistent, isn't he?

PISHCHIK. Two hundred forty rubles . . . the interest on my mortgage.

LYUBOV ANDREEVNA. I haven't any money, dear boy.

PISHCHIK. I'll pay it back, kind lady . . . It's such a small amount.

LYUBOV ANDREEVNA. Oh, all right. Leonid will give it to you . . . Take care of it, Leonid.

GAEV. Right away. Anything he asks for.

LYUBOV ANDREEVNA. No, really. Go ahead. What can we do? . . . He needs it . . . He'll pay it back. [*Exit* LYUBOV ANDREEVNA, TROFIMOV, PISHCHIK, *and* FIRS. *Only* GAEV, VARYA *and* YASHA *remain.*]

GAEV. I see Lyuba hasn't stopped throwing money away. [*To* YASHA.] Stand back a little, Yasha, will you? You smell like a chicken coop.

YASHA. [*With a smirk.*] Haven't changed a bit, Leonid Andreevich.

GAEV. What was that? [*To* VARYA.] What did he say?

VARYA. [*To* YASHA.] Your mother's here from the village. She's been waiting since yesterday in the servants' quarters. She wants to see you.

YASHA. I wish she'd leave me alone.

VARYA. How can you say such a thing!

YASHA. Well, what do I need her for? Couldn't she have waited till tomorrow? [*He exits.*]

VARYA. Mama hasn't changed a bit; she's still the same. She'd give everything away if we let her.

GAEV. Hm . . . [*Pauses.*] When many remedies are prescribed for a disease, it means the disease is incurable. I've given it quite a bit of thought, serious thought; I've come up with all kinds of remedies, all kinds. Which means, basically, none at all. Wouldn't it be nice if someone left us a fortune? Wouldn't it be nice if we could find Anya a rich husband, wouldn't it be nice if one of us went to Yaroslavl and tried his luck with our aunt the countess? She's very, very rich, you know.

VARYA. [*Crying.*] If only God would help.

GAEV. Oh, stop blubbering! She's very rich, but she doesn't like us. In the first place, Lyuba married a lawyer, not a nobleman . . . [ANYA *appears at the door.*] She married beneath her station. And her behavior—well, you can't exactly say she's been virtuous. Oh, she's good, kind, a wonderful woman, and I love her dearly, but after all is said and done, you have to admit her morals are a bit loose. It shows in every move she makes.

VARYA. [*In a whisper.*] Anya's standing at the door.

GAEV. What's that? [*Pause.*] That's funny. I seem to have something in my right eye . . . I can hardly see. Anyway, while I was at the District Court on Thursday . . . [*Enter* ANYA.]

VARYA. Why aren't you in bed, Anya?
ANYA. I can't seem to fall asleep.
GAEV. My little girl. [*He kisses* ANYA's *face and hands.*] My baby . . . [*Almost crying.*] You're not my niece, you're my angel, you're everything to me. Believe me, believe me . . .
ANYA. I do believe you, Uncle Leonid. Everyone loves you, respects you . . . There's only one thing: you have to learn not to talk so much, to keep quiet. Those things you just said about Mama, about your sister—what made you say them?
GAEV. I know, I know . . . [*He covers his face with her hand.*] You're right, it's awful. Lord God, help me! That speech I made today to the bookcase . . . so silly. And it wasn't till it was over I realized how silly it was.
VARYA. She's right, Uncle Leonid. You should learn not to talk so much. Just stop, that's all.
ANYA. You'll feel better if you do.
GAEV. I won't say another word. [*He kisses* ANYA's *and* VARYA's *hands.*] Not another word. But this is important. While I was at the District Court on Thursday, a group of us got together and started talking about this, that, and the other thing, and it looks as though we can borrow enough to pay the bank its interest.
VARYA. With God's help . . .
GAEV. I'm going back in on Tuesday and have another talk with them. [*To* VARYA.] Stop blubbering. [*To* ANYA.] Your mother's going to talk to Lopakhin. He can't possibly refuse . . . And as soon as you feel good and rested, you can pay a visit to your great-aunt the countess in Yaroslavl. That way we'll be tackling it from three different directions. We can't fail. We'll pay the interest, I know we will . . . [*He puts a hard candy into his mouth.*] I give you my word of honor: I swear by anything and everything: the estate shall not be sold! [*Passionately.*] I swear by my happiness! Here is my hand. You can call me a liar and a cheat if I let it come up for auction. I swear by my entire being!
ANYA. [*She is calm again and happy.*] You're so good, Uncle Leonid, so intelligent! [*She hugs her uncle.*] Now I feel better. Calm and happy. [*Enter* FIRS.]
FIRS. [*Reproachfully.*] You ought to be ashamed of yourself, Leonid Andreevich. It's way past your bedtime.
GAEV. Yes, yes, I'm on my way. You can go, Firs. It's all right, I'll undress myself. Well now, little ones, time for bed . . . [*He kisses* ANYA *and* VARYA.] I am a man of the eighties . . . And even if people don't think too much of the eighties, I've suffered for my convictions. Why do you think peasants love me? You have to get to know the peasants. You have to know the way they . . .
ANYA. There you go again, Uncle Leonid.
VARYA. Not now, Uncle Leonid.
FIRS. [*Angrily.*] Leonid Andreevich!
GAEV. Coming. Coming . . . Go to bed. Double bank into the side, [*He exits with* FIRS *hobbling out after him.*]
ANYA. I'm so relieved. I haven't the least desire to go to Yaroslavl. I don't like that great-aunt of ours, but still I'm relieved. Thanks to Uncle Leonid. [*She sits down.*]
VARYA. We'd better get some sleep. I'm going. Oh, by the way, we had some trouble while you were gone. You know, don't you, that only the older people are left in the old servants' quarters: Yefimushka, Polya, Yevstignei, and, of course, Karp. Well, they started letting some tramps sleep there, and at first I closed my eyes to it. But one day I heard a rumor I'd given orders to feed them nothing but dried peas. Because I was so stingy. . . . Yevstignei was the one who started it . . . "All right, then," I said to myself. "If that's the way you want it." So I told him to come see me . . . [*She yawns.*] Well, he came . . . And I said to him, "How could you, Yevstignei? . . . How could you be such a fool? . . ." [*She looks over at* ANYA.] Anechka! . . . [*Pause.*] Asleep! . . . [*She takes* ANYA *by the arm.*] Come to bed now . . . Come with me . . . [*She leads her along.*] My angel is asleep. Come with me . . . [*They walk along slowly.*] [*A shepherd's pipe is heard playing on the far side of the*

orchard. TROFIMOV *starts across the stage, but stops when he sees* VARYA *and* ANYA.]
VARYA. Shh! She's asleep . . . Asleep . . . Come with me, precious.
ANYA. [*Softly, half asleep.*] I'm so tired . . . All those bells . . . Uncle . . . dear . . . Mama and Uncle Leonid . . .
VARYA. Come with me, precious, come with me . . . [*She exits into* ANYA's *room.*]
TROFIMOV. [*Deeply moved.*] My sunshine! My spring!

Act 2

A field. A tumble-down old chapel long since abandoned. It is flanked by a well, some large slabs that must have once been tombstones, and an old bench. A road leads off to GAEV's *estate. A dark strip of tall poplars off to the side marks the beginning of the cherry orchard. There is a row of telegraph poles in the distance, and even farther away, on the horizon, the dim outline of a large town, visible only on the clearest of days. The sun is about to set.* CHARLOTTA, YASHA, *and* DUNYASHA *are sitting on the bench.* YEPIKHODOV *stands nearby playing the guitar. They are all lost in thought.* CHARLOTTA, *who is wearing an old peaked cap, has taken a shotgun off her shoulder and is adjusting the buckle of the strap.*

CHARLOTTA. [*Pensively.*] I don't have any real identity papers, I don't know how old I am, I still feel young. When I was a little girl, my mother and father toured the fairgrounds giving performances, good ones too. I did the salto mortale[1]—stunts like that. And when papa and mama died, a German woman took me in and gave me lessons. And then, well then I grew up and became a governess. But don't ask me where I come from or who I am—I don't know . . . Don't ask who my parents were or even if they were married—I don't know. [*She takes a cucumber out of her pocket and bites into it.*] I don't know a thing. [*Pause.*] I want so much to talk to someone. But who? . . . I'm all alone.
YEPIKHODOV. [*Playing the guitar and singing.*]

What care I for worldly pleasure,
What care I for friend or foe?

I do so enjoy playing the mandolin!
DUNYASHA. That's a guitar, not a mandolin. [*She looks at herself in a hand mirror and ponders her face.*]
YEPIKHODOV. To a fool in love it's a mandolin . . . [*He sings softly.*]

If my heart's most valued treasure,
Keeps our mutual love aglow. [YASHA *joins in.*]

CHARLOTTA. What awful voices they have . . . Ugh! Like jackals.
DUNYASHA. [*To* YASHA.] You're so lucky, going abroad like that.
YASHA. Of course I am. What do you think? [*He yawns, then lights a cigar.*]
YEPIKHODOV. It stands to reason. Everything abroad has long since reached a stage of complete complexion.
YASHA. Absolutely.
YEPIKHODOV. I am a man of culture—I read the most sundry books—but I still can't quite decide what direction to take, what I really want to do—live or shoot myself, so to speak. But just to make sure, I always carry a revolver with me. See? . . . [*He takes out a revolver.*]
CHARLOTTA. Well, that's that. I'm off. [*She slings the gun over her shoulder.*] You're so bright, Yepikhodov, so awe-inspiring—I'll bet all the ladies go crazy over you. Brrr! [*She starts off.*] All these bright lights are so dull. I have no one to talk to . . . Alone, all alone with no one to talk to and . . . and no idea of who I am or why I'm here . . . [*She exits slowly.*]
YEPIKHODOV. When all is said and done and keeping strictly to the point, I can only say that like a boat in a storm, I have received a series of merciless blows. And if, by any chance, I am mistaken, then why did I wake up this morning to find a spider of enormous proportions sit-

ting on my chest? . . . This big. [*He shows its size with both hands.*] Or whenever I pick up a glass of kvass, why is there always something positively indecent floating in it, like a cockroach? [*Pause.*] Have any of you ever read any Buckle?[2] [*Pause.*] May I disturb you with a few words, Avdotya Fyodorovna?

DUNYASHA. Go ahead.

YEPIKHODOV. May I request that we talk in private? . . . [*He sighs.*]

DUNYASHA. [*Embarrassed.*] All right . . . But would you go and bring me back my cape? . . . I left it near the bookshelf . . . It's damp out here . . .

YEPIKHODOV. All right . . . I'll go and get it . . . Now I know what to do with my revolver . . . [*He picks up his guitar and exits strumming it.*]

YASHA. Twenty-two disasters! The man's a fool, if you ask me. [*He yawns.*]

DUNYASHA. I hope to God he doesn't shoot himself. [*Pause.*] I've been so nervous lately, so upset. I was only a little girl when they brought me to the house to work, and now I've completely lost touch with the way other people live. Look how white my hands are—white as a lady's. I'm so delicate, refined, so ladylike, afraid of everything . . . Frightened. And if you ever deceived me, Yasha, I don't know what it would do to my nerves.

YASHA. [*He kisses her.*] A real sugar plum. Of course a girl must keep herself in hand. If there's one thing I disapprove of, it's loose behavior.

DUNYASHA. I'm madly in love with you. You're so well-educated. You can talk about anything. [*Pause.*]

YASHA. [*He yawns.*] Yes . . . Well, the way I see it, if a girl is in love, it means she's immoral. [*Pause.*] What could be more enjoyable than smoking a cigar in the open air? . . . [*He listens.*] Somebody's coming . . . They're coming . . . [DUNYASHA *throws her arms around him.*] Go back to the house and act like you've been out swimming in the river. And don't take the main road or they'll see you and think I asked you here. I'd never live it down.

DUNYASHA. [*She coughs softly.*] That cigar has given me a splitting headache . . . [*She exits.*] [YASHA *stays behind, sitting near the chapel. Enter* LYUBOV ANDREEVNA, GAEV *and* LOPAKHIN.]

LOPAKHIN. You've got to make up your minds once and for all. Time's running out. It's a perfectly simple matter, anyway: either you're willing to lease the land for summer cottages or you're not. Just say the word: yes or no. Say the word.

LYUBOV ANDREEVNA. Who's been smoking those disgusting cigars around here? . . . [*She sits down.*]

GAEV. Now that the railway is finished, it's no trouble at all. [*He sits down.*] Here we took the train into town just for a bite to eat . . . yellow into the side. Think I'll go inside for a game . . .

LYUBOV ANDREEVNA. What's your hurry?

LOPAKHIN. Say the word! [*Pleading with them.*] Tell me, please!

GAEV. [*Yawning.*] What's that?

LYUBOV ANDREEVNA. [*She looks into her purse.*] Yesterday I had lots of money; there's almost none left today. Poor Varya's trying to economize by feeding everybody milk soup, the old servants in the kitchen get nothing but dried peas, and I just throw my money away . . . [*She drops her purse, scattering some gold coins.*] There it goes . . . [*She is annoyed.*]

YASHA. Allow me to pick it up, madam. [*He picks up the coins.*]

LYUBOV ANDREEVNA. Please do, Yasha. And why did I have to go to town for lunch? . . . That pitiful restaurant of yours—the orchestra, the tablecloths smelling of soap . . . Why drink so much, Lyonya? And eat so much? And talk so much? Rambling on like that in the restaurant about the seventies and the symbolists. And to whom? Really now, talking about symbolism to a bunch of waiters!

LOPAKHIN. Hm.

GAEV. [*He dismisses her reproach with a wave of the hand.*] I know, I know. I'm hopeless . . . [*Irritably, to* YASHA.] What are you doing, hanging about all the time?

YASHA. [*He laughs.*] Your voice just makes me laugh.

GAEV. [*To* LYUBOV ANDREEVNA.] Either

he goes or I go . . .

LYUBOV ANDREEVNA. You may leave now, Yasha. Go on . . .

YASHA. [*He hands* LYUBOV ANDREEVNA *her purse.*] Right away. [*He can hardly keep from laughing.*] Right away . . . [*He exits.*]

LOPAKHIN. There's a rich man by the name of Deriganov who's thinking of buying your estate. They say he'll be at the auction in person.

LYUBOV ANDREEVNA. Where did you hear that?

LOPAKHIN. In town. People are talking.

GAEV. Our aunt in Yaroslavl has promised us something, but when or how much—your guess is as good as mine.

LOPAKHIN. About how much? A hundred thousand? Two hundred?

LYUBOV ANDREEVNA. Well . . . More like ten or fifteen—if we've lucky.

LOPAKHIN. I'm sorry, but never in my life have I met anybody so scatterbrained as you or your brother, so impractical and strange. Here I tell you in no uncertain terms that your estate is going up for sale, and you don't seem to understand.

LYUBOV ANDREEVNA. But what can we do? Tell us what to do.

LOPAKHIN. I have told you. I tell you every day. Lease both the cherry orchard and the land for summer cottages, and do it now, right away! The auction will be here in no time. Try to understand. Once you make up your minds in favor of the cottages, you can borrow as much as you like. You'll be saved.

LUYBOV ANDREEVNA. But all those little houses and little people—I'm sorry, it's all so vulgar.

GAEV. I quite agree.

LOPAKHIN. I think I'm going to break down and cry or scream or faint. I can't take it any more. You're too much for me. [*To* GAEV.] You old maid.

GAEV. What was that?

LOPAKHIN. Old maid! [*He starts to go.*]

LYUBOV ANDREEVNA. [*Alarmed.*] No, don't go! Please stay, please. Maybe we can come up with something.

LOPAKHIN. But I *have* come up with something.

LYUBOV ANDREEVNA. Don't go, please! You make things more lively . . . [*Pause.*] I keep expecting something terrible to happen—like the house falling down on us.

GAEV. [*In deep thought.*] Combination into the corner . . . Cross shot into the side . . .

LYUBOV ANDREEVNA. Oh, the sins we have on our conscience . . .

GAEV. [*He puts a hard candy in his mouth.*] People say I've eaten up my fortune in fruit drops . . . [*He laughs.*]

LYUBOV ANDREEVNA. Oh, my sins . . . I've always spent money like water, like a madwoman. And to make things worse, I married a man whose only talent was running up debts, who drank himself to death on champagne. I had the bad luck to fall in love with somebody else right away and just then—it was a cruel blow, but I deserved it—right here in the river . . . my little boy . . . he drowned. And I went abroad, I went away for good, I never wanted to see that river again . . . I shut my eyes and ran, blindly. But *he* came after me . . . brutal, cruel. I bought a place near Menton because *he* came down with something there, and for three years I nursed him day and night. He completely drained me—physically and emotionally. Then last year, when the place had to be sold for debts, I went to Paris, and there he robbed me, ran out on me, took up with another woman. I tried to poison myself . . . It was all so stupid and humiliating . . . And suddenly I felt I couldn't live without Russia, my country, my little girl . . . [*She wipes away her tears.*] O Lord, Lord, be merciful. Forgive my sins! Don't punish me again. [*She takes a telegram out of her pocket.*] This came today from Paris. He begs me to forgive him, implores me to return . . . [*She tears up the telegram.*] Is that music I hear? [*She listens.*]

GAEV. Our famous Jewish orchestra. Remember? Four fiddles, flute, and double bass.

LYUBOV ANDREEVNA. You mean it still exists? We should have them come and play sometime, give a party.

LOPAKHIN. [*He listens.*] I can't hear anything . . . [*He sings softly.*]

> If you pay the Prussians,
> They'll Frenchify us Russians . . . [*He laughs.*]

I saw a really funny play at the theater last night, very funny.

LYUBOV ANDREEVNA. How would you know if it was funny? You people shouldn't go to plays. You should look at yourselves—your gray lives, your empty talk.

LOPAKHIN. It's true, there's no getting away from it: our lives are senseless. [*Pause.*] My father was a peasant, an empty-headed idiot whose only idea of education was to beat me when he was drunk, and with a stick too. When you get down to it, I'm as much of a blockhead and idiot as he was. Never had any schooling. My handwriting is terrible. I'm ashamed to let people see it. A pig could do better.

LYUBOV ANDREEVNA. What you need is a wife, my friend.

LOPAKHIN. Hm . . . True.

LYUBOV ANDREEVNA. Like our Varya. A nice girl.

LOPAKHIN. Hm.

LYUBOV ANDREEVNA. From a nice, simple background too. Works all day long. The main thing is, though, she loves you. And you've been fond of her all these years, haven't you?

LOPAKHIN. Well, it's all right with me . . . She's a nice girl. [*Pause.*]

GAEV. [*To* LYUBOV ANDREEVNA.] Did you know I'd been offered a job at the bank? Six thousand a year . . .

LYUBOV ANDREEVNA. You? In a bank? You stay where you are . . . [*Enter* FIRS *carrying a coat.*]

FIRS. [*To* GAEV.] Put this on now, sir. It's damp out.

GAEV. [*He puts on the coat.*] I wish you'd stop pestering me.

FIRS. Now, now . . . You went off this morning without telling me. [*He looks him over carefully.*]

LYUBOV ANDREEVNA. You look so much older, Firs!

FIRS. Anything you wish, madam.

LOPAKHIN. She says you're looking very old.

FIRS. I *am* old. They were ready to marry me off before your papa was even born . . . [*He laughs.*] I was head footman back when the serfs were freed. I didn't want my freedom, I stayed on with the master and mistress . . . [*Pause.*] I remember how happy they all were at the time—not that they knew why.

LOPAKHIN. Yes, those were the good old days . . . Plenty of floggings.

FIRS. [*Catching his last words.*] Yes, the good old days. The peasants had their masters, the masters had their peasants. Now they're all separate. You don't know where you stand.

GAEV. Quiet, Firs. I'm going into town tomorrow. I've been promised an appointment with some general or other who may let us have a loan.

LOPAKHIN. I wouldn't count on it. And believe me, you couldn't begin to pay the interest.

LYUBOV ANDREEVNA. Don't listen to him. There are no generals. [*Enter* TROFIMOV, ANYA, *and* VARYA.]

GAEV. Ah, here come the children.

ANYA. Look, there's Mama.

LYUBOV ANDREEVNA. [*Tenderly.*] Over here . . . Over here, darlings . . . [*Embracing* ANYA *and* VARYA.] If only the two of you knew how much I love you. Here, sit down next to me. [*They all sit down.*]

LOPAKHIN. Our eternal student here spends all his time with the ladies, I see.

TROFIMOV. Mind your own business.

LOPAKHIN. Going on fifty and still a student.

TROFIMOV. I've had enough of your moronic jokes.

LOPAKHIN. What are you getting so excited about? I can't figure you out.

TROFIMOV. Just leave me alone.

LOPAKHIN. [*He laughs.*] Let me ask you one question: what do you think of me?

TROFIMOV. What do I think of you, Yermolai Alexeevich? Well, you're a rich man, you'll be a millionaire soon, and insofar as beasts of prey are necessary to maintain the cycle of nature by devouring everything in their path, you too are necessary. [*They all laugh.*]

VARYA. Tell us some more about the planets, Petya.

LYUBOV ANDREEVNA. No, let's go back to where we left off yesterday.

TROFIMOV. What were we talking about?

GAEV. Pride.

TROFIMOV. Oh, yes. We did talk a lot. Didn't come to any conclusions, though. From your standpoint there's something mystical about the proud man, and you may be right in a way. But look at the facts—bare, simple facts. Why even talk about pride when man's physiological make-up is so shoddy, when the overwhelming majority of the species is coarse, ignorant, and profoundly unhappy? It's time we stopped admiring ourselves and started working.

GAEV. We're all going to die anyway.

TROFIMOV. Who knows? And who knows what dying means? Maybe man has a hundred senses and loses only the five we're aware of when he dies. That leaves ninety-five to go on living.

LYUBOV ANDREEVNA. You're so clever, Petya! . . .

LOPAKHIN. [*Ironically.*] Brilliant!

TROFIMOV. Mankind marches onward, stronger and stronger. Things that seem impossible to us now will one day be within our reach, commonplace, but only if we work, do all we can to help those who are seeking the truth. Here in Russia hardly anybody works. The overwhelming majority of the intellectuals I know aren't seeking the truth; they aren't doing anything, they're incapable of doing anything. They call themselves the intelligentsia, but they talk down to their servants and treat the peasants like animals. They don't know how to study, they never take their reading seriously, they sit around doing nothing. Science is just an excuse for a chat, and art—a closed book. Oh, they're all very earnest, they all look so solemn, they talk about weighty issues, philosophize—and right under their noses poorly nourished workers sleep without bedding, thirty or forty to a room, plagued by bedbugs, foul damp air, and all kinds of depravity . . . The only reason for all our fine words is clearly to pull the wool over everybody's eyes—our own included. Show me the public nurseries everyone shouts about. Show me the public libraries. You may find them in novels, but you won't find a one in real life. Real life is all filth, vulgarity, Asiatic barbarism . . . I don't like those earnest faces, I'm afraid of them. I'm afraid of earnest words. We'd be better off if we kept our mouths shut.

LOPAKHIN. Well, I'm up every day at four, I work from morning till night. I handle a lot of money—my own and other people's—and I see what makes people tick. Just try to do something—anything—and you'll find out how few honest, decent people there are. Sometimes, when I can't fall asleep, I think to myself, "Lord, you gave us monumental forests, boundless plains, sweeping horizons, and we, who live in their midst, should be as giants . . ."

LYUBOV ANDREEVINA. Why giants? . . . They may be all right in fairy tales, but in real life they're awfully frightening. [YEPIKHODOV *crosses the back of the stage strumming his guitar.*] [*Dreamily.*] There goes Yepikhodov.

ANYA. [*Dreamily.*] There goes Yepikhodov.

GAEV. The sun has set, ladies and gentlemen.

TROFIMOV. Hm.

GAEV. [*In a subdued voice, as if reciting.*] Oh nature, glorious nature, glowing with eternal radiance, so beautiful, so indifferent, thou, whom we call Mother, in whom the quick and the dead are joined together, thou, who givest life and takest it away . . .

VARYA. [*Imploringly.*] Uncle Leonid! . . .

ANYA. Uncle Leonid, you're at it again.

TROFIMOV. You'd do better with a combination off the red into the side.

GAEV. Not another word. I won't say another word. [*They all sit deep in thought. This silence is broken only by* FIRS' *muttering. Then suddenly they hear a distant sound that seems to come from the sky, the sound of a string that has snapped. It dies away mournfully.*]

LYUBOV ANDREEVNA. What was that?

LOPAKHIN. I don't know. A bucket must have snapped loose somewhere off in the mines, a long way off.
GAEV. Maybe it's a bird of some kind . . . A heron . . .
TROFIMOV. Or an owl.
LYUBOV ANDREEVNA. [*She shudders.*] There was something upsetting about it. [*Pause.*]
FIRS. The same things happened just before the big disaster: the owl hooting and the samovar humming.
GAEV. What disaster?
FIRS. Emancipation. [*Pause.*]
LYUBOV ANDREEVNA. Come, let's go in, everybody. It's getting late. [*To* ANYA.] You have tears in your eyes. What is it, child? [*She puts her arms around her.*]
ANYA. Nothing, Mama. I'm all right.
TROFIMOV. Somebody's coming. [*A* PASSERBY *appears wearing a battered white cap and an overcoat. He is slightly drunk.*]
PASSERBY. Excuse me, but can you tell me if I can get to the station this way?
GAEV. Yes, just follow that road.
PASSERBY. Much obliged. [*With a cough.*] Nice weather we're having . . . [*He begins reciting a poem*]

Brother, long suffering brother! Come down to the Volga with me . . . [*To* VARYA.]

Would you have thirty kopeks for a starving Russian, mam'selle? . . . [VARYA *is frightened and cries out.*]
LOPAKHIN. [*Angrily.*] That's enough of that!
LYUBOV ANDREEVNA. [*Ruffled.*] Here . . . This is for you . . . [*She looks around in her purse.*] No silver . . . Oh well . . . Here's a gold piece . . .
PASSERBY. Much obliged! [*He exits.*] [*Laughter.*]
VARYA. [*Still frightened.*] I'm leaving, going away, for good . . . Mama, how could you! The servants have nothing to eat, and you give him gold.
LYUBOV ANDREEVNA. Well, what can you do with a fool like me? I'll give you everything I have when we get back to the house. You'll let me have another loan, won't you, Yermolai Alexeevich? . . .

LOPAKHIN. At your service.
LYUBOV ANDREEVNA. Let's go, everyone. Time to go. By the way, Varya, we've settled the matchmaking. Congratulations.
VARYA. [*Almost crying.*] Please, Mama, it's not a laughing matter.
LOPAKHIN. Get thee to a nunnery, Ovarya.[3]
GAEV. Look, my hands are shaking. What I need is a good game of billiards.
LOPAKHIN. Ovarya, nymph, in thine orisons be all my sins remembered.[3]
LYUBOV ANDREEVNA. Come along, everybody. It's almost time for supper.
VARYA. Did he scare me! My heart's still pounding.
LOPAKHIN. May I remind you all that the cherry orchard's going up for auction on the twenty-second of August? Just keep it in mind. Keep it in mind . . . [*They all exit except* TROFIMOV *and* ANYA.]
ANYA. [*Laughing.*] We ought to have thanked the stranger for frightening Varya like that. Now we're alone.
TROFIMOV. Varya's afraid we'll fall in love. She won't let us out of her sight. She's too narrow-minded to see we're above all that. The only purpose to our life, it's only meaning is to do away with all the petty and illusory concerns that keep us from being happy and free. Onward! On we go! Inexorable. Our goal—that bright star burning in the distance! Onward! Don't fall behind, friends!
ANYA. [*Flinging up her arms.*] How beautifully you put things! [*Pause.*] Isn't it heavenly here today?
TROFIMOV. Yes, the weather's excellent.
ANYA. What have you done to me, Petya? Why don't I love the cherry orchard the way I used to? I used to love it so dearly. I thought it was the best place on earth, our orchard.
TROFIMOV. All Russia is our orchard. The earth is vast and beautiful, filled with wonderful places. [*Pause.*] Think of it, Anya. Your grandfather, great-grandfather, all your ancestors were serf-owners, they owned live souls. Can't you see them—human beings staring out at you from every tree in the orchard, from every leaf, every

trunk? Can't you hear their voices? . . . Owning live souls—it's done something to you, your whole family, past and present. You, your mother, your uncle—you don't even realize you're living on credit, at the expense of others, people you don't let past your front door . . . We're at least two hundred years behind the times, so destitute we lack even a sense of the past. All we do is philosophize, complain about how depressing life is, and drink vodka. But it's perfectly clear that to live in the present we've got to expiate our past, make a clean break with it. And the only way we can do that is by suffering—suffering and relentless hard work. Can you see that, Anya?

ANYA. The house we live in hasn't been ours for a long time now, and I'm going to leave, I swear I am.

TROFIMOV. If you have the keys to the house, then fling them down the well and come away, free as the wind!

ANYA. [*In a state of rapture.*] How beautifully you put it!

TROFIMOV. Take my word for it, Anya! Take my word! I'm not thirty yet, I'm young, I'm still a student, but the things I've been through! As soon as winter comes, I'm hungry, sick, plagued with anxieties, poor as a pauper. The places I've been, the people I've seen. But through it all, every minute of it, every day and every night, I've been haunted by strange premonitions, premonitions of happiness, Anya, I can see it coming . . .

ANYA. [*In a state of reverie.*] The moon is rising. [YEPIKHODOV *is heard playing the same sad song as before. The moon rises. Somewhere over by the poplars* VARYA *is looking for* ANYA *and calling,* "*Anya! Where are you?*"]

TROFIMOV. Yes, the moon is rising. [*Pause.*] There it is—happiness. Here it comes, closer and closer. I can hear its footsteps. And if *we* never get to see it or know it, well, that's all right too. Others will! [VARYA's *voice:* "*Anya! Where are you?*"] Varya again? [*Angrily.*] Impossible!

ANYA. Don't mind her. Let's go down to the river. It's so lovely there.

TROFIMOV. Yes, let's. [VARYA's *voice:* "*Anya! Anya!*"]

Act 3

The drawing room. An arch opens onto the ballroom. The chandelier is lit. The Jewish orchestra mentioned in act 2 is playing in the entrance hall. It is evening. The guests are dancing a grand rond[4] *in the ballroom.* SIMEONOV-PISHCHIK *calls out,* "Promenade à une paire!" PISHCHIK *and* CHARLOTTA IVANOVNA *are the first couple to enter,* TROFIMOV *and* LYUBOV ANDREEVNA *the second,* ANYA *and the* POSTMASTER *the third,* VARYA *and the* STATIONMASTER *the fourth, and so on.* VARYA *is crying quietly and dries her eyes while dancing.* DUNYASHA *is in the last couple. They cross the drawing room with* PISHCHIK *calling out,* "Grand rond, balancez!" *and* "Les cavaliers à genoux et remerciez vos dames." FIRS, *wearing a frock coat, carries in a tray of soda water.* PISHCHIK *and* TROFIMOV *reenter the drawing room.*

PISHCHIK. With my high blood pressure and my two strokes, dancing's no laughing matter, but you know what they say—if you run with the pack, then at least wag your tail. I'm strong as a horse, though. My dear departed father used to say—he liked a good joke—that the ancient line of Simeonov-Pishchik descended from the horse that Caligula made a senator . . . [*He sits down.*] My only problem is money. A hungry dog has meat on the brain. [*He begins to snore, but wakes up immediately.*] And I . . . I have money on the brain . . .

TROFIMOV. Come to think of it, there is something horsy about you.

PISHCHIK. Well . . . A horse is a perfectly good animal . . . You can always sell a horse . . . [*The sound of people playing billards comes from an adjoining room.* VARYA *appears in the ballroom.*]

TROFIMOV. [*He teases her.*] Madame Lopakhina! Madame Lopakhina! . . .

VARYA. [*Angrily.*] Moth-eaten gentleman!
TROFIMOV. Moth-eaten and proud of it!
VARYA. [*Musing bitterly.*] Hiring musicians! What are we going to pay them with? [*She exits.*]
TROFIMOV. [*To* PISHCHIK.] If the energy you've wasted in a lifetime of scrounging for interest payments had been put to better use, you'd have turned the world upside down by now.
PISHCHIK. Nietzsche . . . the philosopher . . . a great man, world renowned, a man of the intellect . . . Nietzsche says it's all right to counterfeit money.
TROFIMOV. So you've read Nietzsche.
PISHCHIK. Well, no . . . My Dashenka told me. But the way things look now, it's my only out . . . Three hundred and ten rubles due the day after tomorrow . . . I've already got a hundred and thirty . . . [*He feels his pockets in alarm.*] It's gone! The money! I've lost it! [*Almost crying.*] Where can it be? [*Joyfully.*] Oh, here it is! In the lining . . . Look at me, sweating all over . . . [*Enter* LYUBOV ANDREEVNA *and* CHARLOTTA IVANOVNA.]
LUYBOV ANDREEVNA. [*She is humming a lively Caucasian dance melody.*] Why isn't Leonid back yet? What can he be doing in town? [*To* DUNYASHA.] See if the musicians want some tea, Dunyasha . . .
TROFIMOV. The auction probably never took place.
LYUBOV ANDREEVNA. This wasn't the right time to have musicians. It wasn't the right time to have a party . . . Oh well, never mind. [*She sits down and hums quietly.*]
CHARLOTTA. [*She hands* PISHCHIK *a deck of cards.*] Pick a card, any card.
PISHCHIK. All right, I have one.
CHARLOTTA. Now shuffle the deck. Fine. And give it back to me, kind sir. Eins, zwei, drei! Take a look in your coat pocket. Is that your card?
PISHCHIK. [*He pulls a card out of his pocket.*] The eight of spades. Absolutely right! [*Amazed.*] Unbelievable.
CHARLOTTA. [*She holds the deck out to* TROFIMOV *in the palm of her hand.*] Quickly—tell me what the top card is.
TROFIMOV. Well, say, the queen of spades.
CHARLOTTA. Right you are! [*To* PISHCHIK.] What's the top card now?
PISHCHIK. The ace of hearts.
CHARLOTTA. Right again! [*She claps her hands, and the cards disappear.*] Nice weather we're having. [*A mysterious woman's* VOICE *that seems to come from underground answers,* "Yes, Madame, marvelous weather."] You're everything I've always hoped for. [*The* VOICE: *"I'm quite taken with you myself."*]
STATIONMASTER. [*Clapping.*] Bravo, Madame ventriloquist.
PISHCHIK. [*Amazed.*] Unbelievable! You're a real charmer, Charlotta Ivanovna . . . I'm in love . . .
CHARLOTTA. In love? [*Shrugging her shoulders.*] You in love? Guter Mensch, aber schlechter Musikant.
TROFIMOV. [*Slapping* PISHCHIK *on the back.*] There's a good horse . . .
CHARLOTTA. Attention, please! One more trick. [*She picks up a plaid traveling blanket from a chair.*] Now here's a fine specimen of plaid. I think I'll sell it . . . [*She shakes it out.*] Any customers?
PISHCHIK. [*Amazed.*] Unbelievable!
CHARLOTTA. Eins, zwei, drei! [*She lifts the blanket with a flourish and out steps* ANYA. ANYA *curtsies, runs over to her mother, gives her a hug, and runs back into the ballroom amidst the oh's and ah's of the crowd.*]
LYUBOV ANDREEVNA. [*Clapping.*] Bravo! Bravo!
CHARLOTTA. And for an encore: Eins, zwei, drei. [*She lifts the blanket and out comes* VARYA *and curtsies.*]
PISHCHIK. [*Amazed.*] Unbelievable.
CHARLOTTA. That's it for today. [*She throws the blanket at* PISHCHIK, *curtsies, and runs off into the ballroom.*]
PISHCHIK. [*Rushing after her.*] Naughty, naughty . . . What a woman! What a woman! [*He exits.*]
LYUBOV ANDREEVNA. Still no sign of Leonid. What can he be doing in town so long? I don't understand it. It must be over by now. Either the estate's been sold or the auction didn't take place. Why keep us in suspense?
VARYA. [*Trying to comfort her.*] Uncle

Leonid's bought it. I'm sure he has.
TROFIMOV. [*Sarcastically.*] Of course he has.
VARYA. Our great-aunt gave him power of attorney to buy it in her name and have the mortgage made over to her. She's doing it for Anya's sake. And God will help us, I'm sure He will. Uncle Leonid's got to buy it.
LYUBOV ANDREEVNA. Your great-aunt gave him fifteen thousand rubles to buy back the estate in her name—she doesn't trust us. Well, that won't even cover the interest. [*She puts her hands over her face.*] My future is in the balance today, my fate . . .
TROFIMOV. [*Teasing* VARYA.] Madame Lopakhina!
VARYA. [*Angrily.*] Eternal student! Thrown out of the university twice.
LYUBOV ANDREEVNA. Don't get so upset, Varya. What if he does tease you about Lopakhin? Go ahead and marry him—he's a nice, attractive man—of course, you don't have to if you don't want to. Nobody's forcing you, darling.
VARYA. I've given it serious thought, Mama. Really I have. He's a nice man, and I like him.
LYUBOV ANDREEVNA. Then marry him. What are you waiting for? I don't understand.
VARYA. I can't very well propose to him, can I? For two years now everybody's been talking about it. Everybody but him. He either avoids the subject or turns it into a joke. Oh, I know. He's busy getting rich, he hasn't got time for me. If I had any money—even a hundred rubles—I'd drop everything and go away from here, the farther the better. Enter a convent.
TROFIMOV. Ah paradise!
VARYA. [*To* TROFIMOV.] The student has to show how clever he is. [*In a gentle, teary voice.*] You're so much uglier than you used to be, Petya. And older. [*To* LYUBOV ANDREEVNA, *no longer crying.*] What I need is to be busy all the time; I need something to do every minute. [*Enter* YASHA.]
YASHA. [*Scarcely able to keep from laughing.*] Yepikhodov's broken a billiard cue. [*He exits.*]
VARYA. What is Yepikhodov doing here? Who said he could play billiards? I can't understand these people . . . [*She exits.*]
LYUBOV ANDREEVNA. Don't tease her, Petya. Can't you see she's miserable enough as it is?
TROFIMOV. Well, I just wish she wouldn't be so prying, such a busybody. She hasn't left Anya or me alone all summer. She's afraid we'll have an affair. Well, what business is that of hers? And anyway, I've never given her the least cause to think so. I'm beyond such trivialities. Love? We're above that kind of thing.
LYUBOV ANDREEVNA. Which means, I suppose, that I'm beneath it. [*Greatly agitated.*] Why isn't Leonid back? All I want to know is whether the estate's been sold. The whole thing is so inconceivable. I don't know what to think. I'm at my wits' end . . . Help me, Petya, or I'll scream, I'll make a fool of myself . . . Say something, anything . . .
TROFIMOV. Does it really matter whether the estate is sold today or not? It's all over and done with, dead and buried. You can't turn back the clock. Try to be calm, try to be honest with yourself. For once in your life look the truth in the face.
LYUBOV ANDREEVNA. What truth? You see so clearly what's true and what's false. I must be going blind. I don't see a thing. You know all the answers, but isn't that because you're young and haven't suffered the consequences of what you preach? You look ahead so boldly, but isn't that because you're sheltered and don't imagine or expect anything terrible to happen? You may be bolder, purer, deeper than we are, but put yourself in my place, show a little generosity, give me the benefit of the doubt. I was born here; my mother and father, my grandfather all lived here. I love this house. Life means nothing to me without the cherry orchard, and if it has to be sold, you might as well sell me along with it . . . [*She embraces* TROFIMOV *and kisses him on the forehead.*] My little boy drowned here . . . [*She weeps.*] Don't be too hard on me. You're so good,

so kind.

TROFIMOV. You know you have my deepest sympathy.

LYUBOV ANDREEVNA. No, I'm putting it all wrong, all wrong . . . [*She takes out a handkerchief. A telegram falls to the floor.*] I'm so depressed today, you can't imagine. I can't stand the noise. I jump at every sound, I'm trembling all over. But I can't go to my room. I'm terrified of the silence and being alone. Don't look down on me, Petya . . . I love you like my own child. I'd gladly let Anya marry you, believe me I would, only you really must go back and finish your studies. You don't do anything, you just drift from place to place. Don't you see how peculiar that is . . . Well, don't you? And you've got to do something about that beard, make it grow or something . . . [*She laughs.*] You look so funny.

TROFIMOV. [*He picks up the telegram.*] I have no desire to be a dandy.

LYUBOV ANDREEVNA. A telegram from Paris. I get one every day. One yesterday, one today. That wild man is sick again, in trouble again . . . He asks me to forgive him, begs me to come. I really should go back and take care of him for a while. I see you don't approve, Petya, but what else can I do, dear, what else can I do? He's sick, he's lonely, unhappy. Who'll look after him, keeping him from making a fool of himself, give him his medicine on time? And anyway—why not come out and say it? . . . I love him. It's obvious. I love him, I love him . . . He's a millstone around my neck, he's dragging me down with him, but I love my millstone, I can't live without it. [*She presses* TROFIMOV'*s hand.*] Don't hold it against me, Petya. Don't say anything at all, not a word . . .

TROFIMOV. [*Almost crying.*] Forgive me for being so blunt, but he's robbed you blind!

LYUBOV ANDREEVNA. No, no, no, you mustn't say things like that . . . [*She puts her hands over her ears.*]

TROFIMOV. But the man's a swindler. You're the only one who doesn't see it! A no-good swindler, a nobody . . .

LYUBOV ANDREEVNA. [*Angry, but in control of herself.*] Here you are, twenty-six, twenty-seven, and still a schoolboy . . .

TROFIMOV. Well, what if I am!

LYUBOV ANDREEVNA. Why aren't you more of a man? At your age you should understand what it means to be in love. You should be in love yourself . . . you should fall in love! [*Angrily.*] That's right! What's so pure about you? You're just a prude, that's all. An oddball, a freak . . .

TROFIMOV. [*Horrified.*] How can you say those things!

LYUBOV ANDREEVNA. So you're "beyond love." You're not beyond love, you're what our Firs would call a silly galoot. Not having a mistress at your age! . . .

TROFIMOV. [*Horrified.*] This is awful! How can she be saying these things? [*He rushes off into the ballroom clutching his head.*] This is awful! . . . I can't stand it, I've got to get away . . . [*He exits, but returns immediately.*] I never want to see you again. [*He exits into the entrance hall.*]

LYUBOV ANDREEVNA. [*She shouts after him.*] Wait, Petya, wait! Don't be silly. I was only joking. Petya! [*There is a sound of rapid footsteps on the stairs in the entrance hall followed by the crash of a fall.* ANYA *and* VARYA *scream and then burst out laughing.*] What's going on out there? [ANYA *runs in.*]

ANYA. [*Laughing.*] Petya's fallen down the stairs!

LYUBOV ANDREEVNA. He's a real character, that Petya . . . [*The* STATIONMASTER *goes and stands in the middle of the ballroom and begins to recite* "*The Sinner Woman*" *by Alexei Tolstoy.*[5] *The others listen for a few lines, but when the strains of a waltz reach them from the entrance hall, the recitation breaks off, and everyone starts dancing.* TROFIMOV, ANYA, VARYA *and* LYUBOV ANDREEVNA *enter from the hall.*] Now, now, Petya . . . Poor, pure Petya . . . I apologize . . . Come, let's dance . . . [*She dances with* PETYA. ANYA *and* VARYA *dance.*] [*Enter* FIRS. *He stands his cane near the side door.* YASHA *has also entered from the drawing room and is watching the dancers.*]

YASHA. How's it going there, Firs?
FIRS. Not feeling too well. We used to have generals and barons and admirals at our parties, and now what do we get—the postmaster, the stationmaster. And even they have to be begged. I've been a little weak lately. The old master, their grandfather, he used to give us sealing wax whenever we got sick. I've been taking sealing wax every day for the last twenty years or more. Maybe that's what keeps me alive.
YASHA. You know, I'm sick of you, Firs. [*He yawns.*] Why don't you just curl up and die?
FIRS. [*He mutters.*] Silly galoot . . . [TROFIMOV *and* LYUBOV ANDREEVNA *dance first in the ballroom, then in the drawing room.*]
LYUBOV ANDREEVNA. Merci. I think I'll sit down for a while . . . [*She sits down.*] I'm tired. [*Enter* ANYA.]
ANYA. [*Shaken.*] Just now in the kitchen there was a man saying the cherry orchard had been sold today.
LYUBOV ANDREEVNA. To whom?
ANYA. He didn't say. He's gone now. [*She dances with* TROFIMOV.] [*Both exit into the ballroom.*]
YASHA. Just some old man jabbering away. A stranger.
FIRS. Leonid Andreevich isn't back yet, isn't home. He's wearing a light coat too. Too light for this weather. He'll catch cold. These young people!
LYUBOV ANDREEVNA. This is killing me. Go and find out. Go and find out who bought it, will you, Yasha?
YASHA. But he's gone. The old man's gone. [*He laughs.*]
LYUBOV ANDREEVNA. [*Slightly annoyed.*] What's so funny? Why are you in such a good mood?
YASHA. It's Yepikhodov. He's so funny, so silly. Twenty-two disasters.
LYUBOV ANDREEVNA. Firs, where will you go if the estate has been sold?
FIRS. Wherever you say.
LYUBOV ANDREEVNA. What is that look on your face? Are you feeling all right? You ought to be in bed, you know.
FIRS. Hm. . . . [*With a trace of a smile.*] If I went to bed, who'd do the serving, who'd take care of things? There's no one in the house but me.
YASHA. [*To* LYUBOV ANDREEVNA.] May I ask you a favor, please, Lyubov Andreevna? If you go back to Paris, will you take me with you? I can't stay here anymore. It's out of the question. [*Looking around and lowering his voice.*] I don't need to tell you. You can see for yourself. The whole country is uncivilized, the people immoral, the life is boring, you can't even get a decent meal in the kitchen, and on top of it all Firs here is always in the way, always mumbling about something or other. Take me with you, please! [*Enter* PISHCHIK.]
PISHCHIK. May I have the pleasure of this waltz . . . beautiful lady . . . [LYUBOV ANDREEVNA *gets up to go with him.*] I'll get those hundred and eighty rubles from you yet, you charmer . . . Just you wait . . . [*He dances.*] A hundred and eighty rubles, that's all . . . [*They dance into the ballroom.*]
YASHA. [*He sings softly.*] "If thou couldst grasp the torments of my heart . . ." [*In the ballroom a figure in a gray top hat and checked trousers is jumping up and down and waving her arms. There are cries of "Bravo, Charlotta Ivanovna!"*]
DUNYASHA. [*She stops to powder her nose.*] The young mistress told me to dance—there are lots of gentlemen and not enough ladies to go around—but dancing makes my head spin, my heart pound. You should have heard what the postmaster said to me just now, Firs Nikolaevich. It took my breath away. [*The music stops.*]
FIRS. What did he tell you?
DUNYASHA. He said I was like a flower.
YASHA. [*He yawns.*] The ignorance of these people. [*He exits.*]
DUNYASHA. Like a flower . . . I'm so sensitive. I just love tender words . . .
FIRS. They'll be your undoing. [*Enter* YEPIKHODOV.]
YEPIKHODOV. You've been avoiding me, Avdotya Fyodorovna . . . as if I were an insect. [*He sighs.*] Ah, life.
DUNYASHA. What is it you want?
YEPIKHODOV. Of course, you may undoubtedly be right. [*He sighs.*] But on

the other hand, if you look at things from a point of view, then, I hope you won't mind my putting it this way, you've reduced me—forgive me for being so blunt—you've reduced me to a state of mind. I know I'm doomed to a disaster a day, but I don't care, I face each day with a smile. You gave me your word, and even though I . . .

DUNYASHA. I'm sorry, but couldn't we talk about it some other time? And would you please leave me alone for now? I'm dreaming. [*She plays with her fan.*]

YEPIKHODOV. A disaster a day, and if you don't mind my putting it this way, all I do is smile. Sometimes I even laugh. [*Enter* VARYA *from the ballroom.*]

VARYA. What, you still here, Semyon? How disrespectful can you be, really! [*To* DUNYASHA.] You may go now, Dunyasha. [*To* YEPIKHODOV.] First you play billiards and break a cue, then you parade up and down the drawing room like a guest.

YEPIKHODOV. You have no right to lecture me, if you don't mind my putting it that way.

VARYA. I'm not lecturing you, I'm just telling you. All you do is wander from one place to another, you never do a stroke of work. I sometimes wonder why we ever hired a clerk.

YEPIKHODOV. [*Offended.*] The only people qualified to judge my working or wandering or eating or billiard playing are older and wiser than you.

VARYA. How dare you talk to me like that! [*Furiously.*] How dare you! So I'm not "wise" enough for you. Well, then, get out of here! Get out of here this instant!

YEPIKHODOV. [*Cowed.*] Might I ask you to be a bit more refined in your choice of words?

VARYA. [*Beside herself.*] Out! Out! This instant! [*He goes over to the door. She follows on his heels.*] Twenty-two disasters. Don't you set foot in here again! I never want to see you again! [YEPIKHODOV *goes out. He calls out from behind the door, "I'm going to lodge a complaint against you!"*] Oh, so you're coming back in, are you?

[*She picks up the cane* FIRS *left by the door.*] All right, come on, come on . . . Come on, I'll show you . . . [*She swings the stick.*] [*Enter* LOPAKHIN *as she is swinging it.*]

LOPAKHIN. Much obliged.

VARYA. [*Angrily and sarcastically.*] Quite sorry, I'm sure.

LOPAKHIN. That's all right. Thank you for the warm welcome.

VARYA. Don't mention it. [*She walks away, then turns around and asks gently.*] I didn't hurt you, did I?

LOPAKHIN. No, not at all. The bump's going to be gigantic, though. [VOICES *in the ballroom are saying, "Lopakhin is back! Yermolai Alexeevich!"*]

PISHCHIK. Well, what do you know! His nibs in person! . . . [*He kisses* LOPAKHIN.] Had a few snorts of cognac, eh, my friend? Well, we've been having a good time too. [*Enter* LYUBOV ANDREEVNA.]

LYUBOV ANDREEVNA. Is that you, Yermolai Alexeevich? Why did it take so long? Where's Leonid?

LOPAKHIN. He came back with me, he'll be right here . . .

LYUBOV ANDREEVNA. [*Agitated.*] Well, what happened? Did the auction take place? Say something!

LOPAKHIN. [*Embarrassed and afraid of showing his joy.*] The auction was over by four . . . We missed our train and had to wait until nine-thirty. [*Sighing deeply.*] Oh dear, my head is spinning. [*Enter* GAEV. *He is carrying some packages in his right hand and wiping away tears with his left.*]

LYUBOV ANDREEVNA. Well, what happened, Lyonya? Lyonya! [*Impatiently, beginning to cry.*] Out with it, for heaven's sake!

GAEV. [*Instead of answering, he makes a helpless gesture. To* FIRS, *weeping.*] Here, take these . . . Some anchovies and herring . . . I haven't had a thing to eat all day . . . Oh, what I've been through! [*The door to the billiard room is open. We hear billiard balls clicking and* YASHA's *voice saying "Seven and eighteen."* GAEV's *expression changes. He stops crying.*] I'm terribly tired. Come and find something for me to change into, Firs. [*He exits, going through the ballroom to his room.* FIRS *follows.*]

PISHCHIK. Well, what happened at the auction? Tell us.

LYUBOV ANDREEVNA. Was the cherry orchard sold?

LOPAKHIN. It was.

LYUBOV ANDREEVNA. Who bought it?

LOPAKHIN. I did. [*Pause.*] [LYUBOV ANDREEVNA *is stunned. She would have fallen if she had not been standing next to an armchair and table.* VARYA *undoes the ring of keys from her belt, throws it on the floor in the middle of the drawing room and exits.*]

LOPAKHIN. I bought it. Wait a minute, everybody, please. I still can't think straight, I don't know what to say . . . [*He laughs.*] We arrived at the auction. Deriganov was already there. Leonid Andreevich had only fifteen thousand, and Deriganov starts off the bidding at thity, over and above the arrears on the mortgage. I can see he means business, so I take the bull by the horns and bid forty. He goes to forty-five, I go to fifty-five. He jumps by fives, I jump by tens . . . And suddenly it's over. I bid ninety thousand over and above the arrears, and I got it. The cherry orchard is mine! Mine! [*He gives a loud laugh.*] Good God in heaven, the cherry orchard's mine! Tell me I'm drunk, out of my mind. Tell me it's only a dream . . . [*He stamps his feet.*] Don't laugh at me. If my father and grandfather could rise up from their graves and see me now—the little boy everybody picked on, who never learned to read, who ran around barefoot in winter. Little Yermolai—the owner of the cherry orchard, the most beautiful place on earth! I have bought the estate where my grandfather and father were slaves, where they weren't even allowed in the kitchen . . . I must be dreaming, I must be inventing it all, it can't be true . . . It's an illusion, a figment of my imagination, it just seems to be happening . . . [*He picks up the keys, smiling fondly.*] She's thrown down the keys to show she's not in charge here anymore. [*He jangles the keys.*] Well, that's not important . . . [*The orchestra begins tuning up offstage.*] Hey, let's have some music out there! Everybody come and watch Yermolai Lopakhin take an ax to the cherry orchard. Watch those trees come down! See the cottages we'll build! Our grandchildren and great-grandchildren will live to see a new life here . . . Hey, let's hear that music! [*The orchestra plays.* LYUBOV ANDREEVNA *has collapsed into a chair and is weeping bitterly.*] [*Reproachfully.*] Why, oh why didn't you listen to me? It's too late dear friend, poor friend. [*Tearfully.*] I wish this were over and done with, I wish our miserable, muddled lives would change somehow.

PISHCHIK. [*He takes* LOPAKHIN *by the arm and speaks softly.*] She's crying. Let's go out into the ballroom and leave her alone . . . Come on . . . [*He takes him by the arm and tries to lead him into the ballroom.*]

LOPAKHIN. What's the matter in there? Can't you play any louder? Louder! I'm the one who gives the orders here now! [*With irony.*] Here comes the new master, the new owner of the cherry orchard! [*He bumps into a small table, nearly knocking over some candlesticks.*] I can pay for everything! [*He exits with* PISHCHIK.] [*There is no one left in the ballroom or drawing room but* LYUBOV ANDREEVNA, *who is huddled up in her chair, weeping bitterly. The orchestra is playing softly.* ANYA *goes over to her mother and kneels down in front of her.* TROFIMOV *remains standing at the entrance to the ballroom.*]

ANYA. Mama! . . . Mama, are you crying? Good, kind, sweet Mama, precious Mama, bless you. I love you . . . Yes, the cherry orchard is sold, gone, true, but don't cry, Mama. You still have your life ahead of you, you still have your good, kind, innocent heart . . . Come with me, Mama, come away with me, come! . . . We'll plant a new orchard, finer than this one. When you see it, you'll understand, and joy—deep, silent joy—will fill your heart, just as the setting sun fills the evening sky, and you will smile again, Mama. Come, Mama, come! . . .

Act 4

The same setting as in act 1. There are no curtains on the windows or pictures on the walls. What little furniture remains is stacked up in one corner as if for sale. There is a sense of emptiness. Upstage, near the main entrance, is a pile of suitcases, traveling bags, and the like. VARY's *and* ANYA's *voices come through the open door on the left.* LOPAKHIN *is standing and waiting.* YASHA *is holding a tray with glasses of champagne.* YEPIKHODOV *is tying up a box in the entrance hall. Offstage there is a low hum of voices: the peasants have come to say their goodbyes.* GAEV *answers, "Thank you, my boys, thank you."*

YASHA. The peasants have come to say goodbye. They mean well, I suppose, Yermolai Alexeevich; they're just so ignorant. [*The hum dies down.* LYUBOV ANDREEVNA *and* GAEV *enter through the hall. Although she is not crying, her face is pale and trembling. She is unable to speak.*]

GAEV. Giving them your purse, Lyuba. How could you? How could you?

LYUBOV ANDREEVNA. I couldn't help it. I couldn't help it. [*They both exit.*]

LOPAKHIN. [*At the door, calling after them.*] Please have some champagne before you go. Just one farewell glass. I didn't think of ordering any from town, but I did find a bottle at the station. Have some, please. [*Pause.*] [*He comes away from the door.*] If I'd known, I wouldn't have bought it. Oh well, I won't have any either. [YASHA *carefully puts the tray down on a chair.*] You have some, Yasha. Nobody else will.

YASHA. To those who are going and those who are staying! [*He drinks.*] That's not real champagne, believe me.

LOPAKHIN. Eight rubles a bottle. [*Pause.*] It's cold as the devil in here.

YASHA. Why light the stoves? We're leaving. [*He laughs.*]

LOPAKHIN. What's so funny?

YASHA. Just happy, that's all.

LOPAKHIN. It's too sunny and calm for October, more like summer. Good building weather. [*He glances at his watch and then the door.*] Don't forget, everybody, the train pulls out in forty-six minutes. That means leaving for the station in twenty minutes. Better hurry up. [TROFIMOV *enters from outside in a coat.*]

TROFIMOV. It must be time to go. The carriages are waiting. Where are my galoshes, damn it? They've disappeared. [*Through the door.*] Anya, my galoshes are gone. I can't find them anywhere.

LOPAKHIN. I'm going to Kharkov. I'll be taking the same train as you. I'm spending the winter there. It's torture sitting around here doing nothing all the time. I can't live without work. I don't know what to do with my hands. They just hang there, like somebody else's.

TROFIMOV. As soon as we're gone, you can get back to work and be useful again.

LOPAKHIN. Come on, have a glass.

TROFIMOV. No thanks.

LOPAKHIN. So you're going to Moscow.

TROFIMOV. Yes, today I'm going with them into town, and tomorrow I leave for Moscow.

LOPAKHIN. I see . . . I suppose your professors are waiting for you to arrive before they start lecturing.

TROFIMOV. Oh, mind your own business.

LOPAKHIN. How many years have you been at the university now?

TROFIMOV. How about thinking up something original for a change? You can do better than that. [*He looks for his galoshes.*] You know, this may be the last time we ever see each other, and before we say goodbye, let me give you a piece of advice. Don't wave your arms about so much. Try to stop waving your arms. And you know, building all those summer houses and expecting the residents to till the soil—well, that's just arm waving too . . . But even so, I like you, really. You've got fine, sensitive fingers, the fingers of an artist; you're a fine, sensitive person . . .

LOPAKHIN. [*Embracing him.*] Goodbye, my boy. Thanks for everything. Let me give you some money for the road. You may need it.

TROFIMOV. No, what for?
LOPAKHIN. But you haven't got any.
TROFIMOV. Yes, I have. I got some for a translation. It's here in my pocket. [*Anxiously.*] Now, where are those galoshes?
VARYA [*From the room next door.*] Here are your filthy galoshes! [*She throws them on the stage.*]
TROFIMOV. What are you so upset about, Varya? Hm . . . these aren't my galoshes!
LOPAKHIN. I planted nearly three thousand acres of poppies in the spring, and now I've made forty thousand rubles on it. And when my poppies were in bloom, that was a sight for sore eyes! Anyway, I've just made forty thousand, so I can afford to offer you a loan. Why turn your nose up at it? I'm a peasant . . . I don't beat around the bush.
TROFIMOV. Your father was a peasant, mine a pharmacist. What difference does that make? [LOPAKHIN *takes out his wallet.*] Stop, stop . . . Even if you offered me two hundred thousand, I wouldn't take it. I'm a free man, and everything people set such great store by—rich and poor alike—has no hold on me whatsoever. It's like a piece of fluff wafting through the air. I can do without you, I can make my own way. I'm strong, I'm proud. Mankind is moving toward a higher truth, the greatest possible happiness on earth, and I am in the forefront.
LOPAKHIN. Will you ever get there?
TROFIMOV. I will. [*Pause.*] I'll get there myself or show others the way. [*The sound of an ax striking a tree comes from far off.*]
LOPAKHIN. Well, goodbye, my boy. Time to go. You talk big to me, I talk big to you, and life goes on. When I work for long stretches at a time, I feel calmer, I feel I know why I'm alive. But think of all the people in Russia with nothing to live for. Oh well, that's not what makes the world go round. I hear Leonid Andreevich has taken that job at the bank. Six thousand a year . . . He'll never stick it out. He's too lazy . . .
ANYA. [*At the door.*] Mama wondered if you'd wait till she goes before you start chopping down the orchard.
TROFIMOV. That wasn't very tactful . . . [*He exits through the hall.*]
LOPAKHIN. I'll stop them immediately . . . the fools! [*He follows* TROFIMOV *out.*]
ANYA. Have they taken Firs to the hospital yet?
YASHA. I told them to this morning. They must have.
ANYA. [*To* YEPIKHODOV, *who is passing through the ballroom.*] Semyon Panteleevich, please see if Firs has been taken to the hospital.
YASHA. [*Offended.*] I told Yegor this morning. How many times do you have to ask?
YEPIKHODOV. Immemorial Firs, in my utter opinion, is beyond repair. It is time he joined his ancestors. I can only envy him. [*He puts a suitcase down on a hatbox and squashes it.*] There, you see? Of course. I knew it. [*He exits.*]
YASHA. [*Sarcastically.*] Twenty-two disasters.
VARYA. [*From behind the door.*] Have they taken Firs to the hospital?
ANYA. Yes, they have.
VARYA. Then, why didn't they take the letter to the doctor?
ANYA. We'd better send somebody over with it now . . . [*She exits.*]
VARYA. [*From the next room.*] Where's Yasha? Tell him his mother's come to say goodbye.
YASHA. [*With a gesture of annoyance.*] Won't they ever leave me alone? [*All this time* DUNYASHA *has been busy with the baggage. Now that* YASHA *is alone, she goes up to him.*]
DUNYASHA. You might at least look in my direction once or twice, Yasha. Going away like this . . . Deserting me . . . [*She throws herself on his neck in tears.*]
YASHA. No use crying. [*He drinks champagne.*] Paris again in six days. Tomorrow we take the express, and we're off in a cloud of smoke. I can hardly believe it. Vive la France! . . . This isn't the place for me. I can't live here, that's all. I've seen enough ignorance to last me a lifetime. [*He drinks champagne.*] It's no use crying. Behave yourself, and you won't have

anything to cry about.
DUNYASHA. [*She powders her nose and looks into a pocket mirror.*] Send me a letter from Paris. I loved you, Yasha, loved you so much! I'm so delicate, Yasha!
YASHA. They're coming. [*He pretends to be taking care of the suitcases, and sings softly to himself.*] [*Enter* LYUBOV ANDREEVNA, GAEV, ANYA *and* CHARLOTTA IVANOVNA.]
GAEV. We'd better be on our way. Not much time left. [*Looking at* YASHA.] Who smells of herring in here?
LYUBOV ANDREEVNA. Everybody seated in the carriages in ten minutes . . . [*She looks around the room.*] Goodbye, dear old house, dear old grandfather. Winter will pass, spring will come, and you'll be gone, demolished. The things these walls have seen! [*She kisses her daughter with great feeling.*] You're radiant, my treasure. Your eyes are like diamonds. Are you happy? Very happy?
ANYA. Very! This is the start of a new life, Mama!
GAEV. [*Cheerfully.*] It's true. Everything's going to be just fine now. Before the cherry orchard was sold, we were all worried and upset, but now that everything's settled once and for all, we've calmed down, we can even laugh again . . . I'm a loyal bank employee, a financier . . . Yellow into the side. You look better too, Lyuba. Really you do.
LYUBOV ANDREEVNA. Yes. My nerves are calmer, it's true. [*They help her on with her hat and coat.*] And I've been sleeping well. You can take my things out now, Yasha. It's time. [*To* ANYA.] My little girl. I'll see you again soon . . . I'll live on the money your great-aunt sent to buy back the estate. Three cheers for auntie from Yaroslavl! The money won't last long. Not in Paris.
ANYA. You'll come back soon, won't you, Mama? . . . Very soon. I'm going to study and take my exams, and then I'll go to work and be able to help you. We'll read all kinds of books together, won't we? . . . [*She kisses her mother's hands.*] We'll read our way through the long autumn evenings, and a wonderful new world will open to us . . . [*Dreamily.*] You will come back, Mama, won't you? . . .
LYUBOV ANDREEVNA. Yes, precious, I'll come. [*She embraces her daughter.*] [*Enter* LOPAKHIN. CHARLOTTA *is singing to herself.*]
GAEV. Lucky Charlotta. She's singing.
CHARLOTTA. [*She picks up a bundle that looks like a baby in swaddling clothes.*] Hush-a-bye, baby . . . [*The sound of a baby crying is heard.*] Hush, my darling. Hush, my dearest. [*The "crying" picks up again.*] You're breaking my heart. [*She throws the bundle down.*] Find me another job, please. I must have a job.
LOPAKHIN. We'll find you something, Charlotta Ivanovna. Don't worry.
GAEV. Everyone's abandoning us. Varya's going off on her own . . . Suddenly nobody needs us.
CHARLOTTA. There's no place for me to live in town. I have to go somewhere else . . . [*She sings to herself.*] Oh well, it doesn't matter. [*Enter* PISHCHIK.]
LOPAKHIN. Well, look who's here! . . .
PISHCHIK. [*Out of breath.*] Phew, just let me catch my breath . . . I'm ready to drop . . . Good people . . . Give me some water . . .
GAEV. After another loan, I'll bet. No thanks, I think I'll go while the going's good . . . [*He exits.*]
PISHCHIK. It's been so long . . . beautiful lady . . . [*To* LOPAKHIN.] You here too? Glad to see you . . . You've got a good head on your shoulders . . . Here . . . Take this . . . [*He gives* LOPAKHIN *some money.*] Four hundred rubles . . . Now all I owe you is eight hundred forty.
LOPAKHIN. [*He shrugs his shoulders in bewilderment.*] I must be dreaming . . . Where did you get it?
PISHCHIK. Just a second . . . It's so hot in here . . . Great event . . . Some Englishmen have discovered a kind of white clay on my land . . . [*To* LYUBOV ANDREEVNA.] And four hundred for you . . . you ravishing creature. [*He hands her the money.*] The rest will come later. [*He drinks down the water.*] Just now on the train a young fellow was saying . . . a great philosopher has been advising people to jump off the roof . . . That's his whole message. Jump. [*Amazed.*] Now

what do you think of that? More water! . . .
LOPAKHIN. Who are those Englishmen?
PISHCHIK. I've leased them the land with the clay for twenty-four years . . . But now forgive me. I'm very busy . . . Lots of stops to make . . . First there's Znoikov . . . then Kardamonov . . . I owe everybody money . . . [*He takes a drink of water.*] Best of health to you all . . . I'll be back on Thursday . . .
LYUBOV ANDREEVNA. We're moving into town today, and tomorrow I'm going abroad.
PISHCHIK. What? [*Alarmed.*] Why? What for? Oh, I see . . . The furniture, the suitcases . . . Oh, well, that's all right . . . [*Almost crying.*] That's all right . . . Very bright, those Englishmen . . . That's all right . . . Well, I wish you all the best . . . God be with you . . . It's all right . . . All good things must come to an end . . . [*He kisses* LYUBOV ANDREEVNA's *hand.*] And if you ever happen to hear my end has come, then think of . . . you know . . . that horse, and say, "There once was a man . . . named Simeonov-Pishchik . . . May he rest in peace . . ." Wonderful weather we're having . . . Hm . . . [*He exits, overcome with embarrassment, but then returns right away and speaks from the doorway.*] Dashenka sends her regards! [*He exits.*]
LYUBOV ANDREEVNA. Well, now we can go. There are two worries I'm taking with me, though. The first is poor Firs. [*Looking at her watch.*] We still have five minutes . . .
ANYA. Firs has been taken to the hospital, Mama. Yasha took him this morning.
LYUBOV ANDREEVNA. My other worry is Varya. She's used to getting up early and working. Now that there's nothing to do, she's like a fish out of water. The poor dear's so thin and pale, always crying . . . [*Pause.*] You know very well, Yermolai Alexeevich, I've dreamed of seeing the two of you married, and it did look as if you were going to propose. [*She whispers to* ANYA, ANYA *nods to* CHARLOTTA, *and they both exit.*] She loves you, you like her, and I just can't see why you always seem to be avoiding each other. I don't understand it!
LOPAKHIN. Neither do I, to tell you the truth. The whole thing is so strange. I don't mind going through with it, though, if it's not too late . . . Let's just get it over with. Once you're gone, I don't think I'll ever ask her.
LYUBOV ANDREEVNA. Fine. It does only take a minute. I'll go and call her . . .
LOPAKHIN. We even have some champagne. [*Looking over at the glasses.*] Empty. Somebody's drunk it all. [YASHA *coughs.*] Or should I say guzzled it all . . .
LYUBOV ANDREEVNA. [*Excitedly.*] Perfect. We'll leave the room . . . Yasha, allez! I'll go and call her . . . [*At the door.*] Varya! Drop what you're doing and come here. Come here at once! [*She exits with* YASHA.]
LOPAKHIN. [*Looking at his watch.*] Hm . . . [*Pause.*] [*Stifled laughter and whispering come from behind the door. After some time* VARYA *enters.*]
VARYA. [*She looks through the luggage carefully.*] That's funny. I can't find it anywhere.
LOPAKHIN. What are you looking for?
VARYA. I packed it myself, and can't remember where. [*Pause.*]
LOPAKHIN. Where will you be going now, Varvara Mikhailovna?
VARYA. Me? To the Ragulins' . . . I've arranged with them to look after their house . . . be a kind of housekeeper there.
LOPAKHIN. That's in Yashnevo, isn't it? About fifty miles from here. [*Pause.*] So life in this house has come to an end.
VARYA. [*Looking through the luggage.*] Where can it be? . . . Maybe I put it in the trunk . . . Yes, that's the end of life in the house . . . And never more shall be . . .
LOPAHKIN. Well, I'm on my way to Kharkov now . . . On the next train. There's a lot to do. I'm leaving Yepikhodov here . . . I've hired him . . .
VARYA. You have?
LOPAKHIN. Last year we had snow by this time, remember? And now it's calm and sunny. Cold, though . . .

Three degrees below freezing.
VARYA. I hadn't noticed. [*Pause.*] The thermometer's broken. [*Pause.*] [*A* VOICE *from the courtyard calls out,* "*Yermolai Alexeevich!*"]
LOPAKHIN. [*As if he had long been expecting the call.*] I'll be right there! [*He exits in a hurry.*] [VARYA *sits on the floor with her head on a bundle of clothes and sobs softly. The door opens, and* LYUBOV ANDREEVNA *enters cautiously.*]
LYUBOV ANDREEVNA. Well? [*Pause.*] We're leaving now.
VARYA. [*She has stopped crying and wiped her eyes.*] Yes, Mama, time to go. I can be at the Ragulins' today if we don't miss the train . . .
LYUBOV ANDREEVNA. [*Calling out the door.*] Anya! Put your things on! [*Enter* ANYA, *then* GAEV *and* CHARLOTTA IVANOVNA. GAEV *is wearing a heavy coat with a hood. The* SERVANTS *and* COACHMEN *come in.* YEPIKHODOV *fusses with the luggage.*]
ANYA. [*Joyfully.*] On our way!
GAEV. Friends, good friends, kind friends . . . As we leave this house forever, I feel compelled to speak out, to express the feelings welling up within me . . .
ANYA. [*Beseechingly.*] Uncle Leonid!
VARYA. Please, Uncle Leonid!
GAEV. [*Despondently.*] Combination off the yellow into the side . . . Not another word. [*Enter* TROFIMOV *followed by* LOPAKHIN.]
TROFIMOV. Come on, everybody, time to go!
LOPAKHIN. My coat, Yepikhodov!
LYUBOV ANDREEVNA. Just one minute more . . . It's as though I'd never seen what the walls in the house were like, or the ceiling, and now I can't take my eyes off them, I love them so much . . .
GAEV. I remember when I was six, sitting in this window on Trinity Sunday and watching Father go off to church.
LYUBOV ANDREEVNA. Is everything outside?
LOPAKHIN. I think so, yes. [*Putting on his coat, to* YEPIKHODOV.] Keep an eye on everything, Yepikhodov.
YEPIKHODOV. [*In a hoarse voice.*] Don't worry, Yermolai Alexeevich!

LOPAKHIN. What's the matter with your voice?
YEPIKHODOV. I was just drinking some water. Must have swallowed something.
YASHA. The ignorance of these people . . .
LYUBOV ANDREEVNA. When we leave, there won't be a soul left . . .
LOPAKHIN. Until spring.
VARYA. [*She pulls an umbrella out of a bundle in such a way that she seems about to strike him;* LOPAKHIN *pretends to be frightened.*] Oh, don't be silly. It never entered my mind.
TROFIMOV. Everyone into the carriages now . . . It's time! The train will be in soon!
VARYA. There are your galoshes, Petya. Right next to that suitcase. [*Tearfully.*] They're so old and dirty . . .
TROFIMOV. [*Putting on his galoshes.*] Let's go, everybody . . .
GAEV. [*Overwrought, afraid of bursting into tears.*] The train . . . The station . . . Cross shot into the side, combination off the white into the corner.
LYUBOV ANDREEVNA. Let's go.
LOPAKHIN. Is everybody here? No one left behind? [*He locks up the side door, left.*] I have some things stored in here. Better lock up. Let's go . . .
ANYA. Goodbye, house! Goodbye, old life!
TROFIMOV. Hello, new life . . . [*He exits with* ANYA.] [VARYA *looks around the room and goes out slowly.* YASHA *and* CHARLOTTA, *with her dog, follow.*]
LOPAKHIN. See you next spring. Don't be too long now . . . See you soon . . . [*He exits.*] [LYUBOV ANDREEVNA *and* GAEV *are left alone. As if waiting for this moment, they throw themselves into one another's arms and sob quietly, holding back, afraid to be heard.*]
GAEV. [*In despair.*] Oh, my sister, my sister . . .
LYUBOV ANDREEVNA. Oh, my dear, my sweet, my beautiful orchard! . . . My life, my youth, my happiness—goodbye! . . . Goodbye! . . . [ANYA *calls out cheerfully,* "*Mama!*" TROFIMOV *calls out cheerfully and excitedly,* "*Yoo Hoo!* . . ."] One last look at the walls, the windows . . . Mother dear used to love walking around this room . . .

GAEV. My sister, my sister . . . [ANYA *calls out, "Mama! . . ."* TROFIMOV *calls out "Yoo Hoo! . . . ."*]

LYUBOV ANDREEVNA. Coming! [*They exit.*] [*The stage is empty. We hear the doors being locked and the carriages driving off. Then it is quiet. The dull thud of an ax coming down on a tree breaks the silence. It is a sad and lonely sound. Suddenly there is a sound of footsteps.* FIRS *appears at the door, right. As usual he is wearing a jacket, a white vest, and slippers. He looks sick.*]

FIRS. [*He goes over to the door and tries the handle.*] Locked. They're gone . . . [*He sits on the couch.*] Forgot about me . . . Oh well . . . I'll just sit here a while . . . I bet Leonid Andreevich didn't wear his fur coat, bet he put on that topcoat instead. . . . [*He heaves a worried sigh.*] And I didn't even look to see . . . Oh, these young people! [*He mutters something unintelligible.*] Life is over before you live it. [*He lies down.*] Think I'll lie down a second . . . No strength left, nothing . . . Silly galoot. [*He lies there motionless.*] [*A distant sound is heard. It seems to come from the sky. It is the sound of a string that has snapped. It dies away mournfully. The silence that sets in is disturbed only by the thud of an ax striking a tree far away in the orchard.*]

1. The "leap of death," a circus stunt.
2. A nineteenth-century English historian. Yepikhodov probably has not read him either.
3. A garbling of Hamlet's injunction to Ophelia (*Hamlet*, 3.1).
4. A dance resembling several American folk dances in which a caller identifies each new step and the couples execute it.
5. The stationmaster announces, "'The Sinner Woman' by Alexei Tolstoy," then launches into the first few lines:

A swarming crowd: gay laughter's clang,
The crash of gongs, the lutes' clear twang,
Flowers and green'ry scattered round . . .